SQUEAK: OPEN PERSONAL COMPUTING AND MULTIMEDIA

SQUEAK: OPEN PERSONAL COMPUTING AND MULTIMEDIA

Mark Guzdial

CVU Center and EduTech Institute
College of Computing
Georgia Institute of Technology

Kim Rose

Walt Disney Imagineering
Research & Development

An Alan R. Apt Book

Prentice Hall
Prentice Hall
Upper Saddle River, New Jersey 07458

Library of Congress Cataloging-in-Publication Data

Guzdial, Mark
Squeak : object-oriented design with multimedia applications / Mark Guzdial.
    p. cm.
  "An Alan R. Apt Book"
  ISBN 0–13–0280917
  1. Object-oriented programming (Computer science).   2. Multimedia systems
  3. Squeak.   I. Title.
QA76.64.G89 2000
006.7'6dc21   00–046951

Vice President and Editorial Director, ECS: *Marcia J. Horton*
Publisher: *Alan R. Apt*
Associate Editor: *Toni D. Holm*
Editorial Assistant: *Amy K. Todd*
Vice-president and Director of Production and Manufacturing, ESM: *David W. Riccardi*
Executive Managing Editor: *Vince O'Brien*
Managing Editor: *David A. George*
Production Editor: *Lakshmi Balasubramanian*
Director of Creative Services: *Paul Belfanti*
Creative Director: *Carole Anson*
Art Director and Cover Designer: *Heather Scott*
Art Editor: *Adam Velthaus*
Manufacturing Manager: *Trudy Pisciotti*
Manufacturing Buyer: *Lisa McDowell*
Senior Marketing Manager: *Jennie Burger*
Composition: *PreTEX, Inc.*

© 2002 Prentice Hall
Prentice Hall, Inc.
Upper Saddle River, New Jersey 07458

10 9 8 7 6 5 4 3 2 1

ISBN 0-13-0280917

Prentice-Hall International (UK) Limited, *London*
Prentice-Hall of Australia Pty. Limited, *Sydney*
Prentice-Hall Canada Inc., *Toronto*
Prentice-Hall Hispanoamericana, S.A., *Mexico City*
Prentice-Hall of India Private Limited, *New Delhi*
Prentice-Hall of Japan, Inc., *Tokyo*
Pearson Education Asia Pte. Ltd., *Singapore*
Editora Prentice-Hall do Brasil, Ltda., *Rio de Janeiro*

Foreword

It Should Be Active, But Where (and When) Will It Be?

Why is this foreword so short? It is mainly because (a) we have been working on explaining complex ideas through active media for more than 30 years, (b) we are starting to realize this goal better and better through Squeak (this, after all, was one of the main reasons we decided to create Squeak), and (c) the best idea I could come up with for a foreword involved an "active essay" example requiring a kind of dynamic collaboration between what I write, you the "reader/constructor," and Squeak, the "dynamic medium for creative thought" that turns your computer into a real "dynabook."

If we pause to think about this for a minute, having these wonderful chapters of examples in this book are indeed very useful, but it would be far better for them to be online and active (and I hope all shall be by the time you have this book in your hands). The examples are also far more likely to be up to date and relevant than when stuck in this book.

So, in part to make this point, I thought I would be stubborn and only publish my contribution online. But now I have a problem. How can I ensure that any reader of this book any time in the future will be able to find my real foreword with my active example and be able to read/coconstruct it?

- Is there some place on the net where I can put it so I can give the URL here and it can be found—even 100 years from now (as a historical curiosity)?

- Can it be found and retrieved?

- Can it run (or be easily made to run) on your current computer—even 100 years from now?

Please note that this paper book will indeed be findable and readable 100 years from now. The active foreword that is online explains how this can be achieved with digital media.

I can't give you a URL that will work for all time. Unfortunately, URLs are tied much too much to particular servers, and these may change over time. A content search is much better, and we can be pretty confident that if the Internet survives (as it no doubt will) then content searches will only get more comprehensive and accurate.

So, here is an official reference to this foreword that any good content search engine should be able to find even 100 years from now:

"It Should Be Active, But Where (and When) Will It Be?"
Alan Kay
Active Essay first written for *Squeak: Open-Source for Computing and Multimedia* and published on `http://www.squeakland.org`.

As you explore the active essay and read the rest of this book, please don't forget to help make computing better, richer, and deeper than it is now. Best wishes,

ALAN C. KAY
VP of Research and Fellow
Walt Disney Imagineering R&D

Preface

Squeak is an open programming language designed especially for personal computing and multimedia. It's certainly the most cross-platform multimedia platform in existence. What's especially interesting is that Squeak is written almost entirely in terms of itself — for example, it is possible to extend Squeak with the speed of native processor primitives without ever writing a line of C code. This book provides a guide to some of the exciting potential of Squeak. It's not a tutorial (though there are some tutorial chapters), but instead, the book offers a path into some of Squeak's unique features:

- For programmers and others interested in Squeak, this book provides in-depth presentations of some of the most exciting aspects of Squeak, such as Morphic and the internals of Squeak. The final chapters point toward the future of Squeak and where it might be used.

- For multimedia developers, there are chapters here on a range of the multimedia capabilities available in Squeak, from advanced graphics and networking, through specific applications like computer music and streaming audio.

- For application developers who want to build on Squeak, the chapters on how to port and extend Squeak explain the process, and several of the chapters point to examples of development on top of Squeak (including examples of applying new development methodologies like *eXtreme Programming*).

- For students and others interested in virtual machines (e.g., for embedded systems), the chapters on Squeak's virtual machine (especially *Back to the Future* and the tour of the object engine), how to port it, and how to extend it provide some of the best writing available yet on an increasingly important technology.

We (the editors and authors of this book) have been living Squeak for some five years now, but for many of you, this book will be your introduction to the wonderful world of Squeak. In another sense, though, if you have used a personal computer in the last twenty years, you *have* already been introduced to Squeak. Squeak is quite literally the direct descendant of the original *Smalltalk* work through which the desktop personal computer was invented. The legendary demonstration of Smalltalk to Steve Jobs of Apple Computer by Adele Goldberg and her team at Xerox Parc in 1979 (based on which Apple developed the Lisa and then the Macintosh) was running much of the exact same code that you're running when you run Squeak.

Of course, Squeak has been advanced considerably from that base system, but mostly just in the last five years. The technical story of how Squeak came to be and how it was developed from that original Smalltalk is told in the reprinted chapter *Back to the Future* in this volume. The challenge posed by that story, though, is made throughout this book.

What if those who developed the desktop personal computer from the original Smalltalk work *missed* something? The developers of the Apple Macintosh operating system, the Microsoft Windows operating system, and all the other desktop systems didn't start from the actual work at Xerox PARC, but from impressions and demonstrations. What if the fifteen years of the development of the desktop personal computer between 1980 and the start of Squeak *went down the wrong path* (or at least, didn't go down the *right* path)?

That's the question that Squeak allows us to ask. Squeak offers us the opportunity to start at the same place as Steve Jobs and others did some twenty years ago, but to explore a different future for personal computers. The researchers at Xerox PARC are hailed for inventing and integrating the *w*indows, *i*cons, *m*enus, and mouse *p*ointer into the "WIMP" desktop user interface that we all know today, but their vision *also* included:

- the computer as a *meta-medium*

- that's completely personalizable

- with software that's portable anywhere (from embedded and handheld devices to mainframe computers)

- and could (and should!) be programmed by "the rest of us."

What would a personal computer be like if those ideas (and the others inherent in the vision of the Dynabook) were integrated at the heart of the desktop interface that we all use, and weren't just add-ons? This book invites you to explore the challenge of an alternate future for personal computers. The chapters of this volume were selected not only to serve as a tutorial and invitation to explore Squeak, but also to pose challenges, opportunities, and intriguing glimpses into a future of personal computing different from that posed by existing systems. Please do accept the challenge, see what Apple and Microsoft saw at the dawn of personal computing, and see what future you and your own vision can make for personal computing.

Acknowledgments

A book like this is a large undertaking that is only possible through the efforts of many.

Our first thanks go to Ian Piumarta, who volunteered to be our LATEXpert when it came time to integrate all the chapters — most of which were in Microsoft

Word! Ian designed the look-and-feel of the book, answered our many questions, and repaired many bugs, for which we owe him great thanks.

We also thank Stephen Pope who edited and assembled the CD for the book. He did a marvelous job of assembling some of the most exciting new work in Squeak.

We are deeply indebted to "Squeak Central," especially Alan Kay for his foreword, Dan Ingalls for updating the seminal *Back to the Future* paper and allowing us to reprint *Back to the Future* here, and John Maloney who allowed us to ask him at a very late date to write the chapter on Morphic. Thanks also to the Association for Computing Machinery (ACM) which gave us permission to reprint *Back to the Future* from the *Proceedings of OOPSLA '97*.

Special thanks to Alan Apt, Toni Holm, and Amy Todd of Prentice-Hall. Alan showed great faith in being willing to publish books on a relatively unknown language by first-time authors and editors. Thanks to Robert Tinney for his willingness to revisit the Smalltalk issue of *Byte* (August, 1981) in producing the cover art for this volume.

The whole Squeak community has joined us in creating this book, through a review Swiki where chapters were checked-out by everyone.[1] In particular, we wish to thank the following reviewers, several of whom read multiple chapters and all of whom provided us with terrific feedback:

Stefan Matthias Aust	Ed Luwish
John Cherniavsky	John Maloney
Kendall Clark	John McIntosh
Stephane Ducasse	David Mitchell
Jörn Eyrich	Chris Norton
Jerome Garcia	Mats Nygren
Joshua Gargus	Bruce O'Neel
Henrik Gedenryd	Bijan Parsia
Robert Hirschfeld	Helge Horch
Andreas Raab	Dwight Hughes
Stephan Rudlof	Andreas Kuckartz
Danny Sharpe	T. M. N. Irish
Lex Spoon	Alan Kay
Jeff Szuhay	Ned Konz
Juan Manuel Vuletich	David Lewis
Sebastian Wain	Doug Way

Mark Guzdial wants to thank the "Georgia Tech Squeakers" (his students and colleagues at Georgia Institute of Technology) for their support and their never-ending stream of new ideas; and his ever-patient family (wife Barbara, and children Matthew, Katherine, and Jennifer) for putting up with Daddy's crazy idea of doing *two* Squeak books at the same time.

---

[1] http://coweb.cc.gatech.edu/squeakbook

Kim Rose wishes to acknowledge the community building power of the internet. Many wonderful relationships have formed out of the collective building of Squeak. Squeak's range, depth, and ability to run on a wide variety of platforms, would not be if not for this amazing communications vehicle. The internet has enabled the romance of Squeak to spread rapidly around the world. Thanks to all of the book's contributors (many of whom Kim and Mark have never met face to face) for their hard work, their good humor, and their effort to bring a particularly special vision of personal computing into the present.

MARK GUZDIAL
Georgia Institute of Technology

KIM ROSE
Walt Disney Imagineering Research & Development

Contents

SQUEAK: OPEN PERSONAL COMPUTING AND MULTIMEDIA

Part One

Squeak for the Programmer and Media Developer

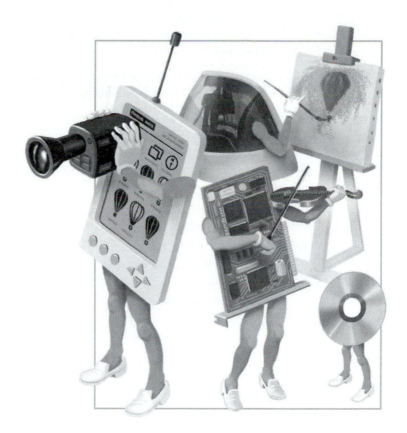

The first part of the book is "for the rest of us"—it's about using Squeak for programming and developing media. In the vision that drove the development of Smalltalk and Squeak, *everyone* is expected to program and develop media. It's not an activity reserved for a priesthood but a form of expression that can be started as a craft and developed into high art.

The chapters in this part are introducing Squeak as it currently is, not as it might be when programming and media development are commonplace activities. This is the starting point for a Dynabook.

- Noel Rappin begins the book by introducing Squeak to the reader already familiar with object-oriented programming.[1] He lays down the basic framework of how one gets around in Squeak.

- John Maloney, one of the original developers of Squeak and of its *Morphic* user interface, provides a tour of Morphic. His chapter includes examples and an exposition of the philosophy behind Morphic.

- Jeff Pierce describes Squeak Alice, the 3-D end-user scripting environment that he implemented while visiting Squeak Central on an internship. *Wonderland* is the kind of programming and media development environment that aims squarely "for the rest of us" and directly addresses the Dynabook vision.

- Bijan Parsia, Lex Spoon, and Bolot Kerimbaev give a grand tour of the networking capabilities in Squeak, from client to server, from HTTP to IRC. The ease of networking and the cross-platform accessibility of Squeak make it a wonderful environment for building networking tools.

---

[1] For an introduction to Squeak for those readers *not* familiar with objects and classes, see the companion book *Squeak: Object-oriented design with multimedia applications* also from Prentice-Hall.

1

Squeak for Nonnative Speakers

Noel Rappin
Openwave Systems

Introduction

Welcome to Squeak! If you are reading this book, it means that you are interested in learning more about the exciting range of applications and activities that are being built in Squeak. If you are reading this chapter, it means that you'd like a quick tour of the basics of using Squeak before learning about its internal implementation or seeing how it can be applied as a web server, 3-D graphics engine, sound synthesizer, handwriting recognizer, cheese grater, and so on.[1] As you'll see demonstrated in the later chapters of this book, it's very hard to start talking about all the features of Squeak without sounding like the host of a late-night infomercial. (It's an object-oriented programming language; not one, but two interface packages; a programming environment; and a web server! Now how much would you pay? Did we mention it's completely cross-platform?)

If you have never programmed in Squeak before, a short introduction is in order before you move on to the advanced topics. The goal of this chapter is to provide enough information about Squeak for you to understand the code samples and design principles in the later chapters, and to experiment with the language on your own—experimentation is a major part of the Squeak world view. You won't leave this chapter knowing every keyboard shortcut and message in Squeak—there's just too much. You will come out of this chapter with (1) a place to start your own Squeak experience and (2) an understanding of the design principles behind Squeak and how they differ from other languages with which you may be familiar.

You are a member of the target audience for this chapter if you are an intermediate to advanced programmer, completely comfortable with basic concepts like function, conditional, loop, variable, and type. I assume that you've completed

---

[1] Okay, just kidding about the cheese grater. All the other ones, though, are real.

at least enough object-oriented programming to be familiar with concepts such as class, instance, method, and inheritance. It will be helpful if at least some of that object-oriented experience is in C++ or Java—I'll be using those as comparisons. (Previous Smalltalk experience is a plus, but not a requirement.) It's entirely possible that even though you've completed some OO programming, you've never really understood what all the fuss was about. Hopefully, we'll show you the reason here.

If that describes you, then this chapter should be at exactly the right place to help you jump to Squeak. If you've never completed any object-oriented programming before, you might want to start with a general introduction to OOP before diving in here.

Feeling Right at Home

The first thing to show you in the tour of Squeak is how to get it and how to feel at home in the environment. Squeak's programming environment is a direct ancestor of the first Smalltalk programming environments written at Xerox PARC. While it is still in many ways more powerful than most programming environments created since, Squeak also takes a little getting used to if you are more comfortable with, say, CodeWarrior or Visual C++.

Getting, Having, Playing

The first step to using Squeak is to download it off the internet or off the book CD and start it on your system. The initial implementation of Squeak was written for the MacOS. Within weeks of the first release, it was ported to several varieties of UNIX. Since then, Squeak has been ported to Windows, BeOS, DOS, a number of flavors of Windows CE, a Motorola chip running without an OS, and so on. The process of starting Squeak is broadly similar across platforms—any operating system quirks not discussed here should be available from the main Squeak web site at `http://www.squeak.org`.

To download Squeak, first head to `http://www.squeak.org` and click on the link for downloading. In most cases, you will find an archive (ZIP, StuffIt, or tar) matching your OS of choice.[2] Download that archive in *binary* mode, and expand it into a directory on your machine. You must perform the download in binary mode, or some of the files may be corrupted by your download program reinterpreting the line endings incorrectly. The CD accompanying this book also contains a Squeak package for several operating systems, which includes the code discussed throughout this book.

---

[2]Some of the less common UNIX and other OS versions distribute VM source code, rather than binary. Compiling the VM is beyond this chapter, but the resources linked from Squeak.org should get you started.

The archive contains at least four files, three of which are identical no matter which platform you are running. Much of the cross-platform power of Squeak comes from the fact that over 90% of the data you download in your archive is common to all platforms.

As of this writing, the current release of Squeak is 2.8, and your archive will contain the following files (file names may vary slightly from operating system to operating system, or from Squeak version to Squeak version):

- An image file: **squeak2.8.image**. The image file contains the entire binary state of your Squeak system. This includes the complete state of all objects known to the system, as well as all compiled code, and various global preferences that have been set. The image file can be thought of as a complete memory dump of the entire Squeak system. In many respects, the image **is** the system. Images are completely compatible across platform—you can save an image in one platform and load it in another. You can also have more than one image saved under different names—if, for example, you have two different Squeak projects with different needs.

- A sources file: **squeakV2.sources**. The sources file contains all of the text source code that was part of the Squeak system at the time of the Squeak 2.0 release. Don't change the name of this file—Squeak will look for it when it's time to display source code.

- A changes file: **squeak2.8.changes**. The changes file contains all the text source code that has been added or changed in Squeak since the 2.0 release. All the changes you make in Squeak by adding or modifying code will also be stored in the changes file. The changes file belongs to the image file of the same name—if you save your image under a new name, you will get a new changes file. The implication of this for you is that all the changes you make to your Squeak system can be viewed, undone, and shared.

- An executable virtual machine (VM) file. The exact name of this file changes from platform to platform. The VM file, which for most purposes you won't have to look at, performs the background grunt work of converting platform independent Squeak code into platform dependent machine code. If this sounds familiar to you Java folks, well, where do you think they got the idea? Compared to the Java VM, the Squeak VM is much smaller (in fact, much of it is written in Squeak code translated by Squeak to C)—which is one of the reasons why Squeak has been so easy to port.[3]

In addition to the above files, your Squeak package may include optional, platform-dependent plug-ins. These files provide support for other OS-dependent features such as 3-D graphics and sound.

---

[3]Squeak's small VM increases flexibility at some cost in speed. Performance is increased by including native machine language versions of the most common or core functions in the VM, called a *primitive*. If the native primitive fails, the system executes the Squeak version instead.

Once you've downloaded the files and dropped them all into a directory, starting up Squeak is a simple matter of running the VM executable with an image file as an argument. In the MacOS, simply double-clicking on an image file is enough. On Win32 machines, dragging the image file over the VM file works, as does using the Explorer to bind .image files to the VM executable file. On UNIX systems, the VM file can be invoked from the command line, with the image file as an argument.

Once you've launched Squeak in whatever OS, you will be treated to a main window in a particularly memorable shade of light green (Figure 1.1). There will be two open windows on top of that—one labeled "Welcome to Squeak 2.7" and the other labeled "Getting Started." Along the left side are a series of minimized windows labeled "Play With Me" numbered 1 through 8.

Now, having launched Squeak successfully, you're probably wondering how you actually do anything. Time for the next section...

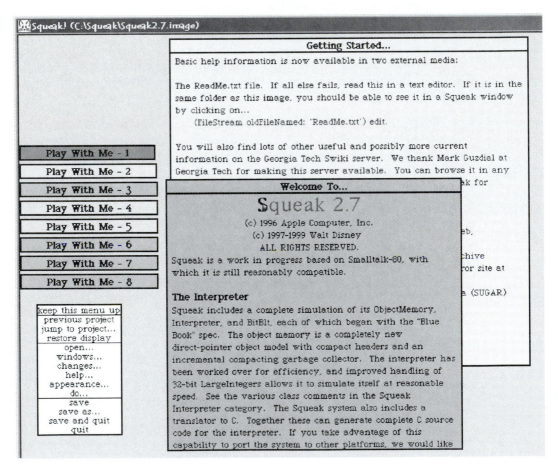

Figure 1.1   Squeak Welcome Screen

Environmental Concerns

Squeak's interface and environment are direct descendents of the original Smalltalk-80 system, itself one of the progenitors of all the window- and mouse-based interfaces you see on your desktop today. That said, Squeak is likely to seem slightly different from your standard Windows or Mac program—you'll immediately notice that Squeak doesn't use menu bars, for one thing. In fact, it's more useful to think of Squeak as its own operating system piggybacking on your existing system rather than merely a program running on whatever OS is controlling the rest of your desktop—many Squeakers stay within Squeak for nearly all their daily computing tasks.

The keyboard and mouse are still the basic modes of interaction with Squeak. The keyboard works pretty much the way keyboards work. As for the mouse, it will almost work the way you expect. Squeak assumes you have a three-button mouse, regardless of how many buttons your mouse actually has. The left button is used for pointing and selecting. The right button brings up a context-specific menu for whatever window you are in, and the center button brings up a menu of window activities (close, resize, and change label) for the currently active window. In practice, you'll rarely use the center button—most of its features are available separately in the title bar of the window. If you are stuck with a Windows two-button mouse, center clicks are simulated with alt-left click.[4] On a Mac, right clicks are represented with cmd-click, and center clicks are opt-click. Occasionally, you'll see references to the three buttons as "red, yellow, and blue," a reference to the names used for the mouse buttons on the original Xerox Alto, but those names are not common anymore. Table 1.1 has a quick-reference chart of the buttons and their common meanings.

Button:	Left	Center	Right
Also Known As:	Red	Yellow	Blue
Generally Used For:	Pointing, selecting	Window manipulation	Context-sensitive menu
Windows 2-Button Equivalent:	Left Click	Alt-Left Click	Right Click
Mac 1-Button Equivalent:	Click	Opt-Click	Cmd-Click

Table 1.1   Squeak Mouse Buttons

---

[4]If you do have a three-button mouse in Windows, you can get the third button to work by right-clicking on the Squeak window toolbar (or its button in the system tray), going to VM Preferences, and selecting "Use 3 Button Mouse Mapping."

Playing around with the Squeak opening window, you'll notice that clicking on either of the large windows makes the window active and also causes a scroll-bar to be displayed to the left of the window. Clicking on the desktop brings up a menu of common system functions including saving and quitting that I'll refer to as the World Menu (also known as the Desktop menu, depending on which GUI you are using, but World Menu is so much cooler sounding).

Clicking on the smaller windows on the side will make them active and display a close box on their left and a maximize box on the right. (Don't close them yet, we're not done with them—if you do accidentally close them, click anywhere on the desktop not covered by a window, and select quit. When prompted to save before quitting, select no. Then restart Squeak—your image will appear just as before.[5]

Now, click on the window labeled "Play With Me 1" and maximize it. Your computer will display a window with some scroll bars and lists. Clicking on this desktop causes a menu to display that looks slightly different from the World Menu on the background desktop because Squeak actually has two completely distinct graphics/interface packages. The initial desktop uses MVC, which is based on Smalltalk-80's original Model, View, Controller framework. However, the Play With Me's (Figure 1.2) and most of the newer Squeak interface work are in Morphic (see Chapter 2), an interface package based on a system originally created for the Self language. From the user perspective of viewing and displaying code, the two packages are similar (Morphic is somewhat jazzier graphically and more fully featured), and most of the topics here will be applicable to both unless otherwise noted.

Now open "Play With Me 3." It opens into a thumbnail sketch of a Squeak desktop—a fact you can confirm by clicking on it and choosing "enter project." Play With Me 3 is an example of a Squeak *project*. Projects are separate environments within Squeak that allow you to maintain a separate desktop and a separate set of code changes for each one. Being able to specify different screen preferences for different projects is nice. (I usually give different projects different background colors, so I can tell what I'm working on at a glance.) The real benefit of projects, however, is that the changes made to the image in each project are stored separately, allowing code in a project to be transferred more easily. We'll see more about this when we discuss change sets.

You get out of a project by clicking on the desktop to get the World Menu and selecting either "previous project," which takes you back to the project you just left, or "jump to project," which gives you a list of all projects in the system and lets you choose which one to go to.

Saving and quitting are also tasks that you'd like to do once in a while from your programming environment (even if the following chapters make a compelling case for never quitting Squeak, saving frequently is recommended). In Squeak, saving is an action you perform on the image as a whole—not on individual methods or classes of code. Individual methods or classes of code can be *filed out* as text,

---

[5]This is an important point that will be discussed later—ordinarily you do save your image when quitting, otherwise changes you make are not saved.

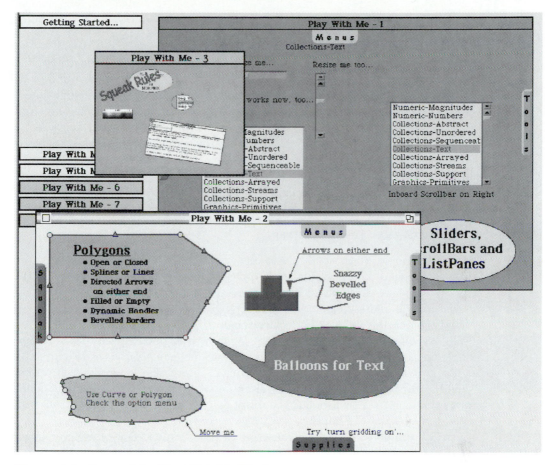

Figure 1.2   Some of the Play With Me Windows

for storage or as a way to package software for distribution. New code methods are accepted into the image, and the image is then saved to disk. Storing the image to disk saves not only the code but also the state of any global variables in the system. Not saving the image to disk means that any changes you've made in the image are gone. (Code changes are usually accessible in the `.changes` file, but must be reaccepted.) To avoid this, you should get in the habit of saving the image frequently.

Given the preceding discussion, the bottom items on the World Menu (Save, Save As..., Save and Quit and Quit) behave as you'd expect. Save As... allows you to create a clone of your image file. Quit will prompt you for a save before actually quitting. Windows users should take care not to exit Squeak by using the upper-right close box—that box will not give you the save prompt, rather, it will ask you if you want to quit Squeak *without* saving. Generally, you should resist this temptation.

Open Some Windows, Feel the Breeze

The Squeak user interface has a variety of specialized windows for code browsing, evaluation, and inspection. However, you'll likely spend the majority of your Squeak time in three windows, the System Browser, the Workspace, and the Transcript.

To start your exploration of these windows, access the World Menu from whatever project you happen to be in. Select "Open." From the submenu, first select a Workspace, then select a Transcript. You are rewarded with two blank windows—one a pale yellow and the other a burnt orange. It seems modest, but this is the beginning of Squeaking.

Select the Workspace (but make sure the Transcript is visible) and type the following (capitalization and parentheses are important):

```
Transcript show: (2 + 2) asString
```

With the cursor at the end of the line, right-click the mouse and select "do it" from the menu. If everything went correctly, you'll see a "4" show up in the Transcript window. If things don't go correctly you'll see an error window. For now, just close it and try again.

What's happening? The Workspace window is a text editor that allows you to evaluate Squeak code. The Transcript Window is a global space that is always available and is used for returning values and for debugging purposes (Figure 1.3). The "do it" command sends text to the Squeak interpreter for evaluation (either the line the cursor is on or a multiline group of selected text). This particular line of code is adding $2 + 2$, converting the result to a string, and asking the Transcript to display the result (4, I hope).

Actually, you don't need the Transcript to show results. On a fresh workspace line, type the following:

```
2 squared.
```

Again, right-click with the cursor at the end of that line, but this time select "print it." The result (who didn't get 4 again?) will appear in the workspace. The "print it" command causes the code to be sent to the interpreter, and then the result returned by that code is written to the window at the end of the selection. Notice that the result is selected so that it can be easily overwritten by the next words you type.

Go to another fresh line and type

```
'abc' reversed.
```

Be sure to use single quotes and not double quotes. This time, right-click and select "inspect it." A new window opens, titled "String," with "self, all inst vars, 1, 2, 3" along the left side. "Inspect it" causes Squeak to evaluate code and open an *inspector window* on the result. Inspector windows show the values of all the component variables of an object and can be opened on any Squeak object. In

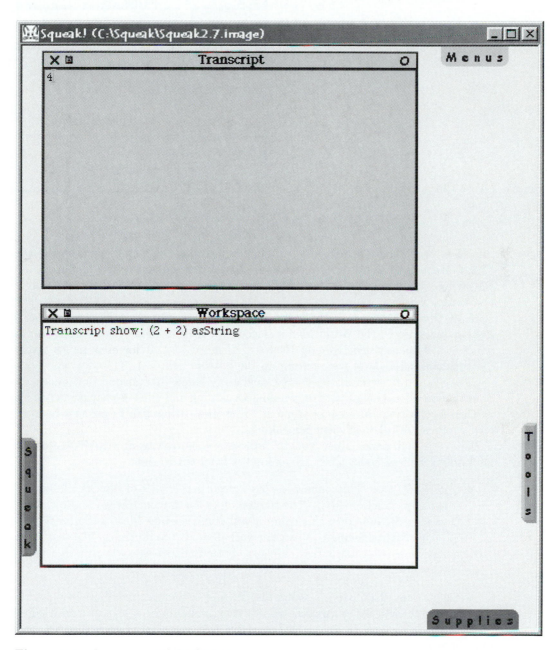

Figure 1.3   Transcript and Workspace

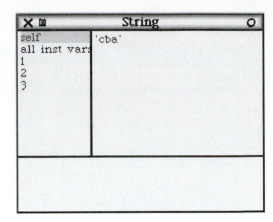

Figure 1.4   An Inspector Window

this case, "self" shows the resulting object as a whole, the string "cba," while the "1,2,3" listings show the ASCII values for the individual characters that make up the string. (See Figure 1.4.) Inspector windows are very helpful in debugging large and complex Squeak objects.

Now that you've seen individual lines of code, it's time to take a peek at the mother lode. Go to the World Menu, select "open," and then select "browser." A window will open, titled "System Browser" (Figure 1.5). It has four panes across the top half and a single pane taking up the bottom half.

The System Browser allows you to view every single line of code that makes up Squeak, as well as being the main window for adding and editing your own code. It is, therefore, a bit of an understatement to say that being able to use this browser effectively is critical to efficient Squeaking.

The top four panes allow you to browse and narrow your search to specific methods of Squeak code. They are as follows from left to right:

- Category Pane: This pane presents *categories*, groups of Squeak classes arranged by functionality. (The arranging is for human categorization only.) Browsing up and down this column will give you some idea of the breadth of Squeak. Right-clicking in this pane will allow you to do things like search for a specific class or add a new category. Selecting a category brings up a list of classes in the...

- Class Pane: This pane presents all the classes that are members of a particular category. These are the classes that make up Squeak's object-oriented hierarchy. Right-clicking in this pane will bring up a menu of options for more information about the selected class. Pressing the "?" button will bring up a comment about the class. The "class" and "instance" buttons control what kind of information about the class is displayed. Selecting a class brings up a list of method categories in the...

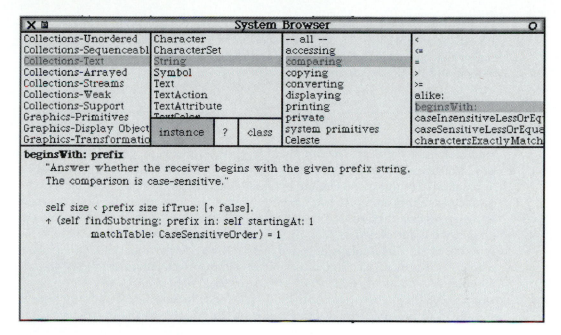

Figure 1.5   The System Browser

- Method Category Pane: This pane presents a list of method categories for a particular class. The categories, which are for human readability only, divide the functionality of a class into more easily browsed chunks. Right-clicking on this menu allows you to add, rename, or organize categories. Selecting a category brings up a list of methods in the...

- Method Pane: This pane gives you a list of methods in the selected category of the selected class. Right-clicking here gives you a menu of more information about the selected method. Selecting a method allows you to see the code in the code pane.

The code pane takes up the bottom half of the System Browser and allows you to view and edit Squeak code. From here you can also create new classes and methods.

As I mentioned, the System Browser contains all the code that runs Squeak, as well as the code that you will write. Since over 95% of Squeak is written in Squeak that includes just about everything: The code that displays the System Browser, interprets and evaluates text, the file system, all the examples you'll see in this book. Some of the code covers the most current cutting-edge multimedia formats, like Flash. Some of the code is so old that the comments refer to the Xerox Alto. Feeling a little overwhelmed is a common first reaction. Feeling empowered is a common second one.

This run through the basics of the Squeak interface is necessarily brief, and I've left out pages of things like keyboard shortcuts and how to change the colors. The end of this chapter will tell you where to look for that information. Now it's time to look at Squeak, the programming language, in more detail.

Think Small

Smalltalk has a different structure than the object-oriented programming languages with which you are most likely to be familiar. Unlike C++ or Java, all variables in Smalltalk are objects, including integers, Booleans, floating point numbers, and characters. There are no "basic types" to clutter up the syntax. In addition, most of the structures that we traditionally think of as syntax, such as loops and conditionals, are implemented as part of the Smalltalk object library and are not special syntactic forms. Smalltalk is designed around a very few syntax rules, applied consistently throughout the language, and provides for maximum flexibility for the programmer. Most of the language issues in this chapter also apply to other dialects of Smalltalk, but a few of them do not (and the interface details are Squeak specific). To minimize confusion, I will continue to refer to the environment and language as Squeak, rather than Smalltalk.

Squeak in a Note Card (Who needs a whole nutshell?)

The basic syntax of Squeak can be summarized easily on a 3×5 note card. Every line of Squeak code is evaluated in exactly the same way.

- Every variable is an object. As in C++ and Java, every object is an instance of a class and has its instance variables and methods determined by that class. Unlike C++ and Java, there are no basic types that are not objects.

- All Squeak code is triggered by a message being sent to a specific object. The object replies to a message by evaluating a method of the same name. If the object does not have such a method, its parent object is checked for the method and so on until either the method is found, or an error is raised.

- All methods return a value.

- There are three types of messages.

  - unary messages, such as **3 negated**. The syntax of a unary message is <object> <messagename>.
  - binary messages, such as **a + b**. The syntax of a binary message is <object> <messagename> <object>.

> – keyword messages such as Transcript show: a. The syntax of a keyword message is <object> <messagepart>: <object>, where there can be multiple <messagepart>: <object> pairs that make up a single message.

- All code is evaluated from left to right, unary messages first, binary messages second, and keyword messages last. Parentheses are used as in other programming languages to force order of evaluation, and are frequently used to mark the boundaries of keyword messages in which that boundary might not be clear from the unparenthesized code.

- In an assignment statement, the right-hand side is evaluated, and the symbol on the left hand side is assigned the resulting value.

And that's it. Every line of Squeak code follows that exact pattern.[6]

Applying the Rules

The next thing you need to understand about Squeak's syntax rules is that there are no exceptions for things such as, say, traditional operator precedence. Operator precedence in Squeak is strictly left to right. So, for example: 2 + 3 * 6 will evaluate to 30, not 20 as you would expect in most languages. If you want it to evaluate to 20, you need 2 + (3 * 6). Most Squeakers consider this a small price to pay for the consistency and readability of Smalltalk code.

The following is an incorrect line of code for computing the length of the hypotenuse of a right triangle:[7]

    hypotenuse := 3 squared + 4 squared sqrt.

The sequence of messages evaluated in this example is as follows:

1. On the right-hand side of the equation, the interpreter evaluates the unary messages from left to right before it can evaluate the binary message +. The first unary message is 3 squared, which returns the integer object 9.

2. The second unary message is 4 squared, which returns 16.

3. At this point we have 9 + 16 sqrt, and the interpreter still has a unary message to evaluate before it can perform the addition. 16 sqrt returns 4.

4. Now the addition is performed, returning 13.

5. Hypotenuse is set to 13.

---

[6]Okay, one exception—the syntax ↑object for returning the result of a method. Alan Kay explains that this can be thought of as a message sent back to the calling object.

[7]Squeak currently uses two separate symbols for assignment—the more familiar := syntax, as well as the underscore character _, which is displayed as a left-pointing arrow (←). The two are functionally identical.

It's not uncommon to have this kind of message traffic jam in Squeak. Parentheses are the traffic cops of choice, turning the line of code into

hypotenuse := (3 squared + 4 squared) sqrt.

The sequence of messages is the same until message number 2, after which the sequence becomes as follows:

1. At this point we have (9 + 16) sqrt. The system can perform the addition, which returns 25.

2. The interpreter now has 25 sqrt, which returns 5.

3. Hypotenuse is set to 5.

Object Orientation

The object-oriented semantics of Squeak are geared toward simplicity, elegance, and flexibility, without the syntactic clutter of C++ and Java. To a programmer coming to Squeak from either of those languages, the Squeak object-oriented structures may seem to be missing features. After working with Squeak for a while, though, you are more likely to realize that the ease of working in Squeak more than makes up for the more complex and rarely used feature set of other object-oriented languages.

Creating Objects

To start, Squeak's object-oriented hierarchy allows only single inheritance. Multiple inheritance is not supported,[8] and there is no feature analogous to Java interfaces[9] or C++ templates. (The dynamic nature of ordinary Squeak objects is what templates are trying to emulate.) All classes in Squeak inherit from the class Object, which has more functionality than its Java counterpart.

To create a new class of your own, open a System Browser and select any category in the first pane. The code pane will show the following:

```
Object subclass: #NameOfClass
    instanceVariableNames: 'instVarName1 instVarName2'
    classVariableNames: 'ClassVarName1 ClassVarName2'
    poolDictionaries: ''
    category: 'Kernel—Methods'
```

---

[8]Although it's not actually hard at all to hack it into the Squeak system by modifying the Object class—it's just rarely worth the trouble.

[9]Some Smalltalk dialects do have features similar to interfaces, and it's not out of the question that Squeak will have one someday.

This is a template for class creation. All you need to do is replace each slot with your needed values. Replace Object with the expected superclass of the new class. Replace NameOfClass with the name of the new class. (However, leave the pound sign—that tells Squeak to consider the name a symbol literal rather than a variable.) By complier-enforced convention, class names begin with capital letters. Replace 'instVarName1 instVarName2' with the list of instance variables in this class, separated by spaces. Replace 'ClassVarName1 ClassVarName2' with the list of class variables. We'll create a class called Person for the rest of these examples. Change the code so that it reads

```
Object subclass: #Person
    instanceVariableNames: 'firstName lastName'
    classVariableNames: 'Population'
    poolDictionaries: "
    category: 'Tutorial'
```

When you are done, right-click in the code pane and select "accept." And just like that, you have created a new class that you can select in the System Browser. You may need to right-click in the category pane and select "update" to see the new category. There is nothing special about this code—it's just a Squeak message being sent to the class Object and creating a new subclass.

Each Squeak class defines instance variables and instance methods. Each instance, as you might expect, gets its own copy of the instance variables and can respond to the messages corresponding to the instance methods. By convention, instance variables start with lowercase letters and are mixed upper and lower case, i.e., "firstName." Any instance variable can be assigned any Squeak object as a value—there is no static typing in Squeak.

A Squeak instance variable can only be accessed from within that class or one of its subclasses. In C++ terminology, all Squeak instance variables are *protected*. (Java's protected keyword also includes access within packages—there is no similar access path in Squeak). All access to the variable from outside the class must go through accessor methods. By convention, the getter method is just the name of the variable, and the setter method is a keyword message using the name of the variable and taking one parameter. For example, to get the firstName of an instance of a class Person, you would type

```
aPerson firstName.
```

To set the variable, you would use

```
aPerson firstName: 'noel'.
```

which shows another piece of Squeak syntax—the use of single quotes around string literals.

Note that you do have to write the getter and setter methods explicitly.[10] To do that, select Person in the class pane, and select one of the elements in the method category pane. The code pane should read

```
message selector and argument names
    "comment stating purpose of message"
    | temporary variable names |
    statements
```

This is a template for method code. The name of the method and keywords goes in the first line. A comment is inserted into the double quotes. A list of temporary variables for the method goes between the pipe characters, separated by spaces, and the code itself goes after that. When you are done typing code into the code pane, right-click in that pane and select "accept." If correct, the code is compiled into the Squeak image—if not, error messages will appear in the code pane at the location of the error.

The code for the getter message looks like this

```
firstName
    ↑firstName
```

And the setter looks like this

```
firstName: aString
    firstName := aString
```

The ↑ symbol indicates a returned value. It's typed as "^." The aString in the header, and first line of the setter is the local name for the object passed as the argument. All Squeak methods return a value—if the message doesn't specify the value, it returns the object that received the message.

By the way, you don't need to go all the way back to the message template to write a new method. If you change the method name in the first line of the code pane, the method will be accepted under the new name without affecting the old method name. This can be a quick way to write a number of similar methods.

Instances and Classes

Classes, like everything else in Squeak, are objects—in this case, instances of the class **Class**. Object manipulation in Squeak is performed by sending messages to the class **Object**—for example, the creation of a subclass, as shown above.

A Squeak class creates a new instance by being passed the message new, as in

```
newPerson := Person new.
```

---

[10]There is a Squeak preference you can set that will automatically create them when called, but it's best to get in the habit of just writing them—it's easier to maintain encapsulation that way.

The new message acts very much like a default constructor in C++ or Java; it returns a new instance. By default, all the instance variables of the new instance are set to nil. The usual idiom is to create an instance method called initialize and refer to it as follows:

newPerson := Person new initialize.

Tracing the Squeak interpreter shows that the first message Person new returns a new instance of the Person class. That new instance is then sent the initialize message. The initialized instance is then assigned to newPerson.

You can create variables that belong to the class, rather to the instances, by putting class variable names in the subclass creation template. Class variable names are capitalized. Class variables behave similarly to static variables in C++ and Java. However, like Squeak instance variables, they are all protected and can only be accessed within instances of that class.

Classes can also have methods. To view and create them, select the class button in the class pane of the system browser. One use for class methods is to create constructors that take parameters, for example, the message Array with: anObject, which creates a new array and populates the first index of that array with anObject. Another use is to provide accessor methods for class variables.

Squeak has no explicit destructor methods. The Squeak garbage collector periodically removes all instances with no external references.

Inheriting the Wealth

Squeak objects inherit all the instance variables and methods of their ancestors all the way up to the class Object. Unlike C++ and Java, Squeak is completely late-binding and performs no compile-time type checking to determine if the object actually answers the message being sent. (Although you will get an error if no object anywhere in the image defines that message.) The method that is invoked from a message is based on the identity of the receiving object at run time. The flexibility of this is shown when you see a line of code that sends a message defined by a number of Objects across the hierarchy:

anObject asString.

Any Squeak object that defines (or has an ancestor which defines) the message asString can legally be assigned to anObject before this line is run. The specific asString method that is run depends on the identity of anObject. Squeak first attempts to see if there is an asString instance method in anObject's class. If yes, that method is invoked. If not, Squeak works up the hierarchy until an asString method is encountered. If the method is not encountered, then Squeak will return a doesNotUnderstand error.

To override a method in a parent class, just define a method of the same name in the child class. If you need to call the parent method to extend it, Squeak provides the pseudo-variable super, which responds to the message sent as if starting one level up on the hierarchy. To refer to the current instance itself, Squeak uses the pseudo-variable self, which can be used either to send other messages to the same object or to pass the object as a parameter in a message, analogous to C++ and Java's use of *this*. The variable self can also be used as an argument to a message, as in anotherObject doSomethingWith: self.

Another important message for the Squeak object-oriented framework is sub-classResponsibilty, which is used similarly to the C++ and Java keyword *abstract*. If you wish to declare a method in a superclass without a definition, with the intent that all subclasses will need to define it, then you create the method with the message body self subclassResponsibility. You can still create instances of the class with that method, but trying to invoke that method will result in an error.

Finding What You Need, Keeping What You Write

Most programmers coming to Squeak for the first time are used to programming environments in which the code is stored in a series of text files, one for each class or module. The transition to Squeak's image based system can be jarring—it's an entirely different way of organizing and managing code. New Squeakers frequently struggle with finding existing code, maintaining their new code, and sharing code with other programmers. Squeak has a number of features that will assist with all of these needs.

The Art of Browsing

The System Browser is where you will most likely spend the majority of your time as a Squeaker. Each of the top panes in the browser window has menu items that allow you to better find or organize code at that level of detail. This section will cover most of them—there are other menu items that have little to do with organization and navigation and will not be covered here. Many of these menu items call up windows that are cousins to the System Browser—the same idea, but organized around a different (usually smaller) structure. They all work essentially the same way, however, and code can be created or edited in any of them just as it is in the main System Browser.

Starting at the top left of the System Browser again, the category pane is by itself a structure for navigation and organization. As mentioned previously, the categories here are solely for human readability—the compiler pays no attention to them. There is no better way to get a feel for what Squeak provides than to browse the category headings. To best use that power for yourself, you should give each of your projects a separate category. It's also common to maintain a category or two of common utility code that you would use in several projects. Large projects are often broken into more than one category. Separating interface code from back end code is common.

Among the menu items available by right clicking on this pane are the following:

find class   Presents you with a dialog box where you can enter a class name or name fragment and get a list of all classes in the current image that match. Since most classes in the Squeak image have names that roughly correspond to their functionality, this can be extremely useful.

recent classes Lists the last 16 classes selected in a System Browser and allows you to go directly to the one you choose.

browse all   Gives you a System Browser cousin that has no category pane. Instead, the class pane lists all classes in the Squeak image alphabetically.

browse   Presents you a System Browser cousin that only displays classes in the category selected.

reorganize   Causes the code pane to become a series of lists corresponding to the current relationship between categories and classes. With a little judicious editing, cutting, and pasting, you can move classes around to different categories. This method is easier than editing each class if you are going to change several classes at once.

update   Updates the System Browser to take notice of category additions or edits made in other System Browsers.

The class pane has quite a few menu items to help you find related classes and methods:

browse class   Opens a new System Browser cousin with just the method categories and methods of the selected class.

browse full   Opens a new System Browser, with the selected class selected.

hierarchy   Puts, in the code pane, a text representation of the object hierarchy containing the selected class.

spawn hierarchy   Opens a new browser window. The class pane of this window includes the object hierarchy containing the selected class.

spawn protocol   Opens a new browser window with only one pane on top that contains the methods of this class in alphabetical order.

inst var refs   Gives you a menu of instance variables in this class. Selecting one returns a browser with all methods in the class which use that instance variable.

inst var defs	Gives menu as above, but returns all methods in the class which define (assign a value to) that instance variable.
class var refs	Displays menu as "inst var refs..." but with class variables.
class vars	Shows an inspector window that allows you to see the current values of all class variables of the selected class.
class refs	Opens a browser with a list of all methods that explicitly reference (usually by creating instances of) the selected class.
unsent methods	Generates a menu of all methods in the current class that are never sent by any object anywhere in the current image.
find method	Generates a menu of the methods of the current class. Selecting an item in that menu takes the current browser to that method.

The method category pane has relatively few menu items for navigation. Like the class category pane, it is not used by the compiler and interpreter. You should take advantage of it, however, to help organize classes that have multiple methods. Perusing the Squeak image, you will see that certain category names are used by convention, including initialize (or initialize-release), adding, accessing, testing, converting, and printing. Using category names that are already enshrined in the image will make it easier for others to read and use your code.

browse	Opens a code browser with all the methods in the selected category.
reorganize	Allows you to use text editing to organize the methods into categories. Similar to the item in the class category pane.
alphabetize	Alphabetizes the categories in the pane.
remove empty	Removes categories in the pane that have no methods.

The code pane has a very large menu attached to it. (The bottom entry "more..." opens a second page of the menu.) Many of these items are duplicates of items in the category pane, and I'm not going to repeat those.

senders of...	Returns a code browser with a list of all methods in the image that send the selected message. However, not all of these methods are necessarily sending it to this class all the time—if you are searching on a common message such as add: it's likely that most of the messages are not aimed at the class you are in—but they potentially could be.

implementers of. . .	Returns a code browser with a list of every method in the image that implements the same message in other classes. This is where you would find all the other **add:** messages in the image.
method inheritance	Walks up the object hierarchy by returning a browser that shows you all the superclasses of this object that also define this message.
versions	Shows you a browser of the previous versions of this method. The Squeak change facility keeps track of every accepted version of a method until specifically purged.
implementers of sent messages	Shows you every method of class that implements any message sent in the selected method. In other words, it's anyplace in the image that could be called from this code. Note that it does not take into account any information in the code about what classes are expected—it displays everything. This item is otherwise known as "what code can I break."
change sets with this method	Lists all change sets currently being maintained in the image that contain this method.
inspect instances	Gives you an inspector window with all instances of the selected class currently living in the image.
inspect subinstances	Is similar to inspect instances, but also includes instances of subclasses of the selected class.

Saving, Loading and Sharing

The easiest mechanism for saving Squeak code is merely to continuously save the image. Using the image as your code repository has many advantages. It stores the values of global and class variables, stores all previous versions, and requires no particular attention to detail beyond remembering to save every time you leave Squeak.

Unfortunately, there are a few drawbacks to relying on images. Although it doesn't happen often, it's possible that an image can become corrupted. Although the '.changes' file means you don't actually lose anything, recovering from an image crash can be a pain. Image files are rather large, and maintaining regular backups will eat up space more quickly than strictly necessary. Also, it's difficult to share code in an image file with another programmer who wants to install the code in their image.

Squeak provides two related mechanisms for saving code as text for easy backup and sharing. The simpler mechanism is called a *file out*. To create a file out, right-click on any of the top panes of the System Browser or related code browser and select the "file out" menu option. A file is created in your Squeak directory containing the contents of the selected category, class, method category, or method, depending on what pane you started in. You do not get a dialog to choose the name—the name of the selected item is used (for methods and method categories, it's the name of the class followed by the name of the method or category). The extension on file outs is ".st." The file is text and is more or less human readable—it includes some delimiter characters to allow the compiler to read the file back in.

To load a file out into your Squeak image, you open a file list by selecting "open" from the main World Menu and then selecting "file list." A file list lets you browse your system's hard drive and has three panes. See Figure 1.6. The top-right pane contains a list of the files and subdirectories in the directory being browsed. The top-left pane has the file tree down to the current directory, and the bottom pane shows the contents of the current file. To file in a ".st" file, browse to it so that the contents of the file are showing in the bottom pane, right-click, and select "file it in" from the menu. Ordinarily, you'll see a progress bar. You may also see some warnings in a Transcript window, if classes are loaded with dependencies to classes that have not yet been loaded. Don't worry—assuming all the classes are in the file out at all, it will all be fine as soon as everything loads. After filing in the ".st" file, do an update on the category pane of a System Browser. You will see that the new code has been loaded into the image.

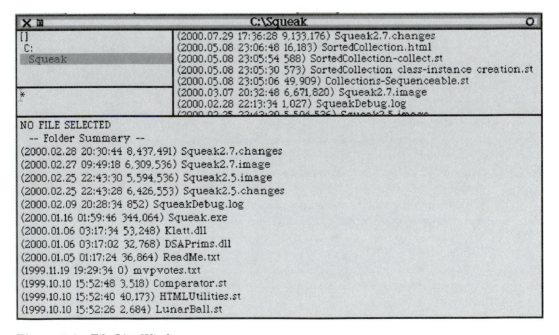

Figure 1.6 File List Window

File outs are limited, however, to only saving entire categories or classes and only one per file. To work around that limitation, you can use a change set. Every change you make to the Squeak image is stored in one or more change sets, and these sets can be saved as text and loaded just like file outs (only with a ".cs" extension). So, any combination of changes you have made at any time to the current image can be combined into a change set, saved, and shared.

This is easily said, but you do have to manage the change sets a little bit to make sure the right changes are in the set you want. The easiest way to do this is to create a Squeak project. By default, all changes made inside a project are stored to a change set of the same name. So all the changes in a project can be saved together, which is often good enough to distribute code.

For a more targeted change set, you can use a change sorter. Change sorters allow you to see the contents of change sets and to modify them. You create a change sorter from the World Menu open command or from the World Menu changes submenu, and they come in two flavors, Simple and Dual.

A simple change sorter (Figure 1.7) shows you all the change sets in the system—that's the top-left pane. The top-right pane is a list of all classes that have changes in the selected change set. The middle pane contains a list of methods in the selected class that are in the change set (not necessarily a list of all methods in the class). The bottom pane shows the code of the selected method, and you can edit and accept code within it.

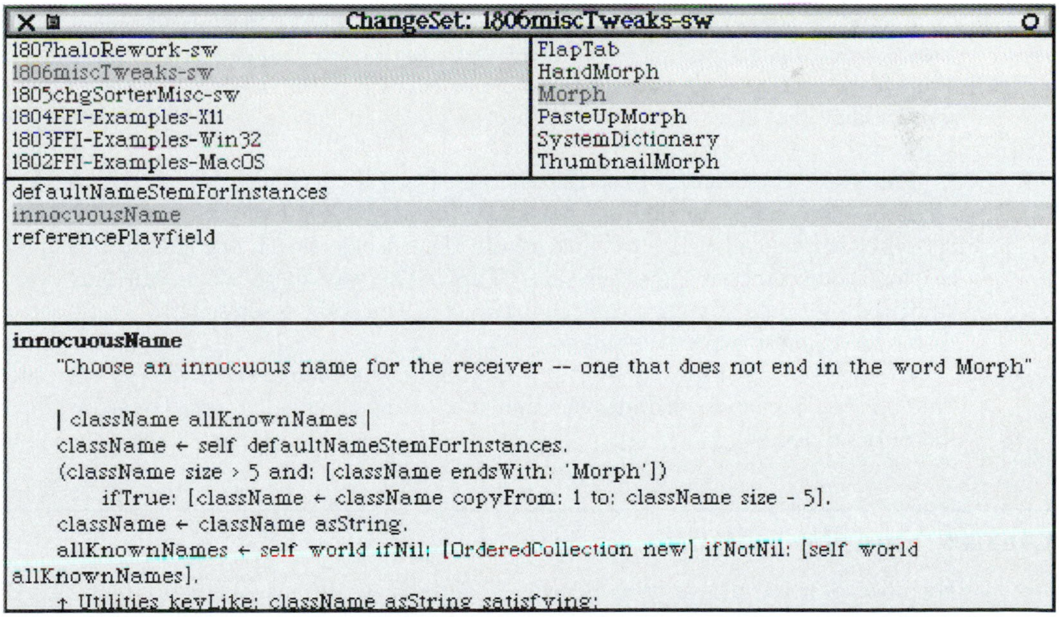

Figure 1.7 Simple Change Sorter

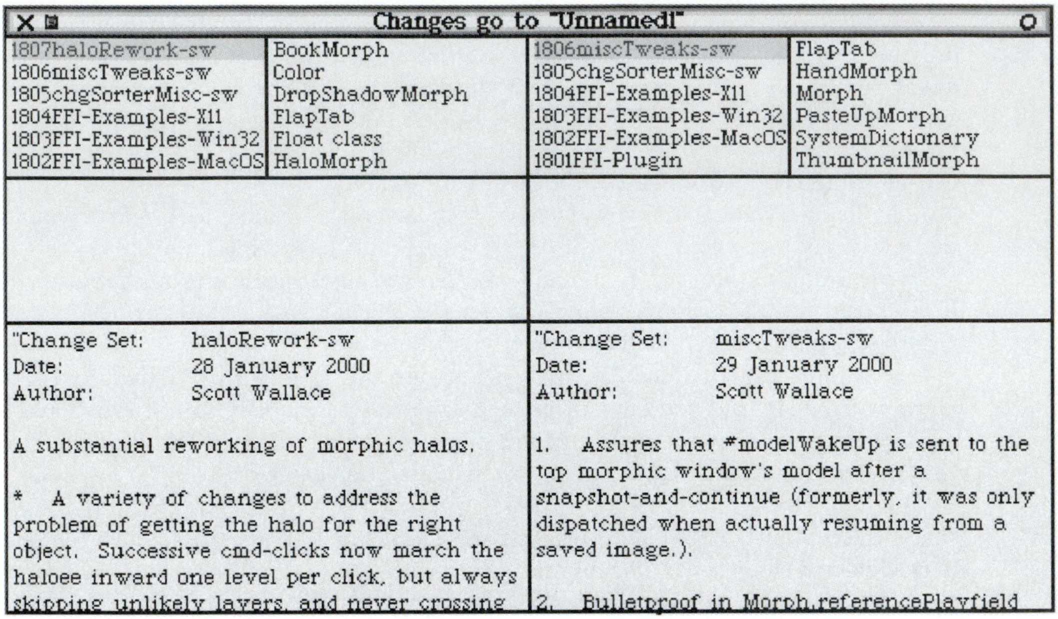

X ▣	Changes go to "Unnamed1"		○
1807haloRework-sw 1806miscTweaks-sw 1805chgSorterMisc-sw 1804FFI-Examples-X11 1803FFI-Examples-Win32 1802FFI-Examples-MacOS	BookMorph Color DropShadowMorph FlapTab Float class HaloMorph	1806miscTweaks-sw 1805chgSorterMisc-sw 1804FFI-Examples-X11 1803FFI-Examples-Win32 1802FFI-Examples-MacOS 1801FFI-Plugin	FlapTab HandMorph Morph PasteUpMorph SystemDictionary ThumbnailMorph

"Change Set: haloRework-sw
Date: 28 January 2000
Author: Scott Wallace

A substantial reworking of morphic halos.

*   A variety of changes to address the problem of getting the halo for the right object. Successive cmd-clicks now march the haloee inward one level per click, but always skipping unlikely layers, and never crossing

"Change Set: miscTweaks-sw
Date: 29 January 2000
Author: Scott Wallace

1.   Assures that #modelWakeUp is sent to the top morphic window's model after a snapshot-and-continue (formerly, it was only dispatched when actually resuming from a saved image.).

2.   Bulletproof in Morph.referencePlayfield

Figure 1.8 Dual Change Sorter

From the top-left pane, you can right-click and select "new change set..." to create a new change set, select it, right-click, and select "make changes go to me." From that point on, all changes in that project will go to that change set. This is particularly nice if you know you are only going to have a few changes that you want saved or distributed.

For even more control over the change set, a dual change sorter (Figure 1.8) looks like two simple change sorters glued together. You can create a new change set on either side, and direct changes from the selected set on one side to be copied to the selected set on the other side. This is the way to go when you only want to distribute some of your recent changes, or if you want to distribute a number of disparate changes across the image.

Change sets are filed out by right-clicking on the change set pane and selecting "file out." They are loaded into the image by using the file list, exactly as ordinary file outs are loaded.

Classes You Should Know

By now, you are probably wondering exactly how all this plays out in terms of things that you actually do during your day-to-day existence as a programmer. There are several Squeak classes that you should be acquainted with to support common programming structures.

Building with Blocks

Nearly all of Squeak's structured programming constructs depend on a class called BlockContext, which has no direct analogue in C++ or Java. A BlockContext (usually just called a block) is a lump of compiled Smalltalk code that can be passed to or returned from methods just like any other object. The block can then be executed at any time.

You create a block by enclosing the code to be blocked inside brackets. For example, type the following into a workspace:

```
[2 + 3]
```

Performing a printIt on that line of code gives you: [] in UndefinedObject>>DoIt, which mostly means that you have an unevaluated BlockContext. In order to get the block to do anything you have to pass it the value message:

```
[2 + 3] value
```

Performing a printIt on that line of code gives you "5." You can also assign the block to an object:

```
a := [2 + 3].
a value.
```

This will also evaluate to "5."

Blocks can also have variables with scope local to the block, which you create like so:[11]

```
[ :a :b | a + b ]
```

and evaluate by passing the message value: with parameters. For example,

```
[ :a :b | a + b ] value: 2 value: 3
```

will also evaluate to "5."

Currently in the Squeak image you can have up to four value: in a row. If you have more temporaries than that, you can (a) seriously consider refactoring, (b) add the message you want, or (c) use valueWithArguments: anArray.

Big deal, right? I mean, we just came up with a really convoluted way of doing things that we could already do anyway. The block concept is very powerful, however, and allows Squeak objects to have much more flexible behavior than their C++ or Java counterparts.

---

[11] It's actually a long-standing issue in the Squeak implementation that the scope of block variable is actually larger than the block itself. However, for reasons of good programming practice and compatibility with future versions of Squeak, you should never depend on a block variable being available outside the block.

Consider, for example, the problem of maintaining a sorted list. Typically this is managed by comparing new objects in the list to the existing objects. In Java 1.1 and in most C++ implementation, you have to roll this functionality on your own. In Java 1.2, which partially replicates the Smalltalk collection classes, this can be accomplished by having your class implement the comparable interface and adding a new method to every class you want sorted. Or you can mess with inner classes. Forget about easily sorting objects of different classes.

In Squeak, as we will see in more detail, the same functionality is accomplished quite easily in the class SortedCollection by the simple application of a block. SortedCollection has as an instance variable called sortBlock that you can see by looking at the class method SortedCollection>>new defaults to [:x :y | x <= y]. This deftly handles any object that implements the <= method. If you want to sort on some more complex set of values, you just send a sortBlock: message to your collection and pass it any complicated block that you want. (Well, it does have to have the two temporary variables.)

Blocks are commonly used to provide "pluggable" behavior to classes, where as a class might be called upon to provide the same kind of behavior in many different contexts. As we'll see below, control structures such as loops and conditionals are prime examples—an if statement always does the same thing structurally, even though the specific code being executed changes each time. You can also easily create your own customized control structures that take blocks as arguments.

Conditionals, Loops, and Other Programmer Type Things

Structured constructs such as conditionals and loops show off the elegance of Squeak's pure object-oriented system. A standard if/then statement is handled in Squeak using the ifTrue:ifFalse message, such as:

```
( a = b )
    ifTrue: [ Transcript show: 'equal' ]
    ifFalse: [ Transcript show: 'not equal' ].
```

The parameters passed to the ifTrue: and ifFalse: keywords are blocks, and as discussed in the previous section they can either be typed out as shown above or be variables previously set to block values. When the message is evaluated, one block or the other is evaluated based on the value of the Boolean expression.

You may have noticed some hand waving in the previous sentence. After all, I had made a point of saying that everything in Squeak is a message sent to an object, and there are no syntactic special forms. What object, then, receives the ifTrue:ifFalse: message?

Tracing out the receiver of the message shows that the = message is sent to the object a. The = message returns either true or false, which means that the message is actually being sent to either **true** or **false**. And, if you point your System Browser at the "Kernel—Objects" category, you'll see a class called **False** and a class called **True**. Each of these classes is a *Singleton,* meaning that they each have only one instance object—**false** and **true** respectively. (If I haven't mentioned that Squeak is case-sensitive so far, now would be a good time to squeeze that in—capital "T" True is the class, lowercase "t" true is the value.) Further browsing in the **True** class, shows that **True≫ifTrue:ifFalse:** is simply evaluated as follows:

    ifTrue: trueAlternativeBlock ifFalse: falseAlternativeBlock
        ↑trueAlternativeBlock value

In other words, to evaluate if-then statements, Squeak depends on the principles of object and message dispatch to control which branch is chosen.[12]

    False≫ifTrue:ifFalse: is the exact same one-liner, except that it is the **falseAlternativeBlock** that is sent the variable message. The messages **ifFalse:ifTrue**, **ifTrue:**, and **ifFalse:** are also available and are implemented analogously.

    Looping constructs in Squeak start similarly, with the **whileTrue:** and **whileFalse:** messages. They are, as you would expect, Squeak's while loop messages. There is, however, one significant "gotcha" compared to the if messages discussed above. Unlike the if messages, which are sent to Boolean objects, the while messages are sent to blocks that return Booleans, such as:

    [x < 3] whileTrue: [x := x + 1].

    There is a reason for this oddity, only I had to stare at my Squeak screen for a few minutes before I remembered what it was. The block allows the receiver of the message to be re-evaluated before each potential loop iteration, whereas a static **Boolean** object would not be re-evaluated. The argument block of the **whileTrue:** in this case, [x := x + 1], is evaluated every time through the loop, for as long as the receiver block continues to evaluate to true.

    Squeak has two mechanisms that give for loop functionality. The simplest is the **timesRepeat: aBlock** message which is sent to an Integer:

    4 timesRepeat: [Transcript print: 'Hi'].

    The block is repeated the value of the integer times. The times repeat construct does not give you access to the index variable within the block. To do that, you need the **to:do:** message, which looks like this.

    1 to: 4 do: [:index | index + 1]

---

[12]In practice, actually, the Squeak compiler usually inlines **Boolean** calls into the method body for performance purposes.

The to:do: message is sent to any integer[13] and is defined thusly in the Squeak image (although, usually compiled inline in practice).

```
to: stop do: aBlock
    |nextValue |
    nextValue := self.
    [nextValue <= stop]
        whileTrue:
            [aBlock value: nextValue.
             nextValue := nextValue + 1]
```

We've already discussed all the Squeak constructs in this code. The first line creates a temporary value, which is then set to self—in this case the number that receives the message (1 in the above call). Line 3 defines the block that is the loop condition, while line 4 sets up the loop itself. Inside the loop, the argument block [:index | index + 1] is sent the value: message with the index of that pass through the loop, and then the counter is incremented. This means that the argument block must have exactly one temporary variable defined to accept the index value.

Squeak also offers the to:by:do: message, which allows you to increment (or decrement) by integers other than one (but not zero). Given the definition of to:do: it shouldn't be hard to figure out how to:by:do: is written—or you could just look it up in the **Number** class.

Collecting Objects

Just about every programming language created since about 1945 has included some mechanism for manipulating a group of variables, most commonly by using a numerically indexed array of values. Few languages, however, offer as rich and varied a set of collection options as Smalltalk. Of all the features of Smalltalk, the collection classes are the ones that I most frequently miss when I'm programming in other languages—it's only in recent years that other languages have even come close to the depth of the Smalltalk collection hierarchy.

In Squeak, the collection classes are defined in the seven categories prefixed with "Collection," and yes, that's seven categories, not seven classes. In fact, it's 65 classes in Squeak 2.7, if I'm counting right (admittedly some of them are support classes, not actually collections). Luckily, we only need to go through a few of them in order to get the general idea. The majority of your collection class use in Squeak will probably be in one of the concrete classes discussed in this section.

Usually, I find it easier to discuss the Squeak collection classes by starting at the top of the hierarchy—the abstract class **Collection**—and discussing the common

---

[13]Technically the message can be sent to any number—it's defined in the **Number** superclass of all numbers. However, it's really only meaningful for integers. The general behavior of these kinds of intervals for non-integers was a raging topic of debate on the Squeak mailing list a few months back.

features of all Squeak collections, then moving to the concrete classes and discussing their specific functionality. If you find the next few paragraphs a little too abstract, it might be helpful to skip down a little bit to the discussion of a specific collection, then come back.

A Squeak collection is... well, there's no getting around the word collection... a Squeak collection is a collection of Squeak objects. Collections are not restricted as to the type or class of Squeak objects that they can contain and, unlike arrays in many other programming languages, are not restricted to holding only objects of a single class at a time. Nor are you required to specify the class of objects to be contained when defining or using the collection.[14]

The class Collection, which is abstract, defines the general protocol for all collections. Collection defines many messages that can be sent to any of the collection subclasses. Some of the most common, important, or interesting include size, which returns the number of elements in the collection. The method isEmpty, returns true or false based on whether there are any elements in the collection. The message includes: anObject returns true or false based on whether the argument is included in the collection. Collections can be converted from one type to another by using a method of the form asSortedCollection or asSet.

The most useful features of the collection class are the enumeration classes that perform actions on each element of the collection. The general form is exemplified by the do: aBlock message, which takes as an argument a single variable block and sends each individual element in the collection to the block. do: returns the original collection, so it is usually called for its side effects. For example, size is defined as

```
size
    | tally |
    tally := 0.
    self do: [:each | tally := tally + 1].
    ↑tally
```

This message simply runs a counter and increments it once for every element in the collection. Notice that in this case, although the block takes an argument, the argument is not used. It is needed, however, because the implementations of do: will send the one argument value: message to the block.

If you want to return a changed list, then you can use the collect: aBlock message. Like do:, it takes a one argument block and applies it to each element. However, rather than returning the original collection, it returns the new collection formed by the result of each block application in order. You can also filter a list using select: aBlock, which takes a one argument block and returns a collection containing all the elements for which the block evaluates to true. And most fun of all, there is inject: thisValue into: binaryBlock. It's actually easier to display the code for inject:into:

---

[14]And having made that bold statement, I admit in the fine print that, while it's true for most collections, certain collections do limit themselves to specific classes for performance reasons or for other logical reasons. Strings, for example, are strictly collections of characters.

then it is to describe it, so here goes.[15] (I'll give examples of inject:into: and the other enumeration methods in a moment.)

```
inject: thisValue into: binaryBlock
    | nextValue |
    nextValue := thisValue.
    self do: [:each |
        nextValue := binaryBlock value: nextValue value: each].
    ↑nextValue
```

This is useful, really, and you'll see how in just a moment.

The specific subclass of Collection that is most similar to what you have likely done before is Array. Arrays in Squeak work quite similarly to arrays in other programming languages. They have a fixed size, although in Squeak that size is set at run time and not at compile time. Like other Squeak collections, any array can have any kind of objects as components.

Arrays are created in a variety of ways. Literal arrays are created with a hash sign and parentheses: #(1 2 3) is a three element array. They can also be created using the class method with: and its variants. Array with: 1 with: 2 with: 3 creates the same three-element array. So, as promised, some enumeration examples are

$$\#(1\ 2\ 3)\ \text{collect: [:each | each squared]} \qquad \Rightarrow (1\ 4\ 9)$$

$$\#(1\ 2\ 3)\ \text{select: [:each | each even]} \qquad \Rightarrow (2)$$

$$\#(1\ 2\ 3)\ \text{inject: 0 into: [:subTotal :next | subTotal + next]} \Rightarrow 6$$

The inject one is the trickiest. Looking at the implementation of inject:into: above, we can see that on the first pass through the loop, the block is sent the arguments 0 and 1. It sums them and returns 1. Next time through, the arguments are the running total 1 and the next list element 2, returning 3. Finally, the arguments are 3 and 3, returning 6. It sums the collection.

Arrays are accessed using the at: message: #(1 2 3) at: 2 returns 2. This points out a large difference between Squeak arrays and C and Java—the first element of a Squeak array has the index 1, not the index 0. Array indices are set using the at: put: message: #(1 2 3) at: 2 put: 4 returns #(1 4 3). There are also handy messages like first and last, that return what they say they return.

Arrays are actually only one of the subclasses of Collection that also inherits from SequenceableCollection—essentially any collection in which the elements have a sequence, and thus integer indices. Another useful subclass of SequenceableCollection is OrderedCollection, which is an array without the fixed size restriction. In addition to the array access messages, an OrderedCollection also responds to add:, which adds an object to the end of the collection, and addFirst:, which adds one to the

---

[15]Okay, if you do want it explained, here's the method comment, "Accumulate a running value associated with evaluating the argument, binaryBlock, with the current value of the argument, thisValue, and the receiver as block arguments."

beginning. The combination makes OrderedCollection useful for mimicking stacks or queues. And, as mentioned in the section on blocks, there is SortedCollection, which maintains the sequence in sorted order based on a comparison block. Unlike Array and OrderedCollection, SortedCollection does not respond to the message at: put:, since the sorted collection insists on controlling where in the sequence a new member belongs.

The sequenceable collection that you are likely to use most often, however, is String, which is defined as an ArrayedCollection of characters. String literals are enclosed in single quotes. (Double quotes are reserved for comments.) Strings in Squeak are mutable in content, but not in length, and can be changed using the same basic methods discussed for arrays. Strings are concatenated using the comma (,) operator—a method that actually also works for all sequenceable collections, should you have need of it. In addition to the existing methods for arrays, the String class has quite a few utility methods, including, but hardly limited to, methods for finding substrings and characters, and comparison methods, including methods for comparing the beginning and end of strings, conversions to date, number, HTML, and Postscript, correction against a dictionary, enumeration over the lines of the string, and so on. A complete listing is obviously beyond the scope of this chapter, but most of the methods are short and well commented—digging through them is a good way to get a handle on some simple, useful Squeak code. Before you try to write some fancy utility on strings, take a look here, since there's a good chance that somebody has beaten you to it.

The ordered collections are similar to what you are probably used to from other programming collections; however, the unordered collections don't have related functionality in most languages. The simplest of these is Bag. Bag is about as simple as a collection gets. It stores anything you put in it, as many times as you put it in, in no particular order.[16] Items are added to the bag using the add: anObject message and are retrieved using... Well, items in a bag aren't usually retrieved the way that items in an array are—bags have no order and thus no index to grab the item. However, you do have access to the full power of the enumeration methods such as do: and select:.

If you come from a C background, you are probably wondering why you would ever use a bag. Often, however, the enumeration routines are everything you need in a collection—think of how many times you create an array and only access it in the context of looping through it. (And if you do need it sorted, there's always asSortedCollection.) In addition, using a bag when you don't need the indexes leads to time and space efficiencies—owing to the implementation of bags, testing for inclusion is particularly fast, compared with arrays. Perhaps more importantly, it provide a comment on the programmer's intentions and the expected use of the collection.

---

[16]In practice, each element of a Bag is only stored once, with a dictionary keeping track of how many times it's in the bag—it's more space efficient.

More structured than the Bag is Set, which mimics a mathematical set—an unordered collection of objects, each of which appears exactly once. Set enforces this by overwriting the add: anObject message to only add the new item if it does not already exist in the set. Converting a collection to a set using asSet and then converting it back can be a useful mechanism for removing duplicates from a collection.

The most useful unordered collection is Dictionary. A dictionary is a collection of associations—a key and a value. Both the key and the value can be any Squeak object. The keys are unique within a specific dictionary, while the values need not be. Objects are placed in the dictionary using at: anObject put: anObject and are retrieved using at: anObject. Therefore

```
sample := Dictionary new.
sample at: 'abc' put: 123.
sample at: 'abc'
```

The last line will return 123. A subsequent at:put: call to sample with 'abc' as the key will replace the 123 value with the new value. You may be familiar with this kind of functionality through Java Hashtables (without, of course, having to typecast everything) or Perl associative arrays (which are limited to string keys only).

Dictionary objects have additional enumeration functions—the standard do: function enumerates over the values in the dictionary, but there are also keysDo:, which takes a one-element block and enumerates over the keys in the dictionary, and keysAndValuesDo:, which takes a two-element block and enumerates over the set of keys and values. The key is the first argument to the block, and the value is the second. There is also associationsDo:, which takes a one argument block and applies it to all the association objects in the dictionary. There are also functions for testing and removing keys that are similar to the existing ones for handling values in other collections.

You Should Also Know the Debugger...

Despite the myriad of tools Squeak has to help you in your programming, it is nevertheless inevitable that you will have the occasional bug or two in your code as you write it. In order to help you find your way through that bug, here is a brief introduction to the Squeak debugger.

The debugger, in addition to being invoked by errors in the code, can also be invoked at any point in the code by including the message self halt.[17] In order to show a typical use of the debugger, set up an example using the person class defined above. (This example assumes you have getter and setter messages set for both the firstName and lastName instance variables.)

---

[17]Remember, though, that everything in Squeak is an Object, including errors. Both user defined halt messages (class Halt) and inadvertent MessageNotUnderstood errors share the same superclass and invoke the debugger through the same entry point.

Let's define the following method to display a person's full name. This method should concatenate three strings, the first name of the person, a space, and the last name of the person.

fullName
    ↑firstName , ' ' , lastName

Unfortunately, I seem to have forgotten the commas between the space and the last name—a potential syntax error. Let's see what happens if the code is evaluated. In the workspace, type

```
a := Person new.
a firstName: 'Noel'.
a lastName: 'Rappin'.
a fullName
```

Now, select and doIt for the entire chunk. You should get a message like the one in Figure 1.9.

The error message box describes the error and provides a stack trace of all the messages leading to the error. It offers the following three options:

- Proceed: Just keep going as though the halt had never been called. Usually only useful after a programmer placed halt.

- Abandon: Stops the message processing at that point.

- Debug: Opens the debugger window.

The debugger window (Figure 1.10) allows you to track the behavior of your errant program to a fine level of detail. The top pane of the window provides a stack trace, starting from the beginning of execution and ending in the message that actually invoked the error. Note, that as in this example, the top message Object≫ doesNotUnderstand: is not the message with the actual error, rather, it's the message invoked by Squeak in response to the condition of asking an object to reply to a message that is not defined. It's not unusual to have to scroll down through one or two messages to reach the method that actually contains the defect. Right-clicking on the top pane gives you a menu that has both instructions for the debugger, such as step forward one message, and also some of the method search functionality that is in the method pane of the system browser.

Figure 1.9 Error Message Box

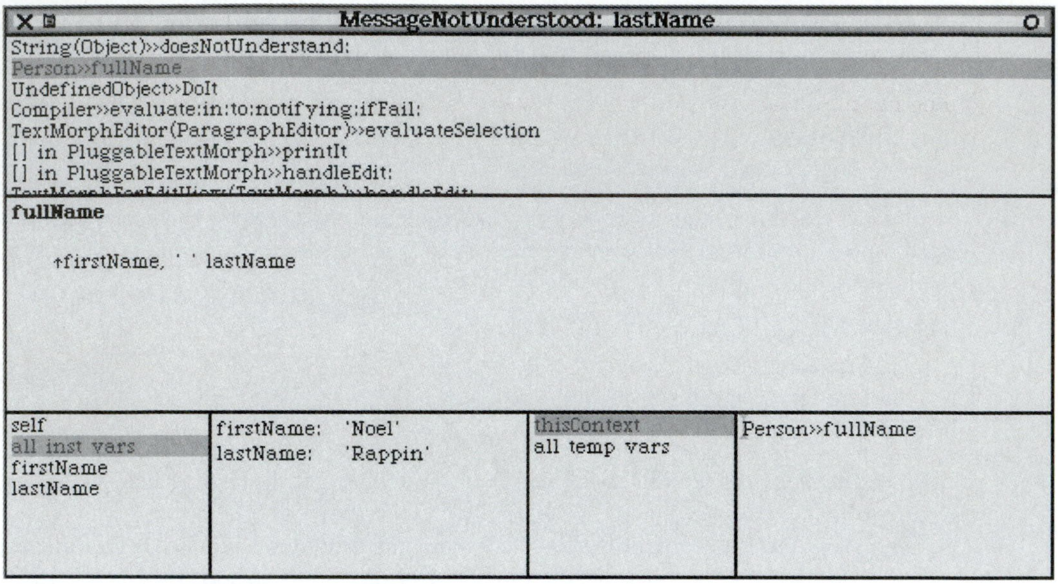

```
MessageNotUnderstood: lastName
String(Object)>>doesNotUnderstand:
Person>>fullName
UndefinedObject>>DoIt
Compiler>>evaluate:in:to:notifying:ifFail:
TextMorphEditor(ParagraphEditor)>>evaluateSelection
[] in PluggableTextMorph>>printIt
[] in PluggableTextMorph>>handleEdit:
```

fullName

    ↑firstName, ' ' lastName

self	firstName: 'Noel'	thisContext	Person>>fullName
all inst vars	lastName: 'Rappin'	all temp vars	
firstName			
lastName			

Figure 1.10   Squeak Debugger

The middle pane is an ordinary code editor. The last message to begin evaluation is highlighted. Right-clicking on this pane gives you everything you would expect in a code editor, including the ability to edit and accept code right in the debugger (and then, of course, continue onward as if nothing had ever gone wrong).

The bottom pane is split in half. The left half contains a mini-inspector window for the object that is executing the message in the pane (in other words, the object returned by evaluating self inside that message). The top two entries are always "self" and "all inst vars" followed by a list of all instance variables in that object. Selecting one of the items in the list shows its value in the next pane. Right-clicking on one of them opens a menu with many of the search functions we have seen before and the opportunity to open a full blown inspector window on the selected object.

The right half of the pane contains a similar list, but for the context of the message send itself, and the values of any variables temporary to the method. In this case, there are none, so all we see are the entries for "thisContext," and "all temp vars." Again, you have the opportunity to open full inspector windows on any of the objects listed.

Looking at the values in Object>>doesNotUnderstand:, you can see that in that context self is "—a string containing only a space, and the message is a Message with selector: lastName and arguments: (). In other words, without the comma, Squeak is evaluating the code: "lastName as (what else) a message send. In this case the string "doesn't have a message called lastName, triggering the error.

For More Information. . .

The main Squeak web site at `http://www.squeak.org` is relatively small, but contains pointers to all the current versions in all operating systems currently supported and information about the Squeak mailing list. Much of the other information on the site is not updated frequently.

The Squeak Swiki at `http://minnow.cc.gatech.edu/squeak` is updated frequently, however. The Swiki is a communal, editable web site, maintained by the Squeak community and powered by Squeak—you'll read about it later in this book. The Swiki has all kinds of useful information posted by Squeakers.

To get on the Squeak mailing list, send an email message to `squeak-request@cs.uiuc.edu` with a subject of "Subscribe." The Squeak mailing list runs at about 50 messages per day, and is archived at `http://macos.tuwien.ac.at:9009/Server.home` and `http://www.egroups.com/list/squeak/`. Topics of discussion on the list vary widely from the newest of newbie questions, to the arcane details of the virtual machine, to Squeak Central messages about the future of Squeak.

A very useful quick reference of Squeak, containing full lists of menus, keyboard shortcuts, and documentation of key classes, is available on-line at `http://www.mucow.com/squeak-qref.html`.

Several Squeak specialties, including the Personal Web Server and Siren, maintain their own mailing lists. More information about these is available on the Swiki.

Updates to the main Squeak image are available from within Squeak, assuming you have an internet connection. Select help from the World Menu, then select "update code from server." A series of change sets will be loaded onto your system. (This will likely take several minutes.) These changes contain enhancements and bug fixes that have been added to the core image by Squeak Central. (Many of them appear on the Squeak mailing list first.) Announcements of new updates are made to the Squeak mailing list. Note that updates only affect the image itself, changes to the Virtual Machine must be downloaded separately.

Happy Squeaking!

Noel Rappin is a Principal Software Engineer at Openwave, where he works on developer tools and training. He has a Ph.D. from the Georgia Institute of Technology, where he worked on educational technology and user-interface design.

2

An Introduction to Morphic: The Squeak User Interface Framework

John Maloney
Walt Disney Imagineering R&D

Introduction

Morphic is a user-interface framework that makes it easy and fun to build lively interactive user interfaces. Morphic handles most of the drudgery of display updating, event dispatching, drag and drop, animation, and automatic layout, thus freeing the programmer to focus on design instead of mechanics. Some user interface frameworks require a lot of boilerplate code to do even simple things. In morphic, a little code goes a long way, and there is hardly any wasted effort.

Morphic facilitates building user interfaces at many levels. At its most basic level, morphic makes it easy to create custom widgets. For example, a math teacher might create a morph that continuously shows the x and y components of a vector as the head of the vector is dragged around (Figure 2.1). To try this for yourself, evaluate HeadingMorph new openInWorld in a workspace.

The HeadingMorph widget can be implemented in just five methods: two for display, two for mouse input, and one for initialization. (The version in the Squeak image includes five additional methods that are not essential.) The process of creating a new morph is easy, because the different aspects of its behavior—its appearance, its response to user inputs, its menu, its drag and drop behavior, and so forth—can be added one at a time. Since the class Morph implements reasonable defaults for every aspect of morph behavior, one can start with an empty subclass of Morph and extend its behavior incrementally, testing along the way.

At another level, one can work by assembling morphs from the existing library, perhaps using an AlignmentMorph or SystemWindow to arrange them into a single tidy package. Most of the tools of the Squeak programming environment are built

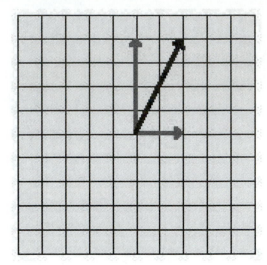

Figure 2.1 HeadingMorph, a custom widget for showing the x and y components of a vector. This morph can be implemented in just five methods.

by assembling just a few elements—scrolling lists and text editors—into multi-paned windows in a manner similar to the way such tools were created in the old Smalltalk Model-View-Controller framework. Another example is ScorePlayerMorph (Figure 2.2), which consists of some sliders, buttons, and strings glued together with AlignmentMorphs. In all these cases, tools are created by assembling instances of pre-existing morph classes. Typically, the component morphs are assembled by the initialization code of the top-level morph. One could imagine constructing this kind of tool graphically by dragging and dropping components from a library. Indeed, morphic was designed with that in mind, but the environmental support needed for this style of tool construction is currently incomplete.

At a more ambitious level, morphic can be used to create viewers and editors for all sorts of information. Examples include SpectrumAnalyzerMorph, which shows a time-varying frequency spectrum of a sound signal (in real time, on a reasonably fast computer), and PianoRollMorph, a graphical representation of a musical score that scrolls as the music plays (Figure 2.3). The relative ease with which such viewers and editors can be created is one of the things that sets morphic apart.

At the final level, the Squeak windowing system is itself built using morphic. An experienced morphic programmer could replace all the familiar windows, scroll bars, menus, flaps, and dialogs of Squeak's windowing system with an entirely new look and feel. Similarly, one could replace the window system with a custom user interface for a dedicated application such as a game or a personal information manager. In short, morphic was designed to support the full range of user interface construction activities, from assembling pre-existing widgets to replacing the window system.

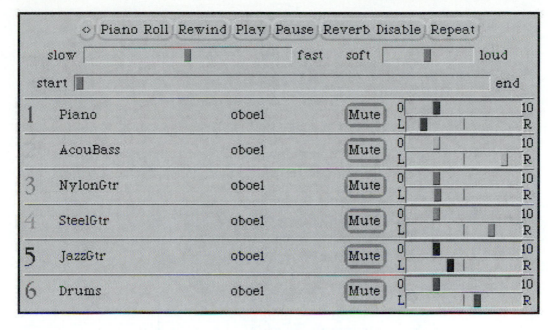

Figure 2.2   A ScorePlayerMorph, a composite morph assembled from sliders, buttons, strings, and pop-up menu widgets using AlignmentMorphs.

Morphic has two faces. The obvious one is the look and feel of the Squeak development environment itself. This is the face it presents to the user. This chapter focuses on the hidden face of morphic: the one that it presents to the morphic programmer. The first part of this chapter explains the key concepts of morphic from a practical standpoint and works through several examples. The second part describes the deeper principles that guided its design.

Once the concepts and principles underlying morphic are understood, it becomes easy to create custom widgets, tools, viewers, and editors in morphic—or perhaps even an entirely new windowing system.

Morphs

The central abstraction of morphic is the graphical object or *morph*. Morphic takes its name from the Greek word for "shape" or "form." The reader may have come across the word "morph" in other contexts, where it is used as a verb meaning "to change shape or form over time." Clearly, both uses of the word "morph" stem from the same Greek root, and although there may be a moment of confusion, the difference between the noun and verb forms of the word quickly becomes clear.

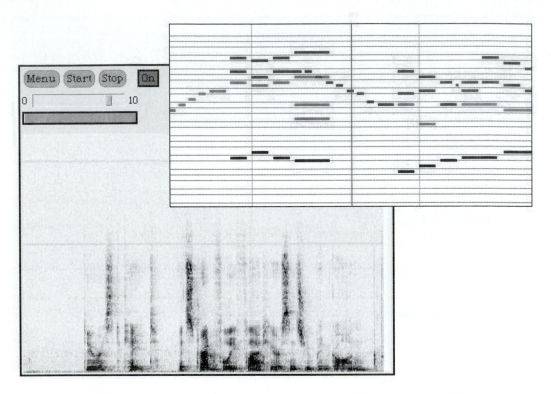

Figure 2.3 A SpectrumAnalyzerMorph and a PianoRollMorph. These viewers go beyond text by presenting dynamic graphical displays of domain-specific data such as sound spectra or a musical score. The PianoRollMorph is a simple editor as well as a viewer.

A morph has a visual representation that creates the illusion of a tangible object that can be picked up, moved, dropped on other morphs, resized, rotated, or deleted. Morphs are flat objects that can be stacked and layered like a bunch of shapes cut out of paper. When two morphs overlap, one of them covers part of the other morph, creating the illusion that it lies in front of that morph; if a morph has a hole in it, morphs behind it are visible through the hole. This layering of overlapping morphs creates a sense of depth, sometimes called "two-and-a-half-dimensions." Morphic encourages this illusion by providing a drop shadow when a morph is picked up by the user. The drop shadow helps to create the illusion that one is manipulating concrete, tangible objects.

In morphic, the programmer is encouraged to create a new kind of morph incrementally. One might start by defining the morph's appearance, then adding interaction, animation, or drag and drop behavior as desired. At each step in this process, the morph can be tested and modified. In this section, we will illustrate this incremental development process through an extended example. We will create a new kind of morph and then add methods to define each aspect of its behavior. While this presentation is not quite detailed enough to be called a tutorial, the code presented is complete. Interested readers are invited to work through the example on their own. The animation, especially, is much more fun to see than to read about.

Defining a New Morph Class

The first step in creating a custom morph is to define a new empty subclass of Morph:

```
Morph subclass: #TestMorph
    instanceVariableNames: 'angle'
    classVariableNames: ''
    poolDictionaries: ''
    category: 'Morphic—Fun'
```

The angle instance variable will be used later; ignore it for now. Because the class Morph defines default behavior for everything a morph must do, one can immediately create an instance of TestMorph by evaluating

```
TestMorph new openInWorld
```

The new morph appears as a simple blue rectangle that can be dragged around. Note that even such a simple morph can be moved, resized, rotated, copied, or deleted. In short, it is a full-fledged morph merely by virtue of being a subclass of Morph. That's because Morph is a concrete class, as opposed to an abstract class (such as Collection) which requires that a subclass supply concrete implementations of various methods to make it complete and operational.

Adding Appearance

The programmer can customize the appearance of this new morph by implementing a single method, the drawOn: method. In morphic, all drawing is done by sending messages to a drawing engine called a *canvas*. The canvas abstraction hides the details of the underlying graphics system, thus both simplifying programming and providing device independence. While morphic's most heavily used canvas, FormCanvas (a subclass of Canvas), uses BitBlt for drawing, it is possible to create subclasses of Canvas that send graphics commands over a socket for rendering on a remote machine or that send Postscript commands to a printer. If color is not available on a device, the canvas can map colors to shades of gray or stipple patterns. Once the drawOn: method is written, all these rendering options are available without any additional work; the same drawOn: method works with any kind of canvas.

Many graphic systems use a *graphics context* object to store such drawing properties as the foreground color and font. This reduces the number of parameters that must be passed in each graphics call. In such a system, the command "fillCircle" might get its fill color, border color, and border width parameters from the context object. While the graphics context style of programming might save a bit on parameter passing overhead, it makes many of the parameters that control a given graphic command implicit, making it harder to understand the code. Furthermore, since the context state depends on the history of the computation, different execution paths can leave the context in different states, making debugging difficult. In morphic, however, the parameters that control the behavior of a given drawing command—such as the fill color or border width—are passed as explicit parameters to the drawing operations. This property makes the code easier to understand and debug.

The best way to learn what graphical operations are available to morphs is to browse the class FormCanvas, which includes methods that

- outline or fill rectangles, polygons, curves, and ellipses

- draw lines and single pixels

- draw pixel-based images of any depth

- draw text in any available font and color

You can make your TestMorph into a colorful oval by drawing it as eight concentric ovals with rainbow colors:

```
drawOn: aCanvas
    | colors |
    colors := color wheel: 6.
    colors withIndexDo: [:c :i |
        aCanvas fillOval: (self bounds insetBy: 4 * i) color: c].
```

The wheel: message is sent to the morph's base color to produce an array of colors with the same brightness and saturation but with six hues spaced evenly around the color wheel. For example, if the morph's base color is blue, this produces the colors blue, magenta, red, yellow, green, and cyan. The next two lines step through this color array painting concentric ovals, each one inset four pixels from the last. To force the morph to redraw itself so you can see the result of this new draw method, just pick it up. When you do this, you'll also see that its drop shadow is now an oval matching its new shape. (See Figure 2.4.)

Note that the result of self bounds controls the size of the largest oval. A morph's bounds is a rectangle that completely encloses that morph. It is used by morphic to support incremental display updates and hit detection. A morph should never draw outside its bounds. Leaving tracks is probably a symptom of a bug in the morph's drawOn: method.

Figure 2.4 A TestMorph after the drawOn: method has been defined. It has been picked up with the mouse, causing it to cast a shadow.

What else can we do to this morph? In morphic, the morph *halo* provides a way to manipulate many aspects of a morph directly (Figure 2.5). The halo is a constellation of control handles around the morph to be manipulated. Some of these handles can be dragged to change the position or shape of the morph, others perform operations such as copying, deleting, or presenting a menu. The morph halo appears when you hold down the alt key (the command or Apple key on a Macintosh) while clicking the mouse on the morph. Leave the cursor over a halo handle for a few seconds to get a help balloon that explains what the handle does.

Try changing the morph's size using its yellow (lower right) halo handle. Try changing its color by pressing on the red halo handle to pop up a menu and selecting the *change color* command. Since the morph's base color is being used as the start of the color wheel, you'll see the entire sequence of colors change. Try duplicating the morph and deleting the duplicate. (If you accidentally delete the original morph, you can make a new instance by evaluating TestMorph new openInWorld again.)

Adding Interaction

Morphic represents user actions such as keystrokes and mouse movements using instances of MorphicEvent. A MorphicEvent records both the event type, such as "mouse down," and a snapshot of the state of the mouse buttons and the keyboard modifier keys (shift, control, and ALT or command) at the time that the event occurred. This allows a program to tell, for example, if the shift key was being held down when the mouse button was pressed.

Figure 2.5 A TestMorph with its halo. The cursor has lingered over a handle for a few seconds, causing the help balloon to appear. Moving the cursor away from the handle will cause the balloon to disappear. Clicking on the background will make the halo itself go away.

A morph can handle a given kind of event by implementing one of the following messages:

- mouseDown: evt

- mouseUp: evt

- mouseMove: evt

- keyStroke: evt

The event is supplied as an argument so that its state can be examined. To demonstrate interaction in the context of our example, add the following two methods to TestMorph:

mouseDown: evt
    self position: self position + (10@0).

handlesMouseDown: evt
    ↑ true

The first method makes the morph jump 10 pixels to the right when it receives a mouse down event. The second method tells morphic that TestMorph accepts the event. In this case, it accepts all events, but it could accept events selectively based on its internal state or information from the event, such as the shift key state. After adding both methods, click on the morph to try it.

After a few clicks, you'll need to pick up the morph to move it back to it original position. Surprise! You can't just pick up the morph anymore, because it now handles mouse events itself, overriding the default grabbing response. You can use the black halo handle (middle-top) to pick up the morph. (This works for any morph that has its own mouse down behavior.) Another way to handle this problem is to make TestMorph reject mouse down events if the shift key is down:

handlesMouseDown: evt
    ↑ evt shiftPressed not

Now you can just hold down the shift key when you want to pick up the morph.

In addition to the basic mouse events, morphs can handle events when the cursor enters and leaves a morph, either with or without the mouse down, or they can elect to get click and double-click events. To learn more about these kinds of events, browse the "event handling" category of Morph.

Adding Drag and Drop

A morph can perform some action when another morph is dropped onto it, and it can decide which dropped morphs it wishes to accept. To accept dropped morphs, a morph must answer true to the following message:

    wantsDroppedMorph: aMorph event: evt

The morph being dropped is supplied as an argument to allow the receiving morph to decide if it wishes to accept it. For example, a printer icon morph in a desktop publishing application might accept only morphs representing printable documents. The event is supplied so that the modifier keys at the time of the drop are available. If the receiving morph agrees to accept the dropped morph, it is sent the message

    acceptDroppingMorph: aMorph event: evt

to actually perform the drop action. For example, a printer morph might queue a print request when a document morph is dropped onto it.

After the recipient of the dropped morph has processed the drop action, the dropped morph itself might need to perform some action. The dropped morph is informed that it has been dropped by sending it the message

    justDroppedInto: aMorph event: evt

The morph that accepted the drop is provided as an argument and the triggering event (typically a mouse up event) is provided so that the modifier keys at the time of the drop are available. Most of the time, the default behavior is appropriate, so the programmer need not implement this method.

To demonstrate drag and drop in the context of the example, add the following two methods to TestMorph:

acceptDroppingMorph: aMorph event: evt
    self color: aMorph color.

wantsDroppedMorph: aMorph event: evt
    ↑ true

To test it, create several RectangleMorphs (using the *new morph...* command of the background menu), give them various colors (using the *change color...* command in the *fill style* submenu of the red halo menu), and drop them on your TestMorph.

Adding Liveness

Animation makes an interactive application come alive and can convey valuable information. However, graphical animation—objects moving and changing their appearance over time—is just one aspect of a more general user-interface goal we call *liveness*. Other examples of liveness include user-interface objects that update themselves dynamically—such as inspectors, clocks, or stock quote displays—and controls that act continuously on their targets, like the morphic color picker.

Animation in a user interface can be annoying if the user is locked out while the animation runs. In morphic, liveness and user actions are concurrent: Any number of morphs can be animated and alive, even while the user drags a scroll bar or responds to a system query. In the early 1980s, user interface designers realized that the system should not lock the user into a mode. Morphic goes one step further: It also keeps the user from locking the system into a mode.

Let's animate our TestMorph example by making it go in a circle when clicked. Add the following three methods:

initialize
```
super initialize.
angle := 0.
```

mouseDown: evt
```
angle := 0.
self startStepping.
```

step
```
angle := angle + 5.
angle > 360 ifTrue: [↑ self stopStepping].
self position: self position + (Point r: 8 degrees: angle).
```

Now you see why we needed the angle instance variable: to store the current direction for this animation. The mouseDown: method initializes the angle to zero degrees and asks morphic to start sending step messages to the morph. Since we've only now added the initialize method to set the initial value of angle, any instances of this morph you already have on your screen will have nil in their angle instance variable; that will be fixed when you mouse down on the morph.

The liveness of a morph is defined by its step method. In this case, the step method advances the angle by five degrees. It then checks to see if the circle is complete, and if so, it tells morphic to stop sending step messages to this morph. If the circle isn't complete, the morph updates its position by moving eight pixels in the direction of the current angle.

Click on the morph to try this. You'll notice that it moves, but very slowly. In fact, step is being sent to it at the default rate of once per second. To make the morph go faster, add the method:

stepTime
```
↑ 20
```

On a fast enough machine, the morph will be sent step every 20 milliseconds, or 50 times a second, and it will really zip. Here's one more thing to try: Make several copies of the morph (using the green halo handle) and quickly click on all of them. You will see that multiple animations can proceed concurrently and that you can still interact with morphs while animations run.

There are several things to keep in mind about step methods. First, since they may run often, the methods should be as efficient as possible. Second, it is good to use an appropriate stepping rate. A clock morph that only displays hours and minutes need not be stepped more often than once a minute (i.e., a step time of 60,000 milliseconds). Finally, the stepTime method defines only the minimum desired time between steps; there is no guarantee that the time between steps won't be longer. Morphs that must pace themselves in real-world time can do interpolation based on Squeak's millisecond clock. Squeak's Alice 3-D system does exactly this in order to support time-based animations such as "turn in a complete circle in three seconds."

Example: PicoPaint

As a final example, this section shows how the core of the simple sketch editor shown in Figure 2.6 can be implemented in only six methods totaling about 30 lines of code.

The first step is, as usual, to create an empty subclass of Morph using the following:

```
Morph subclass: #PicoPaintMorph
    instanceVariableNames: 'form brush lastMouse '
    classVariableNames: ''
    poolDictionaries: ''
    category: 'Morphic—Fun'
```

The instance variable form will hold the sketch being edited (an instance of Form), brush will be a Pen on that Form, and lastMouse will be used during pen strokes.

The following extent: method allows the user to make the sketch whatever size he or she likes:

```
extent: aPoint
    | newForm |
    super extent: aPoint.
    newForm := Form extent: self extent depth: 16.
    newForm fillColor: Color veryLightGray.
    form ifNotNil: [form displayOn: newForm].
    form := newForm.
```

Figure 2.6 Drawing a picture with Pico-PaintMorph, a simple sketch editor.

This method is invoked whenever the morph is resized, such as when the user drags the yellow halo handle. A Form of the new size is created and filled with a background gray color. The contents of the old sketch, if any, are copied into it (using displayOn:). If we didn't do this, we'd lose our sketch when the morph was resized. The nil test allows this method to be called at initialization time, before the form instance variable has been initialized.

To make sure that we start off with a sketch of some default size, we implement the initialize method and invoke extent: from it as follows:

```
initialize
    super initialize.
    self extent: 200@150.
```

Note that both extent: and initialize start by invoking the default versions of these methods inherited from Morph. These inherited methods handle all the morphic bookkeeping details so that the programmer of the subclass doesn't have to worry about them.

Now that the form instance variable is initialized and maintained across size changes, adding the draw method is trivial:

```
drawOn: aCanvas
    aCanvas image: form at: bounds origin.
```

At this point, if you create an instance of PicoPaintMorph, it will appear as a light gray rectangle that can be resized. To make it into a sketch editor, we just need to add user input behavior to draw a stroke when the mouse is dragged on the morph. This requires the following three methods:

```
handlesMouseDown: evt
    ↑ true
```

```
mouseDown: evt
    brush := Pen newOnForm: form.
    brush roundNib: 3.
    brush color: Color red.
    lastMouse := evt cursorPoint − bounds origin.
    brush drawFrom: lastMouse to: lastMouse.
    self changed.
```

```
mouseMove: evt
    | p |
    p := evt cursorPoint − bounds origin.
    p = lastMouse ifTrue: [↑ self].
    brush drawFrom: lastMouse to: p.
    lastMouse := p.
    self changed.
```

The mouseDown: method creates a Pen on the sketch and draws a single point at the place where the mouse went down. Note that mouse event positions are in world coordinates that must be converted into points relative to the origin of the sketch Form before using them to position the pen. The mouseMove: method uses the lastMouse instance variable to decide what to do. If the mouse hasn't moved, it does nothing. If the mouse has moved, it draws a stroke from the previous mouse position to the new mouse position and updates the lastMouse instance variable.

In this case, we don't need to implement the mouseUp: method because a default implementation is inherited from Morph. In another situation, we could add a mouseUp: method to take some final action at the end of the mouse interaction.

Note that both the mouseDown: and mouseMove: methods end with **self changed**. This tells morphic that the morph's appearance has changed so it must be redrawn. But if you make the sketch large and draw a circle quickly, you will notice that the circle drawn by the pen is not smooth, but a rather coarse approximation made of straight line segments. The problem is more pronounced on slower computers. Yet if the sketch is small, the problem is less severe. What is going on?

This is a performance problem stemming from the fact that morphic's incremental screen updating is redrawing the entire area of the display covered by the sketch. As the sketch gets larger, the display updating takes more time, and thus the morph can't process as many mouse events per second. Fortunately, it is easy to improve matters by noticing that only a portion of the sketch must be updated with each mouse event: namely, the rectangle spanning the last mouse position (if any) and the current one. If the mouse only moves a few pixels between events, the portion of the display to be updated is small. By reporting only this small area, rather than the area of the entire sketch, we can make drawing performance be independent of the size of the sketch as follows:

```
mouseDown: evt
    brush := Pen newOnForm: form.
    brush roundNib: 3.
    brush color: Color red.
    lastMouse := evt cursorPoint − bounds origin.
    brush drawFrom: lastMouse to: lastMouse.
    self invalidRect:
        ((lastMouse − brush sourceForm extent corner:
            lastMouse + brush sourceForm extent) translateBy: bounds origin).

mouseMove: evt
    | p |
    p := evt cursorPoint − bounds origin.
    p = lastMouse ifTrue: [↑ self].
    brush drawFrom: lastMouse to: p.
    self invalidRect: ((
        ((lastMouse min: p) − brush sourceForm extent) corner:
        ((lastMouse max: p) + brush sourceForm extent)) translateBy: bounds origin).
    lastMouse := p.
```

The invalidRect: method reports that a portion of the display is no longer valid and must be re-drawn. It takes a rectangle in screen coordinates. This rectangle is expanded on all sides by the size of the pen nib. (Actually, a square nib extends down and to the right of its position, while a circular nib is centered at its position. For the sake of simplicity, this code reports a slightly larger rectangle than strictly necessary, but it doesn't hurt to redraw a few extra pixels.)

Adding Menu Commands

It's easy to extend this sketch editor with menu commands to change the pen size and color, clear the sketch (actually, this can be done already by using the yellow halo handle to shrink and re-expand the sketch editor), fill outlines with a color, read and write sketch files, and so on. To get started, add the following methods:

addCustomMenuItems: aCustomMenu hand: aHandMorph
    super addCustomMenuItems: aCustomMenu hand: aHandMorph.
    aCustomMenu add: 'clear' action: #clear.

clear
    form fillColor: Color veryLightGray.
    self changed.

The first method adds a new item to the menu that is presented when the red halo handle is pressed. The first line of this method adds the menu items inherited from Morph, the next line appends the clear command. The clear method simply fills the sketch with a neutral color. You can now clear your painting using the red halo handle menu. If you make this menu persistent by selecting *keep this menu up* and keep it handy, you can get to the clear command with a single mouse click.

Composite Morphs

Like most user interface tool kits and graphic editors, morphic has a way to create composite graphical structures from simpler pieces. Morphic does this using *embedding*: Any morph can embed other morphs to create a composite morph. Figure 2.7 shows the result of embedding button, string, and star morphs in a rectangle morph.

A composite morph structure behaves like a single object—if you pick it up and move it, you pick up and move the entire composite morph. If you copy or delete it, the entire composite morph is copied or deleted.

The glue that binds objects together in many graphics editors is intangible, merely the lingering after-effect of applying the "group" command to a set of objects. In contrast, the binding agents in a composite morph are the morphs themselves. If a composite morph is disassembled, each of its component morphs is a concrete morph that can be seen and manipulated. This allows composite morphs to be assembled and disassembled almost like physical objects.

Figure 2.7 A composite morph created by embedding various morphs in a rectangle morph. The composite morph is being moved. The embedded morphs stick out past the edge of the rectangle, as reflected by the drop shadow.

Morphic could have been designed to have two kinds of morphs: atomic morphs and grouping morphs. But in a sense, this would be like the "grouping command" approach. What would be the visual manifestation of a group morph? If it were visible, say as an outline around its submorphs, it would be a visual distraction. This suggests that group morphs should be invisible. Yet if all the morphs were removed from a group morph, the group morph would need some sort of visual manifestation so it could be seen and manipulated. Morphic neatly avoids this quandary by having *every* morph be a group morph. For example, to create a lollipop, one can just embed a circle morph on the end of a thin rectangle morph. Reversing that operation makes the two morphs independent again. It feels concrete, simple, and obvious.

At this point, some terminology is useful. The morphs embedded in a composite morph are called its *submorphs*. The morph in which a submorph is embedded is the *owner*. The terms submorph and owner describe relationships between morphs, not kinds of morphs. Any morph can have submorphs, be a submorph, or do both at once. The base of a composite morph structure is called its *root*.

Of course, readers with computer science backgrounds will immediately realize that the structure of a composite morph is a tree. Each morph in this tree knows both its owner morph and all of its submorphs. While morphic could have been designed so that morphs did not know their owners, one of morphic's design goals was that a morph should be able to find out about its context. This makes it simpler for objects in a simulation to find out about—and perhaps respond to—their environment. For example, in a billiards simulation, the morph representing the cue stick might search up its owner chain to find the billiards table morph, and from there find all the billiard balls on the table.

The morphs on the screen are actually just submorphs of a morph called the *world* (actually, an instance of PasteUpMorph). The object representing the user's cursor is a morph called the *hand* (HandMorph). A morph is picked up by removing it from the world and adding it to the hand. Dropping the morph reverses this process. When a morph is deleted, it is removed from its owner and its owner is set to nil. The message root can be sent to a morph to discover the root of the composite morph that contains it. The owner chain is traversed until it gets to a morph whose owner is a world, hand, or nil; that morph is the root.

How does one construct a composite morph? In the morphic programming environment, it is easy. One just places one morph over another and invokes the *embed* command from the halo. This makes the front morph become a submorph of the morph immediately behind it. When writing code, the addMorph: operation is used. In either case, adding a submorph updates both the owner slot of the submorph and the submorph lists of its old and new owner. For example, adding morph B to morph A adds B to A's submorph list, removes B from its old owner's submorph list, and sets B's owner to A. The positions of the two morphs is not changed by this operation unless the new owner does some kind of automatic layout.

Automatic Layout

Automatic layout relieves the programmer from much of the burden of laying out the components of a large composite morph such as the ScorePlayerMorph shown in Figure 2.2. By allowing morphic to handle the details of placing and resizing, the programmer can focus on the topology of the layout—the ordering and nesting of submorphs in their rows and columns—without worrying about their exact positions and sizes. Automatic layout allows composite morphs to adapt gracefully to size changes, including font size changes. Without some form of automatic layout, changing the label font of a button might require the programmer to manually change the size of the button and the placement of all the submorphs around it.

Layout Morphs

Most morphs leave their submorphs alone; the submorphs just stay where they are put. However, *layout morphs* actively control the placement and size of their submorphs. The most common layout morph, AlignmentMorph, employs a simple layout strategy: linear, non-overlapping packing of its submorphs along a single dimension. A given AlignmentMorph can be set to pack either from left-to-right or from top-to-bottom, making it behave like either a row or column. Although this layout strategy does not handle every conceivable layout problem, it does cover a surprisingly wide range of common layout problems. A morphic programmer can also create layout morphs using entirely different layout strategies if necessary, as described later.

Linear packing is best explained procedurally. The task of a horizontal AlignmentMorph is to arrange its submorphs in a row such that the left edge of each morph just touches the right edge of the preceding morph. Submorphs are processed in order: The first submorph is placed at the left end of the row, the second submorph is placed just to the right of the first, and so on. Notice that packing is done only along one dimension—the horizontal dimension in this case. Placement along the other dimension is controlled by the centering attribute of the AlignmentMorph. In the case of a row, the centering attribute determines whether submorphs are placed at the top, bottom, or center of the row.

Space Filling and Shrink Wrapping

For simplicity, the packing strategy was described as if the submorphs being packed were all rigid. In order to support stretchable layouts, an AlignmentMorph can be designated as space-filling. When there is extra space available during packing, a space-filling AlignmentMorph submorph expands to fill it. When there is no extra space, it shrinks to its minimum size. If there are several space-filling morphs in a single row or column, any extra space is divided evenly among them.

Space-filling AlignmentMorphs can be used to control the placement of other submorphs within a row or column. For example, suppose one wanted a row with three buttons, one at the left end, one at the right end, and one in the middle. This can be accomplished by inserting space-filling AlignmentMorphs between the buttons as follows:

<button one> <space-filler> <button two> <space-filler> <button three>

The code to create this row is:

```
r := AlignmentMorph newRow color: Color darkGray.
r addMorphBack: (SimpleButtonMorph new label: 'One').
r addMorphBack: (AlignmentMorph newSpacer: Color white).
r addMorphBack: (SimpleButtonMorph new label: 'Two').
r addMorphBack: (AlignmentMorph newSpacer: Color white).
r addMorphBack: (SimpleButtonMorph new label: 'Three').
r inset: 4.
r centering: #center.
r openInWorld
```

The result is shown in Figure 2.8. When the row is stretched, the extra space is divided evenly between the two space-filling morphs, so that button one stays at the left end, button two is centered, and button three gets pushed to the right end.

It is sometimes desirable for the size of an AlignmentMorph to depend on the size of its submorphs. For example, a labeled box should depend on the size of its label so that it automatically resizes itself when its label changes. An AlignmentMorph designated as shrink-wrap grows or contracts to the smallest size that accommodates

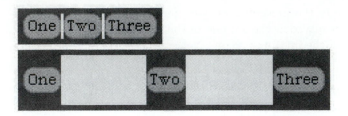

Figure 2.8   Using space-filling AlignmentMorphs (white) to distribute button morphs evenly within a row. The inset attribute of the row was set to leave a little extra space around its edges. The row is shown at its minimum size and at a larger size. For clarity, the space-filling morphs have been made a contrasting color; normally, they would be the same color as the row, making them effectively invisible.

the space requirements of its submorphs. Here's an example to try:

```
r := AlignmentMorph newRow.
r borderWidth: 1.
r hResizing: #shrinkWrap.
r vResizing: #shrinkWrap.
r addMorph: (StringMorph contents: 'Edit this text!').
r openInWorld
```

Shift-click on the label to edit it. Note that the enclosing AlignmentMorph grows and shrinks as you change the length of the label string.

Layout Attributes

As we've just seen, AlignmentMorph has several attributes that control how layout is done. The **orientation** attribute, which determines whether the AlignmentMorph lays out its submorphs in a row or column, can be set to either **horizontal** or **vertical**.

The **centering** attribute controls centering in the non-layout dimension. It can be set to the following:

center Submorphs are centered within the row or column.

topLeft Submorphs are aligned along the top of a row or the left edge of a column.

bottomRight Submorphs are aligned along the bottom of a row or the right edge of a column.

AlignmentMorph has separate resize attributes for the horizontal (hResizing) and vertical (vResizing) dimension; the two dimensions are completely independent in their resizing behavior. These attributes can be set to:

rigid This morph is never resized automatically.

spaceFill When this morph is the submorph of another AlignmentMorph, this morph expands or shrinks depending on the space available. Extra space is distributed evenly among all space-filling morphs in a row or column.

shrinkWrap This morph is shrunk to just fit around its submorphs, or to its minimum size, whichever is larger. Any enclosed space-filling morphs are shrunk as needed.

Custom Layout Policies

AlignmentMorph covers many layout situations, but sometimes a different layout policy is desired. For example, you might wish to create a table of cells for a calendar or spreadsheet, or you might want a layout policy that allowed morphs that didn't fit into one row to move down to the following row, the way words wrap to the next line in many text editors.

In fact, the latter policy is available as an option of PasteUpMorph. To try it, create a new PasteUpMorph and invoke the *start doing auto-line-layout* command from the *playfield options...* menu. Then drop some morphs into it and see how the layout changes. The layout also adapts as you resize the PasteUpMorph with the yellow halo handle.

Implementing custom layout policies, while not difficult, is beyond the scope of this chapter. However, a more advanced morphic programmer might want to study the method fixLayout in PasteUpMorph. The code to implement wrapping rows of morphs is straightforward. The hook that invokes fixLayout is in the method full-Bounds. The comment in AlignmentMorph's implementation of fullBounds explains how the mechanism works. As with many things in morphic, once a custom layout policy is installed, morphic does the rest. The fixLayout method will be invoked when morphs are added or removed from the morph, when a submorph changes size, or when the morph itself is resized—in short, anything that could possibly affect the layout.

How Morphic Works

This section gives an overview of how morphic works in just enough detail to help the morphic programmer get the most out of the system.

The UI Loop

At the heart of every interactive user interface framework lies the modern equivalent of the read-evaluate-print loop of the earliest interactive computer systems. However, in this modern version, "read" processes events instead of characters and "print" performs drawing operations to update a graphical display instead of outputting text. Morphic's version of this loop adds two additional steps to provide hooks for liveness and automatic layout:

do forever:
    process inputs
    send **step** to all active morphs
    update morph layouts
    update the display

Sometimes, none of these steps will have anything to do; there are no events to process, no morph that needs to be stepped, no layout updates, and no display updates. In such cases, morphic sleeps for a few milliseconds so that it doesn't hog the CPU when it's idle.

Input Processing

Input processing is a matter of dispatching incoming events to the appropriate morphs. Keystroke events are sent to the current keyboard focus morph, which is typically established by a mouse click. If no keyboard focus has been established, the keystroke event is discarded. There is at most one keyboard focus morph at any time.

Mouse down events are dispatched by location; the front-most morph at the event location gets to handle the event. Events do not pass through morphs—you can't accidentally press a button that's hidden behind some other morph. Morphic needs to know which morphs are interested in getting mouse events. It does this by sending each candidate morph the **handlesMouseDown:** message. The event is supplied so that a morph can decide if it wants to handle the event based on which mouse button was pressed and which modifier keys were held when the event occurred. If no morph can be found to handle the event, the default behavior is to pick up the front-most morph under the cursor.

Within a composite morph, its front-most submorph is given the first chance to handle an event, consistent with the fact that submorphs appear in front of their owner. If that submorph does not want to handle the event, its owner is given a chance. If its owner doesn't want it, then the owner's owner gets a chance, and so on, up the owner chain. This policy allows a mouse-sensitive morph, such as a button, to be decorated with a label or graphic and still get mouse clicks. In our first attempt at event dispatching, mouse clicks on a submorph were not passed on to its owner, so clicks that hit a button's label were blocked. It is not so easy to click on a button without hitting its label!

What about mouse move and mouse up events? Consider what happens when the user drags the handle of a scroll bar. When the mouse goes down on the scroll bar, the scroll bar starts tracking the mouse as it is dragged. It continues to track the mouse if the cursor moves outside of the scroll bar and even if the cursor is dragged over a button or some other scroll bar. That is because morphic considers the entire sequence of mouse down, repeated mouse moves, and mouse up to be a single transaction. Whichever morph accepts the mouse down event is considered the *mouse focus* until the mouse goes up again. The mouse focus morph is guaranteed to get the entire mouse drag transaction: a mouse down event, at least one mouse move event, and a mouse up event. Thus, a morph can perform some initialization on mouse down and cleanup on mouse up, and be assured that the initialization and cleanup will always get done.

Liveness

Liveness is handled by keeping a list of morphs that need to be stepped, along with their desired next step time. Every cycle, the step message is sent to any morphs that are due for stepping and their next step time is updated. Deleted morphs are pruned from the step list, both to avoid stepping morphs that are no longer on the screen and to allow those morphs to be garbage collected.

Layout Updating

Morphic maintains morph layout incrementally. When a morph is changed in a way that could influence layout (e.g., when a new submorph is added to it), the message layoutChanged is sent to it. This triggers a chain of activity. First, the layout of the changed morph is updated. This may change the amount of space given to some of its submorphs, causing their layouts to be updated. Then, if the space requirements of the changed morph have changed (e.g., if it needs more space to accommodate a newly added submorph), the layout of its owner is updated and possibly its owner's owner and so on. In some cases, the layout of every submorph in a deeply nested composite morph may need to be updated. Fortunately, there are many cases in which layout updates can be localized, thus saving a great deal of work.

As with changed messages, morph clients usually need not send layoutChanged explicitly, since the most common operations that affect the layout of a morph—such as adding and removing submorphs or changing the morph's size—do this already. The alert reader might worry that updating the layout after adding a morph might slow things down when building a row or column with lots of submorphs. In fact, since the cost of updating the layout is proportional to the number of morphs already in the row or column, then adding N morphs one at a time and updating the layout after every morph would have a cost proportional to N^2. This cost would mount up fast when building a complex morph like a ScorePlayerMorph. To avoid this problem, morphic defers all layout updates until the next display cycle. After all, the user can't see any layout changes until the screen is next repainted. Thus, a program can perform any number of layout-changing operations on a given morph between display cycles and morphic will only update that morph's layout once.

Display Updating

Morphic uses a double-buffered, incremental algorithm to keep the screen updated. This algorithm is efficient—it tries to do as little work as possible to update the screen after a change—and high quality—the user does not see the screen being repainted. It is also mostly automatic; many applications can be built without the programmer ever being aware of how the display is maintained. The description here is mostly for the benefit of those readers curious about how the system works.

Morphic keeps a list, called the *damage list* of those portions of the screen that must be redrawn. Every morph has a *bounds* rectangle that encloses its entire visible representation. When a morph changes any aspect of its appearance (for example, its color), it sends itself the message `changed`, which adds its bounds rectangle to the damage list. The display update phase of the morphic UI loop is responsible for bringing the screen up to date. For each rectangle in the damage list, it redraws (in back-to-front order) all the morphs intersecting the damage rectangle. This redrawing is done in an off-screen buffer that is then copied to the screen. Since individual morphs are drawn off screen, the user never sees the intermediate stages of the drawing process, and the final copy from the off-screen buffer to the screen is quite fast. The result is the smooth animation of objects that seem solid regardless of the sequence of individual drawing operations. When all the damage rectangles have been processed, morphic clears the damage list to prepare for the next cycle.

Design Principles behind Morphic

The design principles behind a system—why things are done one way and not some other way—are often not manifest in the system itself. Yet understanding the design philosophy behind a system like morphic can help programmers extend the system in ways that are harmonious with the original design. This section articulates three important design principles underlying morphic: concreteness, liveness, and uniformity.

Concreteness and Directness

We live in a world of physical objects that we constantly manipulate. We take a book from a shelf, we shuffle through stacks of papers, we pack a bag. These things seem easy because we've internalized the laws of the physical world: Objects are persistent, they can be moved around, and if one is careful about how one stacks things, they generally stay where they are put. Morphic strives to create an illusion of concrete objects within the computer that has some of the properties of objects the physical world. We call this principle *concreteness*. Concreteness helps the morphic user understand what happens on the screen by analogy with the physical world. For example, the page sorter shown in Figure 2.9 allows the pages of a

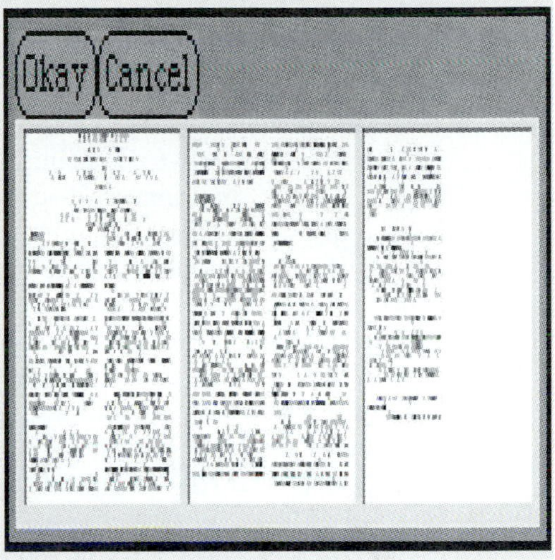

Figure 2.9 Re-ordering the pages of a Book-Morph using a page sorter. Each page is represented by a small thumbnail image. A page is moved by dragging its thumbnail to the desired place in the sequence. The page sorter is handy for sorting "slides" for a Squeak-based presentation.

BookMorph to be re-ordered simply by dragging and dropping thumbnail images of the pages. Since most people have sorted pieces of paper in the physical world, the concreteness of the page sorter makes the process of sorting book pages feel familiar and obvious.

The user quickly realizes that everything on the screen is a morph that can be touched and manipulated. Compound morphs can be disassembled and individual morphs can be inspected, browsed, and changed. Since all these actions begin by pointing directly at the morph in question, we sometimes say that *directness* is another morphic design principle. Concreteness and directness create a strong sense of confidence and empowerment; users quickly gain the ability to reason about morphs the same way they do about physical objects.

Morphic achieves concreteness and directness in several ways. First, the display is updated using double-buffering, so the user never sees morphs in the process of being redrawn. Unlike user interfaces that show an object being moved only as an outline, morphic always shows the full object. In addition, when an object is picked up, it throws a translucent drop shadow the exact shape as itself. Taken together, these display techniques create the sense that morphs are flat physical objects, like shapes cut out of paper, lying on a horizontal surface until picked up by the user. Like pieces of paper, morphs can overlap and hide parts of each other, and they can have holes that allow morphs behind them to show through.

Second, pixels are not dribbled onto the screen by some transient process or procedure; rather, the agent that displayed a given pixel is always a morph that is still present and can be investigated and manipulated. Since a morph draws only within its bounds and those bounds are known, it is always possible to find the morph responsible for something drawn on the display by pointing at it. (Of course, in Squeak it is always possible to draw directly on the Display, but the concreteness of morphs is so nice that there is high incentive to write code that plays by the morphic rules.)

Halos allow many aspects of a morph—its size, position, rotation, and composite morph structure—to be manipulated directly by dragging handles on the morph itself. This is sometimes called *action-by-contact*. In contrast, some user interfaces require the user to manipulate objects through menus or dialog boxes that are physically remote from the object being manipulated, which might be called *action-at-a-distance*. Action-by-contact reinforces directness and concreteness; in the physical world, we usually manipulate objects by contact. Action-at-a-distance is possible in the real world—you can blow out a candle without touching it, for example—but such cases are less common and feel like magic.

Finally, as discussed earlier, concrete morphs combine directly to produce composite morphs. If you remove all the submorphs from a composite morph, the parent morph is still there. No invisible "container" or "glue" objects hold submorphs together; all the pieces are concrete, and the composite morph can be re-assembled again by direct manipulation. The same is true for automatic layout—layout is done by morphs that have a tangible existence independent of the morphs they contain. Thus, there is a place one can go to understand and change the layout properties. We say that morphic *reifies* composite structure and automatic layout behavior.

Liveness

Morphic is inspired by another property of the physical world: *liveness*. Many objects in the physical world are active: clocks tick, traffic lights change, phones ring. Similarly, in morphic any morph can have a life of its own: Object inspectors update, piano rolls scroll, and movies play. Just as in the real world, morphs can continue to run while the user does other things. In stark contrast to user interfaces that wait passively for the next user action, morphic becomes an equal partner in what happens on the screen. Instead of manipulating dead objects, the user interacts with live ones. Liveness makes morphic fun.

Liveness supports the use of animation, both for its own sake and to enhance the user experience. For example, if one drops an object on something that doesn't accept it, it can animate smoothly back to its original position to show that the drop was rejected. This animation does not get in the way, because the user can perform other actions while the animation completes.

Liveness also supports a useful technique called *observing*, in which some morph presents a live display of some value. For example, the following code creates an observer to monitor the amount of free space in the Squeak object memory.

```
spaceWatcher := UpdatingStringMorph new.
spaceWatcher stepTime: 1000.
spaceWatcher target: Smalltalk.
spaceWatcher getSelector: #garbageCollectMost.
spaceWatcher openInWorld.
```

In a notification-based scheme like the Model-View-Controller framework, views watch models that have been carefully instrumented to broadcast change reports to their views. In contrast, observing can watch things that were not designed to be watched. For example, while debugging a memory-hungry multimedia application, one might wish to monitor the total number of bytes used by all graphic objects in memory. While this is not a quantity that is already maintained by the system, it can be computed and observed. Even things outside of the Squeak system can be observed, such as the number of new mail messages on a mail server.

Observing is a polling technique—the observer periodically compares its current observation with the previous observation and performs some action when they differ. This does not necessarily mean it is inefficient. First, the observer only updates the display when the observed value changes, so there are no display update or layout costs when the value doesn't change. Second, the polling frequency of the observer can be adjusted. Let us suppose it took a full tenth of a second to compute the number of bytes used by all graphic objects in memory. If this computation is done only once a minute, it will consume well under one percent of the CPU cycles. Of course, a low polling rate creates a time lag before the display reflects a change, but this loose coupling also allows rapidly changing data to be observed (sampled, actually) without reducing the speed of computation to the screen update rate.

A programming environment for children built using morphic shows several examples of liveness (Figure 2.10). The viewer on the right updates its display of the

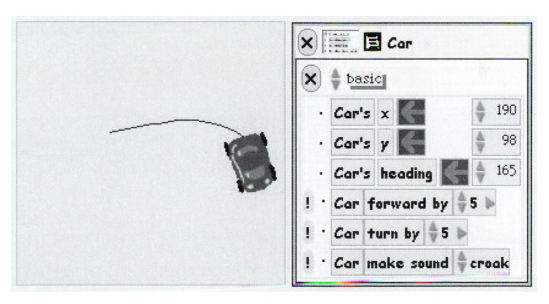

Figure 2.10 Liveness in a programming environment for children. The car's script runs and the x, y, and **heading** fields of the viewer update, even as the child writes another script or performs other activities.

car's position and heading continuously (an application of observing) as the child manipulates the car. This helps the child connect the numbers representing x and y with the car's physical location. The car can be animated by a script written by the child using commands dragged from the viewer. The script can be changed even as it runs, allowing the child to see the effect of script changes immediately. Individual scripts can be turned on and off independently.

Stepping

The primary mechanism used to achieve liveness is the *stepping* mechanism. As we saw, any morph can implement the step message and can define its desired step frequency. This gives morphs a heartbeat that they can use for animation, observing, or other autonomous behavior. It is surprising that such a simple mechanism is so powerful. Liveness is also enabled by morphic's incremental display management, which allows multiple morphs to be stepping at once without worrying about how to sequence their screen updates. Morphic's support for drag and drop and mouse over behaviors further adds to the sense of system liveness.

Morphic avoids the global run/edit switch found in many other systems. Just as you don't have to (and can't!) turn off the laws of physics before manipulating an object in the real world, you needn't suspend stepping before manipulating a morph or even editing its code. Things just keep running. When you pop up a menu or halo on an animating morph, it goes right on animating. When you change the color of a morph using the color palette, its color updates continuously. If you're quick enough, you can click or drop something on an animating morph as it moves across the screen. All these things support the principle of liveness.

Uniformity

Yet another inspiring property of the physical world is its uniformity. No matter where you go and what you do, physical objects obey the same physical laws. We use this uniformity every day to predict how things will behave in new situations. If you drop an object, it falls; you needn't test every object you come across to know that it obeys the law of gravity.

Morphic strives to create a similar uniformity for objects on the screen, a kind of "physics" of morph interactions. This helps users reason about the system and helps them put morphs together in ways not anticipated by the designers. For example, since menus in morphic are just composite morphs, one can extract a few handy commands from a menu and embed them in some other morph to make a custom control panel.

Uniformity is achieved in morphic by striving to avoid special cases. Everything on the screen is a morph, all morphs inherit from Morph, any morph can have submorphs or be a submorph, and composite morphs behave like atomic morphs. In these and other design choices, morphic seeks to merge different things under a single general model and avoids making distinctions that would undermine uniformity.

The Past and Future of Morphic

The first version of morphic was developed by John Maloney and Randy Smith at Sun Microsystems Laboratories as the user-interface construction environment for the Self 4.0 system. Self is a prototype-based language, similar to Smalltalk but without classes or assignment. Randy Smith's previous work with the Alternate Reality Kit and his passion for concreteness and uniformity contributed strongly to morphic's design. For Squeak, morphic was re-written from scratch in Smalltalk. While the details differ, the Squeak version retains the spirit and feel of the original morphic, and it is important to acknowledge the debt it owes to the Self project.

Morphic versus the Model-View-Controller Framework

How does morphic differ from the traditional Smalltalk Model-View-Controller (MVC) framework? One difference is that a morph combines the roles of the controller and view objects by handling both user input and display. This design arose from a desire to simplify and from the observation that most view and controller classes were so interdependent that they had to be used as an inseparable pair.

What about the model? Many morphs are stand-alone graphical objects that need no model, and some morphs are their own model. For example, a StringMorph holds its own string, rather than a reference to a potentially shared StringHolder model. However, morphic also supports MVC's ability to have multiple views on the same model, using the update mechanism to inform all views of changes to the model. The morphic browser and other programming tools interface to their models exactly the same way their MVC counterparts do.

Morphic also differs from MVC in its liveness goal. In MVC, only one top view (i.e., window) is in control at any given time. Only that view can draw on the display, and it must only draw within its own bounds. If it displays anything outside those bounds, by popping up a menu or scroll bar for instance, then it must save and restore the display pixels below the popped-up object. This display management design is more efficient than morphic's incremental redisplay mechanism, since nothing behind the front-most window is ever redrawn while that window retains control. This was an excellent choice for the relatively slow machines on which MVC was developed. However, the MVC design makes it hard to support liveness because there's no easy way for several live views to interleave their screen updates without drawing over each other. In contrast, Morphic's centralization of damage reporting and incremental screen updating makes liveness easy.

Morphic's concreteness is also a departure from MVC. In MVC, feedback for moving or resizing a window is provided as a hollow rectangle, as opposed to a solid object. Again, this is more efficient—only a few screen pixels are updated as the feedback rectangle is dragged around, and no view display code must be run— the right choice for slower machines. In fact, morphic itself supports outline-only window dragging and resizing as an option for slow machines.

The Future of Morphic

What lies ahead for morphic? The Squeak system evolves so rapidly that it is likely that any predictions about its future will be old news by the time of publication. Nevertheless, several directions are worth mentioning.

First, morphic badly needs an overhaul in its handling of rotation and scaling— features that were retrofitted into it long after the initial design and implementation were complete. The original design decision to have a uniform, global coordinate system should probably be reversed; each morph would then provide the coordinate system for its submorphs with optional rotation and scaling.

Morphic is so good at direct manipulation of graphical objects that it seems natural to use morphic itself to assemble tools such as ScorePlayerMorph by dragging and dropping components. In fact, this can be done already, although the current tools are rather crude. The real issue is what to do with a morph once it is built. Where is it stored, how is it instantiated, and how are updates and improvements to it propagated, both within an image and to the larger user community? None of these problems is intractable, but they all need to be addressed as part of making morph construction via direct manipulation a practical reality.

The Self version of morphic supported multiple users working together in a large, flat space called "Kansas." From the beginning, it was planned to add this capability to Squeak morphic, but aside from an early experiment called "telemorphic," not much was done. Recently, however, interest in this area has revived, and it should soon be possible for several users to share a morphic world across the internet.

Efforts are underway to support hardware acceleration of 3-D, and to allow external software packages such as MPEG movie players to display as morphs. These goals require that morphic share the screen with other agents. As 3-D performance improves, morphic may completely integrate the 3-D and 2-D worlds. Instead of a 3-D world being displayed inside a 2-D morph, today's 2-D morphs may become just some unusually flat objects in a 3-D environment.

Further Reading

The following two articles discuss the earlier version of morphic that was part of the Self project at Sun Microsystems Laboratories. Both papers discuss design issues and cite previous work that influenced the design of morphic. The first paper also describes implementation techniques, while the second focuses on morphic's role in creating an integrated programming experience that reinforces Self's prototype-based object model.

J. Maloney and R. Smith, "Directness and Liveness in the Morphic User Interface Construction Environment," *Proc. UIST'95*, pp. 21–28, November 1995.

R. Smith, J. Maloney, and D. Ungar, "The Self-4.0 User Interface: Manifesting the System-wide Vision of Concreteness, Uniformity, and Flexibility," *Proc. OOPSLA'95*, pp. 47–60, October 1995.

John Maloney is one of the original Squeak team. John's contributions to the effort include the Smalltalk-to-C translator (key to Squeak's portability), the Macintosh virtual machine, sockets, the sound and music facilities, and the Morphic user-interface framework.

Before he joined the Squeak team, John worked at Sun Microsystems Laboratories, where he and Randy Smith built the first version of morphic for the Self programming environment. John got his Ph.D. from the University of Washington where, as a student of Alan Borning, he developed a fast, constraint-based user-interface toolkit written in Smalltalk ("Thinglab II"). Earlier in his graduate school career, he spent a summer in the Smalltalk group at Xerox PARC and eight months working on real-time music accompaniment at Carnegie-Mellon.

In the late 1970s, while John was at M.I.T., he worked as a co-op student at DEC's research lab. It was there that he first saw an early implementation of Smalltalk and fell in love with the language. He still has a faded, illicit photocopy of "Dreams and Schemes," a draft of what eventually became the Smalltalk Blue Book.

John loves Renaissance music. He plays recorders, sings with the Stanford Early Music Singers, and for the past several years has been learning to play the sackbut, an early version of the slide trombone.

3

Alice in a Squeak Wonderland

Jeff Pierce
Computer Science Department
Carnegie Mellon University

About This Chapter

This chapter is an introduction to Squeak Alice, an authoring tool for building interactive 3-D worlds in Squeak. The first part of this chapter introduces some of the commands that Squeak Alice provides, as well as the ideas behind them. This part of the chapter does not require any previous knowledge of 3-D graphics and should be accessible to everyone from Squeak novices to Squeak experts. The second part of this chapter describes the implementation of Squeak Alice and requires a more advanced understanding of Squeak classes and 3-D graphics.

What Is Alice?

Printed text, radio, and motion pictures are all different types of media. Although each medium has different strengths and weaknesses, one factor common to all of them is that people use the medium for *storytelling*. Storytelling is one of the oldest and most persistent professions: Sooner or later, people attempt to use every new medium for storytelling.

Interactive 3-D graphics is a new medium that people are still experimenting with for storytelling. The need for expensive and specialized hardware used to be a barrier for potential 3-D authors, but the development of inexpensive graphics accelerator cards has largely eliminated this barrier. A significant barrier that still remains is the *authoring* problem: Creating an interactive 3-D world requires specialized training that most people interested in telling stories do not possess. Working with 3-D graphics typically requires experience with the C or C++ programming languages, as well as familiarity with linear algebra (e.g., 4×4 homogeneous matrix transformations). Unfortunately, the people who possess the skills to work with 3-D graphics are not typically the same people who want to use the medium to tell new kinds of stories. To allow the latter group of people to work with interactive 3-D graphics you need a new type of 3-D authoring tool. The goal of the Alice project was to create an authoring tool for building interactive 3-D worlds that is easy for novices to learn and use.

Where Did Alice Come From?

Randy Pausch and his research group started the Alice project at the University of Virginia. The stated goal of the project was to make it possible for a sophomore Art or English major with little or no programming experience to build an interactive 3-D world. We actually surpassed this goal: We commonly find that motivated high school students, and even some elementary school students, can use Alice.

The first version of Alice ran on Silicon Graphics workstations, but increasingly powerful hardware made it possible for us to port Alice to Windows PC computers at the end of 1995. We made the first public release of Alice at SIGGRAPH 1996, and to date over 100,000 people have downloaded Alice and tried it out for themselves. The current version of Alice is available free from `http://www.alice.org` for Windows 95, 98, and NT.

In 1997, Randy Pausch and some of the original Alice team moved to Carnegie Mellon University (CMU) to form the Stage 3 Research Group.[1] At CMU we continue to develop Alice and learn how to make interactive 3-D graphics even more accessible. Our current goal is to make Alice easier for younger children by eliminating as much of the typing as possible.

How Squeak Alice Got Started

The impetus for the Squeak version of Alice, or simply Squeak Alice, was born when Randy Pausch, the director of the Alice project, and Alan Kay, the leader of the Squeak development team, met and exchanged views on how to make authoring in different media more accessible to children. As a result of that meeting, Alan decided that he wanted to take the lessons we learned from developing Alice and implement them in Squeak. To accomplish that goal, he asked me to spend a semester interning at Disney Imagineering to implement a Squeak version of Alice. As a Ph.D. student working with Randy and a member of the Alice design team, I was familiar with both the lessons we learned from Alice and the structure of the system itself. I leaped at the chance to work with Alan, and after 3 1/2 months of hard work during the 1999 spring semester the first version of Squeak Alice was born.

---

[1] `http://www.cs.cmu.edu/~stage3`

Using Alice in Squeak

To use Squeak Alice, you first need to create a Wonderland. A Wonderland is essentially the collection of all the things you will need to create your own interactive 3-D world: a camera window to give you a view into your world and a script editor that allows you to load actors into your world, give them commands, and create behaviors for them.

How to Create a Wonderland

To create a Wonderland, you first need to make sure you are in a Morphic project. Then you must open a Workspace. To open a workspace, display the World menu by left-clicking your mouse, select *open...*, and, in the new menu that appears, select *workspace*. In the workspace that appears, type

    Wonderland new

and tell Squeak to DoIt (by hitting alt-D for PC users, cmd-D for Mac users). A number of windows will pop up as Squeak creates your Wonderland.

The window on the left is the camera window (Figure 3.1). This window is your view into the 3-D world. In this window, you will see the effects of the commands you execute. You can also "reach through" this window to manipulate 3-D objects in your world using the mouse.

The window on the right is the Wonderland script editor. The editor is composed of four different parts. On the far left is the object tree, which lists the objects in

Figure 3.1   The Camera Window.

your scene. (Later in this chapter you will learn more about the object tree.) To the right of the object tree at the top of the window are three buttons. These buttons choose which part of the editor is active: the script tab, the actor info tab, or the quick reference tab.

The script tab is where you type commands to Squeak Alice and execute scripts (Figure 3.2). This tab is very similar to a Workspace (DoIt will execute commands, while PrintIt will print out results), but also pre-defines names (e.g., left, green, and camera) for the Wonderland. This chapter will provide a lot of sample commands to try. To try a command, type it into the script tab and execute it using DoIt.

The actor info tab provides a view of the actor and some current information about that actor (Figure 3.3). Left-clicking on an actor in the object tree determines what actor the actor info tab will display information about.

The quick reference tab provides examples for many of the commands that Squeak Alice provides (Figure 3.4). If you forget how to format a command you can check this tab.

Changing the Display Depth

To run faster and conserve memory, Squeak initially uses a low *display depth*. The display depth is the number of bits Squeak uses to represent the color for each

Figure 3.2   The Script Editor Showing the Script Tab.

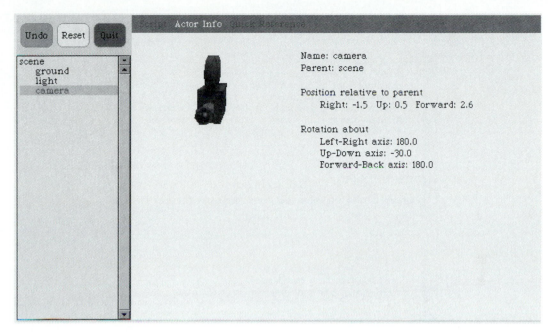

Figure 3.3 The Actor Info Tab.

pixel. You will probably want to change the display depth to 16 or 32 bits, since 3-D graphics. 3-D graphics generally require a higher display depth to look nice. To do this, left-click to open the World menu, select *appearance...*, then *set display depth...*, and finally, choose *16* or *32*.

Creating an Actor

Now that you have created your Wonderland, you need to add some 3-D objects to it. In Squeak Alice, 3-D objects are known as *actors*. Squeak Alice can create actors from a variety of 3-D file formats, including Alice MDL files, 3-DS files, and VRML files. To create an actor, you need to tell the Wonderland what file to use. For example, to create an actor from the Alice MDL file **bunny.mdl**, you would type and execute the following command in the script tab (Figure 3.5 shows the result):

```
w makeActorFrom: 'path/to/file/bunny.mdl'
```

This tells the Wonderland (w is the name for your Wonderland in the script tab) to create an actor using the **bunny.mdl** file. By default, Squeak Alice will try to name the actor using the file name; in this case it will create an actor named "bunny." If an actor with this name already exists (for example, if you already

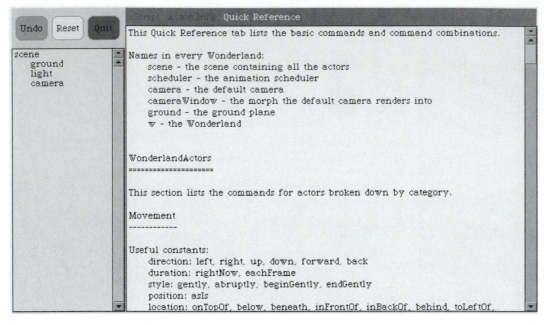

Figure 3.4   The Quick Reference Tab.

Figure 3.5   The Wonderland after Loading a Bunny.

created an actor using the **bunny.mdl** file), Squeak Alice will try to name the actor bunny2, bunny3, etc.

As a public service, the CMU Alice team has made its library of 3-D objects available to the Squeak community free of charge. You can download these objects from[2]

```
http://www.cs.cmu.edu/~jpierce/squeak/SqueakObjects.zip
```

The only restriction is that you must acknowledge that these objects are copyright CMU if you choose to use them.

You can also create actors from other file formats by using the methods makeActorFrom3−DS: and makeActorFromVRML:. One thing to remember when loading 3-DS or VRML files is that these formats specify the size of 3-D objects using an abstract "unit," so your 3-DS model of a car might be, for example, 200 units tall. However, Squeak Alice specifies size in meters rather than some abstract unit, so if you load your car into Squeak Alice it will be 200 meters tall. Luckily you can quickly bring your 3-D object down (or up) to size using the resize: method that you will encounter later in this chapter.

Simple Commands

One of the key lessons we learned from the Alice project is that *vocabulary matters*. Many 3-D authoring tools use commands like "translate" and "rotate" to manipulate objects. Unfortunately, these are not the best commands for novices. Consider that, for our target audience, *translate* is usually thought of as something you do to a language (e.g., translating from English to French) rather than a 3-D object.

Thus, instead of translate and rotate, Squeak Alice users "move" and "turn" objects. However, this only solves part of the problem. Other authoring tools usually require users to specify directions in terms of the X, Y, and Z axes, yet most people generally do not think in terms of moving objects in the X direction. In Squeak Alice, we instead allow users to specify directions using left, right, forward, back, up, and down (Figure 3.6). Each object then defines its own coordinate system (e.g. the bunny has built in forward, left, and up directions). While not all objects have an intrinsic forward direction, we note that no object has an intrinsic X direction. If an object has no intrinsic forward direction, then we assign one arbitrarily.

Type the following commands into the Wonderland script window and execute them to try moving and turning an actor:

```
bunny move: forward.
bunny turn: left
```

---

[2]The Alice objects are also included on the CD-ROM, in the folder `Packages/AliceObjects`.

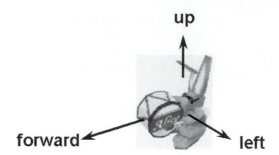

Figure 3.6   The Bunny's Built-in Directions.

Both of these commands provide a default amount to move or turn. By default, actors will move one meter or turn a quarter turn. Users can also specify the desired amount themselves. For the move: command users specify the distance in meters, while for the turn: command they specify the number of turns. This is another lesson we learned from Alice: Novices do not think about turning objects in terms of radians or degrees. Instead, they prefer to think about quarter, half, or full turns. Try the following commands for yourself and see what happens when you change the distance or number of turns.

```
bunny move: forward distance: 2.
bunny turn: left turns: 1/2
```

Working with the Mouse

Rather than type commands to objects, users can also manipulate them with the mouse. Simply clicking and dragging with the left mouse button on an actor moves the actor parallel to the ground plane. To move the actor up or down, the user first left-clicks on the actor and then holds down the shift key before dragging. Left-clicking and then holding down the control key and dragging will turn the actor left or right (around the scene's up vector). Finally, the user can left-click on the actor and then hold down both the shift and control keys to rotate the actor without any constraints.

Users can also access a menu of commonly used commands. To access this menu, the user first left-clicks on the actor's name in the object tree to select it and then right-clicks on the object tree. This will bring up a menu of useful commands that will turn the selected object around once, point the camera at it, and make it grow, shrink, etc.

Squeak Alice also makes it possible for users to create new responses for actors when users click on them. We will cover how to change an actor's responses later in this chapter.

Camera Controls

By default, every Wonderland contains a camera, and users can give this camera commands using the commands for actors. For example, try the following:

```
camera move: back distance: 3.
camera turn: left
```

Users can also maneuver the camera around the world using the mouse. To do this, they first need to show the controls for the camera. You can complete this task by evaluating

```
cameraWindow showCameraControls
```

(see Figure 3.7 for result).

To hide the camera controls again, evaluate

```
cameraWindow hideCameraControls
```

Displaying the camera controls will show a small morph beneath the camera window that depicts four arrows. To move the camera around the scene, you left-click in the camera controls morph and then drag the mouse. Moving the mouse up relative to the center of the controls morph will move the camera forward; the

Figure 3.7 The Camera Window and Camera Controls.

further the mouse pointer is from the center, the faster the camera will move. To move the camera backward you move the mouse down from the center, while to turn the camera left or right you simply move the mouse pointer left or right of the center. Note that you do not need to release and then reclick to change direction. While holding the left mouse button down you just move the mouse pointer to a different position relative to the center of the camera controls morph.

You can change the way the camera moves by holding down one of the modifier keys. To move the camera up or down, hold down the shift key. To force the camera to only rotate left or right, hold down the control key. Because Squeak interprets a left-click while you are holding down the control key as a different command, you will need to click on the camera controls first and then press the control key. Finally, you can tilt the camera up or down by holding down both the shift and control keys and then left-clicking on the controls and dragging the mouse.

Ubiquitous Animation

If you are experimenting with Squeak Alice as you read through this chapter, you have no doubt noticed that the commands to move and turn the bunny animated over time. All commands in Squeak Alice animate by default over one second whenever it makes sense to do so. This is actually based on a psychological principle: People take a second or two to assimilate any instantaneous change. Given this fact, we can make use of that second to animate the command so that users can watch the command unfold. We find that this tends to make scripts easier for users to debug. For example, rather than instantaneously disappearing off the screen, an actor might move out of view to the left, letting the user know where the actor went.

Squeak Alice also allows users to specify durations other than one second. Any command that animates by default also allows the user to explicitly set the duration, for example, in

```
bunny move: left distance: 2 duration: 4.
bunny turn: forward turns: 1 duration: 10
```

There is something else interesting about animations in Squeak Alice. Specifically, these animations are *time* based rather than *frame* based. Users specify how many seconds an animation lasts, rather than the number of frames. There are two reasons for this. First, novices intuitively think about duration in terms of seconds. The notion of a *frame* requires a more detailed understanding of how computer graphics works. Second, the frame-based animation depends upon the speed of the computer you run it on. On a computer that can render at 30 frames per second, a 30-frame animation will last one second. However, on a computer that can render at 60 frames per second that same 30-frame animation will only last half a second. Animations with a duration specified in seconds, by contrast, will last the same amount of time on both computers.

Zero-Duration Animations and rightNow

Squeak Alice allows you to create an animation with a duration of zero seconds by setting the duration to 0:

```
bunny move: forward distance: 2 duration: 0
```

However, this does not actually cause the command to happen instantaneously. When you evaluate a command with a zero duration, Squeak Alice still creates an Animation object for that command. This means that Squeak Alice will not evaluate the command until the next time it processes animations, which will be slightly later. This can cause problems if the next line in your script assumes that the bunny has already moved.

To make Squeak Alice execute a command instantaneously, you need to use the rightNow primitive. This tells Squeak Alice to execute the command right away, without creating an animation object. You use rightNow like this:

```
bunny move: forward distance: 2 duration: rightNow
```

Styles of Animation

By default Squeak Alice animates commands using an ease-in / ease-out (also known as slow in / slow out) animation style. Therefore, if you tell the bunny to move one meter over one second it will not move at a constant speed; instead, the bunny will accelerate to a maximum velocity and then decelerate.

Although this is the default animation style, you can also specify other animation styles using the style: keyword. In addition to the default style (known as *gently*), you can also use the beginGently, endGently, or abruptly animation styles. The beginGently style will accelerate to the maximum velocity but will not decelerate gradually. The endGently style will start at the maximum velocity and then decelerate smoothly. The abruptly style will cause the animation to progess at a constant velocity. The following are examples of the use of the style: keyword:

```
bunny move: forward distance: 2 duration: 2 style: abruptly.
bunny move: forward distance: 4 duration: 8 style: endGently
```

Ubiquitous Undo

Part of the goal of the Alice project is to encourage users to explore the possibilities of 3-D graphics. Before users will explore, however, they need to feel safe. Specifically, they need to feel like actions will not have irrevocable consequences, so that they can eliminate any changes they do not like. One of the ways we accomplish this is by providing a ubiquitous undo mechanism, so that users can always roll back to a safe state.

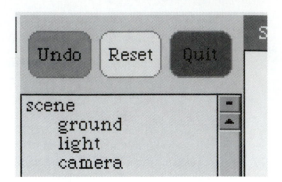

Figure 3.8 The Undo Button.

Squeak Alice provides a big, green Undo button in the Wonderland Editor (Figure 3.8). Each time you click on this button, Squeak will undo one action or command, starting with the most recent. The Wonderland actually keeps track of all of your previous commands, so if you click the Undo button five times Squeak will undo your last five actions. In keeping with our philosophy of ubiquitous animation, Squeak Alice animates the undo operation over one second as well.

Parent-Child Relationships

Alice actors are hierarchical objects, which means that they are divided into different parts with a *parent–child* relationship. This parent–child relationship is important because commands that you give to the parent actor can affect its children. For example, because the head is a child of the bunny, the head will move if you move the bunny.

In Squeak Alice, the *object tree*, located underneath the Undo button in the Wonderland Editor, depicts the parent-child relationships between the different actors (Figure 3.9). The scene, located on the top left, is the parent of all the actors in the Wonderland. The ground, camera, light, and bunny are the immediate children of the scene, so Squeak Alice displays them one level down and to the right of the scene. The bunny actor is also composed of different parts (a head, body, and drum) that are in turn built of more parts.

Because these constituent parts are actors, we use the same Alice commands that we do with the whole actor. Try out the following commands:

```
bunny turn: left.
bunny head turn: left turns: 1.
bunny drum move: forward distance: 2
```

The effect of some commands on an actor's children depends on whether a given child actor is a *first class* or *part* object. The easiest way to think about the distinction is as follows: A first class object is a complete, separate entity like a table or a book, while a part is a piece of an object (e.g., a table leg).

Figure 3.9   The Object Tree.

The reason we created this distinction is that we needed a way for users to be able to decide whether property changes to an actor would affect the actor's children. Thus, a book might be a child of a table, so that the book moves when the table does, but if the user changes the color of the table the book should remain the same color. The user can create this behavior by making the book a child of the table and setting both actors to be first class. You can see for yourself how this works by changing the first class or part status of an actor. Try the following:

    bunny setColor: green.
    bunny head becomeFirstClass.
    bunny setColor: red.
    bunny head becomePart.
    bunny setColor: blue

The first class or part status of an actor also affects how that actor handles events, as we will see shortly.

In addition to changing the first class or part status of an actor, you can change the parent of the actor. The following makes the bunny's head a child of the ground:

    bunny head becomeChildOf: ground

Now if you click on the bunny and drag, you will move the bunny's body and drum. However, his head will remain in place. The bunny's head is now a part of the ground. This also causes the name of the head actor to change. Because the head is a child of the ground, the actor's name changes to **ground head**. You can give it commands using this new name:

    ground head turn: left

Advanced Commands

The Move and Turn commands are both the simplest and the most commonly used commands in Alice. Squeak Alice also provides some useful higher level commands for users to work with.

- Squeak Alice provides an animated destroy command that removes objects from the Wonderland:

    ```
    bunny destroy.
    bunny destroy: 4
    ```

    As with all other Alice commands, users can Undo this operation if they destroy an object accidentally.

- The resize: command allows users to change the size of objects. Many 3-D authoring tools refer to this operation as scaling, but we found that users tend to associate the word "scale" with the notion of weighing. The basic version of resize allows users to specify an amount and duration. More advanced versions allow the user to specify nonuniform resizing and a volume preserving resize. (See Figure 3.10.) The following are examples of the use of the resize: command:

    ```
    bunny resize: 2.
    bunny resize: 1/2 duration: 4.
    bunny resizeTopToBottom: 2 leftToRight: 1 frontToBack: 3.
    bunny resizeLikeRubber: 2 dimension: topToBottom
    ```

- We found that users intuitively understood using turn: to specify yaw (left/right) and pitch (up/down). However, there was no direction that users associated with turn: to describe roll. We implemented the roll: command for this operation:

    ```
    bunny roll: right
    ```

- Squeak Alice provides moveTo: and turnTo: commands that allow users to specify motion to an absolute position or orientation. The user can specify an absolute position or orientation using either a numerical triple or a reference object. The triples use a {Left. Up. Forward} notation and describe positions or orientations in the actor's *parent's* reference frame. For example, for the bunny, {0. 2. 0} is the point two meters above the origin of the scene's coordinate system, while for the bunny's head, this same triple is two meters above the bunny's origin. Try the following commands:

Figure 3.10 The Bunny after a resizeLikeRubber.

```
bunny moveTo: {0. 2. 0}.
bunny turn: left.
bunny turnTo: {0. 0. 0} duration: 3.
bunny moveTo: camera duration: 2.
bunny turnTo: camera
```

- Although users can tell an actor to align with another actor using the turnTo: command, we also provide an alignWith: command:

  ```
  bunny alignWith: camera
  ```

- Sometimes, rather than aligning one actor with another, you want to turn one actor to face the other. The pointAt: command provides this functionality: The command rotates the actor so that it is pointed at the specified target. Note that you can specify either another actor or a {Left. Up. Forward} triple as the target:

  ```
  camera pointAt: bunny.
  camera pointAt: {0. 0. 0} duration: 3
  ```

- The place: command moves actors to a specific position relative to another actor. The positions that Place supports are inFrontOf, inBackOf, onTopOf, onBottomOf, toRightOf, toLeftOf, onCeilingOf, and onFloorOf, as illustrated in the following code:

  ```
  light place: onTopOf object: bunny.
  light place: inFrontOf object: bunny duration: 4
  ```

- After you have been turning and rolling an actor or the camera, you occasionally want to realign the actor with the Wonderland's up vector. This is especially true for the camera, as we found that users quickly become disoriented when the camera is rolled too far left or right. We created the standUp command to provide this functionality:

    ```
    camera standUp.
    camera standUpWithDuration: 4
    ```

- The nudge: command moves actors in multiples of their length, width, or height:

    ```
    bunny nudge: forward.
    bunny nudge: up distance: 2 duration: 2
    ```

- Occasionally, users need to hide an actor temporarily in their Wonderland. The hide command will stop Squeak from drawing an object, while show makes Squeak start drawing it again:

    ```
    bunny hide.
    bunny show
    ```

- The playSound: command will make an actor play a specified WAV file:

    ```
    bunny playSound: 'bangdrum.wav'
    ```

Squeak Alice creates an animation object that controls the playback.

These are, of course, not all of the commands that Squeak Alice provides for actors. For a more comprehensive listing, you can look at the Quick Reference tab in the Wonderland Editor, or you can look at the WonderlandActor implementation itself.

Beyond Time-Dependent Animations

Although the majority of the commands in Squeak Alice create time-dependent animations, you can also use Squeak Alice to create more persistent actions. First, you can use the speed: keyword to cause actors to move at a constant rate. When you add the speed: keyword to the move: command, Squeak Alice will move the object at the specified velocity in meters per second. If you specify a distance:, the actor will move that distance and then stop. If you do not, then the actor will move at the constant rate forever (or until explicitly stopped). The speed: keyword works similarly with the turn: command, but the associated quantity is rotations per second. The following code is illustrative:

```
bunny move: forward distance: 5 speed: 1.
bunny move: forward speed: 1.
bunny turn: left turns: 2 speed: 1/2.
bunny turn: left speed: 1/2.
```

We found that using speed to create a persistent action involving moving or turning made sense to our users. Unfortunately, not all commands naturally involve a speed. We needed a way for users to be able to establish simple constraints like making the bunny's head always point at the camera. For this type of action, we created the eachFrame parameter. You can use eachFrame as the duration to create an action that occurs every time Squeak redraws the Wonderland, as in the command

```
bunny head pointAt: camera duration: eachFrame
```

In addition to allowing users to supply eachFrame as the duration, Squeak Alice also provides eachFrameUntil: and eachFrameFor: keywords that users can add to commands. The eachFrameUntil: command allows users to provide a block context that returns true or false; the command will repeat until the block returns true. The eachFrameFor: keyword makes the command repeat for the specified number of seconds. The following command makes use of another parameter, asIs, to constrain the bunny to only move along the ground for 10 seconds:

```
bunny moveTo: {asIs. 0. asIs} eachFrameFor: 10
```

The asIs parameter tells Squeak Alice to leave the current value "as is." Note that this does *not* prevent the value from changing at all, it merely prevents *that command* from changing the value. Thus, while the previous command is active the user can left-click on the bunny to drag it around. (The moveTo: command will not cause any change in the bunny's left or forward position.) However, if the user holds down shift while dragging to move the bunny up or down then the moveTo: command will always reset the bunny's up position to 0.

Frames of Reference

By giving each actor its own reference frame, we make it very easy to talk about moving actors forward, up, etc. However, another way that people talk about moving objects in the real world is relative to other objects (e.g., move it to your left). Users can move actors in Wonderlands relative to other actors using the asSeenBy: keyword. The following command will move the bunny one meter to the *camera's* left:

```
bunny move: left distance: 1 asSeenBy: camera
```

You can also move an actor to an absolute position relative to another actor. The following command moves the bunny to a position one meter in front of the camera and one meter above it:

```
bunny moveTo: {0. 1. 1} asSeenBy: camera
```

Controlled Exposure to Power

One of the basic design principles we used in the creation of Alice was the notion of *controlled exposure to power*. This principle in essence states that commands should have sensible defaults, so that the user can work with them in their simplest forms and still be able to accomplish useful work. Then, as the user becomes more sophisticated, he or she learns how to specify values explicitly rather than relying on these defaults. The user continues to work with the same commands, but those commands advance with the user. For example, the move: command can take all of the following forms:

```
bunny move: forward.
bunny move: forward distance: 1.
bunny move: forward distance: 1 duration: 1.
bunny move: forward distance: 1 speed: 1/2.
bunny move: forward speed: 1/2.
bunny move: forward speed: 1/2 for: 5.
bunny move: forward asSeenBy: camera.
bunny move: forward distance: 1 asSeenBy: camera.
bunny move: forward distance: 1/10 duration: eachFrame
```

These are only *some* of the forms move: can take. Even though users can start out by simply specifying a direction, there are a lot of different ways they can use move: as they become more advanced users.

Animation Methods

When you give a command to an Actor in a Wonderland, Squeak creates a WonderlandAnimation instance that governs the time-dependent behavior of that command. You can assign this instance to a variable and access the methods defined on animations. Four useful methods that animations provide are pause, resume, stop, and start. pause will temporarily stop an animation until you resume it. stop will stop that animation altogether, while start will run the animation again from scratch. Examine the following code:

```
spin := bunny turn: left turns: 20 duration: 40.
spin pause.
spin resume.
spin stop.
spin start.
```

You can also cause an animation to repeat using the loop command. If you supply a number with loop:, the animation will repeat that number of times. Otherwise the animation will repeat forever until explicitly stopped. If you want the animation to finish the current iteration before stopping, you can use stopLooping, as in the following code:

```
flip := bunny turn: forward turns: 1 duration: 2.
flip loop: 2.
flip loop.
flip stopLooping
```

Composing Animations

Squeak Alice provides a set of primitive commands (e.g., move: and turn:) as well as a set of more advanced commands (e.g., pointAt: and alignWith:). During the initial design of Alice, we realized that these commands alone did not provide the user with the control and flexibility that we wished. We therefore provided a way for users to compose primitive animations to create more complex animations. There are two ways to compose animations: doTogether:, which causes the animations to run at the same time, and doInOrder:, which runs the animations one after another. These commands are defined by the Wonderland itself, rather than by the WonderlandActors. With the doInOrder: command we can, for example, create an animation the causes the bunny to hop up and down:

```
jump := bunny move: up distance: 1 duration: 1/2.
fall := bunny move: down distance: 1 duration: 1/2.
hop := w doInOrder: {jump. fall}.
hop start
```

You can also compose the animations that you create with doInOrder: and doTogether: with other animations:

```
spinJump := w doTogether:
    {hop. bunny turn: left turns: 1 duration: 1}.
spinJump loop.
```

Setting Alarms

Because commands in Squeak Alice are animated over time, each Wonderland needs to keep track of the passage of time. To do this, each Wonderland has a Scheduler instance responsible for keeping track of the passage of time and for updating the animations of commands. When you create a Wonderland, the scheduler sets the time to zero and then updates this time every frame. You can find out the current time (in seconds) in a Wonderland by printing the result of

```
scheduler getTime
```

Squeak Alice makes use of the fact that Scheduler keeps track of the passage of time by allowing you to set *Alarms*. An Alarm is some action (a BlockContext) that you want the Wonderland to execute at a specific time or after some specified time has elapsed.

The two commands the Alarm class provides for this feature are do:at:inScheduler: and do:in:inScheduler:. The first takes a BlockContext, the time to execute the action, and the scheduler to add the alarm to:

```
Alarm
    do: [bunny turn: left turns: 1]
    at: (scheduler getTime + 10)
    inScheduler: scheduler
```

The second command takes a BlockContext, how time much to wait (in seconds) before executing the action, and the scheduler to add the alarm to:

```
myAlarm := Alarm
    do: [bunny turn: left turns: 1]
    in: 5
    inScheduler: scheduler.
```

Both commands return an Alarm instance.

The Alarm instance has a checkTime command that you can use to determine when the alarm will go off and a stop command you can use to stop the alarm before it goes off.

Making Objects React to the User

All of the commands that I have covered so far are useful for creating behaviors for objects, but they do not make the Wonderland interactive. To create interactive behaviors for the actors in a Wonderland, you need to use the respondWith:to: or addResponse:to: methods.

These methods allow you to specify what you want the actor to respond to, and how you want it to respond. Actors can respond to leftMouseDown, leftMouseUp, leftMouseClick, rightMouseDown, rightMouseUp, rightMouseClick, and keyPress events. Responses then take the form of a BlockContext that accepts a single parameter. This parameter is a WonderlandEvent instance that Squeak generates to encapsulate data about the event (e.g., which key the user pressed).

The respondWith:to: method tells the actor to respond to the event with only the specified response; the actor ignores all other previously defined responses for that event. The following command will make the bunny spin around once every time you click on it with the left mouse button:

```
bunny
    respondWith: [:event | bunny turn: left turns: 1]
    to: leftMouseClick
```

Notice that clicking and dragging the bunny will no longer move it around.

The addResponse:to: method will add the new response to any other defined responses for the specified event. The method returns the new reaction, so that you can later remove the reaction using the removeResponse:to: method. The following code illustrates:

```
newReaction := bunny
    addResponse: [:event | bunny turn: left turns: 1]
    to: leftMouseClick.
bunny
    addResponse: [:event | bunny move: forward distance: 2]
    to: leftMouseClick
```

Now you can click and drag the bunny around, and when you let up on the left mouse button, the bunny will move in a small circle. If you now remove the first response you added, the bunny will move forward only when you let up on the button:

```
bunny removeResponse: newReaction to: leftMouseClick
```

Helper Actors

Most of the time users work with actors that have geometry (a polygonal mesh that Squeak Alice uses to create the visual depiction of the actor). When writing scripts, though, users will occasionally need to describe the motion or behavior of an object relative to some arbitrary position or orientation. Consider as a simple example trying to make the bunny orbit around the scene coordinate {0. 0. 2}. The simplest way to do this is to create an actor without any geometry (informally dubbed a *helper actor*) as follows:

```
helper := w makeActor
```

Move that helper to the desired position:

```
helper moveTo: {0. 0. 2} duration: rightNow
```

Then rotate the bunny around that point:

```
bunny turn: left turns: 1 asSeenBy: helper
```

Multiple Cameras

Although Squeak Alice provides only a single camera by default, you can create new cameras to provide multiple views into the Wonderland. There is a drawback to creating new cameras: because your processing resources are finite, each new camera decreases the overall frame rate for all camera views. If your frame rate with one camera is F, then your frame rate with N cameras will be approximately F / N.

Despite this drawback, users often find it useful to provide multiple views onto a scene. For example, multiple views can make it easier to find and manipulate actors in the scene. The syntax for making a new camera is

```
w makeCamera
```

When you execute this command, Squeak Alice will create a new camera (named camera2 for the second camera you create, camera3 for the third, etc.) and add it to the scene. New camera windows all start in the same default position, so you may need to move one camera window to see the other. You can either move the camera window morph with your mouse, or you can actually issue Squeak Alice commands to the camera window morphs themselves. The distance units for morphs are pixels.

```
cameraWindow move: down distance: 50 duration: 2
```

Squeak Alice actually represents the position of a camera in a Wonderland using a 3-D camera model. Although with a single camera you will never see this model, with two or more cameras you can actually position one camera to view another. You can even left-click on a camera model in a Wonderland to move that camera around with the mouse like any other 3-D object. (See Figure 3.11.)

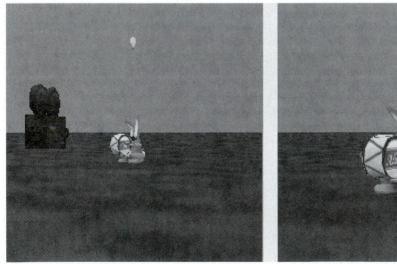

Figure 3.11 Multiple Cameras Providing Multiple Views.

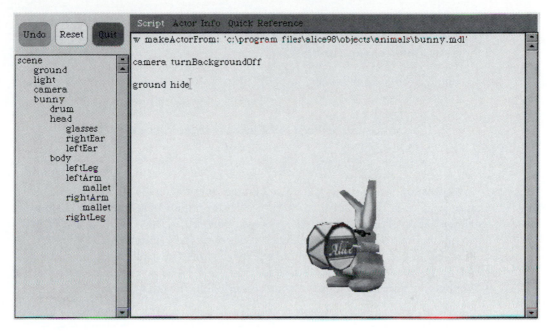

Figure 3.12 The Bunny Blended with the Script Editor.

Blending 2-D and 3-D

Unlike other 3-D authoring tools (including the CMU version of Alice), Squeak Alice allows you to smoothly integrate a 3-D Wonderland with other 2-D content in Squeak. To do this, you simply turn off the background in the camera window:

    cameraWindow turnBackgroundOff

You may also want to hide the ground to focus more on composing the actor with the current Project:

    ground hide

Assuming you pointed the camera at an actor in the Wonderland, you should now see that character blended smoothly with the Project. To move the actor around the project, you need to move the camera window, not the actor itself. Try the following one at a time to see the difference:

    cameraWindow move: right distance: 50.
    bunny move: right distance: 5

Now that you have created a 3-D character integrated with your 2-D project, you can make that actor interact with the project. Squeak Alice provides commands for converting 2-D points to 3-D points, as well as commands to change the Z ordering of the camera window morph in the Project. Thus you can, for example, make the bunny's head watch your cursor:

```
bunny head doEachFrame:
    [bunny head
        pointAt: (camera
            transformScreenPointToScenePoint: (Sensor mousePoint)
            using: bunny)
        duration: rightNow].
```

This example introduces the doEachFrame: method, which allows you to send a snippet of code to an actor to execute each frame, and the camera transformScreenPointToScenePoint:using: method, which converts a 2-D point to a 3-D point using the bunny to determine the relative depth of the 3-D point.

Two other useful methods are the sendInFrontOf: and sendBehind: methods provided by the camera window. These methods allow you to (for instance) make a 3-D character wander around (in front of and behind) a 2-D morph.

Active Textures

Andreas Raab implemented a method of drawing the contents of a morph on a 3-D object in a Wonderland that he calls active textures. To create an active texture you need to open the camera window morph to drag and drop, enable active textures for a particular 3-D object, and then drop a morph on it.

To open a camera window morph to drag and drop, you need to show its menu by holding down Control and left clicking on the camera window morph. Select "open to drag and drop" from this menu.

Next, create a 3-D object that you want to draw the morph on. It's usually easiest to use a 2-D plane. Wonderlands provide a shortcut for creating a simple flat square:

```
w makePlaneNamed: 'myPlane'
```

Now you need to enable active textures for your object. Hold down alt (option for Mac users) and left-click on the plane to show its halos. Click on the red halo to show the plane's menu and select "enable active texture." Repeat these steps to show the plane's menu again, but this time select "auto adjust to texture."

You can create a sample morph to use as your active texture by left-clicking in your project to show the World menu and selecting *new morph*. In the new menu select Demo → BouncingAtomsMorph. Squeak should create a new morph and attach it to your cursor. Now just left-click on the plane to drop the morph on top of it, and you should see the bouncing atoms morph appear on the plane inside your Wonderland. (See Figure 3.13.)

Figure 3.13   An Active Texture in a Wonderland.

Quitting a Wonderland

Squeak creates classes that are specific to each Wonderland and are only used within that Wonderland. As a result, when you want to delete a Wonderland you need to make sure Squeak removes those classes correctly. To do this, you click on the red Quit button in the Wonderland Editor; Squeak will delete the Wonderland for you and clean up after it properly.

Instead of deleting a Wonderland you can pause it by exiting the project containing that Wonderland. You can also reset the Wonderland to its initial condition (but keep the script you have written in the Editor) by clicking the yellow Reset button.

The Squeak Alice Implementation

This part of the chapter provides a brief overview of how I implemented Alice in Squeak. My intention is to provide a high-level understanding of how Squeak Alice works. Advanced Squeak developers who want a more detailed understanding of how Squeak Alice works should find that this discussion at least provides a framework for reading and understanding the actual code.

Balloon3-D

Balloon3-D is an *immediate mode* 3-D renderer written by Andreas Raab. Balloon3-D provides the necessary primitives (lighting, shading, texturing, mesh and matrix transformations, compositing operations, etc.) that are needed to draw a single frame of a 3-D scene. However, Balloon3-D does not provide any continuity between frames, nor does it have any notion of a hierarchical, persistent scene. Put simply, Balloon 3-D knows how to draw triangles, not objects.

Squeak Alice uses Balloon3-D to create a scene graph-based *retained mode* renderer. This means that Squeak Alice knows how to draw objects: it creates a 3-D world that persists from frame to frame. Squeak Alice organizes the objects in the 3-D world (lights, cameras, and actors) in a scene graph. A scene graph is a hierarchical structure that describes the relationships between objects in the scene and their properties (color, lighting, texture, position, etc.). By incrementally modifying the properties of objects in the scene, graph each frame Squeak Alice can animate the 3-D world.

Scheduler

Each Wonderland has a Scheduler instance. The scheduler keeps lists of active animations, actions (e.g., BlockContexts that should be executed each frame), and Alarms. The scheduler causes time to pass in Wonderlands by iterating through these lists.

The scheduler updates itself as often as possible (using the Morphic step method). Each time the scheduler updates, it first determines how much time has elapsed and what the current time in the Wonderland should be. The scheduler then processes the lists of active actions, alarms, and animations.

The scheduler executes any current actions and checks to see if the actions should be removed from the active list. The scheduler removes an action if the action's for: time has expired or its associated until: condition is true.

The scheduler next checks to see if any alarm times have passed. If the scheduler finds an alarm whose time has passed, the scheduler executes the BlockContext associated with the alarm and then removes it from the list of current alarms.

The scheduler's last step is to update the active animations. Animations know their start state and time, end state and time, and the interpolation function to use to move between states. The scheduler thus merely needs to tell an animation the current time to cause the animation to update to the next intermediate state. The scheduler ends by removing any animation whose end time is earlier than the current time. Note that it does update these animations first to make sure that they actually reach their end state.

WonderlandActor

The WonderlandActor class is the most important Squeak Alice class. This class encapsulates the mesh and texture that comprise the visual representation of an actor and defines the core behaviors that you use to interact with actors. Internally, the WonderlandActor class uses 4×4 homogeneous matrices to represent the position, orientation, and size of objects. However, this internal representation is hidden from the user; part of the design philosophy for Alice is to present the user with an interface based on ease of use, not on implementation details.

The behaviors that the WonderlandActor class provides all work in a similar manner. If the user specifies that the behavior should occur rightNow, then the effect of the behavior is instantaneous. Otherwise the behavior method actually creates an animation that encapsulates the current (start) state, the desired target (end) state, the duration, and the interpolation function to use (usually gently, or slow-in/slow-out). In either case the behavior method also creates an undo animation and pushes it on the WonderlandUndoStack instance for that Wonderland.

WonderlandCamera

The WonderlandCamera class defines a special type of WonderlandActor. In addition to possessing the same behaviors as actors, cameras know how to render a frame of the Wonderland from their current point of view. A camera creates an offset for drawing the scene based on its current position and orientation and then tells the Wonderland to walk the scene graph. Walking the scene graph involves setting the background color and then telling the top-level actors (immediate children of the scene) to draw themselves. Each child actor draws itself (using its position, orientation, mesh, and texture) and then tells any of its children to draw themselves.

Each WonderlandCamera instance has a WonderlandCameraMorph instance that it actually renders into. You can access this morph using the getCameraWindow method on cameras. This morph uses the Morphic step method to re-render the view into the Wonderland as often as possible.

Wonderland

The Wonderland class is the container for the 3-D world. This class contains lists of the cameras, lights, and actors in the world and provides methods for creating or loading these objects. The Wonderland class is also responsible for cleanly initializing a new Wonderland instance when you create it (e.g., creating a scheduler and undo stack), as well as cleaning up after a Wonderland instance when you delete it (by quitting the Wonderland).

The Future of Squeak Alice

Very little has changed with Squeak Alice since I completed my internship with Alan's group. While I believe that Squeak Alice has great potential, at least in the short term my time is focused on completing my Ph.D. However, when I next have time to turn my attention to Squeak Alice (or the next time another of the Alice team interns with Alan and his group) there should be many possibilities for its development. Andreas will have finished a new version of Balloon3-D that is capable of taking advantage of hardware 3-D acceleration, and the Alice team at CMU will have learned a whole new set of lessons about making 3-D graphics easy for novices. In addition I hope that the next generation of Squeak Alice will be able to take advantage of feedback directly from its intended audience, novices to 3-D graphics.

Further Reading

To learn more about the Alice project visit the Alice web page at `http://www.alice.org`. For more information on the lessons we learned from Alice, try these references:

Matthew J. Conway. *Alice: Interactive 3-D Scripting for Novices.* Ph.D. dissertation, University of Virginia, May 1998.

Matthew Conway, Steve Audia, Tommy Burnette, Dennis Cosgrove, Kevin Christiansen, Rob Deline, Jim Durbin, Rich Gossweiler, Shuichi Koga, Chris Long, Beth Mallory, Steve Miale, Kristen Monkaitis, James Patten, Jeff Pierce, Joe Shochet, David Staack, Brian Stearns, Richard Stoakley, Chris Sturgill, John Viega, Jeff White, George Williams, Randy Pausch. *Alice: Lessons Learned from Building a 3-D System For Novices.* Proceedings of CHI 2000, pages 486–493.

Jeff Pierce is working on his Ph.D. in computer science at Carnegie Mellon University. During his Ph.D. student career, he has worked on the Alice project, consulted for Disney Imagineering on DisneyQuest, worked at Microsoft Research on handheld devices and 3-D interaction, and implemented Squeak Alice for Alan Kay and his team. Currently, he is busily trying to complete his dissertation on novel 3-D interaction techniques. Jeff can be reached at `jpierce@cs.cmu.edu`. For more information visit `http://www.cs.cmu.edu/~jpierce`.

4

Networking Squeak

Bijan Parsia

Bolot Kerimbaev

Lex Spoon

University of North Carolina at Chapel Hill (Parsia)

Georgia Institute of Technology (Kerimbaev and Spoon)

Introduction

There is an apparent split in the Squeak worldview between the intensely individualistic and the thoroughly social. Squeak itself aspires to be a complete personal computing environment (with the single user in both computational and intellectual control from top to bottom) *and* a tool for collaborative development, exploration, and experimentation. This conception is akin to the notion of a networked personal computer—neither a thin client dependent on the network and server nor an isolated workstation, but a node among peers; server, client, and neither in turn; distinguishable but connected. The ideal Squeaker is not merely autonomous but autokoenonous.[1]

To support Squeaky autokeonony, Squeak has an extensive and varied set of networking facilities, applications, and frameworks and a correspondingly extensive and varied community.

---

[1] "... 'autokeonony' which I take from the Greek 'auto' ("self") and 'koinonia' ("community, or any group whose members have something in common"). What I mean by 'autokeonony' is "the self in community." pp. 145 Sarah Lucia Hoagland, *Lesbian Ethics*.

Why Use Squeak for Networking?

You're looking around for a web server or maybe a new email client. Or perhaps you want to write a web crawler. Why use Squeak? After all, Squeak networking apps tend to lack maturity—no surprise in so young a system. For example, Scamper, the web browser bundled with Squeak, is neither compliant with the latest specs, nor particularly polished, nor dramatically quick (though it is quite snappy for many purposes). If what you wanted was the best or neatest or most powerful web browser as such, Scamper wouldn't fit the bill.

But Scamper and every other Squeak networking[2] app derive some compelling advantages *simply* from being written in Squeak:

First, they share Squeak's hyperportability. Squeak images run (nearly) identically wherever there is a Squeak VM; no converting, recompiling, or tweaking needed. And since the Squeak's VM is very portable,[3] it has, in fact, been ported nearly everywhere. For general networking purposes, all that must be ported above the raw VM are the file primitives and the socket primitives.[4] Conceivably (and it has been proposed on occasion) this dependence on the host platform's networking capabilities could be eliminated by writing a TCP/IP stack in Squeak proper.

Second, they share Squeak's malleability. Given the power and flexibility of Squeak's language and integrated development tools, it's very easy to program clients or servers, and even easier to tweak or extend existing ones. As a Squeak, Smalltalk, and programming novice, I was, nevertheless, able to profitably modify the Pluggable Web Server and the built-in IRC client with very little effort. Combined with its portability, Squeak's bone deep malleability—from network protocol to user interface—makes it almost uniquely ideal for making custom, compact clients.[5]

Finally, they share Squeak's seamless systematicity. Every application—web browser, web server, mail client, what have you—is simply a collection of classes that can be combined and reused in myriad and sometimes stunning ways.[6]

In Squeak, you can be a programming dabbler and still have control over your tools and environment. Right now, you give up a certain level of maturity and functionality that exists in current commercial programs and most longer standing Free/Open Source software. But using Squeak now is like having been in on the ground floor of Linux—it's usable, it's only getting better, and it's getting better fast.

---

[2]I generally use "networking" as a synonym for "TCP/IP based networking," although there's nothing inherent in Squeak that limits it this way. It's simply that TCP/IP protocols are the most popular.

[3]See Chapter 8 on porting Squeak.

[4]At the time of this writing, socket primitives are themselves in some flux.

[5]Rebol is emerging as a competitor on this front, with the release of a beta of Rebol/view, its lightweight portable graphical user interface library. Ported everywhere, *tiny*, and very flexible, it's definitely a system to watch.

[6]Lovers of Cyberdog, Apple Computer's defunct component-based Internet suite, can find much to like about Squeak.

Why Use Networking in Squeak?

You're a Smalltalk veteran. You love hacking the compiler and the VM. You mess with meta-objects and pounce on primitives. Why muck with this mundane networking stuff?

Squeak aims to be a comfortable computing home. We should be able to do in Squeak just about anything we'd care to do, and, of course, one thing most of us want to do is play on the Internet. So, we should be able to browse the web, send and read email, chat, or publish a web site without leaving Squeak, and it should range from pleasant to delightful to do so. Alas, while often pleasant and sometimes delightful, Squeak is not quite paradise. But it certainly has the potential to be paradise. That's a good reason to use Squeak for networking: to help realize that potential.

Squeak also aims to be a cutting-edge research environment. Though some might say that "multimedia" is Squeak's focus, that's too narrow a description. Multimedia is important to Squeak, at least in part, because the various media are crucial to *communication* and, more generally, to *interaction* (not just "with the machine," but with ideas, other people, or tools). Squeak is a good place to do serious and seriously fun exploration of various forms of collaboration, both with standard and with novel tools.[7]

At the time of this writing, most publicly known commercial projects using Squeak are focused on Squeaking the web. In general, there are a lot of projects for which using Squeak to build a web site (for example) is an easy sell. Web apps are high profile and (with Squeak!) quite fun.

Also, there are more folks who know something about HTML, HTTP, FTP, and other TCP/IP services than who know something about Squeak, which makes networking fertile ground for evangelism and instruction. I've found, both when learning and teaching Squeak, that having that solid ground to work from is very helpful. More than just providing some self-confidence and orientation, there's typically immediate gratification in using Squeak for networking tasks. Furthermore, people often have many little networking jobs that they'd love to automate, which gives an immediate, pragmatic focus to an impromptu Squeak demonstration. It's quite pleasant to write little classes, or even just a bit of workspace code, to do the job that your disciple might have otherwise written a Python or Perl[8] script for—it gives your Python- or Perl-wielding friends a very nice taste of Squeak.

Historically, Squeak networking has had a delightful community of novice programmers, new Squeakers, gurus, and plain old end users. The people involved are a joy to be around. They also are an exhaustingly productive bunch. If "Net time" is quick and "Squeak time" is quicker, then it should be no surprise that "Squeak net time" is blindingly fast.

---

[7]See section entitled "Into the Blue."

[8]Python and Perl are both "scripting" languages often used for system administration, as well as for ad hoc, and not so ad hoc, networking tasks.

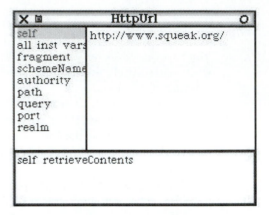

Figure 4.1   Note the various instance varibles corresponding to the proper parts of a URL.

Some Simple SqueakWorking

So, you're ready to jump into the wonderful world of Squeak networking, and you want to know where to begin. For your introductory pleasure, there is the Slick Demo and the Sober Overview. (Note: Start with the Slick Demo.)

A Slick Demo

Most of the popular demos of Squeak involve doing crazy things with graphics, animation, 3-D, or sound, but I've found that for many folks certain simple tricks have the biggest impact.[9] Especially when those tricks give them a different angle on something they take for granted.

To follow the demo script presented shortly, all you need is a Workspace, a basic handle on navigating the Squeak interface,[10] a net connection, and the **netchap.cs** change set filed into your image.

Start off by typing and inspecting the following in the Workspace:

'http://www.squeak.org/' asUrl.

Cool! A URL is an object (hey, this *is* Smalltalk), and scanning the instance variables reveals the structure of URLs. When I first discovered this, I was grabbing URLs left and right just to see what Squeak would make of them. (It works for ftp:, file:, and mailto: URLs as well.)

---

[9]See Mark Guzdial's "Squeak demo for blowing students' minds" story at `http://minnow.cc.gatech.edu/squeak/52`.

[10]See Chapter 1, which introduces Squeak. You need to be able to open a workspace, enter text, select the text and be able to *do it* (alt/cmd-d, or the "do it" menu command), *inspect it* (alt/cmd-i, or the "inspect" menu command), or *explore* (alt/cmd-shift-i). A bit of familiarity with inspectors and explorers is also helpful.

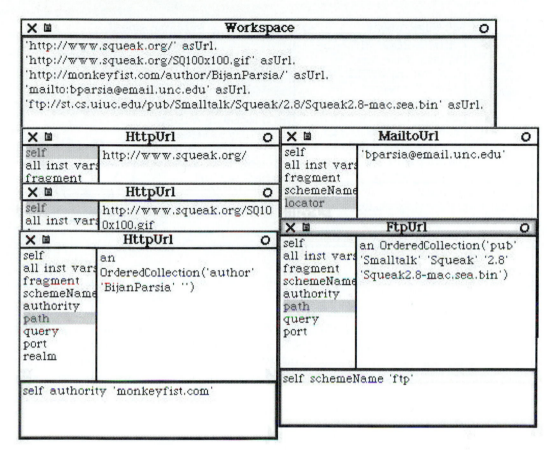

Figure 4.2 OK, perhaps this is going overboard. But it is interesting to notice the different properties of different sorts of URL.

When the charms of URL parsing wear thin, grab one of these URL inspectors, then enter and inspect following line in its "code pane":[11]

    self retrieveContents.

Whoa! Not only did Squeak go out and grab the web page at the end of the URL, but it doesn't just pop out the text—it represents the page as a **MIMEDocument**. Huh? HTML files delivered over the web are **MIMEDocuments**? Okay, I remember that now. In fact, inspecting

    'http://www.squeak.org/SQ100x100.gif' asUrl retrieveContents.

---

[11]Alternatively, you can inspect 'http://www.squeak.org/' asUrl retrieveContents from a workspace. I find working in inspectors and explorers more congenial.

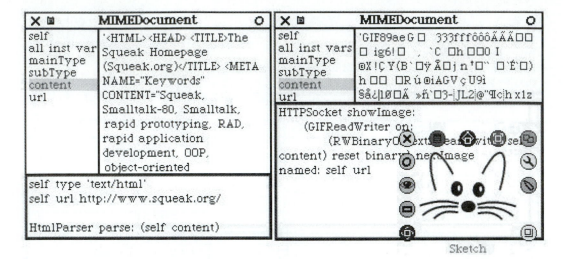

Figure 4.3   The two MIMEDocuments inspectors.

will give me another **MIMEDocument**, only this time it's of type 'image/gif'. That sure beats guessing the type of the content from the filename extension.

But, when we get down to it, the **MIMEDocument** version of the HTML is just a pretty wrapper around some text (the main MIME type *is* text, after all). Can't Squeak do better than that?

Of course, it can. Enter the following text in the code pane of an inspector of an HMTL **MIMEDocument**:

```
HtmlParser parse: (self content).
```

Then explore (cmd/alt-shift-i) the text.[12]

(Incidentally, if you have a GIF **MIMEDocument** handy, you can try doing the following, uglier code:

```
HTTPSocket showImage:
    (GIFReadWriter on:
        (RWBinaryOrTextStream with: self content)
            reset binary) nextImage
    named: self url
```

You can drag the picture around, scale it, or rotate it.)

Getting back to the Explorer, after poking around the parse tree, and examining some of the parse nodes, "do"

```
self openAsMorph.
```

---

[12]I find that using the ObjectExplorer is more fun than inspectors for parse trees; I showed the ObjectExplorer to a friend, and he shouted out, "Python should have this!"

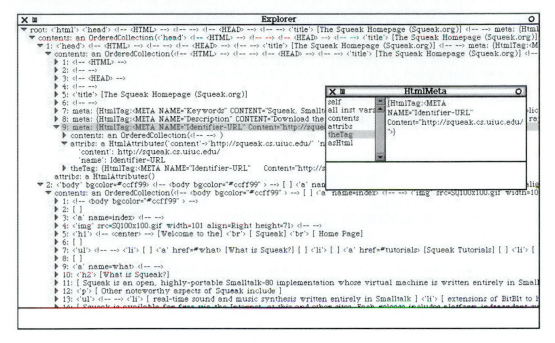

Figure 4.4 The ObjectExplorer makes it easy to dig down into the parse tree.

Now click on some blue text to open Scamper onto a new page. Yes, folks, those links are *live*.

This kind of demonstration shows the following important points even, I hope, to the most skeptical:

- First, and always, Squeak is dramatically cool—and not just for multimedia whiz-bangitry:

- Squeak is remarkably net-savvy, with a sensible understanding of URLs, MIME types, HTML, etc.

- Squeak's net-savvy is accessible through a variety of powerful and interesting tools. There's something compelling about browsing through an HTML parse tree one moment and viewing the rendered HTML the next. In Squeak, the line between "programming tool" and "networking app" is rather thin, and this is an *advantage*, not a failing.

- This advantage isn't just productive, it's also didactic. What you know about networking guides you through the tools and the code. And one can learn about network "objects" (e.g., the structure of URLs) by using the Squeak development tools. Squeak provides a *uniform perspective* on your computing world. Opening an inspector on a URL is very much like opening an inspector

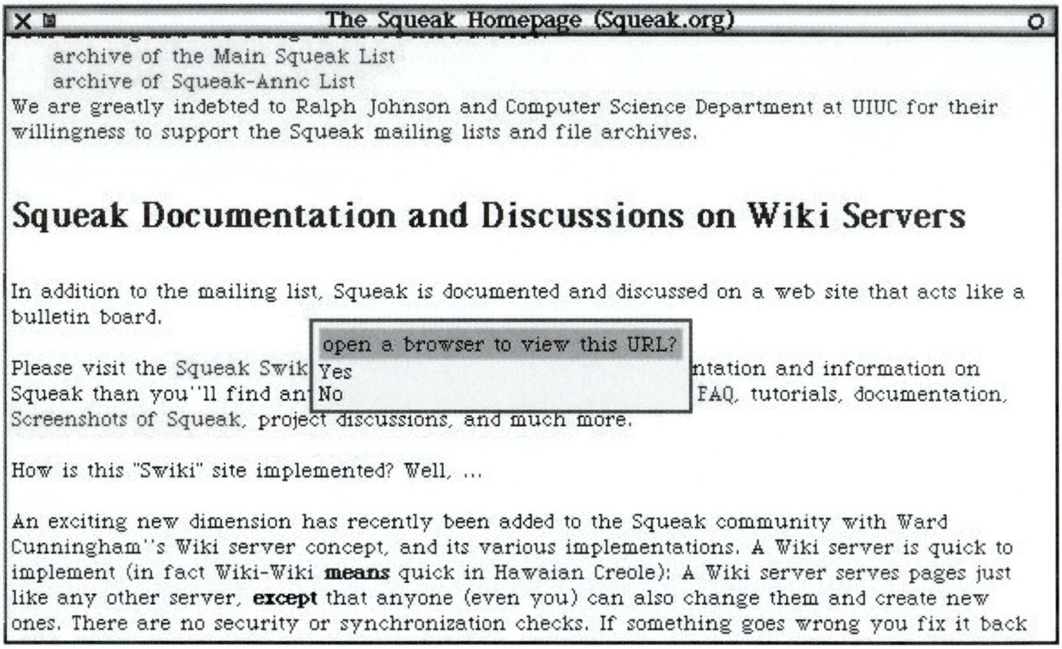

```
X ▪              The Squeak Homepage (Squeak.org)                    O
     archive of the Main Squeak List
     archive of Squeak-Annc List
We are greatly indebted to Ralph Johnson and Computer Science Department at UIUC for their
willingness to support the Squeak mailing lists and file archives.


Squeak Documentation and Discussions on Wiki Servers


In addition to the mailing list, Squeak is documented and discussed on a web site that acts like a
bulletin board.
                              ┌────────────────────────────┐
                              │ open a browser to view this URL? │
Please visit the Squeak Swik │ Yes                        │ ntation and information on
Squeak than you'll find an   │ No                         │ FAQ, tutorials, documentation,
Screenshots of Squeak, proje └────────────────────────────┘

How is this "Swiki" site implemented? Well, ...

An exciting new dimension has recently been added to the Squeak community with Ward
Cunningham''s Wiki server concept, and its various implementations. A Wiki server is quick to
implement (in fact Wiki-Wiki means quick in Hawaian Creole); A Wiki server serves pages just
like any other server, except that anyone (even you) can also change them and create new
ones. There are no security or synchronization checks. If something goes wrong you fix it back
```

Figure 4.5 Notice that the window is *not* a Scamper window. Its contents were merely generated by Scamper's rendering engine. However, the hyperlinks will trigger Scamper to open on that link.

on a SmallInteger. This uniformity, of course, is a driving design principle behind Squeak: *everything*, from the top to the bottom, from the interface to the virtual machine, should be accessible or, perhaps, *transparent* to the same set of tools and techniques.[13]

- The final point is that, no matter how slick the demo, some of those skeptical types only yield to whiz-bang multimedia extravaganzas. Fortunately, Squeak can oblige them with a networking twist.

A Sober Overview

The State of Things

Through at least version 2.8, the core distribution of Squeak contains 15 "Network-" categories comprising nearly 200 classes. Fortunately, a number of these classes are either low-level, mere node-style classes for HTML parsing, or support

[13]I intentionally focused on using the standard IDE tools in the Slick Demo to bring home this point.

classes for applications, so the actual number of interesting, relevant, and distinct classes one needs to master is comparatively small. Furthermore, the whole shebang is reasonably layered, allowing for a strong, task-specific focus. Unfortunately, there are several network-useful, indeed crucial, classes and methods scattered throughout the image (e.g., there are several relevant **Stream** classes and many important **String** methods). When writing network stuff, it's often worth investigating the image before plunging ahead with writing a slew of utility methods.

It's reasonable to divide, in a rough and ready way, the "Network-" categorized classes into three basic groups:

1. basic infrastructure, primarily the Network-Kernel and Network-Protocol classes;

2. middleware/support classes, such as those found in Network-Url, and such classes as **HtmlParser**, **HtmlFormatter**, and **MailMessage**; and

3. end user applications classes (e.g., **Scamper**, **Celeste**, and **PWS**) and their immediate helper classes (e.g., **CelesteComposition**).

The networking primitives are concentrated in two classes: **Socket** and **NetNameResolver**. **NetNameResolver** is a stand-alone utility class, which provides some address and hostname lookup methods on the class side (e.g., **NetNameResolver class≫ addressForString:**). If you are using a dial-up connection (or in some other situation, where your IP address may change frequently) when developing network applications, **NetNameResolver≫localAddressString** is very handy. Otherwise, you can leave **NetNameResolver** alone.

Even if you are mainly using higher level frameworks, some familiarity with **Socket** is useful for debugging and profiling. In particular, many fall into a classic pitfall. Before one can successfully use any network service, the networking primitives must be initialized, typically with **Socket class≫initializeNetwork**. This needs to be done every time you launch the image; doing it more than once causes no harm, but it must be done at least once. Unfortunately, some platforms in some situations don't respond well to the initialization process if, for example, one does it before firing up the PPP connection.[14] To avoid these problems, Squeak doesn't call **initializeNetwork** at start up, which means that you must remember to do so before trying to do any networking. The end-user apps all do this, but not everything else does. (So, be careful with Workspace experiments.)[15]

Socket provides a fairly standard suite of methods for doing normal socket tasks like, among others, connecting, waiting, reading and writing bytes, and listening

---

[14]VisualWorks initializes its network primitives at startup, and "Why does launching VisualWorks try to start up my PPP connection?" is a very common question from Mac users of Cincom's VisualWorks.

[15]It may be that this issue has been resolved by the time you read this book. We can, at least, hope so.

Protocol	Middleware	End User/ high level
FTP	ServerDirectory, ServerFile, RemoteFileStream, FtpUrl	FileList
HTTP (Client)	Some HTTPSocket class methods, HttpUrl	Scamper
POP	No really convenient wrappers.	Celeste
SMTP	No really convenient wrappers.	Celeste

Table 4.1 A view of the built-in networking classes, and their relationships.

on ports. While it's perfectly reasonable to do these things directly with Socket, there are facilities available, even for reading/writing bytes, that are more in the spirit of Smalltalk. Both the Comanche web/application server and the Flow internet/streaming framework[16] provide stream-style access to sockets (and there are other SocketStream implementations floating about). I expect that, in the near future, one of these will make it into the base distribution.

In the current image, subclasses of Socket (in particular, its subclass SimpleClientSocket) are used to provide basic access to a set of Internet services, namely, FTP, HTTP, SMTP, and POP.[17] HTTPSocket and SMTPSocket have some useful utility methods (mostly on the class side). For example, after opening an SMTPSocket on a mail server (using SMTPSocket class»usingServer:), one can send arbitrary mail messages using mailFrom:to:text:. The downside of this method is that you have to be aware of the textual format of mail message, and include *all* the headers (including "From:" and "To:," which might seem redundant).[18] Similarly, while HTTPSocket class does have several convenience methods for fetching web pages (httpShowPage:, httpFileIn:, etc.), most of these methods require some real knowledge of HTTP header formats. Telnet and IRC are a bit different, which is no surprise since they were written much later[19] with a somewhat different sensibility. Both are somewhat tied to Morphic, and not only for the GUI, and thus present a somewhat different programming interface (e.g., the IO loops are implemented using Morphic's "stepping" feature).[20]

The URL classes (in "Network-Url") provide the beginnings of a nicer mode of access to various network services. Developed for Scamper, they do best for retrieving documents, but are easily extended to other tasks.

---

[16]Both reading/writing bytes and the internet/streaming framework are discussed later in this chapter.

[17]The relevant classes are all in Network-Protocols.

[18]Curiously, the standard SMTP stuff in Python has *exactly* this problem, so it isn't a Squeak weakness *per se*, or, at least, not merely a Squeak weakness. Thanks to Kendall G. Clark for pointing this out to me.

[19]By Lex Spoon at the same summer internship where he wrote Scamper.

[20]More on IRC to follow.

Flow into the Future

There is considerable interest in refactoring Squeak's networking system,[21] and several projects working on different aspects. For example, at the time of this writing, there has been an extensive debate on the Squeak mailing list to determine the best semantics and implementation for the networking primitives including such issues as how to finesse the differences between different platforms, the advantages of pushing certain things down into the primitives, and how to ensure certain performance characteristics. At the other end of the spectrum, there has been considerable work done on Celeste; Comanche is gearing up to replace the Pluggable Web Server (PWS); a new Swiki framework, the ComSwiki, has just reached beta 12; new chat and collaboration systems (including audio chat and drag and drop Morph sharing) are in the update stream; and much, much more.[22]

There is also Flow, a comprehensive replacement for everything in between the super low level of the socket primitives and the rarefied heights of applications.[23]

Flow is derived from a Squeak fork developed for a home-networking research project. Thus, Flow is a mature framework that was pounded on for several years as the substratum of a variety of networking applications.[24] Unlike the current system, Flow was developed by one person, Craig Latta, and so lacks the piecemeal feel that the current classes have. Flow is also quite complete, with support for sockets, files, MIDI, serial ports, and a full range of networking protocols. As of this writing, only the basic infrastructure has been ported and released, but that's enough to get a feel for Flow.[25]

The other significant fact about Flow is that it is the basis for a "Camp Smalltalk" project to provide a cross-Smalltalk internet/networking framework. Essentially, Flow *is* that framework, so it is highly likely that it will show up in Squeak in some form.

Flow comprises three class hierarchies: a refactored **Stream** hierarchy, the **ExternalResource** hierarchy, and the **Correspondent** classes.[26] **ExternalResource**s are the low-level classes that encapsulate hardware details and OS facilities. "External" here should be thought of as roughly "external to the Squeak image" (i.e., files,

---

[21]To be fair, there is considerable interest in refactoring everything. *That's the XP (eXtreme Programming) way.*

[22]See section entitled "Into the Blue."

[23]Flow includes its own set of primitives, but it's been modified by John M. McIntosh to use the existing primitives.

[24]Including a very spiffy web browser that also is being back-ported to the main Squeak distribution.

[25]Currently released is "Flow 1," which covers sockets, but lacks support for the various network protocols. Flow 2 does files, Flow 3 MIDI, and Flow 4 serial ports. All these were present and used in the Squeak port. Flow 5 is projected to handle FireWire/ILink connections. In what follows, unless otherwise specified, read "Flow 1" for "Flow."

[26]Flow 2 introduces a fourth hierarchy rooted in **URL**, which handles, as one might expect, URL style references to external resources. They are roughly comparable to the current **URL**-rooted classes.

sockets, serial ports, USB, etc.). These classes also wrap the requisite primitives, much as Socket and NetNameResolver do. Thus, unless you are implementing access to a new sort of input/output interface (e.g., IRDA), you should not need to modify, subclass, or even mess much with the ExternalResource classes. In general, you are better off reading and writing to them via the streaming protocols.

Indeed, streams are the heart and rationale of Flow, and, in some ways, the least obvious aspect. In general, streams provide a uniform interface for multiple and interruptible writing to, modifying, reading from, and enumerating collections of objects. For "internal streams" (e.g., on Collections), streams abstract away from the idiosyncratic access details of the particular collection types. For example, Array and its subclasses (including, most notably, String) are of fixed size, whereas OrderedCollection is of variable size. Thus, without streams, to append a new object to the end of an Array requires copying the contents of the Array to a new Array whose size is greater by one and then putting the new element in the last position of the new Array. Or, one could convert the Array to an OrderedCollection, add: the element, and then convert back.

Clearly, none of these strategies are really sensible. They are error prone, performance poor, and just plain tedious. Fortunately, you can simply open a stream on the Array and start adding or inserting elements at will. Even better, you don't need to care whether the streamed-over collection *is* an Array—the same stream methods will work for an OrderedCollection.[27]

Traditionally, the main external stream has been FileStream, which adds various external resource-specific methods (open, close, finalize, etc.), several file system information methods (fullname, directory, etc.), and "file mode" methods that influence how the underlying "collection of bytes" is to be treated (e.g., read only, write only, as characters with platform-specific line endings, etc.). In Flow 2, FileStream is an ExternalStream on the ExternalResource subclass File. In Flow 1, this basic pattern is repeated[28] for all the various ExternalResources, with one great simplification: Both sockets and hardware ports are treated as kinds of NetResource and have one corresponding stream class, NetStream. Essentially, NetStreams stream over external sequences of bytes that are interactively generated (i.e., via a request, wait, response sequence). In this way, NetStreams are analogous to Random—they are "generating" streams, rather than "iterating" streams.

Adding basic stream support for a new type of NetResource, whether new hardware or a new transport protocol, does not require modifying NetStream at all. You merely must implement in your new NetResource some methods for reading, writ-

---

[27]The performance advantage of streams is a classic Smalltalk tip. Flow incorporates several performance tunings for external resources, including buffering. One nice thing about Flow's factoring of the Stream hierarchy is that these performance tunings typically come for free for new resources.

[28]There are more sophisticated types of streams you might want to have for reading and writing things other than simple sequences of bytes. For example, NetMessages provide for streaming to structured text message formats (like RFC822). But note how, in Flow, these are orthogonal to the resource streamed over.

ing, and waiting for something to read or write.[29] NetStream does the rest. You may wish to add some convenience methods to NetStream, or a subclass, for managing the streamed over resource (much as FileStream does with binary, text, among others), but nothing more than the core is needed to secure stream functionality.

With these two layers, Flow provides an elegant architecture for accessing and implementing low-level features—even NetStream only deals with reading and writing bytes. It is the third layer, i.e., the Correspondents hierarchy, that supplies aid for implementing (and then using) the various Internet services. It supports sending and receiving email or news (POP and SMTP clients), browsing or serving web pages (HTTP client and server), and interacting with chat servers (IRC) or a Telnet server. Furthermore, Flow makes it easy to add custom net protocols, implement printer drivers, or set up a "connect and synchronize" system for palmtops. Flow separates protocol from transport. While Squeak currently includes behavior for protocols like POP and HTTP in subclasses of Socket, Flow provides it in subclasses of Client and Server. Unfortunately, Flow 1 includes none of the protocol-specific classes, so it is a little hard to say what implementing and using them is like. However, the included abstract classes (Correspondent, Client, and Server) do provide a few hints, at least for implementation issues. Correspondent abstracts transport mechanism, stream creation, and connecting/disconnecting. Client adds support for making requests and sending commands to a server, whereas Server has some support for managing (multiple) client connections and server status and responding to client requests.

Overall, Flow provides a remarkably well-organized approach to dealing both with new low-level system facilities and with new application-level protocols. It works hard to minimize repetition, tedium, and distracting details. It also embodies a coherent *model* of external, and thus network, services with cleanly separated concerns. While this particular model may not be to everyone's taste, clearly it is the standard against which alternative proposals will have to be measured.

Service with a Squeak

I can confidently say that if it had not been for Swikis and the Pluggable Web Server (PWS), I would have taken longer to learn how to program Squeak. When the PWS was first incorporated into the Squeak main distribution, I had been experimenting with various ways to integrate an interactive web site with the classes I was teaching. Perhaps it is needless to say, but a philosophy department at a state university typically does not have enormous technical resources. Furthermore, the IT department was rather inflexible about what CGIs, middleware, or custom servers it would permit me to play with, and the sanctioned tools were so dreadful they could be the subject of a study on how to impede learning through technological innovation.

---

[29]The actual four methods are, respectively, next:into:startingAt:, nextPut:from:startingAt:, waitForReadabilityTimeoutAfter:, and waitForWriteability.

The PWS—with bundled Swiki implementation—came to the rescue on all fronts. The Swiki was simple enough that I could get my students up and running in a single class period. The Swiki came integrated with a web server. Therefore, I didn't have to deal with the IT department at all, and I was able to run my class Swikis *in the background* of a heavily used lab machine (a pokey 486 with 20 megs of RAM, running Windows 95), with Netscape often running in the foreground. This worked adequately for about two years, in which time I was able to tweak the Swiki in numerous ways and tweak my use of it even more (e.g., for one course, all of the non-exam written work consisted of Swiki pages). Compared with hunting down a Windows web server, configuring it, hunting down some sort of collaboration CGIs or what have you, and configuring and maintaining them, this was a breeze. I could evolve and debug my customizations on my Mac at home, and then I could just pop them into the server with nary a twitch.

Web servers have been a prominent—perhaps the most prominent—Squeak application to date. Squeak has long been bundled with a web server (the PWS) and several key server apps (most notably, the Swiki), and many people have used it for nothing else. Furthermore, the PWS has been ported to several other Smalltalk variants (e.g., Dolphin Smalltalk and Smalltalk/X) and served as the inspiration for a server (WikiWorks) written in yet another dialect (VisualWorks). Mark Guzdial's Swiki is, I believe, the first Wiki implemented in Smalltalk, a situation that, post-Swiki, has been rectified with (at least) three Wiki implementations in Squeak alone. The creation of a Squeak-based Wiki and its adoption into the core Squeak release was critical, I believe, in spurring the explosion of Wiki use in the past three or so years and, indeed, was instrumental in introducing Wikis and Wiki values to *many* people—even to those outside the Squeak community. There are now at least 30 medium- to large-scale public Smalltalk-based Wikis (and growing), not counting `swiki.net` (which is a professional Swiki hosting organization), plus countless private ones (including a slew run by yours truly, but I've also heard of Swikis used "in house" at various corporations, in classrooms, and, of course, for single person use).

Servers—and, in particular, HTTP servers—are a surprisingly common and even more surprisingly essential component of modern *everyday* computing.

The Pluggable Web Server

There are three aspects of the PWS's history that I find particularly striking:

1. It evolved in a "feedback triangle": it, at once, served as a *tool* of community building (the main Squeak information site is a Swiki, and the PWS itself has attracted a fair number of people to Squeak), a *focus* of a community (one loosely organized by the PWS mailing list), and a *bridge* between communities (most obviously, between the various Smalltalk implementations' authors and users).

2. It served as an important research and development platform both for web servers and web applications, and as the inspiration and basis for new development.

3. It was written by one very bright guy[30] without much Smalltalk, or web server implementation, experience.

The PWS has its roots in two earlier Squeak web servers[31] that, while having some interesting properties of their own, never achieved the popularity of the PWS, mainly because they didn't have the killer app, the Swiki, which also was a driving factor in getting the PWS into the main distribution.

#howToStart

The PWS[32] comes with a number of sample web applications, including a web chat page, a discussion system, a "SqueakTop cam" (i.e., a screenshot server), and, most prominently, the Swiki. To get things rolling, you need merely execute

```
PWS initializeAll.
PWS serveOnPort: 80 loggingTo: 'log.txt'.
```

(Warning, this will work only if you have an image with the relevant changes to PWS class>>initializeAll found in **netchap.cs**. With those changes, initializeAll will install a "Server" directory in the default directory for that image. Server contains all the necessary support files for the examples and is setup to run a Swiki called "myswiki." If you don't have **netchap.cs** changes, you'll need to get ahold of those files and a few other things to get the examples correctly set up. Detailed instructions are to be found in PWS class>>howToStart.)

Once PWS is serving, you can open a browser onto your server, using your machine's hostname or IP address.[33] The standard default page (what you get by surfing to `http://yourserver/`[34] is, to be sure, appropriately bland. However, `http://yourserver/pws.html` is worth a look (both for its discussion of the PWS and for its demonstration of the discussion board). Finally, `http://yourserver/networkingsqueak.html` contains a nice tour of the sample programs.[35]

To turn off the server, use PWS class>>stopServer. Note that the PWS does *not* keep serving through an image snapshot (i.e., you'll shut down your server if you

---

[30]Namely, Mark Guzdial, who wrote it over the second month of his third child's life, which may provide some clue to some of the peculiarities of PWS's construction.

[31]One by Georg Gollman and the other by Tim Jones.

[32]In general, when "PWS" is not emphasized, I'm referring to "the" PWS system, of which the *class* PWS is a part.

[33]This is one place where NetNameResolver class>>addressForString: (and friends) comes in handy.

[34]It's quite common to use "localhost" as your hostname, but sometimes this is a bit awkward or requires reconfiguration, depending on your operating system and individual setup.

[35]The networkingsqueak.html is bundled in **netchap.cs**, but may not be available in old Server directory downloads.

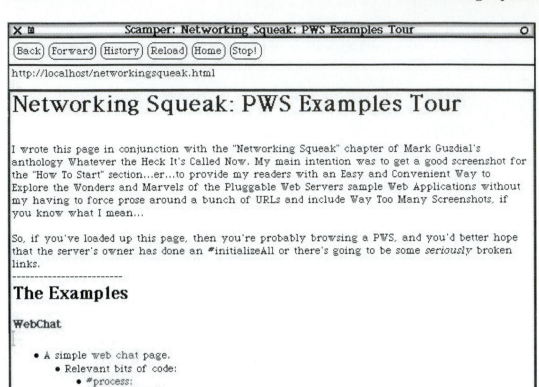

Figure 4.6   The PWS application tour page.

"save" your image). More importantly, it doesn't automatically start up after the save is complete, nor does it (without intervention) begin serving when you launch Squeak—even if you didn't send **stopServer** before you quit. Clearly, the image is *not* a good way to secure persistence for your web app's data.

If you save your image, you'll have to start up the server again manually via **serveOnPort:loggingTo:**. Assuming you've saved your image, there's no need to reinitialize PWS.

The Serving Architecture

A slightly naive, but useful, view of a web server is that it takes in an HTTP request and pops out a page of HTML. What's interesting for the web programmer is what happens in between the request and the response. Ideally, the application author

Class Var	Stores	Facilitates
ServerPort	aConnectionQueue	listening for requests
ServerProcess	aProcess running loopOnPort:loggingTo:	general server behavior
ServerLog	aFileStream	logging
ActionTable	aDictionary	dispatching to ServerActions

Table 4.2 The four key class variables of PWS.

should be isolated from the details of the request and response protocols, either simply so that one might focus on the functionality of one's program or to make it more or less independent of any particular protocol. This isolation is a primary design goal of both the PWS and its successor, Comanche.[36]

The PWS *system* consists of two major components:

1. The web server, which is implemented by the PWS class.

2. The web applications, which are mostly descendants of ServerAction, or instances of SinglePlugServerAction.

PWS has four key class variables that correspond to four key actions of the server (Table 4.2): ServerPort, ServerProcess, and ServerLog are all initialized with

PWS class>>serveOnPort:loggingTo:

and destroyed with

PWS class>>stopServer.

One consequence of the current structure is that you can't have PWS listening on more than one port. If you're trying to understand listening in depth, it helps to have a clear understanding of Squeak's threading model. That clear understanding also will help if you want to try adding multithreading to PWS.

The ServerProcess polls the ServerPort for a connected socket. If there is one, then ServerProcess creates an instance of PWS for that socket (in PWS class>> serve:), which then reads and parses the HTTP request from the socket connection. The instance of PWS (a "request") now dispatches itself (in PWS>>getReply) to a ServerAction for processing (via process:). The ServerAction reads the data out of the request and sends whatever response it has back to the PWS instance (via reply:), which writes it back to the socket and returns control to the listening thread. The ServerPort can, in the default setting, hold a backlog of eight connections, so assuming that your traffic is reasonably light, and your processing isn't too terribly lengthy, all your incoming connections should be handled, and in good time.

---

[36]And of other Smalltalk systems, albeit in different ways. `Cincom'sVisualWave` package, for example, lets you design your program's UI in the normal way and deploy it (however awkwardly) as HTML.

ServerAction dispatching is mediated through the ActionTable, a dictionary of strings onto (normally) instances of various ServerAction classes.[37] One registers an action using PWS class≫link:to:, and there can be an arbitrary number of actions (or names for a single action). While for anything but the simplest web apps, it's probably a good idea to subclass ServerAction, it's quite feasible nonetheless to experiment without creating a new class at all.

Actions

So, first initialize PWS, which puts an empty dictionary in ActionTable.[38] PWS has the notion of a "catchall" action to handle all the requests which aren't directed to any other specific action. This catchall action is named "default," so, since we won't have any other actions in play, we'll let all requests be handled by our little test action.

We now have a name for our action; we need the action to go with it. We're going to use a SinglePlugServerAction. (This is the second way that the "PWS" is "P".) SinglePlugServerAction takes a block that processes any requests it receives and yields a response. For this example, we're going to return the request's URL:

```
PWS initialize.[39]
PWS link: 'default'
    to: (SinglePlugServerAction new
        processBlock: [:request |
            request reply: PWS success;
                reply: PWS contentHTML , PWS crlf.
            request reply:
    '<html><head>
<title>A Really Simple App</title>
</head>
<body><h2>', request url, '</h2></body>
</html>']).
PWS serveOnPort: 80 loggingTo: 'log.txt'.
```

As is clear in Figure 4.7, a PWS instance contains only part of the original URL,[40] but passes the rest to a particular ServerAction to parse and to process as the author sees fit.

---

[37]As long as your class responds to process: you can use it as an action.

[38]PWS class≫initializeAll is worth studying as it sets up a slew of sample actions, including Swikis.

[39]This clears the ActionTable, so if you wish later to play with the sample applications, you must re−initializeAll.

[40]Sadly, the PWS antedates the truly fine URL classes. However, that doesn't mean one can't use them today.

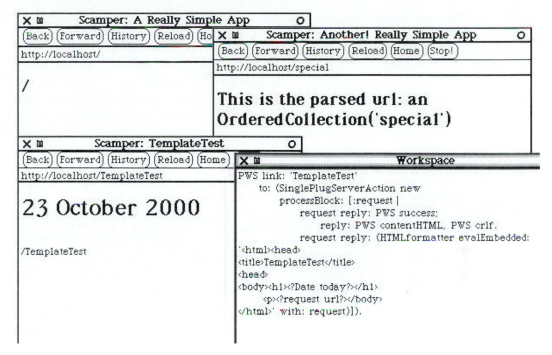

Figure 4.7   I often use Scamper to test out simple web applications.

Changing the block slightly yields

```
PWS link: 'special'
  to: (SinglePlugServerAction new
    processBlock: [:request |
        request reply: PWS success;
          reply: PWS contentHTML , PWS crlf.
        request reply:
    '<html><head>
<title>Another! Really Simple App</title>
</head>
<body>
<h2>This is the parsed url: ',
        request message printString, '</h2>
</body></html>']).
```

and evaluating the result gives us two actions in the ActionTable, with similar, but distinguishable, behavior. Looking at the "Accessing" category of PWS, we find a number of things about the request that we could reflect back in an HTML page—thus giving us a simple way to debug our requests.

There are several things to note about the processBlock:

- A PWS request keeps track of and manages the active connection and its socket. The only thing the action author need do is pass data to it by way of reply:.

- The PWS class has a number of utility methods that come in handy when formulating a response (e.g., success, contentHTML, etc.). This set is rather minimal in some ways (only four of the most common response codes are so encapsulated, for example), but it also gives some clear suggestions for enhancement and extention (e.g., if one were serving tons of JPEG files, it would make sense to have PWS class>>contentJPEG; better yet, one might have the content classes pass their content code to PWS).[41]

- While the PWS might help out with the HTTP parsing and generating, the action author is (thus far) responsible for generating all the HTML. On the other hand, there's nothing *forcing* the return of HTML. Indeed, the Code-Server class will cheerfully serve filed out chunks of Smalltalk code, suitable for being "remotely filed in" to a client Squeak image.

- There are two levels of URL handling: PWS uses the first element of the url-path[42] for selecting the action to handle the request (this is set by PWS class>>link:to: and corresponds to the keys of the ActionTable), but then passes the entire url-path to the selected action (via PWS>>message for the parsed version) for further processing. The action may then interpret the path as it sees fit.

- Given these last two points, it's clear that it's not going to be fun writing SinglePlugServerActions where the block contains anything very complex. Far better to off-load the processing and the generation to a class, to the methods of some existing class, or to *something else entirely*.

Let's start with the something else.

Embedded Code

It's common to have "HTML templates," which are typically files of HTML with interspersed bits of code (in a popular scripting language) set off by special delimiters and which get evaluated at serve time. The PWS has such a mechanism that allows you to embed arbitrary Squeak code in an HTML string or file. The evaluation is done by HTMLformatter (which also has other useful HTML utility functions), in particular by HTMLformatter class>>evalEmbedded:with:. Let us return to our workspace:

---

[41]See section entitled "Comanche—The Next Generation."

[42]Essentially, the url-path is what comes after the hostname, i.e., http://hostname/url-path (with the leading slash actually being part of the url-path).

```
PWS link: 'TemplateTest'
   to: (SinglePlugServerAction new
      processBlock: [:request |
         request reply: PWS success;
            reply: PWS contentHTML , PWS crlf.
         request reply:
            (HTMLformatter evalEmbedded:
   '<html><head>
   <title>Template Test</title>
   </head>
   <body>
      <h1><?Date today?></h1>
      <p><?request url?></p>
   </body>
   </html>'
                     with: request)]).
```

Notice that the template string contains straight HTML save for two bits that appear between the "<?" and "?>" delimiters. The two scripting bits illustrate two key points:

- **<?Date today?>**—This is simply an arbitrary piece of Smalltalk code. Pretty much anything you can do in a workspace, you can evaluate embedded in HTML. One nice bit is that you do not need to return a string—the HTMLformatter acts as if you took the code and "printed-it."

- **<?request url?>:** –A template that is run through HTMLfomatter class>> evalEmbedded is compiled to a two argument block, for example the above template compiles to:[43]

```
[:request :output |
   output nextPutAll:
      '<html><head>
      <title>Template Test</title>
      </head>
      <body>.
   output nextPutAll: [Date today printString] value asString.
   output nextPutAll: '</h1>
      <p>'.
   output nextPutAll: [request url] value asString.
   output nextPutAl l: '</p>
      </body>
      </html>']
```

---

[43] This is easy enough to get if you change the last line of HTMLformatter>>forEvaluatingEmbedded: to return or inspect the uncompiled contents of blockStream (to wit, change the last line to blockStream contents.).

In HTMLformatter, these "format blocks" are passed to the format: method where "output" gets a WriteStream on a String. (It's easy to see that one could have a custom formatter that, for example, wrote more or less directly to the Socket, say, by aliasing reply: with nextPutAll: in PWS, and using the current request as the "output" argument. This might be handy when dealing with complex formatting for timeout-sensitive clients.) In typical PWS usage, "result" gets the second argument of HTMLformatter class≫evalEmbedded:with:, which, as one would expect from the foregoing example, is the PWS instance, but there's no enforcement of that. Indeed, in the PWS's Swiki templates, it's more common to pass a SwikiPage. This, among other things,[44] can make templates rather difficult to debug. My personal horror story: When I first started using a Swiki in the classroom, it would lock up quite often in such a way that necessitated me driving 40 minutes to reset it. The key (discovered after two months) was that a FileStream wasn't getting closed when a page was edited. The offending method was *only* invoked by a template, and, thus, it didn't seem to be getting used.

For the sake of making SinglePlugServerActions more wieldy, this example hasn't helped. But there's no difficulty in popping the template text into a file (e.g., **Test Template.tmp**—the **.tmp** is just for convenience) and evaluating *that*:

```
PWS link: 'TemplateFileTest' to:
   (SinglePlugServerAction new
      processBlock: [:request |
         request reply: PWS success;
            reply: PWS contentHTML , PWS crlf.
         request reply:
            (HTMLformatter evalEmbedded:
               (FileStream readOnlyFileNamed: 'TestTemplate.tmp')
                  with: request)]).
```

From this it's clear that one could set up a method or workspace script that mapped files to certain URLs (well, `url-path` first elements, anyway) quite easily. In the end, I'd say this is mostly useful for debugging templates.

Fortunately, the PWS system has a nice way of turning these *ad hoc* "plugged into" processors into encapsulated, scalable ones: the ServerAction.

Building ServerActions

When PWS has determined which action to dispatch to (in PWS≫getReply), it sends that action a process: message with the PWS reply as the argument. Thus, subclasses of ServerAction need merely override ServerAction≫process: to be ready

---

[44]For example, the fact that templates are typically outside the image and thus not subject to the normal Squeak tools. With a little work, this can be ameliorated.

to be popped into the actions table (via **PWS class»link:to:**).[45] This is, in fact, how the majority of **PWS** applications are implemented.

As an example, I shall construct a simple **PWS** template-based Content Management System (CMS).

The basic idea is the same as in the "TemplateFileTest" workspace code, except instead of manually linking action names to specific files, the class automatically maps URLs into the file system. Fortunately, there's already a **ServerAction** that does this mapping—**ServerAction** itself. (Which is why it's the standard default action.) All we have to do is make sure each **.tmp** file gets run through **HTMLformatter**.

Make a subclass of **ServerAction** called **TemplateServerAction**. Presuming that you have already set up the PWS, you only need to override any of the class methods if you want your "root" directory to be something other than the bundled "server" directory (and you do). Thus, add a class method **serverDirectory**, which returns the path to your root template directory.

If we examine **ServerAction»process:**, we'll see that the actual processing and responding is handed off to a helper method **replyTo:from:**. **process:** itself takes care of what we might call "meta-processing": it checks for authorization,[46] converts the `url-path` string to a file path string, and logs the access. All these we can leave untouched for present purposes.

To switch over from simple serving of files to serving of evaluated templates we'll override **replyTo:with:**[47] so that the file has its embedded code evaluated before returned to the request:

```
TemplateServerAction»replyTo: pieces from: request
    (StandardFileStream isAFileNamed: pieces)
        ifTrue:
        [request reply: PWS success;
            reply: PWS contentHTML , PWS crlf.
            request reply:
                (HTMLformatter evalEmbedded:    The crucial addition.
                    (FileStream fileNamed: pieces) contentsOfEntireFile
                        with: request)]
        ifFalse: [request error: PWS notFound]
```

---

[45]**ServerAction** really is a fairly minimal class, and so long as your class has an instance method **process:** it needn't otherwise be in the **ServerAction** hierarchy; although, for the sake of extensibility, I recommend it.

[46]The PWS and Comanche have various degrees and kinds of security. However, I am by no means a security expert and not particularly interested in being one, so consult someone else about it. I'll note that several of the sample applications that come with PWS, and, indeed, that are setup with **initializeAll**, open the door for some rather nasty exploits (allowing, as they do, the execution of arbitrary Squeak code). If you're going to use the PWS for an open or a production server, take care to evaluate your security situation. Templates, in particular, are not by default run "safely," though you can tighten the screws a bit using **HTMLformatter class» evalEmbedded:with:unlessContains:**. In general, better security methods are on the way.

[47]Clearly, some refactoring is in order here, given the duplication.

That's it. Now we can arrange template files and directories in our template root directory as we see fit, and TemplateServerAction will dish them up.

Turning this from a toy into something useful is straightforward, consisting of the following three simple steps: First, HTMLformatter class>>evalEmbedded:with: can be very slow, which is no surprise since it has to compile the template to a block source text, compile that source text to bytecode, and then evaluate it on the request. So the first step is to avoid it when possible, for example, by discriminating between .html and .tmp files (as well as others) and serving the former straight. More importantly to a template-heavy site, HTMLformatter class >>forEvaluatingEmbedded: returns an instance of HTMLformatter with a compiled version of the template ready to use (via HTMLformatter>>format:).[48] So a simple precompilation/caching system is an important optimization.

Second, there are several kinds of files that one simply doesn't want to run through the HTMLformatter. Image files come immediately to mind, as do straight HTML files. So, some checks for file type before this processing seem in order. Of course, if you do this, you end up with EmbeddedServerAction:[49]

```
replyTo: pieces from: request
    | theLast |
    (StandardFileStream isAFileNamed: pieces)
      ifTrue:
        [theLast := 'gif' ifTrue:
          [↑ self process: request MIMEtype: 'image/gif'].
        theLast = 'jpeg' ifTrue:
          [↑ self process: request MIMEtype: 'image/jpeg'].
        theLast = 'jpg' ifTrue:
          [↑ self process: request MIMEtype: 'image/jpeg'].
        theLast = 'jpe' ifTrue:
          [↑ self process: request MIMEtype: 'image/jpeg'].
        request reply: PWS success;
          reply: PWS contentHTML , PWS crlf.
        request reply: (HTMLformatter evalEmbedded:
          (FileStream fileNamed: pieces)
            contentsOfEntireFile with: request)]
      ifFalse: [request error: PWS notFound]
```

(A worthwhile, and classic, Smalltalk newbie adventure is to refactor the repeated conditionals into a more Smalltalky and extensible style.)

---

[48]This optimization is due to Lex Spoon, and it made a considerable difference in the performance of PWS-based Swikis: from "oh my god" to "quite nippy."

[49]Note: I discovered this fact *after* having invented TemplateServerAction. Ain't it always the way?

Finally, it seems worthwhile to be able to password protect certain pages. Fortunately, the PWS system includes the Authorizer class (which also sees more general use outside of the PWS system). Authorizer allows one to set up named "realms" that have users, usernames, and passwords associated with them. Usernames and passwords are stored encrypted together, according to the scheme detailed in RFC1421.[50] So, one could map certain directories/URLs to certain realms, thus protecting, say, administrative functions. Indeed, one could imagine setting up a form that would take arbitrary Smalltalk code and "doit," like a Workspace. That way, one could perform various administration functions, add or remove users, or change templates remotely, with nothing more than a web browser. One would *definitely* want such a page password protected—it just wouldn't do to have just *anyone* mucking with the server.

And this is exactly what AuthorizedServerAction, in conjunction with the `workspace.html` template, provides.

By examining a bit of the embedded code in `workspace.html`, you can gain some insight into how to handle form data from requests. For example, consider the code

```
. . .
<TEXTAREA NAME="doit" ROWS=10 COLS=80>
   <?request fields notNil
      ifTrue: [request fields at: 'doit' ifAbsent: ['']]
      ifFalse: [' ']?>
</TEXTAREA>. . .
```

This embedded code is expecting the variable "request" to point to a PWS instance. PWS has instance variable "fields," which either contain nil or a Dictionary whose keys are the names of the search fields of the URL (for GET requests) or the POST fields, and whose values are the contents of their respective fields.

Recall that the code between the "<??>" delimiters will be evaluated each time the page is loaded. The first time a client loads the page (say, by requesting `http://yourserver/authorized/workspace.html`), the "fields" of the request will be nil, as this is a straight HTTP GET, with no search fields. Now, suppose the client enters some text in the <textarea> and submits the form: The request is the same URL, but it's a POST with a field entitled "doit" (the name of the <textarea>), which contains the Smalltalk code the client entered. What *the preceding* bit of embedded code does, then, is redisplay the submitted contents of the <textarea>, which duplicates the standard behavior of a workspace (where "doing" a bit of code does not obliterate it).

The actual evaluation of the submitted code takes place further down the template:

---

[50]Authorizer is also used by HttpUrl for storing passwords going out from the browser's perspective.

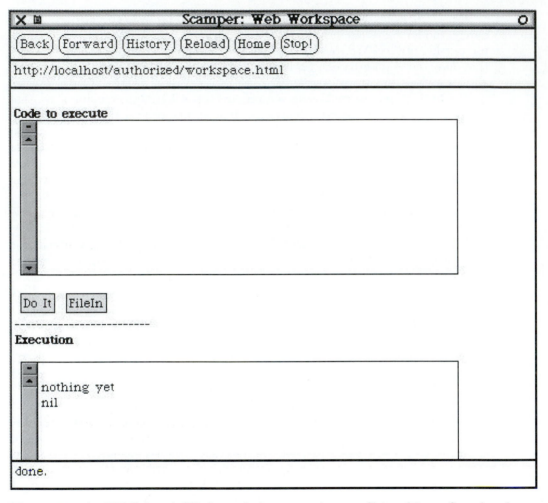

Figure 4.8   An HTML based-"Workspace" that can evaluate or filein arbitrary Squeak code.

```
...
<TEXTAREA NAME="results" ROWS=10 COLS=80>
    <?request fields notNil
        ifTrue: [(request fields at: 'action') = 'Do It'
            ifTrue:
                [(Compiler evaluate:
                    (request fields at: 'doit' ifAbsent: ['nil']))
                        printString]
            ifFalse: [(ReadWriteStream with:
                    (request fields at: 'doit' ifAbsent: ['nil']))
                        reset fileIn. 'done!']]
        ifFalse: ['nothing yet']?>...
```

Thus, depending on which button is selected, either the code will be directly evaluated and the results displayed in the results <textarea>, or it will be filed into the server image and the message "done!" returned.

Embedded code is, as the fact of so many extant variants (ASP, JSP, PHP, eHTML, etc.) testifies, extraordinarily powerful and often quite convenient. Indeed, much of its appeal comes from the "feel" that one is simply extending HTML—a feel that is most powerful in simple examples. Embedded code can go somewhat toward separating presentation design from programming, with the concomitant hope that your non-programming designers can use their old comfy HTML tools. In practice, however, things aren't typically so rosy, since it's very easy to write elaborate "spaghetti" templates that become very difficult for *either* an HTML author *or* a programmer to follow.[51]

Of course, HTMLformatter class>>evalEmbedded:with: isn't *forced* to rely on file-based templates—after all, it's quite happy taking arbitrary strings as its first argument, as it did in the "TestTemplate" example. HTMLformatter is completely decoupled from the PWS, and often a bit of embedded markup is substantially clearer than a series of nextPutAll:s or concatenations. The downside, naturally, is that your templates are still going to be "compiled" at run time unless you cache the format blocks in some manner, which can rather complicate your class's design and implementation. One answer[52] is to have strings with embedded code compiled by the class browser (and compiler) when you accept an "embedded code" method. Squeak Server Pages (SSP) treat the method source of a class as a string with embedded code. SSP methods have a directive at their head that causes them to be sent to a modified parser for compilation (similar to running PWS templates through HTMLformatter class>>forEvaluatingEmbedded:. The user experience is very smooth, and the SSP methods are compiled to an efficient stream-based form.

```
sspTemplateExampleOn: strm
    <ssp on: strm>      This pragma turns on SSP interpetation.
                     Required blank line between pragma and text
    <html><head>
    <title>Template Test</title>
    </head>
    <body>
       <h1><%= Date today %></h1>
       <p><%= request url %></p>
    </body>
    </html>
```

---

[51]Indeed, I have read advice in several books on PHP programming to the effect that one should "generate" all the HTML for a page using print/write-type statements, rather than using embedded code! "Maintainability" is the usual reason given, though, myself, I don't find the examples supplied, or, for that matter, found in the real world, at all convincing.

[52]Explored and variously implemented by Bolot Kerimbaev and Stephen Pair. There are significant differences in the two implementations. I'm focusing on the Pair variant.

For text-heavy methods (and not merely those generating HTML), this can mean greater clarity. Furthermore, SSP methods act just like normal ones and are so regarded by the Squeak IDE, thus changes in SSP methods go to the changes file and can be browsed by the "versions" menu command. Furthermore, code in strings passed to evalEmbedded:with: is seen by the system as part of the string. Thus, commands like "find senders" won't find embedded sendings, which is a serious handicap. SSP methods are also debugger friendly. It's quite easy and often instructive to step through an SSP method watching your output string get built up bit by bit.

A Little Debugging

As with all programming, debugging is the bugaboo of web applications. One of the nasty things about web programming is that you too often end up in an edit-compile-browse cycle *as well as* the edit-save-browse cycle of the HTML author. And you end up using the equivalent of hoary old `println` (or rather, `Transcript>> show:`) in order to stomp bugs. Yuck.

The PWS system, as it stands, doesn't provide any specific debugging support beyond the standard IDE tools (worse, as in the case of embedded code, it sometimes circumvents them). But there are several advantages that come from having the PWS as just another set of objects in your Squeak's image.[53] First, unlike, say, Apache, the web server isn't a black box or even a separate program. It's quite easy to poke around the PWS class and put debugging code in different places. Second, once an HTTP request hits the system, it's converted into an instance of PWS that you can inspect, store in a class, or serialize to disk. Indeed, one of my favorite debugging techniques is to put a judicious `request inspect` or two in my action's method (or even in a template). This is equally handy when debugging custom *clients*, and I've several times evolved a custom client app and matching custom server app hand in hand.[54] Along these lines, it's easy to imagine a tool that, on errors, stashed the offending request for later replay and diagnosis.

Whither PWS?

The Pluggable Web Server has had a lively history, and it remains a workhorse application for many folks. As a core part of the Squeak distribution, it has served both as a stimulus to development and exploration and as a key bit of infrastructure for the Squeak community. While it remains an intriguing system of just the right

---

[53]These advantages accrue equally well to Comanche and other Smalltalk-based servers and to similar systems such as the Python-based Zope.

[54]Or used Scamper to debug a PWS app.

size for beginners to wrap their brains around, it's no longer under active development, nor even acting as the prime web server for the Squeak community. In the course of PWS development, it became clear that the PWS suffered from some design decisions that made it difficult, for example, to improve—or even assess—its performance characteristics in high stress, heavy load installations or to build applications that were cleanly decoupled from PWS details. Furthermore, one way that the PWS is *not* pluggable is with regard to *protocol*.

It soon will be superseded by Comanche, which is a complete rewrite with an eye to solving these problems. Fortunately, Comanche—while not directly compatible with PWS-based apps—does contain a compatibility module. Thus, even if you find yourself more comfortable working with PWS-style design tropes (which I do in many situations), you can rest assured that they won't require even a compatibility revision.

In the end, however, the PWS and Comanche aren't just version 1 and version 2 of the (generically specified) "Squeak bundled web/application server," but instantiations of different approaches to program design. Comanche is a highly factored *framework* that is well integrated into Squeak as a whole. The core of the system is made up of many classes divided into several categories, and even a simple standardly designed Comanche-savvy app will contain three to five classes. The PWS, however, is a single class, with a small number of support and utility classes for writing applications, all of which are well-isolated from the rest of the system.

Comanche—The Next Generation

What would the Web look like if it were a big object system? Current web development technologies offer various approaches to structuring web applications, but most revolve around concepts that are deeply limited by the limitations of HTML. Comanche aims to overcome these limitations through an object-oriented framework. No surprise here; Comanche merely extends Squeak to the Web.

Comanche is a research project, and, as such, it is a tool for answering questions that are yet to be asked. This puts forward special requirements that are not necessarily known in advance. Thus, it was designed to be flexible and modular, allowing easy adjustment to each situation.

Squeak's rich class library is a result of almost three decades of experience in research and practice. Most of Comanche's components have been designed to mesh well with design patterns prevalent in Squeak. Socket communication is wrapped in a stream; polymorphism ensures that other kinds of streams can be used instead of the SocketStream (debugging, for example).

Protocol support is handled in specialized classes: HttpAdaptor, HttpRequest, and HttpResponse. The adaptor takes the appropriate sequence of actions to decode the request and channels it to the application, whose response is encoded into the suitable form.

Layer	Role	Related Classes
Application	Implement the application logic	SwikiModule
Protocol	Interpret the protocol information	HttpAdaptor, HttpRequest, HttpResponse
Server	Handles details of connection, scheduling	ComancheServer
Service	Puts the server and protocol together	ComancheNetService
Network	Already in Squeak, performs low-level data communication	Socket

Table 4.3   Implementation layers in Comanche

Layers

Comanche is implemented in layers that are independent enough to be replaced by alternative implementations (Table 4.3).

The Network and Transport layer is responsible for low-level socket communication. The Service layer manages the server and protocol; in fact, it puts them together (scheduling handler threads, listening to ports, etc.). The Protocol layer translates the streams between network and application. And, the Application performs task-specific actions; that's where most developers will focus.

The most common protocol layer adaptor is HttpAdaptor. It understands HTTP 1.0 (and some 1.1) specifications, such as the format of request and response headers, multipart forms, etc. The HttpAdaptor reads the request and translates it into a ready-to-use form, HttpRequest. An HttpRequest contains a Dictionary of header fields, in which each key is the name of the field (e.g., "content-type"), and the value is the value of the field, such as "text/html." Some common header fields are accessible through accessor methods, contentType, contentLength, etc. Since most applications need to have access to HTTP header fields, the task of processing the header is delegated to HttpAdaptor.

Objects All the Way

Another convention that eases development of applications with Comanche is use of objects all the way. This is not surprising, since Comanche is written in Squeak, in which even arithmetic operations manipulate objects. But beyond just being stuck with objects as atomic entities, Comanche takes advantage of the paradigm. A Comanche application (the top layer) doesn't need to worry about protocol specifics (why be bound to HTTP now if it'll be "yet another protocol" tomorrow?); it just manipulates some objects and returns an object (or a collection of objects) to the protocol adaptor. And, it's the protocol adaptor's role to make sure both parties are happy: The application deals the object and wants to be sure it is properly received on the other end, and the client wants to get the result in a format it understands, such as HTML, GIF, or Flash. Comanche teaches objects to convert themselves into these formats, which are acceptable by web browsers or other standard clients.[55]

Let's do a walkthrough to become familiar with the Comanche application development process. For a minimalist application, just create a class, named MyComancheApp, and implement a single method, process:. This process: takes a request (typically, an HttpRequest, but see information that follows) and replies with an object, or with nil if it doesn't know what to do with the request (or if it wants the request processing to continue, as in multipart form processing).

```
Object subclass: #MyComancheApp
    instanceVariableNames: ''
    classVariableNames: ''
    poolDictionaries: ''
    category: 'Comanche-MyHacking'
```

```
process: request
    ↑'Hello World!'
```

Voilà! The example that binds together all computer-programming books is complete. To make it produce the visible result, start the server by executing the following in the workspace and then open your browser on http://yourserver:8080/:

```
| che |
Socket initializeNetwork.
che := (ComancheNetService named: 'MyComancheApp' onPort: 8080).
che module: (MyComancheApp new).
che start
```

To stop a server, use the following:

```
| che |
che := ComancheServer serverOnPort: 8080 ifAbsent: [].
che ifNotNil: [che stop].
ComancheNetService removeServiceNamed: 'MyComancheApp'
```

How is it possible to return a String and have it served correctly? Each class defines the way it can be converted to a HTTP-compatible form. When an application module returns an object, the Comanche framework channels it through the

---

[55]ObjectWeb, discussed in section "Into the Blue," takes a similar approach, serving Morphic objects to Squeak clients and GIFs of those objects to standard web browsers. For the reverse approach—i.e., teaching standard web browsers to understand Squeak objects—there is the Squeak browser plug-in.

HttpResponse processing, which sends **asHttpResponseTo:** to the returned object. For String, the definition is

  String >> **asHttpResponseTo: request**
   ↑HttpResponse fromString: self

  HttpResponse class >> **fromString: aString:**
   ↑self new
    status: #ok;
    contentType: MIMEDocument contentTypeHtml;
    contents: (ReadStream on: aString);
    yourself

Note that by default, the content type is set to "`text/html`." Lets now look at file serving, which may seem as un-OOP as it gets. However, recall that file manipulation in Squeak is very much OOP. File access is done through FileStream hierarchy. Thus, it is only natural to return an instance of **FileStream**, which would then translate itself into an appropriate form. The code is as follows:

  ReadWriteStream >> **asHttpResponseTo: request**
   "inherited by StandardFileStream"
   ↑HttpResponse fromStream: self

  HttpResponse class >> **fromStream: aStream**
   ↑self new status: #ok;
    contentType: aStream mimeType;
    contents: aStream;
    yourself

  StandardFileStream >> **mimeType**
   ↑MIMEDocument guessTypeFromName: self name.

MIMEDocument contains a database that maps file extensions to appropriate content types; thus, adding support for new content types of files doesn't require changing your methods, but merely adding the new mapping. It is trivial to serve a file without having to worry about headers, content types, etc. (compare to the way PWS handles file serving, in ServerAction >> reply:MIMEtype:). For a complete example of file serving, look at FileServerModule and FileDirectory.

Advanced Application Development

It's easy to write simple applications for Comanche. But suppose we need to create something sophisticated. That's possible, too. To make the most of it, we shouldn't be afraid to step out of the conventional and rely on purely object-oriented design. First, a little revelation: A request doesn't have to be an HttpRequest. This allows us to have an application-specific request, such as WhatTimeIsItRequest.

```
Object subclass: WhatTimeIsItRequest
    instanceVariableNames: 'referenceCity referenceTime queryCity'
    classVariableNames: 'TimeZoneDatabase'
    poolDictionaries: ''
    category: 'Comanche—MyHacking'
```

We define an object that can encapsulate a request, in this case, the time in a time zone, given the time in another zone. Defining a task-specific request object lets us think in terms of the following:

```
WhatTimeIsIt in: 'Berlin' whenIn: 'Boston' itIs: '5:34 pm'
```

A few support methods are necessary to make it work:

WhatTimeIsIt class»in: aRefCity whenIn: aQueryCity itIs: aRefTime
```
    ↑(self new in: aRefCity whenIn: aQueryCity itIs: aRefTime) queryTime
```

WhatTimeIsIt»in: aRefCity whenIn: aQueryCity itIs: aRefTime
```
    referenceCityOffset := TimeZoneDatabase at: aRefCity.
    referenceTime := aRefTime.
    queryCityOffset := TimeZoneDatabase at: aQueryCity.
```

WhatTimeIsIt»queryTime
```
    | timeDelta |
    timeDelta := queryCityOffset − referenceCityOffset.
    ↑referenceTime + timeDelta
```

To make this work over the web, we'll need to write a converter from an HttpRequest and to use those converters in our application:

WhatTimeIsIt class»from: anHttpRequest
```
    | fields aRefCity aRefTime aQueryCity |
    fields ← anHttpRequest getFields.
    aRefCity ← fields at: ?235?referencecity?237? ifAbsent: [].
    aRefTime ← fields at: ?235?referencetime?237? ifAbsent: [].
    aQueryCity ← fields at: ?235?querycity?237? ifAbsent: [].
    ↑self in: aQueryCity whenIn: aRefCity itIs: aRefTime
```

This is a simplified example, of course, since handling time is a complicated matter (for starters, just consider these two words: "daylight savings"), but it demonstrates use of application-specific requests. Properly structured application-specific requests (and responses) provide a protocol-independent interface for the application to the server. With the appropriate conversion methods, the same application could handle HttpRequests, FtpRequests, and PopRequests with no further changes.

Multimedia on the Web

Let's revisit the notion that Comanche operates with objects. Let's also recall that Squeak is a great multimedia environment. Put the two together and you have a powerful multimedia web framework. Need a desktop cam application (the one that shows your Squeak desktop contents)? Easy, just make your application return Display in its **process:** method. Since Display is-a **DisplayScreen**, subclass of **Form**, it knows how to convert itself into a web-friendly image format, such as GIF or JPEG (PNG rendering is on the way). This suggests a very simple way to manipulate images—just use Squeak's rich **Form** class.

Let's see how **Form** handles conversion to **HttpResponse**.

Form ≫ asHttpResponseTo:
↑HttpResponse fromMIMEDocument: self asWebImage

Form ≫ asWebImage
```
"return a MIMEDocument"
| aStream contentType imageWriter |
aStream ← (RWBinaryOrTextStream on: '').
self depth <= 8
    ifTrue: [imageWriter ← GIFReadWriter.
        contentType ← MIMEDocument contentTypeGif]
    ifFalse: [imageWriter ← JPEGReadWriter.
        contentType ← MIMEDocument contentTypeJpeg].
imageWriter putForm: self onStream: aStream.
aStream reset.
↑MIMEDocument contentType: contentType content: aStream
```

Note that the choice of image format is made based on the depth of the image. This approach is a reasonable general solution, but in some cases more control over content type may be desired. For example, you may want to always return GIF images. You could change **Form≫asWebImage** method to accommodate that, but a better approach would be to define a wrapper whose only instance variable would be the form, and which would translate to **HttpResponse** in the desired fashion.

Swikis

The Swiki started out as a Wiki clone. The `WikiWikiWeb` was invented by Ward Cunningham with an eye to making the building of a collaborative web site as fast and easy as possible ("WikiWiki" means "quick" in Hawaiian). A WikiWiki is a *minimally intrusive technology*— if something *gets in the way* of the primary activity (writing and reading), then it should be eliminated, as far as possible.[56]

---
[56]Note: this is a somewhat tendentious view!

The features that *are* added, are done so with an eye to maximizing *easy* flexibility. There are all sorts of web sites that you just won't want to build in a classic WikiWiki, but the kind you *can* make are very interesting indeed.[57] The largest technical barrier, of course, stems from the deep conceptual gap between a web page as a text file and a web page in your browser. This difference standardly requires very different skills, setups, and attitudes for writing and for browsing web pages. Interestingly, Tim Berner-Lee's original web browser unified editing and browsing, and Mosaic itself had the ability to let the user "annotate" a web page with her own (private) comments. Unfortunately, these features disappeared with the rise of Netscape Navigator, Internet Explorer, and the browser wars. There has been a fair bit of effort in recent years to eliminate the writing/browsing divide, but most of these solutions are much more techno-heavy than WikiWiki-style solutions.

The basic Swiki is very lightweight and extremely flexible. Compared to many Wiki clones, it's very easy to setup a complete installation (partially because Squeak is so easy to install). Yet while it's certainly possible to produce an exact duplicate of Ward's WikiWiki, the Swiki has taken a somewhat different turn.

Running a PWS Swiki

While the Swiki is the most complex web application (the most complex one that I know of) bundled with the PWS, it's quite easy to set up, use, and modify.[58]

For each Swiki you intend to run, there must be an eponymous directory in **Server**. So, to have a Swiki named "myswiki,"[59] you must first make a directory named "myswiki" in your **Server**. That Swiki's "Top" page will be at http://your-server/myswiki. With this precondition met, you are ready to register your Swiki with PWS. Unlike in the earlier examples, you should not try to use PWS class>> link:to:, as there are some initialization tasks the SwikiAction must do. To get your Swiki up and running, execute the following in a workspace:

> SwikiAction setUp: 'myswiki'.
> PWS serveOnPort: 80 loggingTo: 'log.txt'. *Unnecessary if it's already running.*

Your new Swiki will contain two pages: the "Front" page and the "Formatting Rules" page. You can start editing your Swiki at will. There's no need to shut the server down when adding a new Swiki. If, however, your server machine should go down, you quit the image without saving, or you re- initialize or initializeAll, you'll leave the SwikiAction (though *not* the Swiki itself) in an inconsistent—or merely non-registered—state. To fix this, do *not* use setUp: again. Instead, you should evaluate

> SwikiAction new restore: 'myswiki'.

---

[57] As in *The WikiWay* (Luefand Cunningham, Addison-Wesley, 2001).
[58] This section presumes that you have read section The Pluggable Web Server.
[59] The classic choice in Swiki example names.

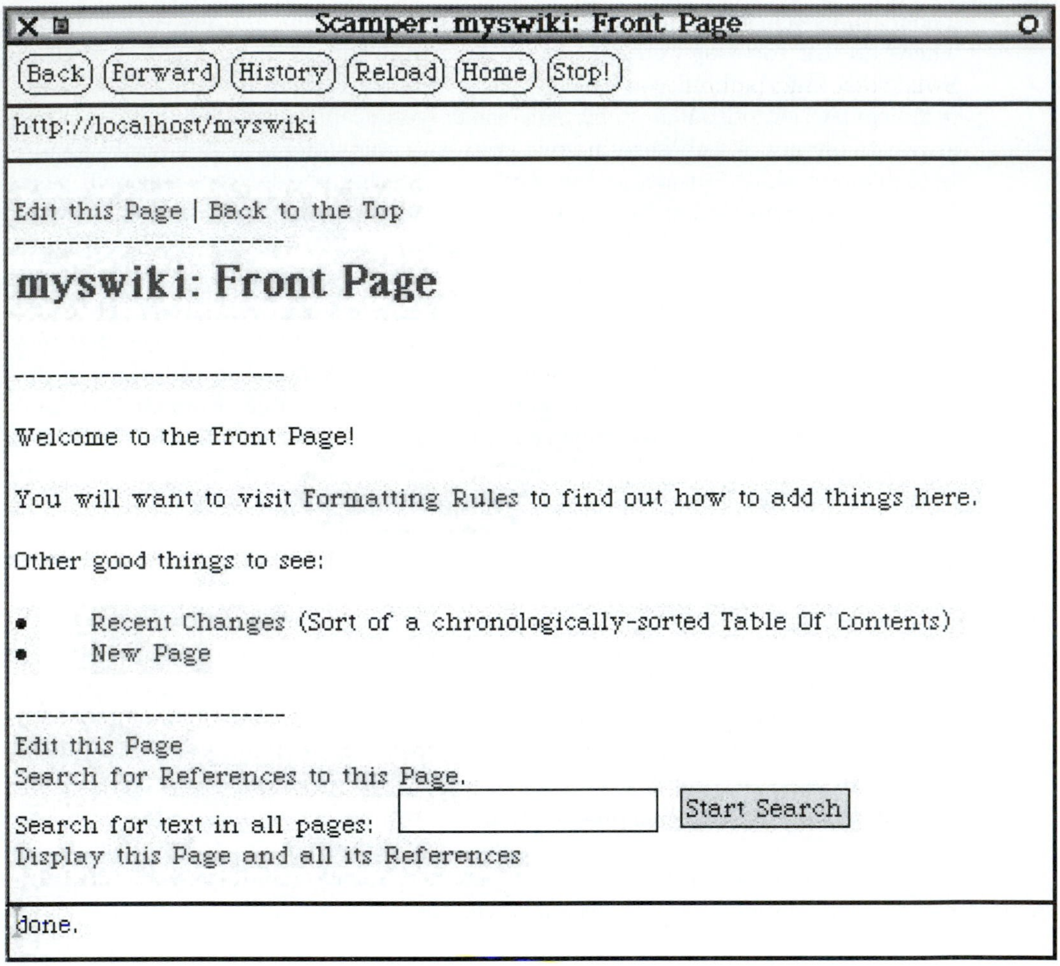

```
┌──────────────────────────────────────────────────────────────┐
│ X ▣            Scamper: myswiki: Front Page                  O │
├──────────────────────────────────────────────────────────────┤
│ (Back) (Forward) (History) (Reload) (Home) (Stop!)            │
├──────────────────────────────────────────────────────────────┤
│ http://localhost/myswiki                                       │
├──────────────────────────────────────────────────────────────┤
│                                                                │
│ Edit this Page | Back to the Top                               │
│ ------------------------                                        │
│ myswiki: Front Page                                            │
│                                                                │
│                                                                │
│ ------------------------                                        │
│                                                                │
│ Welcome to the Front Page!                                     │
│                                                                │
│ You will want to visit Formatting Rules to find out how to add things here. │
│                                                                │
│ Other good things to see:                                      │
│                                                                │
│ •      Recent Changes (Sort of a chronologically-sorted Table Of Contents) │
│ •      New Page                                                 │
│                                                                │
│ ------------------------                                        │
│ Edit this Page                                                 │
│ Search for References to this Page.                            │
│                                                                │
│ Search for text in all pages: [            ]  [ Start Search ] │
│ Display this Page and all its References                       │
│                                                                │
├──────────────────────────────────────────────────────────────┤
│ done.                                                          │
└──────────────────────────────────────────────────────────────┘
```

Figure 4.9   The "Front" page of a new Swiki

This reads in data from your Swiki's folder and sets up the Swiki in PWS's ActionTable. If you have a server that automatically reboots and relaunches Squeak, it's useful to add "restoring" lines to the startup sequence (as well as PWS class>>serverOnPort:loggingTo:)[60] to avoid the need for manual intervention.

Aside from keeping your server running, there's little that a Swiki-webmaster needs to worry about. It's very hard to lose any data, since the SwikiAction writes each edit to disk at submission time and maintains all edits back to the creation of the page. Each page is stored in a separate file in your Swiki's folder, so a simple backup regimen will safeguard your site. One important point: Unless you *really*

---

[60]Details on how to do this are on http://coweb.cc.gatech.edu/squeakbook.

know what you're doing, it's not a good idea to try to edit the page files by hand. Furthermore, there are certain processes that can munge the files and render your Swiki somewhat painful to recover. So, for example, either archive and compress the entire Swiki before FTPing it (or make sure you set the transfer mode to "binary"), otherwise, many FTP programs will automatically "fix" the line endings—a fix which, more likely than not, will mess up your pages.

S/Wikiness

In general, once you have a WikiWiki web site set up, the barriers to being an author on it are extremely minimal. The only technology you need is a web browser with form capability that can connect to the server. The only skills you need above basic web browsing is a mastery of the WikiSyntax and a familiarity with the basic structure of a WikiSite.

The fundamental principles of a Wiki are as follows:

1. Whenever reasonable, prefer *social* solutions to purely techological ones.

2. Anyone can edit any page at any time from anywhere with a web browser. Page creation is as simple as editing a page.

3. The WikiSyntax should be simple to master, and the community should find it easy to be fluent in it.

4. The Wiki is *safe*: If you mess something up, or someone messes up something you like, it's possible to recover.

5. There should be a variety of ways to search the Wiki, including, minimally, a reasonably fast full text search.

6. There should be a reverse chronologically sorted "Recent Changes" page.

The classic WikiSyntax is a simplified, "no-tags," punctuation-based formatting language that makes formatting a web page feel very much like writing an email message. For example, paragraphs are separated by blank lines; two single quotes will *emphasize* text; bullet lists are formed by a collection of lines starting with one or more tabs followed by an asterisk; and internal page links (and new pages) are generated by taking all the words in a phrase, capitalizing them, and removing the spaces to form an InterCapitializedWord. There are more and more complicated formatting commands, but this might well be sufficient for 90% of your WikiNeeds. In no case is HTML allowed.

The base PWS SwikiSyntax is somewhat different due to its specific audience. Mark Guzdial found that his students were almost all HTML fluent and didn't *want* to learn yet another syntax. So, PWS Swikis have only a few bits of "convenience" syntax, to wit:

- Blank lines separate paragraphs, and "returns" inside a block of text generate line breaks (i.e., `<br>`s).

- Both internal and external links are made by enclosing a phrase or a URL in matching asterisks. So

  this would be a link to a Swiki page

  and

  http://www.c2.com/cgi/wiki

  would be a link to the original WikiWikiWeb.

- "*Append Here*" will add a form to the page, wherein a browser can add comments without having to go to the edit page.

Everything else is straight HTML, and you can use any HTML you'd like.

Both of these seeming opposing stands—no HTML vs. mostly HTML—follow the minimally intrusive philosophy, *in the light of* their respective audiences. Mark's students found switching to a custom no-tags syntax *more intrusive* than just using HTML (though they were happy to use the convenience syntax supplied). My philosophy students, on the other hand, were barely computer literate, much less HTML savvy. Indeed, until quite recently, I could depend on the fact that most could scarcely use email (though I admit to being totally thrown off by the one who couldn't type). So I modified the formatter[61] (tabs and <textareas>, for example, are a painful mix). WikiWorks (the VisualWorks-based Wiki clone) uses a different no-tags syntax that's rather pleasant, and ComSwiki offers both a fairly complete WikiWorks-ish style syntax *and* the inclusion of HTML. Much thought has gone toward designing a way to happily handle the profusion of syntaxes, especially in one Swiki, but not much by way of concrete implementation has emerged.[62]

There is one significant danger that an HTML accepting Swiki faces that a no-tags based system does not: The possibility of malicious HTML-based attacks on browsers of your site (e.g., via inserted Javascript).

Tweaking Swikis

The PWS Swiki has two halves: a collection of classes (SwikiAction, UrlMap, and SwikiPage) that control the logic of the Swiki and a collection of templates (found in the "Swiki" directory inside "Server") that determine its appearance (with a little help from HTMLformatter). Thus, an easy way to get started tweaking your Swikis is by twiddling the templates to spruce up the rather utilitarian design (either by

---

[61] By rewriting HTMLformatter >> swikify:linkhandler to use a no-tags syntax somewhat similar to the classic WikiSyntax, but even simpler.

[62] With the exception, in ComSwiki, of the use of `<html></html>` to provide an "escape hatch" into pure HTML.

adding flash and sizzle or by adding yet more utility). The simplest sort of modification is to ignore the embedded code and simply alter the surrounding HTML. For example, perhaps you want to have the name of the Swiki in the title of each page. The page template, `page.html`, has a bit of embedded code generating the page's title, i.e., <TITLE><?request name?></TITLE>. Clearly, simply inserting the desired text (as in, <TITLE>myswiki: <?request name?></TITLE>) will do the trick.

Of course, this sort of hardcoding is terribly inelegant. Furthermore, if you have multiple Swiki's using this template, it will be simply wrong for all but one of them.[63] On the other hand, each SwikiAction knows its own name, so a bit of embedded code will fix things right up with a minimum of fuss. The key to using embedded code is knowing the class of the "request" object. In this case, it is a SwikiPage (indeed, it is the very SwikiPage that corresponds to the requested page) with its contents already converted from SwikiSyntax to HTML. Now, since there's no direct way to get at a SwikiPage's SwikiAction so, we have to go through the page's UrlMap. We end up with

<TITLE><?request map action name?>: <?request name?></TITLE>

which does the job nicely.

This segues nicely into the tweakage possibilities of the Swiki classes. The three Swiki classes neatly divide the duties of a Swiki:

SwikiAction Manages the connection to the PWS and the details of requests and responses. It also handles all the parsing and interpretation of URLs. That is, the SwikiAction knows about HTTP and URLs and which actions to perform given a URL, but nothing about the pages themselves.

UrlMap Determines which page reference goes with which page, whether a SwikiPage like the "Front Page" or a dynamically generated "virtual" page like "Recent Changes" or "Search Results." If you wanted to change how a Swiki URL worked, say using the page title instead of a number, this is the class to focus on.

SwikiPage Is the in-memory representation of the contents and metadata of a page. This is the place to be if you want to change the storage format, for example.

The final piece of the Swiki puzzle is the rendering of SwikiSyntax into HTML (or other formats). This is accomplished in HTMLformatter>>swikify:linkhandler:.

---

[63]It is possible to have Swiki-specific templates. See http://coweb.cc.gatech.edu/squeakbook for details.

With the rise of Comanche, it is natural to ask about the fate of Swikis. Comanche was begun to provide a new base for collaborative web site (a.k.a., Swiki) research, and so the ComSwiki (Comanche Swiki) project was simultaneously launched in order to provide a flexible superstructure for Swiki experiments and development.[64] PWS Swikis proved sufficient for trying out a certain range of new ideas (including per page and per Swiki locking, rendering of Swikis, and system documentation with "active code"), as the plethora of subclasses of the SwikiClasses attests. But, like the PWS, the Swiki is really an application—with plenty of extensibility, to be sure—but nonetheless fairly simple in structure and possibilities. Like Comanche, ComSwiki is a *framework* with many parts and layers, each capable of replacement and extention. Possibilities abound, but a greater effort to learn the framework and how it "thinks" is required.

While that may sound daunting, the average *user* of Swikis, who merely wants to setup and run a few Swikis with a minimum of fuss, should be pleased. ComSwiki comes with a web-based administration utility (as did a certain version of PWS Swiki) that is very easy to use and requires no Smalltalk knowledge and no familiarity with the Squeak user interface.

While both Comanche and ComSwiki are still in beta as of this writing—with ComSwiki going through fairly regular, large upheavals—they have proved to be solid, stable, high-performance systems. They have replaced the PWS as the main Squeak Swiki, and `swiki.net`, a commercial Swiki site-hosting service, is entirely run on a modified Comanche/ComSwiki network. An untuned Comanche has been benchmarked at 30% of Apache's speed for serving straight, static files, which is quite amazing considering that the stock Squeak VM is not a speed burner and that Comanche has been written almost entirely by one graduate student working on it part time. The Comanche/ComSwiki duo are going to be showcase applications of Squeak with at least as much, or perhaps more, impact as the PWS itself.

Squeaky Clients

Squeak is also a wonderful arena for developing network *clients*. Ever wish you could change some small annoying behavior in an application you frequently use? With all Squeak applications you can, networking clients included. This section will describe three networking clients that are built-in to Squeak, and it will describe some ways people have adjusted or extended them for personal use.

Also, networking clients are interesting as programs in themselves. While this section will not make a network specialist out of anyone, it will describe some of the interesting aspects and tradeoffs in programming network clients. Such things are

---

[64]The great PWS/Swiki rewrite made an early split into these two development lines with Bolot specializing in web servers and Jochen Rick concentrating on Swikis.

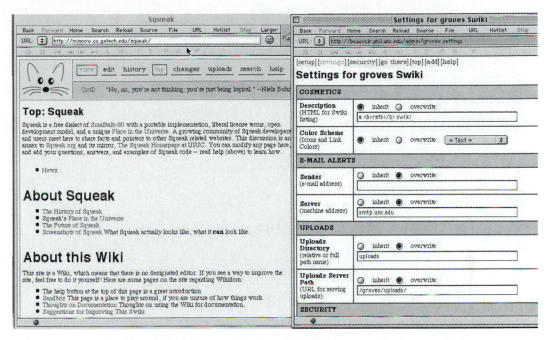

Figure 4.10 Right to left: The Squeak Swiki, an HTML-based class browser built on the Com-Swiki framwork and a bit of the adminstration utility.

especially interesting in Squeak, where the code is so malleable. Many of the decisions a programmer makes, about, say, handling network latency, can be switched in less than an hour's work.

Scamper, the Web Client

Scamper is so named because it allows a Squeaker (i.e., a mouse) to rapidly scamper about the web. To open a new Scamper window, open the world menu and choose "open..." and then "web browser." Using Scamper should be easy for anyone who has used a web browser before—the main operations are scrolling and following a hyperlink by clicking on blue text. What might not be obvious is the Squeak convention of placing menus under the yellow mouse button instead of making them omnipresent. Scamper follows this convention. So to access the Scamper main menu, press and hold the yellow menu button in the middle of the Scamper window.

Scamper handles several common media formats: HTML, plain text, several image formats, and flash animations. The center of this is in the **displayDocument:** method of class **Scamper**. Squeak hackers will commonly customize their web browsing experience by modifying **displayDocument:** or one of its helper methods.

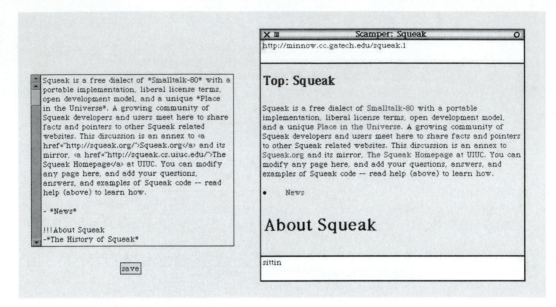

Figure 4.11   The submit button and text area on the left were pulled out of the Scamper window on the right when visiting an earlier page, and they remain functioning even after the browser is being used to view another page.

For example, when Flash support was first added to Squeak, it took only a few minutes to add the necessary line to displayDocument: so that Scamper would properly display Flash pages. Furthermore, various people are experimenting with allowing Squeak morphs to be used as web pages; many of them begin by modifying Scamper, instead of by meddling with the C-based plugins for commercial web browsers.[65]

Scamper can do more than just *display* media, however. In Scamper, web pages are not just displayed, but are rendered with full-blown Squeak objects. The result is that users can interact at a deep level with any object they see, instead of just scrolling around and looking at it. It is extremely simple to make a copy of an image you see in Scamper, modify it with the painting tool, and then save the image to a file and use it as your desktop background.

As a more extreme example, note that the components of an HTML form are themselves Squeak objects. In the example in Figure 4.11, the submit button and the entry field for a Swiki page have been dragged out of Scamper and onto the desktop. This would be useful if a person is planning to make several iterations on a Swiki page, so that they can skip pressing the "Edit this page" link so many times.

---

[65]Of course, the rise of the Squeak browser plug-in may change that.

Programming Notes

The most interesting code in Scamper is probably not Scamper itself, but some of its subsystems. There are several subsystems handy for quickly implementing other web-related programs. For example, the URL classes were developed for Scamper, and, of course, the utility of having an HTML parser is obvious. Furthermore, the ability to render HTML can be useful for building help files deployable both in the image and on the web, and for building other sorts of simple textual user interfaces. Since Scamper uses normal Squeak objects for rendering, a properly tweaked bit of HTML can end up looking pretty much like a standard Morphic UI.

One note of interest in Scamper is its handling of network latency. Network applications have built-in delays that might be arbitrarily long. Thus, it is inappropriate to perform full network requests in the same thread that the user interface uses, because the user interface might stop operation and "freeze." The two general approaches to this problem are to perform network operations in a separate thread or to perform operations one part at a time, so that no single operation will have a long delay.

Scamper takes the approach of using a separate thread for network interactions. The reason is from a combination of factors: First, Scamper's networking interactions are complicated and extensible; working in a background thread means that these operations don't have to be divided into smaller delay-free chunks. Second, there is little communication needed between the networking code and the user-interface code—the network code simply passes a document for the user-interface code to display. The combination of these factors makes using a separate thread a good choice.

Celeste, the Email Client

Celeste is an email client in Squeak. Its precursor was an email reader named Babar (the elephant from the children's stories), and Celeste is Babar's wife.

To try out Celeste, select "open..." from the world menu and then "email reader." A Celeste window will appear. If you choose "fetch mail" from the yellow-button menu in the top-left pane, the system will ask you several questions and then retrieve your email. Don't worry, it won't delete your messages from the server. (If you decide to use Celeste permanently, just choose the "don't leave messages on server" menu item. Celeste will start deleting your messages from the server after it downloads them).

Celeste has two especially powerful capabilities: its mail database and its filters.

Celeste stores messages in a local database that is more sophisticated than that used by most email programs. An email massage may be filed into any number of categories. When a message is initially downloaded, it is placed in the "new" category. This facility is more powerful than the standard folders approach used by most email programs: It allows a message to be in multiple categories simultaneously. You might put certain messages in both a "Squeak" category and a "Networking" category, whereas with regular email systems you have to choose just one. This functionality is accessed with the yellow-button menu on the table of contents.

Second, Celeste allows the visible message list to be filtered. This is especially useful for people who subscribe to mailing lists. The easiest way to access this functionality is to select the "From" or "Subj" buttons. The system will ask for a short string, and then only messages that have a sender or subject matching the string will be displayed.

More powerful are Celeste's custom filters. A custom filter may contain arbitrary Smalltalk code, and thus it may select messages by any criteria, which a computer can decide. Custom filters are saved and retrieved by name and are compiled into a block with a single argument "m," which refers to the message being tested. The object passed to the custom filter block is an IndexFileEntry, which contains various helper methods for filters (e.g., fromHas:, textHas:, etc.). Of course, since filters may contain arbitrary code, you can construct boolean and conditional tests, use other methods of IndexFileEntry, filter messages based on the state of the system (such as time of day), or evaluate code for side effects (to log filter usage, for example). Following are some examples:[66]

```
m participantHas: 'squeak@cs.uiuc.edu'
```

Show messages sent from or to the Squeak list. participantHas: is very handy as it checks the "to," "from," and "cc" mail headers:

```
(m participantHas: 'squeak@cs.uiuc.edu'
      and: [m fromHas: 'your@email.address']
```

Show all those Squeak list messages from you. With more complicated filters, it might well make sense to construct new helper methods in IndexFileEntry or in a separate utility class. The code is

```
Time now hours < 12
   ifTrue:
   [m participantHas: #(squeak pws)]
   ifFalse:
   [m subjectHas: #('[BUG]' '[FIX]')
```

If it's morning, show all Squeak list and PWS list messages, otherwise, show all messages with "[BUG]" or "[FIX]" prefixes. The "filter support" methods of Index-FileEntry will take an array of strings, symbols, or numbers as an argument, do the requisite conversions, and then test for *any* of the members (i.e., it's equivalent to a series of or:s, but considerably more concise).

---

[66]See http://minnow.cc.gatech.edu/squeak/1671 for more cool Celeste filters.

```
(m subjectHas: #(music protest smalltalk))
        ifTrue: [true]
        ifFalse: [Transcript cr;
                        show: 'Rejecting note from ', m from.
                        false]
```

This is a filter with side-effects. Note that you want the whole filter to evaluate to a boolean.

Programming Notes

Regarding network latency, Celeste performs all of its operations in a single operation in the user-interface thread. There is little defense for this choice except that the code is relatively simple.

The Celeste class is, in many ways, a closed system. It is designed to manage the message database and various network operations (such as fetching, sending, queuing, and composing mail) *from a graphical user interface.* It is relatively difficult to access its functions programmatically as it stands, though, of course, adding key accessors and changing certain methods to take an argument rather than relying on direct variable access would go a long way toward alleviating this difficulty.

If you open Celeste using the "email reader" menu command or Celeste class»open, Celeste will open on a message database located in your Squeak directory named "EMAIL"[67] and will prompt you to create one if it's missing. However, you are not restricted to this database. Celeste class»openOn: will let you open a Celeste on a message database of any name, indeed, located anywhere in your filesystem simply by feeding openOn: a fully qualified path to where you keep, or would like to keep, your database, plus its "root" name. You can thereby maintain multiple message database (perhaps for archive purposes) or store your message database in a permanent location distinct from the different Squeak instances or versions you may use. Finally, Celeste (actually, MailDB) is careful to only open a particular database once, no matter how many viewers are open on it.[68]

It is worth exploring the various classes associated with the MailDB. The MailDB class governs three files, each with its own class: the MessageFile, which stores the full text of each message; the IndexFile, which maintains a subset of the headers (i.e., the ones commonly searched for and displayed in the Celeste browsing window), and the CategoriesFile, which maintains the user-defined categories. The messages file is a simple text file with each mail message assigned a unique numerical key and delimited from other messages by a textual separator. The IndexFile maintains the starting position of each message in order to facilitate fetching the message text,

---

[67] In fact, the database comprises three files: a **.messages**, a **.categories**, and an **.index** file. See the next paragraph for further discussion.

[68] At the time of this writing, having multiple Celestes open on a single message database is a little awkward in that changes to one will not automatically be reflected in the other.

which is parsed upon reading into a MailMessage. Both the IndexFile and CategoriesFile are read into memory when Celeste is opened, and searching or filtering operations can be performed very rapidly using the normal enumeration protocols. While Celeste tries very hard not to lose any mail, it's a little more cavalier about indexes and categories. Of course, an IndexFile can be regenerated by scanning over the MessageFile, but categories can't be.

With a little refactoring (mostly to generalize the IndexFileEntry and the fetch-parse cycle of messages), one could easily use the MailDB for various persistence and small database tasks.

MailMessage has undergone a lot of development recently and now handles multipart MIME messages with ease. Talk on the Squeak list is tending toward unifying the MailMessage and MIMEDocument classes in the near future.

Finally, Celeste uses Scamper to render HTML-formatted mail.[69]

IRC Client, the IRC Client

Chatting is one of the most popular activities on the Internet. In a chat network, people may log into the system and send text messages to each other. Typically, there are special interest areas, and participants may send messages to other people who have registered in particular areas.

Squeak includes a client for one particular chat network called "Internet Relay Chat," or IRC for short. IRC was created in 1988 and since has been used for a variety of purposes. Most often it is used for exchanging advice, getting technical support, or simply bantering with other people. However, IRC has also been used for things with larger impact. For example, during the Persian Gulf War, Kuwaiti people broadcast news on IRC more quickly and more personally than television stations did. IRC has been used for classes, for press releases, on-line interviews, publishing, and plain old chewing the fat. Overall, IRC provides communication in a raw form, and people have had no trouble finding applications for it.

To try out IRC yourself, select the "open..." menu again and then select "IRC Chat." Two windows will open. One is for status messages, and one is for messages sent to you personally. Use the yellow-button in the status window (the one labelled "IRC") to choose "connect." Fill in a new nick, and preferably, fill in a username and full name. Then select the big connect button, and the system should connect! You can close the connection window once this is done.

To join a channel, first open a channel list. Choose "channel list" from the yellow-button menu in the main IRC window. Select the "update" button. In a moment, a current list of channels will be displayed. Select a channel and click on "Join Channel" to join it, or select "Create Channel" to create your own channel.

Once in a channel, you may send messages by typing them into the narrow text pane at the bottom of the screen and pressing enter.

---

[69]Not that we would want anyone to think that we *encourage* the sending of HTML mail, heaven forfend!

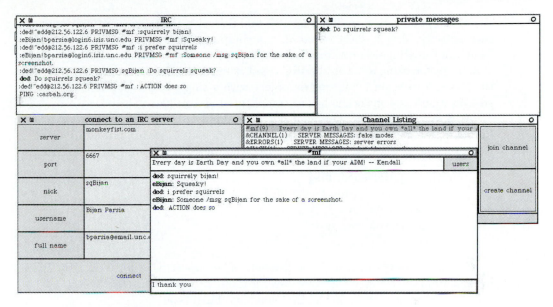

Figure 4.12   A public, private, connect, and channel list.

None of the behavior of the IRC client is complicated, but it does have a large number of interface windows and a large amount of data to keep track of. Thus, for those interested in learning object-oriented programming in Smalltalk, the IRC client would probably serve as a good example.

Programming Notes

The center of the system is the IRCConnection class. This class implements the protocol and parses information sent from the server. It has a handler for various kinds of messages that the server sends, including pings, message-of-the-day updates, channel-list updates, actual IRC messages sent from a human, and many other things. Other classes in the Network-IRC category include classes for maintaining a local copy of the interesting parts of the IRC server's state, for user-interface objects, and for representing messages themselves.

The IRC client handles network latency by dividing the work into small, fast chunks. Instances of IRCConnection expect to have a processIO method sent to them periodically. When this method is called, as much work as possible will be performed without waiting for network responses. The benefit is that there is no thread interaction to worry about—and the IRC does require significant amounts of communication between the networking code and the user-interface code. However, this choice also results in the IRCConnection class having extra instance variables in order to keep track of temporary results between calls to processIO.

Writing "bots" is a tradition in IRC, and Squeak's IRC client certainly supports such activity. A bot, short for *robot*, is a computer-controlled participant on IRC. They are indistinguishable from humans except that they are usually more boring to talk to. Creating a bot in the IRC client is much like implementing an action for the PWS. You begin by writing an object with a single message, and then you can go from there and make the bot as complicated as you like.

As a simple example, here is a bot that simply logs all messages that it sees. In this example, the class will be named LoggingIRCListener. In addition to an initialization method, it will have the following message for interacting on IRC:

```
ircMessageRecieved: msg
    file nextPutAll: (msg sender ifNil: [ 'me' ]);
        nextPutAll: '>>';
        nextPutAll: msg text;
        cr.
```

The next step is to install the listener. The easiest way is to log into IRC as normal and then to use inspectors. After logging into IRC as normal, select "inspect me" from the main menu in the IRC window. Then type

```
(self channelInfo: '#friendly') subscribe:
(LoggingIRCListener new logToFileNamed: 'friendly.log').
```

This code creates a LoggingIRCListener that logs to the file `friendly.log`, and then "subscribes" it to the channel named #friendly.

Into the Blue

Thus far, this chapter has focused on the more traditional networking applications and infrastructure: web servers and mail, HTML, and IRC clients. These sorts of applications are squarely in the "pink plane" of Squeak development—stepwise development of the well-known mostly for the sake of standard use. There are many more interesting pinkish programs out there, e.g., NewsAgent (an "adaptive" news reader), InfoAgent (a bookmark management and link checking utility), and eekMail (a Celeste alternative), among others. In the best of all possible worlds, these sorts of applications and utilities do not merely make the world of internet content and services accessible to the Squeaker, but they present that world in a Squeaky way. Scamper is a fine example of this: It doesn't merely render web pages into a legible form, it turns them into a *collection of objects* that the Squeaker can examine, manipulate, and *think about* in all the standard Squeaky ways. Similarly, Comanche aims to make writing a web application a matter of writing a normal Squeak program, where one spends most of the development "thinking" in objects.

But consider the Web. There is a significant difference in providing a filtering view, or an active model, of the Web as a "sea of objects" and providing a *new* Web that simply *is* that grand ocean. The difference is akin to the difference between implementing object persistence on top a relational database and using an object database.[70] They both can get the job done, but there is an awkwardness in the object-relational mapping case. The shoe pinches in a few places, and there is a tendency to stumble just as you hit your stride.

This is also so with collaboration. The more barriers you have to cross, the more all parties need to do to get "in sync," the more difficult is the collaborating. While there are many reasons for establishing different organizational structures for collaboration, it's important that the tools used do not *force* you into inappropriate structure. This suggests that collaborative tools need to be flexible and scalable: equally well suited to synchronous and asynchronous collaboration in various mixtures—and able to handle just a few people working together in real time, to many working for years. People should be able to fruitfully contribute at all skill levels and the process of working together should enhance both the abilities of those working as well as the project they share.

Once you have a distributed sea of Squeak objects, you have a world of Squeak-based collaboration: If they are truly *Squeak* objects, they must be accessible, intelligible, and transparent to the Squeaker using all the standard Squeak tools.[71] Thus, each Squeaker should experience the Squeakly Web as a giant seamless "virtual image," with objects all about to browse and inspect, to manipulate and mutate, and to save and share.

We ain't there yet.[72] However, there have been several projects and experiments that give some hints of the future. These are the first tentative steps into the blue plane.[73]

The Midwestern States of Sharing

When talking about the "blue" way of dealing with objects we must turn to Morphic.[74] Morphic aims to make objects *concrete* and *directly manipulable* members of a Morphic "world." In the Self project's version of Morphic, worlds were sharable. Each world was very large (albeit flat, hence the name "Kansas") and could contain many objects interacting with many people at the same time, much as in the real world. An early stab at making Squeak Morphic shareable is Telemorphic. Telemorphic has an interesting, if somewhat fragile, way of handling bandwidth restrictions: It transmits only the "actions" performed by each user's "hand."[75] This led, in my experience, to some rather amusing situations where one user thought they were

---

[70]Or, to put it a *bit* more tendentiously, it is like an operating system with a GUI built into the core, and one with a GUI bolted on.

[71]Cue dramatic music.

[72]Abruptly stop dramatic music.

[73]The "pink plane" and "blue plane" terminology gained currency from an early Squeak presentation by Alan Kay. Going into the blue plane entails movement into radically new conceptual spaces.

[74]See Chapter 2 for more discussion of Morphic.

[75]Think "cursor" and read the chapter on Morphic.

picking up an object, whereas in my world they were selecting items from a menu.

In the current Squeak 2.9 alpha versions, there is a new implementation of Kansas, currently dubbed "Midwest Telemorphic."[76] In contrast with "back east" Telemorphic, Midwest Telemorphic captures the drawing commands on the server and broadcasts them across the network to connected clients. Instead of having two sets of Morphs in two different worlds that must be kept in sync, in Midwest Telemorphic the "real" Morphs all live on the server. While the arrangement is more bandwidth heavy than Telemorphic, it's much less confusing to have a single world that is genuinely *shared* rather than two worlds that are only marginally kept in sync.[77]

DirectSqueakSwikis

Midwest Telemorphic and similar technologies work to bring synchronous interaction to Morphic worlds. But such interaction is not the only, and perhaps not even the primary, form of collaboration. Swikis, to pick one example, though highly collaborative, are essentially asynchronous in their interaction. Pretty much only one person can work on a page at a time, and conversations and co-editing occur at a slower (but not necessarily too slow) pace. Following the logic that a minimally intrusive technology takes the audience's skills and experience into account, a Swiki that catered to Morphic users would use Morphic as its "WikiSyntax." Of course, once you have a SwikiPage that is made up of Morphs, you've also got a unified, easy to use, and powerful multimedia design, editing, and production system. Instead of generating a picture, uploading it to a server directory, and including the right tag in the right place in your HTML file, you simply create the picture in your Morphic project and pop it onto the page. So too with a sound. Or an animation.

There are (at least!) three working systems that implement what Alan Kay dubbed "DirectSqueakSwikis": `MuSwiki`,[78] `ObjectWeb`,[79] and "SuperSwikis."[80] MuSwiki's were implemented as part of the Georgia Tech Collaborative Software Group's ongoing experiments with collaborative multimedia and deployed in several classes.[81] It consists of a Squeak-based browser and server using a custom protocol. One of the more interesting uses was in a programming class where students shared CRC[82] card Morphs. Unlike most CRC card software, MuSwiki came close

---

[76]Midwest Telemorphic was originally named "Nebraska," but it was discovered that there was a Java implementation of Kansas with that name. Many thanks to Lex Spoon for pointing this out literally at the last minute.

[77]There are some other projects afoot for remote world interaction, including an implementation of the Virtual Network Computing (`VNC`) protocol.

[78]By Lex Spoon and Mark Guzdial at Georgia Tech.

[79]By Roger Whitney's and Ralph Johnson's eXtreme Programming Workshop at UIUC.

[80]The latest in a line of experiments by Squeak Central; with aid and abetting by Bob Arning.

[81]L. Spoon and M. Guzdial, *MuSwiki: A graphical collaboration tool*, in *Proceedings of CSCL'99*. 1999, p. 590–599.

[82]"Class-Responsibility-Collaborator."

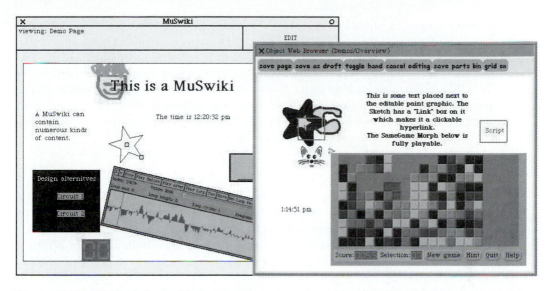

Figure 4.13   To the left is a MuSwiki page, and to the right an ObjectWeb one.

to preserving the feel of sitting at a table with a bunch of index cards—a critical aspect of CRC card practice.

ObjectWeb was an academic project, but a class, rather than a research, project. It's an impressive testimonial to Squeak's ease of programming that a core group of six students working for five weeks with little or no Smalltalk experience and *no* Squeak experience could turn out such a system. ObjectWeb includes an HTTP-based server, a custom Squeak-based client with a specialized Morph editor (MuSwiki, in contrast, relies solely on the normal Morphic tools), and the ability to serve static images of ObjectWeb pages to regular web browsers. The ObjectWeb editor is quite sophisticated, supporting off-line "draft" pages, graphic and text-based hyperlinks, and embedded Smalltalk scripts. Interestingly, ObjectWeb's server is a subclass of PWS, which, no doubt, made it much easier to focus on extra functionality.[83]

SuperSwikis are just starting to emerge from the secret labs of Squeak Central. The (current!) distinguishing feature of SuperSwiki (that I've gleaned) is that they use entire projects as their "page." Since, a standard Squeak image simply *is* a collection of projects, the SuperSwiki conceptually reverses our view of an image: Instead of a system that can be a server or a client or can share and publish objects, Squeak just *is* a Swiki. SuperSwikis combine (as well as subsume) MuSwiki, ObjectWeb, and Midwestern Telemorphic in such a way that there is no difference between working in Squeak and working in a SuperSwiki. With the new web

---

[83]MuSwiki was also prototyped using the PWS system and was only moved to the custom protocol when HTTP proved to be too limited.

browser plugin (a Squeak VM modified to run inside any browser supporting the
Netscape Navigator API) the difference between living in a Squeak-specific web and
in standard World Wide Web narrows. As Alan Kay wrote to the Squeak list, "We
are starting to provide a pretty complete alternative (but a compatible one) to the
WWW." If the Squeak alternative to the World Wide Web is anywhere nearly as
pervasively, if subtly, influential as the orginal Smalltalk project, then if you work
with Squeak and networks today you don't just help invent the future, you live it.

Acknowledgements

I am grateful to Zoe Mulford and Kendall G. Clark for detailed editing and copy-
editing assistance both early and last minute, and enormous moral support. Craig
Latta and John Macintosh reviewed the Flow section for me and let me pump them
for information at Camp Smalltalk 2. Also, at Camp Smalltalk 2, Roger Whitney,
in between helping me with the XML parser project, gave loads of interesting tidbits
about ObjectWeb—not to mention his mind-blowing demo of it. Several folks provided useful feedback of various drafts on the Squeak book website, especially Mark
Guzdial and Mat Nygren. Special thanks to Mark for being very understanding
about deadlines and for getting sick at *just* the right times.

Bijan Parsia is working on his Ph.D. in philosophy at the University of North Carolina at
Chapel Hill. His research areas include epistemology, feminism, early modern philosophy,
logic, philosophy of mathematics, oppression theory, philosophy of mind, early analytic
philosophy, and a bunch of other stuff. His M.A. was on the epistemological status of the
use of computers in the proof of the Four Color Theorem. His dissertation is on cognative
suicide (a.k.a., pragmatically self-defeasible arguments). He has used Squeak and Swikis
in the classroom for many years.

Lex Spoon is working on a Ph.D. in computer science at the Georgia Institute of
Technology. He has been an avid Squeak programmer since it was first offered on the
Internet. He has interned with the Squeak team at Disney. For his Ph.D., he is developing
a system to aid people in understanding Smalltalk programs. If he had a dog or a cat, it
would have a name.

Bolot Kerimbaev is a Ph.D. student at Georgia Tech. When he's not practicing Taido
(the martial art of the 21st century), he's developing Comanche. He worked as an intern
in Alan Kay's Media Research Group on programming with logic in Squeak. He has also
worked at Viant Corporation's Innovation Center focussing on end-user graphics.

Part Two

Squeak for the Systems Programmer

The second part of the book contains the low-level chapters, the ones that explain how Squeak ticks and how to modify that into "tocks," if you so choose. What makes Squeak interesting is that one doesn't shift notation nor semantics as one moves from programming and media development into systems programming. One of the core ideas behind Squeak is *Everything in Squeak*. The virtual machine and all of its add-on components are written in Squeak. You can go as deep as you want into Squeak, and it's all Squeak, all the way down.

These chapters are exciting, both to the Squeak programmer who wants to go deep, but also to the general systems programmer interested in virtual machines (VMs). VMs are central to many modern programming languages (including Java and Python), but with relatively little written explaining how they work and why they work in that way. These chapters help fill that void.

- The first two chapters are written by Squeak Central (led by Dan Ingalls) and by Dan alone, respectively. They present the story of how Squeak came to be, what it really is, and an updating of that story to today.

- Tim Rowledge presents a tour of the Squeak "object engine" (the VM plus a bit more of the core classes). Tim presents not just the Squeak VM, but the general decision points to make about VMs (such as garbage collection methods), and then introduces the Squeak in its decisions (and idiosyncracies).

- Ian Piumarta, who made the first Squeak port outside of the original developers, explains how to port Squeak. His chapter includes some wonderful stories and insights into how things can go awry and how he managed the original port.

- Andrew Greenberg explains how to extend the Squeak VM with pluggable primitives that can be written from *within* Squeak and then translated to C and compiled externally. Using Andrew's chapter, Squeak's capabilities can be expanded to the limits of current hardware.

5

Back to the Future:
The Story of Squeak,
a Practical Smalltalk Written in Itself

Dan Ingalls, Ted Kaehler,
John Maloney, Scott Wallace,
Alan Kay

Walt Disney Imagineering Research and Development

Abstract

Squeak is an open, highly-portable Smalltalk implementation whose virtual machine is written entirely in Smalltalk, making it easy to debug, analyze, and change. To achieve practical performance, a translator produces an equivalent C program whose performance is comparable to commercial Smalltalks.

Other noteworthy aspects of Squeak include a compact object format that typically requires only a single word of overhead per object; a simple yet efficient incremental garbage collector for 32-bit direct pointers; efficient bulk-mutation of objects; extensions of BitBlt to handle color of any depth and anti-aliased image rotation and scaling; and real-time sound and music synthesis written entirely in Smalltalk.

Overview

Squeak is a modern implementation of Smalltalk-80 that is available for free via the Internet, at http://www.squeak.org and other sites. It includes platform-independent support for color, sound, and image processing. Squeak was originally developed on the Macintosh, however, members of its user community have since ported it to numerous platforms including Windows 95 and NT, Windows CE, all common flavors of UNIX, and the Acorn.

151

Squeak stands alone as a practical Smalltalk in which a researcher, professor, or motivated student can examine source code for every part of the system, including graphics primitives and the virtual machine itself, and make changes immediately and without needing to see or deal with any language other than Smalltalk. It also runs bit-identical images across its wide portability base.

Three strands weave through this chapter: (1) the design of the Squeak virtual machine, which differs in several interesting ways from the implementation presented in the Smalltalk "Blue Book" [Gold83] and explored in the "Green Book" [Kras83]; (2) an implementation strategy based on writing the Squeak virtual machine in Smalltalk and translating it into C, using an existing Smalltalk for bootstrapping until Squeak was able to debug and generate its own virtual machine; and (3) the incremental development process through which Squeak was created and evolved over the course of a year.

Background

In December of 1995, the authors found themselves wanting a development environment in which to build educational software that could be used—and even programmed—by non-technical people, and by children. We wanted our software to be effective in mass-access media such as PDAs and the Internet, where download times and power considerations make compactness essential, hardware is diverse, and operating systems may change or be completely absent. Therefore, our ideal system would be a small, portable kernel of simple and uniform design that could be adapted rapidly to new delivery vehicles. We considered using Java but, despite its promise, Java was not yet mature: its libraries were in a state of flux, few commercial implementations were available, and those that were available lacked the hooks required to create the kind of dynamic change that we envisioned.

While Smalltalk met the technical desiderata, none of the available implementations gave us the kind of control we wanted over graphics, sound, and the Smalltalk engine itself, nor the freedom to port and distribute the resulting work, including its host environment, freely over the Internet. Moreover, we felt that we were not alone, that many others in the research community shared our desire for an open, portable, malleable, and yet practical object-oriented programming environment. It became clear that the best way to get what we all wanted was to build a new Smalltalk with these goals and to share it with this wider community.

Project Plan

We did not have to start from scratch, as we had access to the existing Apple Smalltalk-80 implementation, which was a gold mine of useful software. This system consisted of an *image*, or object memory, containing the Smalltalk-80 class library, and a separate *interpreter*, or VM (virtual machine), for running on the

Macintosh. However, the Apple image format was limited by its use of indirect pointers and an object table. Worse yet, the original interpreter consisted of 120 pages of sparsely commented 68020 assembly code that had passed through the hands of seven authors. Portable it was not.

We determined that implementation in C would be key to portability, but none of us wanted to write in C. However, two of us had once adapted the Smalltalk formatter (pretty-printer) to convert a body of code to BCPL. Based on that experience, we determined to write and debug the virtual machine in Smalltalk. Then, in parallel, we would write (also in Smalltalk) a translator from Smalltalk to C, and thus let Smalltalk build its own production interpreter. Out of this decision grew the following plan for building a new Smalltalk system in the shortest possible time:

- Produce a new image

  - Design a new Object Memory and image file format
  - Alter the ST-80 System Tracer to write an image in the new format
  - Eliminate uses of Mac Toolbox calls to restore Smalltalk-80 portability
  - Write a new file system with a simple, portable interface

- Produce a new interpreter written in Smalltalk

  - Type in the Blue Book descriptions for the Interpreter and BitBlt
  - Write a completely new Object Memory class
  - Debug the new Object Memory, Interpreter, and BitBlt

- Compile the interpreter to make it practical

  - Design a translator from a subset of Smalltalk-80 to C
  - Implement this translator
  - Translate the virtual machine to C and compile it
  - Write a small C interface to the Mac OS
  - Run the compiled interpreter with the new image

Through this plan, facilities became available just as they were needed. For example, the interpreter and object memory were debugged using a temporary memory allocator that had no way to reclaim garbage. However, since the system only executed a few byte codes, it never got far enough to run out of memory. Likewise, while the translator was being prepared, most of the bugs in the interpreter and object memory were found and fixed by running them in Smalltalk.

It was easy to stay motivated, because the virtual machine, running inside Apple Smalltalk, was actually simulating the byte codes of the transformed image just five weeks into the project. One week later, we could type "3 + 4" on the screen, compile it, and print the result, and the week after that the entire user interface was working, albeit in slow motion. We were writing the C translator in parallel on a commercial Smalltalk, and by the eighth week, the first translated interpreter displayed a window on the screen. Ten weeks into the project, we "crossed the bridge" and were able to use Squeak to evolve itself, no longer needing to port images forward from Apple Smalltalk. About six weeks later, Squeak's performance had improved to the point that it could simulate its own interpreter and run the C translator, and Squeak became entirely self-supporting.

We attribute the speed with which this initial work was accomplished to the Squeak philosophy: Do everything in Smalltalk so that each improvement makes everything smaller, faster, and better. It has been a pleasant revelation to work on such low-level system facilities as real-time garbage collection and FM music synthesis from within the comfort and convenience of the Smalltalk-80 language and environment.

Once we had a stable, usable interpreter, the focus shifted from creation to evolution. Performance improved steadily and support for color, image transforms, sound synthesis, and networking were added. These improvements were made incrementally, as the need arose, and in parallel with other projects that relied on the stability of the VM. Yet despite the apparent risk of frequent changes to the VM, Squeak has proven as dependable as most commercial Smalltalks we have used. We attribute this success partly to our passion for design simplicity, but mostly to the strategy of implementing the VM in Smalltalk.

The remainder of this chapter discusses various aspects of the Squeak implementation, its memory footprint and performance, the evolution of its user community, and plans for its future.

The Interpreter

We knew that the published Blue Book interpreter description would suffice to get us started. Moreover, we were spared from the tedium of transcription by Mario Wolczko, who had already keyed in the code for use as an on-line reference source for a Smalltalk implementation project at the University of Manchester.

The interpreter is structured as a single class that gets translated to C along with the Object Memory and BitBlt classes. In addition, a subclass (InterpreterSimulator) runs all the same code from within a Smalltalk environment by supporting basic mouse, file, and display operations. This subclass was the basis for debugging the Squeak system into existence. All of this code is included in the Squeak release and it can run its own image, albeit at a snail's pace. (Every memory access, even in BitBlt, runs a Smalltalk method.) Having an interpreter that runs within Smalltalk is invaluable for studying the virtual machine. Any operation can be stopped and inspected, or it can be instrumented to gather timing profiles, exact method counts, and other statistics.

Although we have constantly amended the interpreter to achieve increasing performance, we have stayed pretty close to the Blue Book message interface between the Interpreter and the Object Memory. It is a testament to the original design of that interface that completely changing the Object Memory implementation had almost no impact on the Interpreter.

The Object Memory

The design of an object memory that is general and yet compact is not simple. We all agreed immediately on a number of parameters, though. For efficiency and scalability to large projects, we wanted a 32-bit address space with direct pointers (i.e., a system in which an object reference is just the address of that object in memory). The design had to support all object formats of our existing Smalltalk. It must be amenable to incremental garbage collection and compaction. Finally, it must be able to support the "become" operation (exchange identity of two objects) to the degree required in normal Smalltalk system operation.

While anyone would agree that objects should be stored compactly, every object in Smalltalk requires the following "overhead" information:

- size of the object in bytes, 24 bits or more;

- class of the object, a full 32-bit object pointer;

- hash code for indexing objects, at least 12 bits;

- format of the object (specifying pointer or bits, indexable or not, etc.), 4 bits at least; and

- of course, a few extra bits for storage management needs.

A simple approach would be to allocate three full 32-bit words as the header to every object. However, in a system of 40k objects, this cavalier expenditure of 500k bytes of memory could make the difference between an undeployable prototype and a practical application. Therefore, we designed a variable-length header format that seldom requires more than a single 32-bit word of header information per object. The format is given in Tables 5.1 and 5.2.

Our design is based on the fact that most objects in a typical Smalltalk image are small instances of a relatively small number of classes. The 5-bit compact class index field, if non-zero, is an index into a table of up to 31 classes that are designated as having compact instances; the programmer can change which classes these are. The 6-bit size field, if non-zero, specifies the size of the object in words, accommodating sizes up to 256 bytes (i.e., 64 words, with the additional 2 bits needed to resolve the length of byte-indexable objects encoded in the format field). With only 12 classes designated as compact in the 1.18 Squeak release, around 81% of the objects have only this single word of overhead. Most of the remaining objects need one additional word to store a full class pointer. Only a few remaining objects (1%) are large enough to require a third header word to encode their size, and this extra word of overhead is a tiny fraction of their size.

offset	contents		occurrence
-8	size in words	(30 bits)	
	header type	(2 bits)	1%
-4	full class pointer	(30 bits)	
	header type	(2 bits)	18%
0	base header, as follows:		
	– storage management	(3 bits)	
	– object hash	(12 bits)	
	– compact class index	(5 bits)	
	– object format field (see Table 5.2)	(4 bits)	
	– size in words	(6 bits)	
	– header type	(2 bits)	100%

Table 5.1   Format of a Squeak Object Header.

format	field type
0	no fields
1	fixed pointer fields
2	indexable pointer fields
3	both fixed and indexable pointer fields
4	unused
5	unused
6	indexable word fields (no pointers)
7	unused
8–11	indexable byte fields (no pointers): Low 2 bits are low 2 bits of size in bytes.
12–15	compiled methods: Low 2 bits are low 2 bits of size in bytes. The number of literals is specified in method header, followed by the indexable bytes that store byte codes.

Table 5.2   Encoding of the Object Format Field in a Squeak Object Header.

Storage Management

Apple Smalltalk had achieved good garbage collection behavior with a simple two-generation approach similar to [Unga84]. At startup, and after any full garbage collection (a mark and sweep of the entire image), all surviving objects were considered to be old, and all objects created subsequently (until the next full collection) to be new. All pointer stores were checked and a table maintained of "root" objects—old objects that might contain pointers to new objects. In this way, an incremental mark phase could be achieved by marking all new objects reachable from these roots and sweeping the new object area; unmarked new objects were garbage. Compaction was simple in that system, owing to its use of an object table. Full garbage collection was triggered either by an overflow of the roots table, or by failure of an incremental collection to reclaim a significant amount of space. That system was known to run acceptably with less than 500k of free space and to perform incremental reclamations in under 250 milliseconds on hardware of the 80s (16 MHz 68020).

For Squeak, we determined to apply the same approach to our new system of 32-bit direct pointers. We were faced immediately with a number of challenges. First, we had to write an in-place mark phase capable of dealing with our variable-length headers, including those that did not have an actual class pointer in them. Then there was the need to produce a structure for remapping object pointers during compaction, since we did not have the convenient indirection of an object table. Finally, there was the challenge of rectifying all the object pointers in memory within an acceptable time.

The remapping of object pointers was accomplished by building a number of relocation blocks down from the unused end of memory. A thousand such blocks are reserved outside the object heap, ensuring that at least 1,000 objects can be moved even when there is very little free space. However, if the object heap ends with a free block, that space is also used for relocation blocks. If there is not enough room for the number of relocation blocks needed to do compaction in a single pass (almost never), then the compaction may be done in multiple passes. Each pass generates free space at the end of the object heap that can then be used to create additional relocation blocks for the next pass.

One more issue remained to be dealt with, and that was support of the **become** operation without an object table. (The Smalltalk **become** primitive atomically exchanges the identity of two objects; to Smalltalk code, each object appears to turn into, or "become," the other.) With an object table, the **become** primitive simply exchanges the contents of two object table entries. Without an object table, it requires a full scan of memory to replace every pointer to one object with a pointer to the other. Since full memory scans are relatively costly, we made two changes. First, we eliminated most uses of **become** in the Squeak image by changing certain collection classes to store their elements in separate **array** objects instead of indexed fields. However, **become** operations are essential when adding an instance variable to a class with extant instances, as each instance must mutate into a larger object to accommodate the new variable. So, our second change was to restructure the primitive to one that exchanges the identity of many objects at once. This allows all the instances of a class to be mutated in a single pass through memory. The code for this operation uses the same technique and, in fact, the very same code, as that used to rectify pointers after compaction.

We originally sought to minimize compaction frequency, owing to the overhead associated with rectifying direct addresses. Our strategy was to do a fast mark and sweep, returning objects to a number of free lists, depending on size. Only when memory became overly fragmented would we do a consolidating compaction.

As we studied and optimized the Squeak garbage collector, however, we were able to simplify this approach radically. Since an incremental reclamation only compacts the new object space, it is only necessary to rectify the surviving new objects and any old objects that point to them. The latter are exactly those objects marked as root objects. Since there are typically just a few root objects and not many survivors (most objects die young), we discovered that compaction after an incremental reclamation could be done quickly. In fact, due to the overhead of managing free lists, it turned out to be more efficient to compact after every incremental reclamation and eliminate free lists altogether. This was especially gratifying since issues of fragmentation and coalescing had been a burden in design, analysis, and coding strategy.

Two policy refinements reduced the incremental garbage collection pauses to the point where Squeak became usable for real-time applications such as music and animation. First, a counter is incremented each time an object is allocated. When this counter reaches some threshold, an incremental collection is done even if there is plenty of free space left. This reduces the number of new objects that must be scanned in the sweep phase and also limits the number of surviving objects. By doing a little work often, each incremental collection completes quickly, typically in 5-8 milliseconds. This is within the timing tolerance of even a fairly demanding musician or animator.

The second refinement is to tenure all surviving objects when the number of survivors exceeds a certain threshold, a simplified version of Ungar and Jackson's feedback-mediated tenuring policy [UnJa88]. Tenuring is done as follows. After the incremental garbage collection and compaction, the boundary between the old and new object spaces is moved up to encompass all surviving new objects, as if a full garbage collection had just been done. This "clears the decks" so that future incremental compactions have fewer objects to process. Although in theory this approach could hasten the onset of the next full garbage collection, such full collections are rare in practice. In any case, Squeak's relatively lean image makes full garbage collections less daunting than they might be in a larger system; a full collection typically takes only 250 milliseconds in Squeak.

We have been using this storage manager in support of real-time graphics and music for over a year now with extremely satisfactory results. In our experience, 10 milliseconds is an important threshold for latency in interactive systems, because most of the other critical functions such as mouse polling, sound buffer output and display refresh take place at a commensurate rate.

BitBlt

For BitBlt as well, we began with the Blue Book source code. However, the Blue Book code was written as a simulation in Smalltalk, not as VM code to run on top of the Object Memory. We transformed the code into the latter form and made a few optimizations. This sufficed to get the first Squeak running. The special cases we optimized are as follows:

- the case when there is no source (store constant),

- the case when there is no halftone (store unmasked), and

- the horizontal inner loop (no partial word stores).

Once Squeak became operational, we immediately wanted to give it command over color. We chose to support a wide range of color depths, namely 1-, 2-, 4-, and 8-bit table-based color, as well as 16- and 32-bit direct RGB color (with 5 and 8 bits per color component respectively).

It was relatively simple to extend the internal logic of BitBlt to handle multiple pixel sizes as long as source and destination bit maps are of the same depth. To handle operations between images of different depth, we provided a default conversion and added an optional color map parameter to BitBlt to provide more control when appropriate. The default behavior is simply to extend smaller source pixels to a larger destination size by padding with zeros and to truncate larger source pixels to a smaller destination pixel size. This approach works very well among the table-based colors because the color set for each depth includes the next smaller depth's color set as a subset. In the case of RGB colors, BitBlt performs the zero-fill or truncation independently on each color component.

The real challenge, however, involves operations between RGB and table-based color depths. In such cases, or when wanting more control over the color conversion, the client can supply BitBlt with a color map. This map is sized so that there is one entry for each of the source colors and each entry contains a pixel in the format expected by the destination. It is obvious how to work with this for source pixel sizes of 8 bits or less (map sizes of 256 or less). But it would seem to require a map of 65536 entries for 16 bits or 4294967296 entries for 32-bit color! However, for these cases, Squeak's BitBlt accepts color maps of 512, 4,096, or 32,768 entries, corresponding to 3, 4, and 5 bits per color component, and BitBlt truncates the source pixel's color components to the appropriate number of bits before looking up the pixel in the color map.

Smalltalk to C Translation

We have alluded to the Squeak philosophy of writing everything in Smalltalk. While the Blue Book contains a Smalltalk description of the VM that was actually executed at least once to verify its accuracy, this description was meant to be used only as an explanatory model, not as the source code of a working implementation. In contrast, we needed source code that could be translated into C to produce a reliable and efficient VM.

Our bootstrapping strategy also depended on being able to debug the Smalltalk code for the Squeak VM by running it under an existing Smalltalk implementation,

and this approach was highly successful. Being able to use the powerful tools of
the Smalltalk environment saved us weeks of tedious debugging with a C debugger.
However, useful as it is for debugging, the Squeak VM running on top of Smalltalk is
orders of magnitude too slow for useful work: running in Squeak itself, the Smalltalk
version of the Squeak VM is roughly 450 times slower than the C version. Even
running in the fastest available commercial Smalltalk, the Squeak VM running in
Smalltalk would still be sluggish.

The key to both practical performance and portability is to translate the Smalltalk description of the VM into C. To be able to do this translation without having
to emulate all of Smalltalk in the C runtime system, the VM was written in a
subset of Smalltalk that maps directly onto C constructs. This subset excludes
blocks (except to describe a few control structures), message sending, and even
objects! Methods of the interpreter classes are mapped to C functions and instance
variables are mapped to global variables. For byte code and primitive dispatches,
the special message dispatchOn:in: is mapped to a C switch statement. (When
running in Smalltalk, this construct works by perform:-ing the message selector at
the specified index in a case array. Since a method invocation is much less efficient
than a branch operation, this dispatch is one of the main reasons that the interpreter
runs so much faster when translated to C.)

The translator first translates Smalltalk into parse trees, then uses a simple
table-lookup scheme to generate C code from these parse trees. There are only 42
transformation rules, as shown in Table 5.3. Four of these are for integer operations
that more closely match those of the underlying hardware, such as unsigned shifts,
and the last three are macros for operations so heavily used that they should always
be inlined. All translated code accesses memory through six C macros that read
and write individual bytes, 4-byte words, and 8-byte floats. In the early stages
of development, every such reference was checked against the bounds of object
memory.

Our first translator yielded a two orders of magnitude speedup relative to the
Smalltalk simulation, producing a system that was immediately usable. However,

&	|	and:	or:	not		
+	−	*	//	\\	min:	max:
bitAnd:	bitOr:	bitXor:	bitShift:			
<	<=	=	>	>=	~=	==
isNil	notNil					
whileTrue:	whileFalse:	to:do:	to:by:do:			
ifTrue:	ifFalse:	ifTrue:ifFalse:	ifFalse:ifTrue:			
at:	at:put:					
<<	>>	bitInvert32	preIncrement			
integerValueOf:	integerObjectOf:	isIntegerObject:				

Table 5.3   Operations of Primitive Smalltalk.

one further refinement to the translator yielded a significant additional speedup: inlining. Inlining allows the source code of the VM to be factored into many small, precisely defined methods—thus increasing code-sharing and simplifying debugging—without paying the penalty in extra procedure calls. Inlining is also used to move the byte code service routines into the interpreter byte code dispatch loop, which both reduces byte code dispatch overhead and allows the most critical VM state to be kept in fast, register-based local variables. All told, inlining increases VM performance by a factor of 3.4 while increasing the overall code size of the VM by only 13%.

Sound

Several of us were involved in early experiments with computer music editing and synthesis [Saun77], and it was a disappointment to us that the original Smalltalk-80 release failed to incorporate this vital aspect of any lively computing environment. We determined to right this wrong in the Squeak release.

Early on, we implemented access to the Macintosh sound driver. As the performance of the Squeak system improved, we were delighted to find that we could actually synthesize and mix several voices of music in real time using simple wave table and FM algorithms written entirely in Smalltalk.

Nonetheless, these algorithms are compute-intensive, and we used this application as an opportunity to experiment with using C translation to improve the performance of isolated, time-critical methods. Sound synthesis is an ideal application for this, since nearly all the work is done by small loops with simple arithmetic and array manipulation. The sound generation methods were written so that they could be run directly in Smalltalk or, without changing a line of code, translated into C and linked into the VM as an optional primitive. Since the sound generation code had already been running for weeks in Smalltalk, the translated primitives worked perfectly the first time they ran. Furthermore, we observed nearly a 40-fold increase in performance: from 3 voices sampled at 8 KHz, we jumped to over 20 voices sampled at 44 KHz.

WarpBlt

As we began doing more with general rotation and scaling of images, we found ourselves dissatisfied with the slow speed of non-integer scaling and image rotations by angles other than multiples of 90 degrees. To address this problem in a simple manner, we added a "warp drive" to BitBlt. WarpBlt takes as input a quadrilateral specifying the traversal of the source image corresponding to BitBlt's normal rectangular destination. If the quadrilateral is larger than the destination rectangle, sampling occurs and the image is reduced. If the quadrilateral is smaller than the destination, then interpolation occurs and the image is expanded. If the quadrilateral is a rotated rectangle, then the image is correspondingly rotated. If the source quadrilateral is not rectangular, then the transformation will be correspondingly distorted.

Once we started playing with arbitrarily rotated and scaled images, we began to wish that the results of this crude warp were not so jagged. This led to support for over sampling and smoothing in the warp drive, which does a reasonable job of anti-aliasing in many cases. The approach is to average a number of pixels around a given source coordinate. Averaging colors is not a simple matter with the table-based colors of 8 bits or less. The approach we used is to map from the source color space to RGB colors, average the samples in RGB space, and map the final result back to the nearest indexed color via the normal depth-reducing color map.

As with the sound synthesis work, WarpBlt is completely described in Smalltalk, then translated into C to deliver performance appropriate to interactive graphics.

Code Size and Memory Footprint

Table 5.4 gives the approximate size of the main components of Squeak in lines of code, based on version 1.18 of December 1996. Our measurement includes all comments, but excludes all blank lines. We present these statistics not as rigorous measurement, but more as an order-of-magnitude gauge. For instance, the entire VM is approximately 100 pages. Of that, 6,547 lines are in Smalltalk (translator not included) versus 1,681 lines of OS interface in C that may need to be altered for porting.

The size of the 1.18 Squeak release image, with all development support, including browsers, inspectors, performance analyzers, color graphics, and music support is 968K bytes on the Macintosh. The code for the VM, simulator, and Smalltalk-to-C translator, which are only needed by those engaged in VM development, adds 290K to this figure. The interpreter, when running, requires 300K on a Power PC Macintosh, and the entire Smalltalk environment runs satisfactorily with as little as 200K of free space available. In monochrome, the system runs comfortably in 1.8 MB. We distribute a 650K image with the complete development environment that runs in less than 1MB on the Cassiopeia hand-held computer.

Smalltalk Lines	
Interpreter	3,951
Object Memory	1,283
BitBlt with Warp	1,313
C Lines	
OS interface	1,681

Table 5.4   Lines of Code in Squeak VM.

Performance and Optimization

Thanks to today's fast processors, Squeak's performance was satisfactory from the moment the translator produced its first C translation of the VM. Since this debut, Squeak's performance has improved steadily, and the current version, 1.18, executes about four million byte codes or 173 thousand message sends per second on a 110 MHz Power PC Mac 8100.

Table 5.5 shows the improvement in Squeak's performance over its first year. Two simple benchmarks from the release were used to track the approximate byte code execution rate (**10 benchmark**) and the cost of full-method activation and return (**26 benchFib**). Note that the latter benchmark measures the worst case; not all message sends require a full activation.

The rapid early leaps in performance were due partly to removal of scaffolding—such as assertion checks and range checks on memory references—and partly to improving the runtime model of the translator. For example, object references were originally represented as offsets relative to the base of the object memory rather than as true direct pointers. After May, however, the easy changes had all been made and improvements came in smaller increments, sometimes only a few percent at a time. The most significant of these optimizations include the following features:

- recycling method contexts (This cut the allocation rate by a factor of 10.)

- managing the frequency of checks for user and timer interrupts

- keeping the instruction and stack pointers (IP and SP) in registers

- making the IP and SP be direct pointers, rather than offsets into their base object

- patching the dispatch loop to eliminate an unneeded compiler-generated range check

Date		bytecodes/sec	sends/sec
Apr	14	458K	22,928
May	20	1,111K	60,287
May	23	1,522K	69,319
Jul	9	2,802K	134,717
Aug	1	2,726K	130,945
Sep	23	3,528K	141,155
Nov	12	3,156K	133,164
Dec	12	3,410K	169,617
Jan	21	4,108K	173,360

Table 5.5   Squeak Performance over Time.

- eliminating store-checks when storing into the active and home contexts

- comparing small integers as oops rather than converting them into integers first

- peeking for and doing a jump-if-false byte code that follows a compare

Table 5.6 compares Squeak's current performance over a small suite of benchmarks with that of several commercial Smalltalk implementations that cover a cross-section of implementation technologies, including a bytecode interpreter similar to the original Smalltalk-80 VM (Apple Smalltalk), an aggressively optimized interpreter (ST/V Mac 1.1), and two implementations using dynamic translation to native code (ParcPlace Smalltalk 2.3 and 2.5). In order to draw meaningful comparisons between Squeak and these 68K-based VMs, all timings except those in the last column were taken on a Duo 230 (33Mhz 68030). Since Squeak runs significantly better on modern processors with instruction caches and a generous supply of registers, the final column of the table, SqueakPPC, shows Squeak's performance relative to C on a Power PC-based Macintosh.

So far in the design of Squeak, we have emphasized simplicity, portability, and small memory footprint over high performance. Much better performance is possible. The PP2.3 and PP2.5 columns of Table 5.6 are examples of Deutsch-Schiffman-style dynamic translation (or "JIT") VM [Deut84]. Dynamic translation avoids the overhead of byte code dispatch by translating methods into native instructions kept in a size-bounded cache. The Self project [ChUn91] [Hölz94] broke new ground in high performance by investing more compilation time in heavily used methods, using inlining to eliminate expensive calls and enable further optimizations. This work, which was later extended to Smalltalk and Java [Anim96], shows that one can obtain performance approaching half the speed of optimized C without compromising the semantics of a clean language. Unfortunately, both of these approaches have resulted in VM implementations that are, by Squeak standards, unapproachable and difficult to port.

	AppleST	ST/V	PP2.3	PP2.5	Squeak	SqueakPPC
IntegerSum	185.00	32.00	7.58	6.92	62.34	72.56
VectorSum	99.00	30.00	10.30	11.50	61.70	41.01
PrimeSieve	53.00	40.00	16.07	12.10	70.53	51.57
BubbleSort	88.23	35.29	21.35	13.98	80.29	63.12
TreeSort	43.90	5.00	20.29	1.98	16.33	7.31
MatrixMult	40.79	6.00	22.80	2.94	18.00	36.74
Recurse	28.26	9.47	3.73	2.08	50.26	35.19

Table 5.6 Virtual Machine Performance Relative to Optimized, Platform-Native C for Various Benchmarks. (Smaller numbers are better. A result of 1.0 would indicate that a benchmark ran exactly as fast as optimized C.)

We believe that Squeak can enjoy the same performance as commercial Smalltalk implementations without compromising malleability and portability. In our experience the byte code basis of the Smalltalk-80 standard [Inga78] is hard to beat for compactness and simplicity, and for the programming tools that have grown around it. Therefore, dynamic translation is a natural avenue to high performance. The Squeak philosophy implies that both the dynamic translator and its target code sequences should be written and debugged in Smalltalk, then automatically translated into C to build the production VM. By representing translated methods as ordinary Smalltalk objects, experiments with Self-style inlining and other optimizations could be done at the Smalltalk level. This approach is currently being explored as a way to improve Squeak's performance without adversely affecting its portability.

The Squeak Community

As exciting as the day the interpreter first ran, was the day we released Squeak to the Internet community. In the back of our minds, we all felt that we were finally doing, in September of 1996, what we had failed to do in 1980. However, the code we released ran only on the Macintosh and, although we had worked hard to make it portable, we did not know if we had succeeded.

Three weeks later, we received a message announcing Ian Piumarta's first UNIX port of Squeak. He had ported it to seven additional UNIX platforms two weeks later. At the same time, Andreas Raab announced ports of Squeak for Windows 95 and Windows NT. Neither of these people had even contacted us before starting their porting efforts! A mere five weeks after it was released, Squeak was available on all the major computing platforms except Windows 3.1 and had an active and rapidly growing mailing list. Since that time, Squeak ports have been completed for Linux, the Acorn RISC, and Windows CE, and several other ports are underway.

The Squeak release (including the source code for the VM, C translator, and everything else described in this chapter), as well as all the ports mentioned above, is available through the following sites:

- http://www.squeak.org

- ftp://ftp.create.ucsb.edu

- ftp://alix.inria.fr

- ftp://ftp.cs.uni-magdeburg.de/pub/Smalltalk/free/squeak

The Squeak license agreement explicitly grants the right to use Squeak in commercial applications royalty-free. The only requirement in return is that any ports of Squeak or changes to the base class library must be made available for free on the Internet. New applications and facilities built on Squeak do not need to be shared. We believe that this licensing agreement encourages the continued development and sharing of Squeak by its user community.

Related Work

For the Smalltalk devotee, nothing is more natural than the desire to attack all programming problems with Smalltalk. Thus, there has long been a tradition of using Smalltalk to describe and debug a low-level system before its final implementation. As mentioned earlier, the Blue Book used Smalltalk as a high-level description of a Smalltalk VM, and this description was actually checked for accuracy by running it. In LOOM [Kaeh86], the kernel of a virtual object memory was written and executed in a separate, simplified Smalltalk VM whenever an "object fault" occurred. For better performance, this kernel was later translated into BCPL semiautomatically, then fixed up by hand. This experience planted the seed for the approach taken in Squeak two decades later.

A number of recent systems translate complete Smalltalk programs into lower level languages to gain speed, portability, or application packaging advantages. Smalltalk/X [Gitt95] and SPiCE [YaDo95] generate C code from programs using the full range of Smalltalk semantics, including blocks. Babel [MWH94] translates Smalltalk applications into CLOS and includes a facility for automatically winnowing out unused classes and methods.

Producer [Cox87] translated Smalltalk programs into Objective C, but required the programmer to supply type declarations and rules for mapping dynamically allocated objects such as Points into Objective C record structures. Producer supported only a subset of Smalltalk semantics, because it depended on the Objective C runtime and thus did not support blocks as first-class objects. Squeak's Smalltalk-to-C translator restricts the programmer to an even more limited subset of Smalltalk, but that subset closely mirrors the underlying processor architecture, allowing the translated code to run nearly as efficiently as if it were written in C directly. The difference arises from a difference in goals: The goal of Squeak's translation is merely to support the construction of its own VM, a much simpler task than translating full-blown Smalltalk programs into C.

Squeak's translator is more in the spirit of QUICKTALK [Ball86], a system that used Smalltalk to define new primitive methods for the VM. Another Smalltalk-to-primitive compiler, Hurricane [Atki86], used a combination of user-supplied declarations and simple type inference to eliminate class checks and to inline integer arithmetic. Unlike Squeak's translator, Hurricane allowed the programmer to also use polymorphic arithmetic in the Smalltalk code to be translated. Neither QUICKTALK nor Hurricane attempted to produce an entire VM via translation.

Type information can help a translator produce more efficient code by eliminating runtime type tests and enabling inlining. Typed Smalltalk [JGZ88] added optional type declarations to Smalltalk and used that type information to generate faster code. The quality of its code was comparable to that of QUICKTALK but, to the best of the authors' knowledge, the project's ultimate goal of producing a complete, stand-alone Smalltalk VM was never realized. A different approach is to use type information gathered during program execution to guide on-the-fly optimization, as done in the Self [ChUn91] [Hölz94] and Animorphic [Anim96] VM. Note that using types for optimization is independent of whether the programming language has type declarations. The Self and Animorphic VMs use type information to optimize declaration-free languages, whereas Strongtalk [BrGr93], which augments Smalltalk with an optional type system to support the specification and verification of interfaces, ran on a VM that knew nothing about those types. The subset of Smalltalk used for the Squeak VM maps so directly to the fundamental data types of the hardware that the translator would not benefit from additional type information. However, we have contemplated building a separate primitive compiler that supports polymorphic arithmetic, in which case the declaration-driven optimization techniques of Hurricane and Typed Smalltalk would be beneficial.

Future Work

Work on Squeak continues. We are overhauling Squeak's graphics model to supplant the MVC model with a new one along the lines of Morphic [Malo95] and Fabrik [Inga88]. We also plan to complete Squeak's sound and music facilities by adding sound input and MIDI input and output.

We are collaborating with Ian Piumarta to produce a dynamic translation engine for Squeak, inspired by Eliot Miranda's BrouHaHa Smalltalk [Mira87] and his later work with portable threaded code. A top priority is to build the entire engine in Smalltalk to keep it entirely portable.

Just as we wanted Squeak to be endowed with music and sound capability, we also wanted it to be easily interconnected with the rest of the computing world. To this end, we are adding network stream and datagram support to the system. While not yet complete, the current facilities already support TCP/IP clients and servers on Macintosh and Windows 95/NT, with UNIX support to follow soon.

Conclusions

As far as we know, Squeak is the first practical Smalltalk system written in itself that is complete and self-supporting. Squeak runs the Smalltalk code describing its own VM fast enough for debugging purposes: Although it requires some patience, one can actually interact with menus and windows in this mode. This is no mean feat, considering that every memory reference in the inner loop of BitBlt is running in Smalltalk.

To achieve useful levels of performance, the Smalltalk code of the VM is translated into C, yielding a speedup of approximately 450. Part of this performance gain, a factor of 3.4, can be attributed to the inlining of function calls in the translation process. The translator can also be used to generate primitive methods for computationally intensive inner loops that manipulate fundamental data types of the machine such as bytes, integers, floats, and arrays of these types.

The Squeak VM, since its source code is publicly available, serves as an updated reference implementation for Smalltalk-80. This is especially valuable now that the classic Blue and Green Books [Gold83] [Kras83] are out of print. A number of design choices made in the Blue Book that were appropriate for the slower speed and limited address space of the computer systems of the early 1980s have been revisited, especially those relating to object memory and storage reclamation. Squeak also updates the multimedia components of this reference system by adding color support and image transformation capabilities to BitBlt and by including sound output. While Squeak is not the first Smalltalk to use modern storage management or to support multimedia, it makes a valuable contribution by delivering these capabilities in a small one-language package that is freely available and that runs identically on all platforms.

Final Reflections

While we considered using Java for our project, we still feel that Smalltalk offers a better environment for research and development. At a time when the world is moving toward native host widgets, we still feel that there is power and inspiration in having all of the code for every aspect of computation and display be immediately accessible, changeable, and identical across platforms. Finally, when most development environments fill 100 megabytes of disk space or more, Squeak is a portable, malleable, full-service computing environment, including browsing, split-second recompilation, and source debugging tools, all in a 1-megabyte footprint. Though many of its strengths are rooted in the past, Squeak is suited to the intimate computing potential of PDAs and the Internet, and our work is, now more than ever, inspired by the future.

Acknowledgments

The authors wish to acknowledge the support of Apple Computer throughout this project, especially Jim Spohrer, Don Norman, and Elizabeth Greer. We especially appreciate their wisdom in seeing that Squeak would be worth more if it were made freely available. We also wish to thank the entire Squeak community for their encouragement and support, especially those who have submitted code or donated their time and energy to maintaining Squeak ports and the Squeak mailing list and web sites.

References

[Anim96] Animorphic Systems, *Exhibit at OOPSLA '96*, Animorphic Systems was a small company that included several members of the Self team and produced extremely high performance virtual machines for Smalltalk and Java. The company has since been purchased by Sun Microsystems.

[Atki86] Atkinson, R., *Hurricane: An Optimizing Compiler for Smalltalk*, Proc. of the ACM OOPSLA '86 conf., September 1986, pp. 151–158.

[Ball86] Ballard, M., Maier, D., and Wirffs-Brock, A., *QUICKTALK: A Smalltalk-80 Dialect for Defining Primitive Methods*, Proc. of the ACM OOPSLA '86 conf., September 1986, pp. 140–150.

[BrGr93] Bracha, G. and Griswold, D., *Strongtalk: Typechecking Smalltalk in a Production Environment*, Proc. of the ACM OOPSLA '93 conf., September 1993.

[ChUn91] Chambers, C. and Ungar, D., *Making Pure Object-Oriented Languages Practical*, Proc. of the ACM OOPSLA '91 conf., November 1991, pp. 1–15.

[Cox87] Cox, B. and Schmucker, K., *Producer: A Tool for Translating Smalltalk-80 to Objective-C*, Proc. of the ACM OOPSLA '87 conf., October 1987, pp. 423–429.

[Deut84] Deutsch, L., and Schiffman, A., *Efficient Implementation of the Smalltalk-80 System*, Proc. 11th ACM Symposium on Principles of Programming Languages, January 1984, pp. 297–302.

[Gitt95] Gittinger, C., *Smalltalk/X*, http://www.informatik.uni-stuttgart.de/stx/stx.html, 1995.

[Gold83] Goldberg, A. and Robson, D., *Smalltalk-80: The Language and Its Implementation*, Addison-Wesley, Reading, MA, 1983.

[Hölz94] Hölzle, U., *Adaptive Optimization for Self: Reconciling High Performance with Exploratory Programming*, Ph.D. Thesis, Computer Science Department, Stanford University, 1994.

[Inga78] Ingalls, D., *The Smalltalk-76 Programming System, Design and Implementation*, Proc. 5th ACM Symposium on Principles of Programming Languages, Tucson, AZ, January 1978.

[Inga88] Ingalls, D., Wallace, S., Chow, Y., Ludolph, F., and Doyle, K., *Fabrik: A Visual Programming Environment*, Proc. of the ACM OOPSLA '88 conf., September 1988, pp. 176–190.

[JGZ88] Johnson, R., Graver, J., and Zurawski, L., *TS: An Optimizing Compiler for Smalltalk*, Proc. of the ACM OOPSLA '88 conf., September 1988, pp. 18–26.

[Kaeh86] Kaehler, T., *Virtual Memory on a Narrow Machine for an Object-Oriented Language*, Proc. of the ACM OOPSLA '86 conf., September 1986, pp. 87–106.

[Kras83] Krasner, G., ed., *Smalltalk-80, Bits of History, Words of Advice*, Addison-Wesley, Reading, MA, 1983.

[Malo95] Maloney, J. and Smith, R., *Directness and Liveness in the Morphic User Interface Construction Environment*, UIST '95, November 1995.

[Mira87] Miranda, E., *BrouHaHa—A Portable Smalltalk Interpreter*, Proc. of the ACM OOPSLA '87 conf., October 1987, pp. 354–365.

[MWH94] Moore, I., Wolczko, M., and Hopkins, T., *Babel—A Translator from Smalltalk into CLOS*, TOOLS USA 1994, Prentice Hall, 1994.

[Saun77] Saunders, S., *Improved FM Audio Synthesis Methods for Real-time Digital Music Generation*, in *Computer Music Journal* 1(1), February 1977. Reprinted in *Computer Music*, Roads, C. and Strawn, J., eds., MIT Press, Cambridge, MA, 1985.

[Unga84] Ungar, D., *Generation Scavenging: A Non-Disruptive High Performance Storage Reclamation Algorithm*, Proc. ACM Symposium on Practical Software Development Environments, April 1984, pp. 157–167. Also published as *ACM SIGPLAN Notices* 19(5), May 1984, and *ACM Software Engineering Notes* 9(3), May 1984.

[UnJa88] Ungar, D. and Jackson, F., *Tenuring Policies for Generation-Based Storage Reclamation*, Proc. of the ACM OOPSLA '88 conf., September 1988, pp. 18–26.

[YaDo95] Yasumatsu, K. and Doi, N., *SPiCE: A System for Translating Smalltalk Programs into a C Environment*, IEEE Transactions on Software Engineering 21(11), 1995, pp. 902–912.

6

Back to the Future
Once More

Daniel H. H. Ingalls
Walt Disney Imagineering R&D

Author's note: I began this chapter attempting to duly credit each contributor appropriately. It soon became clear either that the chapter would degenerate to an encyclopedia of credits or it would be full of unfair omissions. I have chosen instead to take the point of view that I write for the entire Squeak community that has worked tirelessly and selflessly to make Squeak what it is. "We" did this together, and so it will be reported here. Most of the important contributions are credited elsewhere.

The structure of this update directly parallels the original paper. You might want to reference back to the previous chapter for context.

Introduction

The purpose of this chapter is to update the paper *Back to the Future—The Story of Squeak, a Practical Smalltalk Written in Itself* (hereinafter simply "BTF") that was presented at the ACM OOPSLA '97 conference, and that is reproduced as Chapter 5 of this volume. As such, the bulk of the text follows the structure of that paper, with comments and new data presented in a parallel sequence. However, a mere update of Squeak's features and performance would not give a sense of the various forces, technical and social, that have guided the evolution of Squeak over the 3 1/2 years since the paper was published. Therefore, we begin with an overview of some of these forces and the effects they have had on the evolution of Squeak since the publication of BTF.

As documented in BTF, Squeak began as a simple bytecode interpreter or VM (virtual machine) written in Smalltalk and translated to C, together with a modernized version of the Apple Smalltalk image. The major changes were to extend the object memory to 32-bit pointers and to extend BitBlt to a flexible color model. The innovation of translating the interpreter made Squeak a practical and portable Smalltalk while being entirely self-contained and self-describing.

Throughout its life so far, Squeak has enjoyed the ministrations of both the core development team at Disney (hereinafter "Squeak Central") and a large and active internet community of developers, academics, and recreational computer scientists. Key to the continuing synergy between these two groups have been Squeak's total openness and the complete portability of Squeak across all major computing platforms, including even simple chip sets with only a BIOS.

The Evolution of Squeak

BTF is mainly about the implementation of Squeak; how it began, how it was carried out, and how it performed. Very little is said about the Squeak image which, in 1996, was simply a classic Smalltalk-80 image, with extensions for color and sound, and the support for simulating and generating the Squeak interpreter.

A major difference between then and now is that most of Squeak's evolution has taken place in the Squeak image (the Smalltalk system class definitions), rather than in the VM. Most of the changes to the VM have come in response to that evolution, to enable or optimize various new capabilities needed along the way. Of all the changes over these years, the areas of greatest impact to Squeak's place in the world so far have been graphics and networking, and the flexible cross-platform support for sound.

Based on experiences with Morphic and Fabrik, we felt a need for a more flexible and concrete graphics model than the existing MVC (Model, View, Controller) view framework, and so, over the next couple of months, we built a reasonable implementation of the Morphic interface used in the Self system. This interface was then put to immediate use as the basis for the EToy experiment—a novice interface to Squeak that allows one to control Morphic objects with halos and active inspectors and to script them by assembling tiles that correspond to Squeak message fragments.

The new Morphic worlds soon cried out for an equivalent to MVC's **Standard-SystemView** so that we could "live" (i.e., integrate all our work) in Morphic as we had lived before in MVC, and this led to the creation of Morphic parallels to the basic MVC views. Similarly, our educational experiments in these new worlds indicated the need for arbitrary scaling and rotation of Morphic objects. Not having anticipated this need so soon, and not having the resources to implement a completely general graphics model at the time, we combined a general transform definition with Squeak's WarpBlt capability to produce the **TransformationMorph**. While Transfomration Morphs are neither a perfect nor a general solution, as one critic has frequently admitted, "You guys sure got a lot of mileage out of that Warp thingy." The advantage of this approach is archetypal of exploratory programming. In a couple of weeks, there was a way to experience and experiment with general scaling and rotation in Morphic, and we could move on to the next most-interesting problem. Moreover, when time actually allows us to rewrite Morphic with a general approach to transformations, we will have several years' worth of working software as examples of what we want and how we need to use it. (For more on this topic, see Chapter 2 on Morphic.)

While WarpBlt actually provides a reasonable anti-aliasing of interior images, the Morphic canvas rendering model had no way to properly combine morphs with anti-aliasing. At this point, we took on the task of designing a new canvas model that would incorporate curve drawing and filling with proper anti-aliasing. This model became the Balloon 2-D rendering engine.

At about this time, two other projects sharpened our focus on 3-D graphics. To begin with, we had just begun a collaboration to port the Alice 3-D system to Squeak. (For more on this project, see Chapter 3 on Alice.) At the same time, for various internal reasons at Disney, we wanted to be able to demonstrate a virtual gallery of computing environments in full 3-D. With the Balloon engine in place, we set about designing a 3-D graphics model that could employ this high-quality rendering onto a general Morphic canvas. This project became the Balloon 3-D engine.

As we used and enhanced the new 3-D facilities, performance inevitably became an issue. The desire to make use of various hardware and software accelerators on different platforms led to a serious reworking of the BitBlt and WarpBlt primitives.

Also crucial to Squeak's coming of age was the implementation of decent network support. By the time BTF was published, Squeak had cross-platform support for client-server protocols for file transfer, worldwide web, and electronic mail. At OOPSLA 97 two Squeaks, one on a Mac and one on a PC, were shown running Telemorphic, a network-integrated version of Morphic (simply using multiple hands) with a multi-user paint program and a multiuser music sequencer application.

The immediate focus at Squeak Central was not on browser access, but rather on leveraging the network to distribute "updates" to anyone participating in the active development of Squeak itself or managing their own collaborative development efforts. The update mechanism is a simple and effective approach to coordinated system development. Each update is a file containing Squeak source code and possibly executable expressions as well. On a server is a list of all updates published so far, and an index of the order in which they were published. Any Squeak system connected to the internet can automatically determine what files have been published since it was last updated and can read them in, thus becoming current with the latest work at Squeak Central or with the image from which the system updates were issued. This mechanism immediately brought the entire Squeak community together and allowed anyone to follow the latest changes with almost no effort at all.

About the time automatic updating became practical, a Pluggable Web Server (PWS) was implemented in Squeak. This software turned out to be a kernel of very high leverage. At about this time, Ward Cunningham's WikiWiki server was being used to coordinate various designs and projects in the Squeak community, and it

suddenly became clear that one could build a server based on Ward's WikiWikiWeb
in almost no time on top of the PWS. Within a month or two, the first so-called
Swiki server was operational, and it soon became a part of the Squeak general
release. Many people downloaded Squeak just to get a free cross-platform Swiki
server!

Over the next year, Squeak's mail (Celeste), browsing (Scamper) and Chat
(IRCMorph) facilities became operational, along with FTP access in the FileList.
Other interesting projects to date include Comanche, a high performance web server,
and Nebraska, a much more flexible approach to multi-user (and remote headless)
applications in Morphic. (For more complete coverage of these topics, see Chapter 4
on networking.)

Many other factors played a role in the progress of Squeak over these four years,
but they are beyond the scope of this summary. With the foregoing sketch as
context, let us now return to BTF and bring the major topics up to date.

The Interpreter

We have been able to retain the original bytecode interpreter design, keeping the
core of the virtual machine relatively simple and yet we have constantly improved
its efficiency through care in compilation (register variables), some shortcuts (at
cache), and some hackery. Also, numerous ancillary "pluggable" primitives, most
of them simply compiled from Squeak, have added greatly to the core computational
power of Squeak.

A number of limitations in the original Squeak interpreter have been improved.
For instance, pluggable primitives allow for essentially unlimited primitive extensions, the maximum number of temporary variables is roughly quadrupled, the
image format has been tested at over 2.5GB, and so on.

The Object Memory

Even more than the interpreter, the original design for Squeak's object memory has
stood the test of time. The basic object format survives unchanged, with only one
extension to support weak array references.

The feature most often criticized is the use of a special header format for one-
word headers. While this typically saves an extra word per object for approximately
90% of the objects in the system, it can require an extra memory access to check the
class of such objects. We have not yielded to this criticism yet because (1) the hard
work has already been done, so moving to a simpler design would not save work at
this point, (2) cleverness can in many cases avoid the extra penalty for looking up
the class, and (3) 4 bytes per object can be a significant savings in small systems.

One interesting capability has been added to the Squeak object memory since
the publication of BTF. This is the ability to extract and install image segments.

One day, while musing about how to deep copy a structure without copying the entire world, it occurred to us that the garbage collector was in a position to solve this problem for us. The idea is to first mark a number of root objects, and then run the normal garbage collection (gc) mark phase. Since gc marking stops at any marked object, the end result would be to mark every object in the system except those "in the shadow" of the root objects. The unmarked objects are, therefore, exactly the objects pointed to by the original roots, but not from anywhere else in the system.

Squeak image segments are produced by a primitive that accepts an array of roots and produces (1) an array of outward pointers from the segment into the rest of the image and (2) a binary object containing a copy of all the objects in the segment. The binary format is identical to that of a Squeak image, except that non-local pointers are represented as indices into the table of outpointers. Extraction of an image segment can be extremely fast, and installation is even faster. For example:

Segment size:	940k segment with 16,403 objects, 6,912 outpointers
Time to extract:	264 milliseconds (mostly marking)
Time to install:	43 milliseconds
Configuration:	8Mb image on a 400MHz Mac

The simplest application of image segments is to perform a fast deepCopy by extracting an image segment and then installing it again as a copy. Another application is segment swapping. For swapping, the extracted segment is written to disk, and then the roots are converted into root stub proxy objects that will read the segment back from disk if they are ever touched. Special care is required to ensure that if a class is a root, it will still be successfully retrieved when a message is sent to one of its instances. When swapping segments, the table of outpointers is retained in the image as part of the root stub complex.

A third valuable application of image segments is for data export. In this case, the binary segment is stored on a file along with a fully externalized representation of the array of outpointers. Such a structure can be transferred from one image to another and can be used for archival data storage as well. A fortuitous discovery about exported segments is that both internal and external pointers in image segments are quite local, and as a result, GZIP compression frequently achieves a factor of four, as opposed to two or less on typical Squeak images.

Storage Management

Squeak's simple two-generation garbage collector has proven to be remarkably well behaved across a wide variety of applications. Its simple approach of incremental collection and compaction without maintaining free lists has provided both high performance and full utilization of available memory. It is still the case that a 600k Squeak image can fit in one megabyte along with the VM and still be happy with the modest 200k of remaining available memory.

As various Squeak applications grow to larger sizes, we have been fortunate to see processor speeds also increase, leaving the typical latency for incremental collection and compaction well below the 10ms threshold that is critical to sound I/O and similar real-time response. A typical Squeak image with a substantial amount of content has the following statistics:

> 20.0Mb   old objects
> 2.2Mb   young objects
> 2.8Mb   free

During a 53-second run, there were 1,400 incremental collections averaging 3.0 ms each, for an overall cost of around 8%.[1]

Squeak now provides access to VM parameters, allowing one to trade latency (time required to perform and incremental GC) against overhead (percent execution time spent in GC). Experimenting with a system similar to that just presented and changing the quota of objects allocated between each GC, we obtained the following results:[2]

Allocation quota	Avg. latency	Avg. overhead
2,000	2ms	11%
4,000	3ms	9%
8,000	4ms	6%
16,000	6ms	6%

In BTF, we reported on Squeak's efficient bulk implementation of object identity reversal known as **become**. The Squeak storage management system now provides both forms of **become**, symmetric and forwarding, both still being done in bulk if appropriate.

BitBlt and WarpBlt

The original design of BitBlt and WarpBlt survives relatively unchanged in the current Squeak release, but it is soon to be supplanted by a completely new implementation dubbed **FXBLT**. This new primitive responds to a number of forces in Squeak's evolution. First is the continued pressure for increased flexibility and low-cost setup when called by the balloon-rendering engine. Second is the ability to take advantage of hardware acceleration. Third is the potential of improved performance in the absence of special hardware by applying some of the dynamic code-generation techniques analogous to those used to accelerate the interpreter. Fourth is the need to reduce latency time which requires that large blts be interruptible. And last but not least is the desire to execute efficient transfers between bitmaps of differing formats, including bits per pixel, bits per color, endianness, and even the order of color components.

---

[1]Configuration: 20Mb image on a 400MHz Mac.
[2]Configuration: 10Mb image on a 400MHz Mac.

Interestingly, while the latency issue is in some cases the most critical one, it is, at the same time amenable to high-level solution by recognizing large blts and breaking them into smaller ones outside of the primitive operation. While we have not applied ourselves seriously to the task of reducing latency in Squeak, we have implemented a limited-latency interface to BitBlt, which did in fact cure interference of large blts with music generation. The extended primitives for text display and line drawing are also potential latency problems, but being optional, they can simply be eliminated at the cost of somewhat slower display of text and lines.

Smalltalk-to-C Translation

The core translator has remained relatively stable since the original release of Squeak. Probably the most significant change introduced since that time is the ability to compile independent primitive modules in conjunction with Squeak's "pluggable primitive" facility.

The pluggable primitive facility allows a method to specify a named primitive implementation. When such a method is executed for the first time, the interpreter attempts to load a module of that name from the directory in which the interpreter exists. If the module is not found, then execution proceeds following the normal rules for primitive failure. If found, the module is loaded, and the specific primitive name is sought within that module. If the name is found, then the appropriate code is executed as a primitive in Squeak. A module can be defined both internally and externally. This means that an interpreter can be shipped with many intensions built in so that no additional plugins are needed. Yet if a new version is present, it will override the code in the interpreter. Note that, after the first lookup, subsequent references to pluggable primitives are resolved with essentially no overhead, whether the module is present or absent (fast failures can be important).

The ability to compile optional plugins from Squeak has spawned a number of extensions of great value to various applications of Squeak. Each of the following plugins enables a significant capability for Squeak applications:

Plugin	Capability
Balloon	2-D vector graphics engine
Squeak3-D	3-D rendering engine
JPEG decoder	Fast JPEG decoder
FFT	Fast fourier transform
FFI	Foreign function interface
KLATT	Speech synthesis
SoundCodecPrims	10:1 ADPCM sound compression/decompression
LargeIntegers	Fast implementation of LargeInteger arithmetic
GZIP	Fast GZIP data compression/decompression

The fast LargeIntegers have enabled practical DSA encryption, and the GZIP compressor is used in many places to save space in Squeak and its external files.

The foreign function interface has enabled a number of interesting experiments and real-world applications, including control of a large real-time 3-D simulator with multiple display screens, a Quicktime toolbox controller capable of displaying QT movies in Morphic, and an interface to the FreeType toolbox. (For more on pluggable primitives, see Chapter 9 on extending the VM.)

Sound

Most of Squeak's sound support is in Squeak itself. However, as described in the original BTF paper, a few primitives are necessary to achieve reasonable performance. The original specification of the primitives has changed somewhat in order to allow fine-grained control over envelope parameters with relatively little computational overhead.

Much more has been done with music in Squeak since the BTF paper. The release image includes a MIDI score player (ScorePlayerMorph) with pan, gain, and mute controls as well as the ability to change the orchestration. A MIDI score piano roll (PianoRollScoreMorph) can display the piece being played in real time, and it supports some very limited editing facilities as well. Sampled timbres can be recorded from a microphone or from other sources, cleaned up and looped in the sample editor (WaveEditor). FM timbres can be edited in the envelope editor (EnvelopeEditorMorph) and tested with an on-screen keyboard (or with another music application). Beyond these primitive but useful facilities, the SIREN system (described in Stephen Pope's chapter in this volume) is a mature application devoted to the creation and manipulation of musical scores in Squeak.

Merely making sound available in a cross-platform and interactive manner has spawned many other interesting capabilities. For instance, the Squeak release includes a real-time speech synthesis facility capable of reading any text intelligibly. It can even sing "Silent Night" as a duet with animated singing faces.

Squeak's 30-line FFT became one of the first pluggable primitives, and a showcase for fast access to Floating-point arrays. Running in Squeak, this routine performed a 4096-point Fourier transform in about 580 milliseconds. The plugin computes the same transform in 3 milliseconds. The FFT plugin has enabled Squeak to display real-time sonograms (SpectrumAnalyzerMorph) and to perform limited speech recognition.

Code Size and Memory Footprint

The size of the kernel interpreter has grown very little, but a number of added primitives have increased the size of the interpreter module by about 50% since the figures were reported in BTF. The Object memory has grown very little since it was first written. BitBlt and the other related graphic routines have nearly doubled in size as a result of the enhancements and other experiments alluded to above.

It is still possible to produce a practical Squeak that will run (interpreter, image, and adequate free space) in one megabyte. Some Squeak releases require massaging to produce an adequately small image (700K) to fit within this constraint.

Performance and Optimization

Table 5 in BTF documents gradual improvements in the efficiency of Squeak's interpreter that achieved an eight-fold improvement over the course of nine months. When that table was written, we had reached version 1.18, and we felt we had squeezed about as much as possible out of a classical bytecode interpreter. We can now compare the 1.18 interpreter with the 2.8 interpreter in use at the time of this writing.

Squeak 1.18	17.7 million bytecodes/sec	907 thousand sends/sec
Squeak 2.8	36.1 million bytecodes/sec	1155 thousand sends/sec[3]

It is gratifying to note that, whereas we thought we had reached the limit of what could easily be done to improve Squeak's performance, we still managed to double the bytecode speed and to squeeze an additional 27% in the time it takes to perform a send. The latter was achieved by doggedly reducing the code executed on each allocation and release of a context, especially eliminating the need to nil out all fields of a context before use by noting the stack pointer in garbage collection. The improvement in bytecode speed came from attention to register allocation in the generated C code, streamlined flow through arithmetic primitives, and the introduction of an "at-cache." The at-cache keeps a small cache (8) of recent objects that can respond primitively to at: and at:put:, along with their size and format (byte, word, pointer, or bits). This cache enables fast treatment of these messages for such objects and also similar speedups for next and nextPut: for streams whose contents satisfy the same conditions.

It must also be noted that during the three years that have elapsed between these two releases, comparable computer speeds have increased fourfold. One could conclude that it is better to put one's time elsewhere than optimization, since next year's silicon will make your efforts seem trivial. However, on slow machines, such as PDA's, every cycle still counts, and on fast machines the results are multiplicative, so it is still important progress.

An entirely separate assault on performance was mounted in 1998. The first attempt, code named Jitter, achieved a significant performance gain (bytecode speed, send speed). However overall benchmarks never made it to the level we sought (2–4 times), and the design seemed to suffer from a number of tuning sensitivities.

Almost before the first Jitter came to life, another design had sprung up in its place. Begun half a year later, and dubbed J3, this design had a much better approach to pointer mapping and worked from a table-driven model of code generation. This time, the performance indications were in the area we had hoped for,

---

[3]Configuration: 10Mb image on a 400MHz Mac.

with still several optimizations yet to be tried. The J3 engine has only run for brief periods of time and has not yet been integrated with the mainline Squeak releases.

It is our hope, looking forward, that J3 technology will finally make it into the mainline Squeak releases. Besides the possibility of 200–400% improvements in execution speed, the move to such a production engine would allow us to actually deconvert some of the tuning of the bytecode interpreter, returning it to a classic didactic model parallel to that in the Blue Book, but exactly true to the Squeak semantics.

The Squeak Community

BTF is a technical paper, and most of the foregoing information serves to bring the reported results up to date. The section entitled "The Squeak Community" is really about the success of Squeak's portability and the remarkable achievements of a couple of outside contributors after Squeak's release. At this point it seems appropriate to balance the technical reports with some of the less technical factors that have made Squeak and the Squeak Community what they are.

If you were to spend time with the principal authors of Squeak, you would find them to be technically competent, but that is not what has made Squeak what it is. What sets this group apart is a further interest in simplicity, leverage, and synergy. Look at Smalltalk itself. A completely different model for computation—sending messages to objects—looks simple and effective. We carry this through an entire system design and find enormous leverage from polymorphism and inheritance in this model. Then extending this out to the world of graphics, it turns out that many things that used to be hard are easy. This feeds back, making the core of the system even more concrete and accessible—the synergy part. It's more than synergy—it's fun.

Thus Squeak, beginning as a Smalltalk system, was already earmarked for the adventurous, but with the added meta-circularity of including its interpreter within itself. Published with complete source code available free over the internet, Squeak was bound to attract an interesting community.

Difficult though it may be, it is probably worth trying to characterize the Squeak community. The two major orientations can best be characterized as "research" and "development." The research group consists of workers similar to the Disney team, whose primary interest in Squeak is as a vehicle for research, a malleable tool that can easily be adapted to serve a wide variety of investigations. The academic members in this group find in Squeak a vast laboratory of interesting experiments in computer science, many comprising the laboratory itself. The commercially oriented developers, on the other hand, see in Squeak a royalty-free Smalltalk base that runs on every major computing platform and can be easily ported to bare chip sets. Both constituents of the Squeak community also share certain fun-loving characteristics. They enjoy the art of programming; they are motivated to improve an open-source facility; and they see it as a sport to reach results comparable to commercial implementations.

As curators of this particular facility, it has been a constant challenge to decide where best to put our effort in the growth, refinement and (hopefully) simplifications that shape the future of Squeak. A classical planner would ask what is our market, what are our strengths, what is the competition, and what comprises, therefore, our best "product" opportunity.

Now we have to look at one more important aspect of this community—the role of Squeak Central. Thus far, Squeak Central has "enjoyed" a central position in shaping the evolution of Squeak. While we have always had an egalitarian attitude toward the community as a whole, we are not a neutral player in the process. Squeak was delivered to the world because (1) we felt that Smalltalk was the most malleable and highest productivity environment to serve as a vehicle for our investigations in personal computing and (2) we felt that only by making it open and free would it garner the kind of intellectual participation needed to become a serious computing environment.

There is, therefore, a distortion in the original characterization of our "market"— a primary drive toward support for what we see as the computational and interactive needs of Squeak Central's "vision" at any given time. We have tried to deal with this asymmetry as much as possible in the manner of a benevolent dictatorship. We make most of the decisions about what is or is not included in the system, but we also try to maximize the synergy with the rest of the Squeak community.

Now we can return to the forces at work in Squeak's "market" as so defined. A number of Squeak's attributes are items that everyone agrees are important. These include cross-platform support, color graphics, and open source distribution. Many others are not. For instance, developers care more about ANSI compliance than anyone else, with academics running a close second. This is because they want to be able to import software from other systems, and they want to be able to use or ship their products with other Smalltalk systems besides Squeak. This can be a matter of performance or one of cooperating with existing software that is tied to a particular Smalltalk host. For similar reasons, developers care a lot about including MVC. However, researchers do not care so much, because many experiments turn out to be simpler to build and easier to demonstrate if written using Morphic.

Squeak Central may not care at all about either ANSI compatibility or support for MVC, because it does not import code from other systems, use MVC in any of its work. However, it is clear that these features are both very important to synergy in the Squeak community. Squeak Central benefits constantly and directly from work done by other members of the community, so concerns such as these are given high regard in all difficult decisions.

As long as the Squeak community is split between developers and researchers, between novices and experts, there will be tension surrounding the makeup and presentation of the system. As long as it makes sense, we try to keep the various forces in balance and maximize the synergy in the results.

Future Work

It is gratifying to see that almost everything we spoke of accomplishing in BTF's "Future Work" section has been done. Given that the scope of BTF was limited to a Smalltalk implementation, this is not surprising. When we look forward from here, in the broader context of general purpose multimedia computing, the challenges seem somewhat more daunting.

Interestingly, one of the future items in BTF was "to supplant the MVC graphics model with a new one along the lines of Morphic and Fabrik." That has all been done and has successfully spawned numerous exciting graphical applications, including the EToy environment, music editors and a complete 3-D gallery of independent Squeak projects. Unfortunately, Morphic grew uncontrollably in response to the differing and demanding masters it was asked to serve, and we are back at the same place a generation later. To paraphrase from four years ago, we now plan to supplant the Morphic graphics model with a new one that incorporates what we have learned so far, that will be simpler and better factored, and that will lend itself better to the support of multiple environments in 3-D and multiple users in those environments.

Much remains to be done to make Squeak more approachable and productive for various classes of users, especially for novices or "internet" programmers. We hope to see in the near future a synthesis of EToy-style environments with the current "serious" software development tools. We also hope to introduce types at both the novice and expert levels, but in a way that is not encumbering to the simplicity and immediacy of coding in Squeak.

At the time of this writing, we are working to bring the various just-in-time compilation experiments into the Squeak mainline release and to support them on all platforms. Improved performance is important to researchers and developers alike, and it should augment the convergent forces in both sides of the Squeak community.

However circuitous the path may seem from time to time, Squeak is destined to follow its authors' vision of the real potential of personal computing. As a personal information appliance it will be simple and convenient. It will be able to store and manipulate many kinds of data from text and numbers to images and sounds and rules for their behavior. Access to different kinds of objects will be simple and uniform, and the system itself will be equally accessible to inspection and manipulation. From whatever perspective you choose to investigate the content or the system itself, the rules for its behavior will be immediately accessible and admit of change and experimentation. All will be so well organized and documented that the motto for learning Squeak would be, *The System is the Curriculum.*

"All" we have to do is organize and document the system as though it were a curriculum.

Dan Ingalls has been the principal architect of five generations of Smalltalk environments. He designed the byte-coded virtual machine that made Smalltalk practical in 1976. He also invented BitBlt, the general-purpose graphical operation that underlies most bitmap graphics systems today, as well as pop-up menus. He received the ACM Grace Hopper Award for Outstanding Young Scientist and the ACM Software Systems Award. Dan's major contributions to the Squeak system include the original concept of a Smalltalk written in itself and made portable and efficient by a Smalltalk-to-C translator. He also designed the early generalizations of BitBlt to arbitrary color depth, with built-in scaling, rotation, and anti-aliasing. He is currently working on an architecture for end-user programming that is tightly coupled to the Squeak object model. Dan received his B.A. in physics from Harvard University and his M.S. in electrical engineering from Stanford University.

7

A Tour of the Squeak Object Engine

Tim Rowledge
exobox

Introduction

This chapter will explain the design and operation of the Squeak Object Engine. The term *Object Engine* is a useful phrase that encompasses both the Smalltalk low-level system code (such as the Context and Process classes) and the Virtual Machine.

We will discuss what a Virtual Machine (VM) is, how it works, what it does for Squeak programmers and users, and how the Squeak VM might develop in the future. Some explanation of system objects such as Contexts and CompiledMethods will be included.

What Is a Virtual Machine?

A Virtual Machine is a software layer that provides us with a pretense of having a machine other than the actual hardware in use. Using one allows systems to run as if on hardware designed explicitly for them.

Object Engine is less commonly used, but is a useful concept that includes the lowest system areas of the language environment running on the VM. Since there is often some flux in the definition of which components are within the actual VM and which are part of the supported environment, Object Engine is useful as a more inclusive term. In Smalltalk we would usually include classes such as Context, Process, Number, InstructionStream, and Class in the definition of Object Engine.

The term Virtual Machine is used in several ways. When IBM refers to VM/CMS, they are referring to a way of making a mainframe behave as if it is many machines, so that programs can assume they have total control even though they do not. Intel systems provide a somewhat similar facility in the x86 architecture, referred to as Virtual Mode. This sort of VM is a complete hardware simulation, often supported at the lowest level by the hardware.

Another sort of VM is the emulator—VirtualPC for the Mac, Acorn's !PC, and Linux's WINE are good examples—where another machine and/or OS is simulated to allow a Mac, an Acorn RiscPC, or a Linux machine to run Windows98 programs and so on. Emulators of games consoles, such as Bleem, are also popular, if a little legally contentious.

Many languages and even applications, such as some popular word processors, are built on a VM. Various implemetations of the BASIC language are probably the most numerous deployed VMs. BASIC interpreters do not just interpret the BASIC language, but have to provide a varying amount of runtime support code depending on the precise system. Perl is another popular language that uses a similar form of VM.

We shall focus in this chapter on the form of VM used for Smalltalk, in particular the Squeak version. Many of the general principles apply equally well to other Smalltalk systems and often to other dynamic languages such as Lisp, Dylan, and even Java.

The Basic Functionality of a Smalltalk Virtual Machine

In a Smalltalk system all we do is

- create objects and

- send them messages which return objects.

In order to send messages, we must execute the bytecode instructions found in the CompiledMethods belonging to the classes making up our system. Some message sends result in the VM calling primitives to perform low-level operations or to interface to the real host operating system. Eventually, most objects are no longer needed, and the system will recover the memory via the garbage collector.

In this section, we will consider the basics of object allocation, message sending, bytecode and primitive execution, and garbage collection.

Creating Objects

Unlike structures in C or records in Pascal, Smalltalk objects are not simply chunks of memory to which we have pointers, and so we need something more sophisticated than the C library malloc() function in order to create new ones.

Smalltalk creates objects by allocating a chunk of the object memory and then building a header that provides the VM with important information such as the class of the object, the size, and some content format description. It also initializes the contents of the newly allocated object to a safe, predetermined value. This is important to the VM since it guarantees that any pointers found inside objects are proper object pointers (or *oops*) and not random memory addresses. Programmers also benefit from being able to rely on the fresh object having nothing unexpected inside it.

Smalltalk allows for the following four kinds of objects:

1. oops, referred to by name. See, for example, class Class.

2. oops, referred to by an index. Optionally there can be named variables as in (1). See OrderedCollection.

3. machine words, usually 32 bit in current implementations, referred to by an index. See Bitmap.

4. bytes, referred to by an index. See String.

If a pointer object (1 or 2 above) were not properly initialized, the garbage collector would be prone to attempting to collect random chunks of memory—any experienced C programmer can tell you tales of the problems that random pointers cause. Objects containing oops are initialized so that all the oops are nil and objects containing words or bytes are filled with zeros.

We cannot mix oops and non-oops in the same object—CompiledMethod appears to do this by an ugly sleight of hand and two special primitives. (See Interpreter primitiveObjectAt and objectAtPut.) Plans exist to correct this situation and to break methods into two normal objects instead of one hybrid.

Message Sending

In order to do anything in Smalltalk, we have to send a message. Sending a message is quite different to calling a function; it is a request to perform some action rather than an order to jump to a particular piece of code. This indirection is what provides much of the power of Object Oriented Programming; it allows for encapsulation and polymorphism by allowing the recipient of the request to decide on the appropriate response. Adele Goldberg has neatly characterized this as "Ask, don't touch."

Message sending involves the following three major components of the Object Engine:

- CompiledMethods

- Contexts

- the VM

A brief explanation of the first two components is required before we can explain the VM details of sending. Smalltalk reifies the executable code that it runs and the execution contexts representing the running state. This guarantees that the system can access that state and manipulate it without recourse to outside programs. Thus, we can implement the Smalltalk debugger in Smalltalk, portably and extensibly.

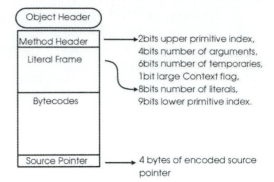

Figure 7.1 Format of CompiledMethod Instances.

CompiledMethod

These are repositories for the fixed part of a Smalltalk program, holding the compiled bytecode instructions and a literal frame, a list of literal objects used to hold message selectors and objects needed by the code that are not receiver instance variables or method temporary variables (see Figure 7.1). They have a header object that encodes important information such as the number of arguments, literals, and temporary variables needed to execute the method as well as an optional primitive number and whether the method requires the normal stack size (16 slots) or the larger stack size (56 slots). All of these quantities are determined by the Compiler when the method code is accepted by the user or filed in from outside.

Context

Contexts are the activation records for Smalltalk, maintaining the program counter and stack pointer, holding pointers to the sending context, the method for which this is appropriate, etc. There are two types of context:

MethodContext. Representing an executing method, MethodContext points back to the context from which it was activated and holds onto its receiver and compiled method. Note how similar it is to a stackframe from a C program (see Figure 7.2).

BlockContext. An active block of code within some method, BlockContext points back to its home context, the MethodContext where it was defined, as well as the caller, the context from where it was activated (see Figure 7.3).

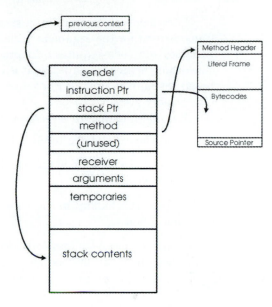

Figure 7.2 Format of MethodContext Instances.

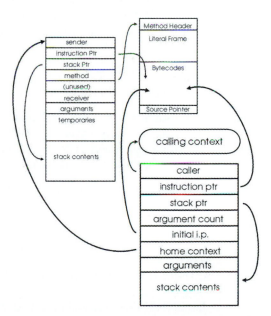

Figure 7.3 Format of BlockContext Instances.

Note that both forms have a stack frame private to their own use. This stack frame is used for the arguments, the local temporary variables and all the working variables the code requires. In practice, the compiler can work out the size of stackframe needed by any code it is compiling, but only two sizes are used in order to aid the implementation of context recycling, which helps reduce the workload on the memory system.

To send a message to a receiver, the VM has to

- find the class of the receiver by examining the object's header

- lookup the message in the list of messages understood by that class (the class's MethodDictionary)

- repeat this lookup in successive superclasses of the receiver if the message is not found

- send the message doesNotUnderstand: to the receiver if no class in the superclass chain can understand the message, so that the error can be handled in a manner appropriate to that object

- extract the appropriate CompiledMethod from the MethodDictionary where the message was found and then

    - check for a primitive (see the later section) associated with the method by reading the method header
    - execute the primitive if there is one
    - if it completes successfully, return the result object directly to the message sender

  otherwise, continue as if there was no primitive called

- establish a new activation record, by creating a new MethodContext and setting up the program counter, stack pointer, message sending, and home contexts, then copy the arguments and receiver from the message sending context's stack to the new stack

- activate that new context and start executing the instructions in the new method

In a typical system, it often turns out that the same message is sent to instances of the same class again and again; consider how often we use arrays of SmallInteger or Character or String. To improve average performance, the VM can cache the found method. If the same combination of the method and the receiver's class is found in the cache, we avoid a repeat of the full search of the MethodDictionary chain. See the method Interpreter>>lookupInMethodCacheSel:class: for the implementation.

VisualWorks and some other commercial Smalltalks use inline cacheing, whereby the cached target and some checking information are included inline with the dynamically translated methods. Although more efficient, it is more complex and has strong interactions with the details of the CPU instruction and data caches.

Bytecodes

When a message has been sent and a new **MethodContext** has been activated, execution continues by executing the bytecodes from the **CompiledMethod**.

The bytecodes are byte-sized tokens that specify the basic operations of the VM such as pushing variables onto the context's stack, branching, popping objects from the stack back into variables, message sending, and returning. Unsurprisingly, they bear a strong resemblance to an instruction set for a stack-oriented CPU.

As the VM is conceptually a simple bytecode interpreter,[1] execution follows this loop:

- fetch bytecode

- increment VM instruction pointer

- branch to appropriate bytecode routine, usually implemented as a 256-way case statement

- execute the bytecode routine

- return to top of loop to fetch next bytecode

Bytecode Categories

Most bytecodes belong to a category where part of the byte is used to specify the basic operation and the rest is used to specify and index of some sort. For example, the Squeak bytecode 34 belongs to the *push literal variable* group that starts at bytecode 32 and pushes the $(34 - 32 = 2)$ second literal variable onto the stack. For up-to-date details on the precise numbering of bytecodes in Squeak, refer to the **Interpreter class>>initializeBytecodeTable** method.

Stack pushes:

Before sending messages, the arguments and the receiver need to be pushed onto the stack. Since the arguments may be receiver variables, temporary variables of the current method, literal variables or constants, or even the current context itself, there are quite a few push bytecodes:

- Push receiver variable 0–15. Fetch the referenced variable of the current receiver and push it.

- Push temporary variable 0–15 from the home context—if the current context is a **BlockContext**, the current home context is the block's home context. See Figure 7.3 above.

---

[1] Virtually all commercial Smalltalks actually take the bytecode list as input to some form of translator that produces a machine-specific subroutine to improve performance. Many techniques both simple and subtle are used. There are plans to incorporate such a dynamic translation or JIT system into Squeak.

- Push literal constant 0–32 from the literal frame of the home context's CompiledMethod.

- Push literal variable 0–32—as before, but assumes that the literal is an Association and pushes the value variable of that instead of the association itself.

- Push special object—receiver, true, false, nil, or the SmallIntegers negative one, zero, one, or two. Since these are very frequently used, it is worth using a few bytecodes on them.

- Extended push—uses the byte following the bytecode to allow a larger index into the receiver, temporary, or literal variables lists.

- Push active context—pushes the actual current context, allowing us to manipulate the execution and build tools such as the debugger, exception handling, and so on.

Stack pops and stores:

The results of message sends need to be popped from the stack and stored into some suitable place. Just as with the push bytecodes, this may mean receiver variables or temporaries, but we do not store into the literal frame nor the current context using bytecodes.

- Store and pop receiver variable 0–8.

- Store and pop temporary variable 0–8.

- Extended pop and store—as before, but uses the next byte to extend the usable index range.

- Extended store—like the preceding pop & store, but does not actually pop the stack.

- Pop stack—just pops the stack.

- Duplicate stack top—pushes the object at the stack top, thus duplicating the stack top.

Jumps:

We need to be able to jump within the bytecodes of a CompiledMethod so that the optimizations applied to control structures, such as ifTrue:ifFalse:, can be supported. Such message sends are short circuited for performance reasons by using test and jump bytecodes along with unconditional jump bytecodes.

- Short unconditional jump—jumps forward by 1 to 8 bytes.

- Short conditional jump—like the short unconditional jumps, but only if the object on the top of the stack is false.

- Long unconditional jump—uses the next byte to extend the jump range to −1024 to +1023. A small but important detail is that backwards branches are taken as a hint that we may be in a loop and so a rapid check is made for any pending interrupts.

- Long jump if true/false—if the object on the top of the stack is true or false as appropriate, use the next byte to give a jump range of 0 to 1023.

Message Sending:

As mentioned earlier, the main activity in a Smalltalk system is message sending. Once the arguments and receiver have been pushed onto the stack, we have to specify the message selector and how many arguments it expects before being able to perform the message lookup. The send bytecodes specify the selector via an index into the CompiledMethod literal frame.

- Send literal selector—can refer to any of the first 16 literals and 0, 1, or 2 arguments.

- Single extended send—uses the next byte to extend the range to the first 32 literals and seven arguments.

- Single extended super send—as before, but implements a super send instead of a normal send, as in the code

      arf := super fribble.

- Second extended send—uses the next byte in a different way to encompass 63 literals and three arguments.

- Double extended do-anything—uses the two next bytes to specify an operation, an argument count, and a literal. For sends, it can cause normal or super sends with up to 31 arguments and a selector anywhere in the first 256 literals. Other operations include pushes, pops and stores. Rumor has it that it can also make tea and butter your toast.

Common selector message sending:

There are a number of messages sent so frequently that it saves space and time to encode them directly as bytecodes. In the current Squeak release they are +, −, <, >, <=, >=, =, ~=, *, /, \\, @, bitShift:, //, bitAnd:, bitOr:, at:, at:put:, size, next, nextPut:, atEnd, ==, class, blockCopy:, value, value:, do:, new, new:, x, and y. Some of these bytecodes simply send the message, some directly implement the most common case(s) (for example, see Interpreter>>bytecodePrimAdd) and have fall-through code to send the general message for any more complex situation.

Returns:

There are two basic forms of return:

- The method return, from a MethodContext back to its sender, commonly seen in code as

    ↑foo.

    The same form of return will return the value of a BlockContext to the sender of its home context, as in the code

    boop ifTrue: [↑self latestAnswer]

    This variety of return is known as a nonlocal return, since it can pass control back to a MethodContext many steps up the context stack. The VM return code has to take some pains to handle this eventuality, particularly if the system uses unwind blocks or exception handling. See the Interpreter≫ returnValue:to: method for details.

- The block return, from a BlockContext to its caller, as in the code

    bar := [thing doThisTo: that] value.

Both return the object at the top of the stack. For performance optimization, there are also direct bytecodes that implement the method return with the receiver, true, false, or nil as the return value. Methods that have no explicit return will use the method return of the receiver as the default.

A good, detailed explanation of the operation of the bytecodes can be found in part 4 of *Smalltalk-80, The Language and its Implementation*, otherwise known as the Blue Book [GoR83], in the section on the operation of the VM and need not be repeated here.

The use of bytecodes as a virtual instruction set is one of the main factors allowing such broad portability of Smalltalk systems. Along with the reified object format applied to the compiled code and activation records, it ensures that any properly implemented VM will provide the proper behaviour.

For those people who are fans of the idea of implementing Smalltalk-specific hardware, it should be noted that the bytecode implementation part of the VM is typically fairly small and simple. A CPU that used Smalltalk bytecodes as its instruction set would still require all the primitives and the object memory code, most of which is quite complex and would probably require a quite different instruction set.

Primitives

Primitives are a good way to improve performance of simple but highly repetitive code or to reach down into the VM for work that can only be done there. This includes the accessing and manipulating of the VM internal state in ways not supported by the bytecode instruction set, interfacing to the world outside the object memory, or functions that must be atomic in order to avoid deadlocks.

Primitives are where a great deal of work gets done, and typically a Smalltalk program might spend around 50% of execution time within primitives. For up-to-date details on the precise numbering of primitives in Squeak, refer to the Interpreter class>>initializePrimitiveTable method.

Primitives are used to handle activities such as those following:

Input

The input of keyboard and mouse events normally requires very platform-specific code and is implemented in primitives such as Interpreter>>primitiveKbdNext and primitiveMouseButtons. In Squeak, these in turn call functions in the platform-specific version of sq{platform}Windows.c and associated files. See Ian Piumarta's chapter on porting Squeak for details.

Output

Traditionally, Smalltalk has relied upon the BitBlt graphics engine to provide all the visual output it needs. Assorted extra primitives have been made available on some platforms in some implementations to provide sound output, serial ports, networking, etc.

Squeak has a plethora of new output and interface capabilities provided via a named primitive mechanism that can dynamically load code at need.

Arithmetic

The basic arithmetic operations for SmallIntegers and Floats are implemented in primitives. Since the machine-level bit representation is hidden from the Smalltalk code, we use primitives to convert the object representation to a CPU-compatible form, to perform the arithmetic operation, and, finally, to convert the result back into a Smalltalk form. It would be possible to implement most arithmetic operations directly in Smalltalk code by providing only a few primitives to access the bits of a number and then performing the appropriate boolean and bit functions to derive the result; the performance would be unacceptable for the most common case of small integers that can be handled efficiently by a typical CPU. This is why Smalltalk has the special class of integer known as SmallInteger; values that can fit within a machine word (along with a tag that allows the VM to discriminate whether the word is an oop or a SmallInteger) can be processed more efficiently than the general case handled by LargePositiveInteger and LargeNegativeInteger. Many arithmetic primitives are also implemented within special bytecodes that can perform the operation if all the arguments are SmallIntegers, passing off the work to more sophisticated code otherwise.

Clearly, it takes many more cycles to perform an apparently simple addition of two plain integers than it would in a compiled C program. Instead of

```
a + b;
```

being compiled to

```
ADD Result, Rarg1, Rarg2
```

which takes an ARM CPU a single cycle, we have

$a + b.$

compiled to the special bytecode for the message #+, which is implemented in the VM as bytecode 176 and presented here in pidgin C code:

```
case 176: /* bytecodePrimAdd */
  t1 = *(int*)(stackpointer - (1 * 4));
  t3 = *(int*)(stackpointer - (0 * 4));
  /* fetch the two arguments off the stack - note that this means
     they must have been pushed before this bytecode! */
  /* test the two objects to make sure both are tagged as
  SmallIntegers, i.e. both have the bottom bit set */
  if (((t1 & t3) & 1) != 0) {
    /* add the two SmallIntegers by shifting each right one place
       to remove the tag bits and then add normally */
    t2 = ((t1 >> 1)) + ((t3 >> 1));
    /* then check the result is a valid SmallInteger value by making
       sure the top two bits are the same - this handles both positive
       and negative results */
    if ((t2 ^ (t2 << 1)) >= 0) {
      /* If the value is ok, convert it back to a SmallInteger by
         shifting one place left and setting the bottom tag bit,
         then push it back onto the Smalltalk stack */
      *(int*)(stackpointer -= (2 - 1) * 4) = ((t2 << 1) | 1));
    }
  } else {
    /* defer to code handling more complex cases */
  }
```

This will take at least 14 operations on most CPUs, even if the memory system can deliver the stack reads and writes in a single cycle. The most plausible time on an ARM is 12 cycles due to the ability to mix shifts and logic operations. The cost of initially pushing the objects onto the stack and of interpreting the bytecodes can be ignored for this example since it makes little overall difference. The important point to make here is that although the costs for adding 1 to 1 and getting 2 seems high, the system will not have any problems adding 24 billion to 5.6×10^{200} and getting a suitable answer, nor in using the #+ message to combine two matrices. Mostly, it demonstrates yet again the limited utility of most benchmark programs.

Storage Handling

In order to create an object, we need a primitive (primitiveNew for objects with only named instance variables and primitiveNew: for objects with indexed variables). These primitives work with the object memory to build the object header and to initialize the contents properly as described earlier. Object creation needs to be atomic so that there is never a time when the garbage collector might have to try to scan malformed memory.

Reading from and writing to arrays with at: and at:put: is done by primitives that access the indexed variables of the object. If used with an object that has no indexed variables, the primitive fails, leaving the backup Smalltalk code to decide what to do. Reading or writing to Streams on Strings or Arrays is very common, and two primitives are provided to improve performance in those cases.

Just as with the simple addition example shown before, the number of CPU cycles required for these primitives seems at first glance to be much higher than you might expect from a compiled C program. In the same way, we gain in flexibility, bounds checking, and reliability.

Process Manipulation

Suspending, resuming, and terminating Processes, as well as the signalling and waiting upon Semaphores are all done in primitives. Changing structures such as the process lists, the VM's idea of the active process and semaphore signal counts needs to be performed atomically, so primitives are used to ensure no deadlocks occur.

Execution Control

Smalltalk has two unusual ways of controlling execution, evaluating blocks and the perform: manner of sending a message.

When a block is sent the message value (or indeed value: or one of its relatives) as in the phrase

    [burp + self wonk] value.

the primitiveValue (or primitiveValueWithArgs) primitive is used to activate the Block-Context; to set the program counter, stack pointer, and caller; and then to copy any arguments into the BlockContext. Execution then proceeds with the bytecodes of the block until either we return to the caller context (the sender of the value message) or the sender of the block's home method (where the block was defined). See also the above section on return bytecodes.

The perform: message, as in

    arkwright perform: #anatomicallyImpossibleAct.

and its siblings, as in

arkwright perform: #ludicrousAct: with: thatThing.

allow us to specify a message at runtime rather than compile time, and so the primitive has to pull the chosen selector from the stack, slide all other arguments down, and then proceed as if the message had been sent in the normal manner.

In general, it is best not to use primitives to do complex or heterogenous things; after all, that is something that Smalltalk is good for. A primitive to fill an array with a certain value might well make sense for performance optimization, but one to fetch, process, and render an entire webpage would not, unless you happened to have the code already available in some shared library. In such a case, we would use the foreign function interface to make use of outside code.

Primitives that do a great deal of bit-twiddling or arithmetic can also make sense, since Smalltalk is not particularly efficient at that (see above). The sound buffer filling primitives (PluckedSound>>mixSampleCount:into:startingAt:leftVol:rightVol: is a good example) are complex vector graphics primitives, such as those in the B3DEnginePlugin 'primitive support' protocol, for example.

Garbage Collection

One of the most useful benefits of a good object memory system is that unwanted, or garbage, objects are collected and killed, and the memory is returned to the system for recycling. There are many schemes for performing this function, and quite a few Ph.D.s have been awarded for work in this area of computer science. Dr. Richard Jones keeps an impressive bibliography of garbage collection literature on his website [Jo99] and is one of the authors of [JoL96], a thoroughly recommended source for further reading.

Garbage collection (GC) is simply a matter of having some way to be able to tell when an object is no longer wanted and then to recycle the memory. Given some known root object(s) it is generally assumed that we can trace all possible accessible objects and then enumerate all those not accessible. If you read [GoR83] you will see that the exemplar system used a reference counting system combined with a mark-sweep system. Most commercial Smalltalks use some variant of a scheme known as Generation Scavenging. Brief explanations of these follow.

Reference Counting

Reference counting relies on checking every store into object memory, incrementing a count field (often contained in the header) of the newly stored object, and decrementing the count of the overwritten object. Any object whose count reaches zero is clearly garbage and must be collected. Any objects that it pointed to must also have their count decremented, with an obvious potential for recursive descent down a long chain of objects.

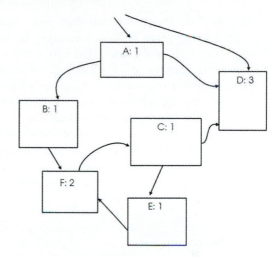

Figure 7.4   Net of objects in initial state.

One problem with a simple reference counting scheme is that cycles of objects can effectively mutually lock a large amount of dead memory, since every object in the cycle has at least one reference. Consider a small web of objects with a cycle composed of C, E and F (see Figure 7.4).

If we now replace the reference from B to F, the cycle is orphaned, but since each object still has a reference count greater than zero, none of them will be garbage collected (see Figure 7.5).

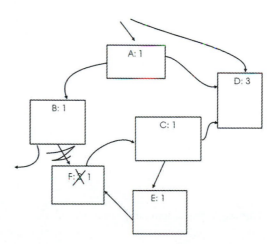

Figure 7.5   Object B no longer points to F—
the cycle F/C/E is orphaned.

Another problem is that every store into object memory will need the reference incrementing and decrementing to be done, even pushes and pops on the stack. Deutsch and Bobrow [Debo76] developed an improved way of dealing with reference counting the stack, known as *deferred reference counting*. This technique allows us to avoid reference counting pushes and pops by keeping a separate table of objects where the reference count might be zero but that might be on the stack—if they are on the stack, then the actual count cannot be zero. At suitable intervals, we scan the stack, correct the count values of the objects in the table, and empty the table. Objects that have a zero count at this stage are definitely dead and are removed. Reference counting is still done for all other stores, and those objects that appear to reach a count of zero are added to the table for later processing as above.

Mark-Sweep Compaction

To avoid completely running out of memory due to cycles, most systems that use reference counting also have a mark-sweep collector that will start at the known important root objects and trace every accessible one, leaving a mark in the object header to check later. In Figure 7.6, the tracing will touch object A and follow its pointer to B and then out of the diagram. Then the trace will follow the pointer from A to D, where it terminates since D points to no other objects. The second pointer to D will also terminate, but this time because the mark bit in the object header is set. Objects F, C, and E will not be marked since no other object points to them.

Once the marking phase is completed, every object marked can be swept up (or down) the memory space, effectively removing all the untouched ones, and the mark removed. There are important details to consider with respect to object cycles,

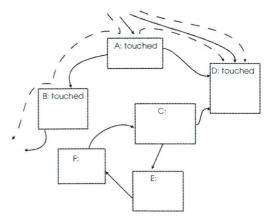

Figure 7.6   Tracing objects in the mark phase.

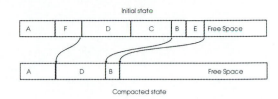

Figure 7.7   Object memory before and after the sweep compaction phase.

which objects are actually roots, how to move the objects memory and update all the references to it, and so on (see Figure 7.7). One useful side effect of the mark-sweep collector is that in compacting all the objects it leaves all the free space in a contiguous lump. In most cases, this can be used to make subsequent memory allocation simpler.

Generation Scavenging

The most commonly used garbage collection scheme in current commercial Smalltalk systems is based on the generation scavenger idea originally developed by David Ungar [Ung87]. He noticed that most new objects live very short lives, and most older objects live effectively forever.

By allocating new objects in a small *eden* area of memory and frequently copying only those still pointed to by a known set of roots into one of a pair of small *survivor* areas, we immediately free the eden area for new allocations. Objects previously in the survivor area that are still live are also copied, leaving one of the survivor spaces empty. Subsequently, we keep copying surviving objects from eden and this survivor area into the other and, eventually, into an *old space* where they are considered tenured. Various refinements in terms of numbers of survivor generations and strategies for moving objects around have been developed.

An important part of a generation scavenger is a table of those old objects (objects existing in old space) into which new objects (objects existing in eden or a survivor space) have been stored. Each time an object is stored into another, a quick check is done to see if the storee is new and the storand is old; this is simpler than the zero count check needed by a reference counting system. If needed, the storand object is added to the table, usually referred to as the *remembered set* or *remembered table*. This table is used as one of the roots when the search for live objects is performed; each of these objects is scanned and new objects they point to are scavenged.

In Figure 7.8, notice that the set of roots and the remembered table both refer to objects in eden and a survivor space. The set of roots may also refer to objects in old space. Eden has partially filled with new objects and survivor space A is near empty. Survivor space B is completely empty and not in use at this point.

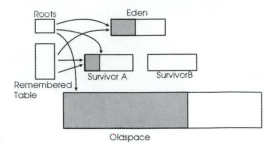

Figure 7.8 Object memory before and after the sweep compaction phase.

To perform a scavenge cycle, we first trace the root objects, moving any that are in eden or survivor space A into survivor space B. Then the objects referred to by the remembered set are traced. Once all the new objects pointed to by the table and other roots have been scavenged, the survivors are also scanned and any new objects found are also scavenged. The process continues until no further surviving objects are found. Any old object that no longer points to new objects can be removed from the remembered table.

In Figure 7.9, we have just completed a scavenge cycle. Eden is completely emptied, with all surviving objects moved to survivor space B. Still-live objects from survivor space A have also been copied to B, or to old space if they met suitable criteria. The remembered table lost some entries as objects died and got left behind. The next scavenge cycle will copy objects into survivor space A.

Note that scavenging a generation is similar to a mark and sweep of the memory in which the generation lives, though the objects get moved to a different space rather than simply compacted within the same space. The chief benefit of scavenging comes from the reduction in amount of memory touched; only a few live objects are moved in most cases, rather than every object being touched to trace through it.

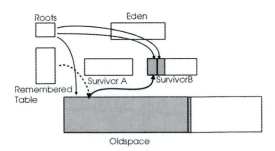

Figure 7.9 Generation scavenging system just after a scavenge.

Why Is an Object Engine Better than C and a Library?

One might reasonably ask why this rather complex-seeming system is better than a "normal" programming environment and a C library.

The most obvious answer is that the message sending support allows, helps, and strongly encourages an object oriented form of programming. Good object-oriented programs form extremely useful libraries that can increase programming productivity greatly. Although it is possible to use almost any language to work in an object-oriented style, doing so without proper support makes it much harder than just "going with the flow" and slipping into procedural programming.

Memory Handling

Much of the code in a complex C program is taken up with storage management: memory allocating, freeing, initializing, checking, and error handling for when it goes wrong. A good VM will handle all this automatically, reliably (making some assumptions about the quality of the VM), and transparently. Although many C programs do not bother to check the bounds of arrays, exceeding those bounds is a major cause of problems. Consider how many computer viruses are spread through or otherwise rely upon buffer overflow and other bounds problems. A Smalltalk VM checks the bounds of any and all accesses to its objects, thus avoiding this problem completely. Furthermore, since an object is absolutely a member of its class (there is no concept of "casting" in Smalltalk), you cannot fool the system into allowing you to write to improper memory locations. This *referential safety* is a very useful property of Smalltalk systems.

Meta-programming Capability

One of the great virtues of a VM is that you can precisely define the lowest-level behavior that the higher level code can see. This allows us to provide a reflective system with meta-programming capabilities and thus to write programs that can reason about the structure of the system and its programs. One good example is the Smalltalk debugger. Since the structure of and interface to the execution records (the BlockContext and MethodContext instances) is defined within Smalltalk, we can manipulate them with a Smalltalk program. We can also store them in memory or in files for later use, which allows for remote debugging and analysis.

Threads and Control Structures Programmer Accessible

When it is possible to cleanly manipulate the contexts, we can add new control structures. See the article *Building Control Structures in the Smalltalk-80 System* by Peter Deutsch in [SCG81] which illustrates this with examples including case statements, generator loops, and coroutining. With only a tiny amount of support in the VM, it is possible to add threads to the system; although they are known as Processes within the class hierarchy.

Portability of the System

In much the same way that the VM allows meta-capability, it can assist in providing high levels of portability. The interface to the machine-specific parts of the VM is uniform, the data structures are uniform, and thus it is possible to make a system that has total binary portability. No recompiling, conversion filters, or other distractions are needed. Squeak, like several commercial Smalltalks, allows you to save an image file on a PC; copy it to a Mac, a BeOS, an Acorn, or almost any Unix machine; and simply run it. The bits are the same and the behavior is the same, barring of course some machine capability peculiarities.

Squeak VM Peculiarities

Squeak's VM departs from the design shown in the Blue Book [GoR83] in quite a few ways. It has a quite different object memory format and uses an interesting variant of mark-sweep garbage collection that approaches generation scavenging in many respects. There are many new primitives, often implemented in dynamically loadable VM plugins, a form of shared library or DLL developed by the Squeak community. A completely new form of graphics engine has been introduced, including 3-D capabilities. There is extensive sound support and full internet connectivity.

Perhaps most radically for the VM per se, the kernel of the VM and most of the code for the assorted plugins is actually implemented as Smalltalk code that is translated to produce C source code to compile and link with the lowest-level platform-specific C code.

Object Format

The Blue Book definition of the ObjectMemory used an Object Table (OT) and a header word for each object to encode the size and some flags. Each OT entry contained some flags (the reference count, for example) and a pointer to the memory address for the body of the object. Any access to the instance variables or class of the object required indirection through the object table to find the body.

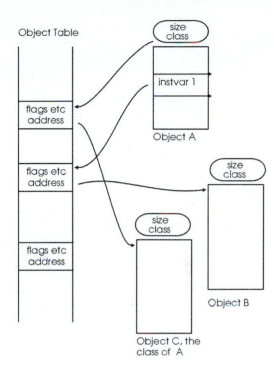

Figure 7.10 Smalltalk-80 Object table mechanism.

In Figure 7.10, we see that to find the class, object C, of object A, we have to use the oop in the object header to be able to read the entry in the OT and thereby find the address of the body of the class. In a similar manner we have to indirect through the OT to find the body of object A's instvar1. When looking up methods as part of a message send, we have to indirect several times in order to find the class of the receiver, the MethodDictionary of that class, and so on.

A sometimes useful attribute of an OT is that objects once created keep the same oop throughout their existence, making the oop a very acceptable hash value for most cases.

Squeak uses a more direct method, whereby the oops are actually the memory addresses of a header word at the front of the object body (see Figure 7.11). This saves a memory indirection when accessing the object. However, it requires a more complicated garbage collection technique, because any object that points to a moved object will need the oop updating.[2]

Since we still need to have the class oop, size, and some flags available for each object, Squeak generally uses a larger header. The canonical header is three words: flags/hash/size, encoded in one word, class oop, size. A high proportion of objects

---

[2]Note the variable object header format described in Figure 7.11.

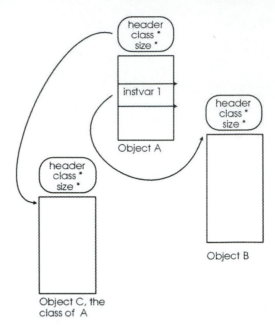

Figure 7.11 Squeak direct pointer object format.

are instances of a small set of common classes, and since few objects are large, it was decided to use three header formats as follows:

- One word—all objects have this header.

    - 3 bits reserved for GC state machine (mark, old, dirty)
    - 12 bits object hash (for hashed Set usage)
    - 5 bits compact class index, nonzero if the class is in a group of classes known as "Compact Classes"
    - 4 bits object format
    - 6 bits object size, in 32-bit words
    - 2 bits header type (0: 3-word, 1: 2-word, 2: free chunk of memory, not an object at all, 3: 1-word)

- Two words—objects that are instances of classes not in the compact classes list. This second word sits in front of the first work of the header.

    - 30 bits oop of the class
    - 2 bits header type, as with one word

- Three words—objects that are too big for the size to be encoded in the one-word header, i.e., more than 255 bytes. This third word sits in front of the other two words of the header.

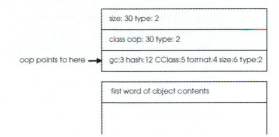

Figure 7.12   Squeak object header layout.

- 30 bits of size
- 2 bits header type, as with one word

Figure 7.12 illustrates the general case three word header.

The set of compact classes that can be used in the compact headers is a Smalltalk array that can be updated dynamically; you can even decide that no classes should qualify. See the methods Behavior≫becomeCompact and becomeUncompact as well as ObjectMemory≫fetchClassOf: and instantiateClass:indexableSize: for illustration. Whether the space savings are worth the complexity of the triple header design is still an open question in the Squeak systems community. With the flexibility to designate classes as compact or not on the fly, definitive experiments can someday answer the question.

Garbage Collection

Squeak uses an interesting hybrid of generation scavenging and mark-sweep collection as its garbage collector (see Figure 7.13). Once the image is loaded into memory the end address of the last object is used as a boundary mark to separate two generations, old objects existing in the lower memory area and new objects are created in the upper memory area.

When the remaining free memory runs low, or a preset number of objects have been allocated, the VM will pause to garbage collect the new object re-

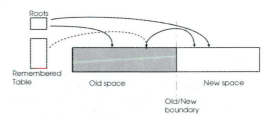

Figure 7.13   Squeak memory organization.

gion (ObjectMemory>>incrementalGC). This is done with a mark-sweep algorithm modified to trace only those objects in the new region, thus touching considerably less memory than an entire-image sweep. As in the generation scavenging scheme described above, the remembered table (the rootTable instance variable in ObjectMemory) is maintained of old objects that might point to new objects for use as roots when tracing which objects still live. These are added to other important root objects such as the active context and the specialObjects array and used as starting points for the depth first tracing implemented by ObjectMemory>> markPhase.

Tracing starts with the root objects, touching A, then B, and stopping there, since F is an old object. D would not be traced since it is also old. When tracing from the remembered table, we would touch C, since it is pointed to by F.

Once the tracing phase has completed, the memory region is swept from bottom to top with each object header being examined to see it has been marked. Those that have not been touched are tagged as free chunks of memory. Then a table of address mappings is built, listing each surviving object and the new address it will have. Once all these mappings are known the survivors are updated so that all their oops are correct, and finally, they are moved down memory to the new addresses. By the end of the compaction, the freed memory is all in one chunk at the top of the new region.

This process might seem complicated, but the use of the two generations means that it can typically run in a very short time; on an Acorn 200MHz StrongARM machine an average figure is 8–9 ms, on an Apple 400MHz G3 PowerBook it is 3 ms. During activities like typing or browsing and coding, the system will run an incremental garbage collect one to five times per second. Obviously, the more garbage that is created, the more time will be spent on collecting it.

One limitation of an incremental collection is that any objects from the old region that are no longer referenced do not get freed and collected. Of course, the observation that lead to generation scavenging tells us that this usually doesn't matter since old objects generally continue to live. However, sometimes we do need to completely clean out the object memory. Many systems that use a generation scavenger for incremental garbage collection also have a secondary collector based on a mark-sweep algorithm. Squeak simply forces the system to believe that the old/new boundary is at the bottom of the old region. Thus, the entire image is now considered to be new objects, and all objects will be fully traced (see Figure 7.14). Look at the ObjectMemory>>fullGC method for details.

Extra Primitives

Squeak has added many primitives to the list given in the Blue Book. They include code for serial ports, sound synthesis and sampling, sockets, MIDI interfaces, file and directory handling, internet access, 3-D graphics, and a general foreign function interface. Most of them are implemented in VM plugins—see the chapter *Extending*

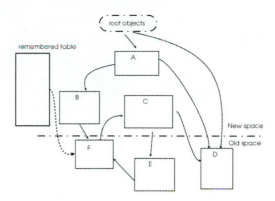

Figure 7.14 Tracing only new objects in Squeak.

the Squeak VM (Chapter 9) for an explanation of the VM plugin mechanism that is used to implement these extra capabilities.

Speeding up at: and at:put:

The messages at: and at:put: are very commonly used—as mentioned, they are both already installed as special bytecode sends. Squeak uses a special cache to further try to speed them up. See Interpreter>>commonAt: and commonAtPut: for the implementation details.

Extended BitBlt and Vector Graphics Extensions

The original BitBlt worked on monochrome bitmaps to provide all the graphics for Smalltalk-80. Squeak has an extended BitBlt that can operate upon multiple bit-per-pixel bitmaps to provide color. It can also handle alpha blending in suitable depth bitmaps, which can, for example, give antialiasing. Different depth bitmaps can be mixed and BitBlt will convert them as required. New extensions to BitBlt allow for mixed pixel endianness, as well as depth, and make external OS bitmaps accessible so that graphics accelerator hardware can be used when provided by the host machine.

WarpBlt is a variant of BitBlt that can perform strange transforms on bitmaps by mapping a source quadrilateral to the destination rectangle and interpolating the pixels as needed. There are demonstration statements in the "Welcome To..." workspace that show some extremes of the distortions possible, but simple scaling and rotation is also possible.

Perhaps most exciting, there is a new geometry-based rendering system known as Balloon, which can be used for 2-D or 3-D graphics. This has introduced sophisticated vector-based graphics to Smalltalk and is the basis of the Alice implementation included in the system. (See the chapter *Alice in a Squeak Wonderland* (Chapter 3).)

VM Kernel Written in Smalltalk

The VM is largely generated from Squeak code that can actually run as a simulation of the VM, which has proven useful in the development of the system. See the Interpreter and ObjectMemory classes for most of the source code.

Note how the VM is written in a fairly stilted style of Smalltalk/C hybrid that has come to be known as *Slang*. Slang requires type information hints that are passed through to the final C source code anytime you need variables that are not C integers. A somewhat more readable dialect of Slang is used in the VM plugins described in the chapter on extending the VM.

You can try out the C code generator by looking at the classes TestCClass1/2 or 3. Printing

```
TestCClass2 test
```

will run a translation on a fairly large example set of methods and return the source code string that would be passed to a C compiler. To build a new VM for your machine, see the chapter on porting Squeak for instructions on how to generate all the files needed and compile them.

Things for the Future

Squeak is not finished and, hopefully, never will be. Already it represents one of the most interesting programming systems in existence, and people are constantly expanding their vision of what it might be used for. The following are some notes on what might be done in pursuit of a few of the author's interests.

Bigger Systems

Probably the largest known Squeak image is the one used by Alan Kay for public demos. Without any special changes to the VM, it was quite happy with over a hundred projects and 160 megabytes of object space. To extend Squeak's range to truly large systems we would probably need to consider changing to a 64-bit architecture and a more sophisticated garbage collection system. Large systems are often very concerned with reliability and data safety—a corporate payroll system ought not crash too often. An object memory that incorporates extra checking, transaction rollbacks, logging, interfaces into secure databases, etc. might be an interesting project.

Smaller Systems, Particularly Embedded Ones

It is possible to squeeze a usable Squeak development image down to approximately 600kb, although there is not very much left by then. Getting to this size involves removing almost everything beyond the most basic development environment and tools—look at the SystemDictionary≫majorShrink method.

Building a small system for an embedded application would involve a more sophisticated tool, such as the SystemTracer, to create the image, but what Object Engine changes would be useful?

Since such a system would not need any of the development tools, we could remove some variables from, or change the structure of, classes, methods, and method dictionaries.

From classes, we could almost certainly remove the following:

- organization—this simply categorizes the class's methods for development tools

- name—it is unlikely that a canned application would have any use for this

- instanceVariables—this is a string of the names of the instance variables

- subclasses—the list of subclasses is rarely accessed.

None of these would require major VM changes except in some debugging routines such as Interpreter≫printCallStack that attempt to extract a class's name.

From compiled methods, we could remove the source code pointer and possibly go so far as to use integers instead of symbols to identify the message selectors. This would work in Squeak, since the method dictionary search code already handles such a possibility. This would reduce the size of the Symbol global table significantly.

MethodDictionary relies on having a size that is a power of two for the purposes of the message lookup algorithm and will double the size of the dictionary anytime it gets to 3/4 full—typically the dictionaries are a little under half full. By changing the system to allow correctly sized dictionaries, we might save some crucial tens of kilobytes.

Depending on the application involved, it might also be possible to make most of the classes in use be compact classes. This would allow most objects to have one-word object headers and reduce the average object overhead in the system.

The VM itself can be shrunk quite simply. In Squeak 2.8, the VM was broken into a number of plugin modules to accompany the kernel. Systems that do not need sound, sockets, or serial ports need not have any of the code present. A Linux VM can be built as small as 300Kb with just the basic kernel capabilities.

Headless Server Systems

If we want to use Squeak as a server program, we need to be able to run headless, which is to say without a GUI.

Most of the changes needed are in the image, in low-level code just outside what we would normally consider part of the object engine. For example, there are methods in the FileStream classes that open dialogues to ask a user whether to overwrite a file or not; clearly this is not appropriate in a server. Proper use of Exceptions and exception handlers would be required to correct this problem, with probable changes to code in the object engine in order to signal errors and to raise some of the appropriate exceptions.

One major change needed in the VM is to avoid attempting to open the main Squeak window as soon as Squeak starts up. Headless systems would not need nor support this window. The Acorn port already handles this by not creating and opening the window until and unless the DisplayScreen>>beDisplay method is executed.

Another important capability would be to communicate with the running system via some suitable channel. Although Squeak already supports sockets, it seems that an interface to Unix style stdin/stdout streams would be useful.

Faster Systems

Although Squeak is amazingly fast—any reasonably modern machine can execute bytecodes faster than most machines could execute native instructions just a few years ago—we would like still more performance.

The Squeak VM is a fairly simple bytecode interpreter, with some neat tricks in the memory manager and primitives to help the speed. To drastically improve performance, we would need to move to a quite different execution model that can remove the bytecode fetch-dispatch loop costs, improve the primitive calling interface speed, reduce the time spent pushing and popping the stack, and reduce the runtime cost of having reified contexts. At the same time, this new system must not break any system invariants, nor reduce the portability.

The overhead of using bytecodes can be almost eliminated by using some form of runtime translation to native machine code [DeS84]. The VM would need extending to provide a subsystem that can use the bytecodes as input to a machine-specific compiler. This has been done in most commercial Smalltalks; it adds a considerable degree of complexity to the VM and particularly to porting the VM to a new machine. The porter has to know the machine CPU architecture and the VM meta-architecture well enough to combine them. Subtleties of the CPU can become major problems—are registers usable for both data and addresses? Does the data cache interact with the instruction cache in a useful manner or not? Do these details change across models of the CPU?

The Squeak execution model is a simple stack-oriented machine, and most modern CPUs are register oriented. Therefore, we lose a lot of time in manipulating a stack instead of filling registers. When code is translated to native instructions, we can avoid a lot of this by taking advantage of the opportunity to optimize out many stack movements. This will likely interact with the use of Contexts with their distinct individual stackframes and potentially non-linear caller/sender relationships; CPUs normally work with a single contiguous stack and a strict call/return convention. Fortunately, most Smalltalk code is quite straightforward, and it is possible to implement a Context caching system that performs almost as well as an ordinary stack and yet handles the exceptional conditions caused by BlockContext returns or references to the activeContext [Mi87].

The best news of all is that by the time this book is published, Squeak will very likely have a VM making use of all these performance improving techniques!

References

[DeBo76] L. Peter Deutsch and Daniel G. Bobrow, *An efficient, incremental, automatic garbage collector*, Comm. ACM, September 1976.

[DeS84] L. Peter Deutsch and Allan M. Schiffman, *Efficient Implementation of the Smalltalk-80 system*, Proc. POPL 1984.

[GoR83] Adele Goldberg and David Robson, *Smalltalk-80: the Language and its Implementation*, Addison-Wesley, May 1983. (Currently out of print. A second, smaller edition was published as: Adele Goldberg & David Robson, *Smalltalk-80: The Language*, Addison-Wesley, 1989. The section on Smalltalk implementation that was removed is available online at `http://users.ipa.net/~dwighth/`.)

[Jo99] Richard Jones, *personal website*, at: `http://www.cs.ukc.ac.uk/people/staff/rej/gcbib/gcbib.html`

[JoL96] Richard Jones and Rafeal Lins, *Garbage collection: algorithms for automatic dynamic memory management*, Wiley, 1996.

[Mi87] Eliot E. Miranda, *BrouHaHa—A portable Smalltalk Interpreter*, Proc. OOPLSA 1987.

[SCG81] Members of the Xerox Palo Alto Research Centre Systems Concepts Group, *Byte Magazine, special edition on Smalltalk-80*, August 1981.

[Ung87] David Ungar, *The Design and Evaluation of a High Performance Smalltalk System*, Addison-Wesley, 1987.

Bibliography: Papers of interest not directly referenced in the text

Patrick J. Caudill and Allen Wirfs-Brock, *A third generation Smalltalk-80 implementation*, Proc. OOPSLA 1986.

Alan C. Kay, *The early history of Smalltalk*, ACM SigPLAN Notices, March 1993.

Glenn Krasner [Ed.], *Smalltalk-80: Bits of History, Words of Advice*, Addison-Wesley, 1983.

David M. Ungar, *Generation Scavenging: A non-disruptive high performance storage reclamation algorithm*, ACM Practical Programming Environments Conference, April 1984, pp. 153–173.

Tim Rowledge is a Mechanical Engineer (gas turbine and motorcycle) turned Industrial Designer. He moved into GUI design as an IBM Research Fellow and discovered Smalltalk. He worked with Smalltalk Express Ltd. for some years, teaching, consulting, and developing a commercial port of BrouHaHa for the Active Book Company. Then he moved to California to join ParcPlace Systems as team lead for non-Unix platforms and later as manager of Smalltalk development. Subsequently, he worked for Interval Research on a Realtime Operating Smalltalk system for a proprietary network/controller/handheld with no OS other than Smalltalk. Currently, Mr. Rowledge is with Exobox, Inc., of San Diego.

8

Porting Squeak

Ian Piumarta

Laboratoire d'Informatique de l'Université Paris VI, and
INRIA Rocquencourt

"Nothing will ever be attempted if all possible objections must first be overcome."
The famous words of Samuel Johnson are particularly relevant to the task of porting
Squeak. As we shall see in this chapter, it is a task where most of the objections
need not be overcome; they can quite cheerfully be left for that proverbial rainy
day...

Introduction

Squeak must be one of the most ubiquitous programming languages to date. In
addition to the original version for Mac OS, Squeak has been ported to a wide
variety of very different platforms: most major flavors of Unix, MacOS-X, several
variations of Windows and Win/CE, OS/2, several "bare hardware" systems, and
so on.

The impressive list of ports has been possible because of the way Squeak cleanly
separates the task of interpreting Smalltalk from the task of communicating with
its host platform. The interpreter is actually a Smalltalk program within the image (in class Interpreter) which is translated into an equivalent C program that can
subsequently be compiled on any system that has an ANSI C compiler. This program makes only one assumption: that pointers and integers are 32 bits wide.[1]
Communication with the host platform is performed through a collection of a hundred or so "support functions," which perform platform-dependent tasks such as
file input/output, updating the screen, and reading keyboard and mouse input.
The generated interpreter code and platform support functions are compiled and

---

[1] This assumption may change in the future as 64-bit systems become more widespread. Existing
64-bit systems sometimes provide compiler options to limit pointers and integers to 32 bits, making
them "Squeak-friendly."

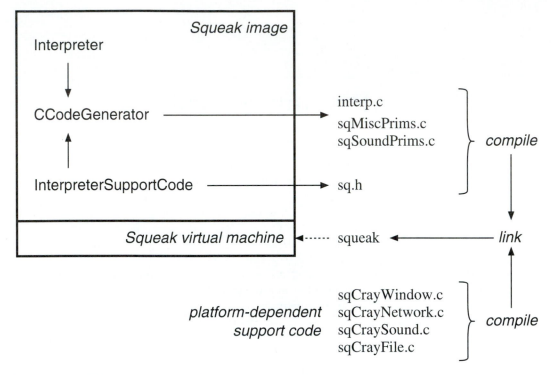

Figure 8.1 The majority of the Squeak virtual machine is generated automatically from an executable specification written in Smalltalk. The class Interpreter is a fully functional implementation of the Squeak interpreter written in a subset of Smalltalk. The CCodeGenerator converts this Smalltalk program into an equivalent C program. The class InterpreterSupportCode adds many primitives (also written in Smalltalk and converted automatically to C) to the generated code, as well as some hand-written header files that are stored as String constants in the image (for convenience). The generated source and header files are compiled and then linked with platform-dependent support code (written by hand) to create the Squeak virtual machine.

then linked together to create the final virtual machine. Figure 8.1 illustrates this division of labor.

Looking at the amount and complexity of support code that comes with Squeak, it may seem that porting it to a new platform is a daunting task. This is not necessarily the case. A couple of points in particular make the task much easier than it might appear.

First is the optional nature of many of the "advanced" features of Squeak (such as support for CD-quality stereo sound recording and output, MIDI, network connectivity, and so on). These features are associated with *primitive methods* in the Squeak image. Each of these primitives calls an associated C function in the support code, which normally implements some "external" action (such as opening a network connection) before returning. However, it is perfectly acceptable for these primitives to "fail" instead of implementing the external actions expected of them. An initial port can therefore avoid an immense amount of complexity by implementing tiny "stubs" in the associated support functions that simply "fail" the primitive from which they were called and then return, without performing any additional work at all. Squeak might be a less exciting place in which to play as a result, but at least it will be "up and running" far sooner because of the optional nature of its advanced features.

Second is the inclusion of the tiny file `sqMacMinimal.c` along with the regular Squeak source code. This file is a kind of "skeleton": It contains a complete set of declarations for both the mandatory and optional support routines, and the simplest possible definitions for the mandatory support that yield a running virtual machine on the Macintosh. (The optional functionality is defined too, but trivially—indicating its absence to the Squeak interpreter.) It is a very good starting point for porting Squeak to a new platform. Generating the Macintosh source files from within the image will also generate a copy of this file. (See the later section, "Generating the Macintosh Support Files.")

About This Chapter

This chapter begins by explaining the structure of the Squeak virtual machine and the process of putting it together based on the various pieces. These pieces are either provided, generated automatically based on Smalltalk code, or written by hand for each supported platform. The mechanism for extracting the provided and generated code from the image is described in "Source Code".

"Getting Started" gives an overview of the steps involved in porting Squeak, and some tips on how to make the process as painless as possible. Following the instructions in this section will yield a minimal, but working, virtual machine for Squeak on a new platform.

Next come some important details about how the generated code interacts with the support code ("Squeak's C Conventions") and how the compilation environment is set up for both generated and support code ("Compilation Environment: `sq.h`"). This last section also describes the additions that must be made to the compilation environment in order to support a port to a new platform.

The next few sections ("Graphical Output" through "Initialization and the Function `main()`") deal mainly with the fine details of each of the mandatory "subsystems" in Squeak and tell the full story behind the outline given earlier (in "Getting Started"). These sections describe functionality that is required for Squeak to work properly and will therefore be a major source of information during an initial porting effort.

The remaining sections ("System Attributes" through ""Headless" Operation") tell the tales of the various optional subsystems such as networking and sound. They describe how to extend Squeak's capabilities in important and interesting ways once an initial port to a new platform is running reliably.

Finally, "Conclusion" offers some closing remarks, including why the significant rate of change in Squeak does not present additional difficulty to the task of porting, before closing the book on the Squeak Porting Story.

This chapter assumes that the reader is already familiar with Smalltalk, and preferably with Squeak. The text refers to several standard Squeak classes without explaining either their purpose or the details of their implementation, except where such explanation is required to understand how they interact with the support code.

Only two typographic conventions are used. Quantities from the C universe (variable and function identifiers, constants, and so on) appear in `fixed-width` font. Quantities from the Squeak universe (expressions and class or method names) appear in sans serif font. Occasionally, a C identifier will be too long to fit onto a single line; in such cases the identifier is split at some convenient point, with the C "continuation character" ('\') indicating the split, like this:

```
returnType someFunctionWhoseIdentifierIsFarTooLong\
        ToFitOnOneLine(arguments...)
```

Source Code

Squeak tries to generate as much of its own implementation as possible automatically. Such code is referred to in this chapter as *generated code*. The code that depends on the host platform, and which is written by hand when porting Squeak to a new platform, is referred to as *support code*.

The generated code can be extracted from any running Squeak system. The next section explains how.

Writing the support code for a new platform is a more difficult task. To make things simpler, the support code is divided into several *subsystems*, each of which deals with a particular aspect of Squeak's connectivity with the "outside world." They include user interaction (screen, keyboard and mouse), networking, sound, serial and MIDI ports, and so on. Some of these subsystems are mandatory: They *must* be implemented (or "mostly implemented") to obtain a working Squeak system. The other subsystems are optional. They represent the parts that can be left for that rainy day.

Generating the Squeak Source Files

The very first task when starting a new port is to generate the platform-independent source files, which will be compiled and then linked with the hand-written support code. These files include the Squeak interpreter itself, automatically generated implementations of various primitive functions, and a few hand-written header files that are stored in image as String constants.

The Squeak interpreter is traditionally called `interp.c`. It is generated automatically by translating a complete, functional implementation written in Smalltalk into an equivalent C program. (See the class Interpreter for details.) This is done by evaluating the expression

> Interpreter translate: 'interp.c' doInlining: true

in a Squeak Workspace. (See the method of the same name in Interpreter class for further details.) This takes a couple of minutes and writes the generated code to the named file in the current working directory.

The automatically generated primitives are created in the same manner as the Squeak interpreter itself—from equivalent Smalltalk implementations that are translated into C. The hand-written header files are stored in the image as constants, just for completeness. Both sets of files can written to the current working directory by evaluating the expression

> InterpreterSupportCode writeSupportFiles

in a Squeak Workspace. (See the method of the same name in InterpreterSupport-Code class for further information.)

Generating the Macintosh Support Files

The Squeak image also contains a complete copy of the support code for the Macintosh, divided into several source files, each of which corresponds to one of the subsystems described in this chapter. Some of these files contain very good documentation and offer much more information (as comments) than could reasonably be included here.

Porting these subsystems to a new platform is, therefore, best accomplished by copying and then modifying the Macintosh version; unless one of the other ports of Squeak already offers support that is similar to the target platform, of course. Evaluating the expression

> InterpreterSupportCode writeMacSourceFiles

in a Squeak Workspace will write these files to the current working directory.

If no file system is available for writing out copies of the hand-written files stored in the image, their contents can be browsed by looking in the "source files" protocol of InterpreterSupportCode class.

Getting Started

This section gives some overall advice about how to go about porting Squeak to a new platform. It begins by outlining which support functions are essential and in what order they might be implemented to obtain a (partially) working Squeak system in the shortest amount of time.

It is very useful to have a running Squeak system available when porting to a new platform.[2] Apart from being able to look inside the image to see how the generated code interacts with the support code, it also affords the possibility of making a "customized" image for use during testing. (For example, such an image might disable the logging of errors to a file until the file system is fully operational in the new port.)

Roadmap to Porting Squeak

Some Smalltalk programmers like write their code in a "demand-driven" style, implementing missing functionality when the Debugger pops open in response to doesNotUnderstand:. This style of development also makes perfect sense for porting Squeak to a new platform.

A copy of the file `sqMacMinimal.c` (extracted from the image, as explained in "Generating the Macintosh Support Files") already contains trivial implementations of the optional functions, that will fail "gracefully" when the image tries to use an unimplemented feature. All that this file is missing are implementations of the "essential" functions.

With just a few minutes' work, trivial implementations of the essential functions can be added to `sqMacMinimal.c`. They can simply print a message (indicating the name of the function) before exiting.

Once this is done, the next step is to try to compile and link the Squeak virtual machine. At the time of writing, the following files are required:

- `interp.c`—automatically generated bytecode interpreter;

- `sqMiscPrims.c`—automatically generated primitives;

- `sqNamedPrims.c`—as generated by the image;

- `sqNamedPrims.h`—modified manually so as to declare no primitives at all ("Plugin Modules");

- `sqFooWindow.c`—the modified copy of `sqMacMinimal.c`, lacking all of the essential support for platform "Foo," but destined eventually to become the "main" program in the "Foo" port of Squeak;

- `sqConfig.h`—a (slightly) modified copy of the original, with an additional section that recognizes the host platform ("Compilation Environment: `sq.h`");

---

[2]This is by no means essential. The very first port of Squeak (to Unix) was made without access to a Macintosh, which at the time was the only platform on which Squeak ran. Apart from 10 minutes spent on a Macintosh right at the start of the porting process (to generate the `interp.c` file and the Macintosh support code for reference purposes), the port was performed entirely "off-line" up to the moment when Unix Squeak could load and run an image for itself.

- `sqPlatformSpecific.h`—a (possibly modified) copy of the original, with any modifications to the compilation environment that might be required ("Compilation Environment: `sq.h`"); plus

- any necessary `C` libraries.

The interpreter code relies only on the following functions from libraries:

- math: `exp()`, `log()`, `atan()`, `sin()`, `sqrt()`, `ldexp()`, `frexp()`, `modf()`;

- standard input/output: `getchar()`, `putchar()`, `printf()`;[3] and

- others: `memcpy()`, `strlen()`, `clock()`.

Given the preceding information, it should be possible to compile and link a Squeak virtual machine. Running this VM should cause an almost immediate exit, after printing the name of the first "essential" support function that is missing. Porting then becomes an iterative process:

- implement the missing "essential" function that caused the exit;

- compile, link, and run; and

- repeat.

If this methodology is followed, the order in which the various essential functions are implemented should be approximately as follows. (Don't worry if some of the comments that follow seem to make little sense right now. When the time comes to implement each particular function, the comments will start to make perfect sense.)

Reading an Image File

`sqImageFileRead()` and friends (see "Reading and Writing the Image File").

Squeak can do nothing without an image file to run, and so the very first thing to get working is the image-loading code.

The virtual machine (VM) keeps track of the full path name of the Squeak image file and the path to the directory containing the virtual machine. In a minimal implementation, the VM path can be the empty string and the image name hard-wired to `squeak.image`. It is assumed that the image file, the changes file, and the system sources file are all in the the same directory and that this directory is the default working directory for any file operations.

The rest of the file system implementation can be left until later.

---

[3]On platforms that have no terminal input/output, even the standard I/O functions could be disabled. They are used only to report fatal errors from within the generated code. (Hopefully, there will still be *some* way for the code to indicate which function caused an exit during the initial "demand driven" development.)

Displaying Bits on Screen

`ioShowDisplay()` and friends (see "Graphical Output"). Once the image-loading code is working, it's time to let Squeak display something. The critical function here is `ioShowDisplay()`, and it's likely that Squeak is now reaching the "stub" that was left in place of this function.

Once this function is working, the latest port of Squeak should actually be displaying something meaningful on the screen.[4] The most likely thing that Squeak will display is a message saying that it can't find the changes file. (This is already not bad, for two relatively simple steps!)

Now is the time to implement a few boring (but critical) user-interface-related functions.

For graphical output: `ioShowDisplay()` is already done, but `ioScreenSize()` is also very useful (and easy to implement). Things like `ioHasDisplayDepth()` can be hard-wired to `1` (after making sure that `squeak.image` is using a depth with which `ioShowDisplay()` can cope.)

The following functions can be made no-ops at this stage of the port:

```
ioProcessEvents(),
ioSetCursor(), and
ioSetCursorWithMask().
```

Handling Time

`ioMSecs()` and friends (see "Time"). Squeak relies heavily on knowing how to tell the time, and in particular on knowing how much time has elapsed since a given event. This step is critical for many ports: Without the timer it is impossible to proceed, since so much of the user interface code relies on it.

The following functions are essential for time-keeping: `ioMSecs()` and `ioMicroMSecs()`.

The function `ioSeconds()` can initially be hard-wired to always return `0`, with the effect that the current date and time will be wrong. On the other hand, the user interface never needs to know the "wall clock" time, and so this will not prevent significant further progress.

Reading the Keyboard and Mouse

`ioGetKeystroke()` and friends (see "Mouse and Keyboard Input").

The following functions are essential for interacting with Squeak:

---

[4]Keep a bottle of champagne handy for this moment: The feeling of achievement that comes with it should not be underestimated.

```
ioGetKeystroke(),
ioGetButtonState(), and
ioPeekKeystroke().
```

The function ioMousePoint() is also needed to track the pointer position.

If the hardware is normally polled to retrieve mouse/keyboard input then io-ProcessEvents() can probably be made a no-op. Otherwise, it might be necessary to implement it, in order to help with the conversion of mouse or keyboard events to a form that Squeak can poll. (See "Reconciling Polling with Event-Driven Input".)

The following functions can be made no-ops at this stage of the port:

```
ioSetCursor(),
ioSetCursorWithMask(), and
ioBeep().
```

And the Rest...

The new port of Squeak is now basically working!

It should be possible to interact with menus, browse the class hierarchy, open a workspace and evaluate expressions in it, and even run some simple benchmarks. Reaching this point is a second good excuse for celebrating.[5]

Now that Squeak can interact, a potentially useful thing to do is to open the "preferences" menu and disable the logging of errors to a file in the current directory—just until the port has a working, writable file system. (Otherwise, the first error of any kind will put the virtual machine into an infinite "fatal error" recursion.)

Note that it is possible to delay implementing the file system for quite a long time, and even then it can initially be made read-only.[6]

One *very* useful thing to get working early in the porting process is the interrupt key (or button). This is especially handy for ports to machines that have no keyboard (such as PDAs), to "escape" from prompts asking for keyboard input.

The rest of the porting process is just a matter of prioritizing which things to implement first. The functions that were mentioned above but left as "no-ops" would be a good starting point, followed by individual "subsystems" as described in the remainder of this chapter.

---

[5]As an indication of how quickly it is possible to arrive at this point, the first port of Squeak (to Unix/X11) was begun late on a Friday evening. After about two days of hacking, sometime during Sunday afternoon, Unix Squeak could be used to browse the class hierarchy and evaluate Smalltalk expressions in a Workspace. Later that same day it successfully saved a renamed .image file (copying the .changes file in the process) and then started up again using the newly saved image. It was only a matter of a few days more before the first "release" of Unix Squeak was publicly available.

[6]Ports to "bare hardware" might also take advantage of the fact that most Flash and CompactFlash cards can be formatted as a FAT-16 MS-DOS file system, which has a published and very simple specification. Any necessary image, changes and sources files can be transferred easily to these cards on a workstation equipped with an appropriate adaptor.

The preceding discussion assumes that the port is being made "in a vacuum." On the other hand, it is possible that an existing port offers a significant, reusable code base on which to build the new port.

Stealing Code from Other Ports

By far the easiest way to get started with a new port is to take an existing port and modify it for the new host. In some cases, a significant amount of work can be avoided by doing this. A good example is the code for updating the physical display.

The Unix/X11 port (at least) contains code to convert 8-, 16-, and 32-bit deep internal Display formats into 8-, 16-, 24-, or 32-bit deep physical screen data, with or without byte order reversal. It also contains a reusable skeleton for reconciling an entirely event-driven graphical, keyboard, and mouse I/O model with Squeak's polled model. The network subsystem should also work with little or no modification on any host that has a BSD-compatible socket library.

Obviously, other ports might offer a more sensible "starting point," depending on the target platform. Certain subsystems (such as sound) are so dependent on the host that they will probably have to be rewritten from scratch in most cases.

An intermediate case concerns hosts that have significant characteristics in common with an an existing port, but which have sufficient differences to warrant an independent existence. In such cases, a serious disadvantage of "forking" a new port is that two sets of essentially identical code must be maintained. Ideally, the code for the new host would be integrated with the existing port, although this also has a disadvantage: It can be accomplished only with the complete cooperation of the maintainer of the existing port (which might have to be reorganized to isolate the incompatible functionality). This situation is probably rare, but examples of both approaches already exist.[7]

Squeak's C Conventions

This section describes several conventions that are used universally by generated code and to which support code must adhere in order to work correctly.

Squeak Does Not Believe in Pointers

Squeak's implementation treats almost everything as an `int`. In particular, pointers that are passed between Squeak and the support code always have type `int`. It is up to the support code to perform any casting that might be required.

---

[7] The Unix version of Squeak was the basis for a significant portion of the (entirely distinct) OS/2 port. The majority of the Unix code is also reused without modification in the Mac OS X version of Squeak. (Mac OS X is essentially BSD Unix, but with a graphics server that is incompatible with X11.)

C Strings vs. Squeak Strings

Squeak and C store strings in fundamentally different ways. In C a string is always terminated with a "null" character (ASCII value 0). Squeak, on the other hand, stores the length of the string and dispenses with any kind of terminating character. This difference is important whenever string data is transferred between Squeak and C. In most cases, such transfers of string data follow the same pattern.

To export a string from Squeak to C, the support function is called with two arguments: a pointer to the string data and the number of bytes in the string. The support function simply copies the given number of bytes (using `memcpy()`, for example) from the given address into its own memory. (If allocating memory dynamically, then it should always add one to the length indicated by Squeak and append a terminating "null" to the copy.)

Importing a string is slightly more complex. In general, Squeak will call two support routines. The first should return the length of the string to be imported from C into Squeak. (This allows Squeak to allocate a new String of the appropriate size, to grow a buffer if necessary, or whatever.) The second routine is called with a pointer to the destination and the actual number of bytes that Squeak expects to be copied. (`strncpy()` is the safest way to actually transfer the bytes into Squeak's memory, to avoid any possibility of trying to copy too many bytes from the point of view of both Squeak and C.)

The clipboard handling routines ("The Clipboard") illustrate perfectly the way Squeak and C exchange string data.

Interacting with Semaphores

Several support routines are required to report asynchronous events to the Squeak interpreter. One example is the networking subsystem, where the completion of a `write()` operation or the availability of data for a `read()` operation must be communicated to the interpreter. This is accomplished by signalling a Semaphore.

Semaphores are identified (to the support code) by an integer index. Signaling a Semaphore is accomplished by calling the (generated) function

```
signalSemaphoreWithIndex(int semaIndex)
```

passing the appropriate Semaphore index as the argument.

Primitive Success and Failure

Some of the support functions are associated directly with a primitive method in the Squeak image. Such functions must indicate whether the primitive operation succeeds or fails. Two generated functions are provided to do this. The first is

```
void primitiveFail(void)
```

which is called to "fail" the primitive. (It does not transfer control back to the Squeak interpreter: The support code must ensure that a `return` is executed at the appropriate moment after failing a primitive.)

The second function is

```
int success(int successFlag)
```

which can be called several times from within a primitive support function. The argument should be either `true` or `false`. This function "composes" successive values of `successFlag`; that is, if a primitive support routine calls this function with `false` as the argument then Squeak will consider the primitive operation to have failed, regardless of how many times (or when) the support function calls it with the argument `true`.

The following sections will indicate when a support function is associated directly with a Squeak primitive. Such functions should "fail" (as described earlier) whenever they cannot complete an operation successfully.

Compilation Environment: `sq.h`

The generated code does not exist in a vacuum—it requires some kind of compilation environment to give it access to a few basic system services on the host platform. Porting Squeak, therefore, also involves defining an appropriate compilation environment for the generated code. This must be done before (or during) the initial attempt to compile and link the first "entirely unimplemented virtual machine" (as described in "Getting Started").

Each of the automatically generated, platform-independent source files begins by including `sq.h`, which establishes a compilation environment for the source file. This header file is also typically included by the (hand-written) platform-dependent source files, since it declares many useful function prototypes—including those for all the functions that should be present in the support code. (Including it routinely in every source file, therefore, helps to detect errors due to incorrect function signatures.) The overall structure of `sq.h` is shown in Figure 8.2.

Generated code makes use of several ANSI and/or POSIX routines that should be available on most platforms that have a Standard C compiler. Since the names of the necessary header files have been standardized, `sq.h` assumes that they are available and `#includes` the following directly: `math.h`, `stdio.h`, `stdlib.h`, `string.h`, and `time.h`.

Unfortunately, the generated code also uses facilities that may or may not be present—or that might be present in different forms depending on the platform. To cope with this, `sq.h` `#includes` two files that will certainly require modification for a new platform.

The first of these is `sqConfig.h`, which is responsible for identifying the host platform. A new port will have to add a corresponding section to `sqConfig.h`.

ANSI/POSIX headers

```
#include <math.h>                              these are assumed to exist on all platforms
#include <stdio.h>
#include <stdlib.h>
#include <string.h>
#include <time.h>

▷ #include "sqConfig.h"                        identifies the host platform
```

defaults for platform-specific definitions

```
#define true   1                               symbolic constants used by generated code
#define false  0
#define null   0

#define EXPORT(type)...                        return type declaration for functions in dynamic li-
                                               braries
#define sqImageFile...                         ANSI/POSIX file types and functions for accessing
#define sqImageFileOpen...                     file streams
  ...

#define sqAllocateMemory...                    interface to memory allocation routines
#define reserveExtraCHeapBytes...

#define storeFloatAtfrom...                    accessing 64-bit IEEE doubles
#define fetchFloatAtinto...

int ioMSecs(void);                             prototypes for fetching millisecond time
int ioLowResMSecs(void);
int ioMicroMSecs(void);

#define ioMSecs()...                           defaults based on ANSI clock() function
#define ioLowResMSecs()...
#define ioMicroMSecs()...

▷ #include "sqPlatformSpecific.h"              redefines zero or more of the above defaults for a
                                               particular host platform
```

prototypes for all support functions

```
/* file i/o */                                 a list of prototypes which declares the set of support
/* directories */                              functions that must be provided by the platform-
  ...                                          dependent support code for each platform on which
                                               Squeak runs
```

variables imported from generated code

```
extern const char *interpreterVersion;         the version string of interp.c
```

Figure 8.2   The structure of the file `sq.h`. The two header files marked with "▷" must be modified when porting to a new platform. The file `sqConfig.h` can define symbols to change the way the two Float access macros are defined. The file `sqPlatformSpecific.h` should redefine any macros that did not receive suitable defaults in `sq.h`. See the text for further details.

(Cut-and-paste from an existing section with minimal modifications will probably do the trick.) The new section must define at least the symbol `SQ_CONFIG_DONE`, to indicate that the platform has been recognized.[8]

---

[8]Some platforms do not have a single, unique predefined preprocessor symbol to aid with their identification. Any disambiguation should be done in `sqConfig.h` and a unique, unambiguous identifying symbol `#define`d for use later on in `sqPlatformSpecific.h`.

symbol/macro	default (ANSI/POSIX) definition
EXPORT(type)	type
sqImageFile	FILE *
sqImageFileOpen(name, mode)	fopen(name, mode)
sqImageFileRead(ptr, sz, count, f)	fread(ptr, sz, count, f)
sqImageFileWrite(ptr, sz, count, f)	fwrite(ptr, sz, count, f)
sqImageFilePosition(f)	ftell(f)
sqImageFileSeek(f, pos)	fseek(f, pos, SEEK_SET)
sqImageFileClose(f)	fclose(f)
reserveExtraCHeapBytes(size, extra)	size
sqAllocateMemory(min, desired)	malloc(desired)
ioMSecs()	((1000 * clock()) / CLOCKS_PER_SEC)
ioLowResMSecs()	((1000 * clock()) / CLOCKS_PER_SEC)
ioMicroMSecs()	((1000 * clock()) / CLOCKS_PER_SEC)

Table 8.1 Default ANSI/POSIX values for the symbols and macros that `sqPlatformSpecific.h` might want to consider redefining.

`sq.h` goes on to define various "sensible" defaults for things that the generated code will need, before including the second of these files: `sqPlatformSpecific.h`. As its name suggests, this file is responsible for providing the generated code with access to basic facilities that differ between platforms. On ANSI/POSIX platforms, it will have almost nothing to do. On more exotic platforms, it will have to "undo" some of the assumptions made in `sq.h`. It does this by selectively redefining the macros previously set up by `sq.h`, in a section of code compiled conditionally according to the host platform (as detected previously in `sqConfig.h`). If any system header files (other than those already included by `sq.h`) are required by the host, then `sqPlatformSpecific.h` is the place in which to `#include` them.

The macros that `sqPlatformSpecific.h` should consider redefining are concerned mainly with declaring functions for dynamically loaded libraries, file access, memory allocation, and keeping track of elapsed time. They are described in the following four sections. Their default "reasonable" ANSI/POSIX definitions (provided by `sq.h`) are shown in Table 8.1.

Declaring Functions for Dynamic Libraries

Some of the generated code is intended to be "pluggable"—compiled separately from the main virtual machine as a dynamically loadable library, to be read into the virtual machine "on-demand" at runtime when first needed. Unfortunately, some compilers and hosts require special declarations for functions that are to be exported from a dynamic library. The macro `EXPORT(type)` is therefore used to declare the return type of any function that might be placed in a dynamic library—for example,

```
EXPORT(int) someDynamicallyLoadedFunction(void) { ... }
```

`sqPlatformSpecific.h` can redefine this macro to provide any additional declaration keywords that might be needed (not forgetting, of course, to include the return type of the function).

Reading and Writing the Image File

Most of the code needed for loading and saving images is generated automatically. This code assumes an ANSI-like interface to the file system. The symbol `sqImage-File` should be defined as the type of a "file handle" on the host platform.

`sqImageFileOpen()` is passed the `name` (a C-style null-terminated string) and `mode` (also a C string) of a file, and should return its handle (of type `sqImageFile`, or `null` if the file does not exist). The `mode` is as specified by ANSI; either `"rb"` (read binary bytes) or `"wb"` (create or truncate and then write binary bytes).[9]

The reading/writing macros are passed a pointer to an area of memory (`ptr`), a file handle (`f`, obtained from `sqImageFileOpen()`) and the number of bytes to transfer expressed as `count` "elements" of size `sz`. These macros should simply transfer `count * sz` "uninterpreted" bytes. (Any "endian" conversions that might be necessary are handled automatically elsewhere.)

Finally, `sqImageFilePosition()` and `sqImageFileSeek()` are responsible for retrieving and setting the "file pointer"—that is, the offset (from the beginning of the file) at which the next read/write operation should commence. (The generated code tacitly assumes that read/write operations will increment the file pointer by the number of bytes read or written.)

Allocating Memory

The generated code needs to know approximately how much space to reserve for the virtual machine's data. This space includes the Smalltalk "heap" (the in-memory copy of the image file) and any additional data space that might be required by dynamically loaded libraries. The macro `reserveExtraCHeapBytes(size, extra)` is used to calculate how much data space should be reserved when the VM starts up. The first argument is the number of bytes required for the image; the second is an estimate of how much additional data space might be needed by dynamic libraries. This macro should return the total amount of data memory that the VM should "reserve" statically. If the host knows how to dynamically allocate more data memory as libraries are loaded (or if it doesn't support dynamic libraries at all), then the correct result is simply the size of the image file (the default definition).

The macro `sqAllocateMemory(min, desired)` is used to allocate the memory for the image (and possibly for the dynamic libraries). The first argument is the minimum acceptable size of memory (measured in bytes), and the second is the

---

[9] "Binary bytes" means that no CR/LF line-end conversion should be attempted when reading/writing the image file.

"ideal" size. This memory allocation macro should return `null` if it cannot allocate at least `min` bytes of memory.

Keeping Track of Elapsed Time

`sq.h` also declares three functions that return the elapsed time (relative to any convenient point of reference):

```
int ioMSecs(void)
int ioLowResMSecs(void)
int ioMicroMSecs(void)
```

(The reason for having three functions to read the time will be explained later, in "Time".) `sq.h` then immediately "hides" these declarations with three macro definitions of the same names that use the ANSI `clock()` function to calculate the time.

`sqPlatformSpecific.h` should seriously consider redefining these macros (or simply undefining them so that real functions can be called in the support code) to improve the accuracy of timing within Squeak. The problem is that `clock()` usually measures elapsed CPU time rather than elapsed wall-clock time. Consequently, whenever Squeak goes to sleep (which it does whenever it runs out of interesting things to do), time will effectively stop passing if the host adheres to the ANSI definition of `clock()`.

The remainder of `sq.h` provides a full set of prototypes for the functions that should be implemented by the platform-support code. Since these declarations should never depend on the host platform (and should, therefore, be identical across all platforms), they appear after the inclusion of `sqPlatformSpecific.h`.

Reading and Writing Floats

Two macros are defined by `sq.h` to copy 64-bit, double-precision, IEEE floating-point values between `C` `doubles` and the data portion of a `Float` object. By default these macros "do the right thing" on big-endian architectures, where the 64 bits of a `double` are stored most significant byte first in memory: The data are transferred in the obvious way, by dereferencing a pointer to `double`.

Two complications might arise with this. The first is that Squeak aligns all data on 32-bit boundaries, *including* the 64 bits of data in a `Float`. If the host imposes 64-bit alignment on `doubles`, then the symbol `DOUBLE_WORD_ALIGNMENT` can be defined in `sqConfig.h` to force these macros to use two 32-bit transfers to move the data. The second complication arises on little-endian machines, where the least significant word is stored first. For these hosts, `sqConfig.h` should define `DOUBLE_WORD_ORDER` to cause the float macros to swap the two 32-bit halves of a double while copying it.

If some other scheme is necessary to copy doubles between C variables and Squeak's object memory, then `sqPlatformSpecific.h` will have to redefine the macros

```
storeFloatAtfrom(i, floatVarName)
fetchFloatAtinto(i, floatVarName)
```

where i is an `int` *expression* giving the address of the data in a Float object, and `floatVarName` is the name of a *variable* of type `double` (whose address can be taken using the `&` operator to effect the transfer).

The two 32-bit halves of a Float's data are automatically byte-swapped to match the local host when the image is loaded. The Float macros, therefore, need not take byte order into account.

Graphical Output

Just like the very first releases of Smalltalk-80 in the mid-1980s, Squeak performs all of its graphical output directly to an object inside the image. This object (called "Display") includes a Bitmap representing what the user should see. The task of rendering Squeak's graphical display is therefore relatively easy. Rather than having to implement a host of different graphical drawing operations directly, the support code simply copies bits out of the Display object and onto the screen at the appropriate moments. The precise nature of "the screen" depends on the platform and might be a window on Mac OS or Unix (which uses the X Window System), or directly to a memory-mapped framebuffer device or even to a tiny LCD panel—which is the case for at least one port of Squeak to "bare hardware."

The "appropriate moments" are determined entirely within Smalltalk, and ultimately result in the calling of the support function `ioShowDisplay()`. This function performs the required copying of bits onto the physical display, according to a "damage rectangle" that is supplied as an argument to the function.

Updating the Display

The support function

```
int ioShowDisplay
  (int dispBitsIndex, int width, int height, int depth,
   int affectedL, int affectedR, int affectedT, int affectedB)
```

is responsible for updating the physical screen, based on a Bitmap representing the display within Squeak.

The first four arguments provide information about the Bitmap data to be transferred to the physical display:

- `dispBitsIndex` is the address of the first byte of the data portion of a `Bitmap` object in Squeak's memory. This address corresponds to the first pixel (top-left corner) of the display.

- `width` is the width of the bitmap's data. The "pitch" of the bitmap (the number of pixels in each scanline) is always rounded up so that each scanline is word-aligned (i.e., it is a multiple of 4 bytes wide).

- `height` is the total number of scanlines in the bitmap data.

- `depth` is the number of bits in a pixel. Currently depths of 1, 2, 4, 8, 16, and 32 bits per pixel are supported.

The final four arguments—`affectedL`, `affectedR`, `affectedT`, and `affectedB`—specify a "damage rectangle." They correspond to the left, right, top, and bottom limits (respectively) of the portion of the display that should be updated.[10]

`Bitmaps` are word objects, and their byte order is swapped automatically if necessary (by generated code) when the image is loaded, to match the natural order of the host. No special action is needed if the host's byte order matches the physical display's byte order.

Display Depths and the Colormap

In 32-bits-per-pixel depth, Squeak really uses 24-bit pixels. The blue component is in the least significant 8 bits of each pixel, followed by 8 bits of green and then 8 bits of red. The most significant 8 bits are unused.

In 16-bits per pixel depth, Squeak really uses 15-bit pixels. The blue component is in the least significant 5 bits of each pixel, followed by 5 bits of green and 5 bits of red. The most significant bit is unused.

In 1-through-8-bits-per-pixel depths, Squeak uses the colormap shown in Table 8.2.

Other Display Functions

```
int ioScreenSize(void)
```

should return the current size of the screen, with the width in the most significant 16 bits and the height in the least significant 16 bits.

---

[10] An initial implementation of `ioShowDisplay()` could ignore the damage rectangle and simply update the entire screen area according to the bitmap. Although slow, this would avoid any possibility of the graphical output appearing to be broken due to misinterpretation of the damage rectangle (yielding an "update area" of zero size) when it is otherwise working perfectly.

pixel	color
0	white (or transparent if bpp > 1)
1	black
2	white (opaque)
3	50% gray
4	red
5	green
6	blue
7	cyan
8	yellow
9	magenta
10	1/8 gray
11	2/8 gray
12	3/8 gray
13	5/8 gray
14	6/8 gray
15	7/8 gray
16–39	1/32–31/32 gray (omitting $n/8$)
$36r + 6b + g + 40$	$6 \times 6 \times 6$ color cube

Table 8.2 Squeak's color map for 1-, 2-, 4-, and 8-bit depths. The *pixel* column refers to the pixel values stored in the **Display Bitmap**. The *color* column specifies the corresponding colors to be rendered on the physical display. For display depths of less than 8 bits, only an initial portion of this table will apply. For example, for depth 2, only the first four lines are relevant (pixel values 0 through 3). For depth 8, the maximum pixel value (according to the table) corresponds to the final entry with $r = 5$, $g = 5$, and $b = 5$; that is, $36 \times 5 + 6 \times 5 + 5 + 40$, which is (rather fortunately) equal to 255. For depths of greater than eight bits Squeak does not use a color map; the bits in the pixel specify the red, green, and blue intensities of the color directly. See the text for further details.

```
int ioHasDisplayDepth(int depth)
```

should return 1 if the host supports a Squeak **Display** of the given **depth**. (This function is used to avoid passing an unsupported depth to `ioShowDisplay()`.)

```
int ioSetFullScreen(int fullScreenFlag)
```

is used to turn "full screen" display on and off. If `fullScreenFlag` is 1, then the function should save the current screen size before resizing the display to occupy the entire screen, removing any window decorations if they are present. (The intention is that Squeak "take over" the entire physical display area.) If `fullScreenFlag` is 0 then the function should restore the physical screen (and any window decorations that might be present by default) to its saved original size.

```
int ioSetDisplayMode(int width, int height, int depth,
                     int fullscreenFlag)
```

is called before Squeak tries to change its Display characteristics. The arguments
have the usual meanings. This function should return 1 to accept the new Display
parameters, or 0 to reject them.

```
int ioForceDisplayUpdate(void)
```

is called from generated code whenever Squeak wants to be certain that its internal
Display and the physical display are "synchronized." If the display is "local" (a
framebuffer connected directly to the host), then nothing special need be done. If
the display is "remote" (a network window system, for example), then this function
should not return until it is certain that any pending display operations (initiated
from ioShowDisplay()) have been completed.

```
int ioSetCursor(int cursorBits, int offsetX, int offsetY)
```

is called whenever Squeak wants to change the visible cursor associated with the
mouse (or other pointing device). cursorBits is the address of a cursor bitmap.
The bitmap is 16 bits wide and 16 bits high. The 16 bits of each "scanline" appear in
the most significant 16 bits of a 32-bit word (the least significant 16 bits are unused).
(Successive "scanlines" are therefore in the most significant halves of consecutive
32-bit words starting at cursorBits.) The host's cursor should be changed to
reflect the bitmap, with a 1 in cursorBitmap being a black pixel in the cursor and
a 0 being transparent (the background shows through the cursor). The "hot spot"
of the cursor is given by the second and third argument, which are measured from
the top-left of the cursor (0, 0) and then *negated*.[11]

```
int ioSetCursorWithMask(int cursorBits, int cursorMask,
        int offsetX, int offsetY)
```

is similar to ioSetCursor(), except that cursorMask points to a bitmap (in the
same format as cursorBits) specifying where the 0 pixels in cursorBits should
be opaque. Wherever cursorMask contains a 1 and cursorBits contains a 0, the
cursor should have an opaque white pixel (obscuring the background) instead of the
normal transparent pixel.

Mouse and Keyboard Input

The interpreter reads keyboard and mouse information with the help of four support
functions. The simplest of these is

---

[11] A hotspot in the top-left corner of the cursor is at offset $(0, 0)$. A hotspot in the bottom-right
corner is at offset $(-15, -15)$. (This, and similar, weirdness comes from Squeak's origins as a
Macintosh application.)

bit	meaning
11	command
10	option
9	control
8	shift
0–7	ASCII code

Table 8.3   Value returned by `ioGetKeystroke()` and `ioPeekKeystroke()`. The low eight bits contain the ASCII code. The next four bits are set to `1`, if the corresponding modifier key was pressed when the keystroke was recorded.

```
int ioMousePoint(void)
```

which should return an `int` representing the current position of the mouse pointer. The top 16 bits contain the x coordinate and the bottom 16 bits the y coordinate. The origin is the top-left corner of the window (or screen, if Squeak is using a raw framebuffer), with x increasing towards the right and y towards the bottom of the window.

The remaining three functions read keyboard input and the state of the "modifier" keys.[12]

```
int ioGetKeystroke(void)
```

reads (and returns) the next character in the keyboard input buffer, removing it from the buffer in the process. The result is a 12-bit integer, in which the least significant eight bits contain the ASCII value of the character, and the next four bits contain the "modifier" keys that were pressed at the time the keystroke was recorded. The bit assignments are shown in Table 8.3. A nondestructive read must also be provided, by the function `ioPeekKeystroke(void)`.

The keyboard handling code should also check for a key code (ASCII character plus the modifier bits) equal to the contents of the variable `interruptKeycode` (declared and defined by generated code). If this key combination (usually "command" plus "."). is pressed then the support code should set the variable `interruptPending` to `true`, and `interruptCheckCounter` to `0` (both variables are declared in generated code). This will cause Squeak to abort its current activity, returning control to the user interface.

The mouse buttons are read by the function

```
int ioGetButtonState(void)
```

[12]On the Macintosh these are "control," "shift," "option," and "command." On other platforms, there are often "meta" and/or "alt" keys that can take the place of either "option" or "command." Other combinations, such as "shift"+"control," can be used if necessary to emulate "command" and/or "option"; the support code should implement whatever mapping seems appropriate or most natural for users accustomed to the platform.

bit	*meaning*
6	command
5	option
3	control
3	shift
2	left mouse button
1	middle mouse button
0	right mouse button

Table 8.4 Value returned by `ioGetButtonState()`. The low three bits indicate which mouse buttons are pressed. The next fours bits are set to `1` if the corresponding modifier key was pressed when the mouse button state was recorded. On systems having a single-button mouse, it should be treated as the left button. The left button should also obey the modifier keys, with "control" transforming it into the middle button and "meta" (or equivalent) transforming it into the right button.

whose result is a 7-bit integer containing three mouse button flags and the four modifier key bits. The bit assignments are shown in Table 8.4.

Reconciling Polling with Event-Driven Input

Unlike most window systems and graphical toolkits (which tend to be event-driven), Squeak "polls" for incoming data from the keyboard, mouse, and other sources. This polling normally occurs whenever the Smalltalk user interface reads the mouse or keyboard state.

Even on systems such as X (which buffer incoming events on behalf of the application), there is a conflict of interests. For example, Squeak expects to be able to read the current position of the mouse at any moment, regardless of how many keyboard events might be waiting in the buffer. This means that the support code must "service" events as soon as possible after they arrive (to keep the mouse position up to date and to check for the "interrupt" key in a timely fashion), while providing some mechanism for "saving up" keyboard events to be delivered at some later time, when Squeak decides to poll for them.

To help reconcile polling with a possibly (or even probably) event-driven platform, the interpreter calls the support function `ioProcessEvents()` before reading the mouse or keyboard state during interactive operation (and approximately two times per second when running a CPU-bound activity, to give the support code chance to set the `interruptPending` flag if necessary).

`ioProcessEvents()` typically has four responsibilities:

- tracking the current position of the mouse based on any "motion" events that might have arrived;

- reading and recording any "keypress" and "buttonpress" events that might have arrived;

- recording the current state of the "modifier" keys along with button and keypress events; and

- setting the `interruptPending` flag to `true`, if the `interruptKeycode` combination has been pressed.

Depending on the precise details of the platform, `ioProcessEvents()` might also be a good place in which to check for other sources of input/output activity (network and sound, for example).

Figure 8.3 shows a "skeleton" for a typical implementation of `ioProcessEvents()`.

If such a scheme is used to match events with Squeak's polling, then the check for the `interruptKeycode` (described in the previous section) should be performed in the event handler, to ensure that user interrupts are caught at the earliest possible moment.[13]

```
int ioProcessEvents(void)
{
  while (/* input event available */)
    {
      event = /* next event */;
      switch (event.type)
        {
          case /* mouse motion */:
            mousePosition.x = event.x;
            mousePosition.y = event.y;
            break;
          case /* keypress */:
            recordKeystroke(event.keycode);      /* the character itself */
            recordModifiers(event.modifiers);    /* shift, control, alt */
            break;
          case /* window expose */:
            fullDisplayUpdate();
            break;
        }
    }
  return 0;
}
```

Figure 8.3   Typical definition of `ioProcessEvents()`.

---

[13] Every platform should try hard to decouple the test for the `interruptKeycode` from the reading of the keyboard via `ioGetKeystroke()`. If Squeak is stuck in an infinite loop, for example, then it is unlikely to ever call `ioGetKeystroke()` again—and Squeak would "freeze," with no possibility of interruption.

Event-Driven Keyboard/Mouse Input

Starting with version 2.9 of Squeak, there is experimental support for true event-driven input. If the image supports event-driven input, then it will call the support function

```
int ioSetInputSemaphore(int inputSemaIndex)
```

once when starting up. The `inputSemaIndex` specifies the index of a Semaphore to be signaled ("Interacting with Semaphores") whenever an input event becomes available. If this function is not called during startup, then the support code should continue to provide "polled" input handling as described previously, to remain compatible with older images.[14]

If the above function is called from generated code during startup, then the support code should arrange for the input Semaphore to be signaled whenever an event arrives. This will cause the interpreter to call the support function

```
ioGetNextEvent(sqInputEvent *evt)
```

shortly afterwards. `evt` is a pointer to an `sqEvent` structure that should be filled in appropriately. The event structures (defined in `sq.h`) are shown in Figure 8.4.

The `type` field should be set to one of the following values (defined symbolically in `sq.h`):

`EventTypeMouse`	for mouse events
`EventTypeKeyboard`	for keyboard events

The `timeStamp` field should be the value of `ioMSecs()` at the time the event arrived.

For mouse events, `x` and `y` give the position of the mouse (relative to the top-left corner of the Squeak window). The `buttons` field details which button caused the event, according to the following constants defined in `sq.h`:[15]

`RedButtonBit`	left mouse button
`BlueButtonBit`	middle mouse button
`YellowButtonBit`	right mouse button

For keyboard events, the `charCode` field contains the character code of the key that was pressed.[16]

---

[14]Backwards compatibility should not be a priority in an initial port of Squeak. The vast majority of Squeak users upgrade to the latest version of the system the instant it becomes available.

[15]The rather colorful names are traditional and come from the colors of the mouse buttons found on the first machines on which Smalltalk ran in the 1970s.

[16]The details of event-driven input are still being debated at the time of writing. No final decision has been made about the way the keyboard characters should be encoded, although the tendency seems to be towards using the 16-bit `keysyms` defined by the X Consortium for use in the X Window System. Conversion to these from an 8-bit ASCII code is trivial (using a lookup table) and avoids discarding potentially interesting information encoded in the `keysyms` on X-based (and similar) systems.

```
typedef struct sqMouseEvent {
  int type;                  /* EventTypeMouse */
  unsigned int timeStamp;    /* time of arrival */
  int x;                     /* mouse X position */
  int y;                     /* mouse Y position */
  int buttons;               /* 'or'ed button bits */
  int modifiers;             /* 'or'ed modifier values */
  int reserved1;             /* reserved for future use */
  int reserved2;             /* reserved for future use */
} sqMouseEvent;
typedef struct sqKeyboardEvent {
  int type;                  /* EventTypeKeyboard */
  unsigned int timeStamp;    /* time of arrival */
  int charCode;              /* character code (see text) */
  int pressCode;             /* EventKey value */
  int modifiers;             /* 'or'ed modifier bits */
  int reserved1;             /* reserved for future use */
  int reserved2;             /* reserved for future use */
  int reserved3;             /* reserved for future use */
} sqKeyboardEvent;
```

Figure 8.4 Squeak mouse and keyboard event structures. Note that the common field `modifiers` is *not* in the same location in the two structures.

The `pressCode` field identifies the physical action that is being reported for the key, according to the following symbolic constants defined in `sq.h`:

> EventKeyDown   key was pressed
> EventKeyUp   key was released

The final `modifiers` field in both mouse and keyboard events reflects the state of the "shift," "control," "alt," and any other kinds of "meta" key that might be present on the keyboard. If a given modifier key is down when an event arrives, the corresponding bit should be set in the event reported to Squeak. As before, from `sq.h`, we have

> ShiftKeyBit   obvious
> CtrlKeyBit   obvious
> CommandKeyBit   "alt" or "meta" key
> OptionKeyBit   "ctrl" + "command" if no distinct key available

The Clipboard

Squeak's editing facilities include the usual "cut," "copy," and "paste" operations. In addition to working with text inside the image, they can be used to exchange

data with other applications. To this effect, Squeak expects the support code to
maintain a "clipboard" holding the text associated with these operations.

The clipboard is the destination for "cut" and "copy" operations. When one of
these operations is performed by the user, the interpreter calls the support function

```
int clipboardWriteFromAt(int count, int base, int offset)
```

which should copy `count` bytes of text from the address `base + offset` into some
suitably allocated external storage.[17] The text is *not* terminated with a "NUL"
character. The return value of this function is ignored.

The clipboard is the source for the "paste" operation. The interpreter first calls
the support function

```
int clipboardSize(void)
```

which should return the number of bytes of text currently stored in the clipboard.
The function

```
int clipboardReadIntoAt(int count, int base, int offset)
```

is then called to transfer `count` bytes of data from the clipboard to the address
`base + offset`. This function must not store more than `count` bytes, should not
attempt to terminate the stored text with a "NUL" character, and should return
the number of bytes actually transferred.

The addresses `base + offset` actually points into the middle of a Smalltalk
`String`, so any text read or written by these functions should use the Smalltalk
line-end convention: a single "CR" character, ASCII value 13.

If the local platform supports copy-and-paste between applications, then the
clipboard is the place where such exchange of data will take place. If the platform's
line-end convention is not the same as Smalltalk's, then the support code will have
to take care of any required conversion when exporting or importing the clipboard
to or from other applications.

Files and Directories

All of Squeak's file primitives are implemented by generated code, which assumes
the existence of the ANSI `stdio` functions. Operations on directories are more
complicated, and a certain amount of support code is necessary. Porting to a new
platform will require the following support functions to be implemented. Unless
otherwise indicated, these functions should return 1 to indicate success and 0 to
indicate failure.

---

[17]On platforms that have the standard `C` library, such storage could by allocated by calling
`malloc()`, for example.

```
int
dir_Delimitor(void)
```

should return the ASCII value of the character used to delimit directories in a pathname.[18]

```
int dir_Create(char *pathString, int pathStringLength)
```

is called to create a new directory.

```
int dir_Delete(char *pathString, int pathStringLength)
```

is called to delete a directory.

```
int dir_Lookup(char *pathString, int pathStringLength,
        int index,
        char *name, int *nameLength,
        int *creationDate, int *modificationDate,
        int *isDirectory, int *sizeIfFile)
```

is called to read information about a file in a directory. The first three arguments are inputs, specifying the path to the directory to be searched and the index of the file within the directory (starting at 1). The remaining arguments are pointers to variables in which the routine should store information about the entry. The creation and modification dates should be in seconds relative to the Squeak epoch. (See "Time".) This function should return a success code as follows:

0 to indicate success (an entry was found in the directory at the given index)

1 to indicate that the index was past the end of the directory

2 to indicate a problem with the **pathString** (for example illegal syntax or a path to some file system object that is not a directory)

Finally,

```
int dir_SetMacFileTypeAndCreator(char *filename,
        int filenameSize, char *fType, char *fCreator)
```

is intended for Mac OS only, can be ignored, and should simply return 1.

---

[18]The absence of this function in the very first port of Squeak caused a certain amount of "entertainment." At the time, the image "remembered" the full paths to its `.changes` and `.sources` files. Since these were originally on a Macintosh file system, the directory delimiter in these paths was a colon ":". It was necessary to make symbolic links (with ridiculously long names) to these files before Squeak would start up correctly. The next step was to change the delimiter to be correct for Unix (a slash "/"), which had the unfortunate side-effect that Squeak began looking for these files in directories that simply did not exist on a Unix system. A painful series of symbolic links (starting at the root of the file system) was needed before Squeak could successfully find the files—at which point the image could be saved from within Squeak, causing it to "remember" a much more "reasonable" set of paths to these files. More than four years after the initial port of Squeak to Unix, the machine that was used *still* had bizarre symbolic links lurking in obscure, seldom-visited corners of the file system. (Removing them had simply been forgotten in the excitement of having a working Squeak system to play with!)

Time

The interpreter needs to recover two kinds of time from the support code. The first is "absolute" time, used for calculating the current date and "wall-clock" time. The second is "relative" time, used for measuring intervals between events.

Absolute time is the responsibility of the function

```
int ioSeconds(void)
```

which should answer the number of seconds that have elapsed since the Squeak "epoch"—midnight on the 1st of January 1901. If the host platform has a different "epoch," then a conversion will be necessary. For example, many systems use 1 January 1970 as their epoch; such systems would have to add 2,177,452,800 seconds (the number of seconds in 17 leap and 52 nonleap years) to the current time.

Three other functions are responsible for "relative" time. It doesn't matter what "epoch" they use (provided that the point of reference doesn't change during a single run of the virtual machine), but greater resolution is required—preferably to the nearest millisecond.

The function

```
int ioMSecs(void)
```

should return the number of milliseconds that have elapsed since some suitable reference time (for example, the number of milliseconds since the virtual machine started running or the number of milliseconds since the machine was booted). The interpreter uses this clock for timing purposes, for example to determine when Delays should expire and for generating MIDI events. Although millisecond resolution is not *required*, the better its resolution the more accurate these timing activities will be. This clock represents a compromise between efficiency and accuracy.

The interpreter can get by with a much lower resolution clock for some activities, particularly when calling ioMSecs() is relatively expensive. For these purposes, it calls

```
int ioLowResMSecs(void)
```

which *must* be fast, even at the expense of accuracy. A resolution as low as a few tenths of a second is acceptable.

Lastly, the function

```
int ioMicroMSecs(void)
```

is called only for profiling purposes. (The slightly peculiar name is meant to suggest that this function could be based on a microsecond clock, even though the answer that it provides is in milliseconds.) It should return the highest resolution of millisecond time available, regardless of how expensive it might be to obtain.

Image Name

The support code is responsible for recovering the pathnames of the virtual machine executable and image files during initialization. The generated code uses the following functions and variables to access this information:

```
int imageNameSize(void)
int vmPathSize(void)
```

should return the length (excluding any terminating nulls) of the absolute paths to the image file and VM executable, respectively.

```
int imageNameGetLength(int sqImageNameIndex, int length)
int vmPathGetLength(int sqVMPathIndex, int length)
```

should copy the name of the image file or virtual machine executable into memory at the address given by their first argument (remember that there are no pointers in Squeak, only `ints`), which should not exceed `length` characters.

```
int imageNamePutLength(int sqImageNameIndex, int length)
```

is called to inform the support code that the name of the image has changed (before saving it with a new name, for example). The support code should update any data that depend on the name of the image, including

```
char imageName[]
```

which should contain the (null terminated) name of the image. (Some generated code refers explicitly to this array.)

Miscellany

```
int ioBeep(void)
```

should ring the keyboard bell. (Since any keyboard manufactured more recently than 1980 will probably not be equipped with a bell, it is acceptable that this function make some appropriate noise emanate from the computer's loudspeaker instead.)

```
int ioExit(void)
```

is called to terminate execution gracefully. This function should never return and (apart from exiting) should perform no action other than releasing any resources that might have been allocated or reserved by the support code during initialization.

```
int ioFormPrint(int bitsAddr,
    int width, int height, int depth,
    double hScale, double vScale, int landscapeFlag)
```

is called to save an area of a Squeak **Bitmap** to a file in whatever the host might consider to be a useful format. Formats used on existing platforms include PostScript and PPM (Portable PixMap, a universal format for bitmapped images that can be converted easily into many tens of other popular formats). `bitsAddr` specifies the address of the first pixel in memory, `depth` the number of bits per pixel, `height` the number of scanlines in the bitmap, and `width` the number of pixels in each scanline.[19] The final three arguments are obvious.

```
int ioRelinquishProcessorForMicroseconds(int microSecs)
```

is called from the generated code whenever Squeak runs out of interesting things to do. This function should "sleep" for the indicated number of `microSecs`. If any of the support code uses polling to check for input/output (network, serial port, and so on), then an "intelligent" implementation of this function would sleep while waiting for input to arrive (or output to complete), with a suitable timeout to ensure that Squeak wakes up again after no more than the given number of `microSecs` have elapsed. (If the host is dedicated to Squeak, then a "stupid" implementation is also possible: The function can return immediately without sleeping. This will cause Squeak to "hog" the CPU. However, on a "dedicated" host, this is presumably not a problem.) This function should return the approximate number of microseconds that were spent sleeping, or `microSecs` if this information is not available.

Initialization and the Function `main()`

The support code is responsible for providing the function `main()` (or whatever function is used for the "standard" entry point of a program on the host). `main()` is responsible for performing the following actions:

- parsing any command line arguments passed to the VM;

- determining the path to the image file either from the command line, from an environment variable, or from some other source (if the VM was started by a graphical manipulation, for example);

- initializing any input/output subsystems that are supported (including the physical display and any colormaps that might be needed);

- loading the image file into memory; and

- starting the Squeak interpreter to "run" the image.

Parsing the command line arguments is relevant only on hosts that support a command-line interface. After parsing the arguments, the absolute paths to the image and VM executable files must be available via the functions described in

---

[19]Remember that the "pitch" of a scanline is always a multiple of four bytes, which means that some correction for the start of successive scanlines might be required if `width * depth` is not a multiple of 32.

"Image Name," and the command-line arguments themselves must be available as system attributes. ("System Attributes" describes system attributes in detail.)

Three kinds of arguments should be distinguished:

- options meant specifically for the VM itself;

- the name of the image to run; and

- options meant specifically for Squeak applications.

The exact format of the command line will depend on the host's conventions, but the above distinction should be respected and the VM should reject unknown VM options, if at all possible. The approach used on Unix-based systems, for example, is to enforce the following order on the command line arguments:

- options intended for the VM, distinguished from the image name by having a "–" prefix;

- the name of the image to run (which lacks the option prefix); and

- "uninterpreted" arguments intended for Squeak applications.

(The VM saves all of these arguments for retrieval using negative system attributes, but saves only the arguments following the image name for retrieval as attributes 2 to 999.)

Initializing the input/output support code depends almost entirely on the platform, and the required actions must be inferred from the support code itself. The only platform-independent part of this initialization is related to the colormap that Squeak uses for 8-bit deep displays. This colormap is described in detail in "Display Depths and the Colormap."

Loading the image file into memory is accomplished by calling the generated function

```
readImageFromFileHeapSize(sqImageFile file, int heapSize)
```

where `file` is a handle on the (already opened) image file (of type `sqImageFile` as explained in "Compilation Environment: `sq.h`") and `heapSize` is the amount of memory requested by the user (possibly from a command line option or environment variable). The return value of this function should be ignored.

A suitable default for `heapSize` should be provided. On a dedicated host this might be the total size of physical memory; otherwise, 20 megabytes is certainly enough for all but the most demanding of Squeak images.

Finally, the `main()` function should call the automatically generated function `interpret()`. This function is the entry point into Squeak's interpreter and never returns to its caller (it's an infinite loop). All further interaction with the support code is made by "callbacks" from the generated interpreter code to the support functions described in this chapter.

System Attributes

Squeak applications are sometimes interested in knowing about the host on which they are running. The support code provides this information through "system attributes," which are strings describing various characteristics of the host platform.[20]

Each attribute is identified by an integer. Generated code uses the usual two-function mechanism to retrieve this information from the support code (as described in "C Strings vs. Squeak Strings").

```
int attributeSize(int id)
```

should return the number of characters in the string representing the attribute with the given identifier.

```
int getAttributeIntoLength(int id, int address, int length)
```

is called subsequently to transfer the string into Squeak's heap at the given address. The support code can assume that the id will not change between the generated code calling the first and second of these functions.

Table 8.5 lists the currently assigned identifiers for system attributes, several of which merit further explanation.

The "raw" command line arguments are exactly as they appeared on the command line when the VM was invoked. They include both arguments intended for the VM and arguments intended to be recovered by Squeak applications. The latter will probably be more interested in the "cooked" command line arguments, which are uniquely those that the VM did not recognize as valid switches or the name of an image file.

id	*meaning of attribute*
-1...-N	"raw" command line arguments that were supplied when starting the VM
0	name of the VM executable
1	name of the image file
2...M	"cooked" command line arguments that were supplied when starting the VM
1001	type of the operating system
1002	name of the operating system
1003	architecture of the host CPU
1004	VM's version string

Table 8.5 Squeak's system attribute identifiers and their corresponding meanings.

---

[20]The functions described in this section are connected directly to the primitive method SystemDictionary>>getSystemAttribute:.

The operating system *type* describes the "class" of operating system running on the host, while the *name* gives the particular OS within that class. (For example, GNU/Linux returns `"unix"` for the type and `"linux-gnu"` for the name, whereas BSD returns `"unix"` and `"bsd"`, respectively.) The processor architecture is a string such as `"68k"` (Motorola 68000 series), `"x86"` (Intel i386 and compatible), `"ppc"` (microprocessors based on the Motorola/IBM Power architecture), and so on.[21]

Finally, the interpreter-version string should be taken from the variable

```
char *interpreterVersion
```

which is declared in, and defined automatically by, the generated code.

Support Subsystems

A significant part of the support code is concerned with input/output subsystems. Any given subsystem `foo` implements at least two support functions: `fooInit()` is called to initialize it, and `fooShutdown()` is called to release any resources that it uses. The arguments to these two functions, and any additional support functions that might be necessary, depend on the subsystem itself.

The Macintosh versions of several subsystems are very well documented, and contain much more information than can (or should) be included here. Table 8.6 lists these subsystems and the names of the corresponding Macintosh source files. They will not be described further here; instead the Macintosh files should be copied and then modified for the new host, according to the copious comments therein. To omit any given subsystem "foo," it is sufficient to "fail" the associated initialization

subsystem	*Macintosh source file*
asynchronous file i/o	`sqMacAsyncFilePrims.c`
file directories	`sqMacDirectory.c`
joystick	`sqMacJoystickAndTablet.c`
graphics tablet	`sqMacJoystickAndTablet.c`
MIDI port	`sqMacSerialAndMIDIPort.c`

Table 8.6 Optional subsystems that are well documented in the Macintosh support code. The comments in each of these files are more than sufficient to modify the code for a new platform.

---

[21] Two possible ways to help determine the correct values of the OS attributes may exist on a given platform. The first is the "UTS" information for the host, which is sometimes available via the command "`uname`"; the OS name should be the same as the UTS "system" and the architecture the same as the UTS "machine." Another possibility exists on hosts that use the GNU compiler. The output of "`gcc -v`" includes the canonical name of the host in the form *cpu-vendor-os* (with possibly a fourth component, which should be considered part of the *os*); the first and third components of this canonical host name correspond to Squeak's architecture and OS name attributes.

primitive from within the function `fooInit()`. "Generating the Macintosh Support Files" describes how to extract the corresponding source files from the Squeak image.

The following sections describe only those optional subsystems that are difficult to implement or that have poor documentation in the corresponding Macintosh source file: networking, sound, and serial port support.

Networking

Networking often proves to be one of the trickiest subsystems to implement, mainly because it inherits some peculiar conventions from the Macintosh origins of Squeak. For example, Squeak assumes that performing an `accept()` on a "listening" socket causes the socket itself to be connected to the peer—regardless of the capabilities of the socket implementation on the host. (On the vast majority of platforms the semantics are those of BSD Unix: The "accepted" socket creates a new connected socket, leaving the original socket listening for new connections. On such hosts, we are obliged to destroy the original listening socket and create a new one, since that is the model adopted in Mac OS.)

The networking support can be divided into two independent services: socket-based communication and host name lookup (using the DNS).

Network Initialization and Shutdown

Generated code calls the support function

        int sqNetworkInit(int resolverSemaIndex)

to initialize the networking subsystem. It should perform any platform-specific initialization and then store the `resolverSemaIndex` in a variable for use by the name lookup routines (which are described in "Host Name Lookup"). It should also compute (and remember somewhere) a unique integer that will be used to identify a network "session" (the period between initializing and shutting down the network subsystem). One possibility is to use the current millisecond time. This "session ID" is intended to help detect any attempt to use a "stale" Socket that was saved in the image and subsequently reloaded into a newly launched Squeak. This function is a primitive and should fail if the network cannot be initialized.

The corresponding shutdown function

        int sqNetworkShutdown(void)

should release any resources that were allocated during network initialization.

Socket Creation and Management

When Squeak creates a Socket it calls a primitive method, associated with the support function

```
void sqSocketCreateNetTypeSocketTypeRecvBytesSendBytes\
    SemaIDReadSemaIDWriteSemaID
  (SocketPtr sptr, int netType, int socketType,
   int recvBufSize, int sendBufSize,
   int semaIndex, int readSemaIndex, int writeSemaIndex)
```

(Note that the identifier has been split simply because it is too long to fit the width of the page.) The `sptr` argument is a pointer to a structure (defined in `sq.h`) containing the following fields that must be initialized directly by the support code:

int sessionID	as computed during network initialization
int socketType	0 streams, 1 for datagrams
void *privateSocketPtr	pointer to the associated privateSocket structure

(Squeak will subsequently identify a Socket to the networking support by its associated SocketPtr pointer. The support code will have to de-reference the `privateSocketPtr` field in this structure to retrieve the address of the `privateSocket` structure associated with the C socket.)

The `privateSocket` structure is defined by the support code, and can contain any information that might be required to manage a socket on the host. (The information in this structure is private to the support code, as implied by the name.) This structure should be allocated by the support code (using `malloc()`, for example) when a Socket is created, and then deallocated (using `free()`, for example) when the Socket is destroyed. Figure 8.5 illustrates the relationship between the Socket object in the image and the associated `privateSocket` structure maintained by the support code.

Most implementations will probably want to define at least the following fields in the `privateSocket` structure:

int connSemaIndex	"connect" completion Semaphore
int readSemaIndex	read completion Semaphore
int writeSemaIndex	write completion Semaphore
int state	the "connection status" of the socket
int error	the error code associated with the last operation performed on the socket

Whatever kind of "handle" the host uses to identify a socket should (of course) also be stored in this structure.[22]

The `netType` parameter is intended to specify alternate network protocols or interfaces, but is currently always 0. Nevertheless, the support code should check this parameter (interpreting 0 as meaning "default") and fail the primitive, if the type is non-zero (indicating that the support code is out of date with respect to the Socket facilities provided in the image). The `socketType` is either 0 for stream-based sockets (e.g., TCP) or 1 for datagram-based sockets (e.g., UDP).

---

[22]The name `privateSocket` is an example only: The implementation can call this structure by any name it likes, since generated code never references it directly.

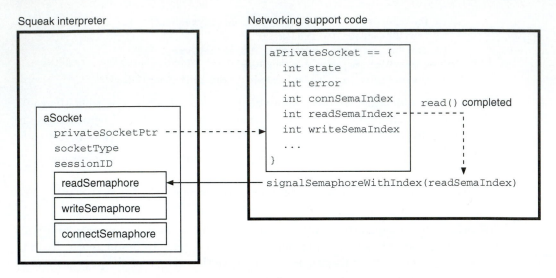

Figure 8.5 The relationship between a Socket object belonging to Squeak and the corresponding `privateSocket` structure belonging to the support code. The three Semaphores are used to signal the completion of operations on the socket: Read and write operations signal the Semaphores corresponding to `readSemaIndex` and `writeSemaIndex`, respectively. Completion of other operations (connecting, accepting, and so on) signal the Semaphore corresponding to `connSemaIndex`. See the text for descriptions of the other fields.

The two buffer size arguments are used to tune the performance of the network code to a particular application. They specify (in bytes) the ideal size of buffer that should be associated with the socket. (These arguments can be ignored if the host does not support changing a socket's buffer sizes.)

The final three arguments specify the indices of Semaphores that are to be signaled ("Interacting with Semaphores") whenever a connection-, read-, or write-related operation is completed for the Socket.

The "connection status" of a socket is read by generated code via the function

```
int sqSocketConnectionStatus(SocketPtr s)
```

which should return one of the following values:

  0   unconnected (the initial state)
  1   waiting for a connection to complete
  2   connected
  3   closed (by the peer)
  4   closed (by the local host)

Similarly, generated code uses the function

```
int  sqSocketError(SocketPtr s)
```

after the failure of a network operation to retrieve a code identifying the problem. The error codes are currently not interpreted by Squeak (since they depend intimately on the host). However, with future expansion in mind, the support code should remember (and provide via this function) whatever error code was indicated by the host operating system.

The support code should also provide the following four functions to retrieve the local and remote host and port numbers associated with a connected socket

```
int  sqSocketLocalAddress(SocketPtr s)
int  sqSocketLocalPort(SocketPtr s)
int  sqSocketRemoteAddress(SocketPtr s)
int  sqSocketRemotePort(SocketPtr s)
```

These functions should return the information in host (not network) byte order, 0 for a socket that is valid but inappropriate (the remote address for an unconnected socket, for example), or -1 if the SocketPtr is invalid (its sessionID is not correct).

Finally, when Squeak destroys a Socket it calls the support function

```
void sqSocketDestroy(SocketPtr s)
```

which should release any private resources (including the privateSocket structure) associated with s. This function is associated with a primitive method and should, therefore, fail the primitive if a problem occurs.

Note that all of the networking support functions that receive a SocketPtr as an argument should perform a minimum of "sanity checking," which means at least verifying that the sessionID stored in the SocketPtr corresponds to the one computed during network initialization.

Connecting and Disconnecting

"Client" and "server" socket connections are implemented by the support functions

```
void sqSocketConnectToPort(SocketPtr s, int addr, int port)
void sqSocketListenOnPort(SocketPtr s, int port)
```

which (as before) use host byte order for addr and port. These functions should also ensure that signalSemaphoreWithIndex() is called for the connection Semaphore associated with s to let Squeak know when a connecting socket is connected or when an accept() has been performed on a listening socket. (It is entirely the responsibility of the support code to detect when a connection request arrives at a listening socket and to perform any subsequent call to accept() that might be required.) Since these functions are associated with primitives, they should fail if a problem occurs during connection.

As mentioned above, listening sockets do not have the usual semantics. After accept()ing a connection, Squeak expects to use the *same* SocketPtr to perform subsequent data transfer on the connected socket. On hosts that use BSD-style sockets, this involves destroying the listening socket and reinitializing the `SocketPtr` and `privateSocket` structures to refer to the newly connected socket.

Connection termination is implemented by the functions

```
void sqSocketCloseConnection(SocketPtr s)
void sqSocketAbortConnection(SocketPtr s)
```

which are associated with primitive methods. The first should fail if the associated socket is not connected; the second should fail only if the `SocketPtr` is invalid for the current session.

Sending and Receiving Data

Data transfer is implemented by the two functions

```
int sqSocketReceiveDataBufCount
    (SocketPtr s, int buf, int bufSize)
```

and

```
int sqSocketSendDataBufCount
    (SocketPtr s, int buf, int bufSize)
```

in which `buf` is the address of the data to be transferred and `bufSize` is the size of the data measured in bytes. These functions should return the actual number of bytes transferred (which can be 0, in the case of an error).

Generated code also requires two support functions that answer whether data transfer can take place.

```
int sqSocketReceiveDataAvailable(SocketPtr s)
```

should return `true` or `false` to indicate whether data is available for `s`; similarly,

```
int sqSocketSendDone(SocketPtr s)
```

indicates whether data can be written without blocking the caller. Both functions should return `-1` if the `SocketPtr` is not valid for the current session.

The support code should also ensure that the read or write **Semaphore** (as appropriate) associated with the socket is signalled, whenever an operation completes.[23] Figure 8.5 illustrates this interaction for the case of a "read" operation that has been completed.

---

[23]Note that these **Semaphores** should always be signalled when an operation completes, even if the operation completes immediately.

Optional BSD-Style Connection Semantics

A recent addition to Squeak supports sockets that implement BSD-style semantics, in which the connected socket does not replace the listening socket when a
connection request is accept()ed. The function

```
void sqSocketListenOnPortBacklogSize
  (SocketPtr s, int port, int backlogSize)
```

is similar to sqListenOnPort(), but should succeed only if the host supports BSD-
style sockets. The backlogSize indicates the number of pending connections that
should be allowed on the listening socket. This function should ensure that the
connection Semaphore associated with s is signaled when an accept() can be performed (but it should *not* perform the accept()). Squeak will subsequently call

```
void sqSocketAcceptFromRecvBytesSendBytes\
    SemaIDReadSemaIDWriteSemaID
  (SocketPtr s, SocketPtr serverSocket,
   int recvBufSize, int sendBufSize,
   int semaIndex, int readSemaIndex, int writeSemaIndex)
```

to perform the accept(), passing the original listening socket as serverSocket and
a newly created SocketPtr as s. This function should initialize s as for any other
newly created socket, including allocating a new privateSocket structure for it.
Both of these functions are primitives, and should fail if an error occurs.

If the host does not support BSD-style semantics for listening sockets, then it
should fail these two primitives, in which case Squeak will revert to the (original,
Macintosh-style) behavior described previously.

Backwards Compatibility

Prior to version 2.8 of Squeak, all socket-based input/output used a single Semaphore
to communicate asynchronous events to the virtual machine. For compatibility with
older images, the support code should therefore implement simplified versions of the
socket creation and accept the following functions:

```
void sqSocketAcceptFromRecvBytesSendBytesSemaID
  (SocketPtr s, SocketPtr serverSocket,
   int recvBufSize, int sendBufSize, int semaIndex);

void sqSocketCreateNetTypeSocketTypeRecvBytesSendBytesSemaID
  (SocketPtr s, int netType, int socketType,
   int recvBufSize, int sendBufSize, int semaIndex)
```

These functions are trivial. They are identical to their "three-semaphore" equiva-
lents, except that they take only a single semaIndex argument. They can simply
call the three-semaphore versions, passing their arguments unmodified and reusing

their single `semaIndex` argument three times as the `semaIndex`, `readSemaIndex`, and `writeSemaIndex` arguments.

Host Name Lookup

Squeak supports host name resolution via the DNS. The interface is a little larger than might be expected, to permit asynchronous lookup on hosts that support it.

Initialization is implicit in the network initialization described earlier. The support code need only store the `resolverSemaIndex` that was passed to `sqNetworkInit()`.

When Squeak wants to convert a host name string into a numeric address, it calls the support function

```
void sqResolverStartNameLookup(char *hostName, int nameSize)
```

where `nameSize` is the length of the (Squeak) string in `hostName`. The support code should signal the `resolverSema` (saved during network initialization) when the lookup has completed. Squeak will then call

```
int sqResolverNameLookupResult(void)
```

to recover the result, which should be a numeric address in host byte order or `-1` to indicate failure.

Reverse lookups (addresses to names) should also be provided by the support code. Squeak calls

```
void sqResolverStartAddrLookup(int address)
```

to begin the lookup, which should cause the `resolverSema` to be signaled when the lookup is finished. To retrieve the result, Squeak uses the usual pair of functions, viz.,

```
int sqResolverAddrLookupResultSize(void)
```

and

```
void sqResolverAddrLookupResult(char *nameForAddress,
                                int nameSize)
```

to recover the length of the result and then perform the actual transfer of bytes into a Squeak String.

Generated code will call the support routine

```
int sqResolverLocalAddress(void)
```

if it decides to abort a lookup operation before it has completed.

The support code should also provide three trivial functions:

```
int sqResolverLocalAddress(void)
```

should return the address of the local host;

```
int sqResolverError(void)
```

should return the operating system error code for the last operation in the case of failure (this value is currently not interpreted by Squeak, but should be correct to allow for future expansion); and finally,

```
int sqResolverStatus(void)
```

should return one of the following values to indicate the current status of the resolver subsystem:

0   the resolver is uninitialized (`sqNetInit()` not yet called)
1   the last lookup was successful
2   a lookup is currently in progress
3   the last lookup failed

Sound

Squeak supports the generation and playback of CD-quality stereo audio.[24] The sound subsystem contains, as always, the usual initialization and shutdown functions:

```
int soundInit(void);
int soundShutdown(void);
```

Sound output is initiated by calling the function

```
int snd_Start
  (int frameCount, int samplesPerSec,
   int stereo, int semaIndex)
```

where `samplesPerSec` is the number of 16-bit samples to be played per second, `stereo` is `true` for stereo or `false` for mono, `semaIndex` refers to a `Semaphore` that should be signaled when sound input/output completes (see "Interacting with Semaphores"), and `frameSize` indicates the amount of buffer space that should be allocated for sound output. The size of output buffer (in bytes) that should be allocated is twice the `frameCount` for mono (two bytes per sample) or four times `frameCount` for stereo (two bytes per channel per sample). This function should return `true` if initialization is successful, `false` if not.

---

[24]An upper limit on sound quality is imposed by the amount of processor power available. Recent machines have no trouble achieving CD quality.

The function

    int snd_AvailableSpace(void)

should return the amount of space available in the output buffer, measured in bytes (not frames).

Three functions are used to insert sound into the output buffer.

    int snd_PlaySilence(void);

is used to fill the output buffer with silence. It should return the number of bytes of space remaining in the output buffer.

    int snd_PlaySamplesFromAtLength
        (int frameCount, int arrayIndex, int startIndex)

is called to insert **frameCount** samples into the output buffer, from memory at the address **arrayIndex + (startIndex * 2)** (mono) or **arrayIndex + (startIndex * 4)** (stereo). The sound should begin playing immediately if possible. This function should return the amount of available space remaining in the output buffer (measured in bytes).

    int snd_InsertSamplesFromLeadTime
        (int frameCount, int srcBufPtr, int samplesOfLeadTime)

is called to insert **frameCount** samples from **srcBufPtr** into the output buffer, with the specified number of samples of lead time (delay) before the sound beings to play. Again, this function should return the amount of remaining available space in the output buffer.

Finally,

    int snd_Stop(void)

is called to abort sound output. It should take appropriate measures to stop sound output as soon as possible.

Sound input is handled via four support functions.

    int snd_SetRecordLevel(int level)

is called to set the input gain to a value between 0 (minimum gain) and 1,000 (maximum gain).

    int snd_StartRecording
        (int desiredSamplesPerSec, int stereo, int semaIndex)

is called to initiate recording, with arguments analogous to those for sound output. The actual input sampling rate should be returned by the function

    double snd_GetRecordingSampleRate(void)

Data transfer from the input buffer to Squeak's memory is the responsibility of

```
int snd_RecordSamplesIntoAtLength
    (int buf, int startSliceIndex, int bufferSize)
```

where `buf` is the destination address, `bufferSize` is measured in bytes, and `start-SliceIndex` is the sample offset in `buf` from which data should be written. Since this offset is measured samples, it should be scaled by two (mono) or four (stereo) to arrive at a byte offset. The routine should take care not to write past the end of `buf` (remembering that `bufferSize` is measured in bytes, not samples). The return value is the number of samples (not bytes) that were actually transferred. Finally,

```
int snd_StopRecording(void)
```

is called to disable recording. The return value is ignored.

Serial Port

As with the other subsystems, serial port support begins with the two functions

```
int serialPortInit(void)
```

and

```
int serialPortShutdown(void)
```

for initialization and subsequent releasing of resources. The first of these is a primitive and should therefore fail if no serial ports are supported. Serial ports are "opened" via the support function

```
int serialPortOpen
    (int portNum,
     int baudRate, int stopBitsType,
     int parityType, int dataBits,
     int inFlowCtrl, int outFlowCtrl,
     int xOnChar, int xOffChar)
```

The possible values of these parameters are shown in Table 8.7. When a serial port is no longer needed, the generated code calls

```
int serialPortClose(int portNum)
```

to release any resources owned by the specified port.

Data transfer is effected by the two support functions

```
int serialPortReadInto(int portNum, int count, int bufferPtr)
```

and

```
int serialPortWriteFrom(int portNum, int count, int bufferPtr)
```

where `bufferPtr` is the address of the data source/destination, and `count` is the number of bytes to be transferred. These functions should return the number of bytes actually read/written and should be immediate (even if no data can be transferred).

portNum	the port number, 0 or 1
baudRate	requested port speed
stopBitsType	0 means 1.5 stop bits
	1 means 1 stop bit
	2 means 2 stop bits
parityType	0 means no parity
	1 means odd parity
	2 means even parity
dataBits	5–8
inFlowCtrl	true to use h/w flow control
outFlowCtrl	true to use h/w flow control
xOnChar	ASCII value of XON character, or 0
xOffChar	ASCII value of XOFF character, or 0

Table 8.7   Parameters passed to `serialPortOpen()`.

Plugin Modules

Many primitives are "hardwired" into interpreter and identified by a numeric index. This arrangement has several drawbacks, including possibly limiting the number of primitives that can be provided[25] and requiring the virtual machine to be recompiled whenever primitives are modified or added.

To circumvent these limitations, Squeak provides a mechanism for assigning names to primitives whose definitions are loaded at runtime from external, dynamically loaded, shared libraries (sometimes called "DLLs"). From within Squeak, these functions appear as "named primitives," and the dynamic libraries in which they are defined are called "modules" (or "plugins"). For this mechanism to work, the support code must provide functions for finding, loading, and resolving names in dynamically loaded libraries.

```
int ioLoadModule(char *pluginName)
```

is called by the generated code to load the dynamic library with the given `pluginName`. This name does not make any assumptions about the host. If there is a standard prefix or suffix for dynamic libraries then the support code must add it to the `pluginName`. Also, if there are several standard places in which to search for the library, then the support code must implement the search explicitly (the `pluginName` is *never* a pathname). This function should answer a unique non-zero integer "handle" that will be used to identify the plugin to the two other plugin support functions. If no library corresponding to the `pluginName` can be found,

---

[25]The primitive "dispatch" mechanism is translated into a `C` `switch` statement in the generated code, and some compilers place a limit on the number of `case` labels that can appear within a `switch`.

then this function should return 0.

```
int ioFindExternalFunctionIn(char *name, int moduleHandle)
```

should search the plugin module (dynamic library) having the given handle (obtained from a previous call to `ioLoadModule()`) for the function corresponding to `name`. `name` is an identifier for a C function, exactly as it appears in the plugin source code. If the host has any special conventions for symbols in binary files (for example, some binary formats prefix all symbols with an underscore "_"), then the support code must take this into account. This function should return the address of the function corresponding to `name`, or 0 if the function is not present in the module.

```
int ioFreeModule(int moduleHandle)
```

is called when Squeak wants to "unload" a plugin module. This function should return 1. If the host does not support the unloading of dynamic libraries or if an error occurs, then it should return 0.

For an initial port of Squeak, all three of these functions can be defined trivially to return 0. They should *not* "fail" the primitive. (This detail is small, but important.)

Profiling

Smalltalk (the SystemDictionary) contains four methods for collecting run-time profiling information. These methods are associated with four optional support functions (their return values are ignored):

`int startProfiling(void)`	turns profiling on
`int stopProfiling(void)`	turns profiling off
`int clearProfile(void)`	should delete any stale profiling information (for example, clearing a buffer of sampled PC values to zero)
`int dumpProfile(void)`	should save the collected profiling information in a form appropriate for the host

Profiling is mainly of interest to the implementors of the Squeak interpreter and should not be considered a priority in a new port.

"Headless" Operation

Squeak provides some impressive "server" capabilities (for Web sites in particular). A Squeak-based server is not normally intended for interactive use, and the usual graphics/keyboard/mouse facilities are at best irrelevant (and at worst a security risk). "Headless" operation refers to running Squeak with these facilities disabled.

Most of the current ports of Squeak support this mode of operation, either in response to a command line option or by using a VM compiled with a special preprocessor symbol to conditionally omit these facilities in the support code.

If appropriate, any new port should try to implement a headless mode of operation. Doing so should require only the following changes in support code behavior:

- The warning beep is disabled. `ioBeep` should, therefore, return 0 without doing anything else.

- Graphical output "succeeds" without actually transferring anything to a physical screen. The following functions should, therefore, do nothing (and return 0):

      ioShowDisplay(),
      ioForceDisplayUpdate(),
      ioSetFullScreen(),
      ioSetDisplayMode(),
      ioSetCursor(), and
      ioSetCursorWithMask().

- Keyboard and mouse input is disabled. `ioGetKeystroke()` and `ioPeekKeystroke()` should return -1 to indicate that there is nothing in the keyboard input buffer. `ioGetButtonState()` and `ioMousePoint()` should return 0 immediately.

- There is no screen, so there is no screen size. `ioScreenSize()` should return some harmless default value, such as `0x00400040` (64 × 64).

- `ioHasDisplayDepth()` should simply answer "yes" (return 1) for all display depths.

- There are no keyboard/mouse input events. `ioProcessEvents()` can return 0 immediately (or possibly after performing any non-interactive polling that it might also be responsible for—network or serial port I/O, for example).

Conclusion

Squeak is a (rapidly) moving target. The user community is adding new features at a furious rate, and it is almost certain that Squeak will include new capabilities—and associated support code—by the time this book appears in print. This need not be a cause for alarm, for two reasons.

First, the fact that most new facilities are "optional" means that they do not affect the initial task of porting Squeak to a new platform; the information presented here should remain relevant (and sufficient) for a long time to come. Truly platform-dependent additions happen rarely and are likely to be limited to very minor details such as provision of additional system attributes.

Second, Squeak's support for adding new primitive methods decouples the support code from many new "low-level" parts of the implementation. Writing new primitives in Smalltalk and then automatically generating the equivalent C is a routine activity for Squeak virtual machine hackers. Such generated primitives, which are necessarily platform independent, are complemented nicely by "plugin modules" for dynamically adding primitives to a running system. These modules can include (and encapsulate) platform-specific details without affecting the "intrinsic" support code for a given platform at all.

Acknowledgments

I am grateful to Andreas Raab and John Maloney for their detailed comments on, and suggestions for improving, the first draft of this chapter.

Ian Piumarta is responsible for the Unix port of Squeak. He has been hooked on Squeak since one week after its initial release, on Smalltalk since meeting ParcPlace's PS2 in 1986, on Unix since scrounging his first account in 1984, and on programming language implementation since reading "K&R" in 1980 (and solving the problem of not having access to a C compiler in a "rather direct" manner). He graduated from the University of Manchester (UK) in 1986 and was later awarded a Ph.D. by the same institution for work on compiling Smalltalk directly to native code.

In 1993, he failed utterly to resist an invitation to move to Paris to work at IRCAM (*Institut de Recherche et Coordination Acoustique/Musique*), the French research institute for contemporary music. He is currently a researcher at the LIP6 (*Laboratoire d'Informatique de l'Université Paris VI*) and INRIA (*Institut National de Recherche en Informatique et Automatique*), where he divides his time between working on highly dynamic/reflexive systems and "infecting" as many of his students and colleagues as possible with the "dynamic language virus."

He can be contacted at `ian.piumarta@inria.fr`

9

Extending the Squeak Virtual Machine

Andrew C. Greenberg
Carlton Fields

Why Extend Squeak?

Extending Squeak's virtual machine assumes an answer to an important threshold question: Why do it? Squeak is an exquisite and highly portable programming environment that is capable of performing most things a programmer might want to do. Squeak has robust memory management and debugging tools that protect the system from catastrophic errors and inform programmers as to their cause. Squeak supports Smalltalk and, therefore, an object-oriented programming paradigm that results in highly reusable and extendable code. Squeak programs are remarkable in their capacity to perform complex applications across many platforms—identically, pixel for pixel.

In contrast, each virtual machine (VM) extension bypasses the Squeak object memory model. Therefore, the extension reintroduces the possibility of hardware crashes due to memory leaks, hanging pointers, address errors, and the panoply of things that can go wrong in traditional programming. VM extensions often rely on fixed assumptions about the internal structure of the objects on which they operate and thus limit the scope of reusability and extensibility of objects that depend on the extension. Otherwise routine operations on Smalltalk objects so extended can result in strange and unpredictable behaviors. Finally, VM extensions tend to introduce machine dependencies.

Notwithstanding all of this, however, there are sometimes compelling reasons to extend the Squeak VM. Among these are to achieve improvements in performance and to obtain enhanced functionality not otherwise possible without an extension.

Squeaking Out More Speed

Squeak programs are not compiled to native machine language, but are compiled to an intermediate representation called bytecodes. Bytecodes are interpreted by the Squeak VM, a computer program that is, in turn, executed on the target machine. Because of this intermediate processing, the overall system typically runs slower, sometimes much slower, than a corresponding C language program that was directly compiled to machine language. Additionally, the Squeak object model carries an unavoidable overhead, since virtually every program operation requires some machine resources to support the Smalltalk message sending and memory management semantics.

In most cases, benefits in portability, power, and safety that derive from the Squeak design decisions may substantially outweigh any cost in speed and other resources. Moreover, as costs plummet for increasingly high-speed processors, demand for "on the metal" speed diminishes. Nevertheless, there are times when the need for speed is paramount—where the lack of speed equates to a lack of functionality.

Modern software design methodologies focus on postponing attention to performance issues until later stages of the system life cycle: "Make it work, make it right, then make it fast." Once a working and sound model of a system exists, traditional "tuning" solutions entirely within Smalltalk often provide adequate performance solutions. Since programs tend to spend the vast majority of their time executing tiny portions of its program code, this approach can often yield excellent and efficient results while permitting a programmer to focus energies on refining only small portions of the code. Using a Squeak profiler to identify program bottlenecks, the particular method or methods can often be identified and improved to a degree sufficient to satisfy a program's requirements.

This approach works well particularly in view of Smalltalk's object-oriented infrastructure. A complete program can often be improved enormously without making changes to the key program logic merely by changing the internal representation and implementation of a single class. Where bottlenecks are not so localized, a program can often be refactored to facilitate speedup efforts. In other cases, straightforward speedups can be obtained by specializing generalized system classes used by the program. For example, a program using the Smalltalk Set classes can often be improved by substituting (without changing the main code) another class that efficiently exploits particular properties of the underlying data.

Sometimes, however, traditional tuning fails to provide speed-up sufficient for an essential function. In such cases, replacing a performance bottleneck with straight-line machine language may make possible functionality that could not be adequately delivered otherwise.

Roaring Like a Mouse: New Power and Functionality

Squeak is extraordinary. The standard image contains arbitrary precision arithmetic, a comprehensive set of collection protocols, several graphic user-interface frameworks, a flexible 3-D graphics engine, a reusable web server, support for most traditional Internet protocols, and powerful sound-processing capabilities, to name just a few of the key built-in "goodies." Underneath, Squeak provides a vast set of primitives providing low-level access to many important machine functions.

Nevertheless, the functional capability of computers continues to increase, and Squeak's designers could not have anticipated every possible need for a system-level primitive. Sometimes, the requirements for access to low-level drivers or local operating system functionality is essential to perform-specific functions. Without the ability to extend Squeak, some hardware might not be usable at all.

In other cases, an existing machine-specific or portable non-Smalltalk library may already exist, providing specific capabilities that would be necessary or helpful for a Squeak application. Particularly where the library is of general utility and effectively maintained by others, it may be desirable to code an extension for Squeak to provide direct access to the functionality of that library, rather than diverting resources unnecessarily to re-invent the wheel in Smalltalk.

These two issues, access to low-level drivers and access to already existing non-Smalltalk libraries, are among the most common reasons for using Squeak extensions.

Anatomy of an Extension

Squeak can be extended in various ways: by rewriting the interpreter, by adding a numbered primitive, or by adding a named primitive. The first two methods require rebuilding the entire Squeak system. By far, the more flexible and adaptable solution—and the primary subject of this chapter—are named, or "pluggable," primitives. On most systems, these named primitives can be implemented as shared libraries, such as Windows DLL libraries.

Once a plugin is made available to the VM using native operating system conventions (in the MacOS, for example, by dragging plugin files into certain folders), a Smalltalk method can call one of its primitives using a specialized extension of the Smalltalk syntax for primitives. This method (the *calling method*) and the primitive function in the plugin communicate in a specialized manner. Ultimately, the primitive returns control to Squeak with a Smalltalk object as its answer.

The process of extending Squeak with named primitives entails

1. creating a Smalltalk interface to the named primitives and

2. creating the Smalltalk plugin and its named primitives.

The Plugin Module

The plugin itself is an external library of machine-language routines, including (1) one or more parameterless functions (the primitive functions) each returning a 32-bit integer result and (2) a separate function taking a single 32-bit parameter, which must be named **setInterpreter**. The primitive functions may be generated in any manner convenient to the author, but are typically generated from source code written in a subset of Smalltalk called *Slang*, which is then translated to C and, in turn, compiled to machine language.

The Interpreter Proxy

Prior to the first call of any primitive in the plugin, the Squeak VM calls setInterpreter, passing to the plugin a pointer to a data structure known as the *interpreter proxy*. The interpreter proxy includes pointers to various internal data structures of the VM and to a subset of the VM's internal subroutines. The plugin saves the interpreter proxy in shared memory for use by the primitives when communicating with Squeak.

Linkage Conventions for Primitive Functions

In operation, the Squeak VM represents every Smalltalk object as a 32-bit integer value, called an *oop*. To call a primitive, the VM creates a stack comprising oops representing the actual parameters and an oop representing the object to which the primitive message was sent. The primitive will thereafter either succeed or fail, and the fact of success or failure is recorded in a global VM variable named **successFlag**. If the primitive succeeds, the primitive is expected to pop the parameter and sender oops from the stack and to put (or leave) in its place a single oop representing the answer to the message. If the primitive fails, then the primitive is expected to leave the stack unchanged. Strict compliance with these linkage conventions is essential to the proper operation of a primitive function.

Key to building extensions, therefore, is an understanding of how Squeak interacts with primitives, and vice-versa. To write a primitive, one must understand in some detail how Squeak represents Smalltalk objects, the workings of the Squeak memory model, and how representations of information can be shared between the VM and the primitive.

The rest of this chapter will discuss the mechanics of building a plugin VM extension. We will begin with a brief introduction to the Slang Smalltalk subset and how to use the Squeak translators and interpreters. We will then detail how Squeak represents Smalltalk data objects and how to use the interpreter proxy to access and manipulate that information. We will then outline the mechanics of how a primitive function can use the interpreter proxy to interact with the Squeak interpreter. Finally, we conclude by putting these pieces together concretely with an example plugin for manipulating large blocks of structured text.

Speaking in Slang

Although named primitive functions may be written in any language capable of generating a shared library with the appropriate linkage conventions, most are written in a subset of Smalltalk known as Slang. Slang code can be written and tested in the Squeak development environment and then translated into C for compilation to a plugin.

A First Plugin

We will begin with a simple example, building a trivial pluggable primitive that answers the SmallInteger instance 17. We begin by creating a subclass of Interpreter-Plugin:

```
InterpreterPlugin subclass: #ExamplePlugin
    instanceVariableNames: ''
    classVariableNames: ''
    poolDictionaries: ''
    category: 'VMConstruction–Plugins'
```

The Primitive Function

InterpreterPlugin provides the essential functionality for constructing a plugin, including code to declare and initialize the interpreter proxy (which will be stored in an instance variable named interpreterProxy) and the infrastructure for translating the plugin to C. To create our primitive function, open a browser on ExamplePlugin, and add the following method:

```
answerSeventeen
    "Extension to answer the SmallInteger seventeen"
    self export: true.
    interpreterProxy
        pop: 1
        thenPush: (interpreterProxy integerObjectOf: 17)
```

The first statement has no effect when interpreted in Smalltalk, but, during translation, identifies the translated procedure as one with an external label in the resulting library. The second statement pops the Smalltalk context stack and then pushes an object handle (called an *oop*) representing the SmallInteger instance 17.

The Smalltalk Interface

Once coded, this method can be tested by executing the following command in a workspace:

ExamplePlugin doPrimitive: 'answerSeventeen'

The statement yields the answer "17." While hardly useful, this code nevertheless illustrates how a primitive might be built. Once the extension is built, the Smalltalk interface can be written. Primitives are conventionally invoked by methods written substantially as follows:

answerSeventeen
     "Answer the SmallInteger seventeen"
     <primitive: 'answerSeventeen' module: 'ExamplePlugin'>
     ↑ExamplePlugin doPrimitive: 'answerSeventeen'

This method, when executed, will seek to invoke the answerSeventeen primitive. However, when the primitive is not available or when the primitive is available but fails during execution, it begins to interpret the remaining Smalltalk code. Assuming that this method were added to class Foo, one would test the primitive by executing the following in a workspace:

Foo new answerSeventeen

We have not yet built the plugin module. Therefore, the primitive will fail, and the result of the interpreted code will be answered.

Translating and Building the Plugin

Once you are satisfied that the Slang program is correct, a plugin library can be created by executing

ExamplePlugin translate

to invoke the Slang translator and generate a file, "ExamplePlugin.c," containing the C code corresponding to the Slang set forth in class ExamplePlugin. That C program may then be compiled using native tools to generate the plugin library.[1]

---

[1] Translated C code may depend upon one or more include files, copies of which are stored in the standard Smalltalk image. You may generate these in text file form by executing the expression InterpreterSupportCode writePluginSupportFiles in a workspace.

Slang: A Brief Summary

Expressions

Slang recognizes Smalltalk literals (including integers, characters, symbols and strings) that are translated into corresponding C-language constants. Symbols are translated into strings. Array literals are not permitted. Assignments from expressions to identifiers are translated into C-language assignments from the translation of the expression to the corresponding identifier.

Unary Message Sends

Unary message sends are generally translated into a procedure call of the procedure identified, passing the receiver as a parameter. Thus,

```
anObject frobosinate
```

is translated to

```
frobosinate(anObject);
```

Binary Message Sends

Binary message sends are generally translated into a procedure call of the procedure identified, passing receiver as a first parameter and the right-most argument as a second parameter. Hence,

```
anObject frobosinateWith: aWidget
```

is translated to

```
frobosinateWith(anObject, aWidget);
```

Keyword Message Sends

Keyword message sends are generally translated into a procedure call of the procedure identified (by conacatenating all of the keywords without colons), passing the receiver as a first parameter and the remaining arguments in order. Thus,

```
anObject frobosinateWith: aWidget andWith: anotherWidget
```

is translated to

```
frobosinateWithandWith(anObject, aWidget, anotherWidget);
```

Message Sends to Self or to InterpreterProxy

An exception to the general rules stated above occurs when messages are sent to either of the "special objects" self or interpreterProxy. Messages sent to *self* are translated as described earlier, but without self as the initial parameter. Messages sent to interpreterProxy are also translated as above, except that the function call will have the string "`interpreterProxy->`" prepended. Therefore,

        self frobosinateWith: a

is translated to

```
frobosinateWith(a);
```

and

        interpreterProxy integerObjectOf: 17

is translated to

```
interpreterProxy->integerObjectOf(17);
```

Builtin Message Sends

Certain messages are not translated in accordance with the preceding rules, but rather to C-language expressions with semantics similar to the corresponding Smalltalk operation: &, |, and:, or:, not, $+$, $-$, $*$, $/$, $//$, $\backslash\backslash$, $<<$, $>>$, min:, max:, bitAnd:, bitOr:, bitXor:, bitShift:, bitInvert32, raisedTo:, $<$, $<=$, $=$, $>$, $>=$, $\sim=$, $==$, and $\sim\sim$. Other messages are also given special meanings, as described shortly.

Arrays

The expression

        foo at: exp

is translated to

```
foo[exp]
```

and the expression

        foo at: exp1 put: exp2

is translated to

```
foo[exp1] = exp2
```

The messages basicAt: and basicAt:put: are translated in the same way.

Control Structures

The following Smalltalk "control structure messages" are translated to C-language statements with similar semantics:

```
[stmtList] whileTrue: [stmtList2]
[stmtList] whileFalse: [stmtList2]
[stmtList] whileTrue
[stmtList] whileFalse
exp1 to: exp2: do: [stmtList]
exp1 to: exp2: by: exp3 do: [stmtList]
exp1 ifTrue: [stmtList]
exp1 ifFalse: [stmtList]
exp1 ifTrue: [stmtList] ifFalse: [stmtList]
exp1 ifFalse: [stmtList] ifTrue: [stmtList]
stmt1. stmt2
```

Note that the square brackets are used here for syntactic purposes only in these control structures. Slang does not support Smalltalk code blocks.

Methods

A method in Smalltalk will be translated to a C-language function returning an integer. If the method is declared in keyword form, the C-language function will be named by concatenating all of the keywords, but without semicolons. Methods may be translated to be called directly as primitives from Smalltalk, as described earlier, or may be translated to be called as subroutines from C-language code, as described later. Temporary variables will be translated as local variables for the function. Thus,

```
frobosinateWith: a andWith: b
    | temp |
    ...Slang code...
```

will be translated as

```
int frobosinateWithandWith(int a, int b)
{
    int temp;
    ...Translated C code...
}
```

If you should want the procedure to return a value with a type other than int, you may use the directive

```
self returnTypeC: 'char *'.
```

C Language Declarations and Coercion of Expressions

Unless you specify otherwise, Slang will translate all method temporaries into C variables defined as integer types. You can declare the variables differently in translated code by using the Slang directive

```
self var: #sPointer declareC: 'char *sPointer'.
```

To satisfy C-type checking semantics, it may be necessary to direct Slang to coerce an expression from one type to another. This can be accomplished with the Slang directive

```
self cCoerce: aSmalltalkExpression to: 'int'
```

Suppose the object at the top of the Smalltalk stack corresponded to an array of characters such as a Smalltalk instance of class **String**. You might use the following Slang code to access its elements:

```
self var: #stringObj declareC: 'int stringObj'.
self var: #stringPtr declareC: 'char *stringPtr'.
self var: #stringSize declareC: 'int stringSize'.
. . .
stringObj ← interpreterProxy stackValue: 0.
stringSize ← interpreterProxy stSizeOf: stringObj.
stringPtr ← self
    cCoerce: (interpreterProxy arrayValueOf: stringObj)
    to: 'char *'.
```

Global Variables

Global variables for a plugin are declared in Smalltalk as instance variables of the InterpreterPlugin subclass and can be further declared for purposes of C-language type definitions by adding a method named declareCVarsIn: to the *class* side of the InterpreterPlugin subclass. With global declarations, however, a string (rather than a symbol) is used as the parameter for the var: keyword. An example follows:

declareCVarsIn: cg
```
    cg var: 'm23ResultX' declareC:'double m23ResultX'.
    cg var: 'm23ResultY' declareC:'double m23ResultY'.
    cg var: 'm23ArgX' declareC:'double m23ArgX'.
    cg var: 'm23ArgY' declareC:'double m23ArgY'.
```

Subroutines

Subroutines are useful in most programming situations. Writing named primitives is no different. For simplicity, many named primitive functions serve only as the "glue" between Smalltalk and the operative subroutines, merely reading and verifying the parameters from the stack and data from the receiver. That information is then passed to the operative subroutine and returned to the glue primitive function, which clears and then pushes the return value back onto the stack in accordance with the linkage conventions.

You may call a Slang subroutine simply by sending the subroutine as a message to the "special object" self, as, for example, in

> self subroutineOn: aFirstValue and: aSecondValue.

In turn, the subroutine might be coded as follows:

> **subroutineOn: aFirstParm and: aSecondParm**
>   self var: #aFirstParm declareC: 'char *'.
>   self var: #aSecondParm declareC: 'float'.
>   self returnTypeC: 'float'.
>   . . . *Slang code for the subroutine* . . .

No special linkage conventions need be followed for these internal Slang subroutines. Those linkage conventions apply only to procedures that will be directly called from Smalltalk using the "<primitive: . . . module: . . . >" mechanism.

The Slang-to-C translator automatically inlines a subroutine if the subroutine is sufficiently short or if it contains, at or near the beginning of its code, a Slang inline: directive of the form

> self inline: true.

Certain subroutines, for example subroutines containing the cCode: directive, will not be inlined even if the subroutine contains an inline: directive.

Inline C-Language Code

Any C-language expression may be inserted into translated code with the expression

> self cCode: 'InternalMemorySystemSubroutine(foo)'.

Of course, this code will not be executed in any way when the code is being interpreted. However, when translated to C, the string will be inserted verbatim, followed by a semicolon.

It is sometimes helpful, particularly when testing, to have certain Smalltalk code executed during translation. For that reason, the expression

> self cCode: 'InternalMemorySystemsubroutine(foo)'
>   inSmalltalk: [. . . *Smalltalk code* . . .]

will be translated as described earlier. However, when it is interpreted, the corresponding Smalltalk code will be executed.

TestInterpreterPlugin

Squeak also provides a second, upwardly compatible, Slang subset translator, the
TestCodeGenerator. TestCodeGenerator is anticipated, in time, to supplant the present Slang interpreter. The TestCodeGenerator provides the same facilities as the
translator described previously, but also provides means for automatically generating plugin linkage code and to greatly facilitate the writing of pluggable primitives.

To use the TestCodeGenerator, define the plugin class as a subclass of TestInterpreterPlugin instead of InterpreterPlugin. A complete description of TestCodeGenerator is beyond the scope of this article. Although documentation is regrettably quite
scant as this article is written, more will be forthcoming in time. In the meanwhile,
the following page from the Squeak Swiki may be helpful:

        http://minnow.cc.gatech.edu/squeak/850

The next section discusses in some depth the internal structure of objects as
they are represented in the Squeak Virtual Machine.

The Shape of a Smalltalk Object

In Smalltalk, everything is an object. Ultimately, however, objects must be represented in hardware as bits and bytes. Unaided by the abstractions of the Smalltalk
model, primitives and the Squeak VM must concern themselves with this uncomfortable reality. To write primitives, a programmer must know that the Squeak VM
represents each and every Smalltalk object with a 32-bit integer value, known as an
oop. The internal representations and interpretations of these oops, however, vary
substantially depending upon the object represented by the oop. It may be helpful
to consider four distinct categories, or "shapes," of Squeak object representations
and how they may be manipulated in Slang and C:

1. Smalltalk SmallInteger objects

2. Other non-indexable Smalltalk objects

3. Smalltalk objects indexable to oops

4. Smalltalk objects indexable to data other than oops

From a Smalltalk point of view, the first category is self-explanatory. The second
category includes, for example, instances of classes Boolean, Fraction, and Object,
but also includes objects that contain indexed objects as instance variables, but are
not themselves indexed, such as instances of classes Form and Set. The third category, objects indexable to oops, include instances of class Array. The last, objects
indexable to things other than oops, include objects indexable to byte or word data,
such as instances of classes LargePositiveInteger, ByteArray, and WordArray.

SmallInteger Objects

Primarily for efficiency reasons, Squeak represents 31-bit signed integer values (Smalltalk SmallInteger objects) with an oop containing that integer data. Oops representing other types of data are pointers to an object "header" stored elsewhere in memory. Since all object headers begin on word boundaries, these pointer oops are even numbers. Squeak exploits this fact by representing SmallIntegers in odd-numbered oops. SmallInteger oops are therefore stored in the following format:

bit index	31 30 29 $\quad$ ... $\quad$ 3 2 1 0
data	... 31-bit SmallInteger data ... 1

While every SmallInteger can be represented by a int-type C variable, the converse is not true. C int variables containing values greater than or equal to 2^{30} or less than -2^{30} will not "fit" into the 31 bits available for SmallInteger data.

Converting between SmallInteger Oops and Values

The interpreter proxy provides two methods to help back and forth between the oop representation of a SmallInteger and the actual numeric value represented:

Smalltalk	C
interpreterProxy integerObjectOf: value	`interpreterProxy->integerObjectOf(value)`
interpreterProxy integerValueOf: oop	`interpreterProxy->integerValueOf(oop)`

If the argument of integerValueOf: is an oop that represents a SmallInteger object, the method will answer a signed C value corresponding to the SmallInteger. The answer will otherwise be undefined, even if the argument does represent an integer object, such as a LargePositiveInteger. Conversely, if an argument to integerObjectOf is within the range of values that can be represented by a SmallInteger, then the method will answer with the corresponding SmallInteger oop. If a SmallInteger cannot represent the value, then the result will be undefined.

Testing for SmallInteger Oops and Values

The isIntegerValue: method answers a Boolean value reflecting whether the argument can be converted into a SmallInteger object. That is, whether the value is within the SmallInteger range. Conversely, isIntegerObject: answers a Boolean value reflecting whether the argument, treated as an oop, represents a SmallInteger. The following examples are illustrative:

interpreterProxy isIntegerObject: oop	`interpreterProxy->isIntegerObject(oop)`
interpreterProxy isIntegerValue: value	`interpreterProxy->isIntegerValue(value)`

Validating Conversion Function

The interpreter proxy provides the following method for validating and loading values that are expected to be SmallIntegers with a single call:

interpreterProxy
    checkedIntegerValue: oop
	interpreterProxy
	    ->checkedIntegerValue (oop)

This method will check whether the oop is a SmallInteger value, and if so, return the corresponding integer value. If the oop is not a SmallInteger value, then the successFlag is set to false, and the result will be undefined.

Long Integer Values outside the SmallInteger Range

On occasion, it is useful to have an extension pass or return a full 32-bit integer value. The interpreter proxy provides the following functions for manipulating unsigned 32-bit values:

interpreterProxy
    positive32BitIntegerFor: value
	interpreterProxy
	    ->positive32BitIntegerFor(value)

interpreterProxy
    positive32BitValueOf: oop
	interpreterProxy
	    ->positive32BitValueOf(oop)

The positive32BitValueOf: method will accept either a SmallInteger or a 4-byte LargePositiveInteger object and answer a value that can be saved into and manipulated as an unsigned long integer. The positive32BitIntegerFor: method will convert a value stored in an unsigned long int C variable and return an oop for a corresponding SmallInteger if the value is within the SmallInteger range, or will return an oop for a LargePositiveInteger.[2]

Other Non-Indexable Objects

All other oops are represented in the VM as pointers to internal data structures containing further descriptions of the oop. The majority of Smalltalk classes have this shape.

Objects without Instance Variables

Some objects with non-indexable shape bear no other data than the class of which they are a member. The only thing that a named primitive can meaningfully do with the oop for such an object is to assign the value to another oop instance "slot"

---

[2]Should a LargePositiveInteger oop be created during a call to positive32BitIntegerOf:, a garbage collection may occur, which in turn might invalidate oops stored in other C variables. See the section entitled "Memory Management and Garbage Collection."

or to compare it with other oops. Oops for some important special objects are provided by the interpreter:

Smalltalk	*C*
interpreterProxy falseObject	`interpreterProxy->falseObject()`
interpreterProxy nilObject	`interpreterProxy->nilObject()`
interpreterProxy trueObject	`interpreterProxy->trueObject()`

It is important to note that since the oop for Smalltalk **true** is likely to be non-zero, it will test as true in a C-language if-statement. However, the same is also true for the oop representing the Smalltalk object **false**. Accordingly, to determine in C whether an oop represents Boolean truth, one should instead code something like the following:

```
if (booleanOop == interpreterProxy->trueObject()) { ... }
```

As an alternative, Smalltalk Boolean objects can be converted to and from C-language Boolean values with the following operations:

interpreterProxy booleanValueOf: oop | `interpreterProxy->booleanValueOf(oop)`

The **booleanValueOf:** method, like **checkedIntegerValue:**, will first check that the oop represents an object of type Boolean and will set the **successFlag** to **false** if it does not. If the oop is valid, then the method will answer a corresponding C-language Boolean value.

As with oops for **true** and **false**, the oop for Smalltalk **nil** will not bear the same integer value as the C language constant **NULL**. The code

```
if (oop == NULL) { ... }
```

will not behave as expected, because the result of the C expression is almost always likely to be false, regardless of whether oop actually represents the Smalltalk object **nil**. To test in C whether an oop represents **nil**, you should instead code something like the following:

```
if (oop == interpreterProxy->nilObject()) { ... }
```

Objects with Named Instance Variables

The vast majority of Smalltalk Classes, however, define non-indexable objects with one or more instance variables. These instance variables are stored in numbered slots, beginning at 0. The slot numbers correspond to the sequence in which those names are listed in the Class definition. The interpreter proxy provides the following functions for manipulating oops corresponding to objects with such a shape:

Smalltalk	*C*

interpreterProxy
    fetchWord: slot ofObject: oop
	`interpreterProxy`
	  `->fetchWordofObject(slot,oop)`

interpreterProxy
    firstFixedField: oop
	`interpreterProxy`
	  `->firstFixedField(oop)`

The value returned by fetchWord:ofObject: is an oop corresponding to the object stored in the corresponding instance variable. The value returned by firstFixedField: is a word-based pointer that can be indexed to return a corresponding instance variable (or in Slang, a Word-based CArrayAccesor). Thus,

```
p ← interpreterProxy firstFixedField: oop.
0 to: numInstVars do: [:i | self foo: (p at: i)]
```
```
int *p;
p = interpreterProxy->firstFixedField(oop);
for (i = 0; i < numInstVars; i++)
  {
    foo(p[i]);
  }
```

will perform the function foo on oops for each instance variable in the object represented by oop.

The interpreter proxy provides the following facilities for extracting the contents of an instance variable from an object, type checking, and, in the case of floats and integers, converting the value at the same time.

interpreterProxy
    fetchInteger: slot ofObject: oop
	interpreterProxy
	    ->fetchIntegerofObject(slot,oop)

interpreterProxy
    fetchPointer: slot ofObject: oop
	interpreterProxy
	    ->fetchPointerofObject(slot, oop)

As side effects, fetchInteger:ofObject: will fail unless the oop corresponds to a SmallInteger, and fetchPointer:ofObject: will fail if the oop corresponds to a Small-Integer.

For example, suppose rcvr contained an oop for an instance of a class that was defined as follows:

```
Object subclass: #Example
    instanceVariableNames: 'instVar0 instVar1'
    classVariableNames: ''
    poolDictionaries: ''
    category: 'Squeak—Plugins'.
```

Then, if instVar0 and instVar1 contain a ByteArray object and a SmallInteger object, respectively, you can load the oop pointers to those objects from rcvr as follows:

```
oop0 ← interpreterProxy fetchPointer: 0 ofObject: rcvr.
oop1 ← interpreterProxy fetchInteger: 1 ofObject: rcvr.
```

Finally, valid Smalltalk values can be stored in slots of an object using the following interpreter proxy methods:

```
interpreterProxy                    interpreterProxy
    storeInteger: slot                  ->storeIntegerofObjectwithValue(slot
    ofObject: oop                                                       oop,
    withValue: integerValue                                     integerValue)

interpreterProxy                    interpreterProxy
    storePointer: slot                  ->storePointerofObjectwithValue(slot,
    ofObject: oop                                                      oop,
    withValue: nonIntegerOop                                  nonIntegerOop)
```

With storeInteger:ofObject:withValue:, the integerValue will be converted to a SmallInteger oop and stored in the specified instance variable (or fail if it cannot be converted). The other method does not convert the oop (but will fail if nonIntegerOop is for a SmallInteger) and stores the object in the specified instance variable.

Objects Indexable to Oops

In addition to named instance variables, objects may contain a variable, indexable number of objects. A principle example is, of course, Smalltalk class Array. Indexable objects may contain oops referring to other Smalltalk objects, or they may contain raw numerical data as bytes or words. Like non-indexable objects, objects that are indexable to Smalltalk objects (but not objects indexable to data!) may also have any number of named instance variables.

Extracting the Indexable Instance Variables

Given an oop, you can obtain the size of the corresponding object (the value the object would answer if sent the message size) using the following code:

```
interpreterProxy stSizeOf: varOop  |  interpreterProxy->stSizeOf(varOop)
```

Or, if you are only interested in the number of bytes consumed by the variable portion of theobject, you may use

```
interpreterProxy byteSizeOf: varOop    interpreterProxy->byteSizeOf(varOop)
```

Given an oop, you can then obtain or change the value of the oop of its elements using

```
interpreterProxy                    interpreterProxy
    stObject: varOop at: index          ->stObjectat(varOop,index)

interpreterProxy                    interpreterProxy
    stObject: varOop at: index put: value   ->stObjectatput(varOop,index,value)
```

You can obtain a C pointer to the first indexable oop stored in the variable portion of the object with the code:

```
p ← self cCoerce: (interpreterProxy firstIndexableField: oop) to: 'int *'
```

```
p = (int *) interpreterProxy->firstIndexableField(oop)
```

after which you can address (or change) individual oops by indexing the array. Whether in Smalltalk or in C, all variable indexed objects referenced through the interpreter proxy are 0 based. Since firstIndexableField: answers objects of type "void *," the result should be coerced to "int *."

Extracting the Named Instance Variables

Objects indexable to oops may have named instance variables in addition to the indexable instance variables. You can test for the presence of such instance variables and manipulate them just as you would for non-indexable instance variables.

Testing for Objects Indexable to Oops

You may test whether an object is indexable (variable) using

interpreterProxy isIndexable: oop | `interpreterProxy->isIndexable(oop)`

which will return true if the **oop** corresponds to any variable object regardless of whether the object is indexable to oops, bytes, or words. You may use

interpreterProxy isPointers: oop | `interpreterProxy->isPointers(oop)`

which will return true if and only if the **oop** corresponds to a variable object indexable to oops.

An Example

The following code reverses, in situ, the order of the objects in the variable Smalltalk object represented by **oop**:

```
a ← self cCoerce: (interpreterProxy firstIndexableField: oop) to: 'int *'.
i ← 0.  j ← (interpreterProxy stSizeOf: oop) − 1.
[i < j] whileTrueDo:
    [t ← a at: i.  a at: i put: (a at: j).  a at: j put: t.
    i ← i + 1.  j ← j − 1].
```

In C, the code would be as follows:

```
a = (int *) interpreterProxy->firstIndexableField(oop);
i = 0;   j = (interpreterProxy->stSizeOf(oop)) - 1;
while(i < j) { t = a[i];   a[i] = a[j];   a[j] = t;   i++;   j--; }
```

Objects Indexable to 1-Byte or 4-Byte Values

Smalltalk permits the creation of objects with indexable instance variables containing binary data, each containing either a single byte or a 4-byte word, each referenced by indexing. Objects of this shape may not contain named instance variable. Therefore, the methods described in the section for named instance variables are inapplicable to such objects.

Unsurprisingly, Smalltalk internally represents the instance variable data as an array of bytes or words. As with objects indexable to oops, pointers to a variable byte or a variable word object's array can be obtained using firstIndexableField:. (In the case of variable byte objects, you should coerce the result to "char *" instead of to "int *".) Likewise, you can obtain the size of such an object using stSizeOf:. (Noting that for word-indexable objects, the message will answer the number of 4-byte words. For byte-indexable objects, the method will answer the number of bytes in the object represented by the oop.) If you desire the number of bytes in the object, regardless of whether it is byte- or word-indexable, you may use byteSizeOf: instead.

You can check the shape of an oop with the following functions:

interpreterProxy isBytes: oop	interpreterProxy->isBytes(oop)
interpreterProxy isWords: oop	interpreterProxy->isWords(oop)
interpreterProxy isWordsOrBytes: oop	interpreterProxy->isWordsOrBytes(oop)

Finally, you can combine validation and conversion byte or word objects in one step using

interpreterProxy
   fetchArray: index ofObject: oop
	interpreterProxy
	   ->fetchArrayofObject(index,oop)

to extract an oop pointer from a named instance variable array. Or you can use

interpreterProxy arrayValueOf: oop	interpreterProxy->arrayValueOf(oop)

to extract an oop pointer from any oop. Both methods will fail if the specified oop is not either byte- or word-indexable and will return a pointer otherwise.

Special Case of a Float

Floating-point values, though in Smalltalk treated as scalar values, are represented as a 64-bit value in the form of an indexable object comprising two 32-bit words. The interpreter proxy converts oops representing Float objects into C values of type double and vice versa with methods analogous to those used for SmallIntegers:

interpreterProxy floatObjectOf: aFloat	interpreterProxy->floatObjectOf(aFloat)
interpreterProxy floatValueOf: oop	interpreterProxy->floatValueOf(oop)

interpreterProxy
   fetchFloat: fieldIndex
   ofObject: objectPointer
	interpreterProxy
	   ->fetchFloatofObject(fieldIndex,
	                        objectPointer)

interpreterProxy isFloatObject: oop	interpreterProxy->isFloatObject(oop)

The Anatomy of a Named Primitive

Primitives are ordinarily invoked in the course of evaluating a Smalltalk expression, when a receiver is sent a message that has been defined as follows

primitiveAccessorNameWith: object1 then: object2 andThen: object3
<primitive: *primitiveName* module: *ExtensionPluginName*>
"Smalltalk Code to be executed if the primitive fails or cannot be loaded"

Of course, the name of the method and the number and names of its parameter may vary. When the message is sent, the oop for the receiver is pushed upon a stack. Each parameter is evaluated and pushed onto the stack in the order they appear in the method's definition. The VM global successFlag is set to true. The stack then looks substantially as follows:

(top) 0	oop for object3
1	oop for object2
2	oop for object1
(bottom) 3	oop for receiver

If the module has not already been loaded, the Squeak VM will attempt to "load" the named plugin, in this case ExtensionPluginName, in a manner that will vary depending upon the operating system. Squeak then attempts to find and execute the function setInterpreter, passing to that function a pointer to the Squeak VM interpreter proxy. (The standard plugin code saves this value in a global variable named interpreterProxy.) If this process succeeds, Squeak will then attempt to locate the pointer for the named primitive function, in this case, primitiveName. Should any part of this process fail, the VM will cease attempting to load the extension and proceed by executing the Smalltalk code that followed the primitive specification.

If all goes well, however, control is passed to the named primitive function. If the primitive fails, that is, sets successFlag to false, the primitive must leave the stack intact (or restore it) before returning. If the primitive does not fail, then the primitive must pop the parameter and receiver oops from the Smalltalk stack and must then push a valid oop thereon to serve as the return value.

This is among the most critical concerns when writing a plugin, and the most common cause of unpredictable behavior. The failure to comply with these linkage conventions can lead to substantial undefined behavior and will likely freeze or crash the Squeak VM.

When the primitive returns from execution, the interpreter will check success-Flag. If the primitive failed, then control is passed to the corresponding Smalltalk code. Otherwise, the Smalltalk stack will be popped once (and only once) to obtain an oop, which will in turn serve as the answer for the primitive message send.

A primitive manipulates the Smalltalk stack (as distinct from the C function and parameter stack) through the interpreter proxy, using the functions described in the next section.

Primitive Access to the Interpreter Stack

The named primitive function may manipulate the stack using the following functions:

interpreterProxy stackValue: offset	`interpreterProxy->stackValue(offset)`
interpreterProxy pop: nItems	`interpreterProxy->pop(nItems)`
interpreterProxy push: oop	`interpreterProxy->push(oop)`

interpreterProxy
    pop: nItems
    thenPush: oop
	`interpreterProxy`
	   `->popthenPush(nItems, oop)`

The method stackValue: offset answers the value on the Smalltalk stack offset slots from the top. Accordingly,

oop ← interpreterProxy stackValue: 0.

returns the value at the top of the stack. The method pop: removes the top nItems elements from the top of the Smalltalk stack, and answers the oop for the last value so removed. Conversely, push: pushes its parameter onto the Smalltalk stack. Method pop:thenPush: removes the nItems and then pushes the specified oop onto the stack.

Since the named primitive rarely knows at the outset whether it will succeed or fail, it is uncommon for the primitive to pop values from the stack, leaving them in place for a "hasty retreat" by a simple return upon identifying a failure condition. The primitive is far more likely, therefore, to use stackValue: rather than the pop-related routines to access its parameters. The interpreter proxy provides various functions that facilitate this process by not only loading the oop at the specified location, but in a single step also validating the shape of and converting the oop to C-friendly values, the parameters and the receiver. These functions are as follows:

interpreterProxy stackIntegerValue: offset	`interpreterProxy` `->stackIntegerValue(offset)`
interpreterProxy stackObjectValue: offset	`interpreterProxy` `->stackObjectValue(offset)`
interpreterProxy stackFloatValue: offset	`interpreterProxy` `->stackFloatValue(offset)`

For variable objects or objects with instance variables important to the primitive, the oop would be loaded using stackValue: and then validated or converted in turn. Finally, the proxy provides a mechanism to ease converting the C-friendly values to oops and pushing the corresponding oops onto the stack in a single step. The mechanism consists of the following functions:

interpreterProxy pushBool: cValue	`interpreterProxy->pushBool(cValue)`
interpreterProxy pushFloat: cDouble	`interpreterProxy->pushFloat(cDouble)`
interpreterProxy pushInteger: intValue	`interpreterProxy->pushInteger(intValue)`

Miscellaneous Plugin Tricks

The interpreter proxy provides a number of additional features useful for developing primitive plugins.

Success and Failure of a Plugin

The following routines are useful for establishing the failure of a primitive:

interpreterProxy failed	`interpreterProxy->failed()`
interpreterProxy primitiveFail	`interpreterProxy->primitiveFail()`
interpreterProxy success: aBoolean	`interpreterProxy->success(aBoolean)`

The first **failed** returns true whenever the primitive has failed. **primitiveFail** establishes that the primitive has failed. **success:** establishes that the primitive has failed if the Boolean expression is false, and does not change the status otherwise.

Strict Type Checking

It is desirable from time to time to verify whether a parameter or receiver is of a specific class, rather than merely to confirm its Smalltalk shape. To determine whether an oop represents an object that is an instance of a particular class, use

interpreterProxy is: oop MemberOf: aString	`interpreterProxy` `    ->isMemberOf(oop, aString)`

To determine whether an oop represents an object that is either an instance of a particular class or one of its subclasses, use

interpreterProxy is: oop KindOf: aString	`interpreterProxy` `    ->isKindOf(oop, aString)`

Determining the Number of Instance Variables

Slang does not provide a method for directly determining the number of instance variables. It does provide the following method for determining the total number of Smalltalk instance slots in an object:

interpreterProxy slotSizeOf: oop | interpreterProxy−>slotSizeOf(oop)

For nonvariable objects, **slotSizeOf:** will return the total number of named instance variables. For variable objects, however, **slotSizeOf:** returns the number of named instance variables *plus* the number of indexable variables. Accordingly, for variable objects, the number of named instance variables is given by

(interpreterProxy slotSizeOf: oop) − (interpreterProxy sizeOf: oop)

```
interpreterProxy->slotSizeOf(oop) - interpreterProxy->sizeOf(oop)
```

Some care must be taken in using this expression, because **sizeOf:** is not defined for most nonvariable objects.

Instantiating Objects inside a Plugin

Since **SmallInteger** objects require no memory other than the oop itself, they can be created, so to speak, on the fly. All other objects require the allocation of memory. While it is typically preferable to allocate objects used in a primitive in Smalltalk with a wrapper around the calling procedure, it is sometimes convenient or necessary to do so inside the primitive. The interpreter proxy provides routines for doing so. Given an oop representing a class, you can instantiate an object of that class and obtain an oop pointing to its object header as follows:

interpreterProxy
    instantiateClass: classPointer
    indexableSize: size
	`interpreterProxy`
	`  ->instantiateClassindexableSize`
	`       (classPointer, size);`

This operation does not execute initialization code typically associated with the object class, however. It merely allocates the space and initializes all instance variables to nil, akin to the **Object>>basicNew** method. To assure that an object is properly initialized, you might instead use

interpreterProxy−>clone(prototype)	`interpreterProxy->clone(prototype);`

which will perform a shallow copy of the object referred to by the prototype oop, as though the **clone** message were sent to the object.

It is fairly straightforward to obtain an oop for a class inside a plugin. At the outset, you can pass the class as a parameter to the function. Alternatively, given an oop, you can obtain the oop for its class using

interpreterProxy fetchClassOf: oop	`interpreterProxy->fetchClassOf(oop);`

Alternatively, you can directly obtain the oop for certain fixed classes using any of the following messages:

classArray	classLargePositiveInteger
classBitmap	classPoint
classByteArray	classSemaphore
classCharacter	classSmallInteger
classFloat	classString

Finally, the interpreterProxy provides a special-purpose function to facilitate the creation of objects of class **Point**.

interpreterProxy
    makePointwithxValue: xValue
    yValue: yValue
	`interpreterProxy`
	`  ->makePointwithxValueyValue(xValue,`
	`                            yValue);`

Memory Management and Garbage Collection

Garbage collection can be provoked from a primitive using the following functions:

```
interpreterProxy fullGC            interpreterProxy->fullGC();
interpreterProxy incrementalGC     interpreterProxy->incrementalGC();
```

These functions are analogous to the similarly-named methods of class **System-Dictionary**. However, garbage collection can also occur whenever a new object is instantiated, either through express instantiation or by using a method that can indirectly create a non-SmallInteger object, such as **positive32BitIntegerOf:**

When that occurs, any oop other than a **SmallInteger** oop stored in a C variable is invalidated and must be "reloaded," for example by obtaining new pointers from the stack or receiver. However, not all oops can be reloaded in this way (e.g., oops that were created by explicit instantiation).

To preserve oops across operations that can cause a garbage collection, the interpreterProxy provides a special *remappable oop* stack, which will hold references to oops that will be remapped during a garbage collection, so that the oop can later be reloaded. The following functions are provided for pushing and popping values from the stack:

```
interpreterProxy                   interpreterProxy
    pushRemappableOop: oop            ->pushRemappableOop(oop);

interpreterProxy                   interpreterProxy
    popRemappableOop                  ->popRemappableOop()
```

For example, if temporaries or globals oop1 and oop2 held oop references to objects, the following Slang code would safely preserve the validity of the objects across a garbage collection:

```
interpreterProxy pushRemappableOop: oop1.
interpreterProxy pushRemappableOop: oop2.
...Smalltalk code that might result in a garbage collection...
oop2 ← interpreterProxy popRemappableOop.
oop1 ← interpreterProxy popRemappableOop.
...references to oop1 and oop2...
```

Callbacks

One of the great weaknesses in the Squeak VM memory model is that the interpreter cannot readily be called from a C-language function. Accordingly, applications requiring callbacks are somewhat difficult to implement. A limited callback capacity can be approximated using the **interpreterProxy** method:

```
interpreterProxy                   interpreterProxy
    signalSemaphoreWithIndex: semaIndex    ->signalSemaphoreWithIndex
                                                (semaIndex);
```

Calling this method sends a signal to a Semaphore that had been registered using the Smalltalk>>registerExternalObject: method.[3] The callback is set up by (1) forking a process that waits on the Semaphore before calling the callback code and (2) registering the Semaphore with the VM. Signaling the Semaphore from a C-language routine using the interpreter Proxy can thereafter trigger the callback.

A Plugin for Swapping Blocks in a Word Processor

Programmers often need to move a blocks of data from one location in a data structure to another. For example, a user of a word processor may wish to move a block of text from one location to another. For example:

1. These
2. Lines
3. Out
4. Of
5. Should
6. Not
7. Be
8. Order

A user might wish to move lines 3 and 4 after line 7, to form the sentence "These Lines Should Not Be Out Of Order." This problem might be described another way, as the problem of "swapping" two unequally sized blocks of words, that is, swapping the two-word block {Out Of} with the three-word block {Should Not Be}. There are many ways to address this problem. For example, data structures such as linked lists can facilitate a speedy implementation of this operation.

If we are constrained, for whatever reason, to chose a more compact data structure, say, a contiguous array of pointers to objects or an array of ASCII bytecodes, the problem becomes somewhat more interesting. A solution attributed to the authors of the TECO text editor is to reverse unequal portions of the string "These Lines Out Of Should Not Be Order" by performing the following steps:

1. reversing the elements of the first block in place; yielding

   "These Lines fO tuO Should Not Be Order"

2. reversing the elements of the second block in place, yielding

   "These Lines fO tuO eB toN dluohS Order"

   and

---

[3]The signalSemaphoreWithIndex: method does not immediately send the signal, but registers a request for the signal with the VM. The VM will send the signal shortly after the primitive returns control to the VM.

3. reversing the elements of the first and second blocks, taken together—yielding

"These Lines Should Not Be Out Of Order."

This approach reduces the problem of swapping unequal blocks to the problem of reversing blocks in place. We might code this approach in Smalltalk by extending OrderedCollection with the following methods:

swapBlockFrom: firstFrom withBlockFrom: secondFrom to: last

```
"Modify me so that my elements from the block beginning with index,
firstFrom, up to but not including the index, secondFrom − 1, are
swapped with the block beginning with index, secondFrom, up to and
including the index, last.  Answer self."
self reverseInPlaceFrom: firstFrom to: secondFrom − 1.
self reverseInPlaceFrom: secondFrom to: last.
self reverseInPlaceFrom: firstFrom to: last
```

reverseInPlaceFrom: from to: to

```
"Modify me so that my elements from the index, from, up to and
including the index, to, are reversed. Assume that I am mutable.
Answer self."
| temp |
0 to: to − from // 2 do:
   [:index |
   temp ← self at: from + index.
   self at: from + index put: (self at: to − index).
   self at: to − index put: temp]
```

These methods work with all mutable subclasses of OrderedCollection, for example, class Array. Executing the DoIt:

```
#(this collection out of should not be order)
   swapBlockFrom: 3 withBlockFrom: 5 to: 8
```

will answer

(this collection should not be out of order)

These methods appear to work well and are general enough to handle all forms of OrderedCollection. However, the code can be noticeably slow when the blocks grow large. Consider a word processor maintaining documents as an Array of objects, each object representing one line. A line object might be an actual String of text in memory; an object representing a proxy to a file or intermediate file in which the text can be found; or some other object of relevance to the program.

Using that representation, one might implement both block moves and line insertions with swapBlockFrom:withBlockFrom:to:. However, for reasonably large files (about 100,000 lines or so), an insertion could take seconds to execute. In an interactive program, such a perceptible pause for a common operation could be intolerably slow. While many alternatives should be weighed to speedily perform this operation, a pluggable primitive is one that may save the day.

Step One: Designing the Interface

Before writing a primitive, it is useful to consider how it will be called. Doing so permits you to better understand the requirements and assumptions under which the primitive can be written. Since the document is represented as an array of objects, we will consider overriding Array>>reverseInPlaceFrom:to:[4] with a primitive. We start by subclassing InterpreterPlugin to hold the plugin and primitive method:

```
InterpreterPlugin subclass: #FlipCollectionPlugin
    instanceVariableNames: ''
    classVariableNames: ''
    poolDictionaries: ''
    category: 'VMConstruction-Plugins'
```

We then create a stub method in FlipCollectionPlugin, named primReverseFromto, and add a primitive interface to class Array as follows:

primitiveReverseFrom: from to: to
    (1) <primitive: 'primReverseFromto' module: 'FlipCollectionPlugin'>
    (2) ↑FlipCollectionPlugin doPrimitive: 'primReverseFromto'

Line (1) identifies the primitive to be called and the module name expected. If the primitive executes properly, the return value (the value at the top of the stack upon completion) will be answered. If (a) the module cannot be loaded; (b) the primitive cannot be found in the module; or (c) the primitive failed when executed, then Line (2) will be executed. Line (2) sets up an environment to simulate in Smalltalk the primitive execution and executes it. The result of that simulation will be returned as the answer to the primitive.

We can then override reverseFrom:to: in class Array with the following call to the primitive:

Array>>reverseFrom: from to: to
    ↑self primitiveReverseFrom: from to: to

This completes the interface. We are now ready to build our primitive.

---

[4]While it may be obvious in this case that the block move spends most of its time in the reverseInPlaceFrom:to: method, this is not always apparent, in general. Squeak provides excellent tools for profiling performance, for example, MessageTally, and these measurements will often inform the question how a plugin should be designed.

Step Two: Coding the Primitive

As discussed previously, the primitive will be a parameterless method, which in this case, we will call primReverseFromto.

primReverseFromto
```
    | from to rcvrOop rcvr t |
(0) self export: true.
(1) self var: #rcvr declareC: 'int *rcvr'.
(2) to ← interpreterProxy stackIntegerValue: 0.
    from ← interpreterProxy stackIntegerValue: 1.
(3) rcvrOop ← interpreterProxy stackObjectValue: 2.
(4) rcvr ← self
    cCoerce: (interpreterProxy firstIndexableField: rcvrOop)
    to: 'int *'.
(5) interpreterProxy success: (from >= 1 and: [from + 1 <= to]).
    interpreterProxy success: (to <= (interpreterProxy stSizeOf: rcvrOop)).
(6) interpreterProxy failed ifTrue: [↑nil].
(7) rcvr ← rcvr − 1.  "adjust for 1−based indexing."
(8) 0 to: to − from / 2 do:
    [:index |
    t ← rcvr at: from + index.
    rcvr at: from + index put: (rcvr at: to − index).
    rcvr at: to − index put: t].
(9) interpreterProxy pop: 3 thenPush: rcvrOop
```

A brief discussion follows:

- Line (0) assures that a C-language function generated from this method will be an exported public reference. All primitives should have this declaration.

- Line (1) assures that the C-language variable associated with the Smalltalk temp **rcvr** will be declared as a pointer to integers. The default is type `int`.

- Lines (2) load the parameters from the stack into temporaries. As you will recall, a method call first pushes the receiver onto the stack, followed by the parameters in ascending order. Thus, parameter **to** will be at the top (index 0) of the stack, followed by parameter **from** and the receiver.

- Line (3) loads the oop for the receiver (an array of objects) into temp **rcvrOop**.

- Lines (4) load **rcvr** with a pointer to a "void *" pointer to the first indexable address of **rcvrOop**, and coerces the result to "int *."

- Lines (5) perform some bounds checking, resetting the success flag on a bounds failure.

- Line (6) checks the success flag. Upon failure, the stack is left as-is, so that the primitive's alternative code can be executed.

- Line (7) adjusts rcvr for 1-based indexing. C-language arrays are 0 based, so by adjusting the pointer, subsequent references may treat the array as though it were a 1-based Smalltalk array.

- Lines (8) perform the actual work. This is the same code set forth in the example code for OrderedCollection>>reverseFrom:to:, except that self is replaced with rcvr. (Without line 20, the code would have to be modified for C's 0-indexed arrays.)

- Line (9) pops the parameters and receiver oops from the stack, and pushes back an oop representing the receiver. (Since we wish to return the rcvr, a simple pop: 2 would have sufficed.)

Step Three: Building the Plugin

Having coded the primitive, we can directly test this code, albeit in slow-motion, using the plugin interpreter. Because the plugin is not installed, the primitive call in primReverseInPlaceFromto will fail and call the interpreter. In this way, you can test most plugin code without actually compiling and installing the plugin.

Once we are satisfied that the code is working correctly, we can build the plugin. The following do-it will generate a C-language file corresponding to the plugin:

FlipCollectionPlugin translate

The generated file can then be compiled, using native system tools, as a shared library and installed as a plugin for testing as live system code, resulting in a substantial and measurable speedup in the block move routines.

After a distinguished career as a technologist, Andrew Greenberg became an intellectual property and patent lawyer. He writes and lectures nationally on issues of law, public policy, and technology. In past lives, he created the *Wizardry* and *Star Saga* computer game series, for which he was inducted into the Computer Gaming World Hall of Fame. He has served as vice-president of engineering, research, and development at Netwolves Technologies, Inc., as president and chief executive officer of Masterplay Publishing Corporation, and as president of Andrew Greenberg, Inc. Andrew lives in Tampa with his wife, Sheila; two beautiful children, Shoshanna and William, a tuba named Lori; and many fuzzy critters too numerous to name.

Part Three

Squeak for the Toolkit Programmer

One of the original goals for Smalltalk was to serve as an environment for building tools for other programmers. The idea was that programmers would build for others, perhaps as often as they built code for themselves.

That's clearly happening with Squeak, as can be seen in the chapters in this part on MathMorphs, Siren, Flow, and XP:

- The first two chapters in this part are about *MathMorphs*, a wonderful mathematics environment built on top of Squeak by students and faculty at the University of Buenos Aires. Luciano Notarfrancesco and Leandro Caniglia present an overview of MathMorphs and how the mathematicians at U.B.A. use it, and then Andres Valloud describes the Function Plotter that he built for MathMorphs. Andres's chapter also serves as a case study for how one build a complex environment in Squeak.

- Stephen Pope has been actively composing music with computers in some variant of Smalltalk since the mid-1980s. When Squeak arrived, he moved his tools and focus there. In his chapter, he describes the path of his work that led to Squeak, presents his *Siren* music composition toolkit, and describes his work in Siren.

- Craig Latta was involved in a large multimedia development project in Squeak, where part of that effort led to the creation of a stream-based view of networking that made easy the development of streaming media. In his chapter, Craig leads us through the thought process of how streaming audio works and how his tools support it.

- John Sarkela, Paul McDonough, and David Caster have been working on tools and techniques to apply the *eXtreme Programming* methodology in Squeak. Their chapter introduces XP for Squeak.

10

MathMorphs: An Environment for Learning and Doing Math

Luciano Notarfrancesco[1] *and*
Leandro Caniglia[2]

University of Buenos Aires
Facultad de Ciencias Exactas y Naturales
Mathematics Department

Introduction

Mathematics comes to life when mathematicians think about a theorem, read a definition, or express their points of view to others. This happens in classrooms and lectures; it's exciting, profound, and beautiful. For centuries, mathematicians have been improving the way they keep their notions and ideas on paper. Style, notations, and terminology have been carefully developed to the highest possible degree of clarity and concision. The result of such enormous effort is a broad and impressive literate repository, which provides help to the new generations that have to absorb this forever-increasing body of knowledge.

Still, writing and reading mathematics is difficult. It demands a great amount of time and effort to translate a clear idea into formal terms. In the writing process, the author must squeeze an alive, ideal world on the inert face of the paper. It is hard, because the author must tell the reader about that world instead of showing it. On the other hand, the reader is supposed to recreate the tale into her own intellect. This two-way process consists of first coding thoughts into a strict notation and later read that austere formalism trying to rebuild the original ideas the formalism is based on.

[1]luciano2@mail.ru
[2]caniglia@dm.uba.ar

The systematic storing and retrieval of cognition is not a simple task. In the meantime, the mathematical objects are reduced to frozen symbols that look the same as mathematics, when in fact they are nothing but notation.

What if mathematicians had a place to keep all their living objects? Not a planar place, but a multidimensional one, with an unlimited capacity to hold things inside. A space with colors and movement. A site where definitions get expressed and instanced without suffering from any kind of hibernation. A space to materialize ideas, letting them evolve into new suggestions to the observer—where the mathematical objects and their relations would coexist, showing new relationships. A comfortable and well-equipped laboratory for mathematical exploration and experimentation. If such a place existed, then it would be a repository of mathematics and not a repository of *texts* about mathematics.

The identification of mathematical objects with their textual (symbolic) description is so deeply rooted in our minds that the distinction we are trying to stress might look obscure. Just think about the difference between the music and the score. Since 1997, the MathMorphs project is the logical consequence of one simple fact: realizing that such a fertile world is possible in the universe of Squeak.

Paradoxically, the description of the MathMorphs work included in this chapter has been written on paper. The following sections attempt to put in words and frozen illustrations the kind of motivation we have experienced in the classroom.

All the projects were worked out and implemented by the students. They are the authors of all this work, and we want to thank them for all the effort and enthusiasm spent in showing us how to get fun with MathMorphs.

Acknowledgments

MathMorphs is the result of the efforts made by several people. Gerardo Richarte has been very creative and is always eager to think about anything. He invented the "type on air" magic and took part in many projects. Daniel Vaisencher made smart contributions and suggestions about MorphicWrappers. Pablo Malavolta proposed visual effects and worked hard in Algebraic Geometry. Andres Valloud programmed the Function Plotters and got involved with MathMorphs from the beginning. Ariel Pacetti devised useful improvements in the implementation of Algebraic Numbers. Alejandro Weil worked with Euclidean Geometry. Eric Maximiliano Guevara implemented Linear Recursive Sequences. Alejandro Tolomei worked on Random Variables and Statistics. Gabriel Stern taught us how to model Metric Spaces and continuous functions. Pablo Schmerkin introduced BiologyMorphs. Ariel Schwartzman worked on PhysicsMorphs integrating many MathMorphs tools. Francisco Garau shared his studies on TypeInference presenting interesting problems to the group and discussing about possible solutions. Valeria Murgia made lots of fruitful suggestions on how to model with Smalltalk. Mathematicians Jorge and Juan Guccione argued deeply about the theoretic aspects of the work. To all these people, we extend our love and gratitude.

MorphicWrappers

Let us begin our MathMorphs tour describing our main tool to play with objects. A MorphicWrapper is a vehicle allowing any object to be included in a Morphic World. This is accomplished by usual techniques: A special kind of morph, the wrapper, acts as an invisible envelope surrounding the ordinary object with the behavior required by Morphic.

What is fun with MorphicWrappers is that they let you take advantage of the amazing potential that Morphic gives to all kinds of users. The MorphicWrapper package also provides a set of tools that further extend the default user-interface capabilities provided by Morphic.

Downloading and Installing the MorphicWrapper package

The MorphicWrapper package is freely available from the following web sites:

    http://dm.uba.ar/mathMorphs

    http://mathMorphs.swiki.net

    http://minnow.cc.gatech.edu/squeak/354

The package's version number is the same as the Squeak version number. It is updated with each Squeak version, so it is a good idea to visit these sites from time to time.

To install the package, proceed as with any other project: (1) Place the change set file MWnn.cs (where 'nn' stands for the version number) in the Squeak folder or directory; (2) open a FileList from the Squeak pop-up menu found in */open.../file list*, and (3) right-click on the MWnn.cs line in the list and choose *"file into new change set."* Versions prior to 2.8 should be filed in from MVC (and not from Morphic).

Advanced users and programmers interested in the development of new features are invited to contact the authors for the last-minute version.

CodeBalloons

Gerardo Richarte first introduced the brilliant concept of "typing on air." Soon, this feature became a distinctive aspect of the MorphicWrappers. A so-called Code-Balloon appears when you start typing "on air." You do not need workspaces any more. Simply type any Squeak expression on the fly, and a CodeBalloon will appear holding the expression as you type it in (Figure 10.1). When you hit the return key or when you click on the receiver, the expression is evaluated and the result is attached to your morphic hand.

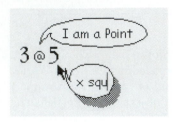
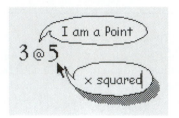

Figure 10.1   A CodeBalloon appears when you start typing.

If the hand is within bounds of a **MorphicWrapper**, then the expression is evaluated in the context of the wrapped object. Thus, when writing the expression, you can use self, super, and any of the instance or class variable names for that object.

Implicit Self

One of the experiments you can try with **CodeBalloons** is the optional omission of "self" when typing on air some expressions. When you have a morph on focus, the contexts make it obvious that the receiver of the message you are about to enter is the morph (Figure 10.2). So, the need to write "self" becomes rather superfluous. The experimental MathMorphs version of implicit self, allows you to include or exclude the starting "self" in expressions where it is the receiver of a message.

The inclusion of "self" assumes that the sender of the message is the same morph. Thus, you are forced to mentally take the place of the morph, when in fact, you are not the morph, but the sender of the message to that morph. This role-shifting can be a good exercise when you go in depth to the object-message paradigm. However, it might be difficult to deal with when you are showing Morphic to children, especially if they do not speak English.

Names

You can use **CodeBalloons** to name objects. These names are meaningful inside the world (Figure 10.3).

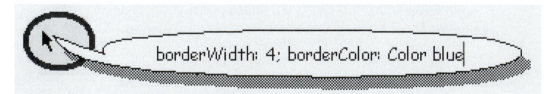

Figure 10.2   Sending messages with implicit self.

  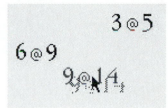

Figure 10.3   Naming objects with MorphicWrappers.

Talking to Normal Morphs

The MorphicWrappers let you talk to any morph using **CodeBalloons** and names. The red dot in the halo of any morph includes the "talk to me" item (Figure 10.4).

You can use the "talk to me" feature to name the morph in just the same way as with MorphicWrappers.

Of course, you can also type any expression on air when the morph is in focus: Place the hand (mouse pointer) on the morph and start typing (additional clicks or gestures are not needed). Be aware, however, that normally no indication makes apparent that the morph has the focus (other than the position of the hand). If the target morph does not eat keyboard events, then the expression will evaluate correctly using "self" as the morph (Figure 10.5). When the keystrokes are captured by the morph, this approach does not work—you should use the "talk to me" item instead.

  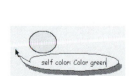 

Figure 10.4   Talking to ordinary morphs.

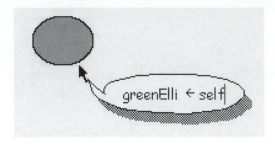

Figure 10.5 Naming an ellipse.

Double-Click Menus

Double-clicking on a **MorphicWrapper** pops up a menu for the object being wrapped (Figure 10.6). This menu shows the object's protocol. The intended message is sent when you select it from the menu.

Typing History

Each wrapper remembers the history of all expressions evaluated in its context. There is one expression history for each class of wrapped objects. The commands in the history can be accessed using the up and down arrows in the keyboard.

Arguments

The double-click menu pops up the unary messages of the protocol, when we have not included any argument. You can add arguments by dragging and dropping them on the receiver. Each argument appears as a **Satellite** flying around the object (Figure 10.7).

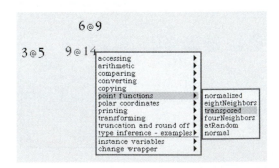

Figure 10.6 Unary protocol of Points.

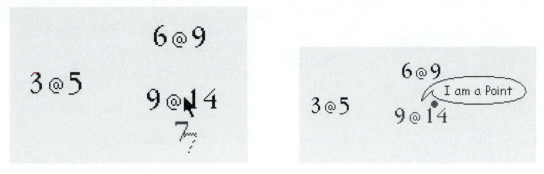

Figure 10.7   Dropped as argument, 7 is represented by a flying satellite (blue dot).

Now the double-click menu shows all the messages with one argument (Figure 10.8). You can drop as many arguments as needed. If you want to get the arguments back, you can use the menu item called "forget arguments." Also, if you let them alone, the satellites will disappear after a few seconds.

Identity

The MorphicWrappers support object identity. This means that no two wrappers will be present for the same object. As an example, suppose you have the string "Squeak" and the character $k. Then you ask "Squeak" for its last element. Since there is only one $k in the system, the answer will be the same $k you already have in the world. When you hit return (or click on "Squeak"), the $k character runs to your hand (Figure 10.9).

This behavior is a very good example of how Morphic makes many properties inherent to objects more apparent. You do not need to tell people about the identity principle; you let the objects perform their roles in the show.

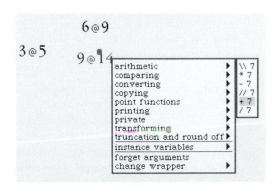

Figure 10.8   Double-click menu with one-argument messages.

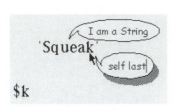 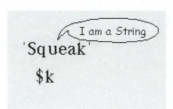 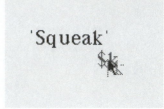

Figure 10.9 The identity principle is illustrated when the $k character runs to assume its role as the answer of the message.

Visual Effects

Once an expression typed on air is evaluated, the answer runs from some undetermined position to the point where the expression was entered. After a short shaking, the answer gets attached to the hand. To drop it, click on the designated place.

A CarryingMorph accomplishes the running effect. This invisible morph takes another morph as its *passenger* and *steps* to the target destination (in this case, the hand), carefully carrying its shipment. By changing the drawOn: method of the CarryingMorph, one could easily add visual effects that would take place during these short trips.

The second visual trick we use is to let the answer of a message *shake* when it is attached to the hand. Here we use a ShakingMorph that moves its target morph with decreasing strength each time it steps.

Direct Manipulation and Requests

Direct manipulation of objects has interesting consequences. The MorphicWrappers enhance the possibilities enabled by Morphic allowing any object to be immediately accessible to the user.

As we saw before, the identity principle is made apparent when the answer of a message runs from its current position to the hand.

Another discovery is that the use of FillInTheBlank becomes superfluous when direct manipulation is enabled. Inside Morphic, we do not need to prompt for strings, because we can prompt for any object.

The conventional approach to ask the user for an input is to offer a widget with some text field and wait for an answer. The user writes some words and hits enter. Then, the requester takes the entered string and tries to figure out the object it represents. As we can see, conventional input boxes are bottlenecks that impose two translation steps: (1) The user must put thoughts in words, and (2) the requester must interpret a description and convert it in an object.

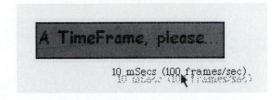

Figure 10.10　RequestBoxes accept any object as input.

With MorphicWrappers, we do not need textual input fields any more. A RequestBox requests an object. When the user has the answer at hand, she drops it into the box. The RequestBox sends the answer back to the requesting object, and the process is done (Figure 10.10). You can cancel the request by throwing it to the trash.

Usually one responds to a RequestBox by typing on air an expression that evaluates to the intended answer.

Programming with MorphicWrappers

The MorphicWrapper package is a framework where more specialized wrappers can be added. With ClassMorphicWrappers, classes and metaclasses behave as morphs. As with any other object, to include an existing class in the world you simply write its name on air. The class pops up attached to the hand (Figure 10.11).

When viewed as morphs, classes show their structure: instance variable names, class variable names, pool dictionaries, and category. The double-click menu exposes the instance and class protocols. Other useful tools are also accessible from this menu.

To edit a method, select it from the double-click menu. A window for the method pops up (Figure 10.12).

Many operations are done by dragging and dropping. For example, instance variables, class variables, pool dictionaries, and class categories are included in the class when a symbol (or string) is dropped on it. Lowercase symbols are interpreted

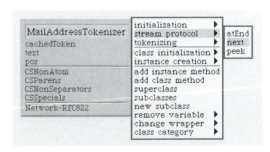

Figure 10.11　The double-click menu exposes all methods.

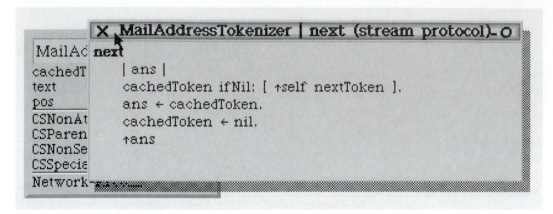

Figure 10.12   Methods can be edited individually.

as instance variable names, while global dictionaries are interpreted as pools. If the symbol contains a dash and begins with an uppercase character, it is taken as the new class category. Other uppercase symbols are included as class variable names. The double-click menu provides an optional way to change the class category; it is useful for category names not containing the dash character.

Dragging and Dropping Objects as Morphs

When an object is dragged out of an Inspector, it is attached as a morph to the hand (Figure 10.13).

If the object being dragged is a morph, then the morph is attached to the hand. Otherwise, a MorphicWrapper on the object appears. The same conversion occurs when dragging classes or methods form a browser or a message list.

The table below provides a tour of MathMorphs in a nutshell. Common tasks and and how to perform them are described.

Figure 10.13   Dragged objects become MorphicWrappers.

How to... A Quick Tour

task	how to	double-click menu	pop-up menu	special keys
Evaluate an expression	Write the expression on air			Use enter or cr to accept
Evaluate an expression without attaching the answer to the hand	Write the expression on air. Be sure to end the expression with a period			Use enter or cr to accept
Name an object (works with most morphs)	Focus on the object and evaluate the expression: name self			
Name a morph (works with every morph)	Find the "talk to me" item and proceed as with normal objects		Use the red dot in the morph's halo	
Recall some expression	Focus the object and hit the up arrow on the keyboard			Up and down arrows
Send a message (I)	Use the name of the object and evaluate the expression associated with the message			
Send a message (II)	Focus the object and evaluate the expression associated with the message using self for the receiver. You may or may not include a leading "self"			
Send a message (III)			Find the message selector as an item in the menu (see also how to add arguments)	
Send a message (IV), opening a debugger			Click on the message selector, an item in the menu, while holding down the shift key	Shift key
Add an argument	Drop the argument on the wrapper			
Forget arguments	Wait, or use the double-click menu, or...	...select the "forget arguments" item		
Answer a RequestBox	Drop the answer on the box			
Cancel a RequestBox	Drop the box on the trash			
Delete a wrapper	Drop the wrapper in the trash or hit backspace when the wrapper has the focus			Backspace
Get a class wrapper	Evaluate the expression consisting of the class name			

continued on next page

task	how to	double-click menu	pop-up menu	special keys
Edit a method	Evaluate the expression Classname #selector or double-click on the class wrapper	Find the selector under the category submenu		Save with alt-s (Cmd-s in the Mac)
Create a new class	Get the superclass for the new class and...	...use the new subclass item		
Add an instance variable to a class	Drop the name of the variable on the class' wrapper			
Remove an instance variable from a class		Use the remove variable item		
Add a class variable to a class	Drop the name of the variable on the class' wrapper			
Add a pool dictionary to a class	Drop the name of the pool (or the pool itself) on the class' wrapper			
Change the class category	Drop the name of the new category, or...	...select the new category item		
Add a new instance or class method (I)		Select the action from the menu		
Add a new instance or class method (II)	Edit any other instance or class method and change the selector before saving it			Save with alt-s
Copy a method from one class to another	Drag and drop the method from the source class on the destination class			Shift while dropping. Save with alt-s
Move a method from one class to another (removing it from the former)	Drag and drop the method from the source class on the destination class			Ctrl + shift while dropping
Change the superclass of a class	Drop the class on the new superclass			Shift while dropping
Remove a method, change its category, run prettyPrint on it, see versions, senders, implementors, etc.	Edit the method and...		...select the proper item in the method's pop-up menu	
Include an object as a morph in the world	Drag the object from an Inspector, Browser, or message list			

Linear Algebra

Expressiveness is a key aspect in MathMorphs' approach. A rich hierarchy of objects allows us to represent the involved entities in Squeak as they are in the mathematical world. The need for spurious conventions on the interpretation of data structures is eliminated. Linear algebra appears everywhere, and so it is a good point of departure to show how our ideas have been accomplished. Let's begin our journey through MathMorphs.

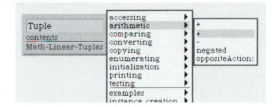

Figure 10.14 Menu fragment showing the instance protocol of tuples.

Tuples

The first linear objects we will consider are tuples. The protocol for these objects includes messages for accessing individual coordinates, for arithmetic operations as addition and scalar action, for testing whether the tuple is null, and for some enumerative messages on the coordinates of the tuple (Figure 10.14).

There is also a rich instance creation class protocol. For example, it is handy to convert a **String** into a **Tuple** (Figure 10.15). It is also convenient to supply a block and a range of indexes, so that the values of the block at the given indexes are collected to build the new tuple.

A subclass of **Tuple** represents sparse, freely indexed tuples. These are appropriate for special purposes in which the indexes are not integers from 1 to n.

Matrixes

The next step in the process of building a linear algebra package is to represent matrixes. The instance protocol includes messages for accessing individual entries, doing arithmetic operations (such as addition and matrix product), as well as product by scalars and tuples (Figure 10.16). To access the entry at row i and column j, the **Point** i@j is used as an index. Elementary operations on rows are implemented as messages.

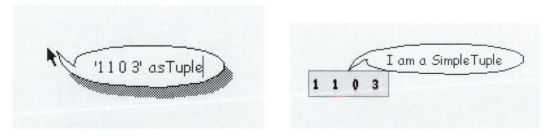

Figure 10.15 Using MorphicWrappers to work with tuples inside Morphic.

Figure 10.16 A fragment of the instance protocol of matrixes.

Basic operations such as transposing or the computation of the trace are also implemented in the instance protocol. On the contrary, more elaborated functions are delegated to external objects. There are **MatrixReducers** (described next), whose responsibility is to compute ranks, determinants, inverses, etc. These objects implement triangulation algorithms. Again, the class protocol includes many useful messages for instance creation (Figure 10.17).

MatrixReducers

A design characteristic of MathMorphs is that algorithms are kept away from the input data. With this idea in mind, we are free to use the same algorithm with different species of inputs and to compare different algorithms when running on the same data. When an algorithm is instanced as an object by itself, one ends up with a machine holding a valuable knowledge about the theoretical aspects of the process and the special characteristics found in any particular run. We can ask the algorithm the time it has taken to run, the final state of any of its variables, etc. Implementations could include recording of special events, loop counters, history of execution, or playback options.

In this case, decoupling the algorithm from the objects it runs on has the beneficial consequence of keeping the implementation and the protocol of matrixes simple (Figure 10.18). Once the **MatrixReducer** has run on its input matrix, we can ask it about the rank, determinant, left inverse, and any other information derived from its work (Figure 10.19).

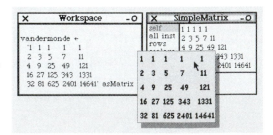

Figure 10.17 Using MorphicWrappers to work with matrixes.

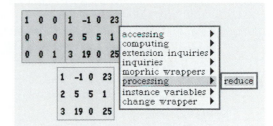

Figure 10.18 A MatrixReducer before processing its input Matrix.

Algebraic Ambients

Linear algebra theory does not require special hypotheses on the field of scalars. The theory is the same regardless of the nature of the coefficients. These may be rationals, reals, complexes, modular integers, algebraic numbers, etc. In MathMorphs, we keep the same degree of generality, implementing all constructions independently from the field of scalars.

One could think that such degree of generality requires a complete implementation of rings and fields. While this kind of objects is interesting by itself, a high degree of dependence between these two frameworks would be contrary to our aims. Fortunately, very little information is needed to implement linear algebra definitions without losing generality. This information is just the zero and the unity of the field of scalars.

We use AlgebraicAmbients to keep independence from the field of scalars. An AlgebraicAmbient is an object that can answer the unit and zero elements of some prime field or ring. Since zero equals unit − unit, these objects only have to remember the unity as an instance variable.

As an example, let us consider the class Tuple. We want instance-creation messages for the canonical vector e_i. When mathematicians say e_i, it is assumed that

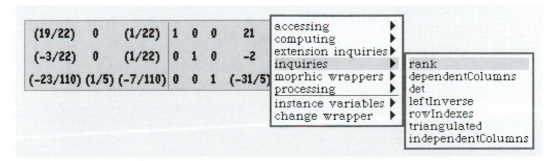

Figure 10.19 The reducer, after processing its input, holds interesting information.

everybody knows the value of n. In other words, they are speaking about $e_{i,n}$. Also, and this is the interesting point, they are assuming that the field of scalars is implied or provided by the context. So, a complete instance creation method should look like this:

Tuple class | e: i dim: n scalars: scalars

where scalars is an AlgebraicAmbient. Since this object knows the unity and zero elements, the message can answer with the desired tuple.

The class AlgebraicAmbient also holds the collection of all available ambients (those that have been used so far). So, the message

AlgebraicAmbient withUnit: unit

answers a previously created ambient with *unit* as the unity, or a newly created instance. Once we have the class, say, IntegerMod5, we can add a new ambient as follows:

AlgebraicAmbient withUnit: (1 mod: 5)

At initialization the class creates a "default" instance withUnit: 1, the SmallInteger. The class also keeps the last scalars used. When a specific scalar argument is not provided, the last scalars are used by default. The framework is unaffected when the scalars change. Moreover, different fields can coexist without having to take special care of them.

This design allows the same code to work regardless of the scalar system. Methods are written without any special considerations about the field of scalars, because they are based on mathematical definitions that do not impose specific restrictions (Figure 10.20). For instance, the matrix reduction algorithms are proven correct in *any* scalar field. These algorithms perform operations based on the properties of fields alone, without ever worrying about any field in particular.

As new numeric systems are added to the image, they can be immediately used as scalars in the package. Examples include real algebraic numbers, complex numbers, modular integers, finite fields, finite extensions of the rationals, etc.

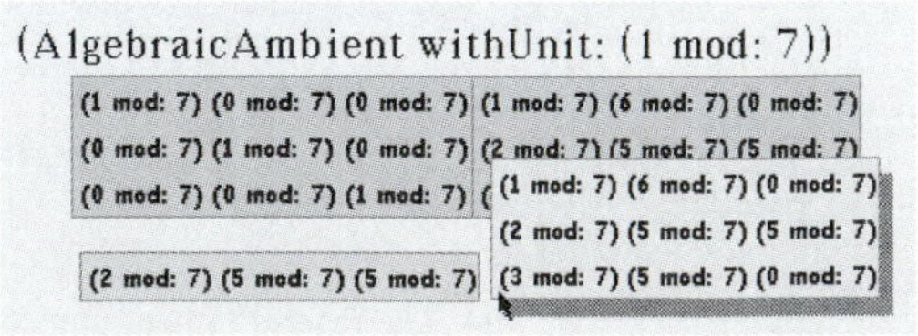

Figure 10.20 The same code works with different scalar systems.

LinearAmbients

We use LinearAmbients to define *abstract* linear spaces and perform functorial operations. These operations include basic ones (such as tensor product, hom, dual, direct sum, etc.) and any combination of them.

When we think about Tuples, Matrixes, LinearForms, LinearEquations, etc., we encounter subspaces and bases. A subspace has a basis, and we usually want to express a vector as a linear combination of the basis.

No matter what algorithm we employ, the fact is that all algorithms assume that we know how to write the coordinates of all involved vectors as tuples. In other words, each time we want to calculate the coordinates of a vector v in some basis B, we need to express the coordinates of the elements of B and v, in terms of another basis.

The problem seems to be circular: To find the coordinates, we must find some other coordinates first. However, it is not circular because all linear spaces are subspaces of a space with a canonical basis. Canonical bases are a clue to break down circularity.

Note that the notion of *canonical* is not mathematically defined. Nevertheless, a canonical basis has an intuitive property: It makes it easy to find the coordinates of any vector. Examples of well-known canonical basis are as follows:

1. Tuples: $e_1 = (1, 0, 0, \ldots)$, $e_2 = (0, 1, 0, \ldots)$, $e_3 = (0, 0, 1, \ldots)$, $\ldots$

2. Matrixes: e_{11}, e_{12}, e_{13}, $\ldots$, e_{ij}, where e_{ij} is the matrix having 1 at i@j and zero everywhere else

3. Single variable polynomials: 1, x, x^2, x^3, $\ldots$

4. Multivariate polynomials: 1, x, y, z, x^2, xy, y^2, yz, z^2, $\ldots$

When we have a canonical basis, we know how to compute the coordinates of any vector.

As we think about canonical bases, we realize that they appear in connection with linear ambients. A "linear ambient" is a linear space that encloses all subspaces in the domain of a given problem. Examples of linear ambients are Q^2, Q^3, Z_p^n, $k[x]$, $k[x]_n$, $k[x, y]$, $k^{n \times m}$, $\ldots$

A linear ambient is not a subspace; it is *the* space. In mathematics, there are spaces and subspaces; the spaces are the ambients where all vectors live.

Each linear ambient has a canonical basis, where "canonical" means that the computation of the coordinates of any given vector is trivial. More precisely, we define the class

LinearAmbient ('basis')

where we have two instance methods:

LinearAmbient | coordinatesOf: vector

and

LinearAmbient | vectorWithCoordiantes: aTuple

Of course, the class **LinearAmbient** is abstract, and the implementation of these methods is a subclass responsibility. Filling up the code for these two methods corresponds exactly to the fact that this task is supposedly easy when we have a canonical basis.

Thus, **LinearAmbient** is a framework that helps us to define concrete ambients. Here are some examples:

TupleAmbient "a number n is given"
Canonical basis: $e_1, e_2, \ldots, e_n$

> **TupleAmbient ≫ coordinatesOf: vector**
> ↑vector

> **TupleAmbient ≫ vectorWithCoordiantes: aTuple**
> ↑aTuple

MatrixAmbient "n and m are given"
Canonical basis: e_{ij} (i running from 1 to n; j running from 1 to m)

> **MatrixAmbient ≫ coordiantesOf: matrix**
> ↑Tuple
> dim: n * m
> fromBlock: [:k | matrix at:
>   (k − 1 // m) + 1 @ (k − 1 \ m) + 1]

> **MatrixAmbient ≫ vectorWithCoordiantes: aTuple**
> ↑ Matrix
> dim: n * m
> fromBlock: [:ij | aTuple at:
>   (ij x − 1) * m + ij y]

DualAmbient: "a subspace V of dim n with a basis is given"
Canonical basis: the dual basis of the given basis of V

> **DualAmbient ≫ coordinatesOf: form**
> ↑ Tuple
> dim: n
> fromBlock: [:k | form at: (basis at: k)]

> **DualAmbient ≫ vectorWithCoordiantes: aTuple**
> | vector |
> vector ← (self canonic: 1) * (aTuple at: 1).
> 2 to: n do: [:k | vector ← (self canonic: k) * (aTuple at: k) + vector].
> ↑ vector

```
Object
  MathFunction
    CompositeFunction
    ConstantFunction
    LinearArrow
      LinearEndomorphism
      LinearForm
      LinearTransformation
    PluggableFunction
    ProductFunction
```

Figure 10.21 Class hierarchy of linear functions.

Following these ideas, it is easy to implement TensorAmbient, HomAmbient, ProductAmbient, PolynomialAmbient, etc. A few classes capture all relevant ambients and their functorial combinations. With the help of ambients, abstract subspaces become naturally integrated. LinearAmbients ensure that all abstract concepts can be modeled and that all algorithms will work.

Arrows

Linear transformations are the arrows in the category of vector spaces. Since these transformations are functions, we have integrated them within the general hierarchy of mathematical functions (Figure 10.21). Our design consists of an abstract superclass named LinearArrow and three concrete subclasses for endomorphisms, linear forms, and general linear transformations.

As with the entire package, linear transformations may use any available algebraic system as the field of scalars. The domain and codomain can be also freely selected. This property gives the freedom to define transformations without worrying about indexes or coordinates (Figure 10.22).

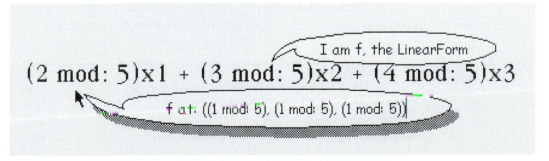

Figure 10.22 A linear form in the field of integers mod 5 is evaluated.

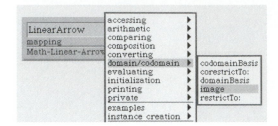

Figure 10.23 Fragment of the LinearArrow instance protocol.

A linear arrow can respond to arithmetic messages such as its sum with another arrow (Figure 10.23). They are also able to compute their images and kernels. The composition method implemented in MathFunction has been redefined taking into account that it must respond with a linear arrow.

Linear Equations and Linear Systems

Once linear forms have been defined, one can consider linear equations by equating the form to a constant value. A collection of linear equations is a linear system. These systems are instances of a special class, namely, LinearSystem. The protocol of LinearSystem includes messages to gather information about the space of solutions. When the system is not homogeneous, the solution set is not a linear subspace, but a linear variety instead (i.e., the displacement of a linear subspace by a particular solution). Thus, LinearSystems are associated with LinearVarieties, a new class of linear objects.

To compute its solutions, a LinearSystem uses an external object having the purpose of solving its equations. Here we have followed the general idea of keeping algorithms away from inputs and outputs. Instances of LinearSystemSolver translate the equations into a matrix and ask an appropriate MatrixReducer to perform the corresponding computations. Finally, they translate the matrix answered by the reducer back to the language of linear varieties and subspaces. The result of this design is a natural coordination of well-defined responsibilities. We have found that this kind of considerations make the work easier and without any loss of generality.

Polynomials

Numerical Analysis and Symbolic Computation show the field of Computational Mathematics from two different points of view. While Numerical Analysis has to do with floating point approximations, errors, and iterative algorithms, Symbolic Algebra employs re-writing techniques and transformation rules to make the relationships among the entities at hand more apparent. Polynomials are a good example where both of these points of view are present. Numerical Analysis is needed to compute the roots of a polynomial up to some error threshold; Symbolic Algebra provides the methods best suited to do arithmetic or calculate derivatives.

In MathMorphs, we think that both points of view should be available at any time. Our ideal is an environment where the desire for any operation, numerical or symbolic, can be satisfied without any additional effort. As an example, consider the polynomial $x^2 - x - 1$. It has two roots: $\varphi = (1+5^{1/2})/2$ and $\varphi' = 1-\varphi$. These roots are algebraic numbers, which means that we can use them in arithmetic expressions without losing precision (i.e., without introducing approximation errors). More clearly, we want to be sure about the accuracy of identities such as $\varphi\varphi' = -1$ and $\varphi + \varphi' = 1$, or any other expression of the same kind. On the other hand, the numbers φ and φ', or any other quantities obtained from them, can be approximated to "real" values going from symbols to floating point numbers. The later we move to real values, the greater precision we achieve. This crucial decision may not be taken beforehand, so we consider convenient the availability of both techniques at any time.

The anatomy of our implementation consists of two main parts: Monomials and Polynomials. Polynomials are built summing up Monomials. In turn, Monomials have a coefficient and a literal part, an instance of MonomialLiteral. For instance, the polynomial $x + 8y^2 + xz = 1$ has four monomials: x^2, $8y^2$, xz, and -1. Here, $8y^2$ is a monomial with coefficient 8 and literal part y^2. Note that -1 is not a SmallInteger, but a Monomial with an empty literal part. However, we can subtract the SmallInteger 1 from the polynomial $x^2 + 8y^2 + xz$. The illustrations that follow show how to create the constituent parts of this polynomial.

The instance creation messages x, y, and z are implemented in MonomialLiteral, Monomial, and Polynomial. In the examples, we have decided to work with Polynomials. Once we have all the monomials we need, we sum them up together in order to get the desired polynomial. Using MorphicWrappers we can easily do this with drop gestures and the double-click menu (Figures 10.24 and 10.25).

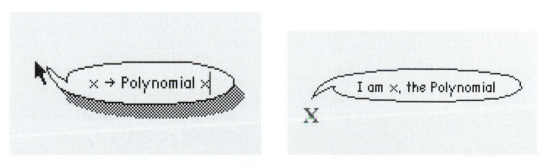

Figure 10.24 The polynomial x is created by sending the #x message.

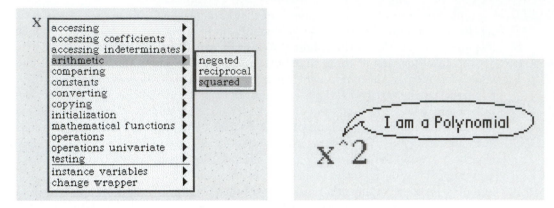

Figure 10.25   Sending the #squared message to x and obtaining the result.

Alternatively, we can write down the expression $x*x + (3*y*y) + (x*z) - 1$ on air. This requires the variables x, y, and z to be previously defined with the messages $x \leftarrow$ Polynomial x, $y \leftarrow$ Polynomial y and $z \leftarrow$ Polynomial z, respectively (Figure 10.26).

Once we have the polynomial, we can perform all ordinary operations, such as the computation of derivatives, GCD, addition, subtraction, multiplication, division and pseudo-division, evaluation, etc. The class protocol also includes an instance-creation message to obtain the interpolation polynomial corresponding to a sequence of values. The division and interpolation operations deserve special consideration.

Division and Pseudo-Division

Since the division of polynomials involves an algorithm with two inputs (dividend and divisor) and two outputs (quotient and remainder) it makes sense to employ objects specialized in the resolution of this problem. Instead of teaching the polynomials how to divide themselves, it is better to put this knowledge in a class by itself. Thus, we have the classes PolynomialDivisor, PolynomialPseudoDivisor, and MultiPolynomialDivisor. PolynomialDivisor implements the standard division algorithm, which works with univariated polynomials over a field. PseudoPolynomialDivisor performs

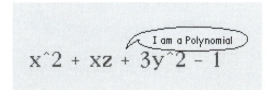

Figure 10.26   The resulting polynomial.

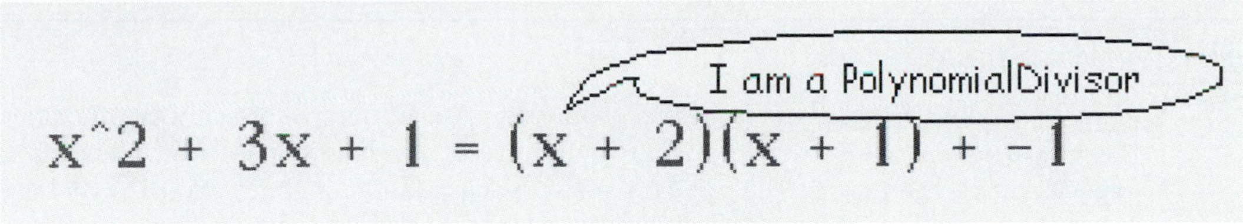

$$x\char`^2 + 3x + 1 = (x + 2)(x + 1) + -1 \quad \boxed{\text{I am a PolynomialDivisor}}$$

Figure 10.27 A PolynomialDivisor showing dividend, divisor, and remainder.

essentially the same algorithm, specialized for polynomials over an Euclidean ring. Finally, MultiPolynomialDivisor implements the algorithm used with *Groebner* bases.

Let us say we need to divide $x^2 + 8x + 1$ by $x + 1$. We create a division algorithm for these polynomials sending the instance creation message divide:by: to PolynomialDivisor. Then, we can ask the division algorithm for the quotient and remainder (Figure 10.27). We proceed in a similar manner to divide multivariate polynomials or polynomials in an Euclidean ring.

Interpolation

PolynomialInterpolators are employed to find a polynomial f satisfying a sequence of conditions of the form $f(x_i) = y_i$. We add new conditions with the message map:to:. The interpolator corrects itself adding a new monomial so as to match the new condition while preserving those previously established (Figure 10.28). Again, our implementation does not depend on the field of coefficients. It works with any available algebraic ambient.

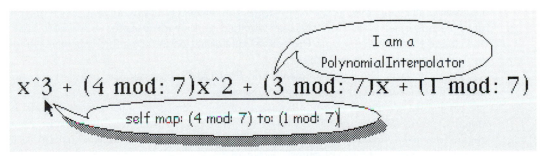

Figure 10.28 A PolynomialInterpolator using arithmetic modulo 7.

Projective Spaces

Linear algebra's geometry is *affine* geometry. An affine space is always included in a *projective* space, but a notion of infinity is needed to describe what affine spaces lack—the part of the projective space they do not include. With projective spaces, we can see affine spaces in a more global and unified way, and properties of affine mathematical objects are better understood when looking at their projective counterparts. For instance, in the affine plane, we have parabolas, hyperbolas, and ellipses, three pretty different kind of curves. But when we look at those curves in the projective plane, they are always ellipses that only differ in how the infinity line crosses them.

Projective Points

The points of a projective space are the lines in a vectorial space (i.e., linear subspaces of dimension 1). We added two methods to LinearAmbient, one to obtain the projective point associated with a vector and the other to get a representative of a projective point. When we associate a projective point with a vector, we are *homogenizing* it; reciprocally, a representative is a nonzero vector such that the point is its homogenization.

> **LinearAmbient » projectiveOf: vector**
> ↑ LinearSubspace basis: (LinearBasis ambient: self; at: 1 put: vector))

> **LinearAmbient » vectorWithProjective: projectivePoint**
> ↑ projectivePoint basis anyOne

Projective points are lines in a vectorial space, so we do not need any special class for them. In the default implementation, LinearSubspaces of dimension 1 are used as projective points. Subclasses may implement the methods, described earlier, if necessary. For example, projective tuples and projective transformations require a more complex behavior than the one provided by LinearSubspace, so we introduced the classes ProjectiveTuple and ProjectiveTransformation and redefined those methods in TupleAmbient and HomAmbient.

There are also ProjectiveAmbients and ProjectiveSubspaces, the projective counterparts of LinearAmbients and LinearSubspaces.

Projective geometry takes advantage of the computational tools available in linear algebra. This benefit is achieved by breaking down the entire space in affine regions named *charts*. The projective points laying outside a chart constitute the infinity hyperplane from the chart's point of view.

Algebraic Numbers

Real numbers are too difficult for the computer. The floating-point approach is illusory in many applications since it is imperfect in nature. Rational numbers and integers offer a more interesting perspective for computer algebra. Also, modular integer arithmetic is a source of examples and counter-examples to play with. Still, for the mathematician, these possibilities are too restrictive. Fortunately, a wider computational horizon is possible if we turn our attention to the field of algebraic numbers. Not only does this field enlarge the range of possibilities; it also brings a rich group of numerical systems such as the finite extensions of the rationals and the finite fields. What is nice about these quantities is that they require linear algebra and polynomials. Thus, algebraic numbers appear in the second layer of our project: the layer that combines basic mathematical objects already modeled.

Algebraic Numbers allow us to deal with irrational numbers without incurring in approximations. As an example, let us consider the square root of 2. Since this number is not rational, its floating-point representation is not accurate. As a consequence, we cannot take for sure that later calculations with such floating-point approximation will lead to the desired result. In order to be *completely sure* about the accuracy of any rational computation, we must adopt a different definition. The square root of 2 can be characterized as the second root of the polynomial $x^2 - 2$.

In general, an algebraic number is given as the ith root of an integer polynomial (i.e., a polynomial with integer coefficients). Hence, two entities are required to define an algebraic number: a polynomial and an integer. Equivalently, the integer identifying the root number may be replaced with an interval such that the polynomial has only one root in it.

The price one pays for this infinite precision is finite. It is necessary to develop more complicated algorithms for the arithmetic operations. For instance, given two algebraic numbers, one must compute the interval and polynomial corresponding to its sum.

The mathematical theory behind algebraic numbers is simple and well known. In order to compute some arithmetic operation, one computes a certain polynomial matrix known as the resultant. Essentially, given the polynomials of two algebraic numbers, one must compute the resultant of some other polynomials derived from them. The determinant of this polynomial matrix is the desired polynomial for the given operation. The way those "other polynomials" are obtained from the original ones depends on the arithmetic operation that must be performed. There is also a rudimentary "interval algebra" that must be defined to isolate the result.

When algebraic numbers are created, they contain a polynomial and an interval. This interval contains only one root of the polynomial, which corresponds to the value of the algebraic number. This interval may be large, but any number of refinements can be applied to get closer and closer to the algebraic number (Figures 10.29 and 10.30).

Figure 10.29 At first glance, the approximation may look poor, but...

The protocol of algebraic numbers includes, of course, all arithmetic operations such as addition, multiplication, division, etc. What is more interesting is that it includes the computation of the square root and, in fact, of any other root. As new algebraic numbers appear, their defining polynomial and isolating interval are always available. The approximation error corresponds to the size of that interval, so it can be arbitrarily reduced with further refinements (Figure 10.31). Furthermore, the length of the interval may be shortened automatically by the number when it is employed as an operand in some operations.

The Sturm's Theorem

The key point of the implementation of Algebraic Numbers is the Sturm's Theorem (1834). This brilliant result gives a surprisingly simple method to find out the isolation interval. The theorem was the subject of study of another MathMorphs project by Eric Rodriguez Guevara.

The idea behind the study of the Sturm's theorem was to illustrate a mathematical proof with an animated morph (Figure 10.32). The theorem states that the number of roots in a given interval, $[-3, \gamma]$ in this example, can be obtained counting the number of sign changes of any *Sturm chain* at both limits of the interval. One way to compute a valid chain is to start with the polynomial and its derivative, and perform successive divisions. The negative remainder of each division replaces the divisor, and the divisor replaces the dividend in the next iteration. The procedure

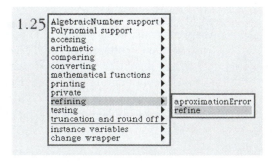

Figure 10.30 ...sending refine one obtains closer results.

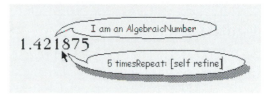

Figure 10.31   Five refinements are applied to the square root of 2.

parallels Euclid's algorithm to compute the *gcd* except that here the remainders are negated. There are other possible chains and all of them give the same result.

The demonstration of the figure shows a chain containing seven polynomials. As the interval's right limit moves from -3 to γ, the red dashes show the signs of the polynomials in the chain when evaluated at the moving end. At any given place, a sign change occurs when the sign goes from $+1$ to -1 or from -1 to $+1$ (zeros do not count).

The Sturm's theorem says that the number of real roots may be obtained as follows: (1) evaluate the polynomials in the chain in the left limit of the interval and count the number of sign changes occurring there; (2) proceed in the same way with the right limit, and (3) subtract the value computed in (2) from the value computed in (1). The result is the number of roots falling in the interval. The only requirement is that the *gcd* between the polynomial and its derivative should be a constant; however, this requirement is easily met dividing, if necessary, the polynomial by the *gcd* with its derivative.

The object responsible for computing all this information is an instance of the class RootFinder. Using the Sturm's theorem it is easy to verify if a given root is isolated in a given interval. It also makes easy to isolate all the real roots. This is the role that this theorem plays in the implementation of Algebraic Numbers.

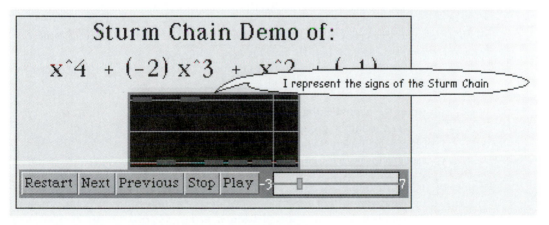

Figure 10.32   A machine showing the sign changes in the Sturm's chain.

Finite Groups

How should we model algebraic structures? Our central interest in MathMorphs is to design environments where mathematical objects are alive. The efforts in computational mathematics seem to be concentrated in the implementation of algorithms. We believe that before the implementation of an algorithm comes the definition of the objects that the algorithm acts on. This way of thinking leads us to model not only the elements, but also the structures such as vectorial spaces, groups, rings, fields, etc.

While Squeak provides, say, the class Fraction to model individual elements, the field of rationals has not been necessary for ordinary applications. But in Mathematics one usually needs the algebraic structures in addition to the elements. This need has been clearly shown in the Linear Algebra package, where we introduced linear spaces and ambients. Finite groups are the simplest example of algebraic structures, so we want to use them as a way to gain more experience on how to model algebraic structures in general.

Subgroups

Finite groups (subgroups) are implemented as the collection of its elements. Methods for enumerative messages have been provided. This makes it possible to define operations on groups just in the same way as they are defined in mathematics. The protocol for operations on groups includes the computation of the *center*, the *commutator*, the *order* of the group, and the *exponent*. The following is an example:

> **Subgroup >> centralizerOf: aCollection**
> ↑self select: [:each |
>   (aCollection detect: [:one |
>   each * one ~= (one * each)] ifNone: []) isNil]

The instance protocol also includes messages testing whether a group is *abelian*, *normal*, or *cyclic*. It also includes methods for computing the translations (cosets), intersections, direct products, and factor groups. The factor group G/N is composed of all the cosets of the form Nx for all x in G:

> **Subgroup >> / normalSubgroup**
> "Answer the factor group of the receiver by the argument."
> ↑self collect: [:each | TranslatedSubgroup
>   subgroup: normalSubgroup translation: each]

Some particular examples of groups are modular integers, quaternions, homomorphisms, direct and semidirect products, permutations, and roots of unity.

A homomorphism is a function f from a group G to a group H such that $f(xy) = f(x)f(y)$ and $f^{-1}(x) = f(x^{-1})$. Homomorphisms are the *arrows* in the

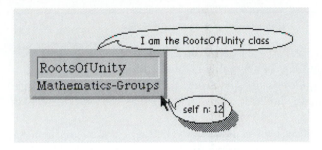

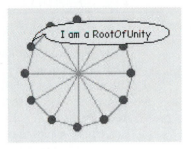

Figure 10.33 The group of 12th roots of unity and its individual roots (the red dots).

theory of groups. In our implementation, they know the domain G, codomain H, and a dictionary that maps x to $f(x)$. The instance protocol includes messages for evaluating; for testing if they are automorphisms, endomorphisms, epimorphisms, or isomorphisms; and for the computation of the inverse, the kernel, and the fiber at a given element.

We can create special classes to represent particular families of groups. For example, we created the RootsOfUnity subclass of Subgroup. An instance of order n in this family represents the group G_n. We customized this subclass with special behavior for instance creation and for the computation of factor groups. In order to create, say G_{12}, we only need to provide the number 12; thus, our instance creation message is RootsOfUnity n: 12 (Figure 10.33).

Since the factor group G_n/G_m is $G_{n/m}$, we redefine the corresponding method in the following way (Figure 10.34):

RootsOfUnity ≫/ aRootsOfUnity
    ↑ self class n: self order / aRootsOfUnity order

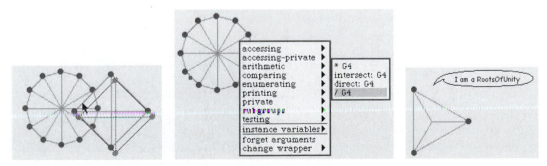

Figure 10.34 The result of dividing G_{12} by G_4 is shown to be G_3.

Algebraic Geometry

In its seminal form, algebraic geometry deals with the set of zeros that are common to a finite collection of polynomials in several variables. These sets consisting of the solutions of polynomial equations are the so-called algebraic varieties. Here, "solutions" means the points in an algebraic closed field, such as the field of complex numbers.

After decades of development and generalization of the theory, some mathematicians realized that all the knowledge accumulated in this domain was not enough for studying algebraic varieties from a computational perspective. The lack of effective methods became apparent, and two new disciplines were born: computational algebraic geometry and computational commutative algebra. Old problems deserved new interest. Suddenly, many mathematicians began to ask themselves how to compute the dimension of a variety, its projective closure, its degree, or in the zero-dimensional case, the concrete points that make up the geometrical set.

Once the first algorithms were rescued from history, it was understood as a matter of fact that the inherent complexity of these problems was too high to be efficiently solved with computers. New methods were needed, and a more careful analysis of the underlying hypotheses had to be formulated. Among the new tools, *Groebner* bases showed to be the most useful.

In this project, we introduce some usual notions studied in computational algebraic geometry and commutative algebra in the form of Squeak objects (Figure 10.35). The computational point of view and its practical limitations are illustrated facing the "Implicitation problem." This problem can be stated as follows: Given an algebraic variety described in rational parametric form, find a system of polynomial equations defining it in implicit form.

Let us see an example for the sake of clarity. Consider the set of all points with coordinates of the form $(x^2/y, y^2/x, x)$. We want to find a set of polynomial equations whose zeros are the topological closure of this set.

The parametric form allows us to deduce some properties of the variety. For example, since it has two parameters (x and y), the variety has a dimension of two.

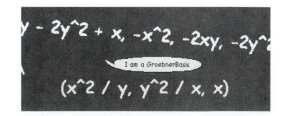

Figure 10.35 Squeak as a blackboard for mathematical thoughts.

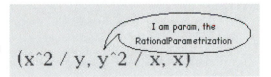

Figure 10.36   A named instance of Rational-
Parametrization.

Still, the implicit form has some advantages. For instance, using the parametric form it is not easy to verify whether a given point belongs to the variety. Also, the parametric form is expressed in terms of rational functions. So, it cannot be evaluated for all possible values of x and y, meaning that some points at the boundary of this surface cannot be expressed in this way. In general, to be able to use the tools provided by commutative algebra, one needs a set of polynomials defining the variety.

In the current implementation, parametric representations of varieties are instances of RationalParametrization. Once such a parametrization has been created, it can be asked for a system of polynomial equations. The solution of this system is the closed variety given by the parametrization. The instance protocol of a RationalParametrization includes the message implicit. This message answers with a proper instance of PolynomialSystem (Figure 10.37).

Having classes to model each of the relevant notions allows us to avoid artificial conventions. Thus, we can go from a RationalParametrization to a PolynomialSystem and then to an AlgebraicVariety. Neither arrays nor other meaningless data structures have any chance to remind us that all this magic takes place in a computer (Figure 10.38).

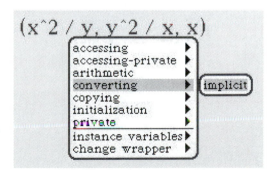

Figure 10.37   Sending the implicit message
to ask for a polynomial system.

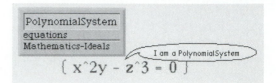

Figure 10.38 The resulting system and its class.

The project also includes classes to represent Groebner bases, ideals, and of course, polynomials (Figure 10.39).

How It Works

We cannot give a mathematical proof here, but we can explain the way we proceed to solve the Implicitation problem. The algorithm starts with the parametric form. It first replaces all variables with new ones. In our example, the parametric form becomes $(u^2/v, v^2/u, u)$. Secondly, new variables are introduced using the standard names. In the example, these are x, y, z. Next, the new variables are used to eliminate denominators from the equation $(x, y, z) = (u^2/v, v^2/u, u)$. We obtain $xv - u^2$, $yu - v^2$, and $z - u$. Now, a last variable is added to eliminate the product of all denominators—in our case, $1 - wuv$. Then a Groebner basis is computed using the lexicographic order defined by $w > v > u > z > y > x$. This is the hard part because of the complexity of the problem. In the worst case, this could be impracticable. Here we have chosen an example that finds the basis within a few seconds. The computation adds three new polynomials: $yz^2w - v$, $xy - zv$, and $x^2y - z^3$. The last step of the algorithm consists of selecting those polynomials in the Groebner basis that contain the variables x, y, and z only. Here, there is only one polynomial with this property: $x^2y - z^3$. Thus, the variety is implicitly defined with the equation $x^2y - z^3 = 0$.

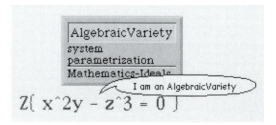

Figure 10.39 An algebraic variety as a set of zeroes.

Tarski Geometry

Classic algebraic geometry works with complex numbers. The same theory is extended to any algebraically closed field. There is a real counterpart of this discipline. When real numbers are used instead of complex numbers, polynomial equations have to be replaced with polynomial inequalities. The real solutions of these new systems are called *semialgebraic sets*. Real geometry (also known as Tarski geometry) and real commutative algebra develop these notions in depth. Again, the computational viewpoint opens new and interesting problems related to algorithmic and complexity. But this time, the geometry and algebraic concepts are enlightened with results and notions coming from logic.

The underlying theory introduced by Tarski is based on the elimination of quantifiers from first-order logical sentences. "First order" means that the variables under the scope of existential or universal quantifiers represent real numbers, not sets. The elimination theorem states that any such sentence is equivalent to another one that is free from quantifiers. The building blocks of these sentences are multivariate polynomial inequalities. Inequalities are combined with disjunctions, conjunctions and implications. The variables occurring in the polynomials are bounded under the scope of existential or universal quantifiers.

As an example consider the sentence the sentence $(\exists x \forall y)[y^2 - x > 0]$. Here we have one inequality and two quantifiers. This sentence turns out to be true, since x can be taken negative. Thus, $1 > 0$, as any other tautology, is a quantifier-free sentence equivalent to the former.

There are circumstances in which the truth of an expression is far from being apparent. But, on the other hand, all quantifier-free sentences containing only bounded variables happen to be trivial since they cannot involve any variable at all. These sentences only include constant inequalities such as $1 > 0$, $1 < 0$ and so on. So, the quantifier elimination can be used as an effective method to find out the truth-value of a sentence, provided that all its variables are bounded (Figure 10.40).

Effective is not the same as efficient. The inherent complexity of the elimination algorithm is exponential. This limitation parallels the one found in algebraic geometry. So, in practice, one cannot expect to solve all possible expressions. However, there are interesting cases to play with. Following our example, let us consider now the semialgebraic set in R^2 consisting of all pairs (x, y) such that $x > 0$. We can create the polynomial inequality sending the message $x > 0$, where x names

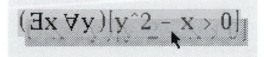

Figure 10.40   An instance of QuantifiedSentence.

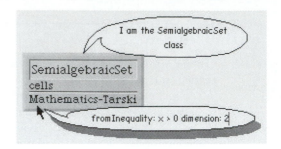

Figure 10.41   Creating the semialgebraic set
$\{(x, y)|x > 0\}$.

the polynomial x. The instance creation message is

> SemialgebraicSet fromInequality: x : 0 dimension: 2.

The dimension must be provided when it is not possible to deduce it from the number of variables occurring in the inequality. The class answers with the corresponding semialgebraic set. (Note from the illustration (Figure 10.41) that when writing the message on air, the name "self" can be omitted. Since the receiver is obviously the class SemialgebraicSet, the use of "self" becomes superfluous.)

Now we are going to use the new semialgebraic set to cause a variation in the logic of our tautological sentence. Instead of asking it for its truth-value, we are going to ask it for the truth restricted to the semialgebraic set. We can do this in two simple steps with the MorphicWrappers. We first drop the set on the sentence (Figure 10.42) and next choose the truthRestrictedTo: method from the double-click menu of the sentence (Figure 10.43).

Surprisingly, the tautology answers with false. At first glance, this could seem to be wrong, since tautologies should be always true. Why is this answer correct? Because a positive value of x less than any squared real value of y does not exist.

As a second example, let us consider the metric definition of continuity. In order to keep it simple, let us think about the concrete case of the continuity of the function x^2 at the point $x = 0$. The formal definition reads as follows:

$$(\forall \epsilon)[\epsilon > 0] \, (\exists \delta)[(\delta > 0) \wedge ((-\delta < x) \wedge (x < \delta)) \Rightarrow (x^2 < \epsilon)].$$

As we can see, this sentence only uses polynomial inequalities in the variables ϵ, δ, and x. Then we can create it as an instance of QuantifiedSentence. In the figure, we have employed the letter u for epsilon and the letter v for delta (Figure 10.44).

Figure 10.42   Step 1: The semialgebraic set
is dropped on the sentence.

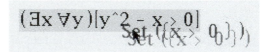

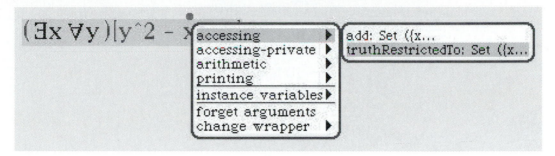

Figure 10.43 Step 2: The message is sent from the double-click menu.

Double-clicking on this sentence, we obtain true (i.e., our QuantifiedSentence is able to ensure us that our function is continuous at 0).

The Tarski geometry project makes use of many of the tools developed in other projects. Here we employ Polynomials, AlgebraicNumbers, Matrixes, and so on. It also introduces new classes, including PolynomialEquation; PolynomialInequality; BooleanConnective with subclasses for Disjunction, Conjunction, and Implication; Quantifier; QuantifiedSentence; SemialgebraicSet; etc.

The hard part relies on the Cylindrical Algebraic Decomposition algorithm (CAD). As usual in the designs we have seen so far, the algorithm takes a class by itself. Objects of this class can decompose R^n into connected components. These components are the so-called *semialgebraic cells*. In such cells, all polynomials from a given set keep their sign invariant. Such a decomposition is called a *cell complex* of R^n.

In our implementation, the connected components are instances of SemialgebraicSet. When $n = 1$, we have the simplest case. A special subclass, SemialgebraicLineCell, takes care of this.

The single variable case is easy. Suppose we have to find the CAD of R with respect to the polynomials $\{f_1, \ldots, f_n\}$. We find all the real roots of $f_1, \ldots, f_n$, say, $a_1 < a_2 < \ldots < a_m$. Then, the CAD we were looking for is

$$[-\infty, a_1), \ [a_1, a_1], \ (a_1, a_2), \ [a_2, a_2], \ (a_2, a_3), \ldots, [a_m, a_m], \ (a_m, +\infty].$$

As we have seen before, when the polynomials have rational coefficients, the roots can be effectively computed using Sturm's theorem. In general, the roots a_i are

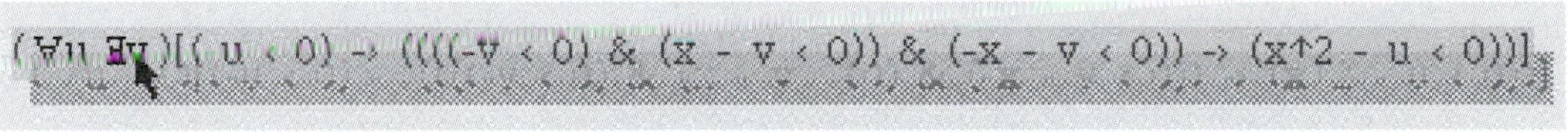

$(\forall u\ \exists v)[(\ u < 0) \rightarrow ((((-v < 0)\ \&\ (x - v < 0))\ \&\ (-x - v < 0)) \rightarrow (x\uparrow2 - u < 0))]$

Figure 10.44 A QuantifiedSentence expressing the continuity of x^2 at 0.

algebraic numbers and we can handle them with infinite precision. Each component can be asked for a sample point laying on it. Sample points are constructed as follows:

- The sample point of $(-\infty, a_1)$ is $a_1 - 1$.

- The sample point of $(a_m, +\infty)$ is $a_m + 1$.

- The sample point of $[a_i, a_i]$ is a_i.

- The sample point of a_i, a_{i+1} is $(a_i + a_i + 1)/2$ (middle point).

Let us illustrate the algorithm with an example: Decide whether the sentence $x^2 - 1 > 0$ is true or false. First, we find the CAD of R with respect to $\{x^2 - 1\}$. The roots of $x^2 - 1$ are -1 and 1, so the CAD is

$$(-\infty, -1), \ [-1, -1], \ (-1, 1), \ [1, 1] \text{ and } (1, +\infty).$$

Sample points are, respectively, -2, -1, 0, 1 and 2.

We know that the polynomial $x^2 - 1$ is sign-invariant over each of the components, so if it is positive in all components, it is positive all over R. We evaluate $x^2 - 1$ at each of the sample points checking the signs. From there, we can conclude whether the sentence is true or false. It turns out to be false, since the values we obtain are

$$(-2)^2 - 1, \ 1^2 - 1, \ 0^2 - 1, \ 1^2 - 1, \text{ and } 2^2 - 1, \text{ or } 3, \ 0, \ -1, 0, \text{ and } 3.$$

Note that while our sentence is not true on R, the CAD shows the cells where it does hold. From the previous evaluation we deduce that the sentence $x^2 - 1 > 0$ defines the semialgebraic set $(-\infty, -1) \cup (1, \infty)$.

The construction of the CAD in the multivariate case works by induction on the dimension. The interested reader will find the mathematical details in [Algorithmic Algebra, B. Mishra, Springer-Verlag]. Suppose we want the CAD of R^k with respect to a set of real polynomials $F = \{f_1, \ldots, f_n\}$ in k indeterminates. We produce another set of polynomials $\Phi(F) = \{g_1, \ldots, g_m\}$ in $k - 1$ indeterminates that have some nice properties. Next, we inductively compute K', the CAD of R^{k-1} with respect to $\Phi(F)$, and name its components as $C_1, \ldots, C_t$. Each component can be asked for a sample point. Let $f = f_1 f_2 \ldots f_n$ be the product of all polynomials in F. Define the function z_j from R^{k-1} to R as follows: $z_j(a1, \ldots, a_{k-1})$ is the jth root of the single variable polynimial $f(a_1, \ldots, a_{k-1}, x)$. The set $\Phi(F)$ is defined to make the number of roots of f invariant over each C in K' and to make each z_j to be a continuous function over each C in K'. Finally, we can construct K, the CAD of R^k. Each cell in K will be of one of two kinds:

1. For each cell C in K', $C \times (-\infty, +\infty)$.

2. For each cell C in K', suppose the number of roots of f is r. Then we have the following cells:

$$
\begin{aligned}
C_0^* &= \{(p,x)|x < z_1(p),\ p \in C\} \\
C_1 &= \{(p,x)|x =< z_1(p),\ p \in C\} \\
C_1^* &= \{(p,x)|z_1(p) < x < z_2(p),\ p \in C\} \\
C_2 &= \{(p,x)|x = z_2(p),\ p \in C\} \\
&\cdots \\
C_m &= \{(p,x)|x = z_m(p),\ p \in C\} \\
C_m^* &= \{(p,x)|z_m(p) < x,\ p \in C\}.
\end{aligned}
$$

Sample points for each of these cells are easily computed.

Let us close stating the Collin's theorem implemented in this project. Given a finite set of multivariate polynomials F in $Q[x_1, \ldots, x_n]$, we can effectively construct the following items:

- A sign-invariant cylindrical algebraic decomposition K of R^n into semialgebraic connected cells. Each cell C in K is homomorphic to R^d for some $0 <= d <= m$.

- A sample algebraic point for each cell in K.

- Defining polynomials for each sample point.

- Quantifier-free sentences defining each of the cells in K.

PhysicsMorphs and BiologyMorphs

The MathMorphs project has motivated some students to start experimenting with other sciences following the spirit initiated in MathMorphs. The first experiments about PhysicsMorphs and BiologyMorphs have given us lots of fun. Kinematics and Wave theory offer good sources of examples. Other projects include Optics and Kalman filters. Let us briefly describe some of them.

A very simple and still representative object to play with is the CannonMorph (Figure 10.45). The cannon obeys the law of gravity. Any other morph can be taken as ammunition. The cannon impels the ammunition with initial velocity proportional to its own extent. In each step, the cannon updates the position of the ammo following Newton's laws. This simple example can be implemented in two different ways. Since the function describing the position is a polynomial in the indeterminate t (time), the computations can be made exact. On the other hand, numerical methods can be used to approximate the derivative of this function (i.e., the velocity) with the quotient of small increments in space and time.

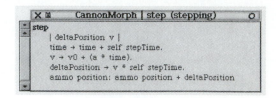

Figure 10.45 Only one simple method gives
the ammo its natural trajectory.

Differential Equations

A more elaborate example involving numerical methods is the solution of differential
equations.

Consider a string under tension (Figure 10.46). When it is separated from its
resting position and then released, as in the case of string musical instruments, a
shaking movement is started along the string. The vibration consists of a wave
phenomenon that can be described with a function $y = f(x, t)$. Here, x and y
are the horizontal and vertical coordinates of a point in the string, and t is the
time. This function satisfies a differential equation known as the *wave* equation.
The general solution of this equation represents all possible functions describing
the position of each point in the string at any given instant t. The exact solution
corresponds to the initial conditions defining the position and velocity of the string
just before it is released.

In many books, such functions are drawn in order to illustrate different waveforms. But since these functions involve three variables, they must be represented
using 3-D graphs. However, one of these dimensions is temporal, not spatial. Thus,
these graphs lack the main characteristic of the object they are describing: movement.

A better way to illustrate a solution is letting the two spatial dimensions change
with time. The whole effect is the one found in "real" strings under similar conditions. To accomplish that, a **VibratingStringMorph** solves the wave equation in each
instant t (i.e., in "real time"). Since the methods to solve this kind of differential
equation are numerical, the positions of a sample of points are computed at regular
intervals. In each step, the **VibratingStringMorph**, a subclass of **CurveMorph**, changes
the points defining it. And, of course, the string oscillates as expected.

Figure 10.46 Two VibratingStringMorphs
moving as waves.

Kalman Filters

High-energy physics studies the fundamental subatomic constituents of the matter. Particle accelerators provide subatomic particles for this study. When, say, protons–antiprotons at high-energy collide, subatomic particles appear. Physicists employ different detectors to determine the trajectory of these particles.

Think of a detector as a set of concentric cylinders. Each cylinder corresponds to a layer. A *hit* is the signal produced by a particle at some point in the detector. Hits occur on different layers. *Tracks* describe the trajectory of the charged particles along a magnetic field. Hence the hits, can be interpreted as the points of intersection of the tracks with each of the layers. The goals of track reconstruction are pattern recognition (track finding) and track fitting.

A Kalman filter (Figure 10.47) is used to predict the position of the particle in layer layer $k + 1$ from its position in layer k. Relevant information comes from the magnetic field. There is also a stochastic process. When a particle goes from layer k to layer $k + 1$ the detector itself introduces a random dispersion.

The method employed to find the tracks is iterative. It uses the notion of *global* track. A global track takes into account the hits, the parameters of the fit, and a bound for the error. The filter combines the predictions for the layer $k + 1$ with the hits detected so far. It takes the best fit and goes on propagating from layer to layer.

Kalman filters allow us to find global tracks, since they resolve track finding and track fitting at the same time. In each iteration, the filter finds the hits corresponding to a given track and the parameters of the fit.

Smooth changes are introduced in the parameters of the tracks. The changes, which are kept under certain threshold error, try to obtain a better fit around the vertexes. The approach is efficient since the matrixes processed by the filter have dimensions of 5×6 or below.

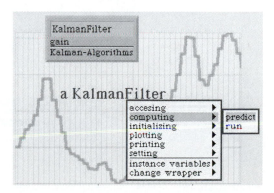

Figure 10.47 A KalmanFilter, its class, and its plot.

This project uses many of the tools developed in MathMorphs such as linear algebra, random variables, numerical integration, and function plotting. It adds the Kalman filters and models for Tracks, Detector, etc. (We want to express our gratitude to Ariel Schwartzman who developed this work, playing long hours with MathMorphs and PhysicsMorphs.)

BiologyMorphs

Pablo Shmerkin came with the idea of developing BiologyMorphs. His main interest is about artificial life. His project is made up from objects of classes such as Genom, GeneticCode, Biomorph, Squeakobe, EcosystemMorph, and BiosphereMorph.

A biosphere can hold more than one ecosystem (Figure 10.48). Each ecosystem has its own set of parameters. These parameters can be altered by the user. If required, the biosphere can collect all genetic information and place it into a BookMorph.

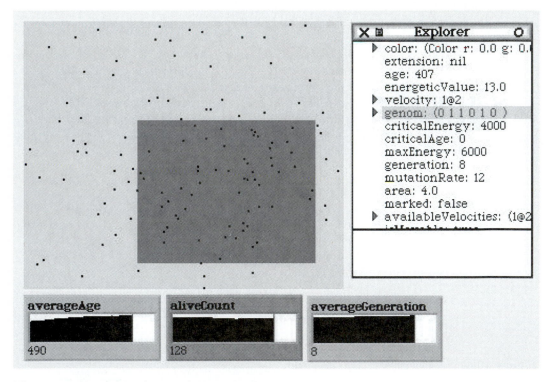

Figure 10.48   A biosphere with two ecosystems.

In the illustration, we see a biosphere with two ecosystems inside it, differentiated by their color. The visual counters show the evolution of the biosphere as natural selection operates on the biomass, and as the user introduces his or her own changes (artificial selection). The dots are moving microbes, each of them having a genom. The object explorer window shows the instance variables of a specific microbe. The green ecosystem is a kind of *Garden of Eden*, so there are a lot of microbes there. As generations goes by, microbes in each ecosystem develop quite different behaviors. Those in the *Garden of Eden* will remain as static as possible, while those in the orange ecosystem, a more hostile ecosystem, will move frenetically in search of food.

Related Projects

MathMorphs, as a collaborative community, has motivated some of its members to initiate individual projects. These projects fall in the boundaries of the group's main interests. They have had the virtue to face the group with new areas and possibilities. On the other hand, the group has acted as a qualified and enthusiastic audience giving valuable feedback to the authors. At the time of this writing, we can name three major projects: Type Inference by Francisco Garau, Arithmetic Coding by Andres Valloud, and Text-to-speech by Luciano Notarfrancesco.

For the sake of brevity, and taking into account that the Text-to-speech system has been incorporated into the base Squeak image, we are not going to describe it in depth here. Still, let us say that the author has extended this system in several directions. For instance, much better and natural voices have been achieved doing *diphones concatenative* synthesis with LPC and Residual Pitch Synchronous LPC diphones. Also, the GesturalVoice is being extended to use a 3-D face with Waters' muscles model, which is specially well suited for the realization of emotions (Figure 10.49).

Type Inference

Mathematics students have few opportunities to work in a Computer Science project from the inside. Frequently, they face computational problems as if the only considerations involving them were the abstract algorithms needed for a program to run. From the viewpoint of the MathMorphs project, the students should be faced with new fields of research where mathematicians and computer scientists could work together sharing the same degree of involvement. Type inference has proven to be a perfect example of such a project.

Type inference is an ambitious project currently under construction. The main person responsible for this project is Francisco Garau. He has studied the problem in detail and has implemented a type inference engine for Squeak. Garau has submitted the work to the University of Buenos Aires in order to get his graduate degree.

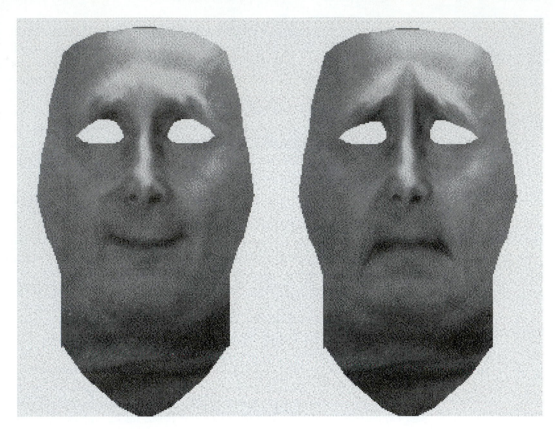

Figure 10.49 Waters' muscles model demonstration.

Type inference is not a new area in Computer Science; it has been widely used in functional languages. But in the past years, there has been an increasing interest to take those ideas to the object-oriented languages. Squeak is no exception.

The main interest behind type inference is to know in advance the types that arbitrary expressions will hold at run-time. There are different approaches to solve this problem. Many of them differ in the formalism and the notion of what a type is.

In this project, the concept of type is heavily biased towards what might be useful to the compiler. These are called *concrete types*. They hold the most precise and detailed information that the compiler would need (i.e., the classes of all objects resulting from an expression in run-time).

In the inferring process, type information is always kept at the most detailed level. As an example, the type of 1@1 is

<Point x: <SmallInteger> y: <SmallInteger>>.

Note that the type of an object knows the types of all its instance variables.

The following very useful applications arise from a type inference engine:

- An image stripper that throws away all the code you do not use. (Thus, a "hello world" application could be minimal.)

- A static checker that warns if a message-not-understood could happen at run-time.

- An optimizing compiler that, when there is no ambiguity, could replace a message send with a direct call to the method (or even inline it).

It should be clear that, in order to infer types, an initial expression must be given. Precisely, that expression, also called "program," is what makes feasible some of the above uses. (Independently, Lex Spoon is also interested in type inference. His "Lucid" system does not need an initial expression; Spoon's main target is program understanding.)

Our work is based on Ole Agesen's thesis, adapting his ideas from Self to Squeak and also making some improvements on the treatment of blocks and instance variables. His ideas about the parallelism between run-time and type inference-time were taken a step further. Thus, you will find classes like TiSystem, TiInterpreter, TiClass, TiCompiledMethod, TiCompiler, TiCompiledBlock, TiPrimitive, and so on.

Coding and Compression

One of the final exams for the course *Objetos Matemáticos en Smalltalk* was a compression project by Andrés Valloud. Its goals were to find a suitable design for modeling data compression and to implement some compression schemes. The basic design followed the guidelines described in the book *Text Compression*, by Timothy C. Bell, John G. Cleary, and Ian H. Witten. This book was published by Prentice Hall in 1990. The book emphasizes the separation of the *model* and the *coder* for any given compressor. The project has shown that in most cases, it is good practice to separate the coder from the model, although this separation should not be too strong.

The project began with an experiment to see if the model proposed by the book *Text Compression* was acceptable in Smalltalk. The book is C oriented, which does not reflect the proposed separation of the model and the coder. This experiment consisted of building a lossless ADPCM compressor with exchangeable models and coders. It showed that there are very concrete benefits that arise from separating the model and the coder. Improvements are easy to obtain, both in terms of efficiency of execution and of compression performance. The ADPCM compressor is consistently better than any combination of Lempel Ziv and Huffman compressors such as Zip. It is also comparable to other proprietary lossless audio compressors such as Ultra Compressor 2 and Rar. It is also extremely efficient. Using only Smalltalk code, this compressor running on a modest machine can process at least 10,000 symbols per second. Modern computers greatly increase this figure. The lossless ADPCM compressor was also the subject of the paper "Lossless Audio Compression and its Implementation," written by the author of the project. It was submitted to and published in a student paper contest for the 28th JAIIO conference, September 9–13, 1999. This event was held at Buenos Aires University.

The second part of the project consisted of an arithmetic coder driven by finite state and finite context models. The independence of the model and the coder was essential for achieving reasonable execution efficiency. This compressor is now undergoing further changes in order to obtain independence of the arithmetic used (fractions, integers, and floating point numbers).

A conclusion arising from this project is that although splitting the coder from the model is a good thing, it is not enough. In most cases, the model could use some information arising from the coder, especially the coding efficiency for each symbol. It has also been found that the way in which the probability intervals are ordered in a finite state model may affect the coding efficiency of the arithmetic coder.

Several side developments were necessary to support this project. They include the BitStream, Tree, Probability, ProbabilityInterval, and BitChunk classes with their associated objects, along with bit-manipulation methods.

Conclusions

It has been said that Squeak is a vehicle. We are trying to make MathMorphs one of the points of departure from which to get the vehicle running.

In 1997, we begun a course of pure mathematics based on Smalltalk at the University of Buenos Aires. Squeak quickly became the natural environment among the students, allowing us to discover new possibilities, for how to teach and learn math. We think this is a good place to present a short report of our exciting experience.

One of the authors of this chapter has been working at the Mathematics Department of the University of Buenos Aires for the last 20 years. He considered himself an innovative teacher. By getting involved with the Squeak idiosyncrasy, he has realized how much the conventional approach was constraining him. The transmission of knowledge to new mathematicians frequently fails in two ways: (1) Brilliant theory dissertations contrast with a lack of interesting examples, and (2) no relevant work is devoted to make the students conceive problems of their own.

In the course "Objetos Matemáticos en Smalltalk," Squeak is used as a laboratory and not merely as a programming tool. The great thing is that Squeak provides a suitable atmosphere where mathematical objects easily become alive.

The communion between Squeak and Mathematics is not an accident. The spirit of Squeak is similar to that found in high Mathematics, where the consequences of fundamental ideas are followed without any loss of generality.

Few and well-established principles naturally correspond to axioms. Precise definitions play a crucial role, both in Squeak and in math. Smalltalk notation is a kind of algebraic notation. Inheritance and polymorphism have algebraic roots, too. Squeak objects and messages resemble the *categorical* objects and arrows found in the underlying structure of mathematical theories. Squeak openness conforms to the mathematical conception of proof.

While object orientation is normally an abstraction task, where real things have to be represented in a virtual space, the same practice has the inverse result when mathematical notions are modeled. The model of a mathematical concept is more tangible than the concept itself. Instead of *abstracting*, one experiences the rather unusual feeling of *concreting*.

During these few years we have also noticed many interesting facts regarding pedagogy. A few of them are as follows:

- The students learn Squeak as a natural consequence of thinking about mathematical ideas.

- "Well-known" mathematical notions suddenly show unsuspected properties.

- Some theorems are naturally generalized in uncommon ways. As a result, deeper than normal understanding is achieved.

- "Living examples" that naively begin as simple forms of code testing, quickly become rich sources of new questions and problems.

- The classical barriers between formal definitions and intuitive ideas are changed into useful and precise specifications on how to move from the paper or blackboard to the Squeak world in a straightforward way.

- Algorithmic thinking and geometry, usually absent in the conventional approach, get included in the whole subject of study.

Squeak has been essential to our project not only for practical reasons (Smalltalk, free, platform-independent, morphic interface, etc.), but also for the presence and spirit of the Squeak community.

We want to share our experience of using Squeak to teach mathematics. Paraphrasing John Maloney, we want to say that nothing makes us happier than enabling students of all ages to gain a deeper, more personal understanding of powerful ideas, and Squeak is showing us how to do that.

Luciano Notarfrancesco (b. 1975, Buenos Aires, Argentina) is an active Squeaker and a member of the MathMorphs group at University of Buenos Aires (`http://mathmorphs.swiki.net`). He is currently working on speech synthesis and physical models of musical instruments. For more information, go to `http://minnow.cc.gatech.edu/squeak/311` or contact him at `lnotarfrancesco@yahoo.com`.

Leandro Caniglia began computer programming in 1975, while he was studying electronic engineering at the University of Buenos Aires (UBA). Later on, in 1982, he worked as a programmer in Banco de la Nación Argentina. At the same, time he studied pure mathematics obtaining a Ph.D. from UBA in 1988. After some years of scientific research and publications in the field of complexity in computational algebra and algebraic geometric held at Consejo Nacional de Investigaciones Cientificas y Tecnicas (CONICET), he and his wife, Valeria Murgia, started a software company. They work full time in VisualSmalltalk and GemStone producing advanced information systems for commercial companies from Argentina, Chile, and Brazil.

Caniglia has been teaching mathematics for the last 20 years at UBA, where he is professor. As an enthusiastic Smalltalk developer, he is one of the founding members of the Smalltalk User's Group of Argentina (SUGAR) and the MathMorphs community.

Presently, he commands the Departamento de Informatica of Superintendencia de Seguros de la Nación, a governmental office regulating the insurance market in Argentina. He also heads the ThinkLab project where professional programmers living at distant places, far from the city of Buenos Aires, learn Squeak and VisualWorks using email and a Swiki.

11

Extending MathMorphs with Function Plotting

Andrés Valloud
Buenos Aires University

Introduction

This chapter describes how to plot mathematical functions in Squeak. It covers and shows the objects involved and how to present the results in Morphic using the MorphicWrappers. It is aimed at Squeakers who desire to develop objects with rich graphic representations.

Historical Notes

The history of the function plotters is interesting. They started with the Math-Morphs project at UBA. The MathMorphs project is led by Leandro Caniglia, Ph.D. in mathematics, and has the goal of introducing mathematical objects in the computer together with their definitions. The result is that mathematical objects come alive on the screen and are much more than a pile of coefficients thrown somewhere in a more or less arbitrary way. The project has grown and expanded itself into areas other than mathematics and computer science, including physics and biology.

Within the focus of MathMorphs, a group of students, including myself, attended the course "Objetos Matemáticos en Smalltalk" (Mathematical Objects in Smalltalk) at UBA. Among other ideas we studied the Sturm theorem, which regards the isolation of real roots of polynomials. By means of an implementation of this theorem, we were able to represent algebraic numbers in a computer with infinite precision. Algebraic numbers are a field composed by the roots of polynomials with integer coefficients. This set of numbers includes the integers, rationals, and their nth roots. The Sturm theorem was interesting by itself, and I decided to make a plotter to see how the theorem reacted to different polynomials. The theorem associates each polynomial with a chain of polynomials that, when evaluated, tells us where the roots of the original polynomial are. The plotter was a plotter for the chain.

After the Sturm plotter was completed, I constructed other simple plotters, especially for Munsell's HSV color system. After that, there was the need for a general function plotter. A compression project I was working on needed the ability to plot histograms. The Sturm plotter was quite simple. It just built the image and pasted it on the screen, using a big, complicated and inelegant main loop. The Munsell plotters were a bit more advanced in the way the plot was drawn, but their architecture was pretty much the one found in the Sturm plotter. This approach lacked enough generality to provide a framework on its own. Therefore, it was necessary to create it first.

The Development of the Function Plotters

In order to build a graph we need a grid to plot it on, the functions we will plot, and some range in which we will evaluate the functions. We also need a procedure to draw our plot on the grid. We will solve each of these problems one by one. We will also leave room for a control entity to come forward, the plotter itself.

An Introduction to Grid Plotting

Our first problem is the grid. If we were to plot on a grid, what color scheme would we like? A grid resembling a blackboard or a notebook's sheet of paper could be interesting. Almost all plots have thicker lines for the axes and thinner lines for the grid, if any grid is present.

Form and ColorForm

Given that we are requested to draw a grid of a certain image size, we need a piece of paper of that size in order to draw the grid. In Squeak, and in other versions of Smalltalk too, the objects that represent such pieces of paper are instances of **Form**. These objects can be created in many ways, but for most purposes the following will be enough:

        Form extent: aPoint depth: anInteger

As a result, we obtain a **Form** that has a size of **aPoint** and that uses **anInteger** bits at each pixel for color-determination purposes. A 640 × 480 size form with a depth of 16 is a high-color form consisting of 640 horizontal pixels by 480 vertical pixels.

Note that Squeak provides both **Form** and **ColorForm** pieces of paper. The first uses a given number of bits per pixel, its depth, to determine the pixel's color immediately using the same number of bits for each color component in the RGB color space. Frequent numbers of bits per color component are 3, 4, 5, and 8. These bits give colors in a fixed color space of 512 (9 bits deep), 4,096 (12 bits deep), 32,768 (15 bits deep), and 16,777,216 colors (24 bits deep), respectively. Note that 16-bit deep forms use 15 bits per pixel to store colors. The extra bit is currently unused and is there to pad the 15 bits into 16 to make handling easier.

On the other hand, instances of **ColorForm** hold a color pallete, and the values at each pixel position are indices to the palette. The maximum size of the palette is 256 colors; hence, instances of **ColorForm** can use up to 8 bits per pixel. The advantage is that if we need an image in true color that uses 256 colors or less, we can get an exact copy in **aColorForm** and thus reduce each pixel entry size from 24 to 8 bits. As a result, the form's memory requirement is divided by approximately three.

Color and TranslucentColor

Instances of **Color** hold 10 bits per RGB component. This avoids propagation of round-off errors when adding, subtracting or mixing colors together. In addition, instances of **TranslucentColor** hold 8 additional bits describing its translucency coefficient. When this coefficient is zero, the color is transparent. If it is maximum, then the color is opaque. The **Color** and **TranslucentColor** interfaces use floating point numbers instead of bit chunks. All the value ranges are normalized to 1.0; therefore, the RGB and alpha values can be anything from 0.0 to 1.0.

Colors can be added and subtracted together, which is component-wise addition and subtraction. They can also be component-wise multiplied by **aNumber**. The result of each individual component after these operations is checked for bounds and forced into [0.0, 1.0]. For example,

Color gray − Color white = Color black

evaluates to **true**. When painting an area with **aTranslucentColor** that has an alpha value of (for example) 0.7, the resulting color will be

(theBackgroundColor ∗ 0.3) + (aTranslucentColor ∗ 0.7)

The component overflow check is not necessary for this expression. It also shows that regular colors are translucent colors with a translucency index of 1.0. Colors in Squeak also support the HSV color system, also known as the Munsell color system. The initials HSV stand for *hue, saturation,* and *value.* It is possible to ask **aColor** about these values and also about its **luminance** and **brightness**.

FormCanvas

When we draw on a piece of paper, a drawing board mimicked by instances of **FormCanvas** can be useful. They are created in the same way as a **Form**, and they hold **aForm** inside them. This form can be requested by sending the message **form**.

Although it is possible to do things with instances of Form alone, instances of FormCanvas provide a more suitable interface for our purposes. Several geometrical shapes can be drawn very easily using aFormCanvas, including lines, circles, rectangles, and ellipses. This separation between the actual graphic and the algorithms that draw things on this data is important. It allows us to change and enhance our algorithms without enlarging the base data class. It also allows very complicated procedures to be encapsulated in their own class without spreading instance variables. Moreover, it encourages polymorphism, since the same algorithm can then be run in different objects without needing to rewrite code.

Let's go back to our problem. We could draw the grid by first filling aFormCanvas with a single background color. Then we could draw lines on top of the background color. In this regard, the protocol of aFormCanvas includes

> line: startPoint to: endPoint width: anInteger color: aColor
>
> fillColor: aColor
>
> fillRectangle: aRectangle color: aColor

The first message instructs aFormCanvas to draw a line of color aColor, from startPoint to endPoint. Each dot drawn will be a square of anInteger by anInteger pixels. The second message tells the formCanvas to fill itself with aColor.

The third message fills aRectangle inside the formCanvas with aColor. This deserves particular attention. First, to build an instance of Rectangle, we can send either the corner: aPoint or the extent: aPoint message to another point. The message corner: b sent to a point named a creates aRectangle whose corners are a and b. On the other hand, the message extent: b creates aRectangle whose corners are a and a+b.

Filling Rectangles in aFormCanvas

Back to FormCanvas and fillRectangle:. The fact that a rectangle is filled with aColor means that to paint a single horizontal line at the y position yStart, we need to use

> aFormCanvas fillRectangle:
>   (xStart @ yStart extent: xEnd @ yStart + 1)

If we did not add + 1 at the end, the rectangle would have an area of zero. When filled with paint, this would indicate that we need no paint, and then nothing would be painted at all. This means that if we had aFormCanvas with a size of 320@200, and we wanted to paint its last horizontal line, we would have to fill the rectangle resulting from

> 0@198 extent: 320@1

Nothing would be painted if the rectangle started at 0@199, because then the rectangle would fall outside aFormCanvas. However, we could also try this rectangle with the desired effect:

> 0@199 corner: 320@198

Next, to draw a grid with thicker x and y axes, we need to know where the axes are. But that information is available only after we evaluate all the functions in their given domains. So, before we build the grid, we need to evaluate the functions.

Function Evaluation

The function evaluation goals are to provide a bound for the functions' images and to calculate the plot's actual points. This problem is different for every plotter. It is not the same to evaluate a function in cartesian as in polar coordinates. Let's take a look at the cartesian case first.

Evaluation in Cartesian Coordinates

Function evaluation is a two-step process. First, the functions are evaluated in their own domain to get their image bound. Then, the calculated points are scaled into points that can be drawn directly over our grid, once it is drawn using the information collected from the first step. To avoid unnecessary complications, we will do all function evaluation and manipulation inside instances of the kind of FunctionPlotterFunction.

Plotter Function Protocol

To create a plotter function, we will use

    aPlotterFunctionClass new: aFunction

Here, aFunction is essentially any object that understands the message valueAt:. Although disguised blocks can serve as functions, objects from a mathematical function hierarchy should be used instead. The basic protocol of plotter functions is as follows:

    domain
    domain: aRegion
    evaluate: anInteger
    evaluate: anInteger timesIn: aRegion
    imageBound
    invalidatePointCache
    scaleTo: aMapping
    scaled

The domain accessors provide access to the function's domain. The imageBound message requests the imageBound for the function. If the function has not been evaluated yet, the answer is nil. To evaluate the function, the evaluate: messages are used. Here, anInteger is the number of samples to take within the domain.

If evaluate:timesIn: is sent, aRegion becomes the domain. Then the function is
evaluated anInteger times. The scaleTo: aMapping message tells the function to take
the values given by the evaluation process and translate them to actual plotting
points over the grid, according to aMapping. In practice, aMapping will be the
grid plotter we still have to describe. After point scaling, the answer to the scaled
message will be true. Finally, plotter functions will hold their scaled points until
told to invalidate their point cache.

In the case of cartesian function plotting, the concrete subclass of FunctionPlotterFunction used will be XYPlotterFunction. The instance variables of these objects
include the domain, the function, the yBound, and the valueCache.

Regions

Domains, bounds, and intervals in general will be represented by instances of ClosedInterval. They are created by evaluating

    ClosedInterval from: anObject to: anotherObject

Their ends are accessed by the start and stop messages. They also implement
the size message, which is implemented by answering stop − start. The protocol
for instances of ClosedInterval includes mutator messages that are very useful for
progressive enclosures. For instance, in order to find the ClosedInterval that best
encloses a set of intervals, we can take a copy of any of them and then send a do:
to the set by means of the following commands:

    answer ← (aSet detect: [:each | true]) copy.
    aSet do: [:some | answer growSoThatEncloses: some]

In the first line, answer becomes the copy of any interval in the set of intervals. In
the second line, it is told to grow so that it encloses every other interval. We will do
this to find the image and domain bounds. The numerical version of this message
is growSoThatIncludes: aNumber. Now, we will go into the evaluation details.

First Step of Cartesian Evaluation

We will assume that we request a plot that has an extent of 640@480 and that the
functions we want to plot have to take values in the range [a, b]. Each function may
have its own particular domain, with the restriction that the closed interval [a, b]
encloses all particular domains exactly. Our strategy will be to take one sample per
horizontal pixel requested within the range that encloses all function domains. In
this case, we could then sample the interval [a, b] 640 times. This can be tricky:
If we take steps of b − a / 640, the final sample will be at a − b / 640 + b, which
is not b! We could then start taking samples at a, incrementing the probing value
by b − a / 639. This causes problems when the plot size has a width of one pixel,
because then we will divide by zero. Hence, we will use b − a / 640 steps, but
evaluate 641 times instead. This produces a harmless extra point, and it also
ensures we will have at least two points to plot, which will be useful later.

This process also allows us to determine a bound for the image of the function. Moreover, it accommodates for each function to have its own domain. Once we have the functions' image bound, we can determine where the x and the y axes are. The following is the method evaluate:

```
evaluate: anInteger
    | deltaX currentX currentY |
    deltaX ← domain size / anInteger.
    valueCache ← (OrderedCollection new: anInteger + 1).
    "We start with an 'empty' interval"
    yBound ← ClosedInterval
        from: (function valueAt: domain start)
        to: (function valueAt: domain start).
    0 to: anInteger do: [:each |
        currentX ← deltaX * each + domain start.
        "We enlarge the interval so that it includes every point"
        yBound growSoThatIncludes: (currentY ← function valueAt: currentX).
        valueCache add: currentX @ currentY]
```

Special care is taken in the currentX assignment to avoid floating point addition problems. This happens when deltaX is not large enough on its own to make domain start change or when addition results in an error of increasing size in currentX.

Second Step of Cartesian Evaluation

There is a second step in function evaluation process. Once the image bounds are determined, we know what our plot will represent—namely, the rectangle of the cartesian plane that has a horizontal span corresponding to the domain bound of all the functions' domains and a vertical span of the bound for all the functions' images. The task we now face is to map our evaluation space into the plotting space, an instance of Form. In this case, this will be done by the "mapping," the grid plotter. In order to do this, functions provide the message scaleTo: aMapping. Mappings, on the other hand, provide scaling messages. Here are the ones we will use for this stage:

```
includes: aPoint
pointFor: aPoint
spanFor: aPoint
transformSpanToGraph: aPoint
transformSpanYToGraph: aValue
yForXAxis
```

The message includes: is answered with true when the evaluation space of the grid includes aPoint. When a grid plotter knows the evaluation space and receives yForXAxis, it can answer the y position in the plot where the x axis is. Furthermore, the grid plotters respond to the message transformSpanYToGraph: by answering the *y* position in the plot that corresponds to a *y* value in the evaluation space.

The message spanFor: is answered with a point in our evaluation space that corresponds to aPoint in the plot. The message pointFor: aPoint, on the other hand, gives as a response a point in the plot that corresponds to aPoint in the evaluation space. (We will also refer to the evaluation space as the *span*.) A mutator version of the message pointFor: aPoint is transformSpanToGraph: aPoint, which changes aPoint into pointFor: aPoint, but without creation of new Point instances. This can be extremely useful when dealing with a lot of points and functions, because this environment promotes the creation of large numbers of points that will become useless quickly. Regarding this issue, creation of Point instances has been a problem in the past. A few simple modifications like the ones described earlier and later in this chapter allowed a performance increase of up to 72%.

Nonreferenced (dead) objects must be detected so they do not take up memory, and this is the job of the garbage collector. Garbage collection can be pretty fast in Squeak. However, that does not mean we are entitled to load it with tons of work, because it is fast anyway. The best way to deal with garbage collection time is to avoid creating garbage in the first place. In addition, if we do not create unnecessary objects, we also avoid the cost of such creation, which is also expensive. We will come back to these issues later.

The CartesianGridPlotter as a Mapping

Let's review the transformSpanToGraph: implementation. In order to do this, we must take a look at the CartesianGridPlotter. This object will provide the grid on which to plot, plus the transformation services between the plotting space and the function evaluation space. For the purposes of the plotter, the evaluation space will be stored as an instance of Rectangle, in the instance variable called span.

The problem now is to map points in the span into points in the grid, thus scaling. The span will be generated from the domain and image bounds calculated using the method growSoThatEncloses: and will be fed to the grid plotter when the function evaluation process is completed. Each function will then be sent scaleTo: aCartesianGridPlotter. This message is implemented as follows:

```
scaleTo: aPlottingGrid
    valueCache do: [:each | aPlottingGrid transformSpanToGraph: each].
    self scaled: true
```

Note that points are mutated inside the valueCache, also avoiding the use of at: and at:put:. This is not recommended as a general rule. However, such tricks help improve the performance so much that their carefully and properly controlled utilization can be considered as a valid alternative for the implementation of critical sections. In this particular case, we employ the trick because point scaling can be extremely time consuming due to the need for creating Point instances and the further management of the created points. Actually, it is interesting to compare how many points are created by this and other more "orthodox" procedures.

Now let's check the calculations necessary to transform aPoint in the span to a point in the grid. We will consider the x coordinate first. In this case, the span and grid extent have, or will usually have, different origin x coordinates. This means that we must shift all numbers before doing the calculations involved in scaling, proceed with zero-based number crunching, and then shift the results as a last step. The first step of this process is to take aPoint x and subtract span origin x from it. Second, we must translate the distance from aPoint x to span origin x into an equivalent distance from aPoint x to the origin point of the grid. This is done by the expression

> aPoint x − span origin x * graphSize x / span width

This expression is correct, but the problem with it is that graphSize x / span width never changes. So, the plotter will cache this value in the instance variable named spanWgSizeX when the span is given. This factor is the ratio between the grid's width and the span's width.

The vertical scaling is a bit tricky, since in graphs higher values of y mean higher position in the graph, whereas in instances of Form, higher values of y mean lower position in the graph. We start, then, with the following expression instead:

> span corner y − aValue * graphSize y / span height

Again, graphSize y / span height does not change; so the plotter will cache it into spanHgSizeY. In order to mutate aPoint, we will use the private method setX: anObject setY: anotherObject. Again, the reason behind this is to avoid unnecessary point creation. Here is the point mutator method in CartesianGridPlotter that translates from span space to graph space:

transformSpanToGraph: aPoint
    aPoint
        setX: (aPoint x − span origin x * spanWgSizeX) rounded
        setY: (span corner y − aPoint y * spanHgSizeY) rounded

We round the new values to create Integer coordinate points.

So, we have now evaluated functions in cartesian coordinates. But what about polar coordinates?

Evaluation in Polar Coordinates

Evaluation in polar coordinates is different, because the goal is to evaluate a function that, given an angle in radians, answers the distance from the origin to a certain point. This point is in the image of the function, at the given angle. It is very much like being in charge of a cannon, and the function, given the direction we aim the cannon, tells us how far to shoot.

Of course, polar functions do not differ a lot from cartesian functions. Instead of a number, we provide an angle; and instead of picking up the oriented distance to the x axis, we pick up the distance to the origin. Thus, both functions behave in the same way, because they take an amount and answer another amount. The interesting thing is to evaluate the functions in the polar space and map the result into the cartesian plane. This can be extremely handy. For example, in comparison with polar coordinates, it is irritating and cumbersome to describe a semicircle in cartesian coordinates. On the other hand, in polar coordinates, a circle becomes a constant, since a circle is a set of points that are at the same given distance from a given point, namely its center. The similarity between cartesian coordinate and polar coordinate functions encourages the implementation of polar coordinate functions by subclassing the classes modeling cartesian coordinate functions. Accordingly, the plotter functions used will be instances of the class ThetaRhoPlotterFunction, which will be a subclass of XYPlotterFunction.

First Step of Evaluation in Polar Coordinates

By far the trickiest thing will be to properly evaluate a function in polar coordinates. This is not because evaluation is hard by itself, but because we are planning to map it into a cartesian plane.

Given a function to plot, how many times should we evaluate it in its domain? If the number of points is too few, the function could look like a polygon instead of a curve. But if the number of points is too large, then we generate too many useless points. These useless points are very expensive in terms of execution time. They involve creation, evaluation, coordinate system mapping, scaling, and then plotting. The worst is that they may turn out to be the same after mapping and scaling. This is especially true if the function takes low values almost all the time, except for a few spikes that alter the scaling in the mapping. The problem is that we do not know the behavior of the function before evaluating it, so we cannot determine a reasonable number of samples to take until it is too late.

Our solution will be to evaluate a safe-and-sound number of times based on the size of the domain and then to eliminate useless points during the scaling process, taking proper care in determining what useless means. Here, it will mean consecutive evaluation points that are equal, or almost equal, after scaling. For instance, the scaling process should leave just two scaled equal points for the constant function zero. We will deal with scaling later.

What is that safe-and-sound number of times? It depends on the function being evaluated. As we do not know, we will use a fixed value to multiply the domain size, namely,

graphSize x / domainBound size * (domainBound size max: 2 * Float pi)

Although it looks quite complicated, it just scales the number of points for the size of each function's domain. Now, evaluation is different from cartesian evaluation, because we need to map one coordinate space into another.

When mapping from polar coordinates into cartesian coordinates, we need the horizontal value bound. We would like a constant function to show a circle touching the horizontal and vertical edges of the graph. That means we will have to scale with respect to x. To do that, we need the bound of the values of x. In cartesian coordinates, the bound was provided by the interval enclosing all the function domains. In polar coordinates, we will have to build that ourselves. The following is the evaluation method for the ThetaRhoPlotterFunction instances:

```
evaluate: anInteger
    | deltaTheta currentTheta rhoTrans thetaTrans cRho |
    valueCache ← (OrderedCollection new: anInteger + 1).
    deltaTheta ← domain size / anInteger.        "Increment between samples"
    currentTheta ← domain start.                 "Samples begin here"
    cRho ← function valueAt: currentTheta.        "This is our first sample"
    "And we translate it to cartesian coordinates"
    thetaTrans ← cRho * currentTheta cos.
    rhoTrans ← cRho * currentTheta sin.
    "We now need bounds for y AND x, since we find out about x after translation"
    xBound ← ClosedInterval from: thetaTrans to: thetaTrans.
    yBound ← ClosedInterval from: rhoTrans to: rhoTrans.
    valueCache add: thetaTrans @ rhoTrans.   "We get our first sample in"
    1 to: anInteger do: [:each |
        currentTheta ← deltaTheta * each + domain start. "New value in domain"
        cRho ← function valueAt: currentTheta.          "New sample"
        "We grow our bounds with translated points"
        xBound growSoThatIncludes: (thetaTrans ← cRho * currentTheta cos).
        yBound growSoThatIncludes: (rhoTrans ← cRho * currentTheta sin).
        "And we add the translated point to the value cache"
        valueCache add: thetaTrans @ rhoTrans]
```

Note the care taken to initialize the bounds. The points are created from translated coordinates. By the time the process ends, the functions originally in the polar coordinate system now can pretend to be functions in the cartesian coordinate system. There is one more step involved, the scaling. Of course, the plotter will first request the xBound from all the polar coordinate functions, then build its domain bound and send it to the grid plotter, which then will initialize its mapping capabilities. After that, the plotter will be able to start the scaling process.

Second Step of Evaluation in Polar Coordinates

Scaling will be done here by means of transformSpanToGraph: aPoint. The scaling method in the plotter functions will get rid of the useless points. A point will be considered useless when the sum of the absolute values of the differences of the coordinates of this point and the last point scaled is less than or equal to 1. The scaling process will begin by mapping all the points into plot space, and then a second filtering pass will be applied. To reduce the burden when the domain size is large, and consequently the number of points scaled is very large, only one collection of points will be used. The source code for the polar coordinate scaling method is as follows:

```
scaleTo: aPlottingGrid
    | lastPosition lastPoint currentPoint |
    "First we map points in the span to points in the graph"
    valueCache do: [:each | aPlottingGrid transformSpanToGraph: each].
    "We will look for similar points, so we initialize some variables"
    lastPosition ← 1.
    lastPoint ← valueCache at: lastPosition.
    2 to: valueCache size do: [:each |
        currentPoint ← valueCache at: each.
        "If the last point we added is similar to the current one..."
        (lastPoint x − currentPoint x) abs +
        (lastPoint y − currentPoint y) abs > 1 ifTrue:
            [lastPosition ← lastPosition + 1. "Then we move it back"
            valueCache at: lastPosition put: currentPoint.
            lastPoint ← currentPoint]].
    "So we are 'compacting' the value cache by eliminating useless points.
    Also, we may have to process the last point in case we did not add it"
    (lastPoint = currentPoint and: [lastPosition > 1]) ifFalse:
        [lastPosition ← lastPosition + 1.
        valueCache at: lastPosition put: lastPoint].
    "We discard the top portion of the value cache"
    valueCache ← valueCache copyFrom: 1 to: lastPosition.
    self scaled: true
```

This completes the scaling process. We are now ready to plot the grid.

Grid Plotting

Our attention will now go to the CartesianGridPlotter class. As we already know, it can translate between points in the span and points in the plot. This knowledge now enables it to determine where the axes are and how to center the grid. It also gives the aspect ratio of the span compared with the aspect ratio of the plot. This is very nice to know, because if the aspect ratio is 1, the grid will be composed of squares, whereas if the aspect ratio was not 1, the grid would be composed of rectangles.

Aspect Ratio

The aspect ratio of a rectangle is defined as its width over its height. Hence, aRectangle that has an extent of 640@480 will have an aspect ratio of 4/3. The idea behind this is that the grid will show how the graph is distorted in the requested plot size. For instance, a circle in a 640@480 plot will look like an ellipse. Accordingly, the grid's units should be rectangles of a 4/3 aspect ratio, because the aspect ratio of a circle's span is 1. And if the aspect ratio of the grid is plotAR, and the span's aspect ratio is spanAR, the combined aspect ratio of the graph inside the plot will be plotAR * spanAR. Now we know what the aspect ratio of the graph is, and so we can draw the grid and the axes properly.

Color Schemes

We will need three colors to plot a grid, namely, the background color, the main axes color, and the grid color. Changing these three colors, we will be able to mimic sheets of notebook paper, blackboards, and blueprint designs. These colors are grouped into color presets; some color presets are already available. Their names are Default, Arte, RecRoll, UBABlack, UBABlackGrid, and UBAGreen. The default color preset can be set by sending resetColors to the grid plotter. The rest can be set by appending their names to colorPreset. For instance, the color preset Arte is set by sending colorPresetArte. Their names deserve some explanation. The preset Arte mimics the paper sheets of the Arte brand notebooks. The RecRoll preset next imitates a brand of recycled paper notebooks called RecRoll. I used those notebooks at UBA. The preset UBABlack models UBA's not-so-black blackboards with chalky axes and grids. The preset UBABlackGrid is a variation with black grids and axes, and it is my favorite. The last preset, UBAGreen, models UBA's green blackboards with chalky grids and axes. These colors may be accessed individually within the plotter by sending the messages backgroundColor, axisColor, and gridColor.

Filling the Background

The first thing we will do in the CartesianGridPlotter will be to prepare our FormCanvas. It is much easier to draw the axes and the grid on top of the background, than to fill the rectangles left between the grid and the axes. Let's simply do the following:

    grid * FormCanvas extent: graphSize depth: 32

But why a depth of 32? That means we will use true color with full support for alpha-blending capabilities. It is possible to use alpha blending with less color depth, but we will choose to do our plots in a 32-bit deep form. If we need a plot that uses less bits per pixel, we can send the message asFormOfDepth: to the form or do something a bit more elaborate such as the Heckbert median cut color-reduction algorithm.

Once we have our grid, it is time to fill it with

    grid fillWith: self backgroundColor

This completes our filling of the grid. What should we draw next? If we draw the main axes first, then we will have to avoid them when drawing the grid. On the other hand, if we draw the grid first, we can safely draw the axes over it. Then, our next step is to draw the grid.

Drawing the Grid

This part is tricky, too. The behavior of the grid is dictated by numerous factors. First, the size of the rectangles drawn depends on the aspect ratio. Their position depends on both axes and the size of the plot. Let's examine this carefully.

The Influence of the Aspect Ratio on the Grid

To distort an initial square of the grid, we need to know how big it is. For our purposes, we will use squares of anInteger pixel's long sides. But which anInteger? We will start with a baseCellSize of 48, and we will let the following procedure adjust this value so that there is a healthy and nice-looking number of grid rectangles.

    calculateBaseCellSize
        baseCellSize ← ((graphSize x max: graphSize y) / 10) rounded max: 8.
        self aspectRatio > 1 ifTrue:
            [baseCellSize * (graphSize y / self aspectRatio / 6) ceiling
                min: baseCellSize max: 4].
        self aspectRatio < 1 ifTrue:
            [baseCellSize * (graphSize x * self aspectRatio / 6) ceiling
                min: baseCellSize max: 4]

This method adjusts the cell size so that there are at least six horizontal and vertical grid lines, and avoids the basic cell side falling below four pixels.

If the aspect ratio of the plot is 1 then the cells, now baseCellSize high and wide, should remain the same. When the aspect ratio is greater than 1, we should have rectangles with an extent of baseCellSize * self aspectRatio @ baseCellSize. Or, the other way around, vertical lines of the grid should be separated by

    baseCellSize * self aspectRatio

pixels. A similar reasoning applies when the aspect ratio is less than 1. Following are the methods that control how far apart horizontal and vertical lines of the grid should be:

gridXInterleave

"Answer the space between x axis guide lines"
self calculateBaseCellSize.
self aspectRatio > 1 ifTrue: [↑(baseCellSize * self aspectRatio) rounded].
↑baseCellSize

gridYInterleave

"Answer the space between y axis guide lines"
self calculateBaseCellSize.
self aspectRatio < 1 ifTrue: [↑(baseCellSize / self aspectRatio) rounded].
↑baseCellSize

The Influence of the Axes' Position on the Grid

At this point, we already have the functions evaluated and scaled. We also know the span and the plotting space. Then, we can certainly verify if the main x and y axes are included or not. These two cases will be handled differently.

If there are no axes in the span, then where should we draw the subgrid? We could follow the 0,0 coordinates and start from there, but then the subgrid could end up not centered in the plot. With no thicker axes to see, this looks odd. So, when there are no axes, we will follow the plot borders and center the subgrid with respect to them. But if the axes are in the plot, we would like the subgrid to be centered with respect to the axes.

That is what we will do for each axis. If an axis is present, then the correspondent vertical or horizontal subgrid is centered at the axis. Otherwise, it is centered from the plot borders. Here is the main grid plotter method:

plotGrid

"Answer the grid generated by the current settings"
| drawX drawY |
grid ← FormCanvas extent: graphSize depth: 32.
grid fillColor: self backgroundColor.
"We first determine what kind of subgrid we need to plot"
(drawX ← self xInterval includes: 0)
    ifTrue: [self generateXZGridOn: grid using: self xInterval]
    ifFalse: [self generateXCGridOn: grid].
(drawY ← self yInterval includes: 0)
    ifTrue: [self generateYZGridOn: grid using: self yInterval]
    ifFalse: [self generateYCGridOn: grid].
"And then we plot the main axes"
drawX ifTrue: [self drawXAxisOn: grid using: self xInterval].
drawY ifTrue: [self drawYAxisOn: grid using: self yInterval].
↑self grid

The axes and grid lines are drawn using the rectangle-filling methods we already saw in the protocol of FormCanvas.

Some of the selector names deserve an explanation. For each coordinate, x and y, there is an axis and a subgrid. The subgrid is a set of lines parallel to the given main axes. What we just discussed means that we have two different ways of drawing the subgrids, either centered around the axes or centered on the plot. Here, these centering methods are referred to by the Z (centering around the axes or around zero) and C letters (plain centering on the plot). For instance, the method name generateYCGridOn: selector means to generate the y subgrid, centered on the plot. Finally, the axes are drawn after the subgrid is drawn. This is done to avoid the subgrid overwriting the main axes, which is not esthetically good.

Introduction to the Plot Engine

So far in our problem, we have evaluated the functions, scaled them, and drawn the grid. It is now time to draw the functions. We have seen that the plotter functions, when scaled, hold a valueCache that contains all the points to be drawn. Actually, these points give us the points of a polygon that we will draw on the grid. The idea is that we play "connect the dots" with such points, and that is why it is important to have at least two points.

Yet, for certain applications, it would be much nicer if we were able to apply some effects to our polygon. For instance, students of calculus know that one interpretation of the value of the integral of a function is a measurement of the area between the function and the x axis. Students of statistics find this very useful when plotting histograms and probability distributions, and they can usually derive a lot of information from those graphs. Students of multivariate calculus are often interested in the contour of certain three-dimensional objects, such as cylinders, cones, paraboloids, and so on. Pie charts and bar graphs, with their variations, would be a great enhancement to our drawn polygon. And hey! We should also keep function colors in mind!

Function Colors and the Munsell Color System

Computers usually follow the RGB color space, in which the red, green, and blue coordinates may take values between 0 and some fixed value like 31, 63, or 255. Each color is then represented by a triplet of those values, one value per color coordinate. The whole RGB color space has the shape of a cube.

Here is a neat little problem. Choose colors such that they are "most" different. How do we do that? Let's get more detailed. We would like colors of the same brightness, yet, as different as possible. But to do that in the RGB cube is not trivial! Things can get messy very quickly because of recursivity in the algorithms. To make things more complicated, the RGB cube does not allow an order relationship between colors as we can find for, say, the real numbers (this can prove to be a very tough problem in connection with the hash value of a color and to color quantization), so we encounter difficulty trying to choose colors sequentially.

Fortunately, it is very easy to solve this problem if we use another coordinate system. Instead of working in the RGB cube, we will work in the HSV color system. Let's examine it.

The Munsell color system space looks like a cylinder. Of course, we will use cylindrical coordinates to describe it. Cylindrical coordinates are an extension of polar coordinates. In polar coordinates, we choose an origin, and for each angle, the function provides the distance to the origin where we should plot a dot. For instance, a circle in polar coordinates is a constant. In general, it is easier to describe circle-like figures in polar coordinates than in any other coordinate system.

But we need to describe a cylinder and not a circle. Thus, we say that the cylinder is the collection of all the parallel, same-radius circles that have their origins in a segment that is perpendicular to all those circles. Then, we can use a height-shift value that lets us move in the segment to choose any particular circle, and then we can use polar coordinates within the circle to reach any point in the cylinder. Cylindrical coordinates are polar coordinates plus a shift axis.

In the Munsell color system cylinder, the segment goes from black to white, and it is referred to as the value component of any given color. Let's get in a circle in particular. The colors are arranged in such a way that all possible colors of the same apparent brightness are together in the circle. Evidently, all the colors in each circle are as bright as the value of the circle in question. Now, to get any color, we use polar coordinates. The angle part is called the hue, and by changing it, we sweep all possible colors. As we get farther away from the center, colors are said to become more saturated or more colorful, so to speak. At the outer perimeter of the circle, we find pure colors. Getting closer to the center mixes each pure hue with the gray color at the center. In a sense, it is doing alpha-blending between any given shade of gray and the pure color at the same brightness. Because each color can be described by their hue, saturation, and value, this color system is also known as HSV. Here you can see the skin of the Munsell cylinder, at saturation 0.9 and with 11 different values, from 0 to 10. Hues run from left to right, and values run from bottom to top. The left corresponds to a hue of 0, while the bottom corresponds to a value of 0. It was plotted by the MunsellTree plotter (Figure 11.1).

Back to our problem. The HSV color system has six familiar hues around its outer perimeter. We could fix the value and saturation, and then choose those basic six hues first. After those run out, we then could choose the hues between each consecutive hue chosen before, and so on. This is exactly what the instances of ColorStream do. They are also the grounds upon which the RainbowMorph is based. The RainbowMorph changes its color over time, by means of the step method. Each time it steps, it will change its color to aColorStream next. At first, it will change coarsely, but as time goes by, the color stream will choose closer and closer colors. After a few minutes, it will smoothly fade from one shade to the next. At all times though, colors chosen will be as far apart as possible from all colors selected previously.

Figure 11.1 The skin of a Munsell Tree at saturation 0.9. The bottom and top of the graph correspond to a value of 0 and 10, respectively. From left to right, all the possible hues are displayed.

We want exactly this behavior for the function color assignment (i.e., to choose colors as far apart from each other as possible). It is also desirable to choose colors with the same brightness, that is, with the same saturation and value. If we allowed different saturations and values, we could end up with very bright colors together with pale ones. Hence, we will assign each function the color given by aColorStream next:

```
next
    | newH |
    newH ← colorStep * colorDelta + colorShift.
    newH >= 1
        ifTrue:
            [colorStep ← 0.
            colorShift = 0
                ifTrue: [colorShift ← colorDelta / 2]
                ifFalse: [colorShift ← colorShift / 2. colorDelta *colorDelta / 2].
            ↑self next]
        ifFalse:
            [colorStep ← colorStep + 1].
    ↑Color h: (h ← newH * 360) s: s v: v
```

The initialization method of ColorStream makes colorDelta to be 1/6, and colorShift and colorStep to be 0. Each time this method is executed, it goes around the outer perimeter of the saturation and value circle chosen in the HSV color system. When the turn is completed, the shift and the delta are updated so that new colors fall between colors already chosen.

Functions and Alpha Blending Colors

Furthermore, functions will get the colors coming out from a ColorStream with a specific alpha-blending value. This allows functions to overlap the grid and other functions, preventing them from overwriting the already existing graphics. Currently, the alpha-blending plot value is 0.08. Other effects, such as area filling, will receive other alpha-blending values, such as 0.02 and even 0.005, to differentiate the effect from the plot itself. These values will be held by the plot engine.

The Plot Engine

We referred to a few things that would enhance our simple polygon plot. Different ways to draw a function will be referred to as plot modes. Each plot mode will draw the polygon and enhance it in some way as it is being drawn. The object that will implement these plot modes is the plot engine.

The plot engine is an object that, taken a mapping for reference and a function to plot, will output the plot to a certain number of plot targets. The mapping will be a grid plotter and it will provide information about the position of the axes. The plotter function will tell the plotter what color and plot mode to use. Plotter functions have a very flexible mechanism to tell the plot engine things. They have attributes that can be set and retrieved by name. Some of them are so important that they have specific accessors, such as the **plotMode**, the width of the plot (called **dotSize**), and the **color**. These are all considered to be attributes of the plotter function.

Plot Targets

About the output, it is very desirable to be able to output the plot to more than one form canvas simultaneously. The first target will be a cache of the plot. We would not like to replot each time the plotter is moved in a Morphic world. On the other hand, it would be nice if we could see the plot being generated in real time. This implies that besides drawing on our cache, we will have to draw directly on the screen. To allow this, we will wrap each form canvas to be drawn on inside an instance of the class **PlotTarget**.

There is an additional benefit arising from using a cache. The plotter will be working in 32 bits and so will the cache. If the screen is set to something less than 32 bits, each draw operation will have its colors truncated. As a result, what is displayed on the screen will be the result of several truncated color operations. At the end, though, we may draw the whole cache, and so we will display the plot with just one color truncation operation. The difference between these is quite noticeable.

Morphic worlds are drawn on a form canvas, but evidently the plotter may not be the only thing present in the display. To allow drawing directly over them as the plot engine works, plot targets will provide an offset to their form canvas. This is done so the plot engine only sees a form canvas on which it has to draw starting at 0@0. Because the plot target will take care of drawing on the form canvas, it will implement a few methods to allow skewing the coordinates by the corresponding offset. For instance, if the function plotter is at 100@100 in the Morphic world, and its grid has an extent of 640@480, the plot target will redirect the rectangle 0@0 corner: 640@480 to 100@100 corner: 740@580. Incidentally, being able to display progress in realtime is also why we will concentrate on synchronous enhancement of the polygon. Special effects look great when they appear on the screen as they are being drawn. Plot targets are given to the plot engine by using the method addTarget: aPlotTarget. The drawing methods implemented by instances of PlotTarget are as follows:

line: startPoint to: endPoint width: aWidth color: aColor

line: startPoint to: endPoint width: aWidth color: aColor withFirstPoint: aBoolean

These are very similar. What they do is draw a line in the form canvas from startPoint + offset to endPoint + offset, with a dot size of aWidth and with color aColor. Furthermore, the first point of the line can be skipped while drawing. This produces better quality plots. Since we will play "connect the dots," we do not need to plot those dots twice (once when we arrive and once when we proceed to the next one).

The Plot Engine's Plot Modes

We will describe the plot modes now, together with some examples of them in action. Some of the illustrations include a few additions to make them more clear. It is a thrilling experience to watch the function plotters draw these pictures on the fly.

The PlotEngine class currently has one concrete subclass, XYPlotEngine. Because the instances of ThetaRhoPlotterFunction translate the points into cartesian coordinates, it is not necessary to have a dedicated ThetaRhoPlotEngine class. The XYPlotEngine provides the following plot modes:

AlphaToOrigin
AlphaToXAxis
DiscreteDerivative
DownVolumeCylinder
DownRightVolumeCone
DownRightVolumeCylinder
OddConical
Standard

We will now describe these eight plot modes.

The Standard Plot Mode

This mode takes the points from the plotter function's valueCache and simply draws a polygon on the plot targets. Following is the implementation:

```
plotStandard
    "Produce a standard plot on the targets"
    | last current |
    last ← toPlot at: 1.
    2 to: toPlot size do: [:each |
        current ← toPlot at: each.
        targets do: [:some | some
            line: current to: last
            width: dotSize color: plotColor
            withFirstPoint: each = toPlot size].
        last ← current]
```

When this method is executed, the plot engine has the function's valueCache stored in toPlot, its plot width in dotSize, and its color in plotColor. The alpha value of plotColor is set to 0.08 by the plot engine. We can see here how each little line of the plot is drawn backwards, so that the withFirstPoint: plot method takes care of plotting the extra point only when necessary.

Examination of Random Sequences

A portion of a previous work regarding compression had to do with the distribution of the absolute values of the difference between pairs of consecutive elements taken from a stream. If the stream is generating numbers at random in a given range, the distribution of these numbers can be proven to have a triangular shape like the one shown in Figure 11.2. In this case, the domain is [0, 255]. The high peak close to zero is 510, and at zero, there are 256 hits. As the difference increases by one, the hits decrease by two. The hit average for a range of width n is $(n + 1)/3$.

Let's suppose for a moment that various common compressors produce a random sequence of bytes (or whatever). We will see how well they perform at their task. For our tests, we will use the zip and rar compression algorithms. Both use the popular Lempel Ziv algorithm for string matching. After LZ, zip uses Huffman, while rar uses a proprietary encoding mechanism. Rar also has dedicated "multimedia" algorithms. The triangular distribution for a random sequence will be left as a reference. We will examine both compressors working on a wav file. The file is an 8-bits, mono, 22khz-sample-rate, 666,108-bytes-long file. The three plots here show the distribution of the uncompressed file, of the zip file (237,902 bytes), and of the rar file (234,000 bytes), left to right. Rar may choose to use its multimedia algorithms.

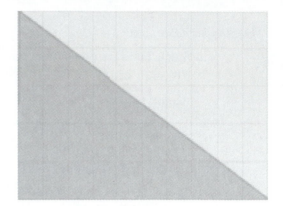

Figure 11.2 Histogram of the absolute difference between consecutive numbers coming from a random number source, in the interval [0, 255].

The histograms in Figure 11.3 are normalized to a maximum hit value of 510. In this case, rar's behavior is closer to random than zip's. Note how the first histogram shows that the absolute values of the differences of consecutive values in this particular wav file are usually small. This behavior is quite common for sound files, regardless of bit depth and channels (even when not de-interleaved). If the histogram were of the difference of consecutive values alone, it would have two spikes at the left and right ends, with a big valley in between.

The Area Filling Plot Modes

Some plot modes will fill an area between the function's graph and the axes, or between the function's graph and a certain fixed point. This is the case of the AlphaToOrigin and AlphaToXAxis plot modes. In the first case, a line is drawn from each point of the function's graph to a fixed point. In the second case, a line is drawn from each point of the function's graph to its x-axis projection. To solve these cases in general, the plot engine implements two private methods called plotFillTo: aBlock and plotFillToPoint: aPoint. The following is the implementation of the first (the other can be obtained by replacing the reference to aBlock value: last by aPoint):

Figure 11.3 Histograms (from left to right) for raw wave, zip compressed, and rar compressed data, compared to random. These particular histograms suggest that PCM data is far from random and that rar does a better job at getting close to the ideal distribution than zip.

plotFillTo: aBlock
    "Produce a standard plot on the targets, and for each point plotted
    fill the line connecting the point plotted with aBlock value: plotted
    point"
    | last current |
    last ← toPlot at: 1.
    "Effect for the first point"
    targets do: [:other | other
        line: last to: (aBlock value: last) width: dotSize color: fillColor].
    2 to: toPlot size do: [:each |
        current ← toPlot at: each.
        "Standard plot"
        targets do: [:some | some
            line: current to: last width: dotSize
            color: plotColor withFirstPoint: each = toPlot size].
        "Effect for each point plotted"
        targets do: [:more | more
            line: current to: (aBlock value: current)
            width: dotSize color: fillColor withFirstPoint: false].
        last ← current]

Here, aBlock is set to: [:each | each x @ xAxisPosition]. The variable xAxisPosition
comes from the context in which the block is created. Its value is aMapping yForX-
Axis. Note the care taken to draw the enhancement from the point referenced by
last. The variable fillColor contains the function's color with an alpha value of 0.02.

An Application of the **ThetaRhoPlotter** in Number Theory

Imagine we took a function that, given an integer, answered the number of prime
factors in the given integer. With that function, we could also find the average prime
factors per integer up to a given integer and get another function. Figures 11.4
and 11.5 show two plots on this topic. Incidentally, the average primes per integer
up to n is asymptotically close to $\log \log n + M$, where M is the Mertens' constant,
whose value is close to 0.57. In the first plot (Figure 11.4), note how the integers
arrange themselves in rings. The innermost ring is the prime ring.

In the second plot (Figure 11.5), we can see how the prime average, in red, gets
flat almost instantly. The blue function here is the green function from the first
illustration. The first illustration is using the **AlphaToOrigin** plot mode, while the
second illustration is using the **AlphaToXAxis** plot mode.

The Discrete Derivative Plot Mode

This plot mode will add small tangent lines to the graph. It is especially designed
to draw such lines only when there has been a considerable variation in the slope

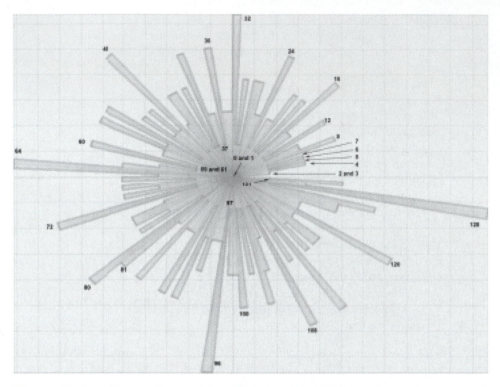

Figure 11.4 Polar coordinate plot of $f(n) =$ number of prime factors in n, in $[0, 131]$ scaled to 0 and 2 * Pi. This plot uses the discrete function adapter to generate a bar-graph plot. The arrows with numbers pointing to the graph indicate which places on the graph correspond to certain integers.

of the curve being plotted. The color of the derivative lines is the function's color with an alpha value of 0.07. Figure 11.6 shows an example of this plot mode with four polynomials. The colors in this plot show the **ColorStream** in action (also note the tangent lines).

The Graph Dragging Plot Modes

The plot modes remaining take the graph and drag it on the targets, leaving some sort of trace while they do so. The idea of these methods came to me by accident. I was trying to get the x-axis area-filling mode to work, but I made several mistakes. Those mistakes showed that a simple process would make a simple plot into something much better. Even more, these effects could be designed such that the plotter would appear to be three dimensional.

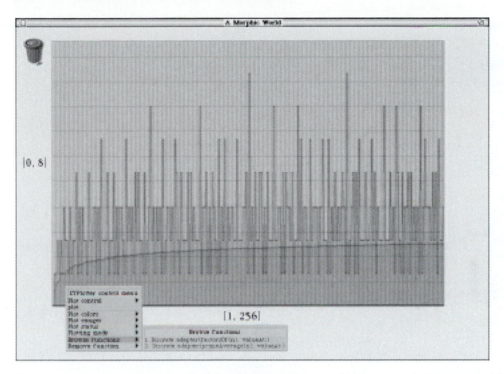

Figure 11.5 Cartesian plot of $f(n)$ = number of prime factors in n, for the interval [1, 256], plotted in blue, with the cumulative average of $f(n)$, plotted in red. This plot features the fill to x-axis plot mode.

In the AlphaToOrigin plot mode, area is filled between the graph and the origin. But it could also be thought of as if the points that form the graph were taken from the center after soaking them with ink. As they move toward their destination, they leave some ink on the way, thus filling the area between the graph and the origin. Graph dragging is a generalization of this thought. Points will be dragged by aPoint, which will be sometimes fixed, sometimes variable. Again, in the plot engine, this is implemented by two methods, one for fixed values and the other for variable values. Their names are plotDraggedBy: aPoint and plotDraggedTo: aBlock. Following is one of them:

```
plotDraggedBy: aPoint
    "Produce a standard plot on the targets, and for each point plotted
    drag from that point by aPoint"
    | last current |
    last ← toPlot at: 1.
    "Effect for first point"
    targets do: [:other | other
        line: last to: last + aPoint width: dotSize color: dragColor].
```

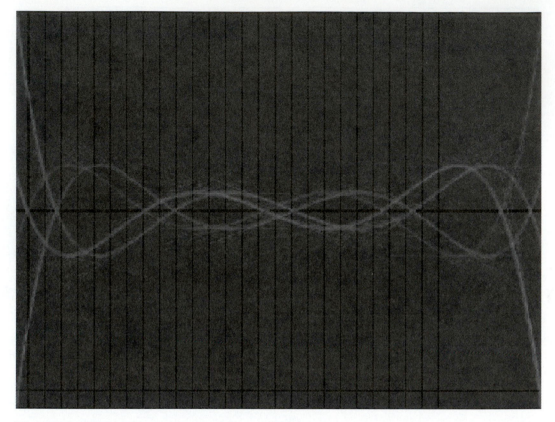

Figure 11.6 Plot of four polynomials featuring the discrete derivative plot mode. At each point of a polynomial's graph, an approximation to the polynomial's derivative is drawn as a line tangent to the polynomial's graph.

```
2 to: toPlot size do: [:each |
    current ← toPlot at: each.
    "Standard plot"
    targets do: [:some | some
        line: current to: last width: dotSize
        color: plotColor withFirstPoint: each = toPlot size].
    "Effect for every plotted point"
    targets do: [:more | more
        line: current to: current + aPoint
        width: dotSize color: dragColor].
    last ← current]
```

In this case, the alpha-blending value for dragColor is 0.005, making the drag plot modes work best with dark grids.

There are four drag modes. Two of them, the cylindrical ones, use fixed drag points. The other two, the conical ones, use a variable drag value. The downVolumeCylinder plot mode drags the graph by

0 @ (self plotSize y * 2 / 3) rounded

and the downRightVolumeCylinder drags by

(self plotSize x / 10) rounded @ (self plotSize y / 3) rounded.

The downRightVolumeCone plot mode works with this block, taken from the method XYPlotEngine≫plot:

```
dragX ← self plotSize x / 14.
dragY ← self plotSize y / 3.
↑self plotDraggedTo: [:each | (each x / 7 − dragX) rounded @ dragY rounded]
```

Finally, the oddConical plot mode works with the following block, also taken from XYPlotEngine≫plot:

```
dragY ← self plotSize y / 3.
↑self plotDraggedTo: [:each |(each x / 5) rounded @ (dragY + each) rounded]
```

Because the drag modes usually create a circular shape, they do their best in polar coordinates.

An Example of the Graph-Dragging Plot Modes with the ThetaRhoPlotter

The functions shown in Figure 11.7 are shifted sine functions. The plotter was instructed to use the downRightVolumeCylinder plot mode. The impression obtained is that the plotter is drawing in 3-D!

Pending Issues

Alas, so much alpha blending could be improved. Right now, and as you can find out after an examination of the illustrations involved, area-filling plot modes suffer from an artifact. This artifact happens when a single pixel suffers several applications of some alpha-blending color mixes. This causes color saturation especially in the alphaToOrigin plot mode, and "holes" in the plot drag modes.

Another artifact happens when several functions force different colors to be alpha blended with one another. Because alpha blending makes the first color drawn less and less important, it simply fades away. Right now, the alpha-blending values are correct mainly because the default dot size is set to 5.

These problems would be fixed if each function were drawn on its own layer form. We would start drawing the functions in their layers, then the effects added to them in other layers, but without using alpha blending. So, we would have two

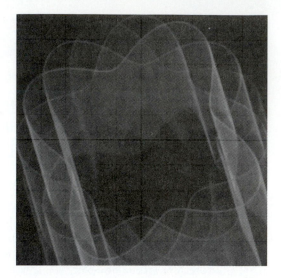

Figure 11.7 Plot of four trigonometric-based functions. This features a cylinder-volume plot mode. The graph of each function leaves a trail creating the veil-like effect.

forms per function. Then, we would add the effects to the function layer using an alpha-blending mask, hence eliminating color saturation and holes. The final phase of this process would be to add the resulting function layers using regular color addition. To make this fast, we would use a very special object, BitBlt. You will find more on BitBlt in the next sections!

Sometimes, though, the artifacts can make the plots look prettier. This is one of the reasons for the artifacts to remain there.

The Function Plotter Itself

Now that we have described the processes by which functions are plotted, we need a controlling entity that will coordinate these processes. These entities will be instances of the **FunctionPlotter** class. Each plotter will have a grid plotter, a plot engine, and a collection of plotter functions.

The most interesting method in a function plotter is its plot method. The following is the plot method found in **XYPlotter**:

```
plot
    "Answer the plot"
    | xBound yBound |
    self functions isEmpty ifTrue: [↑self plotEmptyGrid].
    xBound ← self domainBound.
    xBound isNil ifTrue: [↑self errorOnMissingRegion].
```

This check is to avoid trying to plot inside a nil region. The error is

```
self notify: 'Missing region'
```

With a valid region to plot in, the functions are evaluated if their point cache is invalid:

```
functions do: [:each |
    each valueCache isNil ifTrue:
        [each evaluate:
            (each domain size / xBound size * self plotSize x) floor]].
```

Once they are evaluated, we get the image bound and tell the grid plotter what the span is using:

```
yBound ← self imageBound.
grid span: (xBound start @ yBound start corner: xBound stop @ yBound stop).
answer ← FormCanvas on: grid plotGrid. self updateMorph.
```

The **updateMorph** mechanism implemented by the MorphicWrappers shows the empty grid first if the plotter has its Morphic counterpart through

```
functions do: [:each | each scaled ifFalse: [each scaleTo: grid]].
```

Then, functions are scaled using

```
plotEngine mapping: grid.
plotEngine removeAllTargets.
plotEngine addTarget: answer shift: 0@0.
self directDrawEnable ifTrue:
    [plotEngine
        addTarget: self morphicWrapper
        directDrawTarget shift: self morphicWrapper position].
```

Direct draw is a procedure by which the graph is drawn in Morphic in real time. In order to do that, one of the targets for the plot engine becomes the Morphic world's display, which is an instance of **FormCanvas**. An appropriate shift is given by the morph's position. Now, the plot engine is told to plot each function on all the targets:

```
functions do: [:each | plotEngine plot: each].
```

And finally, if there is a wrapper morph for the plotter, then it is updated. Otherwise, the form is answered with

```
↑self hasMorphicWrapper
    ifTrue: [self updateMorph]
    ifFalse: [self answer]
```

The last **updateMorph** message is sent for a very special reason. The plot is drawn in true color. Yet, if the plot engine is drawing in Morphic, when the display depth is not 32, then things get drawn in special ways that are faster but that also lose some quality. Hence, the last update copies the form drawn in true color to the screen one last time, so that color reduction is applied only once for each pixel of the plot.

The Function Plotter in Morphic

Each plotter has its Morphic counterpart, which are instances of subclasses of the SimplePlotterMorph class. This morph provides basic functionality, such as its extensive double-click menu. The menu controls the addition and removal of functions, the dot sizes, the colors, the plot modes, the plot sizes, the aspect ratio, the invalidation of point caches, etc.

The addition and removal of functions is done by adding submenus to the main menu, namely, Browse Functions and Remove Functions. These submenus have a list of the functions, each one showing in its current color for easy identification. Accordingly, there is a ColoredMenuMorph class, subclass of MenuMorph, to allow for colorful entries.

Most of the parameters for the plotter functions can also be accessed from the double-click menu and its submenus. Plotter properties also have their place. The graph size can be changed, and also the aspect ratio of such sizes can be changed. Suggested plot sizes in the menu are based on several widths, and the heights are calculated using the aspect ratio selected. The basic widths are 320, 400, 512, 640, 720, 800, 896, 960, and 1024, usual widths for standard video modes. Aspect ratios provided in the menu are 1, 6/5, 4/3, and phi. Personally, I do not like the phi aspect ratio. I like the 6/5 one much better.

Other plotter parameters accessible from the double-click menu include the standard values for newly added functions, the color presets, the domain and image bounds, and the status of the direct-draw procedure.

By implementing the click: method, the plotters are also able to catch clicks on them. A click is Morphic event, and it also has a position. We as plotters can ask our mapping where the point we have been clicked on is in the span, and then we can give the result to the hand for everyone to see.

Finally, there is a GIF snapshot facility. This takes the form generated by the plotter and saves a file to the disk. Color reduction is usually needed, because our forms are in true color. The necessary devices for nice color reduction are described in the next section.

Color Reduction

When we described the difference between Form and ColorForm, we mentioned that if we had a true color instance of Form with up to 256 colors, we could put those colors in a color array and generate a ColorForm that would take one-third of the space required by the Form, roughly speaking. (We divide the number of bits per pixel required by 3, but we also add a color table.) Nevertheless, if we had aForm with 257 colors we would not be able to do that, unless we reduced the number of colors used by the form.

By the way, this ColorForm would be useful for many other things. The GIF graphical format allows just 256 colors per image, for instance. Although this format is being replaced by PNG (which is in the public domain, compresses more yet is lossless, and supports more than 256 colors per image), it serves as an example of how color reduction can be useful. Furthermore, there is a GIFReadWriter class in Squeak, so we can use the color reduction to get a nice copy of our image and save a GIF image.

There are many ways to reduce the number of colors used by an image. The simplest and quickest, but by far the least elegant, is to take the bits used to represent each color component in the RGB system and truncate them to a lower amount of bits. If we truncate enough so that our color space has just 256 colors, we win. This can be done by sending the message

> asFormOfDepth: desiredBitsPerPixel

to any form. But in this way, we also lose a lot of density in our color space! We will usually dislike the 256 color space version of a true color image obtained by this method, in comparison to the original. However, we can also use asFormOfDepth: to increase the number of bits per pixel used by a form.

A nice way to reduce the colors used by an image is to implement the Heckbert median-cut color-reduction algorithm. It is implemented and included in the function-plotters package to provide GIF format snapshots of plots.

The Heckbert Color Quantization Algorithm

Paul Heckbert's color quantization median-cut algorithm (median-cut algorithm) is described in a small paragraph of Heckbert's graduation thesis. The idea is simple, and the only factor that makes the algorithm difficult is the structure of the RGB cube, because it does not allow an order relationship between colors that is so nicely behaved as the order relationship in the real numbers.

Boxes and the Minimization Algorithm

We will define a box in the RGB cube to be a subcube of the RGB color space. Boxes may contain a collection of colors. Such colors should be inside the box, in terms of the RGB color system. For instance, the hypothetical box

> Color gray corner: Color white

should not contain Color black. Moreover, we will require that boxes containing colors are minimized, in the sense that a box containing colors must be the smallest box that contains such colors. If not, we see that a procedure similar to the one described for ClosedInterval>>growSoThatIncludes:, done on the colors for each of the colors' RGB coordinates, gives us the minimal box that contains such colors.

Let's think geometrically inside the RGB cube for a minute. Once boxes are minimized, it is natural to ask the boxes about their center. This will be the average between their start and stop colors, and it turns out that we will call this color the representative color for the box. It is also natural to ask boxes for the cube's axis upon which they take more space. We will call this dimension the dominant dimension for the box. If some axes tie, we will choose any of them.

The Median and the Splitting Algorithm

The median of aSortedCollection is

median
```
| pivot |
pivot ← aSortedCollection size // 2.
↑aSortedCollection size odd
    ifTrue: [aSortedCollection at: pivot + 1]
    ifFalse:[(aSortedCollection at: pivot) +
        (aSortedCollection at: pivot + 1) // 2]
```

When colors inside a box are sorted by its dominant dimension, we will define the box's median to be the component corresponding to the dominant dimension of the median of the box's sorted colors.

Now, if the box has more than one color, it is possible to split it by its median. Boxes can be thought of as being determined by a start and a stop color. All colors between start and stop are inside the box. The splitting algorithm generates two boxes from one, as follows:

start corner: (stop copy at: dominantDimension put: self median).

(start copy at: dominantDimension put: self median) corner: stop.

Note that, strictly speaking, this process can generate boxes, rectangles, segments, and points. We will consider them all to be boxes. The splitting algorithm also cuts the sorted collection of the box's colors at the median. The first half of this sorted collection goes into the first box, and the second half goes into the second box. It is important to avoid splitting boxes with a method like includes:, because colors may be unevenly distributed, since boxes may share portions of the RGB cube.

Incidentally, this process implies asking aColor for its red, green, and blue components a very large number of times. If we check the implementation for these messages, we will see that the methods imply doing some bit manipulation. This means colors end up doing a lot of bit shifting, which will give the same results over and over again. This is a bottleneck, which is solved by implementing a ColorProxy object, that holds a color inside and caches its components.

Color Quantization

Now we can do color quantization, based on the pieces we already have. First, we get one box with all the colors we want to quantize, and we minimize it. Then, if we need to get n quantized colors, we apply the splitting algorithm $n-1$ times and then take the representatives from the boxes. Finally, we find the closest representative for each original color, and we are done.

Color Mapping after Quantization

We are done with color quantization, but as you will see, that is the easiest part. Now we have to take all the colors in the form and replace them by their corresponding representatives. That means that we will have to query a mapping from one set of colors to the other a very large number of times. For instance, there are 307,200 pixels in a 640@480 form. Unfortunately, when quantizing from true color there is no other alternative. The complete process should take around 15 seconds. That could be acceptable, but what if we need something faster?

Color Mapping à la *BitBlt*

If we decide to trade true color accuracy for speed, there is another way suggested by Dan Ingalls. There is a very special object in every Smalltalk called BitBlt. Its name comes from BIT BLock Transfer. Note that the actual movement of bits is not the main purpose of BitBlt, rather, it models the transfer itself. Movement of bits happens all the time when something changes on the screen or when something is moved from one buffer to another.

Most transfers are in regard to operations on instances of Form. This transfer can be done in a multitude of ways. Each of these ways is called a combination rule. There is a combination rule that does what we need to do, albeit only in high color. Note that BitBlt is quite bit-level operation oriented. This rule replaces colors using their raw bit values as indices for a replacement table. For instance, the index for Color white would be 32767 (15 bits, 5-5-5). The replacement table is an instance of Bitmap, a subclass of ArrayedCollection. Hence, aBitmap behaves like anArray. The difference is that the objects stored inside aBitmap are small integers. We can get new instances of Bitmap by sending the message new: desiredSize. When created, instances of Bitmap are filled with zeros.

For our color quantization purposes, we need to get a color-replacement table. This table will be accessed with indices resulting from the raw bits of the colors to be replaced. At such indexed positions, it should contain the raw bits of the corresponding replacement color. Here, we see why we have to go to high color: A true color-replacement table would need too much memory! Keep in mind that we need to use these replacement tables, because we want to use BitBlt. We could do with, say, a Dictionary, but that brings the problems of repeated querying and the hash of aColor.

In order to build our replacement table, we first truncate the colors in the original form we are given into high color, if needed. This loss of color information is barely noticeable in most cases, if noticeable at all. After truncation, our form has a depth of 16 bits per pixel at most. Then, we need to build the color-replacement table so that we can replace colors by their corresponding representatives. To do that, we need to know which colors are used in the form. We already have those colors from the quantization process, where we asked aForm for its colorsUsed. We might guess that all colors inside a box are best matched by the box's representative, but this is not always true. Hence, we could try to find the best matching representative.

If we are inclined toward the second option, we can use the three-dimensional Pythagorean theorem inside the RGB cube. The Pythagorean theorem needs a square root. However, as it is not needed to determine whether a color is closer or farther, we can do with distances squared. Also, the interface for color components found in Color is based on floating point numbers generated from the bits stored inside colors. We will do with those bits instead, and, together with other considerations, we end up with a distance measurement ranging from 0 for color equality to 3139587 for total color disparity between black and white.

By implementing the messages we need in Color itself, we avoid asking aColor about its components. The methods to follow are somewhat terse. My current (slow) machine needs 90 nanoseconds to perform an object assignment. Because of the enormous number of times these methods are executed, the toll of extra assignments that would make the code clearer is quite significant.

distanceTo: aColor
```
"Answer the distance to aColor, ranging from 0 to 3139587 in the RGB
cube. This is like || self − aColor ||↑2."
| aRGB blueSummand greenSummand redSummand |
aRGB ← aColor privateRGB.
redSummand ← (rgb bitShift: −20) − (aRGB bitShift: −20).
greenSummand ← ((rgb bitShift: −10) bitAnd: 16r3FF)
    − ((aRGB bitShift: −10) bitAnd: 16r3FF).
blueSummand ← (rgb bitAnd: 16r3FF) − (aRGB bitAnd: 16r3FF).
↑(redSummand * redSummand)
    + (greenSummand * greenSummand)
    + (blueSummand * blueSummand)
```

The previous method computes the distance between two colors.

It is also useful to compute the distance between a color and a 15-bit integer representation of a color. This is done by the following method:

distanceTo5bit: anInteger
```
"Answer the distance to anInteger, ranging from 0 to 3139587 in the
RGB cube. This is like || self − aColor ||↑2.  anInteger is [5 bits
red][5 bits green][5 bits blue]"
```

```
| blueSummand greenSummand redSummand |
redSummand ←
    (rgb bitShift: −20) − ((anInteger bitAnd: 16r7C00) bitShift: −5).
greenSummand ←
    ((rgb bitShift: −10) bitAnd: 16r3FF) − (anInteger bitAnd: 16r3E0).
blueSummand ←
    (rgb bitAnd: 16r3FF) − ((anInteger bitAnd: 16r1F) bitShift: 5)
↑(redSummand * redSummand)
    + (greenSummand * greenSummand)
    + (blueSummand * blueSummand)
```

Once we have our color-replacement table, we need to perform a BitBlt operation. The combination rule used will be Form paint, which overwrites the destination with the source. What is written is the corresponding replacement of the color at the source with the color taken from the replacement table. We collect BitBlt's result in the destination form. We could do as follows to quantize the colors in our source form down to 256 colors:

```
destination ← ColorForm extent: source extent depth: 8.
aBitBlt ← BitBlt toForm: destination.
aBitBlt  sourceForm: source;
    combinationRule: Form paint;
    colorMap: colorMap;
    sourceOrigin: 0@0;
    destOrigin: 0@0;
    destRect: source boundingBox;
    sourceRect: source boundingBox;
    copyBits.
```

In the previous code, source is our form, colorMap is our bitmap, the origin points are an indication of where BitBlt should start to work, the source and destination rectangles are for clipping purposes, and, finally, the message copyBits starts the process. This is about 25 times faster than the form peeking and poking method.

Acknowledgments

Every piece of work done is based on previous work by other people. I would like to thank the Squeak Central for creating Squeak in 1996. Without their hard work, the whole MathMorphs project would not be a reality today.

The Squeak Central is Alan Kay, Dan Ingalls, Ted Kaehler, Scott Wallace, John Maloney, Andreas Raab, Kim Rose, and Pat Brecker. Kim and Mark Guzdial had the idea of making a book about Squeak that would also have the spirit of the original *Smalltalk-80: The Language* book. Mark and Kim have been very helpful in the complex process of writing this present publication. It is a great honor to participate in this book.

I would also thank Dan Ingalls for his help and suggestions on BitBlt so that it would help the Heckbert color-quantization algorithm, and so that it could be used to fix the plotter's artifacts described here. Dan has also been especially supportive about writing this chapter.

My sister, Florencia Valloud, introduced the Munsell tree and color system to me. She helped in the construction of the Munsell plotters and the ColorStream class.

I would like to thank Leandro Caniglia and the members of the MathMorphs project for creating it and for keeping it a healthy environment in which to work. Many thanks go to Luciano Notarfrancesco, Pablo Malavolta, Pablo Shmerkin, Francisco Garau, Gerardo Richarte, Alejandro Weil, Ariel Schwartzman,Valeria Murgia, Eric Rodríguez Guevara, and Ariel Pacetti. I am also grateful toward the Universidad de Mar del Plata (Mar del Plata University), where a MathMorphs presentation was given. It was the first time I gave a lecture to a general audience and the first time I showed the function plotters in public.

Finally, I would like to thank Catana Lucero. Her support and human qualities have been instrumental for this work, both during the months of writing this chapter and also while I was building the function plotters. Catana also read this chapter several times giving valuable suggestions, and her work truly is on every page. I am very glad I met her by means of a random chat program, October 22, 1998. There is no doubt that luck has been on our side.

Andres Valloud is from Buenos Aires, Argentina. Andres was introduced to Smalltalk in 1996 at UBA where he took a Squeak-based mathematics course in 1997 for the Math-Morphs project. He produced a pure object-compression framework for his final exam presentation in 1998 for that course, a 10-month endeavor, which exhibited significant code in unexplored territory for Squeak. In 1999, he wrote and submitted a paper based on his framework regarding lossless ADPCM coding based on finite state models. The paper won acceptance at the 1999, 28th JAIIO (Jornadas Argentinas de Informática e Investigación Operativa) Conference in Buenos Aires, Argentina, and he was asked to present his work at the Conference. Soon after, Andres came to the United States, married, and relocated to San Diego where he now lives with his wife, Catana. He works at Exobox, Inc., where he is able to implement his creativity working with Squeak. You can contact him at sqrmax@prodigy.net.

12

Music and Sound Processing in Squeak Using Siren

Stephen Travis Pope

Center for Research in Electronic Art Technology (CREATE)
University of California, Santa Barbara

Introduction

The Siren system is a general-purpose music composition and production framework integrated with Squeak Smalltalk (1); it is a Smalltalk class library of about 320 classes (about 5,000 methods) for building various music- and sound-related applications. Siren can be used on all Squeak platforms with or without support for MIDI or audio input/output (I/O). The system's Smalltalk source code is available for free on the Internet; see the Siren package home page at the URL `http://www.create.ucsb.edu/Siren`.

This chapter is divided into several sections: (a) the Smoke music description language used within Siren, (b) Siren's real-time MIDI and sound I/O facilities, (c) the graphical user interfaces (GUIs) for Siren objects, and (d) Siren applications— music/sound databases and how a composer might use Siren. The presentation is intended for a Squeak programmer who is interested in music and sound applications or for a computer music enthusiast who is interested in Squeak. Many references are provided to the literature on music software and object-oriented programming.

Why Siren?

The motivation for the development of Siren is to build a powerful, flexible, and portable computer-based composer's tool and instrument. In the past, real-time musical instruments, such as acoustic instruments or electroacoustic synthesizers, have had quite different characteristics from software-based research and production

Characteristic	Tool	Instrument
Typical application	construction	expression
Range of application	(hopefully) broad	narrow is acceptable
User interface	simple, standard	potentially complex, but learnable
Customizability	none or little	per-user customizability
Application mode	for planned tasks	exploratory, experimentation

Table 12.1   Differences between Tools and Instruments.

tools. (There is of course an interesting gray area and also a basic dependency on how the implement is applied—hammer-as-instrument, or piano-as-tool.) One possible description of the basic differences between tools and instruments is given in Table 12.1.

The Siren system is designed to support composition, off-line (i.e., non-interactive) realization, and live performance of electroacoustic music with abstract notations and musical structure representation, as well as sound and score processing. Other desired application areas include music/sound databases, music analysis, and music scholarship and pedagogy. It should ideally be flexible and formal like a tool, and support expression and customizability like an instrument.

The technical goal of the software is to exhibit good object-oriented design principles and elegant state-of-the-art software engineering practice. It needs to be an easily extensible framework for many kinds of intricately structured multimedia data objects, and to provide abstract models of high-level musical constructs and flexible management of very large data sets.

Elements of Siren

There are several packages that make up the Siren system:

- a general-purpose music representation system—the *Smoke* music representation language (the name, suggested by Danny Oppenheim, is derived from "Smallmusic object kernel"), which consists of music magnitudes, events, event lists, generators, functions, and sounds;

- a collection of I/O-related objects such as voices, schedulers, and drivers—real-time and file-based I/O objects for sound and MIDI;

- GUI components for musical applications—an extended GUI framework, widgets, and tools; and

- a collection of built-in end-user application prototypes—Squeak editors and browsers for Siren objects.

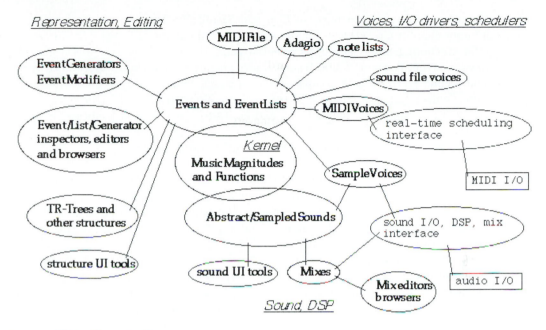

Representation, Editing — Voices, I/O drivers, schedulers

Kernel

Sound, DSP

Figure 12.1 Siren Architecture.

Figure 12.1 shows the basic components of Siren. At the center are the class categories of the Smoke music-and-multimedia-representation language. On the left side are the editors and applications for manipulating Smoke objects in Siren. To the right are the various objects that handle input-output in various formats and real-time drivers. The components on the lower right that are shown in courier typeface are low-level I/O driver interfaces written in C.

History and Relation to Composition

Siren and its direct hardware and software predecessors stem from music systems that developed in the process of my composition. Starting in the mid-1970s, I used non-real-time software sound synthesis programming languages for my composition; I had the very good luck to learn the Music10 language that was based on SAIL (Stanford AI Language) and ran on DEC PDP-10 mainframe computers. This was a very advanced (for its time) and flexible programming language that served as a synthesis and a score-generation language at the same time. I quickly became accustomed to building special representations for each composition and to having flexible high-level tools for music. When I moved onto DEC PDP-11-series mini-computers running UNIX in the late 1970s, I was forced to start writing my own composition tools in the highest-level languages to which I had access. (This led to having to do my own ports of Lisp and Smalltalk virtual machines, but that's another chapter altogether.) The ramification of this is that the software I describe later (including Siren) is always oriented primarily towards the representation of musical structures and compositional algorithms, with real-time performance or actual sound synthesis as secondary considerations. Siren today remains primarily a music-description language and composition structuring tool, with a few MIDI I/O features, simple graphical tools, and hooks to other Squeak facilities for sound generation.

My first generation of object-oriented music software, called *ARA*, was an outgrowth of a Lisp rule-based expert system I wrote between 1980 and 1983 for the composition of *Bat out of Hell* (2). ARA had a rather inflexible music representation (designed for a specific software instrument written in the Music11 sound synthesis language), but allowed the description and manipulation of "middle-level" musical structures such as chords, phrases, and rhythmical patterns in the rules of the expert system.

The next generation was the *DoubleTalk* system (3, 4), which used a Smalltalk-80-based Petri net editing system built (in Berkeley Smalltalk) by Georg Heeg, et al., at the University of Dortmund, Germany. I used DoubleTalk for the composition of *Requiem Aeternam Dona Eis* (1986). This system allowed me to "program" transitions between states of the compositional system using a Prolog-like declarative language that was used to annotate the Petri nets. To execute a DoubleTalk net, one defined its initial "marking"—the placement and types of tokens distributed among the nodes—and then ran the Petri net simulator, the result of which was a score generated by the simulated net's transitions.

In 1986, I started working at Xerox PARC and also at the Stanford University Center for Computer Research in Music and Acoustics (CCRMA). I wrote the first flexible version of a Smalltalk music-description language while there, which served as the foundation for the *HyperScore ToolKit* (5). This package was used (among others) for the composition *Day* (1988), and it was the first to support real-time MIDI I/O as well as graphical notations. (This was the only composition for which I have used MIDI, and the last for which I tried to build graphical tools. I have only done the minimum to support MIDI and GUIs in my tools since 1988.)

Siren's direct predecessor, known as the *MODE* (Musical Object Development Environment) (6, 7), was used for *Kombination XI* (1990/98) (8) and *All Gates Are Open* (1993/95). The MODE was based on ParcPlace Systems' VisualWorks implementation of Smalltalk and supported sound and MIDI I/O, as well as specialized interfaces (via user primitives) to sound analysis/resynthesis packages, such as a phase vocoder, and to special-purpose mixing hardware, such as the Studer/Dyaxis MacMix system.

In each of these cases, some amount of effort was spent—after the completion of a specific composition—to make the tools more general purpose, often making them less useful for any particular task. Siren (9, 10) is a reimplementation of the MODE undertaken in 1997–99; it is based on the representations and tools I am using in the realization of *Ywe Ye, Yi Jr Di* (work in progress). The "clean-up" effort was minimized here; the new Siren package is much more useful, but for a much smaller set of tasks and attitudes about what music representation and composition are. If Siren works well for other composers, it is because of its idiosyncratic approach, rather than its attempted generality (i.e., the instrument approach, rather than the tool approach).

Siren and its predecessors are documented in the book *The Well-Tempered Object: Musical Applications of Object-Oriented Software Technology* (11), in a series of papers in the proceedings of the 1982, 1986, 1987, 1989, 1991, 1992, 1994, 1996, 1997, and 1999 International Computer Music Conferences (ICMCs), in an extended article in *Computer Music Journal* from 1992 (6), and in the 1997 book *Musical Signal Processing* (12). Many of these papers and related documents are available from the Web URL:

```
http://www.create.ucsb.edu/~stp/publ.html
```

Programming Languages for Music

In the computer music literature, the primary programming languages used for advanced experimental systems (to this day) have been Lisp and Smalltalk; this can be traced to several basic concepts. Both languages provide an extremely simple, single-paradigm programming model (i.e., all data are of the same basic "type," and all behavior is accessed in the same way), and both have consistent syntax that scales well to large expressions (a matter of debate among "language bigots"). Both can be interpreted or compiled with ease and are often implemented within development environments based on one or more interactive "read-eval-print loop" objects. The history of the various Lisp machines and Smalltalk-based operating systems demonstrates the scalability of Lisp and Smalltalk both "up" and "down," so that everything from high-level applications frameworks to device drivers can be developed in a single language system. The Smalltalk history shows the independent development of the programming language, the basic class libraries, the user-interface framework, and the delivery platform across at least four full generations.

Two important language features that are common to both Lisp and Smalltalk are *dynamic typing* and *dynamic polymorphism*. Dynamic typing means that data type information is specific to (run-time) values and not to (compile-time) variables, as in many other languages. In Pascal or C, for example, one declares all variables as typed (e.g., int i; means that variable i is an integer) and may not generally assign other kinds of data to a variable after its declaration (e.g., i = "hello"; to assign a string to i). Declaring a variable name in Lisp or Smalltalk says nothing about the types of values that may be assigned to that variable. While this generally implies some additional run-time overhead, dynamic binding is a valuable language asset because of the increase it brings in software flexibility, abstraction, and reusability.

Polymorphism means being able to use the same function name with different types of arguments to evoke different behaviors. Most standard programming

languages allow for some polymorphism in the form of overloading of their arith-
metical operators, meaning that one can say $(3 + 4)$ or $(3.1 + 4.1)$ to add integers
or floating-point numbers. The problem with limited overloading (limited polymorphism) is that one is forced to have many names for the same function applied
to different argument types (e.g., function names like playEvent(), playEventList(),
playSound(), playMix(), etc.). In Lisp and Smalltalk (as well as several other object-
oriented languages), all functions can be overloaded, so that one can create many
types of objects that can be used interchangeably (e.g., many different types of
objects can handle the play message in their own ways). Using polymorphism also
incurs a run-time overhead, but, as with dynamic binding, it can be considered essential for a language that will be used as the base for an exploratory programming
environment for music and multimedia applications.

The 1991 book entitled *The Well-Tempered Object* (11) describes the second
generation of O-O music software systems (mid- to late-1980s, the first generation
having started in the mid-1970s), and there are several third-generation systems
in both LISP (Stanford's CLM or CMU's Nyquist) and Smalltalk (the Symbolic
Sound Kyma system, Dmix, Siren).

Representation of Multimedia Objects

There is a rich and diverse literature related to the representation, manipulation,
and interchange of multimedia data in general, and musical sound and scores in
particular. Two useful surveys are those by Roger Dannenberg (13) and Geraint
Wiggins, et al. (14).

Among the important issues are (1) which media related to sound and music
are to be supported—recorded sound, musical performance, musical structure; (2)
what level of sonic semantics and musical structure is to be supported; and (3)
how exactly the representation is to capture an actual performance or recording.
In many systems, issue (1) is addressed by a small and fixed set of data types
(e.g., sound-only, control-only, or event-only), and a trade-off is seen between issues
(2) and (3), that is, between what Wiggins, et al., call "structural generality" and
"representational completeness."

Many object models for complex domains (musical or not) start by defining a
set of classes of objects that represent the basic "units of measure" or *magnitudes*
of the domain. In the case of sound and music, this means classes to model the
basic properties of sounds and musical events such as time (and/or duration), pitch,
loudness, and spatial dimensions. Along with some model of generic "events" (at
the level of words or musical notes), one must build (1) microlevel functions and
control objects and (2) higher level "event lists" to represent sentences, melodies,
and other composite events. This basic event/event-list design is very similar to the
design patterns found in graphics systems based on display lists.

The Smoke Music Representation Language

The "kernel" of Siren is the set of classes for music magnitudes, functions and sounds, events, event lists, and event structures known as the Smallmusic object kernel, or *Smoke* (15) music representation. Smoke is described in terms of two related description languages (verbose and terse music input languages), a compact binary interchange format, and a mapping onto concrete data structures. All of the high-level packages of Siren—event lists, voices, sound/DSP, compositional structures, and the user-interface framework—interoperate using Smoke events and event lists.

Smoke supports the following kinds of description:

- abstract models of the basic musical quantities (scalar magnitudes, such as pitch, loudness, or duration);

- instrument/note (voice/event or performer/score) pattern for mapping abstract event properties onto concrete parameters of output media or synthesis methods;

- functions of time, sampled sound, granular description, or other (non-note-oriented) description abstractions;

- flexible grain-size of "events" in terms of "notes," "grains," "elements," or "textures";

- event, control, and sampled sound-description levels;

- nested/hierarchical event-tree structures for flexible description of "parts," "tracks," or other parallel/sequential organizations;

- separation of "data" from "interpretation" (what vs. how in terms of providing for interpretation objects called voices);

- abstractions for the description of "middle-level" musical structures (e.g., chords, clusters, or trills);

- annotation of event-tree structures supporting the creation of heterarchies (lattices) and hypermedia networks;

- annotation including graphical data necessary for common-practice notation; and

- description of sampled sound synthesis and processing models, such as sound file mixing or DSP.

Given a flexible and abstract basic object model for Smoke, it should be easy to build converters for many common formats, such as MIDI data, formatted note lists for software sound-synthesis languages (15), DSP code, or mixing scripts. Additionally, it should be possible to parse live performance data (e.g., incoming MIDI streams) into Smoke objects and to interpret or play Siren objects (in some rendition) in real-time.

The "executive summary" of Smoke from (16) is as follows. Music (i.e., a musical surface or structure) can be represented as a series of "events" (which generally last from tens of msec to tens of sec). Events are simply property lists or dictionaries; they can have named properties whose values are arbitrary. These properties may be music-specific objects (such as pitches or spatial positions), and models of many common musical magnitudes are provided. Voice objects and applications determine the interpretation of events' properties and may use "standard" property names, such as pitch, loudness, voice, duration, or position.

Events are grouped into event collections or event lists by their relative start times. Event lists are events themselves and can, therefore, be nested into trees (i.e., an event list can have another event list as one of its events, etc.); they can also map their properties onto their component events. This means that an event can be "shared" by being in more than one event list at different relative start times and with different properties mapped onto it.

Events and event lists are "performed" by the action of a scheduler passing them to an interpretation object or voice. Voices map event properties onto parameters of I/O devices; there can be a rich hierarchy of them. A scheduler expands and/or maps event lists and sends their events to their voices.

Sampled sounds are also describable, by means of synthesis "patches" or signal processing scripts involving a vocabulary of sound-manipulation messages.

Smoke objects also have behaviors for managing several special types of links, which are seen simply as properties where the property name is a symbol such as usedToBe, isTonalAnswerTo, or obeysRubato, and the property value is another Smoke object, for example, an event list. With this facility, one can build multimedia hypermedia navigators for arbitrary Smoke networks. The three example link names described earlier could be used to implement event lists with version history, to embed analytical information in scores, or to attach real-time performance controllers to event lists, respectively.

Music Magnitudes

MusicMagnitude objects are characterized by their *identity*, *class*, *species*, and *value*. For example, the pitch object that represents the note named c3 has its particular object identity, is a member of class SymbolicPitch, of the species Pitch, and has the value 'c3' (a string). MusicMagnitude behaviors distinguish between class membership and species in a multiple-inheritance-like scheme that allows the object representing 440.0 Hz to have pitch-like and limited-precision-real-number-like behaviors. This means that its behavior can depend on what it represents (a pitch), or how its value is stored (a floating-point number).

The mixed-mode music magnitude arithmetic is defined using the technique of species-based coercion, that is, class Pitch knows whether a note name or Hertz value is more general. This provides capabilities similar to those of systems that use the techniques of multiple inheritance and multiple polymorphism (such as C++ and the Common Lisp Object System), but in a much simpler and scalable manner. All meaningful coercion messages—for example, (440.0 Hz asMIDIKeyNumber)—and mixed-mode operations—for example, (1/4 beat + 80 msec)—are defined.

The basic abstract model classes include Pitch, Loudness, and Duration. These classes are abstract and do not even have subclasses; they signify *what* kind of property is being represented. They are used as the species for families of classes that have their own inheritance hierarchy based on *how* they represent their values. This framework is easily extensible for composition- or notation-specific magnitudes.

Figure 12.2 shows the abstract "representation" class hierarchy on the left and the concrete "implementation" hierarchy on the right. The lines between the two sides denote the species relationships, for example, both HertzPitch and SymbolicPitch are of species Pitch and can defer to the species for performing mixed-mode operations such as (#c4 pitch + 12 Hz). The representation hierarchy has abstract classes such as Chroma (species classes representing objects for pitch and

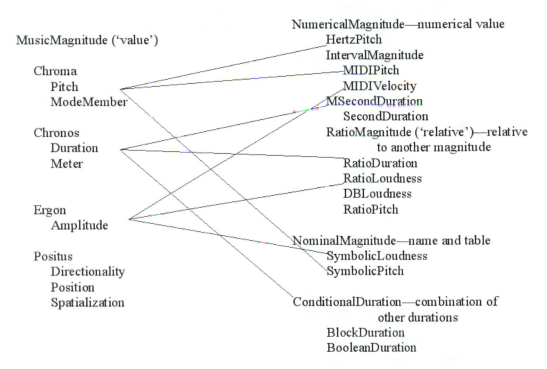

Figure 12.2 Class-Species and Subclass Inheritance Relationships among Siren MusicMagnitudes.

temperament), while the implementation hierarchy has abstract classes such as IntervalMagnitude, which generalizes the concrete classes with fixed numerical ranges.

The handling of time as a parameter is finessed via the abstraction of duration. All times are represented as durations of events, or delays between events, so that no "real" or "absolute" time object is needed. Duration objects can have simple numerical or symbolic values, or they can be conditions (e.g., the duration until some event occurs), Boolean expressions of other durations, or arbitrary blocks of Smalltalk-80 code.

Functions of one or more variables are yet another type of signal-like music magnitude. The Function class hierarchy includes line segment, exponential segment, spline segment, and Fourier summation functions.

In the verbose Smoke format, music magnitudes, events, and event lists are created by instance creation messages sent to the appropriate classes. The first three expressions in the following examples create various music magnitudes and coerce them into other representations:

- **Verbose MusicMagnitude Creation and Coercion Messages**

  (Duration value: 1/16) asMsec   "Answers Duration 62 msec."

  (Pitch value: 60) asHertz   "Answers Pitch 261.623 Hz."

  (Amplitude value: 'ff') asMIDI   "Answers MIDI key velocity 100."

- **Mixed-mode Arithmetic**

  (1/2 beat) + 100 msec   "(0.6 beat)"

  'a4' pitch + 25 Hz   "(465.0 Hz)"

  (#a4 pitch + 100 Hz) asMIDI   "(73 key)"

  'mp' ampl + 3 dB   "(−4.6 dB)"

The terse form for music magnitude creation uses post-operators (unary messages) such as 440 Hz or 250 msec, as shown in the previous examples. Users can extend the music magnitude framework with their own classes that refine the existing models or define totally new kinds of musical metrics.

Events and Event Lists

The AbstractEvent object in Smoke is modeled as a property-list dictionary with a duration. Events have no notion of external time until their durations become active. Event behaviors include duration and property accessing, and "performance," where the semantics of the operation depends on another object—a *voice* or driver as described below.

The primary messages that events understand are

(anEvent duration: someDurationObject)

to set the duration time of the event (to some Duration-type music magnitude), and property-accessing messages such as

    (anEvent color: #blue)

to set the "color" (an arbitrary property) to an arbitrary value (the symbol #blue). This kind of "generic behavior" is implemented by overriding the method doesNot-Understand, which is both very useful and rather dangerous (as it can make broken methods quite difficult to debug).

The meaning of an event's properties is interpreted by voices and user-interface objects; it is obvious that, for example, a pitch property could be mapped differently by a MIDI output voice and a graphical notation editor. It is common to have events with complex objects as properties (e.g., envelope functions, real-time controller maps, DSP scripts, structural annotation, version history, or compositional algorithms) or with more than one copy of some properties (e.g., one event with enharmonic pitch name, key number, and frequency, each of which may be interpreted differently by various voices or structure accessors).

There is no prescribed "level" or "grain size" for events in Smoke. There may be a one-to-one or many-to-one relationship between events and "notes," or single-event objects may be used to represent long complex textures or surfaces.

Note the way that Smoke uses the Smalltalk concatenation message "," to denote the construction of events and event lists; (magnitude, magnitude) means to build an event with the two magnitudes as properties, and (event, event) or ((duration => event), (duration => event)) means to build an event list with the given events as components. (The message "=¿" is similar to the standard Smalltalk "-¿" message except that a special kind of Association [an EventAssociation] is created.) This kind of convenient and compact expression is simply Smalltalk syntax using a few additional implementors of the message "," for concatenation, as shown in Table 12.2.

The classes Siren uses for events are as follows:

- AbstractEvent—Object with a property list (lazily created)

- DurationEvent—adds duration instance variable

- MusicEvent—adds pitch and voice instance variables

- ActionEvent—has a block that it evaluates when scheduled

Receiver class	Answer	Example
MusicMagnitude	MusicEvent	110 Hz, (1/4 beat), 44 dB
MusicEvent	EventList	event1, event2
EventAssociation	EventList	(dur1 => evt1), (dur2 => evt2)

Table 12.2 Interpretations of Concatenation Messages in Smoke.

It is seldom necessary to extend the hierarchy of events. Examples of verbose and terse Siren event-creation messages follow:

- **Verbose Event Creation Messages—Class Messages**

  "Create a 'generic' event."
  MusicEvent duration: 1/4 pitch: 'c3' ampl: 'mf'.
  "Create one with added properties."
  (MusicEvent dur: 1/4 pitch: 'c3') color: #green; accent: #sfz.

- **Terse Event Creation Using Concatenation of Music Magnitudes**

  "Simple event"
  440 Hz, (1/4 beat), 44 dB.
  "with an added (arbitrary) property"
  490 Hz, (1/7 beat), 56 dB, (#voice −> #flute), (#embrochure −> #tight).
  "Event using different syntax"
  (#c4 pitch, 0.21 sec, 64 velocity) voice: Voice default.

EventList objects hold onto collections of events that are tagged and sorted by their start times (represented as the duration between the start time of the event list and that of the event). The event list classes are subclasses of DurationEvent themselves. This means that event lists can behave like events and can, therefore, be arbitrarily deeply nested, that is, one event list can contain another as one of its events.

The primary messages to which event lists respond (in addition to the behavior they inherit by being events) are (anEventList add: anEvent at: aDuration)—to add an event to the list, (anEventList play)—to play the event list on its voice (or a default one), (anEventList edit)—to open a graphical editor in the event list, and Smalltalk-80 collection iteration and enumeration messages such as (anEventList select: [someBlock])—to select the events that satisfy the given (Boolean) function block.

Event lists can map their own properties onto their events in several ways. Properties can be defined as lazy or eager, to signify whether they map themselves when created (eagerly) or when the event list is performed (lazily). This makes it easy to create several event lists that have copies of the same events and map their own properties onto the events at performance time under interactive control. Voices handle mapping of event list properties via event modifiers, as described subsequently.

In a typical hierarchical Smoke score, data structure composition is used to manage the large number of events, event generators, and event modifiers necessary to describe a full performance. The score is a tree—possibly a forest (i.e., with multiple roots) or a lattice (i.e., with cross-branch links between the inner nodes) —of hierarchical event lists representing sections, parts, tracks, phrases, chords, or whatever abstractions the user desires to define. Smoke does not define any fixed event list subclasses for these types; they are all various compositions of parallel or sequential event lists.

Note that events do not know their start times; this is always relative to some outer scope. This means that events can be shared among many event lists, the extreme case being an entire composition where one event is shared and mapped by many different event lists (as described by Carla Scaletti in [17]). The fact that the Smoke text-based event and event list description format consists of executable Smalltalk-80 message expressions (see examples below) means that it can be seen as either a declarative or a procedural description language. The goal is to provide "something of a cross between a music notation and a programming language" as suggested by Roger Dannenberg (13).

The verbose way of creating an event list is to create a named instance and add events explicitly as shown in the following example, which creates a D-major triad (i.e., create a named event list and add three events that all start at the same time):

```
(EventList newNamed: #Chord1)
    add: (1/2 beat, 'd3' pitch, 'mf' ampl) at: 0;
    add: (1/2 beat, 'fs3' pitch, 'mf' ampl) at: 0;
    add: (1/2 beat, 'a4' pitch, 'mf' ampl) at: 0.
```

This same chord (this time anonymous) could be defined more tersely using simple concatenation of event associations as follows (note the comma between the associations):

```
(0 => (1/2 beat, 'd3' pitch, 'mf' ampl)) ,
(0 => (1/2 beat, 'fs3' pitch, 'mf' ampl)) ,
(0 => (1/2 beat, 'a4' pitch, 'mf' ampl)).
```

This chord could have been created even more compactly by using a Chord object (see the discussion of event generators later) as

```
(Chord majorTriadOn: 'd3' inversion: 0) eventList.
```

Terse EventList creation using concatenation of events or (duration, event) associations looks like the following:

```
(440 Hz, (1/2 beat), 44.7 dB) , "comma between events"
(1 => ((1.396 sec, 0.714 ampl) phoneme: #xu)).
```

EventGenerators and EventModifiers

The EventGenerator and EventModifier packages provide for music description and performance using generic or composition-specific middle-level objects. Event generators are used to represent the common structures of the musical vocabulary such as chords, clusters, progressions, or ostinati. Each event generator subclass knows how it is described—for example, a chord with a root and an inversion, or an ostinato with an event list and repeat rate—and can perform itself once or repeatedly, acting like a Smalltalk-80 control structure. EventModifier objects generally hold onto a function and a property name; they can be told to apply their functions to the named property of an event list lazily or eagerly. Event generators/modifiers are described in more detail in (18); some of the other issues are discussed in (19).

EventGenerator Examples

Chords are simple one-dimensional event generators, for example,

> ((Chord majorTetradOn: 'f4' inversion: 1) duration: 1.0) play

To play a loud drum roll at 20 beats/sec (50 msec each) for 2 sec, in middle-C, use

> ((Roll length: 2 sec rhythm: 50 msec note: 60 key) ampl: #ff) play

To create a low 6-second stochastic cloud with five events per second, given interval ranges for the selection of pitch and amplitude, play a constant rhythm with the following code:

```
(Cloud dur: 6            "Cloud lasts 6 sec."
    pitch: (48 to: 60)   "with pitches selected from this range"
    ampl: (80 to: 120)   "and amplitudes in this range"
    voice: (1 to: 8)     "select from these voices"
    density: 5)          "play 5 notes per sec."
```

To play a 6-second cloud that goes from low to high and soft to loud, give starting and ending selection ranges for the properties, as in

```
(DynamicCloud dur: 6                    "6—second DynamicCloud generator"
    pitch: #((30 to: 44) (60 to: 60))   "with starting and ending pitch"
    ampl: #((20 to: 40) (90 to: 120))   "and amplitude ranges
    voice: (1 to: 4)                    "single interval of voices"
    density: 15) play                   "play 15 per second"
```

To edit a dynamic selection cloud that makes a transition from one triad to another, give starting and ending pitch sets for the selection, use the following code:

```
(DynamicSelectionCloud dur: 4           "6—second DynamicSelectionCloud"
    pitch: #( #(48 50 52) #(72 74 76))  "give sets for pitch selection"
    ampl: #(60 80 120)                  "constant selection set"
    voice: #(1 2)                       "2 MIDI voices"
    density: 20) edit                   "20 notes per sec"
```

The result is displayed in Figure 12.3 in a piano-roll-like notation editor.

In the following rubato example, apply a "slow-down" tempo-map to a drum roll by scaling the inter-event delays:

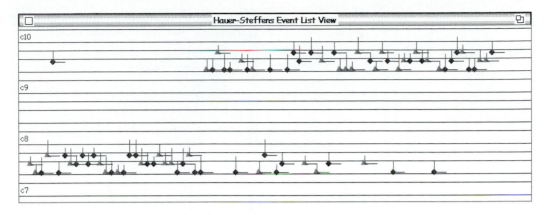

Figure 12.3 DynamicSelectionCloud Chord Cross-Fade.

```
| roll rub |
"Create a drum roll with 10 beats/sec"
roll := ((Roll length: 2000
    rhythm: 100
    note: 60) ampl: 80) eventList.
"Create a modifier to slow down by a factor of 1.5"
rub := Rubato new function: (LinearFunction from: #((0 1) (1 1.5))); scale: 10.
rub applyTo: roll.    "Apply the event modifier to the event list."
roll explore        "Explore the result"
```

The object explorer shown in Figure 12.4 illustrates the inner structure of a Siren event list; the main instance variables are at the top of the property list, and one of the list's event is expanded to show its internal state. The effect of the decellerrando function is visible as the increase of the differences between the relative start times of the events in the list.

Siren I/O

The "performance" of events takes place via IOVoice objects. Event properties are assumed to be independent of the parameters of any synthesis instrument or algorithm. A voice object is a "property-to-parameter mapper" that knows about one or more output or input formats for Smoke data. There are voice "device drivers" for common score file storage formats—such as note lists for various software sound synthesis languages (16), MIDI file format, or phase vocoder scripts—or for use with real-time schedulers connected to MIDI or sampled sound drivers.

These classes can be refined to add new event and signal file formats or multilevel mapping (e.g., for MIDI system exclusive messages) in an abstract way. IOVoice objects can also read input streams (e.g., real-time controller data or output from

Figure 12.4 EventList Result from Applying a Decellerando Tempo Map to a Drum Roll.

a coprocess) and send messages to other voices, schedulers, event modifiers, or event generators. This is how one uses the system for real-time control of complex structures.

Some voices are "timeless" (e.g., MIDI file readers); they operate at full speed regardless of the relative time of the event list they read or write. Others assume that some scheduler hands events to their voices in real time during performance. The EventScheduler (written entirely in Squeak) does just this; it can be used to sequence and synchronize event lists that may include a variety of voices.

IOVoice Examples

To create a random event list and write it out to a cmix-format notelist file, use the following code:

```
file := FileStream named: 'test.out.cmix'.
"This example creates an event list with random notes."
list := EventList randomExample: 64.
"Create a voice to map the list to a cmix—format score file."
voice := CmixVoice newNamed: '1' onStream: file.
"Store the event list on the voice's file."
voice play: list.
file close.          "Close the file."
```

The resulting cmix score file looks like,

```
/* cmix MINC data file created 8 May 2000 */
system("sfcreate -r 44100 -c 1 -i out.snd");
output("out.snd");                    /* output sound file */
makegen(1, 10, 1024, 1)        /* f1 = sine wave */
ins(t,0.0,0.264,79,0.653401229834836,0.4343151734556608,13039);
ins(t,0.264,0.255,74,0.2897873042569436,0.39283562343234,22197);
ins(t,0.519,0.281,75,0.4070028436402803,0.399486889950692,18610);
ins(t,0.8,0.232,77,0.9441084940657525,0.421033562096317,22386);
ins(t,1.032,0.28,73,0.815713333345816,0.431038966901153,22444);
ins(t,1.312,0.298,70,0.900661926670308,0.3880002476591618,12011);
ins(t,1.61,0.248,72,0.05989623258816834,0.4281569774952516,14359);
... etc.
```

Real-time music I/O in Siren is managed by low-level interfaces to the host operating system's device drivers for sound and MIDI; Siren objects use primitive methods that call out to the external functions. The glue code for these primitives is written in Smalltalk and translated to C for linking with the Squeak virtual machine (itself written in Smalltalk and translated). Several sets of primitives exist for Squeak on various platforms, including support for sound synthesis, digital audio signal processing, MIDI event-oriented and continuous controller I/O, and VM-level scheduling.

There are rich class libraries for managing MIDI I/O connections, as shown in the next example of code, which creates a port, a device, and a voice in order to play an event list. Object models for MIDI controllers, extended MIDI commands, and GeneralMIDI channel maps are provided in Siren as well, as demonstrated in the following code fragments.

- Here is the MIDI voice Example:

```
| voice device port scale |
port := MIDIPort default.    "Create a MIDI port"
device := MIDIDevice on: port.   "Create a MIDI device"
voice := MIDIVoice on: device.    "Create a MIDI voice"
"Create an example event list, a scale"
scale := EventList scaleExampleFrom: 24 to: 60 in: 2000.
"Play the event list on the voice"
voice play: scale
```

MIDIPort class≫testBend
```
"Demonstrate pitch−bend by playing two notes and bending them."
"MIDIPort testBend"
| port start |
port := self default.
port open.
"Set the recorder MIDI instrument."
port programChange: 0 to: 'Recorder'.
```

```
port programChange: 1 to: 'Recorder'.
start := Time millisecondClockValue + 150.
"Play two notes."
port play: 76 at: start dur: 5000 amp: 60 voice: 0.
port play: 80 at: start dur: 5000 amp: 60 voice: 1.
"Bend them--one up, one down."
0 to: 500 do:
    [ :i |
        port pitchBend: 0 to: 4096 + (i * 8) at: nil.
        port pitchBend: 1 to: 4096 - (i * 8) at: nil.
        (Delay forMilliseconds: 10) wait ]
```

- An example of GeneralMIDI instrument banks in which one loads channels
  1–16 with tuned percussion instruments is as follows:

```
MIDIPort setEnsembleInOrder:
    #(Agogo 'Tinkle Bell' Timpani Xylophone
        Applause 'Taiko Drum' Glockenspiel 'Synth Drum'
        Gunshot 'Steel Drums' Helicopter Vibraphone
        Woodblock 'Telephone Ring' Kalimba 'Blown Bottle')
```

Applications can have direct access to the Siren real-time I/O scheduler, for
example, to add an event list at a specific future time and kick-start the scheduler,
as in the following example:

```
Siren schedule      "Get the 'global' real-time scheduler."
    "Add an example event list at some future time."
    addAppointment: ActionEvent listExample in: (1000 msec);
    "start the schedule in case it's off."
    runAppointments
```

Because events are medium independent and voices manage all the details of
output channels, we can write the following "multimedia" example:

```
| el |
el := (Cloud dur: 6        "Create a 6-second stochastic cloud."
    pitch: (48 to: 60)     "Choose pitches in this range."
    ampl: (40 to: 70)      "Choose amplitudes in this range."
    "Select from these 2 voices (int 1 means MIDI channel 1)."
    voice: (Array with: 1 with: (SynthVoice default))
    density: 5) eventList.  "Play 5 notes/sec. and get the events."
"Add some 'action' events, this example's events draw ractangles on the screen"
el addAll: ActionEvent listExample2.
el play                    "and play the merged event list"
```

The goal here is to generate and play a mixed-voice event list; a cloud event generator plays alternating notes on a MIDI voice and via the built-in sound synthesis primitives, and a parallel list of action events flashes random screen rectangles in parallel with the sound and MIDI output.

User Interfaces for Music/Sound Processing

Navigator MVC in Siren

The Smalltalk-80 Model-View-Controller (MVC) user-interface paradigm (20) is well known and widely imitated. The traditional three-part MVC architecture involves a model object representing the state and behavior of the domain model—in our case, an event list or signal. The view object presents the state of the model on the display, and the controller object sends messages to the model and/or the view in response to user input.

Many Smalltalk applications extend this design pattern to use a separate object to model the GUI and selection state for the model (giving us four-part MVC); these manager objects are often referred to as browsers, inspectors, or editors.

"Navigator MVC" (21) (see Figure 12.5) is a factoring of the controller/editor and view for higher levels of reuse. The traditional MVC components are still there and are connected by the Smalltalk-dependency mechanism (shown in gray). With this architecture and design pattern for MVC, most applications are modeled as enhanced display list editors (i.e., the generic tool is "smart draw"), with special

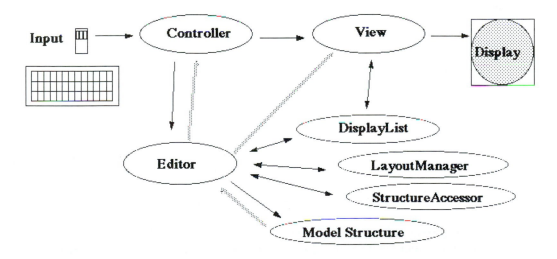

Figure 12.5 Navigator MVC Architecture.

layout manager objects for translating the model structure into a graphical display list representation and for translating structure interaction into model manipulation.

A StructureAccessor is an object that acts as a translator or protocol converter. An example might be an object that responds to the typical messages of a tree node or member of a hierarchy (e.g., What's your name? Do you have and children/subnodes? Who are they? Add this child to them.). One specific, concrete subclass of this might know how to apply that language to navigate through a hierarchical event list (by querying the event list's hierarchy).

The role of the LayoutManager object is central to building Navigator MVC applications. Siren's layout manager objects can take data structures (like event lists) and create display lists for time-sequential (i.e., time running left-to-right or top-to-bottom), hierarchical (i.e., indented list or tree-like), network or graph (e.g., transition diagram), or other layout formats. The editor role of Navigator MVC is played by a smaller number of very generic (and therefore reusable) objects such as EventListEditor or SampledSoundEditor, which are shared by most of the applications in the system.

Much of the work of building a new tool within the Siren system often goes into customizing the interaction and manipulation mechanisms, rather than just the layout of standard pluggable view components. Building a new notation by customizing a layout manager class and (optionally) a view and controller, is relatively easy. Adding new structure accessors to present new perspectives of structures based on properties or link types can be used to extend the range of applications and to construct new hypermedia link navigators. This architecture means that views and controllers are extremely generic (applications are modeled as structured graphics editors), and that the bulk of many applications' special functionality resides in a small number of changes to existing accessor and layout manager classes.

Siren MVC Examples

The example screen in Figure 12.6 shows the simple Siren display list editor running under Squeak MVC; it allows you to manipulate hierarchical structured graphics objects. The pop-up menu in the right of the view shows the default display list controller message. Keyboard commands and mouse interaction support zooming and scrolling. One item is selected in the view and can be dragged or resized using its "selection handles."

The example in Figure 12.7 shows a class inheritance hierarchy presented as a left-bound tree. Color is used to denote class species relationships in the class hierarchies; this is determined by the layout manager used for this example. A refined tree layout manager could do graphical balancing or top-down layout.

A time sequence view is a display list view whose layout manager interprets time as running from left to right. In the example in Figure 12.8, the time sequence is derived from the sentence "Und die Fragen sind die Sätze, die ich nicht aussprechen kann."

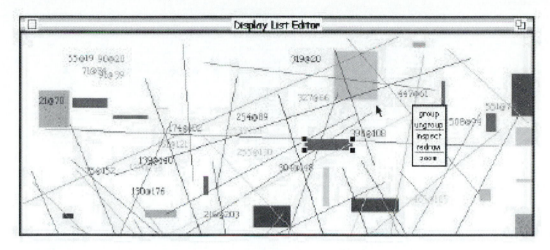

Figure 12.6 Siren DisplayListView Example.

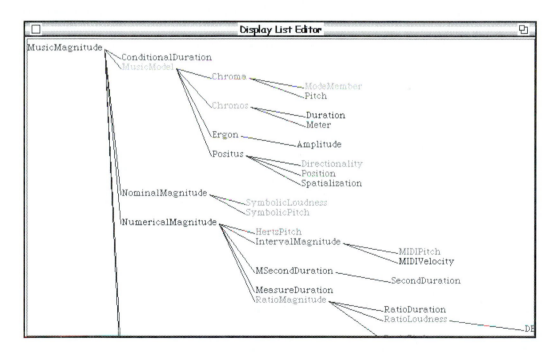

Figure 12.7 Siren LayoutManager Example.

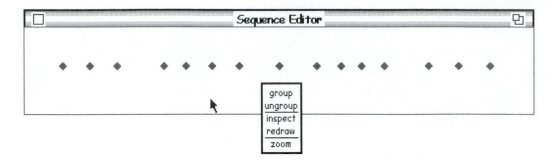

Figure 12.8   Siren TimeSequenceView Example.

In a pitch/time view, time runs left to right, and pitch is displayed from bottom to top. In the example in Figure 12.9, the layout manager creates a separate sub-display list for each note, adding lines to the note head image to show its amplitude and duration, several other properties, and the amplitude envelope.

The multi function view allows the viewing and editing of up to four functions of one variable. The example in Figure 12.10 shows linear break-point functions in red and yellow, an exponential segment function in blue, and a cubic spline function in green. The buttons along the left are for selecting a particular function for editing or file I/O.

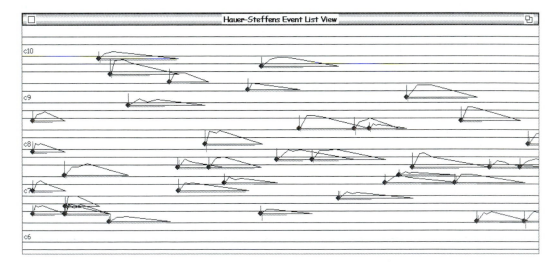

Figure 12.9   Siren Score Editor Example.

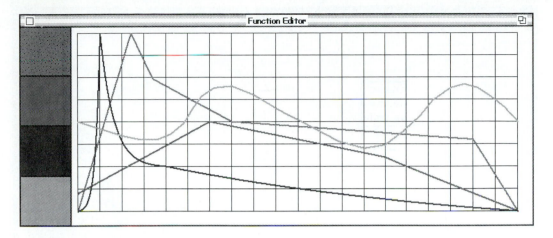

Figure 12.10   Siren Function Editor Example.

The sonogram view displays an FFT-derived spectrum. Figure 12.11 shows the spectrum of a swept sine wave.

Examples of Siren Applications

In this section, we describe two application areas for Siren: (1) a music/sound database project that uses Siren together with other languages and external interfaces and (2) an application of Siren for composition.

Sound/Music Databases: Paleo

Most prior work in sound or music databases has addressed a single kind of data (e.g., MIDI scores or sampled sound effects) and has predefined the types of queries that are to be supported (e.g., queries on fixed sound properties or musical features). Earlier systems also tended to address the needs of music librarians and musicologists, rather than composers and performers. In the Paleo system under development since 1996, we have built a suite of sound and music analysis tools that is integrated with an object-oriented persistency mechanism in Squeak.

The central architectural feature of Paleo is its use of dynamic feature vectors and on-demand indexing. This means that annotational information derived from data analysis can be added to items in the database at any time and that users can develop new analysis or querying techniques and then have them applied to the database's contents on-the-fly within a query. For data that are assumed to be musical sound, this might mean performing envelope detection, spectral analysis, linear prediction, physical model parameter estimation, transient modeling, and

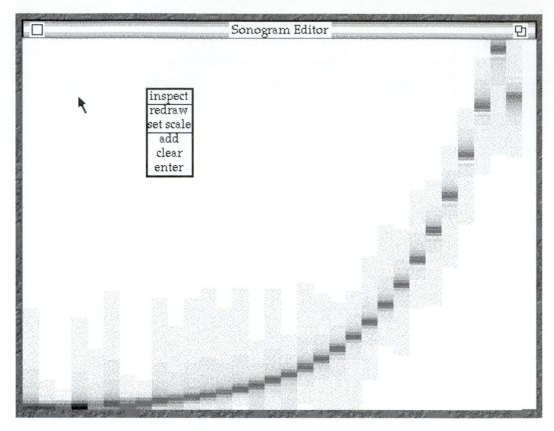

Figure 12.11   Siren Sonogram Example.

so on. For musical performance data (e.g., MIDI), this might entail extraction of expressive timing, phrase analysis, or harmonic analysis.

Paleo content is assumed to be sampled sound, musical scores, or captured musical performances. Scores and performance formats can be simple (e.g., MIDI-derived) or may contain complex annotation and embedded analysis. Paleo is specifically constructed to support multiple sets of captured musical performances (for use in comparing performance expression). This includes the derivation of basic timing and dynamics information from MIDI performances (to be able to separate the performance from the "deadpan" score) and the analysis of timbral information from recorded sounds.

For score analysis, we use a variety of methods, including simple statistical models, rule-based analysis, and constraint derivation. Sampled sound analysis is undertaken using a suite of functions called *NOLib* that is written in the MatLab language and can be accessed from within the Paleo environment over the Net via socket-based MatLab servers. The techniques available in NOLib include all standard time-, frequency-, wavelet modulus-domain analysis operations, as well as pitch detection, instrument classification, and sound segmentation.

The two main applications we envision for Paleo are its uses as an integrated data support system for composers and in a performer's rehearsal workstation. The first set of applications will put the database at the core of a composition-development environment that includes tools for thematic and sonic experimentation and sketch data management. The second platform centers on manipulating rehearsal performance data relative to a "reference" score (which may or may not be a "dead-pan" interpretation). Users can play into the system and then compare their performance to another one of their own or of their teacher's. Query preparation takes place using prebuilt tools such as the composer's sketch browser or by creating direct queries in a simplified declarative query language.

The implementation of the Paleo database persistency and access component is based on the public domain Minnestore object-oriented database package (22), which allows flexible management of data and indices. The Squeak port of Minnestore is called SMS (Squeak Minnestore).

Paleo applications can communicate with an SMS database server over a network and can pass sound sample data or event streams to or from the database. We currently use a simple socket-based protocol, but plan to move to a CORBA-based distribution infrastructure in the near future.

To stress-test Paleo's analysis and query tools against a realistic-sized data set, the test contents included over 1,000 scores of keyboard music (Scarlatti, Bach, Bartok, the Methodist hymnal, etc.), several hundred "world" rhythms, the SHARC database of instrument tone analyses, 100 recorded guitar performance techniques, flute performances, and spoken poetry in five languages. Most of the content is freely available on the Internet.

Paleo Architecture

In Paleo, as in Siren, music and sound data are represented via Smoke objects. In Paleo's SMS data persistency layer, Smoke objects are stored in object sets, which are akin to database tables. Each object set stores one kind of object and can have any number of stored or derived indices. The collection of all defined indices determines the feature vector of the object set. When stored to disk, each object set has its own directory, storage policy, and a group of index files. For performance reasons, there are also cache policies per object set, and methods exist for keeping active object sets in a RAM disk.

Various services can be used by the SMS database server, such as call-outs to the NOLib functions (see the following section) or the use of extra Smalltalk processes for data analysis. The SMS server really only provides the persistency layer and cache policies for open object sets. The overall architecture is as shown in Figure 12.12.

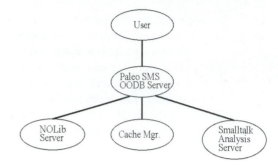

Figure 12.12 Paleo Architecture.

The NOLib Analysis Functions

NOLib is a suite of data analysis and feature extraction routines written by Nicola Orio at CREATE in the MatLab programming language. These functions can be called by analysis scripts (interpreted MatLab programs), which can themselves be started by a network-based "analysis server." We use the public-domain "octave" implementation of MatLab running on UNIX servers. MatLab was chosen for these analysis functions because of the excellent support for signal processing, simple and flexible file I/O, and portability of public-domain MatLab implementations. NOLib functions support sound analysis, recording segmentation, and instrumental timbre feature extraction (e.g., for analyzing the performance technique of instrumental performers).

MIDI File Analysis with Constraints

The purpose of the score analysis framework built for Paleo by Pierre Roy in 1999 is to allow complex queries on various kinds of musical data, including scores, in the spirit of the Humdrum system (23). A large amount of digitized music is available as MIDI files, for instance on any of the many MIDI archives on the Internet.

The MIDI format, however, provides only low-level musical information: It is a performance-oriented, rather than an analysis-oriented, representation of music. Thus, we need to analyze MIDI files to compute additional musical features, such as pitch-classes (by resolving enharmonic ambiguities), voice leading, keys, and harmonies.

The different tasks of analysis—enharmonic, melodic, tonal, and harmonic analysis—are not independent. For instance, the enharmonic analysis depends on tonal analysis, and conversely, the computation of local keys is based on the frequency of the different pitch-classes. Therefore, we need a global strategy in which the different tasks are performed simultaneously.

In the context of our analysis, we often need to perform only a partial analysis, because many queries only involve a few specific elements or incomplete information. Consider the following queries: "How many of Scarlatti's harpsichord sonatas end with a perfect cadence?" or "Are there more minor than major chords in the preludes of Bach's *Well-Tempered Clavichord?*" In such cases, it is useless to perform a complete harmonic analysis of the 555 sonatas by Scarlatti or of the 48 preludes of the *Well-Tempered Clavichord.* This mode of usage demands a scheme allowing partial and incomplete analysis.

What to analyze also depends on various parameters, such as the epoch, the style, and the nature (i.e., form and instrumentation) of the music being considered, for example, the anatomic limitations of human voice compared to a keyboard instrument. Our analysis strategy should be easily adaptable to various situations.

The previous remarks led us to an approach based on constraint satisfaction, instead of using specific algorithms for the different tasks of analysis (24). As a declarative paradigm, constraint satisfaction allows us to build systems that can be easily adapted to specific situations. For instance, adapting the system to vocal or keyboard music analysis is just a matter of using a different set of constraints for the melodies. Constraint resolution can also easily provide partial and incomplete analyses. More precisely, the query "How many sonatas by Scarlatti end with a perfect cadence?" will only require the computation of elements related to the last two chords of each sonata. Finally, constraint resolution is a global process, in which the different elements are progressively computed; thus, interdependent tasks are interlaced in the resolution.

A constraint satisfaction problem or CSP (25) consists of (1) a set of variables (each associated with a set of possible values—its domain), representing the unknown values of the problem, and (2) a set of constraints, expressing relationships between the domain's variables. Solving a CSP consists of instantiating each variable with a value in its domain so that the constraints are satisfied.

Our approach to analyzing a MIDI file is divided into the following steps. First, we quantify the MIDI file to get rid of slight tempo fluctuations, and we segment it into a series of positions. Then, we define a CSP, whose variables represent the different elements of analysis—notes (one for each MIDI note-event), chords (at each position), keys (at each position), and melodies—and whose constraints represent the relationships holding between them. The set of constraints depends on the style and the form of the piece. Then we solve the CSP using standard CSP resolution. We use the BackTalk (26) constraint solver to state and solve the problem.

Paleo I/O Formats

Paleo supports compact and efficient data I/O in the form of methods that work with the Squeak Smalltalk **ReferenceStream** framework, a customizable binary object streaming format. The trade-offs in the design of object storage formats are between size, complexity, and flexibility (pick any two). In Paleo, we opted for a system that is compact, but that also supports the full flexibility of the Smoke music representation, including abstract models for pitch, time, and dynamics; multiple levels of properties and annotation; the attachment of functions of time to events; and hyperlinks between events or event lists.

Data files in this format are on the order of 10–40 times larger than the "corresponding" MIDI files. However, because this notation supports the full Smoke annotation, we can store much richer data. Paleo extensions include simple derived properties such as symbolic pitch (with enharmonic disambiguation) and time (with tempo and meter derivation, rest insertion, and metrical grouping), and higher level properties such as harmonic analysis, performance expression, and others.

Using Paleo

To set up Paleo, we create a database within a storage directory, then create one or more object sets in it (these correspond to classes or tables), and lastly define indices for the object sets (corresponding to instance variables and accessors). One can then add objects to an object set, or retrieve objects based on queries.

Create a New Database of Scores

The first example establishes a new database and adds an object set to it. The objects we add to this set are assumed to respond to the message's composer and style. The examples that follow are in Squeak, and as always, comments are enclosed in double quotes.

```
| dir db |
dir := 'Nomad:Paleo'.              "base directory"
db := SMSDB newOn: dir.            "DB object"
(db addObjectSetNamed: #Scores)    "Add an object−set"
    objectsPerFile: 1;
    storesClass: EventList;        "Stores event lists"
    "Add 2 indices"
    indexOn: #composer domain: String;
    indexOn: #style domain: Symbol.
db save.                           "Save the object set"
"Store objects"
db storeAll: (... collectionOfScores...)
```

Make a Simple Query

To make a simple database query, we reopen the database and create a getOne: message with one or more where: clauses. For example, to get a score by name, we use

```
| db |
db := MinneStoreDB openOn: 'Nomad:Paleo'.
(db getOne: #Scores)        "Create a query on name"
    where: #name eq: #ScarlattiK004;
    execute                 "Get the first response"
```

Add a New Index to an Existing Database

To add a new index to an existing object set, we use (1) the indexOn: message, giving it the name of a "getter" method (i.e., the method that answers the property of the index) or (2) simply a block of Smalltalk code to derive the index value. In the second part of the next example, we create an index of the pitches of the first notes in the score database using a block (the text between the square brackets) that gets the first pitches. This getter block could involve more complex code and/or calls to NOLib functions. The example is as follows:

```
"Add a new index with getter method."
(db objectSetNamed: #Scores)
    indexOn: #name domain: Symbol.
"Add an index with getter block"
(db objectSetNamed: #Scores)
    indexOn: #firstPitch
    domain: SmallInteger
    getter: [ :el | el events first event pitch asMIDI value ].
db save.
```

Make a More Sophisticated Query

To retrieve objects from the database, we use getOne: or getAll:, as described previously, and we can, for example, ask for a range or the derived first-pitch feature:

```
(db getAll: #Scores)
    where: #firstPitch between: 62 and: 65;
    execute
```

Concrete examples of the use of the database in the context of a composition are given in the next section.

Using Siren for Composition

Composition

As stressed at the outset, I develop software tools for use in my own compositions. I documented the use of the earlier MODE system for the piece *Kombination XI* in (8) and (27). One of my current works in progress is called *Ywe Ye, Yi Jr Di* (abbreviated *YYYJD*) and is based on the text of a Chinese poem of the same name by the great T'ang dynasty poet Du Fu. The sound material for the piece is derived from (1) the voice of a man speaking the text (in a 700-year-old Chinese dialect) and (2) the sound of several small bells.

The piece is written for eight or more channels of surround sound, and the effect should be like that of being inside of a huge collection of different, but similar bells that rotate slowly around you and out of which a quiet chant gradually materializes. (The bells are singing to you.)

The bell sounds are processed using a software phase vocoder, a sound analysis/resynthesis package that uses the short-time Fourier transform (STFT) to analyze a sound. One can alter the results of the STFT before resynthesis, allowing, for example, independent control of the pitch and time progress of a sound. For *YYYJD*, I elongate the bell sounds, so that they last several minutes, I also transpose their pitches, so that I can mix together very dense nonharmonic "chords" based on the bell timbres. Lastly, I apply a slight glissando so that the chords are always decreasing in pitch as they rotate and sing.

For the generation of the bell textures, simple Siren event generators are used to create event lists that are then stored onto text files as programs for the phase vocoder, cmix, and/or SuperCollider software sound synthesis languages (16, 28). I use these external languages for historical reasons; the kind of sound file mixing and layering they do could easily be done in Squeak as well. The main reason for using SuperCollider at present is its ease of programming (its source language and class library are close relatives of Smalltalk) and the fact that it supports the ASIO sound interface, so that one can use eight or more channels of sound output.

Extended EventGenerators and User Interfaces for YYYJD

As an example of an extended event generator, I constructed a subclass of Cluster called RotatingBellCluster for *YYYJD*. This class allows me to easily describe and then generate eight-channel textures of inharmonic bell chords where the golden-mean-related "overtones" are placed at separate (related) spatial positions and rotate around the listener at different (slow) rates.

To generate the base sound files (each of which is itself a complex bell timbre), a RotatingBellCluster instance can write a command file for the phase vocoder to process a given sound file (a recorded real bell stored as a sound file with 32-bit floating-point samples) making time-stretched transposed copies whose frequencies are related by multiples of the golden mean. This output looks like the `Makefile` script for the phase vocoder shown in Figure 12.13. The parameters on each line give the time-stretch factors, pitch transposition ratios, and the output file names. This script is run under the shell program on a UNIX compute-server, and often takes several days to process a set of bell samples.

```
# Phase Vocoder script generated by Siren
# rate fftLen win dec int oscPitchFactor ... inFile pipe-to outFile
pv 44100 1024 1024 128 213 0.021286236 0 0 < b.2a.1.float | tosnd -h -f b.2b8.snd
pv 44100 1024 1024 128 213 0.013155617 0 0 < b.2a.1.float | tosnd -h -f b.2b9.snd
pv 44100 1024 1024 128 213 0.008130618 0 0 < b.2a.1.float | tosnd -h -f b.2b0.snd
pv 44100 1024 1024 128 213 1.000000000 0 0 < b.2a.1.float | tosnd -h -f b.2bx.snd
pv 44100 1024 1024 128 213 1.618033988 0 0 < b.2a.1.float | tosnd -h -f b.2ba.snd
pv 44100 1024 1024 128 213 2.618033988 0 0 < b.2a.1.float | tosnd -h -f b.2bb.snd
... many more here ...
```

Figure 12.13 `Makefile` script to generate base sound files.

Given a set of sound files, I need a way to describe precisely how they are mixed and spatialized to generate the desired texture. The basic description of a Rotating-BellCluster is in terms of two components: (1) the collection of files that make up the texture (each of which is represented by an instance of BellPartial), as shown in the first method described next and (2) the three functions that determine the temporal evolution of the bell texture. These functions are shown in the second method. The basic creation method for RotatingBellCluster instances is parameterized with the names of the methods to get these two data sets, so that many different complex instances can be generated and tested.

RotatingBellCluster class methodsFor: 'B2 Bells'

b2Data
"Answer the data for the b2 series of bell partials.
This array is read and turned into a collection of BellPartial objects."
"   Name   Freq   Ampl "
↑#('2ba'   1.6180   15599
        '2bx'   1.0000   21007
        '2b1'   0.6180   8560
    "other partials included here"
        '2b0'   0.0081   21063)

b2aFunctions
"Answer an array of 3 functions for the bell cluster"
↑Array
    "Spectral weighting function"
        with: (LinearFunction from: #((0 1.5) (0.4 0.8) (1 0.5)))
    "Time/density function"
        with: (ExponentialFunction from:
            #((0 20 −2) (0.3 60 −5) (0.7 50 2) (1 30 0)))
    "Mapping of pitch to angular velocity"
        with: (ExponentialFunction from: #((0 0 3) (1 1 0)))

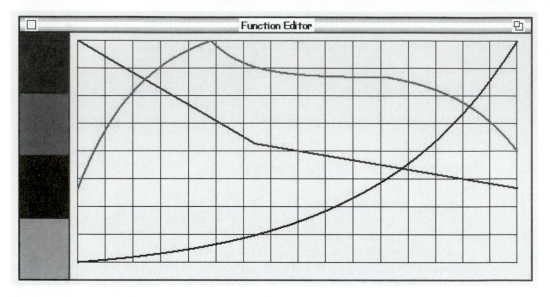

Figure 12.14   Function Editor on a RotatingBellCluster.

The three functions that describe an instance of RotatingBellCluster (as given in the previous method) are (1) the relation between the base frequency of a partial and its amplitude (i.e., the virtual spectrum of the summed complex texture), (2) the density of the texture over time (number of partials active at any moment in time), and (3) the relation between a partial's frequency and its angular (rotational) velocity. The functions defined in the method are shown in the function editor view in Figure 12.14.

To edit RotatingBellCluster instances, I use a TemplateMorph with a few utility methods to support editing functions in place and regenerating the event lists on the fly. This editor is shown in Figure 12.15. The TemplateMorph is a simple object editor that lists the "fields" (typically, though not necessarily, the instance variables) on the left and allows one (where meaningful) to edit them in place on the right.

To actually execute this and create a score for doing the sound file mixing, I first wrote a new subclass (which fits easily on one page) of NoteListVoice (an IOVoice) to support the SuperCollider score file format. This formats the events that are generated by a specific RotatingBellCluster and writes out the result as a score file for further processing in SuperCollider. The method that runs this process is shown in the following example, along with an excerpt of the resulting SuperCollider language score file:

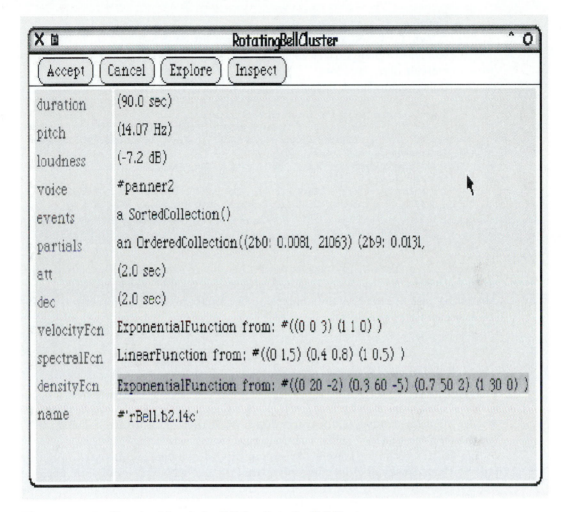

Figure 12.15 TemplateMorph for Editing RotatingBellClusters.

RotatingBellCluster class methodsFor: 'performance'

run
```
"Create, process, and write out a rotating bell cluster from the stored data."
"RotatingBellCluster run"
| list scorefile filename |
list := (RotatingBellCluster      "Instance creation message"
    setup: #b2Data                "which sounds to use"
    functions: #b2aFunctions)     "which functions to use"
        eventList.                "Get the event list"
```

```
filename := 'panner2.sc'.
"Open a voice on a file and play the event list on it."
scorefile := SuperColliderVoice onFileNamed: filename.
scorefile play: list; close.
(FileStream named: filename) edit    "Edit the score file"
```

```
// SuperCollider Score for rotating bell clusters;
//                     generated on 28 July 2000 at 5:04:55 am
// NB: #[ is SuperCollider syntax for a literal array, \x is used for Symbols.
// Instrument command format
// [ delTime , \panner, \file, dur,    att, dec, ampl,    angVel ]
score = #[
    [ 0.5315 ,  \panner , \2bx , 10.7 , 2.0 , 2.0 , 0.8866 , 0.5907 ],
    [ 0.4908 ,  \panner , \2b7 , 10.7 , 2.0 , 2.0 , 1.3346 , 0.0774 ],
    [ 0.4575 ,  \panner , \2b3 , 10.7 , 2.0 , 2.0 , 1.2652 , 0.2520 ],
    ... 414 more lines here ...
];
```

Given these three utility classes (and a couple of methods in TemplateMorph), a total of about four pages of code has provided a flexible tool for describing and generating just the kinds of voluminous and complex textures I wanted to serve as the basis of *YYYJD*.

Framework for Linear Prediction

The next phase of production is to take the recorded spoken Chinese voice, to turn it into a slow singing voice in a lower pitch range, and then to "cross-synthesize" it with the eight-channel bell textures described earlier. This involves (many CPU-months of) the phase vocoder mentioned previously and also a linear prediction coding (LPC) vocoder. I use a library for LPC developed for the cmix language (16) by Paul Lansky at Princeton University (parts of which use even older libraries written in FORTRAN!). For this, I linked the library functions I need into a Squeak plug-in that is accessed via a LinearPredictor object. An example of the inner-most layer of this is primitive calls to the plug-in of the following form:

LinearPredictor methodsFor: 'analysis'

lpcAnalyze: input out: output rate: rate poles: poles framesize: frsize skip: sk dur: dur
    "Call the CmixPlugin's LPC analysis primitive."
    <primitive: 'lpcAnalyzeShort' module:'CmixPlugin'>
    ↑self primitiveFailed

An example of doing the full LPC analysis is given in the following code excerpt, which reads an input sound file and sets up a linear prediction analyzer to process it. The results are returned in the LinearPredictor object, which consists of a series of LPC frame objects.

```
| sndin data lpc |
sndin := StoredSound fromFile: 'Siren:Kombination2a.snd'.
lpc := LinearPredictor on: sndin.
lpc npoles: 24.
lpc framesize: 256.
lpc analyze.
lpc stabilize.
lpc packLPCData.
data := lpc pitchTrackLow: 70 high: 500.
lpc packPitchData: data.
lpc explore
```

In the past, I have built fancy GUI tools for manipulating LPC data (27), but now stick to simpler, text-based methods, generally using event generators to generate LPC processing scripts.

Composition Structuring

To manage the larger-scale construction of *YYYJD*, I built a few extensions to existing Siren and Squeak tools. The most useful extension is a refinement to the (excellent) ObjectExplorer and ObjectExplorerWrapper to support flexible editing of hierarchical event list structures at varying levels of detail. Since Siren events are generic property lists, I need to be able to treat their properties as if they were first-class instance variables and to add new properties and annotations from within the editor. A few pages of extensions to the two classes that make up the explorer made this possible.

Figure 12.16 shows a simple SirenScoreExplorer on the top-level score of *YYYJD*. One can see the hierarchy of the event lists and the comment of the selected list in the text field below the list. This field has several uses, as a do-it field, as an annotation editor, and for adding new properties and relationships.

This editor can be used to "drill down" to arbitrarily low levels of the structure of a composition, as shown in Figure 12.17, which shows the details of the inner structure of the selected (and expanded) RotatingBellCluster.

The most powerful extension to the explorer is the ability to select what to show or hide about a given class of objects. The wrappers hold onto lists of fields and support menu selection for varying levels of detail, as illustrated by Figure 12.18.

Database Integration for Composition

The last new tool in use for *YYYJD* is a browser for the various Paleo data sets. The current version uses a simple multiple list as in traditional code browsers. (I hope to have an explorer-based version running soon.) The left-most list shows the available object sets; when an object set is selected, its indices are shown in the

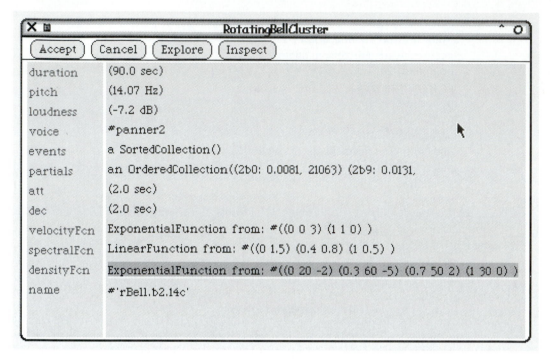

Figure 12.16 SirenScoreExplorer on the Structure of *YYYJD*.

second-level list. Selecting an index allows you to filter the contents of the current object set, and the names of the selected elements are shown in the third list. The buttons to the right allow you to load and store individual object or object sets, or to open various user interfaces (e.g., explorers, template editors, or other tools shown in the following figures) on objects in the database.

The first two examples, given in Figure 12.19, show the database browser on the various object sets related to *YYYJD*. The left-hand screen shot shows an explorer on the top-level score, with the hierarchy expanded down to the level of one of the RotatingBellCluster events. The right-hand view shows a piano-roll-style score for one of the event generators used later in the piece. The browser can have several kinds of explorers, templates, and editors for each of the object sets in a database.

In Figure 12.20, two extended editors are shown, as would be used for editing functions of time (left) and derived spectra (right).

The last example, in Figure 12.21, shows an experimental data set whereby the structural score of Alban Berg's opera *Wozzeck* (stored as a hierarchical event list with annotations, of course) can be used to browse a set of images of the sketches of the score.

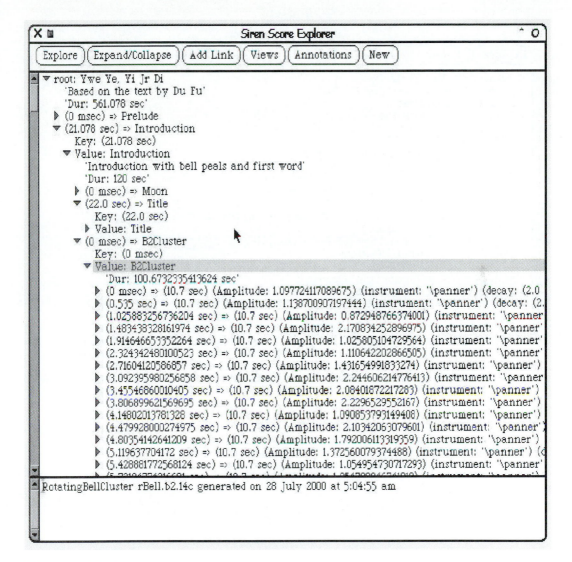

Figure 12.17   Details of a RotatingBellCluster.

The style of the code extensions and new tools described earlier are typical of the way I use Siren in a composition. Programming new event generators and new basic music magnitude models, adding script-like classes, extending the system's graphical tools, and defining new I/O formats are all normal tasks in composition with the system.

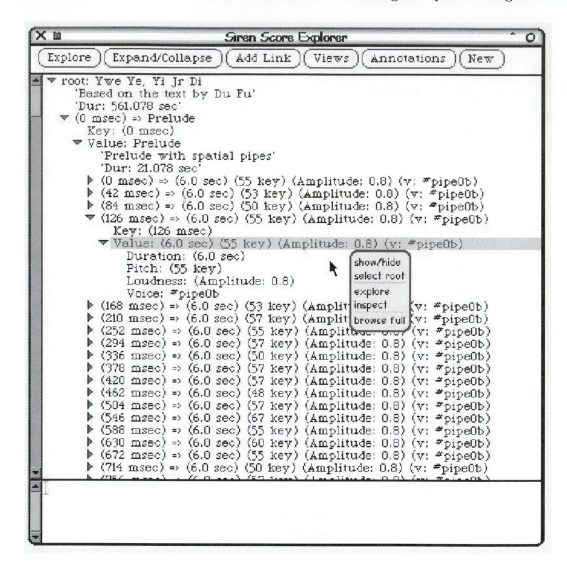

Figure 12.18 Showing/Hiding Fields in the SirenScoreExplorer.

The Future

Let me summarize here where I am now with Siren, what I consider its successes and failures, and where I see taking it in the future.

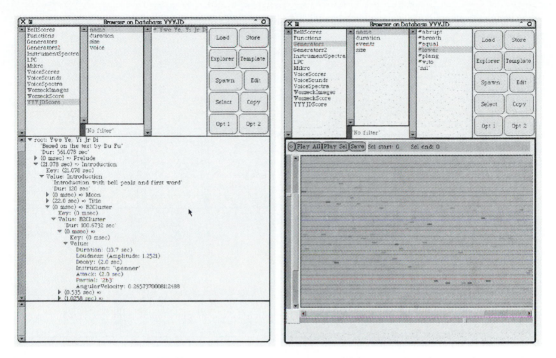

Figure 12.19   Database Browsers Illustrating Structural and Temporal Views of Scores.

Status

I have been making my music tools available since 1978. In 1995, I had pretty much given up on using Smalltalk, largely because of the licensing policy of ParcPlace Systems, Inc. Their VisualWorks system was simply too expensive for composers (or even universities) to use, and I was using a bootleg copy myself. (They have since come out with a free-ware version for noncommercial use.) I had invested several months in porting the MODE classes to Java when I heard about Squeak from Dan Ingalls. Because Squeak is open-source, it is a delight that Siren is freely available in compiled (and portable) form. Several components (such as the LPC plug-in and extended MIDI primitives) are, however, platform specific.

At the beginning of the chapter, I implied that I am the only Siren customer I listen to; this is not entirely true, but is also not entirely untrue. There have been extended periods in which a group of researcher/programmers collaborated on various versions of this software, ranging from the Smoke committee of 1990–92 to the more recent Paleo project team at CREATE. I have enjoyed these collaborations immensely, and the results of the team efforts have generally been incorporated into the system.

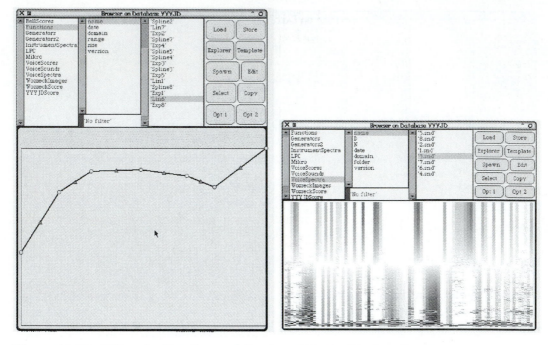

Figure 12.20   Editors for Functions and Spectra within the Database Browser.

Current Siren is available from my website at CREATE, though the full system runs well only on Apple Macintosh computers. (See "Siren 2002.) All of the base Siren system, as well as the SMS database framework and most of the Paleo code, is included.

Successes

It has been a thrill to develop tools for my own use in Smalltalk and to find that they are sometimes of use to other composers. Since what I do is already a pretty elitist effort (contemporary serious music), I am always pleased when someone actually uses Siren and sends me comments (or a bug report). It has been interesting to see what features external users add to the system, and a number of these have been incorporated recently (e.g., Alberto De Campo's microtonal MIDI representation).

Failures

Most of the disappointments for Siren's users (and me) are based on the basic profile of what Siren is intended to do in the first place. I have used MIDI only for one

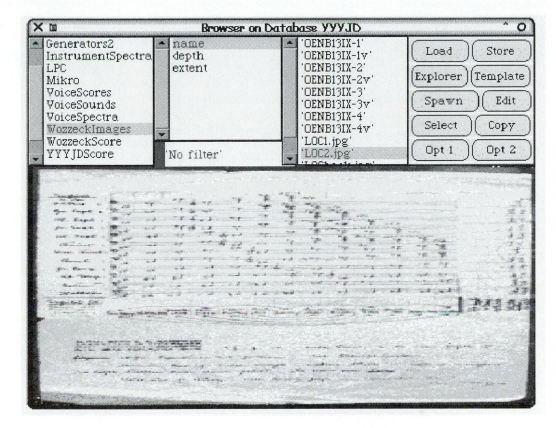

Figure 12.21   Database Browser on the Images of the Opera *Wozzeck*.

experimental composition (that is now played from tape in concerts). I am not a big fan of graphical tools, so many users are disappointed that Siren is not a free MIDI sequencer, a graphical programming language for music, or an object-oriented sound synthesis system. (All of these are available elsewhere.)

While it has been very fulfilling to have active collaborators, there have also been frustrations, such as the difficulty of achieving multi-platform support for a standard set of high-level MIDI I/O functions. The base set of primitives included in Squeak is inappropriate for intensive MIDI-oriented applications, and there appear to be no volunteers to maintain a set of more powerful primitives on multiple platforms.

Siren 2002

When I look ahead to the future, I hope that in two years I have more of the same, only faster and more flexible! My main wishes are related to the hardware I use, rather than weaknesses in Squeak or Siren. (I've given up on ever getting the 32-hour day.) That being said, the main features that I miss in Squeak can be grouped as follows:

- Language issues—Multiple value returns and multiple value assignment, true multiple inheritance (to be used rarely, of course), assertions, and multiple kinds of (nesting) comment characters.

- Library issues—CORBA IDL and ORB integration, probability distributions (a la ST80), very high-precision floating-point numbers, and integrated namespaces and packages.

- Tool issues—Integrated source code control system and configuration management tools, and tools for CORBA distributed applications.

- GUI issues—Native look and feel, and themes.

My primary fear about Squeak is related to "image bloat." The system is growing fast, and we have still not integrated namespaces and packages to the point where image management is easy.

My plans for the next few months (as I work on *YYYJD*), are to integrate the Steinberg ASIO sound libraries (as soon as it is clear what will be supported on the next generation of Macintosh operating systems) and to incorporate more of the LPC vocoder functions into Siren. Medium term, I intend to work on a more powerful synthesis engine (stealing ideas from SuperCollider) and to integrate Siren and SuperCollider as plug-ins to each other. Lastly, I have already composed the follow-on pieces to *YYYJD* (*. . . nor shall my sword sleep in my hand* and *To My Younger Brother*) and hope to start working on them in early 2001.

Acknowledgments

It would be extremely unfair to present this work as mine alone. Siren incorporates the work of many people who have contributed ideas and/or code; they include Paul Alderman, Alberto De Campo, Roger Dannenberg, Lounette Dyer, Adrian Freed, Guy Garnett, Kurt Hebel, Craig Latta, David Leibs, Mark Lentczner, Hitoshi Katta, Alex Kouznetsov, James McCartney, Hans-Martin Mosner, Danny Oppenheim, Nicola Orio, Francois Pachet, Pierre Roy, Carla Scaletti, Bill Schottstaedt, John Tangney, and Bill Walker. Pierre Roy and Nicola Orio also contributed texts to this chapter.

I must also acknowledge here the generous support of my employers and the academic institutions where this software was developed, including PCS/Cadmus GmbH in Munich, Xerox PARC, ParcPlace Systems, Inc., CCRMA/Stanford, the STEIM Foundation in Amsterdam, The Swedish Institute for Computer Science, CMNAT/Berkeley, CREATE/UC Santa Barbara, and the electronic music studio of the Technical University of Berlin. Special thanks for moral and financial support during the writing of this chapter go to CREATE's director JoAnn Kuchera-Morin and the manager of the TU Berlin studio, Folkmar Hein, as well as to the Deutscher Akademischer Austauschdienst (DAAD).

Lastly, Mark Guzdial and Juan Manuel Vuletich read and provided very useful comments on an earlier draft of this text, and Anita Flanzbaum edited the manuscript.

Conclusions

Siren is a framework in Squeak Smalltalk for music and sound processing. The main focus is towards the representation of structured music and musical composition methods. This chapter described the Smoke representation language that serves as the kernel of Siren, introduced its I/O facilities, and presented several extended examples of Siren in action.

References

[1] D. Ingalls, T. Kaehler, J. Maloney, S. Wallace, and A. Kay, *Back to the Future: The Story of Squeak, A Practical Smalltalk Written in Itself*, Proc. ACM OOPSLA 1997.

[2] S. T. Pope, *Bat Out Of Hell*, Perspectives of New Music, V. 24, 1986 (cassette). Also in: Computer Music Journal Sound Anthology, V. 21, 1997 (CD).

[3] S. T. Pope, *Music Notation and the Representation of Musical Structure and Knowledge*, Perspectives of New Music, 24(2), Winter, 1986.

[4] S. T. Pope, *The Development of an Intelligent Composer's Assistant: Interactive Graphics Tools and Knowledge Representation for Composers*, Proc. 1986 International Computer Music Conference. San Francisco: International Computer Music Association.

[5] S. T. Pope, *A Smalltalk-80-based Music Toolkit*, Proc. 1987 International Computer Music Conference. San Francisco: International Computer Music Association.

[6] S. T. Pope, *The Interim DynaPiano: An Integrated Computer Tool and Instrument for Composers*, Computer Music Journal, 16(3), Fall, 1992.

[7] S. T. Pope, *An Introduction to the MODE*, in: The Well-Tempered Object: Musical Applications of Object-Oriented Software Technology, S. T. Pope, ed., MIT Press, 1991.

[8] S. T. Pope, *Kombination XI*, (musical composition), in: Or Some Computer Music, Touch/OR Records, 1999. Also in: The Virtuoso in the Computer Age (CDCM V. 13), Centaur Records, 1993.

[9] S. T. Pope, *Siren: Software for Music Composition and Performance in Squeak*, Proc. 1997 International Computer Music Conference. San Francisco: International Computer Music Association.

[10] S. T. Pope, *The Siren Music/Sound Package for Squeak Smalltalk*, Proc. ACM OOPSLA 1998.

[11] S. T. Pope, ed, *The Well-Tempered Object: Musical Applications of Object-Oriented Software Technology*, MIT Press, 1991.

[12] C. Roads, S. T. Pope, G. DePoli, and A. Piccialli, eds, *Musical Signal Processing*, Swets & Zeitlinger, 1997.

[13] R. Dannenberg, *Music Representation Issues, Techniques, and Systems*, Computer Music Journal, 17(3), Fall, 1993.

[14] G. Wiggins, et al, *A Framework for the Evaluation of Music Representation Systems*, Computer Music Journal, 17(3), Fall, 1993.

[15] S. T. Pope, *Musical Object Representation*, in: Musical Signal Processing, C. Roadds, S. T. Pope, G. DePoli, and A. Piccialli, eds., Swets & Zeitlinger, 1992.

[16] S. T. Pope, *Machine Tongues XV: Three Packages for Software Sound Synthesis*, Computer Music Journal, 17(2), Summer, 1993.

[17] C. Scaletti, *The Kyma/Platypus Computer Music Workstation*, Computer Music Journal, 13(2), Summer, 1989. Reprinted in: The Well-Tempered Object: Musical Applications of Object-Oriented Software Technology, S. T. Pope, ed., MIT Press, 1991.

[18] S. T. Pope, *Modeling Musical Structures as EventGenerators*, Proc. 1989 International Computer Music Conference. San Francisco: International Computer Music Association.

[19] R. Dannenberg, P. Desain, and H-J. Honing, *Programming Language Design for Musical Signal Processing*, in: Musical Signal Processing, C. Roadds, S. T. Pope, G. DePoli, and A. Piccialli, eds., Swets & Zeitlinger, 1992.

[20] G. Krasner and S. T. Pope, *A Cookbook for the Model-View-Controller User Interface Paradigm in Smalltalk-80*, Journal of Object-Oriented Programming, 1(3), 1988.

[21] S. T. Pope, N. Harter and K. Pier, *A Navigator for UNIX*, 1989 ACM SIGCHI video collection.

[22] J. Carlson, *MinneStore OO Database Documentation*, 1998. See http://www.objectcomposition.com

[23] D. Huron, *The Humdrum Toolkit Reference Manual*, Center for Computer Assisted Research in the Humanities, Menlo Park, California, 1994.

[24] R. Mouton, *Outils intelligents pour les musicologues*, Ph.D. Thesis, Université du Maine, Le Mans, France, 1994.

[25] A. Mackworth, *Consistency in Networks of Relations*, Artificial intelligence, 8(1), 1977.

[26] P. Roy, A. Liret, and F. Pachet, *The Framework Approach for Constraint Satisfaction*, ACM Computing Survey Symposium, 1998.

[27] S. T. Pope, *Producing 'Kombination XI': Using Modern Hardware and Software Systems for Composition*, Leonardo Music Journal, 2(1), 1992.

[28] J. McCartney, *SuperCollider Software*, see `www.audiosynth.com`.

Stephen Travis Pope (b. 1955, New Jersey, USA), studied at Cornell University, the Vienna Music Academy, and the "Mozarteum" Academy in Salzburg, Austria, receiving a variety of degrees and certificates in electrical engineering, recording engineering, and music theory and composition. He has taught both music and computer science at the graduate level and has worked as a composer, software engineer, engineering manager, consultant/mentor/trainer, editor, and performing musician. From 1988 through 1997, he served as editor-in-chief of *Computer Music Journal*, published by the MIT Press. He is currently active as a software consultant specializing in object-oriented software and as a senior research specialist at the Center Research in Electronic Art Technology (CREATE) in the Department of Music at the University of California, Santa Barbara.

Stephen has over 80 publications on topics related to music theory and composition, computer music, artificial intelligence, graphics and user interfaces, integrated programming environments, and object-oriented programming. He has been an officer of the International Computer Music Association and was elected a lifetime member in 1990. He has realized his musical works at computer music studios in the USA (CCRMA/Stanford, CNMAT/Berkeley, and CREATE/Santa Barbara) and Europe (IRCAM/Paris, STEIM/Amsterdam, EMS/Stockholm, CMRS/Salzburg, and IEuEM/Vienna). His music is available in recorded form from Centaur Records/CDCM, Perspectives of New Music, Touch Records, SBC Records, and on MIT Press Monograph CD/CD-ROMs.

Stephen lived in Europe (Austria, Germany, and France) from 1977 to 1986 and has spent several years there since then (in Holland and Sweden).

13

Streaming Audio

Craig Latta
The NetJam project
`netjam.org`

Afternoon

It's been a slow day. Browsing through the day's mail over a fresh cup of coffee, you notice your copy of **Squeak: Open-Source for Computing and Multimedia** has arrived. You peruse the covers lazily, noticing that a chapter about streaming audio lies within.

Streaming audio!

Feverishly, you scan the table of contents. A shudder runs down your spine as your eyes alight on the title, and the page number is revealed. The pages fly in a flurry of acid-free abandon, finally revealing page 423.There you read, in letters which shall remain indelibly etched in your psyche, "`netjam.org/flow`." This is all you need to see; there's not a moment to lose. Instantly the book is forgotten as your fingers pound the URL into the nearest keyboard, and instructions flood the screen. A few clicks later, installation is complete. Breathlessly, you... *do it*:

```
(Sound fromHostNamed: 'netjam.org') play
```

One Internet moment later, the strains of a new yet somehow familiar song sift forth from your speakers. You experience a state of giddy bliss. Streaming audio! In Squeak!

A verse goes by, then a chorus. Then another verse. Another chorus. Then... another verse followed by another chorus. But then a bridge! Can a break be far behind?

Indeed, the break has come quite literally. The music has stopped. A notifier stares innocently at you. It's all too much; utterly spent, you pass out.

```
┌────────────────────────────────────────────────────────────┐
│ □                      debug me                          ⊡  │
├────────────────────────────────────────────────────────────┤
│ RingBuffer»basicNext:                                        │
│ RingBuffer»next:                                             │
│ VorbisSound(ExternalSound)»                                  │
│     mixFramesInQuantity:                                     │
│     into:                                                    │
│     startingAt:                                              │
│     leftVolume:                                              │
│     rightVolume:                                             │
│ VorbisSound(Sound)»                                          │
│     playFramesInQuantity:                                    │
│     into:                                                    │
│     startingAt:                                              │
│ [] in SoundPlayer class»playLoop                             │
│                                                              │
└────────────────────────────────────────────────────────────┘
```

Twilight

Some time later, you regain consciousness. An eerie silence fills the room in the twilight, broken occasionally by the gentle swapping of hard disks. Then it hits you. The song…the song was trying to tell you something. You've never really explored the implementation of audio or networking before, but it doesn't matter. You simply must hear the rest of that song. Summoning a new reserve of energy, you reach for the mouse. With a click, the notifier gives way to a debugger. The contexts of the suspended process lay before you.

They deal in receivers you've never seen and messages you've never sent. You decide it's best to start at the beginning, if you're going to understand this. The first thing you notice is that none of the selectors mention the mouse, controllers, or other human-interface elements. This must not be the human interface process. Sure enough, the earliest context is SoundPlayer class»playLoop; this is a process that does nothing but play sounds. This makes sense; other work (such as handling mouse and keyboard events) may continue unaffected in other processes.

You also notice that this method determines the rate at which audio data is played. You realize an important terminological detail: the difference between *sample* and *frame* as they are used here. A sample is an instantaneous measure of sound pressure at a single position. The magnitude of each sample ranges over a power-of-two interval (audio compact discs use signed 16-bit values). A frame is a collection of concurrent samples for one or more waveforms, each of which is transmitted over a *channel*. Your sound is in stereo, so it has two waveforms (one for each ear) and thus two samples for each two-channel frame. The data is played at a certain *frame rate*, also known as the *sampling rate*.

You grab a pen and idly sketch a diagram of the process.

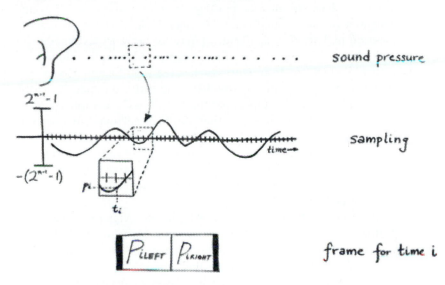

You venture further into SoundPlayer class≫playLoop. Here you see the connection between the sound-playing process and your own beloved sound. SoundPlayer asks each active sound to mix an amount of pending audio samples into a buffer, then plays the buffer. It's your sound's turn to mix, in response to mixFramesInQuantity:into:startingAt:leftVolume:rightVolume:. Another diagram takes shape.

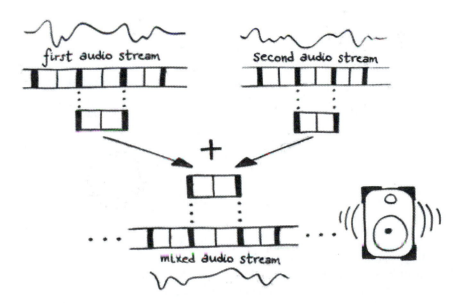

You notice that your sound is an instance of VorbisSound, a subclass of ExternalSound. Since the mixing message is sent to each active sound, it must be implemented by each sound class. A quick look at the implementors of the mixing message highlights a significant difference between ExternalSounds and sounds of other classes. Whereas the others supply their audio samples algorithmically (as with FMSound), or from static caches (as with SampledSound), ExternalSounds supply them from a dynamic cache, fed by an external *packet stream.* The "VorbisSound" name implies support for the Vorbis audio compression format (an open alternative to MP3). So it seems that the ExternalSound hierarchy provides audio "codec" (COder/DECoder) behavior.

At the point of suspension in the mixing message, your sound is fetching its next samples. It gets them from an instance variable named, reasonably enough, samples. But what sort of object is samples, and how is it in a position to be a source of audio data?

Another click reveals that it's a RingBuffer. You read the class comment for RingBuffer and find that its instances are first-in, first-out buffers that respond to stream protocol. You know a bit about streams—the system transcript is one you use often. The basic idea is pretty simple: A stream provides interleaved reading and writing access to a collection, with messages derived from next and nextPut:. A RingBuffer behaves like a stream, via those messages, but elements are discarded after being read, and operations proceed at the beginning of the collection after the end is reached. By "wrapping around" this way, the buffer gives its collection the appearance of a "ring."

Such a structure is quite appropriate for a network data buffer. While one process is consuming elements from the "front," another can write them to the "end." Internally, the buffer uses a fixed-size collection, with two pointers keeping track of where reading and writing take place. This provides a space-efficient way to keep the consuming process from waiting for elements, despite network lapses and any processing overhead incurred by the writing process. This is particularly important for sounds; the overhead of decoding compressed audio could be considerable, and waiting for audio data would result in audible gaps.

It seems that you're experiencing just such a gap, made indefinite by the suspension of the sound-playing process. Moving forward to the most recent context, you see the problem: The samples buffer is empty. The process appears to have been suspended by the line

```
thisContext handle: #noMoreReadableElements
```

Browsing the implementors of handle:, you see that this is an exception-handling expression. Certainly something more useful than halting could happen in response to buffer starvation. Assuming that sample consumption outpaced production, but that production hasn't stopped entirely, simply waiting and attempting to consume again might be a viable solution. You need to handle this exception.

After all this browsing, you finally get to write some code of your own. Where should the handling occur? Probably back in

mixFramesInQuantity:into:startingAt:leftVolume:rightVolume:

where the sound attempted to consume samples. The class comment for Exception suggests looking at the usage examples in BlockContext class. Perusing them, you find restart. This gives you a template for the code you need to write. The expression

samples next: numberOfFramesToPlay * bytesPerFrame

becomes

```
[samples next: numberOfFramesToPlay * bytesPerFrame]
    valueHandling: #noMoreReadableElements
    with: [:exception |
        "Ostensibly, another process is producing samples.
        By this time, there may be space available.
        Simply restart."
        exception restart]
```

That ought to do the trick.

But what is the sample-producing process? You look at the references to **samples**. The first to catch your eye is ExternalSound >> decode:. This is where the sound converts bytes into audio samples and writes to the samples buffer. The default implementation in ExternalSound doesn't actually do any decoding; it just writes given bytes directly to the samples buffer. This would be appropriate for uncompressed audio sample data (e.g., the WAV format), but probably not for anything transmitted over a network. Networks are still relatively slow, at least for sending live raw digital audio. The most common audio frame rate (the one used on audio CDs) is 44,100 frames per second, with each frame consisting of two 16-bit samples. That's 1,411,200 bits per second. Music listeners with network connections faster than 500 kb/s are still relatively rare, and connections as slow as 28.8 kb/s are common.

Compression techniques like MP3 and Vorbis reduce the network bandwidth requirement by roughly a factor of 10, supporting CD-quality audio for those with connections in the 150-kb/s range and convenient downloadable audio for those with slower connections. They do this at a considerable cost of complexity, however. One look at VorbisSound >> decode: dampens your sense of adventure a little; it's complicated. Contemporary audio compression algorithms take advantage of psychoacoustic phenomena, in particular, the way certain sounds "mask" or occlude others in human hearing. For example, a louder tone at a certain pitch will mask quieter tones at nearby pitches. The algorithms attempt to encode a simpler version of their input, giving the illusion of the whole upon decoding. The most readily apparent fact about the implementation is one of terminology: encoded data elements are called *packets*, and decoded elements are called *samples*.

But all you're really concerned with here is that decoding takes time (and that it yields usable samples). Oh, and where do the encoded bytes come from?

You look at the senders of decode:, and find ExternalSound>>on:numberOfChannels:bytesPerFrame:frameRate:. Here's where the buffering process is created. It repeatedly waits for data, then decodes what has become available. Data come from another of the sound's instance variables, named "packets." The variable contains packets, an instance of NetStream, another variation on the stream concept. Browsing the NetStream class, you see that its collection isn't a typical internal collection. As the class name implies, elements come from another machine on the Net.

Looking deeper into NetStream, you see that it uses a "resource" instead of an internal collection. What does packets use? You open an inspector on packets, and select resource. It's an instance of OutgoingClientTCPSocket. This must be where the actual bytes come from. But looking at the instance creation protocol of NetStream, you realize that resource needn't be an "outgoing client TCP socket" or even a socket at all. NetStream can create instances with several different resources. Browsing the OutgoingClientTCPSocket class, you notice it's a subclass of NetResource, which has other subclasses, including UDPSocket and SerialPort. With the same NetSound and NetStream interface, your audio data could just as well come from other external resources, like a serial port or an infrared link.

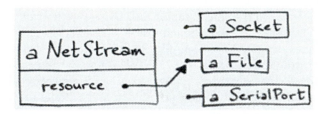

Night

Night has fallen. The room around you has vanished, eclipsed by the glow of the screen. You turn on a torchiere and take stock of your surroundings... There's a dedicated sound player process that continually fills a buffer with audio data, then plays it. It fills the buffer by asking each active sound to mix some quantity of its ensuing frames with the sound buffer's current contents. Your sound gets its frames from a sample buffer, fed by another process which continually fetches and decodes compressed audio packets from a socket connected to a remote machine. A dog barks from somewhere in the distance. Your coffee has long since gone cold. There are four messages waiting on your answering machine, but your trusty pen is still nearby.

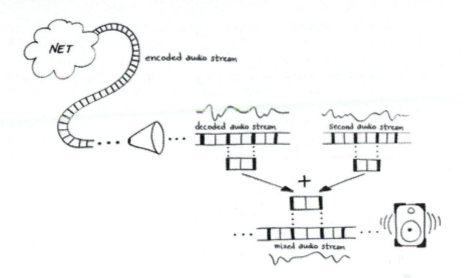

This is all very well, you think, but how does the sound know how many bytes to mix from the sample buffer? How did the sound know what its frame rate was supposed to be? How does it know the number of channels to use, and how many bytes are used by each frame? In the case of other sounds, this information is either implicit (as with FM sounds) or specified "out of band" in a header (as with sounds played from files). Perhaps NetSounds have a means of communicating out-of-band information about the sounds they play.

You go back a few contexts, where your sound is the receiver, and look at the instance variables. Among them is the promisingly named control. Clicking on it for a description, you read that it's an AudioClient, connected to port 7777 of netjam.org, controlling a VorbisSound. You open yet another browser, on AudioClient.

The first thing you notice about AudioClient is that it seems to be part of a larger client/server framework. It's a subclass of Client, which has Server for a sibling and Correspondent for a parent. Client and Correspondent seem to handle the details of connecting to a server and setting resource options (such as whether to communicate in binary or text). Having created an AudioClient with toHostNamed:, an ExternalSound is free to start using it as a sort of remote control. This is just what happens in ExternalSound class>>fromHostNamed:, the first method you ran. ExternalSound creates an AudioClient as a control, selects a track to play, then creates an instance of an appropriate ExternalSound subclass, with a sample stream, channel quantity, frame size, and frame rate obtained from the control.

Looking at the instance behavior of AudioClient, you see how an instance answers these parameters. Using its NetStream, it sends command numbers and answers objects based on the results. For the numerical answers, the server result itself is used. In the case of the audio packet stream, the client answers a new NetStream connected to the remote port indicated by the server result. These commands form the basis for a very simple audio control protocol.

If there's an AudioClient, might there be an AudioServer as well? Sure enough, there is; a quick browse through it confirms the behavior suggested by AudioClient. For each client connected to it, an AudioServer keeps a reference to a sequence of audio frames, and a NetStream onto which it encodes them, in a separate process. Interestingly, as long as source frames are available from a stream in real time or faster, they may come from a file, a synthesized sound, or live acoustic input. Concurrently with writing frames, the server listens for commands from each client. Some of these commands request changes in the writing of the frames. For example, a "pause" command causes the server to suspend a client's writing process.

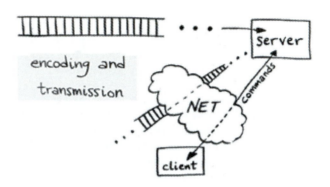

Suddenly, the silence becomes deafening. With a start, you put down your pen, select the mixing method context, and restart it, thus resuming the sound playing process. The music resumes, pulsing hypnotically.

You were right. The song *was* trying to tell you something. You listen attentively, nodding thoughtfully. Truer words you've never heard. That was certainly worth waiting for. Having reached a state of closure, you head sleepily toward bed. On your way, you come across the Squeak book, still open to the streaming audio chapter.

Perhaps tomorrow you'll read it.

Acknowledgments

Craig thanks Gale, for her understanding, love, and support. He also thanks Sam Adams and IBM for their enthusiasm, Interval Research for their ambition, and, of course, Mark Guzdial and Kim Rose for their encouragement (and lenience :). Congratulations!

Further Reading

Calvino, Italo. *If on a Winter's Night a Traveler*. Harcourt Brace, 1982.

Egremont, Carlton III. *Mr. Bunny's Guide to Active X*. Addison-Wesley, 1998.

Montgomery, Christopher. *The Ogg Vorbis audio codec website*. `xiph.org`.

Pohlmann, Ken C. *Principles of Digital Audio*, fourth edition. McGraw-Hill, 2000.

Craig Latta `Craig.Latta@NetJam.ORG` is descended from a long line of itinerant researchers. Asking only for a fast network connection and an occasional glimpse at the sky, he toils endlessly in the hinterlands of experimental computer science and time-varying media. This afternoon he worked for IBM's Watson Research Center. At twilight he went for a nice walk. Now, under cover of night, he pursues the NetJam project (`netjam.org`), a music improvisation network.

14

Embracing Change with Squeak: Extreme Programming (XP)

J. Sarkela, P. McDonough, and D. Caster

Introduction

In the world of sports, one often hears the adjective "extreme" applied to activities that involve high risk, a sense of daring, and a participant who constantly pushes the envelope to achieve the next level of success. Similarly, in the programming world, "extreme" describes a methodology in which teams collaborate on projects that entail risk, explore uncharted territories, and constantly push the envelope of productivity. This is the world of Extreme Programming (XP).

The XP practices embody a set of heuristics for recognizing and adapting to change, for change is the only constant in XP. The XP process values learning as a basic skill for individuals and the team, as the tensions inherent in development stimulate evolutionary growth. In the XP view, setbacks and failures provide essential feedback on which the software development process thrives, where risk is something to be understood and managed, not merely avoided.

In this chapter, we explore the XP methodology and consider how it empowers the Squeak programmer. We introduce enough of the XP process to keep the discussion somewhat self-contained, before exploring a few chosen aspects such as planning and testing in more depth, to facilitate a Squeak developer's first few steps toward adopting XP.[1] We also describe simple ways to use XP in Squeak, exploiting the development tools present in a standard Squeak distribution, as well

---

[1] A thorough treatment of XP can be found in *Extreme Programming Explained,* written by Kent Beck, published by Addison Wesley, 1999.

as the SUnit testing framework.[2] Finally, we conclude with some observations based on our experience with Squeak and the XP process.

XP Overview

Extreme Programming encompasses a set of mutually supporting practices that encourage communication, learning, and a constant emphasis on "the simplest thing that could possibly work." Teamwork among the customer, the development staff, and related business interests is essential to the success of any project. XP concentrates on building an evolving, shared vision of the project rather than promulgating detailed rules of architecture, documentation, and the like. In a sense, all participants agree to a social contract when they decide to "do XP."

XP is an integrated approach, which cannot easily be broken out into its components without losing its essence. Nevertheless, several distinguishing practices within XP stand out: a focus on testing and repeatability, a rapid and iterative approach to software development and delivery, and programming in pairs (two people, one computer terminal, keyboard, and mouse). After the initial planning stage of a project, these quickly become the team's basic, day-to-day working environment. They are also transferable and beneficial to smaller teams or individuals, or to more informal projects that may not be able to access XP in its entirety.

XP's advocacy of close collaboration between technical and business interests does not, of course, change the fact that it is the programmers who write the code. Facilitating the production of code is the most important job, and XP devolves both power and responsibility onto the programmers. An iterative approach, with short production cycles from one code release to the next, leaves the programming team plenty of latitude to revisit and improve existing code. At the same time, this brings a working (if rudimentary) system to the customers as quickly as possible, giving them the opportunity to start with a minimal feature set and then guide the requirements over time in response to actual business needs.

In order to make this work, XP imposes upon programmers the requirement that each new piece of code added to the system must come with a piece of test code to prove its functionality—and that the test code be written *prior* to the writing of the code it will test. Over time, this yields a growing suite of regression tests that represents the expected functionality of the program at any given time. Running the full suite of tests after each introduction of any new code serves both to assure programmers that, in making changes, they have not damaged existing features and to assure the end user that the quality of the system will only improve over time. More subtly, this use of iteration and testing gives teams the courage to revisit and improve their earlier work, a crucial freedom for the long-term health of the code base.

Pair programming is the most visible manifestation of XP's overall emphasis on communication and mutual understanding of the project. Generally, one partner

---

[2]The SUnit framework is available for download at `www.xProgramming.com`, among other places.

will "drive," typing in the code while the other partner reads along. This gives the first partner the confidence that another pair of eyes is watching for any mistakes, and the second partner can also think ahead and be ready to propose a next course of action when the person doing the typing comes to a stopping point. More broadly, the programming pair is the atomic unit of an XP team and is crucial to building a shared understanding of the project's code base. This knowledge will transfer across the code base as team members switch partners from time to time, and as the various project tasks are passed from pair to pair—for in XP, nobody owns code, and each programmer will likely visit at least two parts of the system (different programming tasks) each week. By participating actively in ongoing planning and acceptance testing activities, among others, the end user will also share in the overall understanding of the project and its aims.

By keeping simplicity, reliability, and the rapid delivery of useful functionality at the forefront, XP weaves these practices together into an efficient, practical methodology. In addition to the direct benefits of its component practices, XP also serves a project by eliminating the need for many time-consuming activities prescribed by most approaches to software development. With commonly understood and well-factored code, internal documentation becomes unnecessary. Similarly, as all programming is done in pairs and as each piece of code is revisited repeatedly over the life of the project, formal code reviews are mere redundancies in the XP world. Finally, by sticking to a simple, shared story of how the system works during each planning/development iteration, and by including a customer at all times in the project's day-to-day activities, XP smoothes and rationalizes the management-level communication, allowing programmers to get on with the job at hand.

Planning in XP

XP, as the name implies, focuses first and foremost on programming. Experience has shown it nearly impossible to determine at the beginning of a significant software-development project precisely what features will be in the final system, so XP does not attempt it.

Nevertheless, XP begins with a plan. The plan aims not to detail and control software development far into the future, but rather to set the course for development. In his recent book *Extreme Programming Explained*, Kent Beck compares the practice of XP with the act of driving an automobile—and like a driver at the steering wheel, an XP team expects to correct its course on an ongoing basis. At the outset of development, the plan will be speculative. As the project progresses, collective understanding of the deliverable is refined, and adjustments take place as needed. By revisiting the plan throughout the life of the project, the team also gains a basis against which to calibrate its expectations of itself.

The primary medium of planning and documentation in XP is the humble index card. Customer plans take the form of story cards, and then development tasks appear on task cards. Each story describes a way in which the end user wishes to use the system, and many of the development tasks will correspond directly to one or more user stories. The technical plan takes into account internal quality issues as well as external features, however, other tasks will be related to refinement of the underlying design as much as to the implementation of the system. The cards themselves are short-lived, serving only to set out the aims of a single project iteration (a matter of a few weeks); in future iterations, the source code and the tests form a complete, accurate record of the current state of the project.

XP transforms the process of software development into a continuous learning experience for both customer and developer, and planning serves learning. The team learns what it is capable of and what needs must be met to produce a system of value. It does this by being courageous; by taking small, measured steps; and by carefully evaluating the results it gets. Working in discrete iterations rather than attempting to drive the entire effort from a predefined "master plan" allows the team to accommodate the inevitable changes that take place in technical and business requirements. Taking frequent, small steps insures against making large investments of effort based on assumptions that turn out to be false in actual practice.

Plan Only as Long as Needed

The common practice of finalizing a design before attempting to write code often results in "over-frameworking"—constructing solutions to problems before the problems are actually discovered. In practice, this can lead to brittle, complicated programs that do not address the system requirements. (Since the actual requirements tend to vary over the life of a project anyway, one cannot expect to avoid this problem with ever more exact, detailed requirement specifications.) XP turns the process upside down, spending only enough effort on a given activity during a given production cycle to enable its dependent activities.

In XP, a system release is first planned by identifying a set of "user stories." This activity is the *Planning Game*. In this game, the objective is to identify (from the customer perspective) an increment of system function that either (initially) represents a minimum useful system or (subsequently) adds value to a working system.

One of the purposes of planning is to make schedules predictable. During the Planning Game, each story is estimated by the development team in terms of ideal engineering time—time spent devoted entirely to the task. Projection of a completion date is determined by summing the ideal engineering time represented by the customer selected stories and multiplying by the reciprocal of the loading factor. From this result, a projected delivery date can be determined. A loading factor (always less than or equal to 0.5) is determined for the team by experience. If there is no calibrated (experience-based) value for the loading factor, something less than 0.5 must be used. Why? Because if the loading factor of individuals exceeds 0.5, they are not helping each other enough. Remember that all programming in XP is done in pairs.

The next level of planning, called the *Iteration Planning Game* is now played: The selected stories are decomposed into engineering tasks and estimated in essentially the same way as in the Planning Game. Iterations are increments of work towards completion of the stories selected in the Planning Game. Iteration planning is crucial to tuning the loading factor and providing early feedback on team progress towards completion of the stories. Individual iterations tend to be short, about one to three weeks, whereas release cycles may take several months. The goal is to keep iterations short enough so that steering can take place in a controlled and informed manner.

Testing

In many popular approaches to software development, activities proceed in a linear fashion: from analysis and requirements gathering to design, to coding, to testing, and, finally, to code release. XP regards these phases as artificial barriers, erected to compartmentalize an inherently fluid process. XP, in contrast, leverages the support each "phase" makes available to the others to adopt an iterative approach based upon rapid, repeated deployment of the software.

Once the activities of an iteration are identified, tests are written to validate the features that comprise that deliverable. In order to write tests, enough design is done to identify the key classes and behaviors of the system under construction. When the tests have been implemented, the simplest code that will pass those tests is written. In later iterations (or if the team decides to adopt XP in the course of an ongoing project), this may lead to the discovery of an opportunity to eliminate redundancy and redesign existing code. Such refactoring facilitates future modification and reuse. As a direct consequence, all activities stay focused upon the group's fundamental objective: a working, usable system.

Test Thoroughly and Integrate Continuously

Unit tests give the programmer courage to do the right thing. At times in development, it will become clear that part or all of the system needs radical refactoring (reorganization, simplification, reassignment of responsibilities, or other cleanup). An experienced developer normally feels some trepidation when embarking upon what could turn out to be a significant change. Automated unit tests assure that (tested) program features can be relied upon. After radical refactoring, a click of a button will confirm the fidelity with which we have preserved the system function that predated our changes. In the event that we were not entirely successful in maintaining system quality, the tests point to the areas that require immediate attention before we proceed with new feature implementation.

In modern programming, almost never do we find ourselves working alone on a software project of any significant size. Furthermore, in an XP project, no code is "owned" by a single individual (or pair of individuals). It is, therefore, essential that new work be integrated with the rest of the work of others as often as practical, which is to say, at the end of an episode of development, usually a few hours, or at most a day's worth of work. Integration is not complete until all the tests run correctly. Such integration episodes happen (serially) one at a time. This way, if testing reveals a regression, it is clear which set of changes "broke the build."

Using XP on a Squeak Project

Most of what became XP grew out of the experience of many individuals building object-oriented systems in Smalltalk, making XP a natural for use with Squeak. We now present a sketch of how one might proceed to adopt XP practices on a Squeak-based project.

One of the essential notions to keep in mind when using the XP process is that of scale. XP scales over a large continuum of project sizes. Such scaling may entail reducing or eliminating individual practices for smaller projects, but one must do this carefully. For instance, the planning phases may not require the two-tier approach of Planning Game and Iteration Planning Game. Perhaps a particular project requires only about a week's worth of work, and the stories are few. It may be the case that stories and tasks are in one-to-one correspondence. The iteration period may be shortened to a few days or even hours. These are all examples of projects at the small end of the size spectrum.

If you are working alone, consider getting someone who understands what you are doing to pair program with you. Pair programming skills are good to have, and the other person just might have a suggestion that makes what you are doing better.

Test and Integrate

Probably the best way in which to become familiar with XP is to adopt the practices one at a time. For a software developer, the practice of testing is the place to start. That means making testing the cornerstone of all coding activities.

By writing the unit tests first, even before writing the code to be tested, we are led to consider what the public interface of our object should be, in a form of what Bertrand Meyer has called "Programming by Contract."[3] The tests verify that the object under test does indeed provide the services that we expect of it. The next step is to consider the conditions under which we expect the object to provide service to clients, and what would be reasonable responses to the agreed queries (api). Later on, when we actually begin writing code, we start by running the tests and seeing what works and what doesn't (prior to writing code, obviously,

---

[3]Meyer, Bertrand. *Object-Oriented Software Construction.* Prentice Hall, 1988.

we expect nothing to work at all—which means things can only get better!). We take each success, failure, and error one at a time and extend and modify the code until all of the tests pass. Then and only then does it make sense for us to consider integrating this object or objects into larger systems.

Testing and frequent integration should never be skipped. Even on the smallest project, start by writing tests for the capability you plan to implement. Write tests while fleshing out the design for whatever it is you want the new capability to be. Implement the behavior tested for and ensure that the tests all pass. If you are adding capability to existing code, write tests to verify the continued correct operation of whatever you are extending or reusing.

Frequent integration ensures that collective code updates occur in a sequenced and repeatable manner. While there are many possible approaches, this is one simple suggestion. Identify a machine as the build machine. This machine should be one of the faster machines available to the development team. Create a build directory on the build machine. At least two images are kept in the build directory. The first is a raw, untouched image that is used as the basis for performing full system builds on a periodic basis. The second is the current development base image. This directory also contains a file that has the names of the released change sets—we'll call this a build list file. The released change sets themselves should be stored in a subdirectory.

At the beginning of a code development episode, the programmers copy the current development image from the build machine to the development machine they intend to use. When the image is first started, the programmers create a new change set with a name that identifies the programming task being addressed.

When the code has reached a point where all of the unit tests pass, the change set is filed out. The pair submits this change set file to the system builder, who files it into the current development base image. All of the unit tests for the project are run. If all of the tests pass, then that image is saved as the new development base image, and the change set is placed in a subdirectory of released code changes. The file name of this change set is added as the last line of the build list file.

If less than 100 percent of the unit tests succeed, the image is not saved. The code submission is rejected, and the responsible team grabs the latest development build, loads their changes, and works until all of the tests pass. They then resubmit the new change set to the system builder.

A full system build should be performed after every development iteration, in order to archive a benchmark as a starting point for the next iteration. A full system build consists of starting with a raw image and filing in the changes that are recorded in the build list file. It is important for reasons of repeatability to file in these changes in the order that they are called out in the build list file. After all of the released change sets have been filed in, all tests are run. If any tests fail, the fixes are placed in updated change sets, the build list file updated accordingly, and the build restarted. The next iteration should not begin until all of the unit tests pass, immediately after a complete build is run.

Reusing Previously Developed Code

Squeak comes with a large class library. Very often, the simplest thing that could possibly work implies reusing code that is part of the base class library. Since the Squeak base class library has few SUnit tests, what should a conscientious programming team do?

The answer is, it depends. Squeak is an open source project. This fact is both a blessing and a (mild) curse. Because Squeak is undergoing constant change, individual system behavior may be altered subtly or radically over short intervals of time. Writing tests for the capability being reused will help to defend the integrity of present and future system function added by an XP team using Squeak.

If the code being reused is known to be stable and to have survived extensive reuse, then there may be no compelling need to take the time required to develop an SUnit test. Examples of this would be the core Collection and Magnitude classes.[4] On the other hand, one of the purposes of SUnit tests is to help give us courage when reusing and refactoring code. In the presence of reuse, we would like to have our SUnit test serve as a contract for service with the code being considered for reuse. Rather than writing a comprehensive unit test suite for the classes being reused, it is sufficient to write a test that defines a contract for service. We only need to test for the capabilities of the interface that we need to reuse.

These observations may provoke controversy between the pragmatist and the purist. It is certainly in the interest of all Squeak programmers to have an extensive test suite for the underlying classes of the base distribution. This is true if for no other reason than to insure that ports to other platforms work correctly. Furthermore, an extensive test suite built up over time would help the developers and maintainers of Squeak to improve the base class hierarchy and give them courage when faced with the inevitable need to make fundamental changes. Finally, when packaging Squeak applications for deployment, such tests could help to insure that needed system function is present after the packaging process is completed.

Testing User-Interface Functionality

A basic tenet of XP is that anything that does not have an automated test does not exist. That is an interesting theory in principle, but it is less than satisfactory in practice, especially in a media-rich environment like Squeak. This is a time when the 20-80 rule comes strongly into play. There are times when we cannot afford a solution that addresses 100 percent of our needs. The 20-80 rule asserts that 80 percent of the benefit comes from 20 percent of the work. Thus, even

---

[4]They are not included in the standard Squeak distribution, but the ANSI Smalltalk unit tests released under the aegis of Camp Smalltalk address significant portions of these class hierarchies, among others.

though we cannot effectively automate 100 percent of the user-interface components, automating even a small measure of the user-interface capability yields tangible benefit.

For a first level of testing, there is a distinct benefit to just programmatically creating user-interface components, opening them, and deleting them. This level of testing will identify gross errors. More sophisticated tests can test whether allocated resources and component models are returned to the system after the component has been deleted.

A more comprehensive test may be constructed using the EventRecorderMorph. These tests should ensure exact location and extent of the interface component under test. Once the components are placed, event tapes may be played back that exercise the actual code paths. A caveat is that popups, like notifiers and confirmers, will appear under the active hand and not the hand playing back the remote events. For development that is heavily user interface-centric, it would be well worth defining a programming task to allow these popups to open under the playback hand rather than the user hand.

Example: An Event Framework

How do we adopt XP practices, then? We jump right in and start writing tests, of course. Well, soon, but not quite yet. In order to write tests, we need to understand enough about our design to be able to expect to reuse the end result. We must discover the essential classes involved, the messages they implement, and how these objects collaborate. In this section, we will look at an actual development episode, to introduce the planning and testing practices in the course of retro-fitting XP on to an existing project.

Specifically, we will look at how one might test and (if necessary) modify an event signaling and handling mechanism for Squeak.

The Event Mechanism: Stories and Tasks

The Squeak 2.8 update stream adds an event-based dependency mechanism to the base image. In our example, we will test a similar event mechanism. We intend to reuse this latter event mechanism, an application of the Observer pattern,[5] and depend heavily upon its correct behavior. The mechanism allows a model object to trigger synchronous event notifications, and observer objects may register an action that they will perform when that model object triggers a particular event notification—conceptually, akin to a broadcast form of message send. An event is identified by a unary or keyword symbol. The model object triggering a keyword event will be expected to supply appropriate argument objects for that particular

---

[5]Gamma, et al., *Design Patterns*, Addison-Wesley, 1995.

event. On the other side, the observer object's action is typically specified in terms of a receiver object, a selector, and argument bindings either from a keyword event notification or supplied with the registration. Our prior experience led us to begin with a different interface, so we expect to add method selectors for portability reasons. We may also have to make some adjustments in the implementation.

The key behaviors for the event mechanism are introduced as extensions to the class Object. These behaviors may be categorized as relating to registering, triggering, and releasing events, and we will reflect this in the method protocols we create. As tests reveal missing selectors, we will implement the necessary behavior. At this point, we might want to describe the operation of the event mechanism on a task card. This particular event mechanism is probably about as complex as a single task should get, so we would probably consider it one task for planning purposes.

We intend to implement the following semantics:

Registering—These messages allow an observer to register an action to be performed when an event is triggered. When the receiver triggers <anEvent>, the message <aSelector> is sent to <anObject>. If <anEvent> offers arguments, these will be bound to <aSelector> prior to forwarding to <anObject>. If multiple actions are specified, they will be performed in the order in which they were registered. The messages are as follows:

```
when: anEvent send: aSelector to: anObject
when: anEvent send: aSelector to: anObject with: anArgument
when: anEvent send: aSelector to: anObject withArguments: aSequenceOfArgs
```

Triggering—These messages allow an object to signal that an event named <anEvent> has occurred. All registered actions will have completed before the messages return. The return value of the trigger method is the value returned by the last action performed. The following messages are illustrative:

```
triggerEvent: anEvent
triggerEvent: anEvent with: anArgument
triggerEvent: anEvent withArguments: aSequenceOfArgs
triggerEvent: anEvent ifNotHandled: aBlock
triggerEvent: anEvent with: anArgument ifNotHandled: aBlock
triggerEvent: anEvent withArguments: aSequenceOfArgs ifNotHandled: aBlock
```

Releasing—These messages allow an observer to release event dependencies upon the receiver:

```
removeAllActionsWithReceiver: anObject
removeAllActionsWithReceiver: anObject forEvent: anEvent
removeActionsForEvent: anEvent
```

Writing SUnit Tests for the Event Mechanism

Our task is to build a Unit test that exercises this interface. To build a unit test, we first subclass **TestCase**. To provide reference to the initial conditions that must exist in order for our test to have meaning, we add instance variables to this **TestCase** subclass. We override two methods, #setUp and #tearDown, in order to support the corresponding initialization and finalization (releasing) behavior. With this information at hand, we create a new change set, **KernelEventTests**, to track the development of the test case. As we begin to write the tests for event triggering, we soon discover that the message selector, #triggerEvent:, is not implemented. This is something of a surprise. Upon examination of the class **Object**, we discover that in the Squeak implementation, the designers chose the selector #trigger: rather than #triggerEvent:.

At this point, we pause and put on our redesigners' hats. The folks who made this choice are themselves familiar with yet another implementation of this mechanism that uses slightly different message selectors. On this project, we value portability. If we implement the other selector form, #triggerEvent:, by delegating its implementation to #trigger:, then we can satisfy both interfaces. Further, if we test the outer wrapper methods, we will know for certain that we have tested the inner methods.

As soon as we recognize the need for wrapper methods, that task becomes fairly obvious, and as developers we naturally want to jump right in and create those methods—after all, they're trivially simple, so why not? Well, at this point it behooves us to make a conscious decision. Writing the wrapper methods is a coding task. Developers are always faced with the temptation of blasting ahead and jumping into coding. Fortunately, XP supplies an alternative—remember, there are always two of you at a keyboard. So rather than going off track, the programmer who is not at the keyboard grabs a handy index card and starts a list of things that must be implemented when the tests are done. At the top of that list is the task of writing wrapper methods for the #trigger: family of selectors. The presence of this list will pay off eventually, because the pair of programmers will not have to stop in order to discuss what to do next once the task at hand is complete. In the course of the coding episode that resulted in the creation of this event system and test suite (included on the accompanying CD-ROM), we made the following notations on our to-do task card:

- wrap **trigger:** * methods with **triggerEvent:** * methods

- need *:ifNotHandled: methods

- need to implement **removeActionsForEvent:**

- need to implement **removeAllActionsWithReceiver**

- need to implement **removeAllActionsWithReceiver:forEvent:**

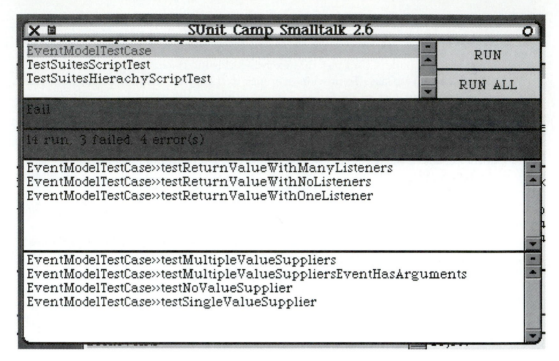

Figure 14.1   Results of Running Our SUnit Test.

Meanwhile, back at test central, we have continued to implement the unit tests for the event mechanism. In that process we noted that the event framework also uses divergent selectors when releasing event dependencies, and we further note the absence of #trigger:ifNotHandled: selectors. In the spirit of our previous decisions, we note on an index card that these selectors need to be implemented for portability reasons. When the tests are completed, we run through the cards of work to be done and implement the missing methods that remove actions.

In Figure 14.1, we see the results of running our SUnit test after implementing the missing selectors that we noted when writing the unit test. Not quite the results we may have hoped for, but very good information. We start by looking at the simpler of the two errors, #testReturnValueWithNoListeners. Upon examination we see that the test expected a nil return value and got instead the object that triggered the event. We read the code in question and see that the mechanism as implemented does not include supporting the notion of events that request information from the dependent. This means that we must rewrite the core #trigger: selectors so that they return the value of the last event handler. In this process, we reassess our earlier design decision to wrap the existing #trigger: methods with our #triggerEvent: methods. If we instead wrap the new triggerEvent: methods with the #trigger: methods, we can remove redundant code in our implementation. The time is taken

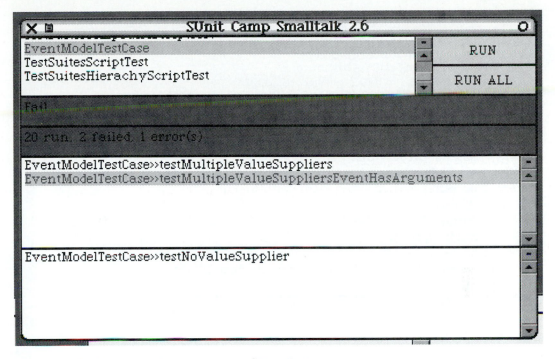

Figure 14.2 Viewing an Improvement in SUnit Tests.

to refactor the code to reflect this new understanding. We then rerun the tests and see a small improvement. (See Figure 14.2.)

We need to examine this failure (Figure 14.3) more closely. Why exactly did this test fail? Selecting the failure will let us open up a debugger on the test in question.

From the debugger, we see that the value being returned is not the value returned from the last action registered. When we look at the code that implements #trigger:, we see that it iterates over the collection of registered event actions and returns the value of the last event action. While looking at this code, we see temporary variables that suggest that the collection of event handlers is a Set. So, we conclude that the underlying collection holding event actions is some kind of unordered collection. Upon examination of the code (see Object>>when:perform: in Squeak 2.8), we discover that it is indeed using a Set. We change this to be an OrderedCollection and rerun the tests. All of the tests pass, and we are ready to use the event mechanism.

What did we learn from this? First, that even though we may see message selectors that we have been using for over a decade in a different dialect of Smalltalk, there may be subtle, but important, differences in the semantics of the implementation. We found no bugs in the implementation, just that it did not conform to

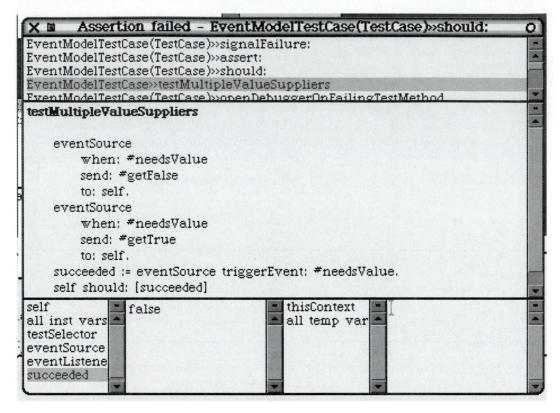

Figure 14.3   Examining the Failure Case.

the expectations that we had based upon prior experience. By codifying the contract for service that we expected as an SUnit test, we discovered this fact earlier and were able to write a compatibility layer that met our expectations and did not perturb the fundamental operation of the system as released.

How much project time was used by writing the tests before coding the implementation? That is hard to assess prior to the actual completion of the project. Our development was very focused and wasted very little effort because the test framework gave us a list of what was not yet working. We could have built some very large systems that appeared to work before discovering the more subtle use of unordered collections to hold event actions. It may have been very much more time consuming to debug a complex system that depended heavily upon events and was failing because of them in ways that pointed away from the event mechanism itself. Our test discovered the discrepancy before any other code could come to depend upon it. So in the last analysis, we did spend more time up front writing tests that reflect our understanding of the reusable component. However, as a consequence, we had a strongly directed implementation effort that revealed deep, but subtle, inconsistencies earlier rather than later.

Programming in Pairs: Two Heads Are Better than One

Each of the XP practices serves a concrete purpose from the technical point of view. What is not as obvious, is the underlying social engineering inherent in XP practices. For example, focusing on testing not only directs us to our goal, but also defuses territorial behavior amongst team members. When all of the code is owned by all of the team, all code ownership questions disappear. If someone changes some code and makes it simpler without breaking any tests, everyone benefits. By making unit tests a first priority, the real issues are brought into focus. Is the code base simpler? Do all of the tests pass?

Since XP is a comprehensive approach to software production, involving managers as much as architects and programmers, it impacts all aspects of a team's work. In effect, the XP approach becomes an unspoken language connecting all stakeholders in a project. The practice of pair programming, more than any other, leaps out to visibly distinguish XP from other methodologies.

It is probably safe to say that the experience of programming with another person at your side is going to be different as a function of who your partner is. Since each partner's responsibility (and personality) is a little different, it is useful to consider some of the skills that make pair programming work and some of the obstacles you may need to overcome to become a good pair programmer.

Most of us are accustomed to working alone when we program. We don't have to worry about someone else following what we are doing when we are typing away at our keyboards, operating browsers, evaluating expressions in a workspace, and all the other activities we engage in when we are "Squeaking." Programming with another individual at your side watching (nearly) your every move might take a little getting used to, but it is worth it.

In XP, the person who has the keyboard and mouse has the immediate responsibility for the programming task, and we will call him or her the driver. The other partner, whom we will refer to as the navigator, has the responsibility of thinking strategically and understanding the story arc represented by the particular code written and entered by the driver. Most of us are not mind readers, and at times it can be difficult to remain coupled to the same train of thought, especially when the partners may at times be thinking at different levels of abstraction. This is where communication (be it visual, spoken, or unspoken) becomes particularly important.

A running dialog between the partners is essential. It will be much easier to see the same pictures in your respective heads if you talk between yourselves about what you are doing. This not only serves the purpose of staying in touch with each other's thoughts, but also leads both individuals to think through what they are doing. Frequently, verbalizing what you think you are doing makes you think more clearly about what you are actually doing. Weaknesses as well as strengths of particular approaches to problems can be considered quickly, resulting in swifter convergence on working code.

If code is a kind of literature, than reading is probably the most important part of communication between a pair. Most of the time we will be reading code and probably executing it in our heads. The person who's "driving" has to allow the partner to read and understand what is being written—in fact its essential. Flashing between windows as fast as you can move your mouse is a sure way to lose somebody, if you are not in constant communication some other way. Quick tangential thoughts can distract us for a moment and cause us to lose contact with our partner. Avoid this by verbalizing the thought at the proper moment or making a note on an index card. If one of you believes exploration is needed, be sure that you say so, whether you are driving or not.

This is another place where courage is essential. Each partner must be unafraid to verbalize their respective feelings about what is being done. If you are afraid of admitting that you are not following what is going on, then you will not be able to recover from those brief lapses of attention to which we fall prey. If you do not understand part of the system that you are working on, admit that, find someone who does, and get them to help you. In the culture of XP, it is a rule that you cannot refuse to help others on the team when they ask for it.

Learning is essential, too. Take the time to understand what someone else is proposing before becoming predisposed to your own approach. Listen carefully and be observant so that you know who to go to when you need to know something, then take the time to learn as much as you can from them. Pair programming is a great way to do that.

XP and Squeak

Squeak is ideally suited to serve the emerging world of remote, media-rich software applications. In such an environment, far more than on a desktop, the efficiency and reliability of the software becomes a crucial consideration. The Squeak programming and deployment environment is rich, powerful, and almost entirely flexible. Further, its nature as an open source project lends it that dynamic character which spawns experimentation and rapid advancement of the state of the art. But there is a price to be paid for this energy. In such a rapidly changing world, anyone who wishes to deliver truly production quality software over more than one or two release cycles ignores notions such as code simplicity and flexibility, not to mention reliability, only at considerable peril.

In navigating these shoals, Squeak will not be sailing uncharted waters. The notion of using defined software practices to address real-world project complexity is hardly new. As a lightweight, but comprehensive, methodology that addresses such concerns, XP is ideally suited for use by Squeakers. Beyond its clear applicability to object-oriented systems and its proven success, it shares with Squeak a fundamental emphasis on the acts of learning and sharing as the background to all activities. More than most formally specified methodologies, XP takes into account the natural creative power inherent in the individual team members and their interactions. And XP gets straight to the point. It aims simply to facilitate the fundamental act of software production—delivering working programs—and to recognize that most of anything else that goes on is ultimately wasted effort.

It seems almost axiomatic that every process invented to improve the chances of success for completing a software project must be remembered for a key feature of that process. To pick just one, or even several, of the practices that make up XP, however, would miss the point entirely. Those practices synergize in a way that causes us to look at the systems development effort in an altogether different light: as a holistic, organic, and yet, ultimately, quite rational process. Such an understanding demands an approach to project direction that aims to set out a clear mechanism for assuring the robustness of the end product, and then guiding and facilitating rather than seeking to proscribe the team's creative efforts.

Perhaps most of all, XP recognizes that each real-world situation will differ slightly from any possible model, so it knows where to stop. Once the team has learned to work together efficiently, without unnecessary noise or backtracking, its members have become experts on the problem at hand. XP does not presume to tell them exactly how to proceed in every situation—the only absolute rule is, no rule is absolute. Besides all the obvious efficiency and impeccable Smalltalk heritage, in its careful accounting for the human factor, XP reveals the world view it shares with Squeak—computers are there to serve people, not vice versa, and by the way, there's no shame in having fun.

A mathematician lured into the practical, concrete world of programming, John Sarkela has worked at various points of time as a kernel hacker, a protocol machine builder, an instructor, a VM builder, and a consultant. Over time, a consistent theme of developing communicating, cooperating systems has emerged. John has enjoyed using Smalltalk since the mid 1980s. His current ambition is to apply the processes of social work to object (re)design. Currently, he works for ReThink Systems in California.

Paul McDonough arrived at Smalltalk by way of control systems engineering with Eurotherm and later got a better idea of how to use it properly while working for Digitalk and ParcPlace-Digitalk. He currently takes care of all kinds of things at ReThink Systems, and has been Squeaking almost full time since 1998. Paul holds bachelor's degrees in electrical engineering and international relations, and a master's degree in international affairs.

David L. Caster is a software engineer with ReThink Systems. David has worked extensively on communications and operating systems, compilers, and software tools of every stripe over the last 27 years. An avid fan of Smalltalk since 1989, David has worked with most of the major dialects and has a passion for instrumentation and measurement of software written in Smalltalk. He particularly enjoys mentoring and working with new talent while traveling and living in different parts of North America. David is currently exploring XML and Smalltalk bindings to other programming languages.

Part Four

Squeak for the Future

The future of Squeak lies in developing the vision of all users who are creating and sharing programs and multimedia. The chapters in this final part of the book explore two aspects of realizing this vision.

- John Steinmetz's chapter talks about Squeak as a tool for learning, as was the original purpose of Smalltalk itself. He critiques the current usefulness of Squeak for learning and conjectures how it can be improved.

- Dan Shafer's chapter predicts how Squeak can affect the developer and commercial worlds. He sees Squeak meeting many of the needs of the Web and post-PC era of development.

15

Computers and Squeak as Environments for Learning

John Steinmetz

Introduction

Computers, although promoted as an all-purpose educational panacea, certainly aren't. The machines do have potential to assist certain learners in specific ways. Computer scientists, software engineers, teachers, parents, and children are using Squeak to explore that potential.[1] Some of Squeak's features are designed (and are being designed) to help non-experts learn programming and to facilitate construction of environments and projects for learning about other subjects.

To promote more thoughtful discussion about computers and learning, and to provide some background before considering Squeak projects, this chapter will begin with general thoughts about children and computers. Part 1 presents some assumptions and persistent misconceptions about computers and learning. Parts 2 and 3 will discuss two ways that computers can assist learning. Part 2 presents their most common current use, simulating older media—such as words on paper or musical sound—while offering extra leverage for working in those media. Part 3

---

[1]The Disney Squeak team developed the infrastructure and ideas for Squeak-based learning environments. Alan Kay originated many of the general concepts and project ideas, and these have been realized and implemented brilliantly by Scott Wallace, Andreas Raab, John Maloney, Ted Kaehler and Dan Ingalls. Kim Rose has organized experiments in classrooms and sought the system improvements needed to make them feasible. B.J. Allen-Conn and Naala Brewer have designed projects specifically for children, and their work has helped the programmers to improve the system. Meanwhile, Mark Guzdial at Georgia Tech has been using Squeak with adult learners. Work with Squeak and learners is not confined to one continent; see the chapters on Mathmorphs in this volume.

considers brand new possibilities offered by computers, with entirely new ways to perceive and understand. Squeakers are developing tools, ideas, and genres to help these new media evolve. The final "Parting Shots" are thoughts about project design and collaboration. The illustrations throughout this chapter come from Squeak projects.

Part 1: Children, Computers, and Learning

Because computers seem so powerful and versatile, people sometimes talk as though using computers can guarantee positive outcomes. This misconception is especially prevalent in discussions of education.[2] In discussing any medium, it is important to remember that outcomes depend on the intentions and assumptions of the people using the medium. Skillful educators and learners can use almost any medium to advantage, but no medium can, by itself, determine what a person will learn.

Nevertheless, schools and households are buying lots of computers for children, often without a clear idea of what the machines are for, but convinced that they will help somehow. The result may be an increase in wasted time, boredom, and frustration for teachers, students, and parents.[3] Worse yet, time spent with computers by both teachers and students may deprive children of the attention and experiences they need in order to learn and grow.[4] Clearer thinking is needed about what computers are good for in education.

I should say right away that, despite the pleasure I have had in using computers for almost 20 years, and after nearly as many years of working with computers and schoolchildren in various research settings, I mostly keep my own children (ages 4 and 11) away from computers.

I want my children to occupy themselves mainly with real stuff, and with virtual stuff from their own imaginations. They need many years of experience contacting the world through their senses and imaginations. I think they need to spend lots of time with older technologies and older kinds of virtuality like language, musical instruments, art supplies, magnifying glasses, books, basketballs, arithmetic, and so on. Children need to develop an inner life, the ability to visualize, imagine, and follow a chain of thought, because reading, mathematics, and other later work require not just the decoding of symbols, but also the generation of inner spaces where the meaning of the symbols can take shape. Media of all kinds can disrupt children's abilities to form their own visual images, create their own stories, and form those crucial inner worlds.

---

[2]See Todd Oppenheim's excellent article, "The Computer Delusion," in the July 1997 issue of the *Atlantic Monthly*, or at `www.theatlantic.com/issues/97jul/computer.htm`. The Web version includes links to other information and organizations. A very helpful review of research on children and computers, "Fool's Gold: A Critical Look at Computers in Childhood" is available from the Alliance for Childhood, `www.allianceforchildhood.net`.

[3]In researching her book *Failure to Connect*, Jane Healy spent months visiting schools that were proud of their use of computers. She reported in a 1999 talk for Whole.org in Los Angeles that hardly any of these programs were contributing significantly to student learning.

[4]Lowell Monke, "Computers in Schools," *Yes!*, #8, Winter 1998–99, p. 33.

Parents and teachers, concerned about childrens' futures, sometimes push children too soon into symbolic and abstract work. Politicians hope to improve reading scores by teaching reading earlier. However, earlier is not necessarily better, and early childhood specialists maintain that the mentality of early childhood is not yet suited to sequential and abstract thought. The main work of early childhood is imaginative play. Nevertheless, many kindergartens now require homework, and I recently heard about a nursery school that devotes a certain number of hours per week to computer activities.

Content aside, some investigators[5] observe that watching video screens may interfere with children's brain development, both by presenting harmful stimuli and by depriving the child of necessary movement and multisensory stimulation. Using computers (as well as television and video games) may harm young children even if the content seems to be beneficial.

After children have a lot of contact with the world, lots of imaginative play, and lots of practice using representation systems, they should be able to profit from the computer's abstractions and simulations. Computer work probably doesn't need to begin until fifth or sixth grade, or maybe later, when children's brains can withstand the neurological impact of screen stimuli and when their minds are ready to grasp cause and effect.

But how should learners use computers? How can computers help? Educational use of computers is frequently colored by unexamined assumptions. Before considering how computers can help learners, let's take a look at how people *think* computers can help.

Examining Assumptions about Computers and Learning

Computers will make learning fun.

Much of the excitement about computers in education has been generated by computer companies, but some of the enthusiasm comes from parents who have seen their children having fun with computers and computer games. (Figure 15.1.) I'm sure that many parents, remembering their own schooling as unhappy and boring, hope that computers will somehow enliven their children's education.

A child's ability to remain attentive to a computer game without becoming bored comes in large part from the constantly shifting visual stimuli that continually re-engage the child's attention, no matter what the content. This is the fun of being entertained—even entrained.

---

[5]Healy, Jane, *Endangered Minds: Why Children Don't Think and What We Can Do About It*, 1990, New York: Simon and Schuster.

Buzzell, Keith, *The Children of Cyclops: The Influence of Television Viewing on the Developing Human Brain*, 1998, California: Association of Waldorf Schools of North America.

Pearce, Joseph Chilton, *Evolution's End: Claiming the Potential of Our Intelligence*, 1992, California: Harper San Francisco.

Winn, Marie, *The Plug-in Drug*, 1985, New York: Penguin Books.

Figure 15.1 Students in a fourth- and fifth-grade classroom working with Squeak. The desks, with the computers inside and windows on top, can be used for computerless work as well. Open Charter School, Los Angeles. (Photo by Kim Rose.)

The fun of learning is of a different kind, having to do with making interior connections between something known and something new—the "aha!" experience. Entertaining stimuli may attract somebody to learn, but the real fun of learning is not the fun of being entertained. Entertainment can get in the way of learning if it prevents the learner from doing his or her part—engaging in a uniquely personal way with the content, with the activity, or with the learning process itself.

Learning requires knowing how to *devote* attention to something; repeatedly allowing one's attention to be *captured* does not teach how to direct and focus attention purposefully. As many teachers have noticed, students who are used to being entertained by video stimulation may be less able to engage, less able to pay the sustained attention required in order to enjoy the learning process.

Fun can be an important component in a learning environment, and fun is often a clue that learning is happening. One helpful question to ask about a learning

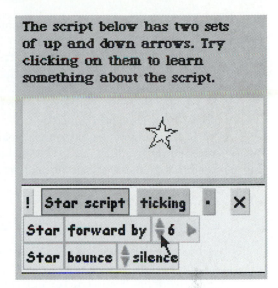

Figure 15.2   A page from a computer activity introducing ideas through simple activities.

activity is "Who's having the fun?"[6] In other words, who is making creative choices, who is thinking, and who is having insights? In some learning situations, teachers think up interesting projects, find relevant information, discover insights, and share their discoveries, while students are merely expected to absorb the results. Those teachers are having most of the fun and doing most of the learning. It can be helpful to think about where the fun is in a subject or a learning activity, and how to share some of that fun with the students.

If computers were to make learning more fun, they would do so not with flashy effects, but by helping learners make personal contact with the heart of a subject or by helping learners activate and develop their own abilities to perceive and understand.

Computers will make learning more efficient.

In many fields computers have been used to reduce the human hours necessary to accomplish tasks. Computers have also taken on many repetitive jobs that formerly had to be done by people. It may seem logical that education could be similarly automated, that teachers and students using computers could teach and learn in less time, that computers could reduce the repetition needed for learning.

Unfortunately for this assumption, the main tasks in learning occur inside the learner, not in any place that can be automated. So far, no computer system has been able to monitor the myriad factors—such as motivation, temperament,

---

[6]Dolores Patton, Leslie Barclay, Doreen Nelson, and I learned to ask this question in a research project of Apple Computer's Vivarium Program, a precursor to the Disney Squeak team.

learning style, previous knowledge, and skills—well enough to help a student learn more efficiently.

Computers do have a role in learning, but their role is not to reduce work time. In fact, computers may make learning more labor-intensive. The most effective computer-using classrooms I have seen require more teacher-hours than other forms of teaching, because students need so much help using the computers and computers need so much support time.

It is certainly possible to make learning more efficient and effective, not through automation but through better understanding of learning processes, and through heightened awareness of the motivations, skills, knowledge, and temperament of individual learners.

Computers will make learning easier.

Behind the assumptions about fun and efficiency is an understandable hope that computers will make learning easier. This hope predates computers, of course, and much work has been done to help learners overcome unnecessary obstacles, whether interior obstacles like fear or incompatible learning style, or external obstacles like poor sequence or negative classroom atmosphere. Much of what has been learned in the last 50 or 100 years about such obstacles has yet to be integrated into mainstream education.

Nevertheless, no amount of removing obstacles can alter the basic truth that some things are difficult to learn. The difficulties need not involve suffering, but learning often requires time, patience, care, and persistence. Some especially worthwhile things are especially difficult: learning to play a musical instrument, learning to make a 3-point shot, learning calculus, learning to get along with people, learning to draw, learning to read, and learning a foreign language.

Learning difficult things has a side-benefit, too: Going through the process can help a person develop a capacity to work through difficulties.

In many cases, removing the hard parts removes the best parts. If computers make things easy by leaving out or glossing over the best parts, they help no one. If they make things easier by helping learners to focus on what's important and stick with it, they could be helpful. If they also remove some unnecessary obstacles, they could be a bigger help.

The main job of schools and teachers and others who help learners is to help learners through the worthwhile hard parts.

Computers will provide information.

Too often people use the word "education" as if it meant "providing information" and "learning" as though it meant "absorbing information." Of course, those definitions are woefully incomplete. Learners usually have access to plenty of information; they need to learn how and why to make use of it. Using computers to increase the amount of available information is not necessarily a help.

It should be obvious that, particularly for children, collecting information is less important than developing ways to transform information into knowledge and understanding. If computers can help with that, then their information providing could be a positive contribution.

Computers will connect children with other people.

Computers can mislead adults as well as children about their ability to connect people meaningfully. Computer teacher Lowell Monke writes in *Yes!* magazine about a classroom of teenagers exchanging email with students in other countries. This special project, which was supposed to help the students develop understanding for people from different cultures, seemed not to help at all in the hallway outside the classroom, where other students from ESL classes, all recent immigrants, were ignored all year long by the students who were supposedly learning to transcend cultural barriers via email.[7] Let's not kid ourselves about what can be learned through correspondence—sometimes you have to tough it out through the difficulties of in-person contact.

As with other computer capabilities, their connectivity is neither positive nor negative. Everything depends on intent, the use to which the capability is put, and the extent to which the activity helps learners integrate what they learn.

The future will be technological, so our children need to know technology.

Until very recently, every computer innovator and everyone using computers at work had learned to use computers in adulthood. During these people's childhoods no computers were available to children, yet as adults they were able to invent, improve, and use computers. You don't need to have a computer as a kid to become a computer expert later in life.

Besides, becoming expert at today's technology will not be much help tomorrow. The most valuable job skills in the future will probably be in the areas of creative and flexible thinking, assimilation of new kinds of information, acquisition of new skills, and ability to recognize what's essential and what's fluff. As always, the advantage will go to those who have cultivated the human skills and knowledge for dealing with the inner and outer world. Learning to understand the purposes and uses of knowledge, skills, and technologies of all kinds—starting with language and crayons—will help children to create their future.

In every culture, people must learn how to use essential technologies. If computers were to help people prepare to use future technologies, they would do so by helping people to become less dependent on any particular technology, more adaptable to different approaches, and more savvy about advantages and pitfalls of any given technology.

---

[7] Lowell Monke, "Computers in Schools," *Yes!*, #8, Winter 1998–99, p. 33. This insightful essay by an experienced computer teacher is also posted at `www.futurenet.org/8Education/monke.html`.

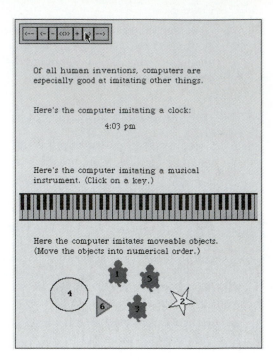

Figure 15.3   A computer imitates a page in a book about how computers can imitate other media.

Part 2: Computer Simulations of Older Media

Although computers are probably inappropriate for young children, they can help older children, adolescents, and adults with learning. Computers can't solve all learning problems, but they can help in particular ways. For people who are developmentally and educationally prepared, working with simulations, virtual environments, and computational representations can play a role in their further growth.

Computers can help learners in two general ways: by simulating older media or by presenting new media that are unique to computers. Parts 2 and 3 discuss these two approaches to learning with computers.

Computers are commonly used in education (and in workplaces and homes as well) to simulate other media that were in existence long before computers. Text editors simulate words on paper; Drawing and painting programs simulate older forms of artmaking. A computer can simulate an ensemble of musical instruments, a model of the solar system, or an ant colony.

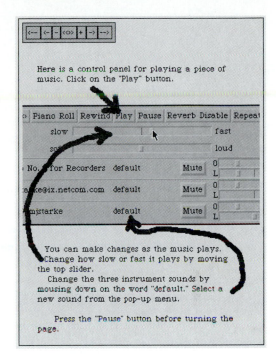

Here is a control panel for playing a piece of
music. Click on the "Play" button.

| ◇ | Piano Roll | Rewind | Play | Pause | Reverb | Disable | Repeat |

slow _____ fast

so_____ loud

No. for Recorders	default	Mute	0 L
a_ke@ix.netcom.com	default	Mute	0 L
mjstarke	default	Mute	0 L

You can make changes as the music plays.
Change how slow or fast it plays by moving
the top slider.
   Change the three instrument sounds by
mousing down on the word "default." Select a
new sound from the pop-up menu.

   Press the "Pause" button before turning the
page.

Figure 15.4 A Squeak interface for affecting
music's loudness, tempo, and instrumentation.

Potential Advantages of Simulating Older Media

Simulations of older media offer leverage.

Computers can open up possibilities that were not available in the original medium.
Text editors allow rewriting without so much retyping or erasing. Drawing programs
allow a drawing to be altered and manipulated in ways that would be impossible
on paper. Computer simulations of music give novices opportunities to try different
orchestrations, change tempos, and otherwise alter the music without having to
spend years practicing a musical instrument.

Novices can jump to an intermediate level.

If you want to compose music nowadays, you don't necessarily have to be a good
performer. You can have a computer play your music for you. The computer may
also offer you compositional assistance, so you don't have to know very much about
composing either.

Computer simulations can facilitate learning by allowing novices to explore a medium at an intermediate level, without having to do the skill building that used to be unavoidable. This means that a novice can start working immediately with essential elements of that medium, the elements that make the medium exciting.

Similarly, desktop publishing software makes all of us potential graphic designers, without the need for specialized equipment and training. Word processing software, by reducing the pain of erasing and retyping, can foster a healthy playfulness toward language and writing, making it easier to try out different ways to say something.

Learners may more easily contact "the good stuff."

Using computer simulations of older media can help novices contact the romance and excitement of a medium before investing in skill building. Having an early experience of a medium's potential may inspire people to stick with the skill-building work.

Learners may be able to see the forest instead of the trees.

Some education methods pay a great deal of attention to skill building without fully exploring what the skills in that medium are for. This is like not being able to see the forest for the trees. For example, some music students become technically competent but unexpressive; some writing students learn to write correctly, but not beautifully; and some science students know scientific principles, but don't know how to think like a scientist. One great promise of computers is that, by putting people in contact right away with some of the power and potential of a given medium, they may help learners stay aware of the forest while working to master the trees.

Computer simulations facilitate hands-on work with symbols.

Currently, only a small percentage of adults understands science and mathematics well enough to participate in discussion of important issues facing our society. One reason so many adults have trouble with math and science is that they have trouble with the symbolic representation systems.

Computers might be able to help more people practice scientific and mathematical thinking by offering opportunities to work in different modes. Approaching the same concept or data visually and kinesthetically, as well as symbolically, might help more people become fluent with the symbols.

Pitfalls of Simulating of Older Media

None of those potential advantages comes automatically. Unless the users are working toward that advantage, it won't come—and for every advantage that a technology offers, there is a flip side with a risk or a loss of some kind.

The following are some of the potential disadvantages of using computers to simulate older media:

Computers don't guarantee seeing the forest.

Computers can't automatically bring people to awareness of a medium's higher level pleasures. Teachers who are good at ignoring the forest may continue to do so even while using computers.

In the mid 1980s, walking down an elementary school hallway, I passed a classroom full of Atari 800s. I had been having lots of fun with my first computer, an Atari 800, learning the word processor and exploring LOGO. Knowing how good kids are at having fun, I was eager to see what they were doing in the computer room.

To my dismay, I found the room full of bored children assigned to an uninspiring task. On the walls were nicely lettered computer terms, and beside each monitor was a card with step-by-step instructions for typing a sentence that said, "My name is ____." I didn't detect any fun, nor any points of contact with the medium's potential.

I shouldn't have been surprised. For generations bad teaching has managed to transform thrilling matters—such as literature, history, and science—into boredom. This particular school had applied a similar transformation to its computers.

Computers present more trees.

When using computers to simulate an older medium, users may become distracted by features. For instance, using a computer to learn about writing requires that the focus be on the writing, not on the computer. The computer may help the learner to manipulate the writing, but it is sometimes hard to tell whether the learner is learning about writing or about the software.

This irony is not unique to computers: The very features that grant easier access to the forest also present more trees.

Power doesn't necessarily lead to insight.

For novices, exercising intermediate-level powers may become distracting. Learning ultimately requires internal change, but making changes to computer representations is so much fun that it can keep going without much learning taking place.

Skipping skills may be limiting.

Without having gone through a skill-building phase, people may be less able to grasp and work with a field's fundamental issues. For instance, part of musicality is in the body, not in the mind, and that physical aspect of musicianship develops through learning to play an instrument or to sing. It might be hard to compose well without getting physical first.

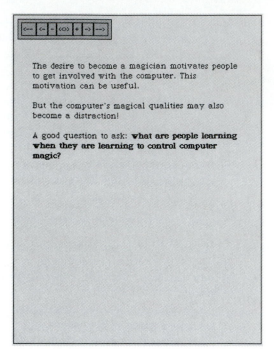

Figure 15.5 This computer "page" asks an important question for those who would use computers for learning. Are users learning useful skills that can be transferred to other domains? Are they learning skills that will grant them access to higher level learning? If they're fiddling around, is it the kind of fiddling that eventually leads to insight? Or is it just fooling around?

Not everything can be discovered by messing around.

Good writing doesn't come about just through playing with words; a writer also needs to be aware of larger issues like pacing and structure—issues that are not explicit in words themselves in word-processing tools. Similarly, one can play around with a page-layout program forever without stumbling across principles of good design.

Skills and knowledge matter in every medium, and jumping to an intermediate level has the potential to mislead novices about what they are really accomplishing.

Skipping skills may erode patience.

Skipping skill building may also increase impatience with complex, difficult, long-term work. If people can sit down at a computer and manipulate complex music, where's the motivation to practice the violin? Yet there seems to be great value in sticking with complex long-term projects like learning to play the violin.

Simulations have weaknesses.

Drawing programs, for all their powers, make it very difficult to produce a line with as much life as any child can create with a crayon. Even an extremely advanced and patient user of music software would have trouble producing a performance as nuanced as a child's singing. Simulations have power because they're not the real thing, and they also lose power because they're not the real thing.

Good news, bad news

Every technology—not just learning technologies—bears good news and bad news. Each technology offers potential advantages and potential pitfalls. Skillful use of technology has always included understanding both sides.

The results depend not just on the user's skills but also on assumptions and intentions. A computer can't guarantee outcomes any more than a pencil can. Computers, like all other technologies for learning, need to be used mindfully.

Part 3: The Computer as a New Medium

Computers are so new that their nature and potential are still unfolding, but the medium offers two unique characteristics: multiple perspectives and the capacity to model dynamic processes. Whatever new genres emerge in this medium will probably exploit those characteristics.

One way to develop a new medium is to create a "literature" of examples to show what the medium can do, to provide fodder for discussion, and to inspire improvements. In a new medium, even bad examples can be helpful, by showing what doesn't work.

Some Squeak projects are examples that exploit and demonstrate the medium's possibilities (and display its weaknesses). Through this work, Squeakers are developing two new genres that are unique to computers while constructing the software infrastructure for building and sharing a literature.

Multiple Perspectives

Because computers are so good at imitating other media, they can manifest a thing (image, concept, relationship, datum, etc.) in several different ways. Computers can present in different visual forms, and they can also address other senses, most often hearing, touch, and the kinesthetic sense. By offering different ways to examine and explore, computers can help a person understand in more than one way.

For learners, the computer's multiple perspectives offer opportunities to engage a topic in different ways. This means that the medium can address different learning styles. It also means that one learner can explore the same issue in a variety of ways—through a variety of senses, with different representations—and thus deepen the learning. With or without computers, good teachers use multiple perspectives to reach different learners and to deepen learning.

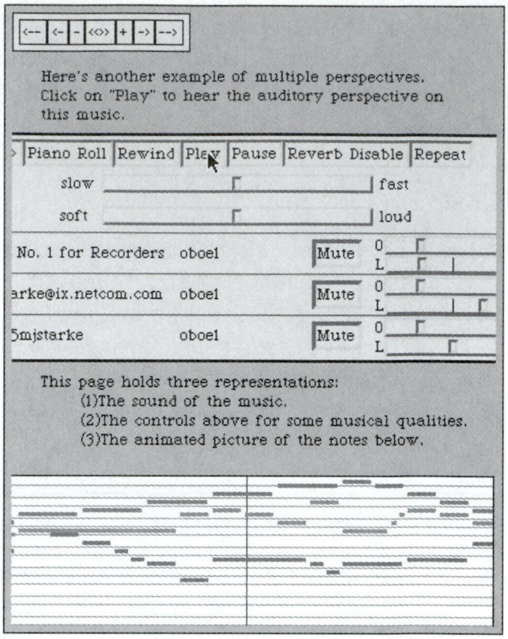

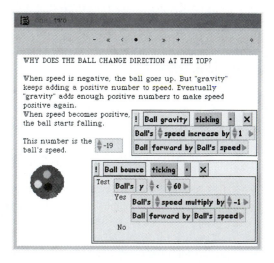

Figure 15.6 Three representations of a piece of music: sound, control settings, and notation.

Figures 15.6 and 15.7 show computer activities that include multiple representations.

The pair of illustrations in Figure 15.8 shows two ways to think about a circle. Working with these representations might foster new perspectives on circles.

Figure 15.7 A Squeak-based lesson in gravity includes text, animation, and the program code controlling the animation. Users can change the animations to learn more about how to program a simulation of gravity. They make changes by manipulating the drawing, by clicking on buttons to alter the code, or by altering the code directly. The representation is textual, visual, and symbolic, and can be engaged physically, visually, textually, or symbolically. (Such a lesson extends, but does not replace, physical and observation activities with real-world objects.)

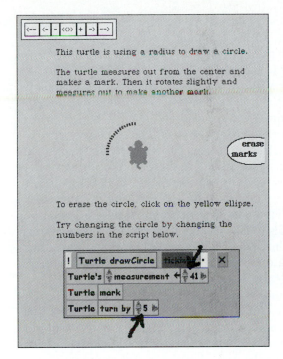
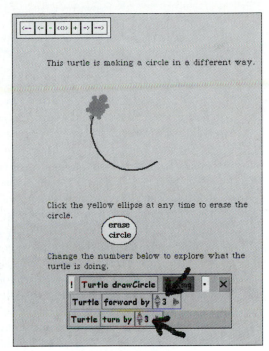

Figure 15.8   Two Ways to Think about Circles.

Both scripts produce circles, yet they are made in different ways. By working with the two scripts, a person might begin to see that a circle can be understood in different ways, with or without reference to a center point.

Another perspective that might emerge from working with these two kinds of circles is that a circle can be seen as a process instead of a thing. Surprisingly, circles can emerge from different processes.

Of course working with multiple perspectives doesn't assure insight or understanding. Such work might even lead to negative outcomes such as reluctance or inability to maintain any point of view long enough for fruitful exploration.

Dynamic Processes

Because they are so good at making changes, computers can facilitate learning about dynamic processes—processes in which change is ongoing. As a time-based medium, computers provide particularly helpful ways to understand processes in time.

Humans have developed many ways to capture changes in time, such as musical notation, mathematical symbols, stories, and plays. More recently, we have developed ways to store and replay time-based phenomena on film, tape, and disk.

Other devices such as oscilloscopes and plotters represent oscillations, waveforms, and other fluctuations in time. Now, with computers, we have ways to link our notations with our stored replays. We can, for instance, link a film's shooting script with the film itself, with a storyboard, and with other ways of understanding the film. We can link a recording of music with the score, with analysis, with simulated performances that can be altered by the user, and so on. We can link oscilloscope-like pictures of waveforms with the equations that describe them. Changing one of the linked representations alters the others, too.

Naturally there are tradeoffs and risks in linking different kinds of representations. In general, notations derive their power by focussing on key phenomena or relationships while disregarding others. Linking notations directly to output must be done carefully, then, because a notation may leave out information or variables that are crucial to the liveliness and vividness of the output. Making the notation more complex may help, but it may also make the notation harder to understand.

For example, music software can link music notation with sound output. However, music notation is not a complete recipe for a performance. Because music notation does not include all of the details that make a performance vivid and soulful (human performers add those details as they perform), computer playback of music notation often sounds mechanical and unmusical. Using a computer to link musical notation to performance may limit the user, omitting crucial elements simply because they can't be notated. Some music software works around this problem by providing ways to add information to the score, but this makes the notation very complicated, dense with information, and difficult to read. (Despite its limitations, computer playback of music can be very useful and even exciting, especially as a compositional tool.)

Linking mathematical symbols to computer animations may help some learners understand mathematics. The math used to describe a motion formerly lay unmoving on the page, eluding the understanding of those who could not make the mental connection between the symbols and the movement. With a computer, the math can be implemented in software to run a simulation. Changes to the math in the program result in immediate changes to the simulation. Changes to the simulation affect the math.

Making direct manipulations to a simulation program might help learners deepen their understanding of phenomena, principles, symbolic representations, and the relationships between them.

Figure 15.10 shows a simple dynamic process. A circle grows until it reaches a certain size, when it collapses and begins growing again. (The original purpose of this example was to illustrate how computers can model dynamic processes, not to teach this particular process.)

Similar examples should help people to grasp higher order fluctuations as well. For instance, if velocity increases by some rate, and that rate also increases over time (an accelerating acceleration), a computer simulation could allow a learner to manipulate both rates of increase and watch what happens to the simulation.

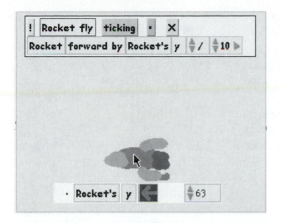
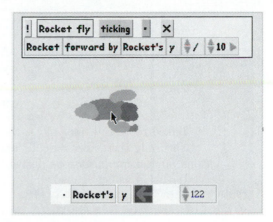

Figure 15.9 In this simulation, the rocket's speed is dependent on its altitude. Moving the rocket higher or lower in the window raises or lowers its velocity. The user can move the rocket by dragging it or by changing the value of its y coordinate. (Note that moving the rocket changes its y-coordinate, and changing the y-coordinate moves the rocket. These changes affect the calculation that determines the rocket's velocity.)

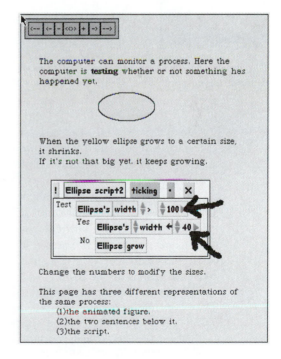

Figure 15.10 A simple dynamic process, offered in three representations: an animation, a description of the animation, and the program that runs it. The user is invited to modify the program.

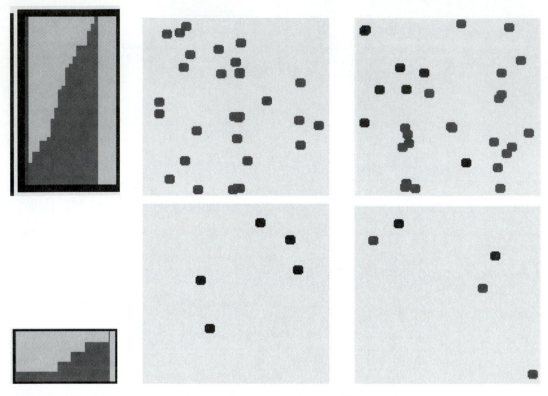

Figure 15.11 Snapshots from an "infection" simulation. The simulation was run twice, with different size populations. Graphs show the rates of infection.

Among important dynamic processes are complex systems with many variables or many objects. Immensely helpful to professional scientists trying to understand complex systems, computers are beginning to help nonprofessionals understand them as well.[8] Figure 15.11 shows the Squeak "bouncing atoms" demonstration, a relatively simple simulation of a complex system. One of the careening dots can "infect" others with a new color when they collide. The simulation continues until all dots have acquired the new color. How long will it take for the whole population to become infected? Users can run the simulation with different conditions and generate graphs of the results.

Of course playing with simulations does not guarantee any particular learning. That depends, as always, on the users' intent and attention.

---

[8]Richard Dawkins' "Blind Watchmaker" program was one of the first programs designed to simulate a complex system for lay people. By modeling the interaction of mutation and selection, the program provided hands-on experience with the forces underlying evolution. Part of the program's effectiveness was that it required the user to play an active role, that of selection forces.

Genres for a New Medium

Every new technology begins life by imitating older technologies. The first piano music was rather like harpsichord music. Early films were rather like filmed plays. The first cars looked like carriages.

As people gain a better understanding of the unique characteristics of a new medium, new genres develop. Liszt wrote piano music that would have been unimaginable a couple of generations earlier. Films developed their own unique grammar. Cars began to take on a different look more suited to their nature.

Genres in the computer medium are still developing. The medium's creators are working to understand its potential, its grammar and syntax, and its limitations and possibilities. The medium's unprecedented flexibility and unceasing technical transformation may make it difficult for stable genres to emerge. However, just as humans eventually figured out what film was all about and what pianos were good for, we will eventually develop genres unique to the computer medium. And, just as piano music, films, and cars have continued to evolve, computer genres, once they appear, will continue to develop.

Some transitional genres have already appeared. Dynamic spreadsheets are a new twist on an old genre. Desktop publishing is a new way to create older genres. Websites, on the other hand, are something new and different, probably a transitional form on the way to becoming a new genre. Video games provide examples of new genres.

New genres in the computer medium will certainly include different kinds of learning environments. The Squeak community is working with two new genres for learning: the Active Essay and the SqueakToy.

Active Essay

An "Active Essay" is a new kind of document combining words, simulations, and programs.[9] The user works directly with multiple ways of representing the concepts under discussion. By "playing with" the simulations and code, the user gets some hands-on experience with the topic.

Squeak's design makes it easy to display functioning code alongside other text, graphics, animations, and simulations, so that the code and its outcome can be observed simultaneously. A window can contain any kind of object, and endusers can examine any object and the code that runs it. Learners who know the Morphic interface can examine objects in an Active Essay to find their names and scripts, and can easily redesign objects and their programs.

Perhaps the main advantage of the Active Essay is that the user is not just a reader of text or an observer of outcomes, but a participant in the activity. The

---

[9] Alan Kay and Ted Kaehler have developed the Active Essay and have constructed some examples. See Ted's Web page, `www.webpage.com/~kaehler2/`, for more information on Active Essays.

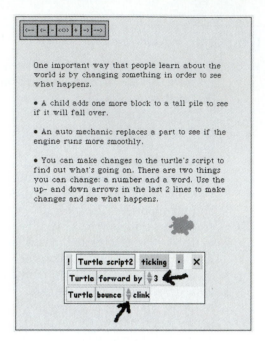

Figure 15.12 Along with words, this Active Essay includes simple programs that can be changed while running. (When this page first appears, the turtle is moving.)

user can be invited to rewrite text, design graphics, write code, or change existing programs. An Active Essay is not just a collection of information and experiences, but a laboratory for experimentation and exploration.

One potential use of the Active Essay is in teaching about Squeak. There is a tantalizing possibility that the computer might replace printed manuals and become the medium for learning about itself, about software, and about programming.

Much remains to be learned about Active Essays, but here are a few observations about strategies and style in this genre:

- The learning that takes place flows from the user's actions and thinking. A good Active Essay would stimulate thinking through appropriate action and exploration. An Active Essay is less a place to display an author's cleverness, than a way to call forth cleverness from the user.

- Computer screens are still not good places to read text. At this point the most exciting thing about Active Essays is not the text, but the participatory activities.

- Fitting everything onto the screen can be a problem. As the medium develops, we will better understand what needs to be visible, what can be hidden away, and where to store hidden elements.

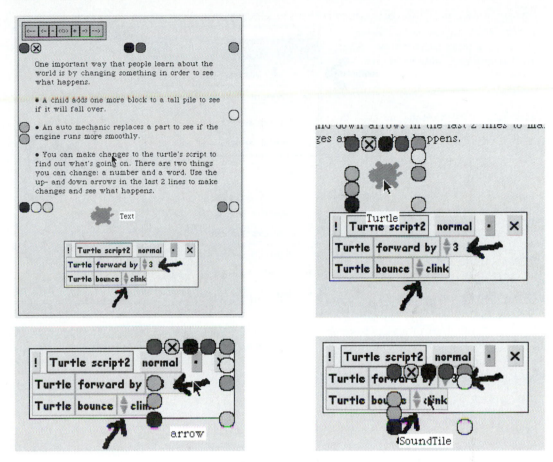

Figure 15.13 A user selects different items on the screen: a block of text, graphic elements (a turtle, an arrow), and a scripting tile. Once selected, any of these objects can be revised, repainted, rewritten, relocated, or rescripted.

- An ongoing problem is how to carry the user through a sequence of actions and make sure that the user did them all correctly. One strategy is to invite the user to make some changes, and then to continue on a new "page" with all of those changes made correctly.[10]

- Instructions and guidance may be given in many ways: in written form, by recorded voice, by animated character, by animated example (i.e., numbers move to show you how to move the numbers), and by video clip. Although early prototypes are rather like books with text and illustrations, the Active Essay will probably develop into something quite different from a book.

---

[10]Thanks to Alan Kay for this insight; he noticed the strategy implemented in a tutorial for the software Alice.

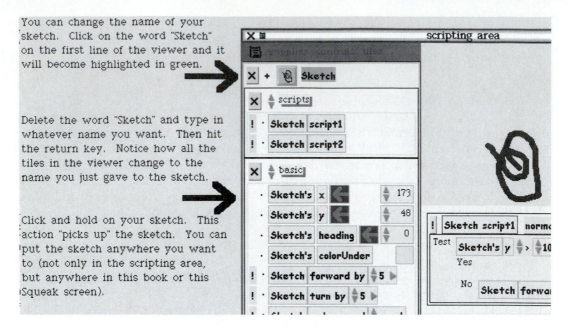

You can change the name of your sketch. Click on the word "Sketch" on the first line of the viewer and it will become highlighted in green.

Delete the word "Sketch" and type in whatever name you want. Then hit the return key. Notice how all the tiles in the viewer change to the name you just gave to the sketch.

Click and hold on your sketch. This action "picks up" the sketch. You can put the sketch anywhere you want to (not only in the scripting area, but anywhere in this book or this Squeak screen).

Figure 15.14 Part of a page from an Active Essay by Naala Brewer, using Morphic to teach about viewers in the Morphic interface. (Naala Brewer constructed a set of lessons about the interface and projects to build while she was a research intern at Disney, working with the Squeak team. Contact her at `Naala.Brewer@disney.com`.)

- Some Active Essays may need to have intelligence, or at least a capacity to track the user's doings in order to suggest next steps.

- Users' levels of experience might determine how they interact with an Active Essay. Novice users would mainly participate in ready-made activities, while more experienced users might want to "look under the hood" to find out why objects behave as they do, and advanced users might want to learn more about how a simulation or the essay itself is constructed.

SqueakToys

While Active Essays dispense information and experiences, SqueakToys[11] are construction projects or kits. Experiences and information are involved, but the center of the activity is making something.

---

[11] The working name for such projects, "eToys," has been scrapped due to trademark conflicts, and a new moniker is needed. I'm calling them "SqueakToys" until we think of something better.

Background: Learning by Making Things.

Although much of what people need and want to learn appears to be informational, the most challenging part of education is to connect new skills and information with what the learner already knows. If new learning is not connected in this way, the learner may not be able to retain it in any usable form. (For example, if education were simply a matter of dispensing information, then the barrage of data about environmental crises would have been sufficient to change Americans' patterns of consumption.) Most learners need help integrating new learning. Facilitating such integration is not trivial, because every learner arrives with a unique set of assumptions, obstacles, previous experiences, skills, motivations, and knowledge.

One great way to learn and to integrate learning is to make something.[12] Whether the something is a sculpture, a house, a musical composition, a performance, a theory, a computer program, or an essay, making it is a way to find out what you know and what you don't know, to provide a context for new learning, to integrate that new learning, and to give form to what you have learned. In an educational setting, the finished product also provides clues about what the maker knows and doesn't know—especially about what knowledge and skills the maker is able to put to use. Educators are increasingly, and appropriately, concerned that learners be able to activate and use what they learn.

When I write an essay, the act of writing helps me—forces me—to see connections between things I know and to discover ways to organize the information and the connections. Writing may help me remember important items I'd forgotten. I may also have to gather new information, and because I need that information for my essay, I am likely to integrate it with what I already know.

A well-designed educational project makes learning exciting and fun precisely because it requires the learner to use new information, skills, or understanding in some meaningful way. The learner must grasp the new learning well enough to assess how it relates to the project, and then make decisions about whether and how to use it. Sometimes this decision-making and learning happens below the threshold of awareness while the learner's attention is focussed on completing the project. Making something is one powerful way to initiate fruitful connections between what a learner already knows and what she is learning.

I also suspect that people learn more easily after activating what they already know. When making something puts a learner's existing knowledge and skills into action, potential connection points become "alive," ready to link with new learning.

Because learners vary in their ability to integrate new learning and in their learning styles, there is no one right way to teach. Learners need flexible facilitation approaches that can help each learner's unique situation. Making things can be one such approach; a well-designed project to make something can provide lots of entry

---

[12]I am indebted to Prof. Doreen Nelson of Cal Poly, Pomona, for her ideas about how constructing things—particularly objects in three dimensions—helps learning. Similar ideas from Seymour Papert and others influenced projects in computation and learning at the M.I.T. Media Lab, and such projects have now spread to other places through the efforts of Mitchel Resnick, Uri Wilensky, Yasmin Kafai, Amy Bruckman, and others.

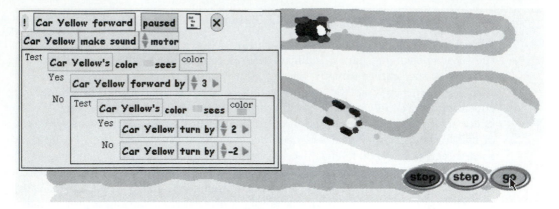

Figure 15.15 "Robot Car" project designed by B.J. Allen-Conn, a teacher in the Los Angeles Unified School District. The cars automatically follow a curving road. The program for the lower car is displayed. Without seeing this script, several of the students were able to program their own simulations to exhibit the same behavior (after a project by Alan Kay).

points, varied learning opportunities, and multiple motivations for engaging with the project.

Learning by Making SqueakToys.

One purpose of Squeak's Morphic interface is for nonexpert adult programmers to design SqueakToys, projects for kids to build in the computer environment. Through making simple animations and simulations, children encounter ideas from mathematics, science, and programming and practice using them. SqueakToys are meant to be fun and fairly easy to build, capable of being mocked up spontaneously, without too much forethought—rather like sketching an idea on the back of an envelope. SqueakToys are meant to be easy to modify and extend. In other words, SqueakToys should be easy to change as their maker's ideas develop.

SqueakToy construction zone.

The SqueakToy endeavor is a multi-level environment for learning. In addition to whatever the children learn from building SqueakToys, adults observe how the children use the SqueakToy projects and how learning takes place. Meanwhile, the adults who design SqueakToy projects learn about programming and about what makes those projects effective. Squeak programmers are learning how to design an interface to facilitate the creative work of adult intermediate programmers, the construction work of children, and the support work of parents and teachers who help their children build SqueakToys. That's a tall order for one interface, so there is much to learn.

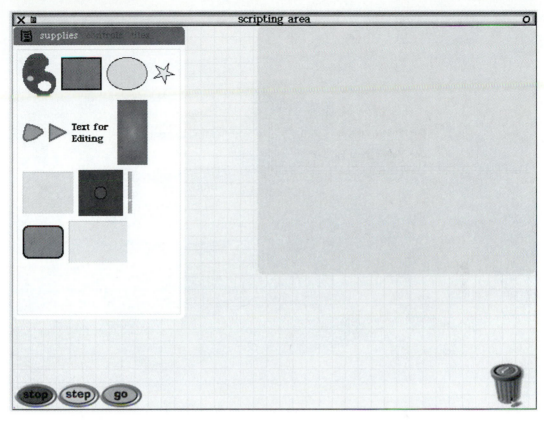

Figure 15.16 Combining features of previous systems that Squeak's designers admired, Morphic includes a simple painting interface and a tiling system for creating scripts for objects. In a basic SqueakToy project, the child draws an object or character and then gives it movement or other behavior by assembling a script from the tiles provided. To create such a project for children, an adult must build it and then figure out how to make the materials and concepts available for a child.

The Disney Squeak team has a long-standing interest in designing systems to help novices learn programming. Squeak, Morphic, and SqueakToys are the latest fruits of that interest, and they are proving to be quite useful, both for the novices and for those attempting to understand how to help them. Squeak's combination of power and flexibility has facilitated prototyping and redesign of interfaces and projects. Facilities for sharing projects and updates make it relatively easy to turn critiques of the system into improvements.

The interface has been sufficient for preliminary experiments with a few parents, teachers, and children building small-scale simulations and animations. For her classroom of fourth- and fifth-graders at the Open Charter School in Los Angeles, B.J. Allen-Conn designed several SqueakToy projects, and at first the children

Figure 15.17 Students absorbed in their work on a SqueakToy. Part of this assignment is to answer questions on paper. Open Charter School, Los Angeles. (Photo by Kim Rose.)

seemed chiefly occupied with learning the interface. Over the several weeks of their work with SqueakToys, several of the children became fluent enough to switch their attention to the mathematical thinking embedded in the projects. Some students, with help from the adults on hand, conceived additions to or variations on the projects and figured out how to implement their ideas.

In fact, the children had so much fun working with Squeak that they frequently had trouble stopping their tinkering long enough to think about their SqueakToy's behavior. Computers can be so compelling, and making changes to them can be so much fun, that users become distracted from the very thinking a project is supposed to foster.

I have also found Morphic useful for constructing Active Essays aimed at adults. Its ability to construct and modify projects on the fly is particularly helpful and enjoyable.

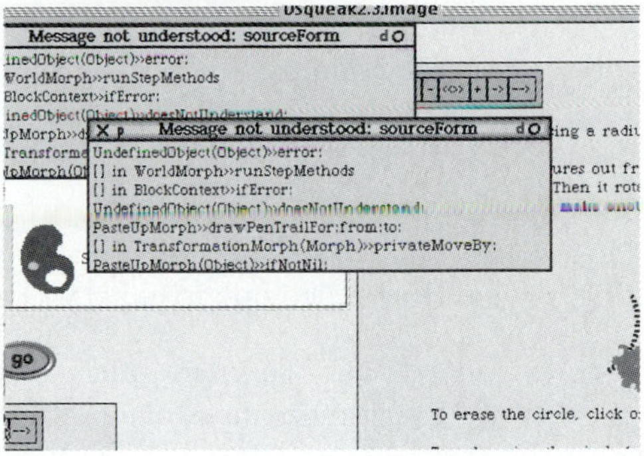

Figure 15.18 Too often, error messages are generated that baffle intermediates and beginners, because they come from outside Morphic and look different from any other SqueakToy messages.

Although much work of simplification and clarification remains, Morphic offers some helpful ways of thinking about what non-expert users might need in order to do some programming, and Squeak makes it possible to implement those ideas so that they can be tested.

Among the remaining challenges, one of the greatest is to make it easier for users to share their projects between machines. Although Squeak works across platforms, the problem of conforming with different versions of a system subject to constant updates has not yet been solved for inexperienced users.

Some other difficulties are inherent to user-interface design, with its constant tradeoffs between conflicting needs. Building SqueakToys requires seeing both the simulation (or animation) and the code that runs it, along with instructions. How to fit everything onto the screen—particularly when it needs to be able to run on any platform—will be an ongoing problem with no single correct solution.

Because reading text from the screen is so unappealing—and early experiments confirm that children don't like to read SqueakToy instructions[13]—SqueakToy designers will need to discover other ways to communicate with users.

All these experiences and observations can contribute to better understanding the computer's potential as a learning environment.

Parting Shots

Let me offer some final ideas about children, learning, and Squeak.

Useful Questions

The following are a few questions to keep in mind when designing computer-based learning environments:

---

[13]In Naala Brewer's experiment at a Saturday drop-in computer class, children enjoyed building SqueakToys but preferred adult coaching over reading the onscreen documentation.

- What is the person learning? How much of the learning is about how to use the computer or the software, and how much is about something else?

- To what extent does the project require thinking and/or imaginative response?

- How many possible right answers are there?

- How much opportunity for design choice does the user have?

- What is the intent of the project from the standpoint of the designer? From the standpoint of the user?

- To complete the project, what will the user need to discover? What will the user need to be given?

- How will the user's attention be drawn to thinking about the phenomena onscreen instead of just making changes or proceeding by trial and error?

- Who's having the fun?

Squeak Learning Communities

Just as Squeak has attracted a far-flung community of users and developers, Squeak-Toys and Active Essays are beginning to attract a community of project designers and teachers. At this writing, the community is tiny. As Morphic's interface improves, that community will probably grow. Another potential community is in homes, where children and parents may work with SqueakToys downloaded from websites. Eventually, a community of children may share their SqueakToy projects via the Internet. For the present, though, Morphic remains a promising and stimulating research system, serving users who have access to support from the system's designers.

For SqueakToys to succeed with a broad cross section of children (not just with those with gifts and inclinations for programming), and particularly for SqueakToys to reach homes successfully via the Internet, Squeakers will need to discover ways to help non-expert adults, such as parents, to facilitate children's use of the projects. Many adults do not know how to coach children's learning by asking questions or directing attention instead of offering answers. Internet-based SqueakToys will need to help the adults help the children.

In classrooms, computer-based projects in older languages like LOGO and HyperCard have stimulated collaborations between children. Because making something with a computer requires a variety of skills, children with different abilities and different learning styles can help each other. Some teachers report that computer projects also foster a more collaborative spirit between teachers and students, because teachers who are computer novices become learners alongside their students.

Figure 15.19 B.J. Allen-Conn and students discuss a SqueakToy project. Open Charter School, Los Angeles. (Photo by Kim Rose.)

In comparison with older languages, Morphic offers an environment in which novices can try ideas with a relatively little pre planning. The tiles and their displays reduce the need to remember names of primitives and what they do, so the system can be learned partly through experimentation. By fostering exploration and improvisation, Morphic may also foster collaboration.

Active Essays and SqueakToys are conceived not just for solitary learners, but also for children or grownups working together in small teams, helping each other to understand, solve problems, and develop solutions. Collaboration seems to suit computer-based construction activities, whether the collaboration is between children gathered around a terminal or between Squeak developers scattered around the world.

John Steinmetz has worked as a consultant to Alan Kay's research groups at Atari, Apple, and Disney. He has progammed experimental software activities for children, he has composed music that uses computers together with live instruments, and he has written essays about new and old technologies for learning and expression. John mainly makes his living as a freelance bassoonist in Los Angeles, performing with Los Angeles Opera and other organizations. His Quintet has been released on CD in a performance by the Borealis Quintet, and his pamphlet "How to Enjoy a Live Concert" is published by Naxos Records. Contact him at johns@cogent.net.

16

The Future of Squeak

Dan Shafer
The WeTalk Network, Inc.

Introduction

Friedrich Nietzsche once said,

> Our destiny exercises its influence over us even when, as yet, we have
> not learned its nature; it is our future that lays down the law of our
> today.

If ever there was a topic to which Nietzsche's thought could be applied, it is
Squeak. We have not yet learned the nature of the destiny of Squeak because that
destiny continues to unfold before our very eyes and because we are about the business of creating that destiny. Yet, to an extent not attained by other programming
languages and environments, Squeak has always been *about* the future. Its future
has in fact determined many of the ways it works and thinks today.

In this chapter, we'll take a look at where Squeak might well be headed over the
next two to five years. To choose a shorter time horizon would result in a chapter
that would be obsolete almost before the book could see the light of day. To project
further would be foolhardy in the extreme given the uncertainty not only of Squeak
but of the world in which it will play its role.

Much of the content of this chapter derives from conversations I have been
privileged to have with the group of Squeak developers and insiders known affec-
tionately as "Squeak Central." Some of it also comes from extensive conversations
I have had with my colleague, Laurence Rozier, who is among the most forward-
thinking object-aware software professionals I have met. Rozier has been carrying
Squeak's message to me and thousands of others for many years, as he carried the
Smalltalk and JavaScript and other object-oriented language message before and
since.

I have also sprinkled a few of my own predictions liberally through the text. What emerges is not a guaranteed future or even a "certified" future bearing the imprimatur of the Squeak Central team or of the Squeak community. Rather, this is an attempt to have some fun speculating about where our favorite programming language and environment might take us and where we might guide it.

The chapter is divided into two major sections. In the first, we'll focus on the future of the Squeak kernel, the heart of the beauty, as it were. In the second, we'll concentrate on applications and implementations that Squeak may facilitate in the relatively near term as the Squeak community broadens, deepens, and learns.

Some Basic Concepts

Because this chapter is about the broad-scoped future of Squeak, I use a couple of terms in ways that are probably not completely technically accurate. Certainly they aren't entirely precise.

When I talk about Squeak in this chapter, I mean to include not only what is clearly and inherently part of what the Squeak Central team is building (i.e., the kernel and virtual machine along with such core additions as Morphic, SqueakToys, and the Swiki), but also important and widely used classes and packages being developed by others. Comanche is one example of this kind of extension that I will bring under the umbrella name of "Squeak," because it feels to me like the future of Squeak with Comanche is richer than its future without that Web server.

The other term that is hard to define and confine not just in Squeak, but in Smalltalk dialects of all types, is "application." Traditionally, this has meant a file on which a user could double-click with a mouse and that ran as a sort of stand-alone piece of functionality from that time forward. The problem is that this kind of analogy doesn't resonate with people. In your real life, you don't have things lying around on your desktop (particularly not a trash can!). You may not even have a desktop.

In the world of Smalltalk and Squeak, though, things are much more natural, though this naturalness means we have to think more carefully about what we are doing than we would have to if we weren't so conditioned to metaphors that don't map to our real lives. In some cases, an application might exist as a set of objects the user simply adds to his or her system and which extend what the user can do. In that scenario, there is presumably an underlying environment, whether a Squeak image, an operating system, or a chip with Squeak embedded. In some cases, transparent background downloads of packages might make the very existence of something even vaguely resembling an application irrelevant. There would be no such thing as a "system" or an "environment"; rather the Squeak "thing" would in fact become the environment or the system. This kind of behavior will be particularly predominant, I suspect, when it comes to portable devices and TV set-top boxes. In still other cases, packaging might well be used to create what looks more like the traditional double-clickable application.

On some levels, this explanation is part of a much larger issue that centers on how humans interact with and perceive computers. In just the past few years, we've seen the perception of a computer as a desktop where stuff (documents and applications, principally) is stored to a sort of transport mechanism. "I just went over to Yahoo! and looked it up" has become such a part of the way we think and talk about our experience that websites like yahoo.com are clearly places in our minds, just like Grandmother's house. In no real sense, of course, do we "go" to Yahoo. But that's what it feels like and it's how we describe the activity. This has deep implications for how we build the user interfaces of the future, how we help people make the shift from the analog world to the digital world of their computers and other electronic devices. Squeak and Morphic are destined to play a major role in that evolution.

The Squeak Kernel in the Future

In speculating about the future of the Squeak kernel, we are in some sense on relatively firm ground, at least as far as prediction itself can ever be on a solid foundation. The kernel, after all, is in the figurative control of Squeak Central. Though its design clearly allows for extension by other members of the Squeak community, Squeak Central plays a sort of central arbiter role akin to that played in other Open Source community projects by those who are ultimately seen as the keepers of the vision.

This is not to suggest, however, that other members of the Squeak community cannot or will not influence the direction of the kernel. They clearly have, and they just as clearly will, continue to do so.

Small Is Good, Modular Is Even Better

The size of the Squeak kernel will ultimately be quite small, almost certainly smaller than 1MB. The Version 1.18 Squeak release image only occupied 968K on the Macintosh, with VM support adding another 290K.

Development work past that early release of the technology bloated the image somewhat, but Squeak Central has repeatedly assured the community that it is intent at some point on getting back to these size parameters if not even smaller.

In a message posted to the Squeak mailing list in late 1999, Dan Ingalls said, "[We] still need to extend our reach ... before we will really know what the kernel should be and how it wants to be seen by users." In that same email message, Ingalls warned, "It's going to get worse before it gets better, but it *will* get better."

The size of the kernel is important and interesting, but even more significant is the concept of Squeak modularity. "The monolithic Squeak environment will go away," predicted Squeak Central's Ted Kaehler. He points to then-recent development of ImageSegments as an important bit of technology in terms of making

Squeak modular. "ImageSegments are capsules of live objects. We are using them to make stand-alone importable projects with their own Internet URLs," Kaehler says.

ImageSegments is a facility that can begin with a defined list of root objects and write to a binary file all of those objects and other objects to which the original objects point. This allows Squeak developers to create remarkably stand-alone pieces of functionality that can be readily imported into a different Squeak image.

Combined with ImageSegments, the Squeak Central team has been perfecting a technique which will allow developers to create Morphic "SqueakPages" that can be saved to a server as external objects and dynamically loaded into a running Squeak image as needed.

In addition to the obvious advantages ImageSegments present for the delivery of Squeak functionality in small packages, they also facilitate the kind of robust project and change management that is essential to the success of environments like the Web, which must be subject to being updated at any given moment.

The Internet and Distributed Computing Models

As Squeak becomes more and more modular, it lends itself increasingly to distributed computing applications. Older, monolithic versions of Smalltalk were notoriously unfriendly to networking; even creating networked applications was a major undertaking. Squeak, by contrast, is coming of age in an era when the Internet, in general, and the World Wide Web, more specifically, are integral parts of the software landscape. It acknowledges this fact and thrives in it.

"We now foresee," Ingalls has said, "the possibility of an extended universe of Squeak worlds, distributed over the Internet as Web pages, downloaded and internalized. . . and swappable in a reasonable memory footprint. . . "

This ability to save, send, store, and dynamically reload segments and pages will allow Smalltalk, for the first time, to play a crucial role in the creative development process where collaboration is important. The implications of this capability, as we will see in the second major part of this chapter, are staggering.

It is almost certain that within the next two years, Squeak will also support a notion very close to that of the Java applet: a bit of relatively stand-alone functionality that can be downloaded, embedded into a Web page (or some similar future form factor) on the client, and executed.

Meanwhile, the Audience Evolves

People encountering Squeak for the first time are often bewildered by the question of whether, in a world of the Internet and Java programming, there is room, let alone a need, for yet another programming language. For those who are already comfortable creating software in Java or C++, Squeak Central has a simple answer: For you, there isn't.

"We expect to grow Squeak in the direction of a significantly broadened user base rather than by attracting or even attempting to attract Java and C++ programmers," Scott Wallace of Squeak Central says.

Expect Squeak's evolution along these lines to focus on the SqueakToy environment and extensions to it, built on top of the Morphic substrate that has emerged as everyone's preferred way of interacting with and managing Squeak development. The idea is to attract an increasing audience of users who are not programmers, but rather multimedia authors and others who can bring to the table contributions that, in Ingalls' words, "are more generally enlightening and educational, enabled by Squeak."

Squeak Central has indicated it plans to focus significant energy on increasing support for first-time users in coming versions of Squeak. Specifically, the team plans to explore the following four aspects of Squeak to see what kinds of improvements can be made to make Squeak more accessible to new users and nonprogrammers:

- experiments with alternative syntaxes;

- easier creation of simple applications;

- a new, streamlined programming framework focusing on an integrated "object operating table"; and

- integration of "SqueakToy" scripting tiles.

Discussions of audience among the members of Squeak Central often devolve to trying to find a word to describe the user base, composed as it inevitably is of both programming users and what have traditionally been called "end" users as if there were in fact a theoretical end point to the use process. Alan Kay and others have begun adopting the word "omni-user" to encompass all types of empowered users accessing Squeak capabilities and services.

Fitting Squeak into Your Hand

One of the most exciting and interesting areas of Squeak development has been the emergence of hand-held devices capable of running (and in some cases even supporting development in) Squeak in small memory footprints and on small form-factor screens. Sharp has two Personal Digital Assistants (PDAs) available only in Japan at this writing that support Squeak and on which Squeak programs operate.

Squeak has also been successfully ported to Microsoft's WinCE platform and the Cassiopeia from Casio, among other small form-factor devices.

"We are," says Wallace, "coming closer and closer to the famed DynaBook dream" of Alan Kay's early career.

The portability of Squeak even to places where no operating system yet exists has been a reality for Squeak Central from early in the product's life. In the first year of its development, the Squeak team brought in an undergraduate college student who had never seen Squeak. They asked him to port Squeak to a bare microprocessor then being developed by one of the major semiconductor firms. That chip had only a minimalist software design kit (SDK) available, and it was purely text-based.

"In three weeks," recalls John Maloney of Squeak Central, "this guy had Squeak ported to this chip. Most of that time was eaten up getting peripheral drivers to work so it could display graphics on a screen in color and respond to keyboard input." The team says that when Kay saw the demo for the first time, he immediately began to demonstrate to others who were present the implications of this. Once you've done the port, a huge body of work and content is suddenly immediately available in the new environment.

He asked the student to let him "drive" the demo and proceeded to astound the audience of semiconductor executives by showing off some of his best demonstrations running on this bare-chip implementation of Squeak.

3-D in Squeak

Three-dimensional graphics are important elements of realistic multimedia and virtual-reality worlds, but creating them on any modern computer platform within the reach of the average person is so difficult that almost nobody attempts the task. The Squeak community has long been interested in overcoming this obstacle to multimedia creation.

It has a strong ally in the person of Randy Pausch (see Chapter 3, "Alice in a Squeak Wonderland," by Jeff Pierce for a detailed discussion of this technology), whose teams first at the University of Virginia and later at Carnegie-Mellon University have created an experimental 3-D tool called Alice. This tool has been ported to Squeak from its origins in Python (an object-oriented Open Source scripting language) and is under active use by dozens of teachers, multimedia developers, and tool designers who are striving to make it as easy to create 3-D objects as it is to create 2-D documents in a word processor.

The Squeak team has felt strongly that 3-D support belongs directly in the kernel, or at least at the heart of the language. In late 1999, Squeak Central integrated the 3-D engine in the language with the Morphic interface technology that is rapidly becoming the core of the Squeak development environment. This allows the projection of 3-D images onto Morphic canvases.

"Our real goal here," explains Maloney, "is to create a place where 2-D and 3-D objects can both play on the same screen or canvas without any performance penalty. When we accomplish that, we will have gone a very long way toward the Holy Grail Pausch and his colleagues envision."

This will allow for the first time the seamless integration of 3-D with existing text and graphical content, a development whose impact on computing it might be difficult to overstate. The entire segment of the software industry that is interested in exploring the 3-D representation and visualization of 2-D data would be greatly accelerated in its efforts by the availability of this functionality.

Taking a page from the book of Macintosh (not coincidentally the OS of choice for Squeak Central, most of whom were part of Apple Computer at some point), the idea of a 3-D Finder has some serious interest among Squeak developers. Rozier has had visions of such a top-level interface for many years, having created an environment called HyperOffice more than 15 years ago. HyperOffice, which Rozier first built in Framework and later redeployed in Digitalk Smalltalk/V and JavaScript, uses the concept of a building with floors dedicated to certain functionality (like the accounting department) and offices or rooms where individuals keep their projects and documents.

In its Framework incarnation, the program used crude 3-D file drawers. However, by the time it reached its Smalltalk/V incarnation under the name CyberTalk, it boasted a strong representation of a 3-D office environment.

Users can "beam" between offices, use other users' computers with appropriate permission, and generally get the feeling of inhabiting a real-world building while they accomplish their work goals.

Rozier is, at this writing, finishing a Morphic project bringing this work up to date and implementing it in Squeak. By the time you read this, it will be available through Rozier's website, The Pattern (`http://www.thepattern.com`).

"Extending the flat [2-D] desktop to a set of rooms and places to navigate among is the next logical step in system user interface design," says Maloney. "Whereas in today's Squeak environment, we switch projects by clicking on icons representing windows and their contents, in the future, we will run down hallways into adjacent and distant rooms containing our various projects."

Major Graphic Changes Coming Soon

In some ways, 3-D graphics implementation alongside 2-D graphics is a subset of a larger future direction Squeak is taking. Squeak Central has indicated it is at this writing close to being able to take full advantage of the graphics acceleration hardware on each kind of machine on which Squeak runs. At the same time, Andreas Raab is finishing up a "Just in Time" version of the graphics engine in Squeak that will compile efficient new, machine-native code for each bitmap movement on the screen. Speed, then, lies just around the bend.

One of the major reasons Squeak Central chose to undertake this step is to permit Squeak to take full advantage of hardware graphics acceleration.

Once this new bitmapped imaging is in place, Squeak Central plans to reconstruct Morphic from scratch, preserving as much of the existing Morphic as possible in the process but making the new Morphs more lightweight objects that can be more easily and compactly manipulated and scripted.

There is also very little doubt that the Squeak community plans to create a blizzard of new widgets for user-interface design and construction, probably on top of Morphic. In early 2000, the Squeak mailing lists were abuzz with conversations on the subject, and several volunteers were already gathering resources and energy to tackle the problem. Once these widgets are available, it will become easier to create business applications that look and feel like native platform applications. (Not everyone believes that this is either good or necessary. However, since Squeak allows for such widget kits, it is guaranteed that they will be built.)

As the new Morphic is completed and widgets are built and ported to the new environment, Ingalls has signaled his intent to create a Squeak version of a 1988 programming concept he and other members of the team presented at the annual Object-Oriented Programming Systems and Languages (OOPSLA) conference called Fabrik. This is a visual "wiring" development environment that would facilitate the assembly of Morphs and widgets into full-blown interfaces and applications.

It is safe to bet that over the next two years, Squeak will become a visually programmable environment in which the creation of easily packaged stand-alone applications with native look-and-feel will become an eminently achievable goal even for a non-programmer.

What Belongs in the Kernel?

In the very early days of Smalltalk, someone suggested that the world of computing had had some of its ideas out of kilter for some time. Asked why there was so much operating-system-like functionality in Smalltalk, Squeak Central's Ingalls replied, "An operating system is a collection of things that don't fit into a language. There shouldn't be one."

Ever since then, the Smalltalk and Squeak worlds have become involved in frequent, largely friendly debates about what should be in the language kernel, what should be in the operating system, and what should be in the language, but not in the kernel.

With modularity emerging as a touchstone of the new versions of Squeak that will emerge in the near future, this discussion merits even closer examination. Before the existence of ImageSegments or any equivalent idea, there was little if any *practical* distinction between a Smalltalk image and the Smalltalk kernel. There were, to be sure, technical differences, but to the application builder or end user, the line was largely indistinct and irrelevant.

Now that we are able to externalize and load on demand major pieces of functionality, it is inevitable that the tendency is going to swing strongly toward eliminating from the kernel anything that doesn't absolutely need to be present all the time.

This will mean that some of the elements contained in today's "basic" or "core" image (which remains for practical purposes indistinguishable from what is technically the kernel) will now be externalized. Multimedia graphics, for example, will probably become an externally loadable set of objects rather than integrated into core Squeak. Similarly, Web servers, Swiki capability, speech recognition and synthesis, MIDI interfaces, and many other pieces of Squeak that veteran Squeakers have come to think of as core elements of the environment will be loaded as needed.

The other side of this coin is that in a connected world—even where that connection might be file-based URLs on local hardware—the distinction between what is contained in the distributed image and what is stored externally to be loaded as needed becomes largely irrelevant. If you use a bit of code that calls some routine that isn't in the current image you or your user is running, Squeak simply uses the URL of the missing object(s) to load the functionality on the fly and completely transparently.

All of this leads to a suggestion that we will almost certainly see a Squeak-based operating system—or, to be somewhat more accurate, Squeak running in the absence of an operating system—in the near future. Indeed, there has already been one abortive attempt at such a project[1] which even empowered the creation of device drivers in Squeak. ("Imagine being able to write device drivers for new peripherals and form factors entirely in Squeak Morphic," Squeak Centralist John Mahoney enthuses.)

Why would one want to create or use a Squeak OS? When asked that question, Maloney said, "I can see a future in which everything you might want to fine-tune or control on your computer is right there for you to access through a Squeak Morphic interface. You can change anything. You are in control."

The advantages of such an approach, Maloney says, "are transitional. You can just sit there in native mode and real time and manage everything. Given a low-latency Squeak, this is entirely feasible. All of the missing elements that used to constitute gaps between Squeak and OS capability are now perfectly capable of being filled."

Some Reasonably Clear Directions

Over the next few years, it is fairly certain that Squeak will be applied to a broad range of problems and needs. Many of these are obvious; either they derive from the use to which computers are already being put, or they have been made clearly a conscious part of the way Squeak works and is being created.

But some of the ways we are almost certain to see Squeak evolve may not be readily apparent from our present vantage point.

---

[1] A project conducted at Interval Research, a product and company incubator, had a working version of a Squeak OS on a handheld device, but the project was shelved in favor of implementing Microsoft's WinCE instead. The outcome was foreseeable given that Interval is funded in large part by Microsoft co-founder Paul Allen, a lifelong friend of Microsoft founder Bill Gates.

Squeak Gets Corporate MIS Buy-In, à la Linux

IBM, if not uniquely at least unusually among large computer companies, understands the ultimate value of Smalltalk. Its VisualAge development environments for Smalltalk, Basic, C++, and Java are all based on work done entirely in Smalltalk several years ago. To this day, the company maintains a very active and moderately large group of Smalltalk developers and related programs and technologies.

At the same time, IBM has more recently become an avid advocate of the Open Source movement of which Squeak is also a part. When in late 1999, Big Blue opened its arms to the Linux world and began supporting that free operating system, the rules of computing began a major upheaval, the entire effect of which has yet to be felt.

But IBM is not alone among large global corporations embracing Linux, which has with blinding speed become all but the *de facto* server operating system of choice. Companies like Red Hat Software, VA Research, and LinuxCare have sprung up around this phenomenon and have enjoyed immense market approval in public stock offerings. At this writing, the Linux train is just leaving the station and it's already traveling at the speed of sound.

Squeak may well enjoy the same kind of success in a few years. Rozier says, "Squeak at this point is very nearly in a parallel position with where Linux was two years ago," and he cites the following criteria as evidence to support his contention:

- It is completely Open Source.

- It is surrounded and enhanced by a small, but fanatical, group of developers and fans.

- It enjoys just enough central management control from Squeak Central to keep it from veering so far off course as to become unusable while allowing for individual creativity.

- It is ubiquitous: It already runs on more platforms today than Linux does, and it seems destined to continue to spread to new chips and operating systems all the time.

- It is in widespread use in academic settings where it can grow and be nurtured without the pressure of productization or profitability.

At the same time, Squeak enjoys the following advantages over where Linux was at relatively the same point in its growth:

- Because it is a language and a development environment and a deployment platform, Squeak is more useful to a much larger audience. Very few people make decisions about operating systems, and even fewer do more than simply run them. Programming environments are a horse of a different color, because they allow mere mortals to create applications, solutions, and projects.

- Built as it is on a very long-term language base going back to Smalltalk-80, Squeak enjoys a legacy of books, experienced programmers, documentation, sample applications, and real programs that form a sound basis for newcomers to learn it.

- It is pre-equipped to deal with the changing world of the Internet and the Web. Whereas it is sometimes difficult to adapt Linux to new technologies as they emerge, Squeak is inherently adaptable and extensible. It includes classes that allow straight forward abstraction to deal with networking and multimedia needs and issues.

- As we have indicated earlier, Squeak's nature supports dynamic management of its configuration. This, in turn, results in a huge win for users and for corporate IS/IT departments supporting those users. As the speed at which business is conducted continues to accelerate, reducing the time to adjust to change is a major economic win. Squeak will play a key role in facilitating this cost-reduction by bringing user-configurable and easily programmable configurators and change mechanisms to the desktop.

Ultimately, for these and a number of other reasons related to some of the specific applications we'll be looking at later in this chapter, Squeak could become the next big story in corporate computing.

If Squeak has a downside in all of this, it is simply that it relies on Squeak Smalltalk syntax, which programmers accustomed to C, C++, and Java often find too cumbersome. Even that problem is relatively easily addressed in the "assimilation" strategy of Squeak, though. Anyone can write a module that shows methods in a particular syntax and accepts changes in that syntax. "We have been experimenting with new looks for Squeak with kids in mind," Kaehler says, "but anyone could create, for example, a C-syntax module."

Squeak's Potential to Alter Education Approaches

From its inception, of course, Squeak has been viewed primarily as a language to enhance and support the education of the world's children. The very first Smalltalk efforts were aimed at developing a language that would be accessible to children; in fact, that goal gives the language its name.

Squeak is, if anything, more clearly deliberate in its aim at education as its primary market space. The Squeak Central team is strongly, if not exclusively, focused on education. Wallace says, "One of our big dreams for Squeak is for it to disconnect learning from the necessity of sitting in rows in a classroom."

Kaehler envisions a time when a small number of hand-held devices in a remote Third World classroom will be able to connect to a collection of the world's great works of literature such as that embodied in Project Gutenberg. "Can you imagine what learning could take place in such a free-form environment where Squeak could be used to open up all those avenues of learning and wisdom?" he says wistfully.

Rozier is a strong believer in the global importance of this kind of distributed education. "Imagine how much the world will be able to learn from those brilliant, sophisticated wise men and women of indigenous populations once we have a language rich and expressive enough with which we can communicate with one another."

Much of the potential for Squeak to alter radically how students are taught rests in its historical roots in Simula and the degree to which an object-oriented architecture lends itself to the creation of simulations. The SqueakToys capability executed in Morphic in the current release of Squeak is an excellent example of how simulation can be brought to bear in a learning environment where students add to their knowledge and wisdom by experimentation and experience rather than by passive reception of lectures and limited feedback loops.

Squeak as Hand-Held OS: At the Amusement Park

Today's cellular phones and PDAs allow their users very little control over their behavior or their appearance. Because of their small memory footprints and their primitive interfaces (Did you ever try to enter a long, complicated email address into a cell phone with its simple keypad?), these devices tend to stay in fixed configurations. If you want a phone with more functionality, you toss your old one and buy a new one.

Squeak has the potential to change that situation dramatically. If Squeak can run on top of a raw semiconductor CPU, it can certainly replace the operating system running in a cell phone or a PDA. And if it can do that, it can open up worlds of possible extensions, enhancements, and unheard-of functionality for users of these small devices.

Imagine, for example, a family going to a theme park in the not-so-distant future. When they arrive at the gate and pay their admission fee, instead of a fistful of tickets or a paper or magnetic badge, each member of the party is given a palm-sized device with a color LCD screen running a Squeak application.

Throughout their stay at the park, the family members can communicate with one another via text messages or short voice data bursts. Built-in global positioning system (GPS) software and hardware will ensure that lost parents can be easily located by their children. Want to ride the most popular attraction at the park? Rather than traipsing a mile over to the ride to find out there's a two-hour line, just tap on your Squeak application's screen and get an instant update on the wait. Want to buy something? Just beam your credit card information into the infrared receiver on the cash register of the vendor.

Oh, by the way, you might not want to leave this wonderful little device behind when you go home. That's OK. You can buy it and take it home with you where you can use it to keep up with the latest news about the amusement park owner's business, new cartoons and movies, cable broadcasts, and video releases, and to keep up with your own personal email account at the home address of some famous rodent.

All of that and more is certainly well within reach with Squeak as an embeddable system.

In fact, Rozier believes that Squeak might enjoy extremely widespread adoption by telecommunications companies and hand-held device manufacturers. "It is, after all," he points out, "the only Open Source technology suitable to meet the needs of creating both servers and devices needed by these companies. The future of small is Squeak Smalltalk."

There is, in fact, another level on which Squeak's potential importance in the world of operating systems is becoming obvious. At its heart, Squeak has a virtual machine (VM). This virtual machine essentially *replaces* the notion of an operating system with the concept of a true computing environment. In the earliest days of Smalltalk, Dan Ingalls described the operating system as a place to put things that didn't fit into the programming language, going so far as to say that there shouldn't even *be* an OS.

Squeak is, in many respects, an operating environment that is at once richer and more malleable than the typical chip-dependent OS. It happens also to have a very powerful and accessible programming language (Smalltalk dialect) in it, but that feature is almost incidental for some purposes and many users.

Squeak Supplants Netscape and Internet Explorer

There is widespread agreement among those who are building content and sites for the World Wide Web that they are being severely hampered by the inability (some would say refusal) of AOL/Netscape and Microsoft to create a Web browser that is even remotely capable of accessing all the kinds of content people would like to experience.

Browsers were first designed to be fairly passive display pieces. They could be pointed at various URLs and from those sites they could retrieve and display static text and graphics. Over the first two or three years of the Web, browsers evolved rapidly so that they supported interaction, form completion, animated graphics, and then even multimedia. But their mechanisms for supporting these additional types of content were primitive and lacked standards support.

To make your browser show you a movie, for example, you have to have the site owner help you figure out what kind of add-on functionality in the form of a browser plug-in you need. It must then guide you to the place where you can obtain that plug-in, download it, and install it. Then, you often have to close your browser application and restart it, remembering where you were when this whole ordeal began.

When the browser manufacturers tried to implement a more standards-based solution to users' expressed desires to have more fluidity and interactivity in their browsers, they fumbled the ball again. They decided to promulgate something called dynamic HTML (DHTML). But DHTML isn't a single technology; it is a term that describes the rather unhappy marriage of JavaScript scripting, HTML markup, and extensions to both the language and the markup that facilitated the creation and manipulation of individual objects in the browser.

This idea, which is at its heart right and helpful, became ensnared in the usual standards battle with the ultimate result that both Microsoft and AOL/Netscape implemented it so differently that it is all but impossible to write truly cross-browser DHTML pages without a lot of experience and much trial-and-error.

Morphic, particularly with its extended Macromedia Flash player, could provide the solution to this browser dilemma. If an Open Source Squeak project were started with the intent of producing a freely distributed browser that would natively understand how to deal with Flash content and which could be easily adapted— programmatically or behaviorally—to deal with other kinds of content, it would fill a huge gap. It could, in fact, become the new browser of choice, first in corporate settings and behind firewalls where the browser decision is centralized, and later in homes and schools interested in the adaptability of this new design.

Rozier says this will happen. "First," he predicts, "we'll see helper applications and browser companions done in Squeak. When people see the unlimited potential for extension and enhancement Squeak tools represent, the move to a Squeak-based browser, perhaps surrounding Flash as a multimedia file format, will be too compelling to resist."

Squeak-Based Comanche Becomes Cross-Platform Personal Web Server of Choice

Today, there is no cross-platform personal Web server. Linux has Apache, Microsoft Windows has Internet Information Server (IIS), Macintosh has WebSTAR, large-scale UNIX machines have Netscape, and there are a number of other variants. However, none of them is cross-platform or ubiquitous.

Why should we want such a beast?

The magic of the Web is the degree to which it allows every individual who owns a node on the Internet to become a publisher of content. Whether the audience for that publishing effort is a group of coworkers on a LAN or the entire known world on the Web, all of us need or want to share information with others.

Historically, the Internet is built on the TCP/IP protocol suite, which in turn was created to prevent single points of failure on a communications network. That means that every node has some important role to play, and that nodes tend to be relatively equal to one another. The Web builds further on those ideas.

Furthermore, people obviously *want* to share or publish information in numbers that were unheard-of before the advent of the Web. How else explain the raging success of such businesses as Geocities and Xoom, which find themselves with *millions* of ordinary people creating and publishing websites for the world to see?

In some ways, however, the idea of requiring people who want to share information with others to upload their information to someone else's computer is anti-Internet. If you want to publish content, you have a personal computer almost by definition. So why can't you just turn your computer into a Web server?

You can.

All major home computers today come with a personal Web server. The problem is that these Web servers are closed, proprietary, and limited.

So along comes Comanche, a Squeak-based, Open Source Web server built on the original Squeak Pluggable Web Server (PWS; see Chapter 4 for full details). Comanche is a project being driven principally by Bolot Kerimbaev and Stephen Pair, with the usual supporting cast of many others helping with debugging and feature enhancement.

For all the reasons that Squeak should gain widespread corporate acceptance similar to that attained by Linux in the recent past, Comanche should become the personal Web server of choice in the future. It is cross-platform, Open Source, infinitely extensible, and eminently usable.

Given the boundless nature of the underlying Squeak environment, Comanche becomes a true Web platform in its own right. It will be trivial for people to publish websites or Swikis (see Chapter 4) on their own local machines and extend those sites with functionality only dreamed about by today's website designers and developers.

Rozier puts it this way: "Linux continues to try to find a suitable client environment at the same time as Windows struggles to become a decent server. Squeak is becoming the first environment to provide the best of both worlds, a truly distributed peer network."

Squeak and the Microsoft.NET Initiative

In mid-2000, Microsoft announced what it characterized as a revolutionary new product strategy that will see all of its products and technologies converge on an interoperable Internet. At the core of this new initiative—which in many ways is not nearly as astounding as Microsoft would have us believe, building as it does on dozens of existing Open Source projects and products—is a language-independent virtual machine. Much of the work on this VM was done by Smalltalk guru David Simmons, who created SmalltalkAgents and Smalltalk 2000. In fact, a Smalltalk-based scripting language called SmallScript will be incorporated into the .NET strategy when it is released some time in the second half of 2001.

This has interesting potential implications for Squeak as well. Simmons has invited the Squeak community to join the SmallScript and .NET initiatives and to port the VM and other technologies to the Squeak platform. At this writing, a number of Squeak advocates are getting ready to do just that.

Ultimately, this could prove to be a huge win for Smalltalk as it enters into a mainstream, widely adopted, new application platform, the interoperable World Wide Web.

Squeak Web Server and Scriptable Intelligent Agents

Mobile agents have been an important area of computer research for a number of years. Like other kinds of objects and components, agents need a backplane, a place from which to be dispatched to undertake their masters' bidding and to which they return with their results. At the same time, their value increases with the network effect of an increasingly diverse collection of nodes on which they can operate.

By providing the platform for a truly distributed peer network (see previous section), Squeak will also become the launch pad for these agents. Rozier has spent the past 15 years perfecting a technology he calls Scriptable Intelligent Agents (SIAs), and he sees Squeak as the ultimate platform on which these agents can be nurtured and trained.

The first place such agents might well find acceptance in the world of the Web will be in the emergence of 24/7 custom pricing. A website called Priceline.com emerged in late 1999 with a custom pricing model that was sufficiently unique that it was granted a U.S. Patent. The concept was simple: Consumers could go to the site and indicate an interest in purchasing, say, an airline ticket to Los Angeles for any time in the week of March 13 (for example) and a desire to be able to buy it for $200 or less. Within an hour, Priceline.com infrastructure would search out and identify a vendor willing to match the user's requirements.

Imagine how powerful this idea becomes if you can dispatch your own SIAs to the Web to locate the best prices—within your parameters—for goods and services you wish to purchase. You are no longer tied to a single site's limited resources, but you are free to have your agent roam cyberspace looking for bargains and deals and partners. The fundamental shift in pricing that this technology represents is ground-shaking in its implications.

And Squeak plays a key role in this development, because of its ease of customization, accessible programmability, and incorporation of personal Web servers as "farms" for agents.

Squeak as a Multimedia Tool and Platform

By its nature and origins, Squeak is intensely graphical. As it has rapidly evolved in the past year or so, Morphic has made it even more graphical. It should come as no real surprise, then, that Squeak has also become a fertile playground for multimedia developers and producers, and that much of its near-term future evolution is likely to concentrate in this area.

We've already touched on the issue of including 3-D capabilities in the kernel and on the implications of the Alice 3-D project being ported to Squeak.

Andreas Raab, at this writing the latest addition to Squeak Central, has been working on multimedia aspects of the language for some time. He implemented the Macromedia Flash player, which was among the first full-scale Squeak tools to demonstrate the feasibility of what Rozier calls "Borg-like assimilation" of external standards and technologies. It is already possible to load any file stored in the publicly documented Macromedia Flash file format into Squeak and play the resulting movie. In the process, we can get our hands on the individual objects within the Flash movie and thus create whole new types and levels of interaction.

But beyond 2-D and 3-D graphics, beyond even the ability to play Flash and Virtual Reality Modeling Language (VRML) files directly in the Squeak environment and in Morphic worlds, the Squeak community has always been strongly interested in sound. The use of music, voice, and sound effects in computing has not been well developed. On the Web and in programming environments like Squeak, even less has been done with determining precisely how audio influences ought to be brought to bear on the user experience.

Stephen T. Pope, one of the early Smalltalkers, has for many years been working on MIDI tools and interfaces. His work is included in the Squeak image as of this writing. It represents some of the most interesting and advanced work being done with incorporating musical capabilities into computers.

Already this work has been built into an interactive MIDI Jukebox and a piano-roll type of interface for composing, arranging, playing, and editing music.

Squeak developers have done much with audio engines. Work will now be focused on the creation of great voices for these engines and in the area of file compression. The SqueakTime asynchronous file reader included in the current releases of Squeak are not very efficient at compression, resulting in large file sizes and often poor playback.

In the near future, expect to see an MPEG player (assuming licensing and royalty issues can be worked out satisfactorily).

Ultimately, its developers expect to see Squeak spawn a successful effort to create a dynamite tool for multimedia development that will allow composers and producers the ease of drag-and-drop incorporation and mixture of 2-D and 3-D graphics, MIDI and compressed sound and music, and animations including Flash movies.

Combining the best of what we've learned from watching thousands of developers use commercial tools, Squeak could form the basis for the creation of a new generation of multimedia development aids by making an infinitely extensible platform core to the success of the tool. Much as Adobe has maintained its leadership in the photo-manipulation market by opening its widely used Photoshop to plug-ins, so Squeak, by allowing extensions to be coded in Morphic and Smalltalk, could allow the end users of a Squeak-based multimedia tool to extend it at will. The results will no doubt be astonishing.

The First Fully Extensible Collaboration Tool?

In building and extending Squeak, the Squeak Central team and the broader community have almost coincidentally managed to create an environment for collaboration that is probably already better than anything on the commercial market.

The sharing of files and live objects between Squeak images is easy and becoming trivially transparent as this is written. The Morphic environment empowers individuals to share graphical representations of their ideas very quickly; the narrow, but enthusiastic and successful, use of "whiteboard" technology will be dwarfed by what is possible in Squeak.

"We are all interested in generic collaborative tools," Wallace says. "We use them all the time and we know where they are strong and where they are weak. A really general-purpose collaborative tool, infinitely extensible in Squeak, of course, is definitely in the offing if for no other reason than that it grows naturally out of the work we are doing."

Clearly, the notion of taking collaboration and its big sibling, online community, to the next level, would greatly benefit from Squeak and Morphic. Not only because it is object-oriented, but also because the components already available to facilitate collaboration—and others to come in the near future—make Squeak a powerful and infinitely extensible platform for the construction of discussion boards and for meaningful real-time interaction with whiteboard-supported chat, graphical instant messaging, and other such feature sets. All of this can be easily integrated into the underlying system because of Squeak's nature as a VM and OS-replacement.

Web-Based Games

The first Web-based game written in Squeak, "Oceanic Panic," made its debut in kiosks at Disney's Epcot Center as this was being written. More are under development.

Games delivered and experienced on the Web would have a number of advantages over those played on either personal computers or dedicated proprietary game-playing platforms:

- They would be easier to install than those on PCs, because they would carry their infrastructure—sound support and the like—around with them.

- They would lend themselves more easily to multi-player scenarios, since they would by nature be networked and sharable.

- They could be personalized, customized, and extended using Smalltalk, Morphic, and other, similar programming and development techniques that are at the core of Squeak.

Expect to see a huge increase in the number, variety, and kinds of Web-based games and fun educational applications as Squeak moves more and more into this arena.

Finally, the Dynabook?

During the early days of Smalltalk, Kay was going around talking about and describing his vision for a new type of device he dubbed the Dynabook (dynamic book). He saw this device as featuring a graphical interface, connected to external links in some then-unknown way and embodying a way for children (its users) to program, or extend, it. His ideas grew out of his early experience with object-manipulation programs during his days at the University of Utah.

It seems that Kay has infected most, if not all, of the Squeak Central team with his notions so that it is difficult to have a conversation with any of them about the future of Squeak without the Dynabook being mentioned repeatedly.

Certainly, Squeak has moved the marker a long way toward the realization of Kay's dream. Out of the Morphic interface has grown Ingalls' and Kaehler's work with ActiveEssays, which in many ways are the content Kay would have chosen as a primary type of information to be presented on the Dynabook.

The facts that Squeak can be deployed on highly portable, even handheld, devices and that such devices are easily connected to wireless networks over which Squeak runs quite efficiently and effectively certainly lead to the conclusion that the Dynabook is finally within reach.

Dan Shafer is the founder and chairman of The WeTalk Network, Inc., creators of a network of online communities including WeTalkSports.com, WeTalkSciFi.com, WeTalkStyle.com, and dozens of others. He has been a member of the Smalltalk community for many years, having authored several introductory programming books as well as a number of systems in various dialects of the language. He is the author of more than 50 books on computers and high technology as well as a frequent speaker and lecturer on technology-related topics. For several years, Dan has chaired and directed the content for CNET's Builder.com Live conference in New Orleans. He lives with his wife Carolyn and their Shiitzu dog Albert Einstein in Belmont, California.

Subject Index

Prentice Hall

YOU SHOULD CAREFULLY READ THE FOLLOWING TERMS AND CONDITIONS BEFORE OPEN-
ING THIS CD PACKAGE. OPENING THIS CD PACKAGE INDICATES YOUR ACCEPTANCE OF
THESE TERMS AND CONDITIONS. IF YOU DO NOT AGREE WITH THEM, YOU SHOULD
PROMPTLY RETURN THE PACKAGE UNOPENED, AND YOUR MONEY WILL BE REFUNDED.

IT IS A VIOLATION OF COPYRIGHT LAWS TO MAKE A COPY OF THE ACCOMPANYING
SOFTWARE EXCEPT FOR BACKUP PURPOSES TO GUARD AGAINST ACCIDENTAL LOSS OR
DAMAGE.

Prentice-Hall, Inc. provides this program and licenses its use. You assume responsibility for the selection
of the program to achieve your intended results, and for the installation, use, and results obtained from
the program. This license extends only to use of the program in the United States or countries in which
the program is marketed by duly authorized distributors.

LICENSE

You may:

a. use the program;

b. copy the program into any machine- readable form without limit;

c. modify the program and/or merge it into another program in support of your use of the program.

LIMITED WARRANTY

THE PROGRAM IS PROVIDED "AS IS" WITHOUT WARRANTY OF ANY KIND, EITHER EX-
PRESSED OR IMPLIED, INCLUDING, BUT NOT LIMITED TO, THE IMPLIED WARRANTIES OF
MERCHANTABILITY AND FITNESS FOR A PARTICULAR PURPOSE. THE ENTIRE RISK AS TO
THE QUALITY AND PERFORMANCE OF THE PROGRAM IS WITH YOU. SHOULD THE PRO-
GRAM PROVE DEFECTIVE, YOU (AND NOT PRENTICE-HALL, INC. OR ANY AUTHORIZED
DISTRIBUTOR) ASSUME THE ENTIRE COST OF ALL NECESSARY SERVICING, REPAIR, OR
CORRECTION.

SOME STATES DO NOT ALLOW THE EXCLUSION OF IMPLIED WARRANTIES, SO THE ABOVE
EXCLUSION MAY NOT APPLY TO YOU. THIS WARRANTY GIVES YOU SPECIFIC LEGAL
RIGHTS AND YOU MAY ALSO HAVE OTHER RIGHTS THAT VARY FROM STATE TO STATE.

Prentice-Hall, Inc. does not warrant that the functions contained in the program will meet your requirements or that the operation of the program will be uninterrupted or error free.

However, Prentice-Hall, Inc., warrants the cd(s) on which the program is furnished to be free from
defects in materials and workmanship under normal use for a period of ninety (90) days from the date
of delivery to you as evidenced by a copy of your receipt.

LIMITATIONS OF REMEDIES

Prentice-Hall's entire liability and your exclusive remedy shall be:

1. the replacement of any cd not meeting Prentice-Hall's "Limited Warranty" and that is returned to
Prentice- Hall with a copy of your purchase order, or

2. if Prentice-Hall is unable to deliver a replacement diskette or cassette that is free of defects in materials
or workmanship, you may terminate this Agreement by returning the program, and your money will be
refunded.

IN NO EVENT WILL PRENTICE-HALL BE LIABLE TO YOU FOR ANY DAMAGES, INCLUD-
ING ANY LOST PROFITS, LOST SAVINGS, OR OTHER INCIDENTAL OR CONSEQUENTIAL
DAMAGES ARISING OUT OF THE USE OR INABILITY TO USE SUCH PROGRAM EVEN IF
PRENTICE-HALL, OR AN AUTHORIZED DISTRIBUTOR HAS BEEN ADVISED OF THE POSSI-
BILITY OF SUCH DAMAGES, OR FOR ANY CLAIM BY ANY OTHER PARTY.

SOME STATES DO NOT ALLOW THE LIMITATION OR EXCLUSION OF LIABILITY FOR IN-
CIDENTAL OR CONSEQUENTIAL DAMAGES, SO THE ABOVE LIMITATION OR EXCLUSION
MAY NOT APPLY TO YOU.

GENERAL

You may not sublicense, assign, or transfer the license or the program except as expressly provided in
this Agreement. Any attempt otherwise to sublicense, assign, or transfer any of the rights, duties, or
obligations hereunder is void.

This Agreement will be governed by the laws of the State of New York.

Should you have any questions concerning this Agreement, you may contact Prentice-Hall, Inc., by
writing to:

Prentice Hall College Division Upper Saddle River, NJ 07458

Should you have any questions concerning technical support you may write to:

YOU ACKNOWLEDGE THAT YOU HAVE READ THIS AGREEMENT, UNDERSTAND IT, AND
AGREE TO BE BOUND BY ITS TERMS AND CONDITIONS. YOU FURTHER AGREE THAT
IT IS THE COMPLETE AND EXCLUSIVE STATEMENT OF THE AGREEMENT BETWEEN US
THAT SUPERSEDES ANY PROPOSAL OR PRIOR AGREEMENT, ORAL OR WRITTEN, AND
ANY OTHER COMMUNICATIONS BETWEEN US RELATING TO THE SUBJECT MATTER OF
THIS AGREEMENT.

ISBN:0-13-0608122